GW01003616

BUYING POWER

BUYING POWER

A History of Consumer Activism in America

LAWRENCE B. GLICKMAN

THE UNIVERSITY OF CHICAGO PRESS · Chicago and London

The University of Chicago Press, Chicago 60637
The University of Chicago Press, Ltd., London
© 2009 by The University of Chicago
All rights reserved. Published 2009.
Paperback edition 2012
Printed in the United States of America

21 20 19 18 17 16 15 14 13 12   2 3 4 5 6

ISBN-13: 978-0-226-29865-8 (cloth)
ISBN-13: 978-0-226-29867-2 (paper)
ISBN-10: 0-226-29865-5 (cloth)
ISBN-10: 0-226-29867-1 (paper)

Library of Congress Cataloging-in-Publication Data
Glickman, Lawrence B., 1963–
    Buying power : a history of consumer activism in America /
    Lawrence B. Glickman.
        p. cm.
    Includes bibliographical references and index.
    ISBN-13: 978-0-226-29865-8 (cloth : alk. paper)
    ISBN-10: 0-226-29865-5 (cloth : alk. paper) 1. Consumers—
United States—Political activity—History. 2. Boycotts—United
States—History. 3. Consumer behavior—Political aspects—United
States—History. 4. Consumer protection—United States—Citizen
participation—History. 5. United States. Consumer Protection
Agency—History. I. Title.
HC110.C6G56 2009
381.3'20973—dc22
                                                        2008050249

♾ This paper meets the requirements of ANSI/NISO Z39.48-1992
(Permanence of Paper).

TO JILL, ALEXANDER, AND ABIGAIL

CONTENTS

PREFACE

In May of 1977 the journalist Nicholas von Hoffman labeled the popularization of the word "consumer" "one of the great non-accomplishments of our times." "Consumer," he complained, "has all but replaced the word 'citizen.'" Unlike the public-oriented citizen, von Hoffman claimed, "the consumer is antisocial." Not only were consumers self-centered; they were not even fully human, but instead were best compared to "low order invertebrate mammals." Raising their ethological status slightly, and grudgingly conceding that they indeed had a backbone, he compared them to pigs: "A nation of consumers is a nation of hogs," he declared. By contrast with the citizen who processed information with his brain via the nervous system, "the seat of the American consumer's . . . sensitivities is his digestive tract." Other than the energy he expended to "feed his face," the consumer was completely passive; he was a "dupe, an organism incapable of making a sound judgement about any choice." Lacking sense and judgment, myopically concerned with their own satiation, consumers were incapable of acting collectively, according to von Hoffman. The "consumer movement" was therefore a non sequitur. Even Ralph Nader, the nation's best-known consumer advocate, was, he declared, "the pluperfect nonconsumer." Nader's lack of materialism, his curiosity, and his skepticism were "all qualities alien to the consumer."[1]

Von Hoffman's lament is familiar. Similar claims about the evils of consumerism had been pronounced countless times before and continue to be echoed. Critics across the ideological spectrum have decried modern consumer society as abetting passivity and selfishness, promoting a lack of concern for the public sphere, and encouraging environmental degradation, the exploitation of labor, and the suffering of our nonhuman fellow animals. To these critics, consumption inures us to evil, insulates us from each other, and inhibits meaningful political participation.

Yet throughout the history of the United States the omnipresent rhetoric of consumer passivity has been consistently accompanied by an equally ubiquitous consumer activism. Activists have understood, and practiced, consumption, not as the negation of citizenship, but as an instrument of solidarity, a mode of ethical agency, and a bridge to healing relationships with both nature and the animate world. Indeed, von Hoffman's opinion column decrying the inability of consumers to act collectively coincided with the engagement of a large number of politicized consumers in a myriad of protests. In the spring of 1977, organized labor was launching three prominent boycotts against nonunion agricultural, textile, and beer-making firms, and gay rights and women's organizations announced boycotts of Florida oranges (because of the homophobic comments of the growers' spokeswoman, Anita Bryant), and also of states that had not yet passed the Equal Rights Amendment. At the same time, several international boycotts dominated the news, including a protest against Japan for its killing of whales and dolphins, an Arab League boycott of Israel, a boycott of South Africa by black athletes at the Commonwealth Games, and a call for a more general boycott of that nation because it endorsed apartheid.[2]

The spring of 1977 also was filled with news and debates about consumer representation in government. Two weeks after von Hoffman's article appeared, a Louis Harris poll revealed broad public support for the consumer movement; the pollster projected the emergence of a "staggeringly" large politicized consumer bloc. In April of that year, Esther Peterson was appointed special assistant for consumer affairs to President Jimmy Carter. In addition, a bill to create a federal "Consumer Protection Agency" was approved by the House Government Operations Committee, making it seem likely that such an agency, strongly supported by Carter, would come into being within the year.[3]

Positing not only that consumption undermines citizenship but that at some unspecified but fairly recent point in our history Americans had acted as public-spirited citizens in large measure because they had not yet adopted a consumer identity, von Hoffman held that civic engagement was more common in the era "before we became a nation of consumers." The view that the age of citizenship has been replaced by the age of consumerism has become conventional wisdom.

Buying Power tells a different story about the relationship between politics and consumption. Demonstrating that boycotting and other politicized forms of organized consumption have a history as long as the United

States, it argues that, from the founding of the nation onward, Americans have often expressed their citizenship in and through acts of consumption. The spring of 1977 was not unusual: consumer activism has been the norm, not the exception.

Historians have told bits of this story before but they have done so in a piecemeal and instrumental fashion, examining particular boycotts, especially those associated with the American Revolution and the modern Civil Rights movement. This has often led to a depiction of boycotting as a sporadic rather than a continuous political tradition, "from the tea dumped in Boston Harbor to the segregated seating in Montgomery, Alabama, buses," in the words of the journalist Lynn Duke in 1991.[4] But this common periodization omits the entire nineteenth century. Treating boycotts as intermittent, it produces a gap not only in our knowledge of the history of consumer activism but also in our understanding of the relationships among the particular named boycotts. The connections among consumer politics both within and across political generations are, as a result, lost.

It is well known that boycotts and other forms of consumer activism have been regularly employed in social movements throughout American history, but we know very little about the meaning and significance of these tactics. What did Americans hope to accomplish through the use of these consumer-based weapons, as opposed to other forms of political action? One of the goals of this book is to show that boycotts and other forms of consumer activism were, among other things, a means to reconcile consumption and citizenship.[5]

✳

Buying Power is structured chronologically and unfolds thematically. After an introductory chapter which offers a thematic overview of the book's main arguments, part 1, "The Birth of Consumer Activism, 1776–1900," comprising chapters 1–4, examines the origins and development of this political tradition. When did consumer activism begin? Activists liked to say that it dated back to "time immemorial." In a sense, as we shall see, this was true. However, what made consumer activism truly original beginning in the late eighteenth century was the invention of long-distance solidarity through acts of consumption. Long-distance solidarity operated in two ways: by making the near distant and the distant near. Beginning in the 1760s, colonial rebels began to publicize local acts of consumer protest so that a nascent community of Americans came to understand these acts to be linked in one movement. Over time, activists used the market and print to aggregate the focus of consumers far and wide on a common enemy. The agents of the movements discussed in the first three chapters—nonimportation, free produce, and nonintercourse—developed these key elements of modern consumer activism. The fourth chapter traces the origins and dissemination of the term "boycott," a practice that soon became synonymous with consumer activism itself.

Part 2, "The Birth of the Consumer Movement, 1900–1945," containing chapters 5–7, explores the crucial period of the first half of the twentieth century, a time when the tradition of consumer activism was modified and sometimes challenged by the rise of the "consumer movement." From the moment they conceived it, consumer activists began adapting it to new conditions. These chapters explore new styles of boycotting that developed in the first four decades of the twentieth century and analyze the origins of the "consumer movement." In this period, boycotting was joined by a novel form of consumer politics. Unlike consumer activists who took consumers to be agents of change, proponents of the consumer movement sought to define what they called the "consumer interest." In this vision, consumers constituted a group to be protected. Just as consumer activism had changed, however, the consumer movement did not remain static. No sooner was the consumer movement created than it divided into quarreling camps.

Part 3, "Advocates and Activists: Consumer Activism since World War II," made up of chapters 8 and 9, looks at the popularity of the consumer movement in the postwar years and analyzes persistent tensions, many of them already apparent in consumer activism's earlier manifestations. These chapters explore the surprising breadth of the consumer movement in the postwar years, highlighting the alliance between consumer advocates and modern liberalism. It is therefore no coincidence that one of the opening salvos in the backlash against postwar liberalism came in the organized attempt to delegitimize the consumer movement. Even when the consumer movement was at its peak, consumer activism in the form of boycotts was a regular feature of the postwar years. With the decline of the consumer movement in the last third of the twentieth century, however, consumer activism regained its former prominence.

Narrating the story of the development and transformation of consumer activism through time, this book explores change and continuity in each iteration of consumer activism, with a special emphasis on the signal contributions of each of the three eras highlighted by the book: the development of the language and philosophy of long-distance solidarity in part 1; the claim that consumers themselves were a group in need of expert assistance in part 2; and the alliance with, and revolt against, postwar liberalism in part 3. The epilogue examines the resurgence of consumer activism in recent years and highlights the ways in which boycotts of the early twenty-first century have (usually unknowingly) replicated many earlier strands of this American political tradition.

This genealogy of consumer activism offers a new interpretation of American history. First, it identifies consumer activism as a long-term and significant political and, indeed, intellectual tradition, marked, despite the diversity of its participants, by continuities in practices and, equally significant, continuities in thought; second, it unearths unexplored aspects of that tradition as well as movements that may have been discussed in other contexts but have not been previously considered under the rubric of consumer activism; third, it reinterprets the meaning of some of the more well-known instances of consumer activism, in large measure by placing the thought and actions of these activists in the context of the achievements of their forgotten predecessors and followers; and fourth, it reframes the significance of the twentieth-century "consumer movement," simultaneously historicizing it as a branch of the broader and more long-term phenomenon of consumer activism, and highlighting its diversity and originality.

Shortly before Nicholas von Hoffman published his critique of American consumers, the conservative columnist George Will seemed to offer a similar view, for he too was critical of a consumer orientation. "Unfortunately, many citizens today think of themselves primarily as consumers," wrote Will, who lamented that too many Americans held that "policy should serve consumption." By acknowledging that consumption was bound up with citizenship for most Americans, however, Will recognized what von Hoffman did not. At the same time, understanding the link between consumption and citizenship was only the beginning of the story. As we will see, while Americans have consistently seen consumption and politics as related, they have understood the connection in strikingly diverse ways.[6]

ACKNOWLEDGMENTS

Writing this book has affirmed a key insight of consumer activism: that people are deeply connected to others through links that are no less powerful for being invisible. This book has linked me to many people and organizations who, though invisible to me in the sense that I have never met them, facilitated the completion of this project by way of their generous support and wisdom. Fellow scholars, librarians, and archivists helpfully responded to my requests by e-mail and telephone, often offering to photocopy and mail me relevant materials. Historians, past and present, have written books and articles which provided inspiration and points of departure. I am grateful to several organizations that encouraged my ambitious goals in research and writing, including the National Endowment for the Humanities for a Fellowship for University Teachers for the 2000–2001 academic year; the American Philosophical Society (especially the directors, Richard Dunn and Mary Maples Dunn) for a sabbatical fellowship during the 2007 calendar year; and the Center for Human Values at Princeton University, where I was a Laurance S. Rockefeller Fellow for the 2006–2007 academic year (where the acting director, Anthony Appiah, and the superb staff including Jan Logan, Erum Syed, Susan Winters, Andrew Perhac, and Kim German, as well as the other fellows, made the center a wonderful and stimulating academic home).

Finding out about the various consumer causes this book explores required travel to many archives. I would like to thank the helpful staff at the following institutions: Consumers Union (especially Kevin Mannion); the Department of Special Collections at Rutgers University, which houses the records of Consumers' Research; the Consumer Movement Archives and the Richard L. D. Morse Collection at Kansas State University, where Tony Crawford generously helped me comb through the rich materials; the

Schlesinger Library at the Radcliffe Institute for Advanced Study, Harvard University, which houses the papers of the Consumers' League of Massachusetts, the League of Women Shoppers, Maud Nathan, and Esther Peterson, among many other invaluable sources; the Sophia Smith Collection at Smith College, which houses other records of the League of Women Shoppers; the Historical Society of Pennsylvania, which holds the Max Weiner Papers, containing much information about the Consumer Education and Protection Association, and the Schomburg Center for Research in Black Culture of the New York Public Library. When travel was not possible, I depended mightily on the superb and efficient Interlibrary Loan Department of the Thomas Cooper Library at the University of South Carolina.

At the University of South Carolina, I am grateful to Dean Mary Anne Fitzpatrick for providing research funds that allowed me to complete the manuscript. During the decade or so of work on this project, I was extremely fortunate to work under two fantastic chairs, who gave me much support, financial and otherwise: Patrick J. Maney and Lacy K. Ford, Jr. I also thank the superb staff of the History Department (especially Beverly Edwards, Melissa Kupfer, Becky Roberts, and Theresa Walling). Among my colleagues, I owe particularly heartfelt appreciation to Tom Brown, Dan Carter, Bobby Donaldson, Lacy Ford, Kent Germany, Karl Gerth, Kasey Grier, Robert Herzstein, Ann Johnson, Paul Johnson, Jessica Kross, Thomas Lekan, Daniel Littlefield, Pat Maney, Ken Perkins, Michael Scardaville, Lauren Sklaroff, Mark Smith, and Robert Weir. Ken Clements deserves special thanks for reading the entire manuscript and offering in his inimitable fashion dozens of useful and creative suggestions. In thinking about this book, I was also instructed and inspired by many excellent graduate students—many of them now graduated—who became colleagues in the exploration of consumer society, including Eric Bargeron, Eric Cheezum, Aaron Haberman, Kathy Hilliard, Adam Mack, Aaron Marrs (who generously provided me with numerous research leads on antebellum consumerism), Becky Miller, Eric Plaag, David Prior, and Michael Reynolds. Special thanks to Robin Copp of the South Caroliniana Library and Bill Sudduth, the head of Documents, Microforms, and Newspapers, for going above and beyond the call of duty to help me out. Finally, this book never would have been completed without the expert research assistance of Laura Foxworth.

A supportive and culinarily gifted group of friends in Columbia asked me about my book and, just as important, engaged me in other edifying activities. Special thanks to Amit Almor, Vered Almor, Amittai Aviram, Bob Bohl, Susan Courtney, Cynthia Davis, Rabbi Hesh Epstein, Chavi Epstein, Greg Forter, Arnie Levine, Nina Levine, Allen Miller, Agnes Mueller, Rabbi

Meir Muller, Sheindal Muller, John Reagle, Ann Poling, and Nicholas Vaz-sonyi (as well as all of their children). Other friends, now scattered far and wide, contributed more than they know to nourishing my soul: Rachelle Abrahami, Michael Berkowitz, Marianne Constable, John Gershman, Bonnie Honig, Cathy Kudlick, Hillary Kunins, Barbara Leckie, Mary Odem, Albert Park, Lucy Salyer, Marc Schachter, Anne Schepens, Stephen Shainbart, Joel Westheimer, Tim Weston, Michael Whinston, Deborah Yasher, Marcia Yonemoto, and Elizabeth Young. Thanks a million to Marc, who read the complete manuscript and offered wonderful suggestions even after I thought I was done.

I have presented portions of my research at many conferences and invited lectures over the last decade, and I am deeply indebted to the audiences at these talks, from whom I learned a great deal. At Harvard's Charles Warren Center for Studies in American History, I presented some of my first thoughts on the topic. Thanks especially to Laurel Thatcher Ulrich for the invitation to speak. At Boston University's Department of American and New England Studies, I received helpful feedback from Marilyn Halter, Bruce Shulman, and Nina Silber. At the history departments of the Davis and Berkeley campuses of the University of California, I got much constructive advice. Thanks especially to Paula Fass, who facilitated my talk at Berkeley. I benefited enormously from my first forays into early nineteenth-century consumer activism at Northwestern University (where Bonnie Honig not only helped arrange my visit but also peppered me with wise comments, as did Dylan Penningroth, Joe Barton, Steve Hahn, and Stephanie McCurry) and at the University of Michigan (where Jay Cook invited me and, along with Rita Chin, hosted, and also offered helpful comments, and where I was very happy to run my ideas by J. Mills Thornton, among many others). Thanks to Marcia Yonemoto and Tim Weston for inviting me to the University of Colorado, Boulder, and to Julie Greene for commenting perceptively. I also benefited from the comments of the audience at the University of Minnesota, Twin Cities. It was a special privilege to present my work to my colleagues at the Center for Human Values at Princeton, and I am particularly grateful to Anthony Appiah for his insightful comments. At a variety of national conferences over the past decade, I benefited from the comments of the late Susan Porter Benson, Lizabeth Cohen, Gary Cross, Gary Gerstle, Roger Horowitz, Daniel Walker Howe, John F. Kasson, Jackson Lears, Nelson Lichtenstein, and Annelise Orleck. I was fortunate to be invited to speak at several international conferences, whose audiences were wonderfully accommodating, interested, and helpful. At "Balancing Public Interest and Community Orientation: Cultural Patterns in the United States and Germany," at the J. W. Goethe

Universität in Frankfurt, I had the opportunity to place U.S. consumer activism in comparative perspective. At the First International Seminar on Political Consumerism at the City University in Stockholm, I was fortunate to be able to discuss the topic with scholars of contemporary consumer politics. Thanks especially to the conference organizer, Michelle Micheletti. At "In the Name of the Consumer," a conference at the Centre de Recherches Historiques of the École des Hautes Études en Science Sociales in Paris, I was delighted to engage with many scholars who shared my interests.

I am grateful to my editor, Robert Devens, and the friendly and efficient staff at the University of Chicago Press, particularly Emilie Sandoz, Megan Marz, and Erik Carlson. One of Robert's many talents was finding the referees for the manuscript, Alexis McCrossen and Daniel Horowitz, both of whom gave the book a thorough and thoughtful going-over and provided a perfect mix of encouragement and lists of things to do. As have so many others, Dan Horowitz has been a mentor and champion of long standing. I am deeply grateful for his generosity. Jean-Christophe Agnew, Lizabeth Cohen, Gary Cross, and Kathy Peiss have also been generous supporters over the years.

I regret that a number of teachers and colleagues did not live to see the publication of a book that they supported and encouraged. I will never forget what I learned from Sue Benson, Jon Gjerde, James Kettner, Reggie Zelnik, and most especially from Lawrence Levine, my dissertation adviser and friend.

My extended family provided invaluable love and support. As this book has progressed, I have enjoyed the growing number of nieces, nephews, cousins, and in-laws who have enriched my life. Special thanks to my in-laws Esther and Hershey Frank for everything over the years. I am fortunate to have two extraordinary brothers, Cliff and Mark, with wonderful families. My parents, Sandra and Ronald Glickman, are simply the best. Their never-ending generosity and love has sustained me and the way they live their life provides a model that I continually seek to follow. Thanks again, Mom and Dad.

This book is dedicated to my amazing family. Thanks so much to my daughter Abigail, who, from an early age, asked me why I was writing about boycotts but not "girlcots." At the time, I did not realize that there had been a debate among consumer activists about the use of this phrase.[7] My son Alexander insisted that both his third- and fourth-grade classes would be interested in learning about my research, fixed my computer problems, and helped with the title. Jill Frank encouraged me, held me to her high standards, and read the manuscript with her careful eye for clarity and argument. Most of all, she is my cherished life partner.

*

I am grateful to the editors and readers (many of them anonymous) who critiqued the articles that form the basis of some of the chapters of this book: Marie Chessel, Matthew Hilton, Joanne Meyerowitz, Kathleen Newman, Peter Stearns, and Marita Sturken. And thanks to the following journals for allowing me to publish material in revised form: *Journal of American History*, *Journal of Social History*, *American Quarterly*, *Sciences de la Société*, and the *OAH Magazine of History*. Thanks also to Berg Publishers for permission to use material from an article that appeared in *The Expert Consumer: Associations and Professionals in the Consumer Society*, edited by Alain Chatriot, Marie-Emmanuelle Chessel, and Matthew Hilton.

AN AMERICAN POLITICAL TRADITION

Throughout their history, Americans have engaged in an almost continuous series of boycotts, demands for leisure and recreation, campaigns for access to the benefits of consumer society, and efforts to promote safe and ethical consumption. From the American Revolution, to the antebellum era, to the sectional crises that culminated in the Civil War, to the rise of the labor movement in the Gilded Age, to the Progressive period, to the Great Depression, to the struggle for African American freedom, to the social movements of the 1960s, through our own time, in which nearly two-thirds of Americans take part in at least one boycott on an annual basis, consumer activism has been an important, although generally underacknowledged tactic of every political generation.[1] This book offers a genealogy and interpretation of what I call the American political tradition of consumer activism.

Tracing this history is illuminating in its own right, as it reveals the persistence with which Americans have understood consumption in political terms and have practiced politics in consumerist terms. Indeed, consumer activism provides a lens through which to analyze almost every important topic and period in political history and culture. But understandings and practices of consumer activism have changed over time and have been contested, even in the same period, and often within the same movement. To recount a history of this American political tradition is therefore to map Americans' evolving, and often conflicting, ethical understandings, moral beliefs, and social practices as they both shaped and were shaped by engagements with consumer society. These understanding, beliefs, and practices mirror central tensions and themes of American history, as consumer activists simultaneously embedded themselves in and challenged key political, social, and economic developments, including capitalism, liberalism, humanitarianism, cosmopolitanism, and, of course, consumer society. A tradition as persistent as the American nation itself, consumer activism in some ways constituted the United States as an independent nation: from the 1760s onward, consumer politics became critical to the independence struggle, and the tensions and complexities in the practices of consumer activism consistently reflected and shaped American history.

In spite of its pervasiveness, consumer activism is an unusual American political tradition for several reasons. First, it has taken a number of forms in the service of a wide variety of causes. Indeed, one of the themes of this book is the contestation over the meaning of, and transformation of, consumer politics during the course of its more-than-two-century history. It was a movement without a name for more than a century, practiced by a diverse group of Revolutionaries, abolitionists, Southern nationalists, and moral reformers. Even after the coining of the word "boycott" in 1880, the diversity of boycotters persisted. In the twentieth century a new and influential form of consumer activism emerged, a "consumer movement" led by experts and elites on behalf of consumers. For a time, the consumer movement threatened to engulf all modes of consumer activism. But consumer activism continued to be practiced and, as we will see, it continued to gain adherents, even as the consumer movement lost momentum in the last decades of the twentieth century.

Second, consumer activists have rarely achieved their immediate objectives. While it is an enduring political tactic and philosophy, consumer activism lacks the signature victory that we associate with such social movements as abolitionism, organized labor, women's suffrage, temperance, and Civil Rights. The story is complicated, however, because consumer tactics played an important role in all of these movements and many others as well, so the successful Revolutionary and Civil Rights boycotts have not always been understood as victories for consumer activism. It is nonetheless indisputably the case that the vast majority of boycotts throughout American history have been putative failures.

Finally, unlike other social movements, in which memory serves an essential function—indeed, activists often invent mythic pasts, full of heroic predecessors on whose shoulders they stand—consumer activists have, by and large, and in almost every generation, acted with no demonstrable knowledge that others before them had fought analogous battles, used similar tactics, and shared an underlying understanding of the ways in which markets linked distant people. They generally preferred to describe themselves not as inheritors and modifiers of venerable traditions but as political pioneers. Even Ralph Nader, who credited his predecessors more than most of his colleagues in the revived consumer movement of the 1960s, underestimated the depth of its history. In a 1971 speech describing the "three stages" of the consumer movement, Nader, seeing himself as a representative of the third stage, highlighted the "muckraking stage" in the Progressive Era as the first, but noted that "by far the most important was the stage in the twenties and thirties, although that's not generally recognized." His evidence for the importance of this "second stage": "It was at that point that the major institutions that should represent consumers were basically forged—for example, the rural electric co-ops, the labor unions, Triple-A motor clubs, the credit unions."[2] Nader's genealogy notably omitted consumer organizations, such as the National Consumers League (NCL), Consumers' Research (CR), and Consumers Union (CU), that were at the heart of both the "muckraking stage" and the period that he labeled "most important." By contrast, leaders of other social movements of the period—say, second-wave feminists, whose very name suggests an awareness of their history, or Civil Rights campaigners—regularly acknowledged the debts they owed to their forerunners.

Despite the wide variety of its forms, the diversity of its practitioners, its overall lack of success in achieving its objectives, and the relative absence of memory and myth that usually characterize social movements, consumer activism has, for more than two centuries, provided a remarkably consistent vision of the power of aggregate consumption and its withdrawal to promote what I call "long-distance solidarity." If solidarity concerns "the inclusive community of the affected," consumer activists expanded the parameters of such communities, by emphasizing the degree to which "the affected" need not be nearby; through communication networks, and markets, consumers could extend what the historian Thomas Haskell has called the "circle of responsibility" via their actions at the cash register.[3] In this way, consumer activists, in spite of their differences, have been political theorists, offering a context and a narrative to educate consumers about the meaning of the goods they buy, or choose not to buy, and the social impact of their shopping choices.

Central to this context and narrative is the claim that purchasing goods, far from being a private decision, is a fundamentally social act, with far-reaching consequences. Ever since the nineteenth century, consumer activists have emphasized the impact of consumption on the hiring of labor to harvest or fashion the desired product, on the employer who manufactured the product, and on the economy of the nation in which the good was produced. Consumers, they argued, bore the ultimate responsibility for the rippling consequences of their purchases. Actions taken at the cash register have a host of effects, most of them invisible to the shopper, who is bound up in a dense and extensive "web" or "chain" (words that consumer activists have used since the early nineteenth century) that was recognized, from the beginning, to be potentially worldwide. The circular for the first "free produce" store in 1826, for example, noted that if "we continue to purchase and consume the labor of slaves . . . their chains [will be] more firmly riveted." It is notable that Benjamin Lundy, the proprietor of this store, addressed the circular "To the Farmers, Planters, Merchants, and others, in the United States, and elsewhere," inviting the web of consumers everywhere to, in Wendell Phillips's words, "melt the slave's chains away." A century later, in the 1930s, Horace Kallen compared consumers to "a web, a network" and Stuart Chase included a chapter, "The Web," on the significance of the invisible but interconnected social bonds of consumption in his book *The Economy of Abundance*. In his 1963 "Letter from Birmingham Jail," the Reverend Martin Luther King, Jr., a few years removed from his leadership of one of the most successful boycotts in U.S. history, announced the "inter-relatedness of all communities" with the following image: "We are caught in an inescapable web of mutuality, tied in a single garment of destiny." Thus, the metaphors of the web and the chain have provided consumer activists and others with a way of conceptualizing what the sociologist Viviana A. Zelizer has called "the means by which people bridge the apparently unbridgeable gap between social solidarity and commercialized transaction."[4]

Over time, consumer activists came to understand this web as bi- and even multidirectional. Not only did consumers affect how products were sold and made, but, in turn, they believed that these goods and their makers and sellers also affected consumers.[5] Beginning in the late nineteenth century, consumer activists stressed the hidden dangers of some products, such as disease-infested meat produced in faraway packing houses, and the equally hidden virtues of others, such as sanitary, inexpensive, standardized brand-name goods. In many cases, they promoted products as ethical because of how they were made. They also emphasized the problems that high costs and inaccurately or falsely labeled and misleadingly advertised products, such as patent medicines, posed for consumers. In thus providing a context for understanding the relationship between goods and people, consumer activists suggested both that individual consumers influenced the entire web of production and, likewise, that the chain of production altered those individual consumers. In this worldview, any actions affecting the radiating links on the "chain" of consumption necessarily impinged on every other one.

This book treats the disparate actions of diverse groups for variegated purposes as a tradition because there are continuities in action and also continuities in patterns of thought among them. This is not to say that theories of the impact of consumption were unchanging: as consumer society matured, as notions of politics and citizenship metamorphosed, as the identity of the participants, and of the groups consumer activists aimed to help, changed, and as the economy and the media mushroomed, understandings of the social impact of organized consumption and nonconsumption transformed as well. Although each iteration of consumer activism was unique in relation to its predecessors, and was itself a site of struggle among its participants, a core set of beliefs about the economic and ethical powers of consumption has linked groups with otherwise different purposes and membership and typically little awareness of those who came before them. Whatever the particularities of their specific political engagements, consumer activists have agreed, and often challenged others in society with the belief, that consumption was inherently *political*, which is to say bound with the use of aggregate purchasing power to promote justice. This is not to suggest that consumer activists agreed about precisely how consumer power operated or about the meaning of justice. For example, antebellum America's abolitionist boycotters of slave-made goods and white Southern proponents of "nonintercourse" with the North employed nearly identical tactics to promote antithetical goals, putting their shared belief in the power of organized consumption to work for opposing causes.

Just as consumer activists have shared understandings about the political power of consumption and sets of tactics, even when these have been used to differing political ends, so too have they been guided by a relatively stable theory of moral action, even as they have disagreed about what constituted morality. Generations of consumer activists have shared a view of the consumer as a potentially robust political actor, whose power extended as far as the factories, distributors, and stores (as well as the people that owned and worked in these facilities) producing and selling the goods he or she bought. Shopping was simultaneously a social, moral, and political act because of the causal impact of purchasing goods. The inescapable consequences of shopping, the fact that buying a good directly affected its makers, sellers, and the environment, necessitated consumer responsibility. Consumer ethics, in the form of an awareness of the consequences of one's actions at the cash register, was, for consumer activists, the necessary corollary to consumer power. Over the course of American history, consumer activists have believed that organized consumption or nonconsumption could sustain (or, conversely, weaken) not just a product but a cause, a people, even a nation. By buying or refusing to buy such diverse products and services as British tea, slave-made goods, holidays at Northern resorts, union-label cigars, rides on Jim Crow streetcars,

Japanese silk, table grapes, Nestle's chocolate, and Nike sneakers, collectivities of consumers have sought not merely to make their preferences known but also to help or to harm materially the producers and sellers of these goods and services. For example, "free produce" advocates believed that slavery existed because people bought slave-made products and they advocated boycotting these goods—and concomitantly increasing demands for goods made by free labor—not just to announce a dislike of the slave system but tangibly to weaken it. Similarly, according to the advocates of the boycott of Japanese goods in the 1930s, to avoid buying or wearing silk was to undermine the Japanese economy and the capacity of its army. Shopping or boycotting, in this view, was not just declarative but performative. Purchasing Japanese silk stockings, according to boycott proponents, was not only to profess indifference to the victims of that country's militarism; it was also directly to harm those victims. "Your stockings kill babies," proclaimed a pamphlet of a group supporting the boycott.[6]

Consumer activists have believed that consumers, more than any other group, could, and indeed necessarily did, exercise the intertwined forces of economic power and moral responsibility. In so doing, they consistently challenged contemporary standards of moral responsibility not, as did most critics, because those standards set the bar too high but because they set it too low. Both humanitarianism in the late eighteenth and nineteenth centuries and philanthropy in the twentieth and twenty-first have urged individuals to feel sympathy for, and to alleviate the suffering of, others, typically through charitable donations. But they have not held the individuals whose donations and support they seek responsible for that suffering. By contrast, consumer activists, from the late eighteenth century onward, posited a more tightly linked world (hence the favored metaphors of the web and the chain), in which there existed no guilt-free observers. If humanitarians and philanthropists urged Good Samaritans to step in after the suffering, consumer activists held shoppers liable for the suffering. Consumer choices, in their view, were inevitably moral choices as well. This concept of long-distance solidarity also challenges a more recent account of morality known as "proximal empathy," or the injunction to be kind to those nearest to us by kin and distance. Unlike utilitarian ethicists, notably Peter Singer, who criticize the notion of proximal empathy because it favors those who happen to live near us (and those we know and can see) rather than strangers, advocates of long-distance solidarity claimed that anyone affected by one's consumption patterns was not really a stranger.[7] Consumer activists proclaimed the "death of moral distance" long before recent debates about "globalization"; indeed, one might say that they invented the concept.[8] No matter how far away physically, victims of deleterious consuming practices were not unrelated to consumers in a moral sense. Consumer activists, in effect, proposed a new physics of time and space, highlighting the real-time effects of consumption and suggesting that in an increasingly global market economy, the moral impact of one's actions was not determined by physical propinquity but by the market-based effects of one's economic actions. Beginning in the late eighteenth century, the logic of consumer activism held that consumption might and probably did influence the morality of one's relationships with distant and unknown workers (as well their employers, environment, and country) who produced the goods they bought, as it did with relations with neighbors.

The distance it potentially traversed and the number of people it potentially encompassed made consumer activism powerful. These features also made it impossible to understand through the senses, since boycotters based their politics on the faraway impact of purchasing choices. One of the key transformations traced in this book is the movement from what I call early modern consumer activism to modern consumer activism. The former, which predominated during the American Revolution, was characterized by face-to-face direct actions. Modern consumer activism, in contrast, which began in nascent form during the Revolutionary era and matured in the nineteenth century, was defined by efforts to coordinate the consumption of like-minded but not necessarily proximate people in order to influence manufacturers and producers, who also often resided in other towns, states, or even countries. Each person, in this vision, was a node on a network that might traverse distances as small as a few city blocks or as large as a continent or an ocean. As a politics of the immediate and the local gave way to one of mediation and distance, as Americans became aware that they were routinely "engaging in relationships with people they did not see," consumer activists recognized that they needed to develop sensory metaphors for their efforts. Colston E. Warne, the leader of CU, spoke in 1936 of the need for consumers to develop a "sixth sense," to prevent the problem of "buy[ing] blindly." Much earlier, in 1882, an Evanston newspaper, invoking a metaphor already well established by consumer activists, described the "pocket nerve" as "the slender, impalpable, but all-sensory thread" that connects the brain with the "pocket book." This nerve did not, of course, have a real physiological existence. But the metaphor suggested that consumer activism had a potent, if invisible, impact. Claiming that the pocket nerve was "the most sensitive nerve in the organism of the Northern people," the *Richmond Enquirer* predicted that a Southern boycott of the North in 1859 was likely to succeed.[9] Consumer activists also used the phrase "medium of the pocket" to suggest that the market provided an effective means to affect potentially distant actors.

A social understanding of goods undergirded the ethical stance of consumer activists, who have long argued that embedded within every good and service was a story: the story of who produced it, under what conditions, and who profited from its sale. This narrative unfolded backward in time from the moment of consumption, like a film playing in reverse, dramatizing the ways in which a good was harvested, manipulated, transformed, packaged, advertised, and sold. Consumer activists also recognized that the story was rarely self-evident. Appearances could, and usually did, deceive. Products did not, as a rule, announce their moral provenance, which, in any case, was often contested. To provide a narrative of these products required instilling an awareness of the invisible social context of products, one that consumer activists tried to disseminate through vivid descriptions of, for example, "blood-stained" British tea or cotton that howled with the cries of its enslaved producers. "Things made in unhappiness carry spiritual infection," according to a member of the NCL.[10] Telling these stories about products required confronting the alternative narratives spun by the makers and sellers of goods and services, who, uninterested in how the goods came into being, were solely concerned with how these goods might affirm or alter one's identity in the future. By the lights of the producers and marketers, goods magically appeared, without a history, prettily packaged, on the shelves of stores—or illustrated in catalogs and, eventually, on the Internet—promising personal satisfaction and sometimes individual transformation and even liberation. Battling against this kind of commodity fetishism, consumer activists argued that goods, services, and commercial amusements were not free-floating signifiers but rather were enmeshed in a web of (usually hidden) labor, markets, and environments. As we shall see, divergent groups of consumer activists conceptualized this web differently, emphasizing varying aspects of the production, distribution, and consumption processes. Some consumer activists, especially those in the twentieth century associated with the new consumer movement, emphasized the cost and quality of goods rather than the conditions of their production. Although they reversed the process, emphasizing the effects of products on consumers, and attending to hidden dangers or flaws of products, the virtues of cheaper substitutes, and the value of comparing similar goods, even advocates of this utilitarian strand of consumerism situated goods socially. Others, who stressed the environmental consequences of consumption, continued to highlight the social impact of purchasing decisions. Whatever their emphasis, all consumer activists have nonetheless understood the imperative to narrate the social life of commodities, to share their story, their history, in effect the autobiography that these commodities would themselves tell if they could speak.

Attending in all these ways to the dynamic interrelationship between the individual and the social, the private and the public, the personal and the political, consumer activists magnify, often to the point of exaggeration, the impact of individual action on the public sphere. They highlight the social implications of relations usually hidden from the public, especially in the form of exploitative employment relationships, from slavery in the nineteenth century to sweatshops in the twenty-first. Over time, and even within eras, consumer activists have offered several interpretations of these relationships, with some placing more emphasis on individual aspects of consumer activism, others on the social.

Even as they have vested extraordinary power in individual consumers, a majority of consumer activists have at the same time denigrated the self and its desires, along with the practices of consumption that mediate that relationship. This strand of thinking holds to the original meaning of consumption as destruction, and emphasizes the dangers of consumption, usually in both personal and social terms. Adherents of this mode of consumer activism have understood consumption as generating unvirtuous, immoral people and injustice. Because, in their view, virtuous people do not consume but rather sacrifice, it is not surprising that the pantheon of consumer activists, from Benjamin Lundy and Lucretia Mott, the Quaker leaders of the free produce movement, to F. J. Schlink, the founder of the first product-testing organization, Consumers' Research, to Ralph Nader, is dominated by exemplars of asceticism. Today's "voluntary simplicity" movement, itself highly suspicious of the practice of consumption, extends this tradition.[11]

Consumer activism, however, is a capacious tradition, and, as we will see, other ways of seeing the relationship between virtue and justice have periodically emerged, and even briefly become dominant. A steady stream of consumer activists has argued that the posture of asceticism undervalues the potentially positive social impact of consumption—indeed, that it denies the very premises that made consumer activism conceivable and a viable form of political engagement in the first place. If individuals eschew the marketplace, they fail to exercise the force that drives political economy. For these consumer activists, individual or coordinated withdrawal, while sometimes necessary, is far less effective than organizing the consuming power of the market to effect change.

Yet another set of consumer activists has pushed the issue of consumer power further, stressing that individual pleasure and group solidarity are consistent with and sometimes necessary for justice to prevail. Calling into question the equation of virtue with sacrifice, they claim that virtue cannot be understood in individual terms, but only by way of the social impact of one's actions. Consumers could thus combine virtue with pleasure, and indeed with the quest for beauty and fashion. Denigrating these pleasurable and aesthetic aspects of consumerism, they argue, has limited the appeal of consumer activism in a society whose dominant culture promised, although it did not necessarily deliver, these as the birthright of all Americans. From the early nineteenth century to the present, a strand of activists has insisted on combining style with substance, and uniting the beautiful and the good. As Marci Zaroff, the founder of Under the Canopy, a line of clothing and home furnishings made from organic cotton and other natural fabrics, recently said, "If you give people fit and style and value, and also appeal to their values, it's not 'Why would I buy it?' It's 'Why wouldn't I buy it?'"[12]

Although they may have differed about the relationship between individual pleasure and social justice, consumer activists have consistently promised shoppers an immediate and extensive capacity to assist others or to support a cause, often from afar. Theirs was a seemingly cosmopolitan form of political engagement, since it linked the consumer, not only with other like-minded consumers, but also with potentially distant workers, employers, landscapes, products, and nations. Theoretically, all manner of elective affinities could be expressed through consumer activism—solidarities that would be difficult, perhaps impossible, to express through conventional understandings of politics and group loyalty. Yet though consumer activists challenged, in these ways, the claim that all politics and all relationships were local, they often made this challenge, perhaps paradoxically, through what I call "identity-affirming" consumption. Their conception of solidarity may have eclipsed distance, making imagined communities actual. Nonetheless, this conception of solidarity often reinforced rather than subverted older loyalties, sometimes old and frequently invented, to clan, race, or nation. Long-distance solidarity did not necessarily weaken particularism, ethnocentrism, or jingoism. On the contrary, it often promoted prejudice because it made possible a potentially worldwide web of commercial chauvinism. Long-distance solidarity thus facilitated the construction of racial and ethnic identities and enabled these constructions to extend beyond a single place. The history of consumer activism as a history of people linking their actions with unseen others is also a history of those very same people who, in linking their actions in this way, claim membership in a group, often through the denigration of a despised other. In this way, much like the Internet does today, consumer activism frequently provided a cosmopolitan forum for particularistic ends.

The nonimportation, nonconsumption movements of the Revolutionary era, for example, helped invent American identity, in large measure by attenuating the colonists' sense of Britishness. Since then, consumer activists have instructed shoppers to, variously, "Buy American," "Buy Native American," "Buy Black," "Buy labor," and, in the heated partisan climate of the early twenty-first century, "Buy Blue State"—and in so doing to support one identity and often to weaken one's personal claim to, or solidarity with, other potential identities.[13] Consumer activism, however, does not always or necessarily promote parochial interests. Consumer activists have invented and reinforced any number of new solidarities, such as that between shoppers and farm workers during the United Farm Workers' grape boycott of the 1960s and 1970s. Consumer activism has also worked on behalf of "others" who are victims of prejudice. African American consumers during the Jim Crow era, for example, often lent their patronage to department stores and the Sears catalog, whose one-price system and anonymity allowed them to purchase goods on the same terms as others and also to avoid mistreatment by racist local merchants.

Consumer activism, all this of suggests, must be studied in the context of consumer society. Consumer activists have frequently understood themselves as opponents of consumer society, and it is true that over time their dominant message of sacrifice, suspicion of pleasure, willingness to challenge prevailing fashions, and attempts to claim the seemingly private act of consumption as eminently political have frequently put them at odds with mainstream manifestations of consumer culture. But, like a photographic negative, they have shed light on consumer society, even as they have criticized and denounced some its key features. They have also participated in, and helped shape, consumer culture in a wide variety of ways. One understudied aspect of consumer activism that this book seeks to emphasize is that many consumer activists have promoted not an ideology of anticonsumption but alternative forms of consumption, including so-called buycotts, which are not a recent development but instead form an integral part of almost every episode of consumer activism from the "free produce" stores run by abolitionists to the many forms of ethical goods marketed to consumers today. Second, rather than taking consumer society to be unchanging and unchangeable, many consumer activists have treated it as a site of contestation. They have not accepted that consumer society necessarily produced a particular kind of politics and in their actions have sought to demonstrate that consumer society could provide resources for the practices of politics they supported. Third, the rhetoric and practices of consumer activism, for the most part market based, owe their very existence to that institution and to the values of consumer society. Even where they have questioned the fundamental premises of mainstream consumer logic, most consumer activists have worked within its constraints and taken advantage of its benefits. Without consumer society there would be no consumer activism. Indeed, the logic of consumer activism has often mirrored, and sometimes anticipated, developments in consumer society. It is no coincidence that the nascent consumer activism of the boycotters of the American Revolution occurred at precisely the same moment as, according to eighteenth-century scholars, its twin, consumer society, was being born. Nor is it surprising that Northern "free produce" and Southern "nonintercourse" occurred during the era of the "market revolution." The first nationwide consumer organization, the NCL, formed in the late nineteenth century, coterminously with national name-brand goods, with which it shared the new corporate, impersonal moniker, like the National Biscuit Company, once again showing that consumer activism mirrored almost precisely the evolution of consumer society, and making it hard to determine which came first. In similar fashion, the Internet (our contemporary "Web") provides a new organizing tool for activists—witness the hundreds of Web sites advocating boycotts of one sort or another—as well as a new advertising venue for corporations. Some commentators emphasize the fundamentally consumer-oriented nature of consumer activists' rhetoric and practices in order to denigrate the activists for lacking purity or for being easily co-opted, a critique that many consumer activists themselves have shared. This moralism is less interesting from the standpoint of the genealogy I offer than consumer activists' creative attempts to find sources of political engagement in the powerful techniques and technologies of consumerism and their refusal to assume a teleology in which adoption of such techniques signaled defeat. Consumer activists have used, and often subverted, the techniques of consumer society for their own political purposes, practicing "culture jamming," for example, long before the contemporary organization, Adbusters, coined the phrase in the 1990s.[14]

By reflecting and also shaping the evolving political and consumer culture, consumer activism provides a window into these transformations and developments. Whether rejecting it or adopting its techniques, consumer activists held up a mirror to consumer society. Similarly, in their use or rejection of the political vocabulary of their era, each generation of consumer activists gives us insight into political trends. Consumer activists in the Revolutionary era, for example, relied primarily on the agency of merchants' associations and political elites. During the age of Jackson, as the politics of deference weakened, ordinary consumers became the chief political actors of activist campaigns. As workers began self-consciously

identifying themselves as a class in society, they called for labor consumerism, a solidarity of working-class shoppers every bit as important as
the producerist solidarity of the shopfloor or the fields. Occasionally, consumer activism presages political and cultural developments. For example,
free produce activists used the word "consumer" at a time when most merchants continued to use the older term "customers." Nonintercourse advocates developed "white lists" of morally sanctioned goods generations before the NCL popularized the idea in the early 1900s. For their part, as we
shall see, NCL activists were Progressives *avant la lettre*. Perhaps most significant, consumer activists promoted a new conception of trust, which
did not require sight and touch, but rather depended on an understanding of how markets worked. Other blocs within consumer society, with different interests, put this notion to different uses. For example, through
his mail-order catalog, Richard Sears sought to make consumers trust him
and his unseen company in Chicago more than local merchants, by inviting customers to visit his Chicago warehouse, by publishing letters from
satisfied customers, and by letting readers in on the tricks of his competitors.[15] At the same time, advertisers began to undermine the visible and
the local by suggesting, for example, that biscuits sanitarily packaged under the national Uneeda brand were safer than one plucked, at one's own
grave risk, out of the germ-infested local grocer's cracker barrel. Of course,
the NCL and its muckraking allies soon became aware that corporate production often generated invisible dangers of its own, witness Upton Sinclair's stomach-churning description of the meatpacking industry in his
classic muckraking novel of 1906, *The Jungle*. The point was not that goods
of distant provenance were inherently more trustworthy than local ones. It
was rather that consumption brought the household into the public sphere
(both near and far) and the public sphere into the home. This is why consumer activists sought to promote knowledge about both, and why the
consumer movement often described itself as engaged in a battle with advertisers to serve as the "eyes and ears" of the consumer.

A historical perspective reveals that, in spite of the continuities in ideology, activists have, over time, understood the meaning of consumption in
very different ways, which has affected how they have practiced the politics
of consumption. These understandings map fairly neatly onto the three
centuries of consumer activism: the eighteenth, nineteenth, and twentieth
(into the early twenty-first). An understanding of consumption as the use of
a good already purchased guided the politics of consumption practiced by
the boycotters of the American Revolution. Following the standard meaning of the term in the late eighteenth century, their pamphlets and dec-
larations called upon citizens to neither "purchase nor consume" British

goods, suggesting that these were separate acts, chronologically and episte-
mologically distinct. For these boycotters, consumption was synonymous
with the use of a good rather than with its purchase (a distinction that was
just being called into question by Adam Smith and the new political economists), and the use of a good, even if it had already been purchased, was
the key act to be avoided. Consumer activism to them was a form of symbolic politics. To wear homespun clothing was primarily to claim a badge of
membership in the new nation and only secondarily to harm British manufacturers. Laying claim to an older moral economy, eighteenth-century
consumer activists took subsistence (in the form of fair prices for bread
and other staples) to be the right of all citizens and their families. This view
occasionally led them, and later generations, to collective action on behalf
of poor consumers in the form of bread riots and demands for an assize on
bread. Their consumer politics was also linked to early modern forms of
consumer activism, such as social ostracism and public embarrassment.
Thus, they emphasized honor and dishonor and sought to wear emblems
of their support and to physically show their enemies to be dishonorable,
most famously through the threat of tar and feathers. Nineteenth-century
consumer activists, the first generation to accept the Smithian revolution
in economic thought, understood consumption essentially as we do today,
as the purchase of a good or service. For them, the politics of consumption
therefore had less to do with the use or nonuse of a good—although this
too was important—and more to do with the prior, and to them fundamental, act of its purchase. Moreover, nineteenth-century consumers generally
aimed to assist not themselves as consumers but those whose lives they believed they could improve through coordinated acts of consumption. In
the early decades of the twentieth century, by contrast, not just consumption, but also consumers themselves became a key focus. Defining consumers as a class in a pluralistic society, consumer activists came to see the
politics of consumption primarily as a means of protecting and defending
the rights of this new class. Whereas the prototypical nineteenth-century
activist used consumption as a tool to help others (the nation, slaves, the
South as a region), a significant strand of twentieth-century consumer activists sought the help of others, mainly experts and politicians, on behalf
of the new category, the "consumer interest."

New modes of consumer activism did not simply replace previous
ones; old and new often overlapped. The symbolic politics of consumption
(wearing Kente cloth, for example) and the moral economy of consumption (say, in the form of the 1966 "housewives' strike" over the high cost
of meat) continue as political forces into the present. Similarly, the view of
consumers as a group needing protection, while an important strand of

twentieth-century activism, coexisted alongside the view of consumption as a mode of solidarity with others. In the 1960s and 1970s, many millions of Americans supported, without any sense of contradiction, Ralph Nader's campaign for a Consumer Protection Agency (CPA) and Cesar Chavez's call for a boycott of table grapes, even as they adopted aesthetic styles that announced their claim to ethnic, racial, political, or countercultural identities.

Consumer activism has had an enduring, if sometimes uneasy, affiliation with liberalism, which is, not coincidentally, a political tradition as long standing, capacious, and protean as consumer activism itself. In the eighteenth century, liberals promoted a new conception of economic virtue, challenging republican suspicions of commerce. In the nineteenth century, liberals stood for a belief in the liberating power of markets and of the social consequences of seemingly private economic activities. And in the twentieth century, liberals began to argue that state protection and regulation was necessary for freedom to flourish. Transformations in consumer activism accorded roughly with liberalism's evolving self-understandings. As liberalism splintered in the mid-twentieth century—a time when one could find left-leaning liberals, interest-group liberals, anticommunist liberals, and fellow-traveling liberals—consumer activists too faced a set of schisms. In the later twentieth century, many liberals embraced consumer activism, and leaders of the consumer movement supported what the historian Robert Collins has called "growth liberalism."[16] CU's agenda accorded with an expanding economic pie and an economy of mass consumption. At the same time, as liberalism separated itself from radicalism in the post–World War II years, liberal consumer groups defined themselves less as radical consumer activists than as reforming consumer advocates, whose chief function was to lobby for laws and business practices that would be favorable to the "consumer interest." Both John F. Kennedy's New Frontier and, more emphatically, Lyndon B. Johnson's Great Society recognized a government role for consumer advocacy. Kennedy and Johnson believed in the need for consumer representation in government; and Kennedy declaimed a Consumer's Bill of Rights. In some ways, the high-water mark of liberalism also marked the acme of popularity for the consumer movement. In the early 1970s, polls showed public sentiment overwhelmingly in favor of the CPA bill, huge numbers of Americans claimed to support the United Farm Workers' grape boycott as well as the incipient environmental movement, and Ralph Nader was consistently on the list of the most popular and admired Americans.

It is probably not coincidental that these interrelated movements began to lose popularity at roughly the same time. Both consumer activism and liberalism faced an organized and formidable set of opponents who succeeded in delegitimating them, in large measure by conflating the two. Coined in the 1920s, the word "consumerism" was reminted in the 1960s not by advocates of the consumer movement but by its opponents in the business world, who aimed to belittle it as a subset of their main enemy, modern liberalism. The origins of the vocabulary and tactics of the New Right can be found in embryonic form in the 1960s and 1970s in conservative opposition to the CPA and to Naderism, both of which they defined as subsets of liberalism. Although these experts called themselves consumer advocates, the critics successfully redefined consumer advocates as arrogant enemies of ordinary consumers.

The critique of what was usually called consumerism in the late twentieth century, however, did not diminish the importance of consumer activism as a political strategy, even to its conservative critics. For not all consumer activists were self-identified liberals. Indeed, in the late twentieth century, critics of liberalism, from both the Left and the Right, seized on consumerist tactics and called for armies of boycotters and economic supporters to promote their causes. Leftist protesters against globalization attacked neoliberalism, in part by critiquing the brands (and sometimes attacking and even defacing the storefronts) of the leading purveyors of global consumption, such as Starbucks coffee and Nike sneakers.[17] Conversely, the Southern Baptist boycotters of the Walt Disney Company decried that company's liberalism, which they defined as a cultural permissivism that signaled a rejection of traditional values. Furthermore, many boycotts now, as in the past, have illiberal justifications and goals. Around the world, boycotts continue to be used to punish unpopular ethnic or racial groups or to promote jingoism. This side of consumer activism, not often acknowledged by its liberal champions, should call into question the idea that there is any natural or permanent alliance between consumer activism and a single, virtuous political stance, including late twentieth-century liberalism. But this does not undermine the claim that there has been a close relationship between consumer activism and philosophical liberalism, which both attribute great collective power to the expression of individual economic preferences.

A history of consumer activism must include the stories of all stripes of consumer activists, not merely those who fit a particular model to whom we may feel personally sympathetic. Such a history must take into account the arguments and strategies of the opponents of consumer activism, both within particular movements and without. Often, the most vocal and effective opposition to specific instances of consumer activism was internal. For example, abolitionists who opposed their colleagues in the "free produce" movement criticized it far more vociferously than did their slaveholding enemies, who largely ignored the movement. Similarly, white Southern opponents of the strategy of "nonintercourse" were more vocal in their criticism than were the movement's ostensible Northern enemies. Indeed, one of the leitmotifs of this book is the internal contestation that has characterized almost every boycott campaign.

External critics of consumer activism existed as well. Often, these were critics of the cause as much as of the tactics of consumer activism, but they typically justified their opposition by condemning consumer politics as immoral, un-American, or both. For example, shortly after the labor movement developed a set of consumer tactics in the late nineteenth century—quickly dubbed the "labor boycott"—their opponents in law and business developed antiboycott leagues, which not only condemned the causes for which labor stood, but successfully defined the tactic as illegal. In 1939 the consumer movement was one of the first charged by the House Committee on Un-American Activities (HUAC) as a key element in the "communist transmission belt." From the late 1930s through the 1950s, the consumer movement was, along with the labor and Civil Rights movements, dogged with the charge that it was communist led and inspired, and, like these other movements, it underwent internal purges as a result of these charges. Later still, as the era of McCarthyism came to an end, critics of the consumer movement focused less on the communism of the consumer movement than on its liberalism. By the 1960s, the charges of anticommunism had become rare and a new and potent form of anticonsumerism had emerged, in which the consumer movement was equated with and served as a metaphor for a kind of big-government, elitist liberalism. More recently, critics of consumer activism, building on this critique of excessive government-sponsored consumer advocacy, have decried boycotters for denying consumers their rights as shoppers in a free market of goods. In recent years, giant and powerful companies, including Microsoft and Wal-Mart, have sought to convince consumers that corporations are better equipped to serve consumers' interests than American consumers themselves. "Wal-Mart acts as a bargaining agent for . . . families—achieving on their behalf a negotiating power they would never have on their own," claimed Lee Scott, the company's chairman in 2005. "*Wal-Mart harnesses the collective clout of ordinary Americans to make their lives better.*"[18] For these firms, consumer activism, understood as the collective aggregation of individual consumer power, is unnecessary and passé, best replaced by a kind of consumer passivism in which Americans, recognizing the might of business's bargaining power, cede to corporations the job that was once their own.

By conventional measures, most of the movements discussed in this book failed to achieve their putative goals. Taking account of their undeniable failures should not, however, blind us to the many successes of consumer activists. For "success" and "failure" are not absolute, but relative terms, and how one defines them makes all the difference. If we call consumer activists failures because they did not unseat an immoral economic system, a giant corporation, or a national economy, perhaps our standards of judgment need to be altered. By this stringent standard, nearly every social movement throughout history must be judged a failure. Consumer activists may not often have succeeded in achieving the ends they desired, but they often helped to publicize, popularize, and politicize causes. More important than any single consumer campaign has been their creation and popularization of both a cognitive framework that encourages individuals to recognize human interdependence, to ponder the distant, even global, consequences of their actions, and a political framework that offers a prescription for collective action. Although unambiguous victory was rare, there were many significant partial victories. Frequently, as this book will show, the most important accomplishments of consumer activists were not ones that they intended or even imagined. Using the hindsight that is the prerogative of the historian, I narrate a history of consumer activism that, far from being only a catalog of failures, is also a story of surprising successes, even if unforeseen by those passing on new elements and frequently unacknowledged by those who make use of them. Not least among these success stories has been the staying power of both the tactics and the philosophy of consumer activism through every generation of American history.

Among the chief reasons for Americans' near-continuous uses of consumer activism are the enormous latitude of the category "consumer" and the low barriers to entry for potential boycotters or buycotters. These may also be its biggest weaknesses. If, as consumer activists in the twentieth century maintained, "everybody" was a consumer, this meant that, while they formed a large, even universal, category, consumers were inherently diffuse and diverse, possessing other, often more salient, identities as well, affiliations often at odds with a person's consumer aspect. It is no wonder then that not only proponents of consumer activism claim the universality of this category; their opponents made this claim just as frequently and they did in order to demonstrate that this identity was too thin a reed on which to build a successful movement. However, many, perhaps most, episodes of consumer activism called on consumers to act not primarily on behalf of a universal consumer identity but because their efforts in this realm could assist a group in need. It was sometimes the case that the consumer belonged to this group; for example, working-class consumers may have been asked to boycott an antiunion employer. Often, however, boycott leaders asked consumers to assist groups to which they did not belong. When consumers themselves were the group in need of assistance (as in a meat boycott or complaints about the high cost of living), this identity was usually defined as in conflict with another group in society (greedy supermarket chains, for example). Although they welcomed all buyers to join the causes they promoted, consumer activists rarely called for action in the service of promoting a universal consumer identity. Instead, consumers participated in an activity about which they had a shared cognitive and moral understanding. Most often activists sought to mobilize consumption in conjunction with other interests—as, for example, African American consumers, working-class consumers, antifascist consumers, or "green consumers."

This suggests that another source of variation—in addition to the shaping fact of changes in the dominant understandings of consumption in a given period—was that consumer activists employed their methods on behalf of a wide range of causes. The methods of consumer activism, as we will see, have been employed by the left, the right, and very often groups whose politics are not easily placed on the traditional political spectrum. Beyond this issue of the application of similar tactics, based on shared underlying theories of moral action—the bidirectional causal impact of consumption and the concomitant long-distance solidarity bred by that understanding—activists have held very different conceptions of the goal and meaning of consumer engagements. This unique and paradoxical combination of unity and diversity, the fact that similar tactics and underlying epistemologies could be put to different, even opposing, uses by pretty much every subset of the American population over the course of the country's history, provide the keys to the staying power and variety of the tradition of consumer activism.

✳

Despite a growing interest in the history of consumer society and its relationship to politics, historians have tended to treat the topic of consumer activism in a piecemeal way and in isolation, focusing on one particular episode or another. Those scholars who have proposed a more systematic understanding of consumer activism have inaccurately characterized it as an episodic twentieth-century development, or as a subset of the broader issue of that century's politics of consumption. After an obligatory mention of the boycotts of the Revolutionary era, historians of consumer activism have, for the most part, leapfrogged the nineteenth century entirely to examine what they take to be the birth of modern consumer activism in the Progressive Era. American consumer activism, in the standard version, is discontinuous: born prematurely in the 1770s, it was dormant for more than a century before emerging in the twentieth century, and even then as a periodic phenomenon of the 1900s, 1930s, 1960s, and 1990s.[19] Moreover, these scholars have frequently conflated consumer activism with something called the "consumer movement," assuming that they are one and the same.

Initially sharing many of these assumptions, I began this book as a study of twentieth-century consumer activism. In the process of researching the topic, I examined the archival records of every major, as well as many minor and evanescent, American consumer organizations, among them (in chronological order of their founding) the NCL, CR, CU, the League of Women Shoppers (LWS), and the Consumer Education and Protection Association. The histories of these organizations—their tactics, philosophies, and disagreements—play a significant role in my story. However, the scope of this book changed and broadened as I explored the minutes, newspapers, and pamphlets of other groups, such as nonimportation clubs, free produce societies, nonintercourse associations, and labor and Civil Rights groups, and as I read newspapers which described hundreds of boycotts for a wide variety of causes throughout the nineteenth century. Members of these groups neither defined themselves as consumer activists nor saw their cause as fighting on behalf of consumers. Nonetheless, they called on their supporters to act in their capacity as consumers and they employed sophisticated consumerist tactics and philosophies. What these records reveal is not only that consumer activism existed well before the twentieth century, but also that eighteenth- and nineteenth-century consumer activists developed a philosophy and vocabulary of consumer activism that twentieth-century (and contemporary) activists, including those in the consumer movement, employed and modified, despite their generally spotty memory of these predecessors. Although it was certainly not their intention, pre-twentieth-century groups set the template of modern consumer activism. These early groups typically failed to achieve their intended goals, whether that was abolition, Southern commercial independence, or the defeat of Jim Crow. But their efforts established a way of thinking about consumption and a mode of action that were themselves enduring, if unintended, achievements. Their understandings of the social consequences of consumption and of the consequent power of long-distance solidarity, while not ends in themselves for these groups, became the means by which citizens (and all those who aspired to take part in meaningful political action) could promote and effect social change. Even as particular movements faded and were forgotten, these means endured as a framework through which future generations conducted their own political efforts. Pre-twentieth-century activists also established a lasting archetype: the persona of the abstemious activist who abjured the pleasures of consumption and whose self-denial was his or her defining characteristic, a style that seemingly made their virtue self-evident.

These early movements also introduced tensions that continue to exist within consumer activism and occasionally to divide consumer activists. For one, even these early activists tended to forget or misremember those who came before them. While most paid obeisance to their Revolutionary forebears, they typically ignored other groups that had used consumer tactics. Second, almost from the beginning a minority of consumer activists challenged the valorization of sacrifice and insisted on assimilating rather than opposing the categories of aesthetics (including pleasure, fashion, and beauty) and justice (including morality, obligations, and ethics). Third, these early consumer activists, like their successors, assigned great power to ordinary consumers but at the same time generally distrusted the ability of these consumers to exercise such power wisely and justly. The tendency to decry the unwillingness of consumers to do either what was good for them or what was good for society has been a defining characteristic of most twentieth-century consumer activists. It followed from the frustrations of the pioneering pre-twentieth-century consumer activists, who were the first to recognize the power of organized consumption or nonconsumption and also the first to believe that ordinary consumers too often ignored the strictures of responsible consumption, thereby undermining causes that these consumers had it in their collective power to promote.

This long-term historical framework helps us to understand precursors to modern consumer activism and enables us to see that the "consumer movement" of the twentieth century had roots in a more-than-century-old political tradition. It also sets into relief what was original about the consumer movement of the twentieth century. The founders of the "consumer movement" did not invent consumer politics; they utilized theories of aggregate consumer power and long-distance solidarity enunciated by their forgotten predecessors. Understanding this context does not undermine the importance or originality of this movement, which took consumers themselves to be the chief beneficiaries of their actions. From the Progressive Era onward, the consumer movement is a central strand of the story of consumer activism. Even this strand, however, needs to be understood in its full diversity. After all, the "consumer movement" consisted of both the activists of the left-wing LWS and their enemies in the conservative product-testing organization CR. Its single most important organization, CU, had multiple and not always consistent agendas. Examining CU in light of the history of consumer activism highlights these diverse and conflicting agendas.

Studying consumer activism over the long term not only allows us to look backward in time; it also broadens the conception of what counts as consumer activism and leads us to recognize that this phenomenon is more complex, diffuse, and contested than a study of twentieth-century consumer organizations alone would suggest. Exclusively examining self-defined consumer groups unnecessarily narrows both the periodization and distorts the meaning and significance of consumer activism. Consumer activism is a continuous, not periodic, as well as a contested, not monolithic, political tradition in American history. By tracing the origins of consumer activism to the eighteenth century and following its development through the nineteenth, twentieth, and twenty-first centuries, this book situates it as a significant, and understudied, strand of American political culture, a durable but flexible mode of political engagement. This long view of consumer activism highlights continuities, transformations, and tensions in the theories and practices of consumer activists. By examining consumer activist movements sequentially, this book shows the ways in which each iteration built, whether consciously or not, on previous movements, how each simultaneously extended the tradition of consumer activism but also modified it and sometimes even squared off against it. It also demonstrates the ways in which consumer activists both reflected and shaped American political and consumer culture.

By providing a typology of consumer activism over time, this book seeks to understand the evolution of an American political tradition. By asking similar questions of each movement, it charts changes and continuities in the tradition, and it also situates each movement in the political and consumer culture of its era. Among the questions the book systematically asks of each movement under consideration (and to which the appendix, a chart labeled "Consumer Movements," provides a brief overview) are the following: Who was doing the work of boycotting or buycotting? Who were the putative beneficiaries of such actions? How were boycotts justified? What were the methods and institutional forms of consumer activists? What was their vision of consumer society? Who opposed the movement and why? How did activists in each movement remember previous consumer activists and what connective tissue linked it to movements that came before and those that followed? In addition to the deeds of consumer activists and their organizations, then, this book traces how consumer activists have justified their actions, what they believed the goal of their organized consumption (or nonconsumption) to be, and how these justifications and beliefs changed over time.

Comparing the answers to these questions across time and among contemporaneous movements provides a gauge of continuities and variations in the tradition of consumer activism and highlights the difficulties of overarching generalizations about this tradition. For example, in the many cases where consumer activists have singled out a representative product to be bought or eschewed—and therefore have appeared to be acting in similar fashion—it is instructive to categorize their reasons for doing so. Did they deem the product to be unhealthy (such as the rat-infested meat discovered by Upton Sinclair) or defective (e.g. the Corvair)? Did they deem it to be overpriced (as in cost-of-living protests)? Was a suitable and less expensive substitute readily available, as product-testing organizations constantly reminded shoppers? Or did they recommend avoiding the product not because it was inherently bad, but because of its association with something they deemed immoral (labor relations, a racially discriminatory system, an employer, a region, or a country one opposed)? Such comparisons reveal that even when the means of protest appears to be similar—in this case, the boycott of a single item—different justifications and understandings make necessary further distinctions among styles of consumer activism.

In comparing and contrasting these narratives and political visions, this book seeks to unravel not just the tactical but also the philosophical strands that have constituted this underacknowledged political tradition. One such strand is what I call "market-based radicalism," the perception that the market was a, perhaps the, key site of political struggle. Few consumer activists believed that the marketplace itself was inherently moral. Rather, they believed the market was a neutral vessel that reflected the morality of its actors and, because of its role in radiating the actions of consumers, the medium that made long-distance solidarity possible. For consumer activists, using the language of the marketplace and invoking its logic, however, did not imply a particular brand of politics. This was a radicalism that cut across ideological lines.

Another element of consumer activist's thought was their attempt to bridge and even to undermine the public-private divide. If, as I argued earlier, consumer activists shared with liberals a belief in the impact of private acts on the public sphere, they also challenged liberal thought by questioning the meaningfulness of the public-private distinction. Consumer activists stressed that shopping, often understood as the quintessentially private act in capitalist society, was in fact an unavoidably public responsibility, and that this was so for at least two reasons. Radiating inward in the web of consumption, goods brought into the home took with them the very real, if undetectable, congeries of relationships and forces that made their production, distribution, and sale possible. So in purchasing a product, one was also in effect mandating the social, environmental, and political system in which that good was produced. More important for most consumer activists was the outward radiation of shopping decisions, their belief that every individual consumer action had powerful social repercussions, which also were generally invisible to consumers but no less their responsibility. In this worldview, few consuming acts qualified as private. Challenging the widely held view of consumption as private and apolitical, consumer activists, while conceding that shopping was in part an expression of personal identity and an instrument of personal pleasure, also claimed that the social nature of goods in a capitalist society meant that shopping could never be reduced to such individual terms. Indeed, one of the reasons for the persistent appeal of consumer activism is it that promises concerned individuals a means of connection to (sometimes faraway) people and concerns.

Other strands revealed by the comparative study of episodes of consumer activism suggest persistent tensions that have existed both across time and within particular movements. The exploration of these tensions does not undermine the tradition of consumer activism; indeed, the tensions are an important part of what makes this political tradition so enduring. The most significant tension, one which continues to bedevil activists, involves the relationship between consumer activists and consumer society. More specifically, it concerns the relationship between the goal of justice, the defining mission of consumer activists (leaving aside for the moment the many different and even contradictory ways that such activists have understood justice), and pleasure, the chief promise of the architects of consumer society (leaving aside for the moment the many possible meanings of pleasure). This has been a conflicted relationship. While consumer society is the medium in which consumer activists have operated, many of them have seen its dominant values as antithetical to their own. As we have seen, consumer activists have put a high premium on virtuous sacrifice, on doing without, on abstention. To the extent they adopted an aesthetic, it was an antistyle, an overt abstemiousness that borders on the ostentatious, a fashion of the unfashionable. Yet, almost from the beginning, a subset of consumer activists has believed it possible to merge justice with pleasure, fashion, and style. This group has seen consumer society not just as the medium in which it operates but as a resource in its struggle to marry virtue and aesthetics. There remains deep suspicion among the majority of consumer activists about whether consuming pleasures accord with social justice. Yet from the "free produce" movement of the nine-teenth century to the "slow food" movement of the twenty-first century, some activists have attempted to enact such a merger, which I call "ethical aestheticism."

Another enduring tension involves the relationship between leaders and followers. Consumer activists have always held the democratic prem-ise that all consumers could be ethical actors. For most of American his-tory, consumer activism has been far more open to participants than that other measure of democratic citizenship, voting, which excluded slaves and, later, under Jim Crow, most African Americans and, until 1920, most women. This is one of the reasons why boycotts and buycotts have appealed especially, if not exclusively, to political outsiders. Purchasing items from the Sears catalog rather than a racist merchant or supporting a "Don't buy where you can't work" effort served as political acts for African Americans. Generally, too, activists welcomed all supporters as allies and comrades. At the same time, leaders of these movements have found their followers to be too few, too irresolute, too ignorant, or just too incompetent to sustain their cause. The twentieth-century culture of expertise exacerbated this ten-sion. Leaders of the NCL, like other Progressives, believed that consumers needed to be protected and led by experts, and often expressed frustration that consumers did not follow their lead. Later in the twentieth-century, this tension between leaders and followers took on a gender dimension, as the mostly male, scientifically trained leaders of the "consumer movement" sought to lead a movement whose ground troops were mostly women. Crit-ics of the consumer movement sought to exploit this tension between lead-ers and followers by charging the leaders with an elitist and undemocratic distrust of the masses they professed to represent.

A third tension relates to the fact that consumer activism was used for different, and sometimes opposing, purposes. Consumer activism was more than a tactic, which by definition can be used for many purposes and causes. If this were all it was, it would not deserve the name of a political tradition. Consumer activists also shared a worldview, an epistemology, and an understanding of the social nature of the making and consumption of goods. Yet in part because the web which connected individuals through goods to people, causes, environments, and nations was so global, so all en-compassing, they could imagine the social impact of shopping in a mul-titude of ways. Or even if they understood it in the same way, they could prize one element of the web over another. Boycotters of Japanese silk, for example, believed that their actions served to weaken that nation's ability to make war. Their opponents did not take issue with the social nature of consumption. Instead, they argued that the most significant victims in the causal web of this boycott were the American workers who converted Japanese silk into full-fashioned hosiery.

A final tension concerns the question of what actions qualify as consumer activism and what sorts of people should be understood as consumer activists. Modifying the motto of the LWS, "Use your buying power for justice," as the title of this book, I define consumer activism as organized consumption or, more often, nonconsumption that is collective, oriented toward the public sphere, grassroots, and conscious of the political impact of print and commerce. Hence, I devote little space to individualized consumer protests, such as irate letters to companies for selling defective or substandard products, Web sites that catalog customer dissatisfaction like www.starbucked.com (whose motto "Consumer activism is for everyone" suggests a different understanding of the phenomenon than I offer) or www.consumerist.com (where "shoppers bite back"), and what I call "personal boycotts," the decisions, frequently idiosyncratic, of individual shoppers not to buy a product or frequent a store. Similarly, I focus on questions of "style"—usually understood by cultural studies scholars as the subversive use of capitalist commodities by individuals or groups— and what Daniel Boorstin has called "consumption communities" (of, for example, Levis wearers, Harley-Davidson riders, or Gap shoppers) only to the extent that such styles and communities are part of a coordinated and conscious effort to affect other groups in the chain of production, distribution, and consumption.[20] My focus is more on bottom-up social movements than on top-down practices, such as state policies (regulation, taxation, and foreign policy) and business methods (including welfare capitalism, Fordism, and "green marketing"). However, because consumer activists, especially in the twentieth century, both shaped and were shaped by such state policies and corporate practices, as, for example, in campaigns for the regulation of food and drugs, I also examine the interaction of the activists with corporate policies and state and federal law. The tradition of consumer activism is a political hybrid, then, taking many forms.

Perhaps the dominant mode of consumer activism has been that practiced by self-identified outsiders within American politics, protesting what they have seen as the problems of the dominant economic system and using their consumer power as what one boycotter in 1899 called a "weapon of the weak against the strong," a form of political resistance outside the realm of electoral politics.[21] Even when they were in fact wealthy and powerful, as were colonial merchants in the 1760s or Southern firebrands on the eve of the Civil War, consumer activists often claimed to be opposing a system perpetuating some sort of inequity—in these cases, British imperialism, or the unholy alliance of Northern political and commercial interests. Other efforts, such as campaigns of working-class women for afford-able meat or of African Americans for discrimination-free public facilities, more accurately fit the description of outsider politics. However, impor-tant episodes of consumer activism did not operate solely in the subaltern mode. The women of the NCL, like the Progressive movement of which they were a part, not only formed alliances with social scientists and poli-ticians; they also saw themselves as experts whose job was not to follow the people, or even necessarily to organize them, but to educate and improve them, and sometimes even to scold them. At the same time, the women of this group were disenfranchised until 1920 and able to operate only in what Robyn Muncy has called the "female dominion" of reform politics.[22] Simi-larly, the "consumer movement" of product-testing organizations and con-sumer educators, which began in the late 1920s, saw its mission as lead-ing ordinary consumers through the complex maze of modern life, via the dissemination of scientifically produced technical knowledge. They too were elites in this sense but outsiders too in that they challenged the pow-erful business lobbies of the era. Advocates of the consumer movement sought a close alliance with the federal government during the world wars, especially in assisting with the conservation and rationing campaigns of World War II. From the 1930s onward, consumer activists fought for the creation of a cabinet-level Department of the Consumer; in the 1960s and 1970s, this energy was directed toward the promotion of legislation for a Consumer Protection Agency. The premise of these efforts was that, even with its powerful allies in government, the consumer interest was insuffi-ciently represented at law or understood by government officials and busi-ness leaders. Such alliances with the state produced consumer regulations and agencies at both the state and federal levels, as well as many frustra-tions, especially in the unsuccessful efforts to enact legislation to form a CPA. Many consumer activists in this period saw lobbying elites, rather than leading grassroots efforts, as their chief and defining duty. Esther Pe-terson, who, after Ralph Nader, was the leading consumer advocate of the postwar era, called herself a consumer activist (accurately in my view) al-though she spent a good part of her career working in the employ of the federal government and the Giant supermarket chain.[23] Consumer activists sought to shape what I call the nation's consumer regime—its taxation, en-vironmental, and regulatory policies—in order to create an environment for a certain type of consumption. These efforts, of necessity, required an engagement with business forces and the state, whose leaders, as Lizabeth Cohen has shown, had their own vision of the politics of consumption.[24] Consumer activists have staked a claim wherever the broad categories of consumption and citizenship, long their defining concerns, intersect.

PART I

THE BIRTH OF CONSUMER ACTIVISM

THE AMERICAN REVOLUTION CONSIDERED AS A CONSUMER MOVEMENT

A puzzle of American consumer activism that this book seeks to explore is the absence of historical memory that uniquely characterizes this political tradition. Whereas other social movements routinely mythologize, aggrandize, and often fictionalize the achievements of their predecessors, most consumer activists of the nineteenth and twentieth centuries made no attempt to do so, and by this omission failed to recognize the degree to which they were part of a continuing tradition.

In the long span of this history of omission and forgetting there is one significant exception: consumer activists, whatever their cause, have memorialized the American Founders, who, from the mid-1760s through independence, made consumer tactics central to their patriotic cause. Beginning in the 1820s, Southern nationalists embarking on a path of "nonintercourse" with the North wore homespun clothing and drank toasts to the surviving members of the founding generation, whom they saw as the pioneering consumerist patriots, and who blazed the path that they claimed to be following. Abolitionist boycotters of slave-made goods of the same period saw themselves as engaged in a mission of sanctifying the nation that also included tributes to the Founders; they proudly linked "antislavery to a beloved history of Revolutionary action." Later generations, no longer surrounded by living veterans of the Revolutionary era, continued to pay obeisance to them, finding in their actions sanction for their own consumerist efforts. Even the generation that first used the word "boycott," which was coined in 1880, was quick to deflect credit for the popularization of the idea to the Founders. Rare was the boycotter of the nineteenth or twentieth century, no matter the cause, who did not compare herself to the generation that defiantly wore homespun, tarred and feathered recalcitrant merchants, and dumped the king's immoral tea into Boston Harbor rather than purchase or drink it. Indeed, consumer activists ever since have restaged the Tea Party to highlight the justice of their cause. In response to the postwar inflation of 1946, the American Veterans Committee staged a mock Boston Tea Party, dumping bales representing overpriced goods into the water. In 1969, supporters of the United Farm Workers–led boycott of grapes enacted what they called a "modern version" of the Tea Party in Boston, dropping grapes into the famous harbor.[1]

Although other more direct and immediate precursors abounded, consumer activists generally hearkened back only to one era, the period between the Stamp Act and the Declaration of Independence. Whenever consumer activists shifted their gaze backward, they generally saw only the caboose and not the many trains between them and their Revolutionary forebears. If they saw themselves as part of a tradition at all, it was as part of a strangely discontinuous one; it was the story of the revival of a dormant form of political engagement. And so consumer activists of the late nineteenth century largely skipped over their antebellum predecessors and instead drew links to the Founders, only, in turn, to be themselves ignored or forgotten by future generations. The consumer movement of the 1930s ignored the nineteenth century entirely and found its roots in the 1770s. The movement of the 1960s, despite the strong continuities and obvious debt to the Depression generation, sought above all to claim the mantle of the men and women who made the nation through their consumer politics. Into the twenty-first century, the nonimporters of colonial America remain the lodestar for contemporary consumer activists.[2]

This selective memory is perhaps not so puzzling. It makes sense to link one's strategies to the movement that within a generation was valorized and whose flaws and divisions had been long forgotten. Drawing a connection to the patriots has long been a way for Americans of different eras to emphasize their virtue. It is also politically expedient, inoculating a movement against charges, frequently directed against consumer activists throughout American history, of irresponsibility or unpatriotic activity.

Embedded in these rememberings and misrememberings is also a claim about the roots of the philosophy and tactics of consumer activism. Consumer activists, in this view, pay tribute to the Founders, and not to other predecessors, because they were not only the developers of democratic politics in the United States but also the originators of American consumer politics. In this view—one which has been shared by both consumer activists and historians—the Founders invented the practice, if not the word, of the boycott as well as the sense of consumer responsibility that assigned consumers important duties as citizens, and the extended solidarity through the cash and print nexus. Just as the Founders' Constitution has been elaborated with amendments, without being fundamentally transformed, so too has their conception of consumer politics been adapted but not altered. The rest of the history of consumer activism is a footnote, a series of adaptations to what the historian T. H. Breen has called the "strikingly original" form of politics invented by the Revolutionaries.[3] Modern consumer activism, in this view, can be understood as the unfolding of a script set in the 1760s and 1770s.

This view of the Revolutionary origins of American consumer activism is incomplete. Through an examination of the forms of consumer activism developed by Americans in the 1760s and 1770s, this chapter argues that the originality of the Revolutionary generation's consumer tactics has been exaggerated and that historians have underestimated the degree to which the Founders drew on earlier traditions of popular protest. The similarities between the practices of modern consumer activists and those of the late eighteenth-century proponents of nonimportation have been overstated. A key to the differences between early modern consumer practices and later generations of consumer activists was that late colonial Americans held different understandings of the meaning of consumption. They lived in a world in which "consumer society" was newly emerging, in which to consume meant "to use" rather than "to purchase," and one which was deeply suspicious of the nascent practices and techniques that became central not only to promoters of modern commercial society but also to proponents of modern consumer activism.

Calling attention to the continuities between Revolutionary consumer activists and their early modern predecessors and noting that many hallmarks of consumer activism emerged only in the nineteenth century, however, should not lead us to underestimate the novelty of the actions and ideas of the 1760s and 1770s. Consumer activism was born in the Revolutionary era, but it had important precursors; and, although born in this era, it did not develop all of its modern characteristics until the nineteenth century. Consumer activism in the Revolutionary era was, in other words, transitional. The characteristics of late eighteenth-century consumer activism reflected a mixture of continuity and change. Revolutionary consumer activism represented both the last act of the early modern tradition of consumer protest and the first stage of modern consumer activism. And this is precisely how many nineteenth-century consumer activists understood the actions of the Revolutionary generation. Those who in 1880 coined the word "boycott," the signature tactic of consumer activism in the United States, maintained that it had a history as old as history itself, but one with special origins in the 1770s. Indeed, throughout the nineteenth century, consumer activists and commentators promoted the seemingly incoherent view that boycotts were a venerable, even ancient form of popular mobilization, and that the American Revolutionaries invented this mode of political protest. "The boycott has been employed against obnoxious individuals from time immemorial," noted the political economist and Christian socialist Richard Ely in 1886, shortly after the controversial term was coined. This was a commonplace observation of the period. As evidence, Ely pointed to a boycott of "the monks of Christ's Church" in 1327 in Canterbury, England. A few sentences later, however, the political economist made a seemingly abrupt and unexplained about-face when he claimed that "the boycott was born in the cradle of American liberty." Several decades later, Samuel Gompers, the leader of the American Federation of Labor, noted in an interview that the "boycott itself—social, political, moral, and economic—is as old as human history." Yet, despite noting that "the name is only a quarter of a century old," he too simultaneously found its American origins in the Boston Tea Party. Ely, Gompers, and the many others who held these opposing views were correct. Consumer activism existed long before the 1760s, but the Revolutionaries remade it, in many cases by elaborating and extending techniques from earlier generations. Many of their techniques, in turn, were further refined by later generations. The decades of the 1760s and 1770s, then, can rightly be called the era in which modern consumer activism was born. I mean this in a sense similar to Neil McKendrick's view that this period marked the birth of consumer society: "To speak of a birth indicates . . . the need for a long preceding period of growth, and the necessity for many further stages before the maturity of 'a society of high mass consumption' would be reached; and yet also indicates the importance, the excitement, the novel sense of a dramatic event." Although consumer activism was conceived earlier and matured later, its nascent modern form emerged in the crucial moment of colonial and Revolutionary America. If it is misleading to say that this group invented consumer activism, the generation of the 1760s did shape it in significant ways, not least because every species of consumer activist that followed employed a similar mix of borrowing and reshaping to create a form of boycotting relevant to its time.[4]

Consumer activism of the Revolutionary period was a mixture of old and new, and it is the job of this chapter to tease out these differences. The new aspects of the Revolutionaries' consumer activism were not all that endured. Just as important were the inheritances which they modified and, in turn, passed on. Many of the beliefs and techniques that they borrowed and adapted, rather than invented, became part and parcel of the consumer activists' toolkit in the nineteenth century, and in many cases remain there to this day. These included many of the signature characteristics of consumer activism, the basic edifice upon which the architecture of consumer activism continues to rest. In their ambivalence about consumption, the tactic at the center of their campaigns, in their suspicion of pleasure, in their valorization of sacrifice, they were not just uncertain early adopters of new tactics, but forerunners of consumer activists' defining ambivalence toward consumer society.

I. Continuities in Revolutionary Consumer Activism

When did consumer activism begin? According to Breen, the "consumer boycott was a brilliantly American invention," an "innovative strategy" that took root during the period leading to the Revolution. Breen is correct to note the importance of America in this period as central to the emergence of consumer activism. His declaration of the "utter novelty" of their actions, however, needs to be qualified.[5] Too often, scholars emphasize only the new and distinctive aspects of the Revolutionary boycotters. They generally do not look backward to find precedents, nor do they look forward to understand deviations from patterns that the consumer activists of the 1760s and 1770s established. In this view, the Revolutionaries are best understood as men and women ahead of their time, so far advanced that their key practice was only named in the nineteenth century. "A boycott was such a novel idea that the very word would not be coined for almost another century," as Adam Hochschild writes.[6] What these views minimize, however, is that the patriots were as much inheritors of an old tradition of consumer activism as inventors of a new one. As Sidney Tarrow, a scholar of American social movements, notes, the "colonists brought with them a repertoire of collective action from early modern Europe, and as the political conflict with the mother country gathered force in the early 1760s, their first responses were traditional." J. Franklin Jameson, whose 1926 book *The American Revolution Considered as a Social Movement* inspired the title of this chapter, concretely illustrated this general point when he observed that during the nonimportation era "the spinning wheel came into renewed use in every household."[7] Consumer politics of the Revolutionary era was poised between traditional forms of consumer protest that long predated it and the modern forms that American consumer activism eventually took.

Revolutionary activists did not invent the tactic of the boycott; that came earlier. Nor did they coin the term; that came later. The colonists who organized and participated in the nonimportation movement beginning in 1764 were not the first to promote the tools of consumer protest, although, as we shall see, they were the first to lead a social movement based on these principles and they also elaborated and publicized those tools in significant new ways, for they established the enduring principle that an unpublicized boycott was not really a boycott at all. We tend to think of consumption as a modern concern and of consumer politics as a recent development. However, consumption was a central mode of political engagement for ordinary people long before other forms of politics, such as voting, became available to them. In the medieval borough, R. H. Tawney writes, consumption "held primacy in the public mind." In the eighteenth century, as E. P. Thompson has noted, "the consumer defended his old notion of right as stubbornly as . . . he defended his craft status as an artisan." Long before the American colonists revolted, some residents of another British colony, Ireland, proposed that their compatriots take up the nonconsumption of British-made goods as a political tactic. The most famous salvo in this aborted campaign was Jonathan Swift's 1720 essay *A Proposal for the Universal Use of Irish Manufacture*. The essayist called upon his compatriots, "Male and Female never to appear with one Single Shred that comes from England." Instead, he promoted a vision in which the Irish would be "universally clad in their own Manufacture." No social movement followed Swift's suggestion, although in the 1770s, Irish societies, imitating the American colonists, formed to enforce nonimportation of British goods.[8] So Americans of the 1760s were not the first to develop the logic of nonimportation, although they were the first to implement it successfully.

Nor were the colonists the first to adopt consumer tactics as political weapons. Throughout the eighteenth century, food riots were common in Europe. These food rioters possessed a "highly-sensitive consumer-consciousness." Such riots were not absent in colonial America, where a series of bread riots took place in Boston, Philadelphia, and other colonial cities in the second and third decades of the seventeenth century. In 1713, for example, a crowd of Bostonians destroyed the grain of the merchant Andrew Belcher, whom many poor residents perceived as charging exorbitant prices.[9]

Similarly, American colonists employed the tactic of ostracism, a practice with roots in classical Greece and ancient Christianity.[10] They continued the tradition of casting out of the community what a group of Boston residents described in 1775 as "villains that are inimical to the cause of liberty."[11] In a communal society that deeply valued the thick bonds of neighborliness, the threat of social isolation was grave. As noted in the *Pennsylvania Gazette* in 1765, the punishment to "let him be alone in the world—let him wish to associate with the wild beasts of some dark, loathsome cave" was literally to excommunicate him or her.[12] Colonists who supported British imperial measures, from the Stamp Act to the Intolerable Acts, routinely faced the wrath of their neighbors, who punished them through isolation. For example, in 1765, citizens in Essex County, New Jersey, declared that they would have "no Communication with any such Person, nor speak to them on any Occasion, unless it be to inform them of their Vileness."[13] A group of Bostonians promised eight years later that those who drank British tea would be "treated as wretches unworthy to live, and will be made the first Victims of our Just Resentment."[14] To be sure, the colonists put an American spin on ostracism and other "rituals of public humiliation," particularly in their use of the tactic of tarring and feathering.[15] But this shaming remained, as it had in earlier societies, a function of face-to-face contact and aimed at personal humiliation and communal condemnation.[16] Later generations grew to embrace less visible, more distant forms of politics that relied upon commercial rather than neighborly networks and devalued symbolic acts, although these never went away entirely.

Practitioners of ostracism and humiliation sought not only to punish but also to induce personal redemption and conversion. Later generations of boycotters, by contrast, aimed to punish malefactors and to force them to change their ways. Caring little or not at all whether their targets had undergone a soul-searing conversion, they sought a tangible change in economic behavior. Not so the Revolutionaries. For example, the residents of several Boston-area communities in 1773 vowed to ostracize Eleazer Bradshaw, an unrepentant tea purchaser, "until there appears a reformation in said *Bradshaw*." Similarly, a group in Augusta County, Virginia, promised "to have no further dealings, connection, or intercourse" with one Alexander Miller, who apparently had impugned the motives of the Continental Congress. They aimed to catalyze "his sincere repentance of his past folly." With these "testimonials of repentance," as the historian Pauline Maier calls them, the protesters drew from the past as much as they pointed to the future. They employed shame-based rather than market-based forms of punishment.[17]

Another link with the past lay in the colonists' understanding of the words "consumer" and "consumption." For them, as for those who preceded them, and distinctly unlike later generations, these words essentially meant "using up" or "using." This connotation drew on the original meaning of the word, to burn up (as in consumed by fire). The colonists used the word "consumption" frequently, "consume and consumer" much less so. With the onset of the nonconsumption movement in 1774, they organized the first political campaign around the term.[18] Yet in contrast to consumer activists in the nineteenth and twentieth centuries, to them consumption meant not purchasing a good but rather the distinct act of using it after it had been obtained. Nor did it connote an economically positive act; it was seen as merely a necessary one, and often simply wasteful. Similarly, for most colonists, the idea of consuming more than the bare necessities seemed a dangerous indulgence. They shared with the Protestants of the Reformation era a deep suspicion of the practice of consumption, especially the purchase of items deemed luxuries.

Yet a mass consumption revolution had begun in the early part of the eighteenth century, and many Americans avidly pursued the conveniences and pleasures of food items and mass-produced goods, newly available, such as sugar, tea, and tea sets. An increasing number of colonists were beginning to understand consumption as a social good, not only because of the domestic comfort it provided but also because the consequences of consumption were economically beneficial.[19] This was the theory that Adam Smith was contemporaneously developing across the Atlantic Ocean. And, drawing on recent economic theorizing, the colonists increasingly understood that their consumption of British goods was an important source of economic strength for the empire. In spite of the negative valence many of them associated with consumption, colonists pioneered the strategic use of mass consumption for political purposes. And they sought, from 1764 until the Revolution, to organize their consuming power for political effect. "By affecting the trade and interest of Great Britain so deeply," a Boston nonimportation committee claimed in 1774, we "shall induce her to withdraw her oppressive hand." For this group, as for many other colonists, "a suspension of all commercial intercourse with the island of Great Britain" was the most effective way to get their "rights restored."[20] The nonimportation agreements in their varying iterations marked a radically new form of political organization, for reasons we will discuss below. They reached their apotheosis with the creation of the Association of the Continental Congress in 1774.

In spite of both their originality as political activists and their prescient recognition of the potential political power of mass consumption, the leaders of the nonimportation (and, later, nonexportation, nonconsumption) movement held what is from the modern perspective a backward-looking interpretation of the word "consumption." The vast majority of nonimportation agreements, signed by colonists all along the Eastern seaboard, used a variation of the phrase "we will neither purchase or consume" British goods, language which defined buying a good and using it as distinct economic actions, with consumption referring to the latter and not the former. Typically, these agreements employed the word "use" as an explicit synonym for "consume," as in the resolution of the Continental Congress that "we will not purchase or use any tea." Other agreements mentioned all three acts, clarifying this distinction, as did the inhabitants of Weathersfield, Connecticut, when they resolved in 1769, "Nor will we purchase or use and consume any Goods imported contrary to said Agreement." When in

1774 the Continental Congress organized the Association to carry out non-consumption, it too distinguished between purchasing and using enumerated goods, particularly British tea. John Dickinson's famous *Farmers' Letters* similarly described "users" and "consumers" as synonyms.[21]

These examples suggest that advocates of nonimportation, even as late as 1774 and 1775, understood consumption as use, although some were beginning to accept emerging definitions of consumption as purchasing and as the linchpin of the modern economy. The ostensible reason for the creation of these patriotic organizations was the adoption of the new theory that consumption, understood as the purchase of goods, was "the sole end and purpose of all production," as Adam Smith would write in *The Wealth of Nations*, published in 1776. But they equally emphasized use, an activity with no discernable economic consequences, since one uses a good only after acquiring it. Consumption, as they understood it, occurred after the relevant economic transactions had taken place. Their agreements and resolutions always included prohibitions against the use of British goods. Indeed, they often invoked the original meaning of consumption—"to burn up"—as in the report of the patriots of Lexington who "brought together every ounce" of British tea "contained in the town, and committed it to one common bonfire." Their goal, they claimed, was to bring "the detestable herb into disuse."[22]

"Disuse" was a telling word, one that emphasized the nature of their goal. The Continental Congress's call for "the total disuse of all EAST INDIA TEAS" was central to the aim of discouraging the "purchase or use" of British goods. Boston residents also promised "totally to abstain from the Use of TEA" and, furthermore, pledged that "we will absolutely refuse it, if it should be offered to us upon any Occasion whatsoever" until "the late Revenue Acts are repealed."[23] Not using goods, as opposed to not buying them, was part of a ritual of purification, a display of personal virtue in the public sphere. The act of disuse—indeed, the performance of disuse—was a means of disclaiming morally objectionable causes. But disuse was not, to the way of thinking of future consumer activists, an effective way to hurt the pocketbook of opponents. Not using goods already acquired would have no impact upon what a later generation would call the all-important "pocket nerve" of merchants.

The most famous act of the colonial rebellion, what came to be known as the Boston Tea Party, centered around use as well. Although patriots urged colonists—and especially merchants—not to buy tea, they vigilantly enforced disuse. On the night of December 23, 1773, the rebels disused British tea by dumping it into Boston Harbor. Accounts of this ritual of communal purification almost uniformly emphasized the efforts by the patriots to ensure that nobody pocketed any of the discarded tea. As the *Massachusetts Gazette* reported, "There was the greatest care taken to prevent the tea from being purloined by the populace; one or two being detected in endeavoring to pocket a small quantity were stripped of their acquisitions and very roughly handled."[24] The recollections of George Robert Twelves Hewes, considered the last surviving member of the group of sixty that stormed the pier and dumped the tea overboard, focus to a surprising extent on his efforts to prevent those charged with dumping the tea and the many hundreds of observers from somehow salvaging the aromatic leaves for personal use. Indeed, in his memoir, published in the 1820s to great acclaim, Hewes devotes many more words to the pursuit of tea thieves than he does to the act of dumping the tea overboard. Almost fifty years after the fact, Hewes' detailed recall of the punishments meted out to those who sought to reclaim the ill-fated tea for personal use suggests the signal importance that the colonists placed on disuse. In Hewes's telling, the Tea Party was the stage setter for the real action, the pursuit of tea thieves. "During the time we were throwing the tea overboard," Hewes recounted, after a cursory one-paragraph discussion of that act, "There were several attempts made by some of the citizens of Boston and its vicinity to carry off small quantities of it for their family use. To effect that object, they would watch their opportunity to snatch up a handful from the deck, where it became plentifully scattered, and put it into their pockets." At this point, Hewes' reminiscence turns to detailed descriptions of three instances of attempted theft of the tea that he witnessed.

In the first case, Hewes proudly recalls fingering an acquaintance who was guilty of seeking to purloin the dumped tea: "One Captain O'Connor, whom I well knew, came on board for that purpose, and when he supposed he was not noticed, filled his pockets, and also the lining of his coat. But I had detected him and gave information to the captain of what he was doing. We were ordered to take him into custody, and just as he was stepping from the vessel, I seized him by the skirt of his coat, and in attempting to pull him back, I tore it off; but, springing forward, by a rapid effort he made his escape. He had, however, to run a gauntlet through the crowd upon the wharf nine each one, as he passed, giving him a kick or a stroke." Public and physical humiliation was the penalty for unauthorized use. Hewes witnessed the next incident of theft catching with amusement: "Another attempt was made to save a little tea from the ruins of the cargo by a tall, aged man who wore a large cocked hat and white wig, which was fashionable at that time. He had slightly slipped a little into his pocket, but being detected, they seized him and, taking his hat and wig from his head, threw them, together with the tea, of which they had emptied his pockets, into the water. In consideration of his advanced age, he was permitted to escape, with now and then a slight kick." To Hewes's satisfaction, the theft of tea was met with physical violence and public humiliation.

Hewes picked up his recollections of the next morning, when he helped catch more tea embezzlers: "The next morning, after we had cleared the ships of the tea, it was discovered that very considerable quantities of it were floating upon the surface of the water; and to prevent the possibility of any of its being saved for use, a number of small boats were manned by sailors and citizens, who rowed them into those parts of the harbor wherever the tea was visible, and by beating it with oars and paddles so thoroughly drenched it as to render its entire destruction inevitable." In his memoirs, Hewes also offers instances of punishments for those who improperly sold the tea, including a graphic description of an accused woman whose house was smeared with excrement as punishment for her reuse of the tainted tea.[25]

Even those who came upon tea that had washed ashore weeks later faced severe consequences. One such unlucky person was Ebenezer Withington, who, in January of 1774, came upon "half a chest" of tea in the marshes of his hometown of Dorchester. The Sons of Liberty caught wind of Withington's scheme to sell the tea. Ultimately, patriots took Withington's stolen tea and brought it to Boston Common, where they "committed it to flames."[26] The patriots consumed it in the old sense, rather than consuming it in the emerging sense of the word. For this group, consumption meant use or destruction.

The Tea Party was both the high point and the endgame for consumer activists who understood use as the crucial category of action. It marked the last moment in which consumption as use predominated over consumption as purchase in political importance. Later generations of consumer activists understood the moment of purchase as the crucial point, the act that set off a wide-ranging causal chain for which the consumer was ultimately responsible. While recognizing this point—and instantiating it in their movement with the prohibition against the purchase of tea and other British products—most colonists, as we will see, assumed that the most relevant actors were merchants rather than ordinary individuals, since merchants bought goods directly from British brokers. Later generations of Americans would claim this mantle of relevance for themselves, but in the Revolutionary era, politicized purchasing was still the prerogative of a particular and relatively small (and elite) class.

If the Revolutionary boycotters clung to an older conception of the literal meaning of the word "consumption," they also shared an inherited view about its dangerous moral consequences. Leaders of the nonimportation movement held an equally traditional view about the moral valence of consumption. Although the nonimporters recognized the power of mass consumption—and here we can agree with T. H. Breen that they did so in pioneering ways—we should remember that what they usually demanded was *nonconsumption*. Where consumption was necessary, they sought to ensure that it was a particularly constricted kind of virtuous consumption, pleasurable only in the sense that it supported domestic production and denied the English revenue. It seems a great contradiction that the founders of this form of commercial politics appeared to be, as the historian Barbara Clark Smith has argued, "profoundly anticommercial."[27] As we will see, however, this was no irony. Nor was it a deviation from the norms of the consumer movement as it developed over time: consumer activists have, throughout American history, organized social movements based on a recognition of the power of consumption and conducted these movements on the basis of a profound ambivalence about the morality of consumption. That ambivalence, as in the case of the Founders, often turned into an abiding suspicion of the act of consumption. Yet being suspicious of consumption is not the same as being "anticommercial," and we will see in the next section that the patriots believed deeply in the power of commerce and markets, even if they disliked some of the consequences of an increasingly commercialized world.

Although, for reasons offered below, I would reject the label "anticommercial," it is clear that the nonimporters favored an "ascetic morality," in which they prized sacrifice, self-denial, and frugality and condemned extravagance, luxury, and most forms of commercial amusement. The organizations promoting nonimportation and nonconsumption, which culminated in the Association of the Continental Congress in 1774, uniformly condemned all forms of conspicuous consumption, such as betting on horse races and cockfights, and they even inveighed against the practice of wearing fashionable clothes to funerals. They may have embraced consumer tactics, but they rejected what a later generation would label consumerism, the idea that it was virtuous in and of itself to buy and enjoy goods. Instead, the Boston Town Meeting dismissed purchasing in 1767 as the acquisition of "superfluities" and "luxuries." As the eighth article of the Association stated, "We will in our several stations encourage frugality, oeconomy and industry; and promote agriculture, arts and the manufactures of this country, especially that of wool; and will discountenance and discourage every species of extravagance and dissipation, especially all horse racing, and all kinds of gaming, cock fighting, exhibitions of shows, plays, and other expensive diversions and entertainments. And on the death of any relation or friend, none of us, or any of our families, will

go into any further mourning dress, than a black crape or ribbon and neck-
lace for Ladies, and we will discontinue the giving of gloves and scarfs at
funerals." Note that the Association did not reject manufacturing; it proposed developing domestic industry and agriculture. At the same time, the
colonists who supported the Association placed limits on the extent and
type of manufacturing—and, in turn, the kinds of consumption—they favored. They supported the production and consumption of necessities but
rejected the making or buying of anything that smacked of luxury.[28]

Revolutionaries described enemies of the movement as greedy and
overly materialistic. They persistently identified England itself as effeminate, fashion conscious, and perversely interested in consumption and often used the same terms to describe their Tory neighbors. (In chapter 3, we
will see that antebellum Southern nationalists portrayed Northerners in
precisely the same way.) A number of Connecticut delegates to the consti-
tutional convention decried the "avaricious men" who violated the terms of
nonimportation. By standing firmly in favor of what Edmund Morgan calls
"patriotic frugality," the colonists sought to renew what they took to be the
"ancestral virtues." The reality, of course, was more complicated. Dreams
of leisure and plenitude were as deeply rooted in Western civilization as
was the veneration of work, if not more so. From the Horn of Plenty to the
dreams of the land of Cockaigne through what in nineteenth-century song
came to be called the "Big Rock Candy Mountain," abundance and pleasure have long been central to ordinary people's dreams of the good life.[29]
The values of hard work, deferred gratification, and the celebration of sacrifice—what Max Weber later identified as the hallmark of the "Protestant
ethic"—did not enjoy hegemony even in so Protestant a place as colonial
America. By and large, however, the colonial consumer activists sided with
Sparta rather than Athens and took asceticism and sacrifice to be the highest virtues. Most later generations of consumer activists, as we will see,
continued this tradition of equating sacrifice with virtue. But, even in the
Revolutionary generation, we can see some elements of a politics of pleasure that would emerge as an important minority strand in modern consumer activism.

Like later generations of consumer activists, the nonimporters posited
an equivalence between private actions and the public good. They defined
sacrifice as the essence of personal and public virtue. The personal was political: personal actions were an emblem of virtuousness. So was enforcing
such norms on the community, which included regulating and monitoring
the behavior of neighbors. Members of groups that embraced nonimportation, from the Sons of Liberty to the Solemn League and Covenant to the
Association of the Continental Congress, not only did not consume (use)

Bohea tea, they made it publicly known that they would not countenance its use by neighbors. Nonimportation groups publicized nonuse and ensured that it was universally upheld through the media of petitions, pamphlets, and newspaper articles, which named members of the Association. They published notices asking compatriots not to buy from merchants who violated their rules, such as the 1768 demand that Sons and Daughters of Liberty "not buy any one thing of" William Jackson, an importer in Boston, for such a purchase "will bring Disgrace upon themselves, and their Posterity, for ever and ever" (see fig. 1.1). They also published apologies by repentant violators of nonimportation, such as the New Yorker Abraham H. Van Vleck, who in 1775 publicly acknowledged committing "a most atrocious Crime against my Country, by contravening one of the Recommendations of the Honorable Continental Congress, in Shipping Provisions to Nantucket."[30] They encouraged compliance and solidarity through public displays of nonconsumption, which ranged from bonfires to the use of alternative goods (homespun wool, sassafras rather than tea) to the public and humiliating punishments of neighbors who, in using banned products, violated these holy compacts.

All of this suggests that the goals of nonimportation associations were twofold: first, to weaken the British economy and therefore to force a change in the king's and Parliament's imperial policy; and second, to organize, publicize, and systematize the types of symbolic politics that had taken place in local communities throughout the early modern era. The colonists believed that they were responsible for the second and took matters into their own hands as they demonstrated their virtue through displays of sacrifice, community censure, and membership in a local branch of the increasingly national nonimportation movement. They generally understood the first task to be the job of a specific class, the merchants. Ordinary colonists took their role in this matter to be coercing merchants into behaving in a morally acceptable and politically expedient manner.

A final way in which the colonists reflected the past more than they anticipated the future of consumer activism, then, is in their conception of the duty of the citizen-activist. Whereas later generations understood consumption itself as an important, even defining act of citizenship, the colonists saw their role primarily as enforcers of nonconsumption. The boycotting colonists, Breen has powerfully shown, created the idea of a democratic public. Although initially led by merchants, over time ordinary men and women saw themselves as part of the nonimportation movement. By the 1770s, ordinary Americans had claimed a new and powerful role for themselves as members of the public, as signers of petitions, and as participants in the consumer politics of the nonimportation, nonconsumption movement. This process

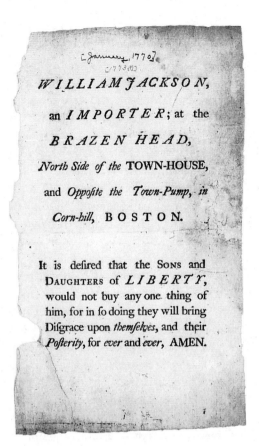

[January, 1770]
[1773?]

WILLIAM JACKSON,

an *IMPORTER*; at the

BRAZEN HEAD,

North Side of the TOWN-HOUSE,

and *Oppofite the Town-Pump, in*

Corn-hill, BOSTON.

It is defired that the SONS and
DAUGHTERS of *LIBERTY*,
would not buy any one thing of
him, for in fo doing they will bring
Difgrace upon *themfelves*, and their
Pofterity, for *ever* and *ever*, AMEN.

Figure 1.1. A 1768 broad-
side announcing the public
dishonoring of the importer
William Jackson. (Library of
Congress Prints and Photographs Division, Washington
DC. LC-USZ62-43568. Image
courtesy of newsbank.com.)

was a key element of the radicalism of the American Revolution. The colonists forcefully inserted themselves into politics, previously the domain of
elites. And yet, in critical ways, they enlisted as deputies, rather than as leaders, whose primary task was to force merchants to stop importing and selling
goods enumerated for boycott. They saw their job as crucially important, but
it was a second order of importance in that they assigned primary agency to
merchants. A later generation would see the consumer as the fulcrum of the
economic system; the Revolutionary consumer activists placed merchants in
that role. They aimed more to enforce the boycott than to themselves be the
boycotters. Often this called for what later came to be known as a secondary
boycott of recalcitrant merchants, as when South Carolina's Christopher Gadsden called for planters and artisans to force merchants to join a boycott "by
refusing to deal with those who failed to cooperate." The task of the colonists
was to take on recalcitrant merchants and others who, they believed, according to Gary Nash, "had to be admonished, cajoled, scorned, ostracized, condemned, threatened, bullied and often punished." This was a novel form of

popular politics, to be sure, but it largely focused on the "popular intimidation against those who broke the nonimportation ban," rather than on engagement in acts of nonimportation themselves. The "patriotic inhabitants of Lexington," for example, called on citizens to "enjoin their Selectmen to deny licences to all houses of entertainment, who were known to afford tea to their guests."[31] Enjoining Selectmen was not the same as taking direct action.

The colonists' twin jobs were keeping the merchants in line and participating in the private and public politics of nonuse. Whereas they recognized the transatlantic significance of the former action, they tended to understand the latter as a combination of a personal statement and an act of communal solidarity. The former initiated ripples that extended throughout the Atlantic world; the latter stayed in the community. The advocates of nonimportation, as Edmund Morgan has noted, "made very little of the effect that their self-denial would have on the British government." Most colonists had not yet made the cognitive leap that posited consumption as the initiator of all economic activity, nor had they concluded that their own economic actions had inexorable and far-reaching economic effects. But they had imbibed enough of the new economics to recognize that the actions of merchants in the New World would necessarily have a pronounced effect on the Old. This is why "the nonimportation associations only gradually involved the nonmercantile population." Indeed, the resolutions of the nonimportation groups typically spoke in the voice of the merchants or defined merchants or manufacturers as the crucial actors. Article 6, for example, aimed at "owners of vessels," while 9 (directed toward "vendors of goods or merchandise"), 10 (threatening "any merchant, trader or other person" who imported goods), and 13 (aimed at "manufacturers") all targeted business leaders. Breen is correct to call the boycott the "distinguishing mark of colonial protest" if we understand the boycott as the actions of a stratum of society (encouraged and enforced, to be sure, by the broader society), rather than a tactic available to the entire populace, a definition different from how it came to be understood from the nineteenth century onward. In an 1892 article, Richard Henry Dana, a lawyer and civil service reformer, answered the question of whether there had been any boycotting in the Revolutionary era in the affirmative ("surely there was"). But his summary of the nonimporters' goals pointed to the differences: "Circulars were printed and notices posted warning persons not to trade with such and such merchants who had imported goods from England." Rather than boycotting England directly, the colonists, in Dana's understanding, boycotted the merchants in the hopes that they, in turn, would mount an effectual economic campaign. It is probably the case that, as Roy Raphael speculates, "the nonimportation movement . . . involved the majority of free Americans in one manner or another."[32] To label colonial protest popular, however, is not the same as to say that all popular actions were of equal import or impact. The "public" was invoked in new ways during the Revolution; but the birth of democratic politics in this period did not precisely coincide with the view that individual citizens had it in their power (provided they acted collectively) to alter the economy and the polity in a direct way. The colonists understood their actions as important—indeed central—but the scale and scope of these actions did not generally extend beyond the local community. They were only beginning to grasp the long-range consequences of their actions.

A characteristic aspect of modern consumer activism as it developed in the nineteenth century was a denigration of the importance of the senses, since these could only tell you about the proximate and the visible. The force of one's actions as a consumer, as later activists came to understand it, typically extended far beyond the local, making it necessary to relegate the senses to a lesser order power, in favor of an understanding of the causal impact of consumption along the axis of distant markets. In their emphasis on primacy of the senses, the Revolutionaries took up the worldview of early modern consumer activists. They sought what one witness to the Boston Tea Party called "ocular demonstration" of phenomena, eyewitness evidence of the efficacy of their actions that were generally unavailable to later boycotters.[33] They practiced close surveillance of merchants and others suspected of violating nonimportation. And members of communities closely watched each other for signs of slippage from Revolutionary principles—a fancier-than-necessary English garment perhaps, or suspected use of Bohea tea. Theirs was a culture of constant vigilance—one in which people and things were closely watched (see fig. 1.2). Their punishments too were far more sensory—and physically painful—than later generations of consumer activists meted out. Rather than the metaphorical *pocket nerve* at which later generations of consumer activists aimed, they hurled their brickbats at merchants windows and their tar and feathers at the bodies of those they sought to dishonor. Whereas later generations were content to disrupt the business of an immoral merchant, the Revolutionaries insisted on rituals of public humiliation.

The colonists conceived of political agency as based upon a division of labor between citizens and merchants. The division followed geographic lines of causality: the former were responsible for the local and the latter were responsible for the distant, and the transatlantic. Citizens were in charge of the visible, what could be apprehended by the senses, social relations. Merchants, in turn, were responsible for the relations that could not

Figure 1.2. "The Alternative of Williams-Burg." A crowd forces a merchant to sign the Continental Association, which enforced nonimportation. (The Colonial Williamsburg Foundation.)

be seen, the relations of the market. Citizens demonstrated their virtue in plain sight of their neighbors; merchants aimed to weaken the economy and, in turn, to disrupt the politics of the British Empire.

Initially, many colonists believed that republics could not exist over extensive areas for the same reasons.[34] Distance made it impossible to be vigilant and made displays of personal purity unworkable (since such displays could not be seen at a distance). These were the signal characteristics of consumer virtue, as they understood it. The nonimporting colonists posited a strong relationship between private and public, but understood this relation differently from the way future generations would. Private actions molded the public sphere through the edifying display of virtue or the portentous threats of a neighbor practicing surveillance. They did not yet promote the idea that private actions would automatically alter the public sphere.

II. Novelty

In spite of the significant, and usually overlooked, elements of continuity, the Revolutionary era marks an important transitional moment in the history of consumer activism. As the Revolution approached, consumer activism took on increasing scale and breadth. In this process, notwithstanding the deployment of many older techniques and the persistence of inherited values, activists questioned some older ideas and developed new techniques. Even during the Boston Tea Party, when, as we have seen, most participants understood use (not purchase) as the crucial political act, some colonists challenged this assumption. According to one eyewitness account of the event, "A BACHELOR wondered what the point was in burning even English tea, since the duty had already been paid, provided no more was to be imported from England, while the duty continued." Future consumer activists would accept the premises of this question as they adopted the assumption that the moment of purchase, not use, was critical. By the 1780s, it was becoming increasingly common for "consumption" to connote purchasing. The understanding of consumption as use persisted well into the nineteenth century, but it was increasingly supplanted by the new, modern conception of consumption.[35]

Consumer activists of the Revolutionary era did not change the nature of their mission primarily by rejecting older ideas or by embracing new ones. They used a mixed vocabulary, sometimes backward oriented and sometimes forward looking, and sometimes both at the same time. The newness of consumer activism of the 1760s and 1770s was a function of the extension, rather than invention, of ideas and practices already in circulation. Yet many of these extensions ultimately resulted in differences in kind. For the very idea of extension—the belief that local actions could have a far-reaching impact—amounted to a radical transformation and partial repudiation of the previous spirit of consumer activism. By expanding the range of older forms of economic coercion, the Revolutionaries (often inadvertently) altered the meaning of these activities. In elaborating and adapting, the Revolutionaries transformed the meaning of consumer activism, practiced it in fundamentally new ways, and presaged, even if they did not practice, the forms that it took in the nineteenth and twentieth centuries. In the course of attempting to "adapt the traditional, classical republican impulse to modern commercial society," they inadvertently discovered that elemental aspects of modern commercial society provided a new basis upon which to uphold those republican impulses.[36] They thus set consumer activism on the paradoxical course it has followed ever since—one beholden to consumer society for providing its signature tactics while at the same time fundamentally opposed to central aspects of consumer society. Theirs was a politics and a morality both made by and undermined by consumer society. During the Revolutionary era we see much more of the opposition, but omens of the embrace are present as well. In the process, the nonimporters transformed consumer activism from a localistic form of politics to one that extended as far and wide as the web of print and commerce could carry it.

The central extension developed by the Revolutionary activists was, in fact, a literal extension, in the sense of a geographic expansion, of the central concepts and practices of early modern consumer activism. In almost every aspect, this was their main innovation: taking techniques that had been understood as inherently local and that were applied in face-to-face contexts, and rethinking them, and in the process reanimating them, as practices that could cover potentially great distances. They reimagined the world as a lattice consisting of invisible but very real filaments that connected disparate parts. In transcending space, they sought, to some extent, to conquer it. The expanded field of play for consumer activists meant that distance no longer prevented membership in a social movement or stunted effective political action. To be sure, the Founders continued and elaborated many of the local, direct, and interpersonal practices that had long been the hallmark of early modern consumer activism. Indeed, the majority of their efforts highlighted standards of purity in the self as well as the community and ensured, through coercion and even violence, that others, particularly merchants, obeyed these standards. The Revolutionaries supplemented these not so much with fundamentally different techniques as with new conceptions of the range for which these practices could be applied by means of print and markets. By converting local practices to national and even international ones, they laid the groundwork for modern consumer activism, whose essence ever since has been long-distance solidarity and whose central metaphor has been the chain or the web linking far-flung goods and people.

The logic of these extensions worked in two complementary ways. It expanded the number of people who could be linked in a common struggle, since propinquity was no longer a prerequisite for making common cause. The pool of consumer activists working simultaneously for a cause could now be drawn from like-minded thinkers all over the colonies, since their deeds could be coordinated and aimed at a shared target or targets and publicized nationally. It also expanded the number of people who were affected by the actions of individual consumers, or by the collective behavior of large numbers of consumers. By virtue of the newly described powers of market-based activity, consumers believed that they could affect those who provided the goods that they bought, or refused to buy. But here too was something new, the use of print to coincide with consumer actions. Ever since, boycotts have been characterized by such publications.

The Revolutionaries tentatively but increasingly mixed their faith in the local with a new recognition of the power of distance. Article 11 of the Association, for example, emphasized both traditional forms of surveillance and new modes of publicity. It began by calling upon colonists to select representatives "whose business it shall be attentively to observe the conduct of all persons touching this association." At the same time, it promised that those who "violated this association" would have their names "published in the gazette," as a result of which their names would be "publicly known and universally contemned as enemies of American liberty; and thenceforth we respectively will break off all dealings with him or her." After a promise of expansion through publicity, the last clause, reflecting the mixture of methods both old and new, sanctions the traditional punishment of ostracism.[37]

The Revolutionaries developed a vocabulary to reflect their new conception of the geographic expansion of human agency and responsibility. They used a language of networks, grids, and circuits that grew out of emerging patterns of trade, developments in economic thought, new experiences of intra- and even intercontinental community and agency, and, of course, evolving conceptions of politics. Reflecting what a French encyclopedia called "bonds of commerce" and what Thomas Jefferson described as "political bands" in the first sentence of the Declaration of Independence, the Founders introduced linkages that united disparate peoples across distances. Volitional, the result of individual agency, not geography, these bands could be, as the declaration declared, dissolved. This political understanding mirrored an emergent economic language and practice of long-distance commerce, which Stephen Hopkins, the Rhode Island governor, called the "circuitry of commerce"—the trade upon which both metropole and colony depended—that was disrupted by the Stamp Act and other unjust imperial edicts. As the Committee of Merchants of Philadelphia wrote to their English counterparts in 1769, "We consider the merchants here and in England as the Links of the Chain that binds both Countries together." What Arthur M. Schlesinger called the "impalpable but sinewy bonds" of transatlantic commerce came to alter the ways in which the Revolutionaries imagined politics. William Henry Drayton of South Carolina believed that "organizing the nonimportation movement was substantially equivalent to erecting a new political structure."[38] This was so to the extent that these commercial bands led them to imagine new relations to each other and the world, and new means of altering those relations.

The great innovation of the Revolutionary era consumer activists, then, was to redefine, by dramatically expanding, their scope of influence. They did so by promoting the idea that people were linked not just through proximity and the bonds of community (and not just as British colonial subjects) but equally and in some ways more importantly by new kinds of relations that attached the interests of people across potentially great distances. Indeed, sometimes they attenuated neighborly bonds in favor of cosmopolitan ones.[39] These bonds, unlike those among neighbors, were invisible but real. The key here was their understanding of market relations and the media—the cash nexus and the print nexus—as enabling new kinds of imagined communities. In particular, they redefined moral communities to include not just neighborly relations but the union of any group of people with shared interests and the ability to influence the moral life of others. These people formed a group by virtue of shared consumer practices and also through shared information about their actions via placard, sandwich board, petition, or newspaper.

Another element of their expansion of the concept and practice of consumer activism in the Revolutionary era was the colonists' partial acceptance of consumption as a political force. Even as many colonists remained steadfast in their negative view of the morality of consumption, a growing number came around to accepting a new view of the phenomenology of consumption, a new understanding of how consumption operated. The key here was a novel and robust conception of consumer causation. Economic thinkers beginning in the late seventeenth century had argued that consumption was a productive activity, one that set off economic activity. One consequence of this view is that producers were dependent upon consumers. As Adam Smith put it in The Wealth of Nations, the "artificer is the servant of customers, from whom he derives subsistence." Several years later, in his Notes on the State of Virginia, Thomas Jefferson claimed that the producers depend for their subsistence "on the casualties and caprices of customers." Like many other colonists, Jefferson bemoaned rather than celebrated this newly recognized power of consumers. But backhanded recognition of this sort became increasingly common in the Revolutionary era. The politicized colonists began to apply this thinking about consumer causality to their relationship to the British metropole, arguing that as American consumers enriched British merchants, they could also weaken them by not purchasing. Some patriots began to argue that Americans should embrace this power and use consumption as a political weapon in the imperial battle.[40]

The colonists might have continued to disapprove of the act of consumption and harbor suspicion about the motives of consumers, but they also began to conceive of coordinated acts of collective consumption as a powerful force, one capable of operating over long distance. Although Barbara Clark Smith is correct that at some level the "boycotters rejected integration into and dependence upon the world market," their campaigns were built upon a framework of commercial integration. The colonists also recognized the necessity of market-based transactions, even as they did not yet fully place consumers as the linchpin of these processes. Indeed, the Revolutionary boycotters rejected trade with Britain precisely because they posited the economic and political power of consumption. To be sure, they celebrated self-sufficiency and sacrifice as virtuous actions. But they also celebrated what Drew McCoy has called a "burgeoning and invigorating intercourse with the rest of the world."[41]

The key innovation of the American patriots, then, was not so much their use of consumer tactics as their belief that such tools could be extended beyond a particular locale. The leaders of the nonimportation movement did not invent consumer politics so much through new techniques as through the coordination of consumer politics across cities and towns throughout the thirteen colonies. Although the practices themselves were not typically new, this process of coordination reflected a crucial shift from the micropolitics of consumption to the movement politics of consumption, a shift abetted by the knowledge, spread through the print media, that each action would not only occur but be publicized. Previously, consumer actions were commonplace, part of the texture of daily life in many communities but remaining unknown outside of those communities because they were so rarely publicized. Publicity accorded such actions new meaning. Reflecting on the American Revolution, John Adams declared that "thirteen clocks were made to strike together—a perfection of mechanism which no artist has ever before effected." Adams suggested that individual actions in a particular place were, for the first time, part of a broader, unified, and coordinated campaign. The creation of the Association by the Continental Congress in 1774 gave this view organizational sanction.[42]

Print culture, in the form of newspapers, handbills, and petitions, helped make these clocks strike as one, by connecting distant people into a virtual community, by excluding others from that community, and by serving as a medium for the exchange of goods and information. As we have seen, Richard Henry Dana argued that the web of print and commerce made the Revolutionary's actions important precursors to later political organizing. What the historian Kevin Gilmartin has observed of early nineteenth-century British popular consumer politics was equally true of the American colonists at an earlier period: these actions "were organized through the press and enlisted the participation of active readers." Part of what made these Revolutionary actions worthy of the label "boycott" was their use of print to spread the word. And the printed word did not mean only newspapers. Charlestonians used handbills as a means of "inviting all the inhabitants, without exception, particularly the landholders, to assemble in the Great hall over the Exchange, at 3 on Friday afternoon." Newspapers nonetheless served several purposes for the Revolutionary consumer activists and made their actions distinctive. For one thing, they spread news rapidly. News of the Bostonians' tea dump into the harbor appeared in newspapers in New York and Philadelphia within days. They also accelerated the process through which, as Breen puts it, "private decisions in the consumer marketplace came to be widely reinterpreted as acts meriting public scrutiny." They served as a virtual public space through which communities constructed and formed coalitions. Newspapers articles listed the names of the members of nonimportation groups, enumerated prohibited goods, and noted the people who bought them—"their names may be published, their conduct exposed, and their persons avoided," according to an article in the *Pennsylvania Gazette*. In so doing, they turned "distant strangers" into political comrades and, conversely, transformed some neighbors into political enemies.[43]

The characteristics promoted by the media and the market—publicity, agency, the publicizing of the private, connections across space—transformed the meaning of consumer activism. Take ostracism, for example, which traditionally took the form of studiously ignoring, and sometimes even exiling, one's neighbors; it was the severest punishment a member of a community faced for violating its rules. Its purpose was to sever the personal and social connections that linked people in community. The Revolutionaries continued to practice ostracism, but they also added a new twist by seeking to break not just personal bonds but also what they called "commercial connexions" with merchants and others who defied the nonimportation ban. For example, Bostonians called for withholding from those who committed unpatriotic acts "not only all commercial Dealings, but every Act and Office of Common Civility." This was an ostracism of the person and the purse. This innovation of moving the action beyond a specific place expanded the field of ostracism and made the modern boycott possible. Markets turned strangers into virtual neighbors, morally responsible to each other. By expanding the field of ethics and action, the patriots suggested not only that the colonists could ostracize a distant malefactor but that they had both the moral obligation and the power to do so. Moreover, even local acts of neighborly ostracism took on national significance. As article 11 of the Association proclaimed, once names were publicized, those people, wherever their locale, became "universally known." Similarly, punishment of those outside the moral pale became increasingly understood as economic as well as social. Thus, colonists threatened the avaricious "mercenary wretches" who violated the "non-consumption agreement" with the promise that "we will not purchase any merchandize of them, or transact any business for them, or suffer them to transact any for us, but will wholly withdraw from them, and leave them to the consolation of possessing and contemplating the curious moments of British industry and American slavery, which they would so greedily amass to themselves for such sordid wicked purposes; and shall consider in the same light, and treat in the same manner, every Person that shall purchase any such goods of them, or do business for them, or employ them in their business."[44] Here was a call for commercial ostracism, driven as much by the desire to harm the pocketbook as to inflict dishonor.

The colonists' conception of ostracism expanded in other ways as well. The announcement by a group in Charleston that "we will not purchase any goods of any person or persons whosoever, that shall hereafter import, buy or sell, any such teas" was standard operating procedure by late 1773. But the members added in explanation that commercial ostracism was aimed not only at the person being ostracized but also at the system upheld by immoral commerce: "And this we do, because we conceive, that the payment of such duties will be acknowledging a power, which the British Parliament hath assumed, and which we deny them to have under our excellent constitution, [to] tax us against our consent." Resolving to have "no trade, commerce, dealings, or intercourse whatsoever," article 14 of the Association produced similar sentiments, but the authors added another component of expansion. This was not a call for a boycott of an individual but of "any colony or province in North America which shall not accede to, or which shall hereafter violate this association." No longer was the boycott a tool used solely against individuals. The association applied it to larger institutions and even countries. What is interesting is that they continued to use the older language of personal ostracism, claiming, for example, that it "will hold them unworthy of the rights of freeman and as inimical to the liberties of their country."[45] This was another instance of the transitional nature of Revolutionary consumer activism. The "freeman" in this case was not a person but rather a state or province.

Another element of the newness of Revolutionary consumer activism came in their promotion of substitutes to boycotted goods. Although most patriots emphasized sacrifice as the ultimate good, others began to argue for the benefits of alternative modes of moral consumption. They promoted substitutes for many products imported from England, such as coffee, tea, and clothing. Calls for American versions of British products began almost as soon as the imperial crisis started in 1763 and intensified over the next decade. One element in the campaign for alternatives to British goods was the appearance and celebration of homespun clothing. Harvard students appeared at commencement in homespun, and homespun weddings became a popular fashion. Although nonimporters envisioned homespun as a means of avoiding commerce, stores also began to sell American cloth. Many Americans pledged to eschew lamb as a way to increase the number of sheep available for shearing. In addition, colonists promoted alternatives to coffee (rye) and tea (sassafras, balm, and sage). Others eschewed imported beer "in order to encourage the local brewing industry." These alternatives were halfway and transitional measures, since the patriots often stressed noncommercial substitutes, such as home-grown wool. However, the promotion of alternative products was significant because the promoters for the first time assigned consumption (as purchase) a positive valence. It was a challenge to the reigning style of "conspicuous non-consumption," because alternative, moral commerce could hardly be described as "profoundly anticommercial," except insofar as the emphasis was on noncommercial substitutes.[46]

The Revolutionaries presaged the end of the era of the food riot and the moral economy of village coercion—what Charles Tilly has called the "food riot's rise and fall" by the early nineteenth century—even as they embraced these forms of early modern consumer activism. This cohort practiced its politics in the midst of the momentous shift that E. P. Thompson has described from the "bread nexus" to the "cash nexus." The world they were simultaneously living in and leaving behind was one of face-to-face contact, a world in which commerce proceeded with "little intermediate processing." Beginning in the 1740s and thereafter with increasing rapidity, colonists bought clothing and household items from distant markets, making the world of goods seem increasingly impersonal. British items, such as cloth, tea, and tea service—and other products from different sources—became affordable not just for the wealthy but for ordinary colonists. The context of the eighteenth-century consumer revolution doubtless contributed to the expanded sense of causality and community. Yet these same markets served to integrate distant communities, leading many consumers to ponder their relationship to people and places that they would never see. Although they were far away, a growing number of colonists began to argue that they were intimately connected to the places and peoples who fashioned the goods they bought. While many scholars represent this transformation as one of "diminished human reciprocities," consumer activists in this period suggested the opposite: namely, that the market expanded both the reality and the possibilities of human reciprocity. There is a parallel with contemporaneous development of the nation-state, which was being understood as an imagined community, one in which, in Benedict Anderson's famous formulation, "the members of even the smallest nation will never know most of their fellow-members, meet them, or even hear of them, yet in the minds of each lives the image of their communion." The key shift here could be described in a number of ways: from the local to the distant, from the visible to the invisible, from the market as a place to the market as a placeless but powerful force.[47]

The colonists did not abandon the concept of community, nor did they disclaim the importance of virtue. Rather, they reconceptualized them. The colonists new idea of community, based less on physical proximity than on commercial and media pathways, rested on a conception of moral impact and shared philosophies, and the possibility of maintaining the spirit of republicanism in a much-enlarged country. All these forms of expansion hinged on new conceptions of the public sphere, whose boundaries expanded as the imaginary space covered by communities grew with the evolving cash and media nexus.

In the emergent view of some of the Revolutionaries, these extensions—both commercial and journalistic—provided the underpinnings for new conceptions of agency and of the bonds of community and hence new ways to think about political and economic morality. One major political implication that followed from this changing worldview was the rejection of the idea that healthy republics could exist only over small areas. Whereas some Americans came to accept that geographically expansive republics could, in fact, flourish, the consumerist Revolutionaries came to an even more radical conclusion. Since markets and media expanded the framework and capacity for morally relevant actions, the American republic, increasingly crosshatched with a grid of commerce and print culture, was not, in fact, big in morally relevant ways. Rather than undermining virtue, an extensive republic could promote it because its geographic range would be no bar to moral actions. Indeed, a linked republic facilitated the exercise of virtue.

This view had implications for the understandings of the moral status of consumption in early national America. The rise of consumer society in this period is oftentimes narrated as a tale of decline. "The virtuous citizenry dedicated to lean austerity . . . disintegrated shortly after the Revolution into autonomous consumers engulfed in the desire for possessions," writes the historian Anne Fairfax Withington. Like contemporary Americans, she laments, they began to "revel in materialism" rather than uphold the "ascetic morality" of the Revolutionary period. Although he is less critical of this shift, Gordon Wood similarly claims that after the Revolution, America was "taken over by moneymaking and the pursuit of individual interest." These interpretations underestimate the ways in which the Revolutionary consumer activists and their descendants understood the relationship between consumption and the public sphere. While many of the patriots continued to decry aspects of consumption—and continued to associate it with degeneration and lack of virtue—others were beginning to develop a view of consumers as citizens and of consumption as collective and political. Beginning to explore the "liberating possibilities of the marketplace," they did so not in the individualist sense suggested by Withington and Wood, but largely in collectivist terms. In other words, as T. H. Breen as shown, they began to understand consumption as a social glue. As Samuel Blodget, an early American economist, argued in the first decade of the nineteenth century, commerce and business were the "golden chains" that held society together. They provided, he claimed, a way to "enlarge society." The Revolutionary activists promoted consumption as a source of unity in a distended society, a possible answer to the quest for what Wood has called the search for "new adhesives and attachments to hold people together" in post-Revolutionary America.[48]

The historian Cary Carson poses an important question: how did the consumer revolution of the eighteenth century affect "social relationships"? Typically, we think of consumption as attenuating personal relationships, as promoting privatized individuals rather than socially conscious citizens. But many Americans began to argue that consumption creates new social bonds, and that commerce, as Joseph Priestley wrote, "brings us into closer and more extensive connections with our own species." While modern consumption privatized some aspects of life previously public, it also promoted the reverse—what we might call the politicizing of personal life. Those who embraced the integrative logic of consumption challenged the private-public divide: private actions, in their understanding, had inexorable public consequences.[49]

The claim that the Revolutionaries "invented" consumer activism, this chapter has argued, is not entirely accurate. This is so because, as a general rule, they used techniques already in circulation, understood consumption in traditional terms, entrusted merchants with consumer agency, and embraced the local and the visible as the main venues for their political work. Although "all the individual elements existed in the United States by 1783," Charles Tilly writes, "it still took decades for the full social movement apparatus to become widely available to popular claimants." But to view Revolutionary era consumer activism as "premodern" is a mistake as well. For one thing, the rituals of the Revolutionary boycotters endured and became central to the style of modern consumer activism. Many of the characteristics of American consumer activism—indeed, of our style of symbolic politics writ large—are rooted in the era. It was the Revolutionary boycotters who began the practice of wearing their conscience literally on their sleeves. The Harvard students who wore homespun at their commencement ceremony during the Stamp Act crisis set off a practice that generations of Americans have followed, adopted by Southern nationalists in the antebellum period, by farmers protesting against the "jute trust" in the 1880s, and by boycotters of Japanese silk in the 1930s. As one scholar noted in 1917, "the use of homespun appears to have been the favored of these weapons drawn from the quiver of ancient days."[50] Moreover, the quest for simplicity, usually understood as a purifying and bracing asceticism, has guided most consumer activists ever since the 1760s. This decade witnessed the birth of the fashion of unfashionableness, one of the defining characteristics of consumer activism up to Ralph Nader. Similarly, the valorization of sacrifice, of what the Revolutionaries called "disusing," hardly ceased with the eighteenth-century activists. Finally, the coercion and humiliation of neighbors and potential allies remains a thread in an activist style that seeks not only to enforce personal morality but to equate that morality with the public good. Neither the activists nor their followers abandoned the intimate politics of community, the distrust of consumption, and a faith in thrift. All these remained part of modern consumer activism. Indeed, it was the tension between these older traditions and the newer ideas that gave consumer activism its animating force.

Even if patriots did not embrace or invent all of the elements that came to characterize it later, they initiated the key element of modern consumer activism, which was the embrace of distance. The sociologists Charles Tilly and Sidney Tarrow note a fundamental change in the practice of social movements late in the eighteenth century. In this period, Tilly writes, there was a move away from "the more parochial attachments to local settings involved in Rough Music, effigy burning, and house sacking." Instead, he argues, Americans began to develop "quick-moving modular tactics" which became "a hallmark of social movement activity."[51] Tarrow further notes that the Revolutionary era marked "the beginning of a more organized, general and nonphysical form of collective action—the boycott." The emphasis on "nonphysical" is crucial; Americans came to believe that their new political practices were not dependent on proximity. Moreover, these "modular" weapons were typically consumer practices.[52] The combination of the extension of previous practices and rejection of some older beliefs laid the groundwork for future consumer activism.

The nonimporters and nonconsumers of the Revolutionary generation were undoubtedly key transitional figures in the history of consumer activism. But what precisely was their legacy? Later generations of consumer activists invented new techniques based on different understandings of consumption, and where they borrowed tactics of the Revolutionary generation, they adapted, transformed, and modernized them. Yet in important ways, this generation remained central to the later history of consumer activism. For one thing, unlike other consumer activists, they lived on in memory. Whatever cause they stood for, groups of consumer activists sought to portray themselves as inspired by, and the logical heirs of, the first generation of political consumers. In addition, while not abandoning venerable community policing tactics—indeed, community surveillance was central to Revolutionary consumer activism—practitioners of nonimportation and other such tactics presaged modern consumer activism in a number of ways. Their call for alternative modes of moral commerce was adopted by later generations of consumer activists. In a new age of publicity, American consumer activists of the Revolutionary generation were the first to advertise and publicize their actions to create public lists of friends and enemies. Using the networks that made their actions possible in the first place, they characteristically circulated news of their actions, as a way both of announcing them and gaining adherents. Finally, as this chapter has argued, they helped redefine virtue in new ways, seeking to make it consonant with consumer society. Consumer activists continued to wrestle with the question of whether virtue and consumption could be paired, as they continued to valorize sacrifice. But in raising the issue, the nonimporters set the parameters of modern consumer activism. Tempering claims for the originality of their actions and the singular importance of their legacy, then, should not lead us to underestimate the monumental importance of this period in the history of American consumer activism.

BUY FOR THE SAKE OF THE SLAVE

I. "Through the Medium of Their Pockets"

For those accustomed to thinking that the nineteenth century marked a long dormant period between the consumer activism of the 1760s and 1770s and that of the twentieth century, it would come as a surprise to read the minutes, newspapers, and pamphlets of organizations, such as "free produce" societies, "nonintercourse" associations, and Sabbatarian groups, all of which made their initial appearance in the late 1820s and persisted throughout the antebellum period. Free produce advocates called upon abolitionists to eschew goods made by slave labor and, alternatively, to purchase only "free labor" produce made by nonslave workers. White Southern advocates of nonintercourse used precisely the same methods—the boycott and buycott—and very similar rhetoric for the exact opposite cause: the maintenance of a slave labor economy and the weakening of the free labor North. Sabbatarians, inspired by the evangelical fervor of the Second Great Awakening, called on Christians, North and South, to uphold the sanctity of the Sabbath by boycotting businesses that violated the fourth commandment. I stumbled upon these groups, starting with free produce, when I came across brief but suggestive references to their consumer politics, almost always in works that were in the field of antebellum American history rather than consumer history. These campaigns are not unknown to specialists in antebellum American history, but the extensive use of consumer tactics, while noted by several historians, has not been the source of sustained commentary. It is a paradox that scholars of the antebellum period, who have done so much to highlight the political significance of the "market revolution," have had very little to say about the relation of the developments that fall under this rubric to the other economic revolution that began roughly at the same time, the "consumer revolution." The result is that free produce and nonintercourse (and to a lesser extent,

Sabbatarianism and other moral reform efforts, such as temperance), which played a foundational role of the American tradition of consumer activism, have, when they have been studied at all, been shunted into other historiographical categories. At the same time, twentieth-century scholars have frequently conflated consumer activism with the "consumer movement," the product-testing movement on behalf of ordinary consumers that began in the late 1920s, thus cutting off an exploration of important precursors. And consumer activists themselves, when they have invoked their history at all, have, as we have seen, after acknowledging their debt to the Revolutionaries, skipped the nineteenth century entirely. Noting that "consumer boycotts have been used as tools for change for literally hundreds of years," for example, Todd Putnam, the editor of the *National Boycott News*, sought to provide a long genealogy of the movement he hoped to revive in 1989. When he got down to cases, however, Putnam skipped from the Boston Tea Party in 1773 to the 1930s, omitting the century in which the groundwork of modern consumer activism was formed and in which the word "boycott" was coined.[1]

Although the 1820s marked a—perhaps the—key turning point, it is important to note that this period is not discontinuous with previous developments in the history of consumer activism. Like every episode of consumer activism in every era of U.S. history, the boycotters of this period drew, both explicitly and implicitly, on the theories and actions of previous groups. All of these antebellum movements linked their efforts to the nonimportation campaigns of the Revolutionary generation. The free produce abolitionists in particular built on a nearly continuous tradition of consumer protest that long preceded their movement. Many of them were inspired by the example of John Woolman (1720–1772), the Quaker who, as a young man, made the decision to eschew all commercial connections with slavery; for example, he wore undyed clothing because slaves made dyes. Woolman's journals, first published in 1774, provided a personal model of the eschewal of slave-made goods. As the poet and free labor advocate John Greenleaf Whittier wrote in an introduction to an edition of Woolman's journals that also nicely describes the broader phenomenology of the spread of consumer activism, "We are often surprised to find the initial link in the chain of causes to be some comparatively obscure individual, the divine commission and significance of whose life were scarcely understood by his contemporaries, and perhaps not even by himself. The little one has become a thousand; the handful of corn shakes like Lebanon." Free produce advocates were also inspired by the Quaker Elias Hicks's *Observations on the Slavery of the Africans* (1811). Hicks went beyond Woolman's personal politics by imploring other Quakers to avoid slave-produced goods. In addition, American abolitionists were well aware of the organized and popular boycotts of slave-produced sugar that began in Britain in the 1790s and continued sporadically through the 1820s. Finally, many free producers were doubtless aware of the maple sugar craze of the early 1790s, in which Benjamin Franklin and others encouraged entrepreneurial Americans to market the sweet sap of the maple tree as an alternative to slave-grown cane sugar. The successful marketing of maple sugar, claimed one advocate, would "diminish so many strokes of the whip, which our luxury draws upon the blacks." The Southern nonintercourse movement of the antebellum era drew its name from the nonintercourse policy during the War of 1812. These antebellum movements all made use of older forms of consumer activism discussed in chapter 1, including ostracism, although, as we will see, they adapted them in significant ways.[2]

Sabbatarians, nonintercourse advocates, and free produce proponents supported distinct, and even opposing, causes, and advocates of each effort certainly did not see themselves as part of a like-minded coalition (even though a good number of Northern evangelicals, including William Lloyd Garrison, supported the boycott as a moral tool against both slavery and alcohol).[3] Supporters of these causes neither defined themselves as consumer activists nor understood themselves to be fighting on behalf of consumers. Nonetheless, they called on citizens to act in their capacity as consumers, and they invented sophisticated and enduring consumerist tactics and philosophies. These movements, to the chagrin of their leaders, neither launched boycotts that damaged the economy of their enemies nor sustained alternative businesses long enough for the greater public to take much notice of them, except perhaps as a source of ridicule due to the yawning chasm between their bold plans to use commerce in the service of a moral revolution and their generally short-lived, unprofitable, business ventures.

Yet in the late 1820s each of these groups, almost coterminously, developed a distinctly modern form of consumer politics. The history of these groups is not a mere preface to modern consumer activism or even its prehistory. If, as we argued in the last chapter, consumer activism was born in the Revolutionary era, it grew into early adulthood in the half century before the Civil War. This first generation of modern consumer activists, set, in inchoate form, the terms for the consumer activism that was to follow. Sabbatarians, free producers, and advocates of nonintercourse should be viewed as modern consumer activists because their ideologies and actions lie closer to their twentieth-century counterparts, to whom they were generally unknown—groups that we will examine in later chapters, such as the National Consumers League and the League of Women Shoppers—than to their eighteenth-century forebears, the Revolutionary boycotters of British goods and wearers of native homespun clothing, to whom they paid regular tribute. What their histories reveal is not only that consumer activism existed well before the twentieth century, but that nineteenth-century consumer activists developed a philosophy, practice, and vocabulary of consumer activism that twentieth-century (and contemporary) activists, including those in the consumer movement, employed and modified. Typically failing to achieve their intended goals, whether that was the abolition of chattel slavery, Southern commercial independence, or the protection of the Sabbath from commercial encroachments, these consumer activists established a way of thinking about consumption and a mode of action that were themselves enduring, if unintended, achievements. Their understandings of the social consequences of consumption and of the consequent power of long-distance solidarity, while not ends in themselves for these groups, became the means by which modern citizens (and all those who aspired to take part in meaningful political action via consumption) believed that they could promote social change. Even as particular movements faded and were forgotten, these means endured as a framework through which future generations made their own political efforts.

In the past, most famously during the American Revolution, consumers had been called upon to withhold their patronage from unsavory merchants who sold goods of British origin as a form of economic and moral protest and to ostracize and even to harass fellow citizens who did not. In the vision represented by these new enterprises, consumption was a key pressure point not only negatively but positively: not only were consumers asked to boycott certain products or companies; they were also asked to spend their money at morally sanctioned venues. They celebrated the "purchase of that which comes through clean hands," as the abolitionist newspaper the *Liberator* put it in 1831. This celebration of consumption had implications for the ways in which these groups understood the relationship between virtue and sacrifice. With the advent of moral commerce, virtue was no longer automatically twinned with sacrifice, as it had been for the Revolutionary boycotters as well as for abolitionist sugar boycotters. Indeed, the new class of moral entrepreneurs who opened free produce stores and other such businesses argued that consumers best actualized their ethical views through the consumption of the goods they sold. By severing the link between virtue and sacrifice, they opened the possibility for a new kind of ethical consumption. It was now possible to "buy for the sake of the slave." Others agreed that one could consume rather than sacrifice to enact other ethical commitments. To be sure, there were advocates of moral consumption prior to the 1820s. However, for most of them—for example, the maple sugar entrepreneurs of the 1790s—the moral cause they supported was a happy by-product rather than the raison d'être of the enterprise. By contrast, the free producers and other antebellum consumer activists aimed to, as Augusta Rohrbach has written of William Lloyd Garrison's newspaper the *Liberator*, "make the cause a commercial venture."[4]

Free producers, advocates of nonintercourse with the North, and Sabbatarians developed a conception of political action that took place within, rather than outside of, the marketplace. Their imagined community of political actors, extending far beyond their locality, included not only those who avoided products deemed immoral but equally those who purchased the new morally sanctioned products that they purveyed. Rather than being thought of a discrete and bounded place, each point of consumption began to be conceived of as a node linking individual shoppers to what was becoming a nationwide (and, in some cases, even worldwide) web of producers, manufacturers, other consumers, environments and even nation-states. What Adam Hochschild observes of the British abolitionists is equally true of the free producers on both sides of the Atlantic: they drew "connections between the near and the distant." We tend to think of the networked world as a new thing, but the linked nature of the United States, and much of the rest of the world, was the condition through which these groups sought to build a new politics of solidarity.[5]

One phrase that activists in all of these causes used suggests this new conception of the networked world. "We believe their conscience to be most easily affected through the medium of their pockets," wrote one abolitionist in 1859. Sabbatarians too were convinced that they could change "owners of steamboats, stages, canal boats, and livery stables" by acting "through the medium of their pockets." Proslavery ideologues also spoke of the effectiveness of this medium. The medium of the pocket. Just so. This phrase suggested that it was the economy, driven by consumer power, that motivated people to change.[6]

The early movements introduced tensions that continue to exist within consumer activism, occasionally divide consumer activists, and persist in frustrating their opponents both within and outside the cause. For example, there were no fiercer critics of the free produce efforts than fellow abolitionists, no angrier opponents of Sabbatarian boycotts than other evangelicals, no harsher denouncers of nonintercourse with the North than other Southern nationalists. The attempts of these consumer activists to marry economics and morality, particularly the use of the free market for moral improvement, struck their critics as not only impractical but also, in a certain capitalistic sense, immoral. Something about their self-righteousness (a characteristic attributed to each of these groups, and practically all

subsequent consumer activists, and which most have borne with pride)—
a self-righteousness that was a product of their magnification of individual action and their belief that buying or boycotting was a performative
moral action—meant that they were often singled out for the special scorn
that society heaps on the sanctimonious. These early consumer activists,
like their successors, assigned great power to ordinary consumers, but at
the same time generally distrusted the ability of these consumers to exercise such power wisely and justly. The practice of ranting against the unwillingness of consumers to do either what was good for them or what was
good for society, a defining characteristic of most twentieth-century consumer activists, has its roots in the frustrations of these pioneering consumer activists, who recognized the power of organized consumption or
nonconsumption and also believed that ordinary consumers, ignoring the
strictures of responsible consumption, undermined their cause through
ignorance, indifference, or other moral failings.

II. The Rise of Antebellum Consumer Activism

Sometime around 1826 human nature may not have transformed, but at
that time a sea change occurred in the ways in which people believed that
they could organize for and promote social change. In 1826, the first "free
produce" store opened in Baltimore. Within two years of this date, the
first advocates of Southern "nonintercourse" with the North called for a
consumer-driven commercial declaration of independence, and several
Northern evangelicals founded the first Sabbath-upholding commercial
freight company. Suddenly, in a variety of realms, a new practice joined
the two-generation-old tactic of the boycott, the withholding of pecuniary
support from a business, product, or nation deemed immoral: an alternative means of commerce which provided consumers with a positive way to
exercise their ethical views. In 1826, a group of Presbyterians, for example,
urged "all our ministers and church members when traveling, to give preference to such livery establishments, steamboats, canal boats, and other
public vehicles, as do not violate" the Sabbath. The ferment of the Second
Great Awakening produced many similar consumer-based moral reforms,
which, by adding the option of purchasing morally sanctioned goods, offered concerned citizens another choice—fitting for a nascent consumer
society—in addition to the boycott, about how to act economically on their
moral beliefs. Temperance advocates called for Christians to boycott saloons, and some even opened alcohol-free inns. Advocates of the coloniza-
tion movement, the campaign to transfer American slaves to Africa, sought
to organize a packet line to Liberia. Christian bookstores opened in compe-

tition with secular ones. The evangelical reforming brothers Lewis and Arthur Tappan founded a newspaper, the *Journal of Commerce*, that, they announced, would strictly observe the Sabbath and "avoid all participation
in the gain of those fashionable vices which sap the foundations of morality and religion" by refusing advertisements for the sale of alcohol or theatrical events.[7]

One of the first observers to take stock of this "new power brought to
bear on society" was the acclaimed Unitarian minster William Ellery Channing. In an 1829 essay, the Boston theologian highlighted the newness and
the underlying similarities, as well as the dangers, of the styles of politics that had suddenly appeared in various quarters of the country in support of a variety of causes. Taking note of the "immense facility given to
intercourse by modern improvements, by increased commerce and traveling, by the post-office, by the steam-boat, and especially by the press,
by newspapers, periodicals, tracts, and other publications," Channing saw
that, via this communications infrastructure, the people of a "whole country" could "easily understand one another, and easily act together." No longer was physical proximity the necessary precondition for effective political action. The market, communication, and transportation revolutions
had made it possible for "immense and widely separated multitudes" to
unite and act effectively on behalf of causes they held dear. Invoking a military metaphor, Channing observed: "The grand manoeuvre to which Na-
poleon owed his victories, we mean the concentration of great numbers on
a single point, is now placed within the reach of all parties and sects." Not
only could people from different parts of the nation with no connection
other than a shared "elective affinity" be enlisted "with the uniformity of a
disciplined army" in a new kind of battle, but "facilities of intercourse" also
made it possible for them to do so with unprecedented speed. "So extensive
have coalitions become . . . and so various and rapid are the means of communication, that when a few leaders have agreed on an object, an impulse
may be given in a month to the whole country." In noting the ways in which
imagined communities of activists acted through the medium of a new infrastructure, Channing taxonomized not only the methods and techniques
of the Sabbatarians he disliked but also the many other moral causes that
built on this new conception of long-distance solidarity.[8]

What Channing left unsaid is that what made these new social movements tick was a vision of the consumer as a powerful moral, political, and
economic actor. Sabbatarians, nonintercourse supporters, and proponents
of free produce were the first groups to construct movements built on a new
understanding of consumers as what one free produce advocate called "the
original cause, the first mover" of economic activity. This view, as we have

seen, was most famously promulgated by Adam Smith, who wrote that "consumption is the sole end of all production." These groups in the 1820s were the first to attempt to build political movements upon this assumption. In their view, consumers were like billiard players, setting off and orchestrating a chain reaction of economic activity. This vision of the power of ordinary consumers is what sets them apart from previous boycotters, including those of the Revolutionary era, and makes them the key shapers of modern consumer activism. The activists of the 1820s were also the first to define consumers—rather than agrarian patriarchs, or the producing classes, or, for that matter, elite merchants, the leaders of the nonimportation campaigns of the 1770s—as representative citizens and the moral center of the republic. Theirs were the first bottom-up consumer movements, the first to focus on individual consumers as agents of moral and economic change, and the first to use the word "consumer" in its positive, modern sense, long before most scholars assume that it was coined. The modern-sounding phrase "conscientious consumer" originated with the free produce movement. As the phrase implies, these early consumer activists understood consumer power as inevitably a moral and ethical force, since in this worldview consumers were responsible for the far-reaching impact of their actions. They often used the metaphor of a chain to refer to the binding relationships which linked individual consumers to producers of the goods they bought as well as other consumers.[9]

In his prescient comments, Channing, seizing on the open-ended nature of market relations, pointed out that the "spirit of association, which characterizes our time," could potentially empower any cause, including distasteful ones, and warned citizens of the need "to secure this powerful instrument against perversion." From Channing's point of view, the Sabbatarian effort to shut down Sunday commerce revealed the dangers of consumer politics. In his estimation, the national network of commerce and communications had provided overzealous moralists not only with a platform but the ability to attempt to enforce their vision unfairly on the rest of the country. Their claims that people who did not support the boycotts they sanctioned were, in the words of a New York Sabbatarian, "involved in the guilt" raised the bar of political participation, since neutrality or even tacit support for the cause was no longer an option. From the point of view of Sabbatarians, in the newly connected world, in which shopping was social action—and it was Channing's signal observation to note that this would be true of all consumerist associations—citizens could not passively observe the great social struggles of the age from the sidelines. Rather than soliciting the assistance of a committed minority, Sabbatarians believed that it was their duty to enlist all consumers in their cause, in part by informing those consumers that neutrality was not possible. Since every point of consumption was a node in a national system, an entry point that produced an immediate economic impact, every shopper's purchases were as much a moral mandate as an economic decision. For Lyman Beecher, the founder of the leading Sabbatarian organization, the General Union for Promoting the Observance of the Christian Sabbath, the choice was stark: consumers either sanctioned the "perpetuation of evil," or they promoted a worthy cause. In response, the wealthy evangelicals Arthur Tappan and Josiah Bissell set up a Sabbath-observing freight company based in Rochester, New York, the Pioneer Line. Founding this line and asking Christian consumers to support other businesses that obeyed the fourth commandment made the option of consuming preferable to the boycott of businesses deemed immoral.[10]

The remainder of this chapter will examine the free produce movement; the next chapter will take up the "nonintercourse" campaigns, highlighting Channing's view that opposing causes could use the same new tools.

III. The Rise of Free Produce

The "free produce" movement, led by Quaker and free black abolitionists, encouraged consumers to avoid slave-made goods and to purchase products made by "free labor." Consciously adopting the strategies of the British antislavery sugar boycotters of the 1790s, free produce supporters became active in the United States in the 1820s. They described boycotting slave-made goods as a necessary but insufficient response to the evil of slavery and promoted a "free labor" alternative. To this end, they organized "free produce" stores, the first of which opened in 1826 in Baltimore. Most stores sold clothing and dry goods but some also offered free labor shoes, soaps, ice cream, and candy (see figs. 2.1, 2.2). Philadelphia was the capital of free produce agitation, but, over time, more than fifty stores opened in eight other states, including Ohio, Indiana, and New York, and in England as well. The last free produce store closed its doors in 1867, two years after the abolition of American chattel slavery.[11]

Free produce was based on a new set of ideas about consumption. It was also a business. From harvesting raw materials to producing, distributing, and marketing goods, free produce entrepreneurs sought to develop alternatives to an economy that, even in the northern United States, was thoroughly intertwined with the system of slave labor. Many abolitionists, attracted to this bold entrepreneurial vision, became supporters, consumers, and even investors in free labor enterprises, especially in the late 1830s and early 1840s, the height of abolitionist unity. Benjamin Lundy, the editor of

FREE LABOR.

Pine Apple, Strawberry, and Raspberry Ice Creams,

MADE directly from the JUICES which are so put up as to preserve the FULL FLAVOR of FRESH FRUIT for any length of time, not made into Syrup, which destroys the flavor, warranted superior to any to be found elsewhere, at

S. P. McBURNEY'S,
Ice Cream and Fine Cake Establishment,
No. 89 North Sixth Street,
East side, below Race.

FREE LABOR STORE.

TH᷄ subscriber having purchased the stock and fixtures of the store at the N. W. corner of 5th and Cherry Sts. of Lydia White, would respectfully inform his friends and those who prefer using the produce of free labor, that he will continue the business as heretofore, and hopes by attention thereto, to merit and receive a continuance of the patronage bestowed upon the former occupant.

JOEL FISHER.

FREE LABOR BOOT AND SHOE STORE,
Wholesale and Retail.

THE subscriber notifies his friends and the public generally, that he keeps constantly on hand, at the most reasonable prices, a large assortment of

Women's and Children's Boots and Shoes,

of every description, and best materials, and entirely free from the contamination of slave labor.

Country Merchants will do well to call and examine for themselves, before purchasing elsewhere.

All orders punctually executed, and at the shortest notice.   JAMES WILLIS,
No. 241 Arch street, one door below 7th.

N. B. Marking on linen in durable ink done to order by Marv A. Willis.   Jan 18—1y.

Figure 2.1. A free produce store in Mount Pleasant, Ohio. This store, which operated from 1848 to 1857, was in the former home of Benjamin Lundy, a founder of the free produce idea. (Ohio Historical Society.)

Figure 2.2. Advertisements for "free labor" stores and products in an abolitionist newspaper. (*Pennsylvania Freeman*, Feb 5, 1836, 4.)

the *Genius of Universal Emancipation*, and mentor to William Lloyd Garrison, opened the first free produce store. (Lundy himself had been converted to the idea when he apprenticed to Charles Osbourne, the editor of the Ohio newspaper, *The Philanthropist*, founded in 1816, the first newspaper to promote the nonconsumption of slave-made goods.) The feminist Quaker Lucretia Mott and her husband James ran a free produce store in Philadelphia. David Lee Child, the husband of the famous writer Lydia Marie Child, traveled to France in 1837 to study sugar beet production in the hopes of finding a free labor alternative to the Louisiana and Cuban cane fields. The poet John Greenleaf Whittier edited the *Non-Slaveholder*, the most important free produce journal. Many well-known black abolitionists, including Henry Highland Garnet, William Wells Brown, and Frances Harper, supported free produce in their writings and on transatlantic lecture tours. Several African Americans, among them Lydia White and William Whipper, ran free produce stores, as did several dozen Quaker abolitionists. Other prominent abolitionists supported the precepts of the free produce movement, including Frederick Douglass, Gerrit Smith (who served as vice president of the American Free Produce Association), the Grimké sisters (the 1838 wedding reception for Angelina Grimké and Theodore Weld featured free-sugar desserts made by a black confectioner), Harriet Beecher Stowe and her minister husband, Calvin, as well as, for a time, William Lloyd Garrison, the editor of the *Liberator*, which in its early years included extensive coverage of and editorial support for the free produce movement.[12]

Despite this impressive roster of supporters, free produce stores were generally short-lived enterprises. Finding "free labor" cotton and sugar proved to be the biggest challenge facing free produce supporters. Efforts to seek free labor sources in the slaveholding South failed. Emancipation in the British empire in 1838 spurred a search for free labor goods in the West Indies, but high tariff duties stymied this option. The business correspondence of merchants suggests that running a free produce store was often an exercise in frustration. In his twenty years as a proprietor, George Washington Taylor, who ran one of the most successful and, by the standards of the movement, long-lasting stores, not infrequently received sugar "with a very disagreeable taste and odor" and "very poor, dark and dirty" rice. As if difficulties in the supply chain were not daunting enough, free produce merchants also faced problems on the demand side from customers who complained about the quality and cost of the merchandise. In addition, notes Ruth Nuermberger, hyperconscientious consumers "constantly questioned the genuineness of free labor goods offered to them." By the late 1840s, as we will see, many prominent abolitionists who had initially supported the free produce idea had come to oppose it. In the 1850s, free produce advertisements, a staple of the American abolitionist press in the previous two decades, appeared rarely, and the movement's few remaining supporters became increasingly embittered and resigned. "It is painful and humiliating to be obliged to chronicle among ourselves, an apparent decline of interest in this deeply interesting and important cause," admitted the disconsolate managers of a New York free produce organization in 1853. Unlike the British antislavery boycotts of the 1790s, free produce never became a mass movement, even among abolitionists.[13]

The fact that it failed as a business venture and indeed as a social movement should not lead us to underestimate the significance of free produce for the history of American consumer activism. Adopting and also transforming the rhetoric and tactics established during the nonimportation campaigns of the 1770s and the sugar boycotts of the 1790s, free produce activists laid the template of modern consumer activism. Like the nonimportation leaders, they castigated purchasers of goods of immoral provenance. But they heightened the rhetoric and made it more corporeal. Like their predecessors of the Revolutionary era, they understood fashion and aesthetics as domains of morality. But instead of treating aesthetics as immoral, they debated the meaning of the relationship between aesthetics and virtue. Stressing the importance of a commercial alternative to nonconsumption, free produce activists viewed the market as a contested terrain and an important arena of moral influence subject to their agency, rather than as an evil to be suffered and, if possible, avoided. They were the first consumer activists to propose what scholars today call the "buycott," a commercial alternative to abstention, and the first to suggest labeling ethical goods. As in many consumer movements of the twentieth century—and in the Revolutionary era—women played a key role as leaders and even as proprietors of free produce stores. Viewing consumers as agents of moral and economic change and using the word "consumer" in its positive, modern sense, free produce was the first bottom-up consumer movement. As we have seen, during the nonimportation movement, consumers were partially mobilized to watch over merchants to make sure that they did not violate nonimportation agreements and to disuse British goods. But leaders of these efforts did not stress to the degree that free producers and later generations of consumer activists did the extent to which consumption itself was the key political act. Indeed, in contrast to Revolutionary boycotters, free produce activists rejected the claim that they should discard the "slave-produced goods in your possession; for if it was sinful to buy them, it is sinful to use them." As Lewis Gunn remarked in 1838, "To throw away the articles, would as much encourage slavery, as to use them. If their price has gone into the hands of the slave-holder, all the support which slavery can derive from them has already been secured." For the free produce activists, individual consumption—not the actions of merchants, nor the use of things already bought, nor the symbolism of ostentatious disuse—was the key link in the causal chain. In all these ways, the free produce movement established a model for modern consumer activism, one every bit as significant as that developed by their much-better-remembered predecessors of the Revolutionary era.[14]

The template laid by the free produce movement was not only positive. Many of the criticisms made against contemporary consumer activists were first leveled at the free produce campaigners. For example, William Lloyd Garrison, among others, criticized the movement he had once supported for self-righteous holier-than-thou posturing. Critics charged free produce supporters with reducing politics to personal morality, with being fashionably antifashion and conspicuously self-denying, and for overemphasizing what William's son, Wendell Phillips Garrison, called "outward style," that is, practicing an ostentatious and pretentious simplicity. Critics accused free produce activists of overvaluing private rectitude to the point where it had little connection with the public good.[15]

Developing the philosophies and techniques and even the vocabulary that continue to guide consumer activism, the movement inaugurated the utilitarian, antiaesthetic strain that runs deep in this tradition, but a minority in it saw the need to develop a politics of consumption that was simultaneously moral and fashionable. Largely forgotten, not only by its heirs in the National Consumers League and other twentieth-century consumer groups but also by historians of consumer politics and antebellum reform, the free produce movement should be remembered both as a telling precursor to modern consumer activism and as an illuminating lens through which to view key issues in antebellum American historiography, including, as we will see, the growth of consumer society, "free labor" ideology, humanitarianism, and the market revolution.

IV. Consumer Power and Responsibility

"IF THERE WERE NO CONSUMERS OF SLAVE-PRODUCE THERE WOULD BE NO SLAVES." Variations of this claim, endlessly repeated by free produce advocates, built on a new understanding of consumers as engine of economic activity. Organizing the first social movement upon this insight, free produce proponents believed that consumers determined the fortunes of the entire economic food chain. Consumers were thus agents—indeed, moral agents—responsible for the plight of the workers, and this included not only the products they would make but also whether the workers themselves were to be enslaved or free. Consumers of slave-made goods, became, according to one activist, "one indispensable link in the chain of causes which perpetuates the system." In the moral economy of the free produce movement, consumers of slave-made products, especially cotton and sugar, were implicated in the crime of slavery, since "slave-grown produce tends . . . to rivet the chains and add to the labour and misery of the Slave."[16]

Unlike their Revolutionary forebears, then, free produce advocates took it as a matter of course that consumers had become the nation's principle economic and moral agent. In 1831, Lundy's newspaper, the *Genius of Universal Emancipation*, published one of the first American articles with the title "Consumers," and the word appeared repeatedly in abolitionist journals and speeches in this period. While Lundy and other free producers noted the capacity of consumers for good, and encouraged them to act on it, they also warned this newly empowered class of their equally powerful capacity for supporting slavery and other immoral causes. It was "an axiom too self-evident," wrote Lundy that consumers of slave-made goods bore the "guilty responsibility" for slavery, not the slave owners who merely served their interests.[17]

Free produce supporters placed an unprecedented emphasis on consumption because they believed that consumers alone possessed the power to promote "free labor," a concept that was central to their cause. A truly free market, they claimed, would reveal free labor to be cheaper and more efficient than slave labor; as one supporter wrote, "slave labour is gradually exterminated when brought into competition with free labour." Indeed, the genesis of the free produce movement was the idea—articulated by Benjamin Lundy in his 1825 pamphlet *A Plan for the Gradual Abolition of Slavery in the United States*—of bringing free labor "into direct competition" with slave labor. The next year, having conceived of a way to make this competition a reality, Lundy opened his "free labor" store; the phrase "free produce" emerged several years later. Free labor stores, thus, would do far more than allow purchasers to avoid the taint of slavery; they would also provide a market for free produce to compete with slave-made goods, a competition that, by the lights of their economic theory, free labor was sure to win. The high-water mark of the free produce movement, the Requited Labor Convention held in Philadelphia in 1838, attended by Garrison and many other abolitionist leaders, led to the formation of the American Free Produce Association. A resolution at the convention declared, "As slaves are robbed of the fruits of their toil, all who partake of those fruits are participants in the robbery." The growing number of free produce stores, the delegates added, made this form of consumerist criminal activity unnecessary.[18]

Free produce advocates believed that most Northerners, despite their ostensible faith in free labor, sustained slavery through their "use [of] the productions of the bondman's constrained and unpaid toil." Free produce supporters described all purchasers of slave-made goods as partners in robbery: "participants," "accessories," "aggrandizers," "enrichers," "countenancers," and "abettors." If these words appeared to imply that consumers merely enabled a crime whose main perpetrator lay elsewhere, this was not the position of the free produce activists, who understood consumers to be, as one free produce activist put it, "the ultimatum of the whole system" of slavery. Similarly, the free produce advocate Joseph A. Dugdale described "the consumer of slave-grown produce" as the de facto employer of slave owners. "It is clear to those who will take the trouble to examine the subject," according to another free produce campaigner, "that the northern merchant who purchases the cotton, sugar and rice of the southern planter . . . the auctioneer who cries his human wares in the market, and sell those helpless victims of cupidity . . . yea, even the heartless, murderous slave-trader, are each and all of them, only so many AGENTS, employed by and for the CONSUMER in extracting and transferring the products of the unrequited toil, of the poor down trodden suffering slave." This was, to put it mildly, a strong version of consumer sovereignty, in which all other actors in the economic system, particularly slave owners, owed their existence to the shoppers who, in a fundamental sense, created them. In his defense of the accused fugitive slaves at the "rescue trials" of 1851, the New Hampshire Senator John P. Hale made this analogy explicit, when he described the slaveholders as salesmen: "Why, gentlemen, he sells agony! Torture is his stock-in-trade! He is a walking scourge! He hawks, peddles, retails, groans and tears about the streets of Norfolk!" Quoting this passage in her *Key to Uncle Tom's Cabin*, Harriet Beecher Stowe pointed out that since it was shoppers who kept the peddlers in business, consumers bore the responsibility for this agony and torture. This is why she concluded that "the roots of the poison-tree [of slavery] have run under the very hearth-stone of New England families." *Uncle Tom's Cabin* itself can be read as Stowe's endorsement of the view that the "public sentiment" that allowed for unthinking consumption of the products of slavery made the entire system of slavery, even the odious slave trader, possible.[19]

Free produce activists thus turned the fundamental conceit of abolition on its head, shifting the focus away from the South and its slaveholders to the North and its consumers of slave-made products. Whereas Ralph Waldo Emerson famously said, "Who makes the abolitionist? The Slaveholder," free produce supporters reversed the sequence, charging abolitionists with making the slaveholder, through their unthinking purchase of slave-made goods. As an article in the form of wisdom dispensed from a fictitious slaveholder to a Northern consumer declared, "You don't technically hold the slave, but you give the gold which makes him to be held! We are but your servants!" In this view, those seemingly far more directly involved in slavery than Northern (or British) shoppers, were, in effect, servants of those consumers. As the free produce supporter Henry Grew asked the attendees at the New England Antislavery convention of 1850, what did the abolitionist slogan "No union with slaveholders" mean if they abetted slavery? Properly understood, one activist claimed, the phrase had to mean "No *social, religious, political, or commercial* Union with slaveholders." Two years earlier, Benjamin Kent and Lydia C. Hambleton, members of the Union Free-Produce Society, similarly claimed that for the phrase "No union with slaveholders" to have any teeth, it must be applied "commercially as well as ecclesiastically." Abolitionists condemned hypocritical Northern politicians who compromised with the "slave power." But this was precisely the charge leveled at them by the free produce activists, on the ground that their purchase of slave-made goods financed slavery. In labeling slaveholders the servants of consumers, free produce activists analogized northern consumers to the group they most despised, slave owners, and slave owners to the people for whom they felt the most sympathy, slaves. If abolitionists routinely identified with the suffering slaves, free produce activists identified them with slave owners through their consumption of slave-made goods. Since "demand is the main prop and stay of slavery," wrote one free produce advocate, it follows that the "slaveholder is comparatively innocent." The consumer, after all, set off the chain of events that, to use a favorite word of free produce activists, "stimulated" the slaveholder to act. Thus, claimed one free producer, consumers are "in a more guilty condition than the slaveholders."[20]

This interpretation of slavery as a system that existed, as one free produce activist put it, for the "express purpose of furnishing products to the consumer" challenged the premises of the prevailing humanitarian discourse, which urged people to alleviate suffering once they were made aware of it and to identify with the sufferer. Abolitionists typically understood themselves as bystanders to suffering, who once having learned of it, were obligated to act to relieve such suffering. They graphically highlighted and magnified the pain of slaves that needed to be ameliorated and urged citizens to identify with suffering slaves. By depicting Northerners not as observers of suffering but as causes of it, free produce campaigners radically extended and relocated the concepts of obligation and responsibility. Slavery was not merely a moral wrong, they maintained, but a moral wrong that Northern consumers sustained through their purchases. If, in the standard trope, the humanitarian was the sympathetic observer, a good Samaritan aiding a "starving stranger" and identifying with his or her travails, in the hands of the free produce activists, the "sympathetic observer" was better understood as a thief and a slave owner, and the sufferer was not a stranger but a victim of a crime, one perpetrated by the consumer of slave goods, who turned out to be the sympathetic observer himself. This robust conception of humanitarianism well illustrates what the historian Thomas Haskell has called the "power of market discipline to inculcate altered perceptions of causation in human affairs." Markets allowed free producers to project their ability to end suffering in distant places, but they also, and in ways willfully ignored by mainstream and even many radical abolitionists, identified consumers as perpetrators of far-flung and morally hideous crimes.[21]

What enabled free produce activists to attribute such power to consumers was their vision of the world and especially of the growing part of it connected by market relations as what the *Non-Slaveholder* called "one connected and dependent whole." In this interconnected world, every purchase affected other links of the chain; the manufacturers, distributors and, especially, the laborers, whose jobs were all initiated by the first cause of consumer demand. This new and radical understanding of consumer agency followed from the free produce conception of the market as a potentially revolutionary force and an ideal conduit for the expression of consumers' desires. If earlier movements had focused on merchants, not consumers—angry colonists, for example, threatened not consumers but shopkeepers for violating the cause—free produce activists espoused an unshakable belief in consumers as the market's driving force. If the market was the world's connective tissue, the consumer directed and shaped the links formed by this tissue. The need to ensure that markets worked for the betterment of enslaved people, according to the Vermont free produce leader Henry Miles, highlighted the "necessity of making his practice and his profession agree." In this view, shopping was politics by other means, enabling the activist to put theoretical beliefs into practice. The potent forces of market relations ensured that the abolitionist who carried her principles into commercial as well as political forums would serve their ultimate goal. "Our moral influence against slavery must be weakened, our testimony diluted, if while we denounce slavery as robbery of the basest kind," observed the black abolitionist Frances Ellen Watkins, "we are constantly demanding rice from the swamps, cotton from the plantations and sugar from the deadly mills."[22]

Unlike many celebrants of the market, however, free produce campaigners did not ascribe morality to the market itself. While they fervently held that, as L. W. Gause claimed, "commerce is indispensable to the welfare of society," they also recognized, as one Quaker abstainer put it, that "commerce is without a conscience of its own." They believed that markets magnified the range and scope of good and bad behavior, since actions that previously might have made only a neighbor happy or unhappy could now spread misery or joy to innumerable people in distant places. So while power inhered in markets, this force could be used for good or for ill. This made the market both powerful and dangerous. The key was to harness the market's power without triggering what Gause called "unrighteous commerce." As Samuel Rhoads reminded the readers of the *Liberator* in 1850, slavery "is sustained by commercial union."[23]

According to free produce advocates, markets were not themselves moral but, if used properly, they provided a potentially powerful engine for moral change. Using the market, consumers could abet the crime of slavery or eliminate it. Market forces could themselves solve the problems of which free produce proprietors and customers complained, including high prices and the narrow range of goods. If only a critical mass of consumers demanded moral sugar and cotton, one free produce proponent claimed with confidence, "Free Enterprize would rush to the task of meeting their wants." Because free produce brought "free into competition with slave labor, in every article of cultivation" it was "the great lever, by which this Colossus is to be overturned!" This market-oriented worldview led free produce activists to treat slaveholders as profit maximizers who would respond to the stimulus of consumers exactly as did other capitalist merchants: "The slaveholders are not such devoted worshippers of slavery, as to make voluntary sacrifices of their own interests upon her altar." Recognizing that "the market, though shut to the productions of slave labor, will still be opened to the productions of requited labor," slave owners would change course and become suppliers of free produce. Indeed, claimed Samuel Rhoads, "emancipation would become the interest of the planters." The inevitable result, as William Henry Hobbey confidently predicted, would be a turn toward free labor: "As abstainers increase in number, the demand for free labour produce will be greater. Consequently there will be a greater effort on the part of the producer to supply the demand; and the direct result would be thus, that all the free negroes in the slave states would receive employment, and there would be many plantations conducted wholly by freemen." This was consistent with the view free producers put forward of slaveholders as "agents" of consumers and of consumers, rather than workers, as the primary bulwark of free labor.[24]

To combat the reifying effects of global markets, free produce campaigners sought to humanize the people and the forces that brought goods into their shopping cart. Market relations, free producers stressed end-lessly, were as real and as consequential as face-to-face relations. But this was not a reality that one could ascertain through the senses; the con-sumer of slave-made goods, far from the scene of subjugation, could not see a slave suffer or hear the crack of an overseer's whip. As the author of an article entitled "How Do You Know?" claimed, physical distance from the production of goods too often blinded consumers to their moral ob-ligations to the slave: "Let us remember that . . . however far removed we may be from the *scene of their sufferings in the physical world*, in the moral world we are standing beside them." To highlight the moral, if not physical, proximity of buyer to maker, free produce activists sought to create in the minds of prospective purchasers of slave-made goods what Charlotte Suss-man has called "a moment of literalization when the bodies of both pro-ducers and consumers are physically connected with a commodity." One rhetorical strategy to overcome the alienation created by distance was, as we have seen, to describe the consumer as the employer of slave labor, and therefore the person responsible not just for slavery in general, which is a rather abstract charge, but for the labor of a specific enslaved person. "Ev-ery one who buys a pound of Southern sugar or a yard of Southern cotton," in the words of W. J. Snelling, "virtually approves and sanctions an hour or more of slave-labour."[25]

Another technique to make the crime of slavery tangible to the con-sumer operated at the level of perception and affect. In order to show "in true colors, the affliction to which the slave is subjected" free produce cam-paigners overlaid, through metonymy, seemingly neutral and even beauti-ful slave-made products with graphic and disturbing images of suffering. Activists sought to teach consumers not only to apprehend what appeared before them—a cup of sugar or a cotton dress—but, through their under-standing of the slave's unseen suffering, also to see a blood-stained prod-uct and to hear the groans of its maker. As Henry Highland Garnet declared in 1851, "The sugar with which we sweetened our tea, and the rice which we ate, were actually spread with the sweat of the slaves, sprinkled with their tears, and fanned by their sighs." Garnet and others wished, through such imagery, to convey the bad behind the good. "If we would open our ears to hear, we might hear the response, or open our eyes to see, we might see [slavery] branded upon every barrel of Southern sugar," wrote a columnist in the *Non-Slaveholder*. "Go to yonder store, and the products of oppression will stare you in the face. Look! And you will see the pro-slavery pictures there exhibited." Proslavery pictures were not literally displayed on prod-ucts. Nor did they speak. Yet Frances Ellen Watkins urged abolitionists to hear their cries of pain: "We enter the wardrobe and the sighs and groans of the slave are lingering around the seams of our clothes and floating amid the folds of our garments." Free produce activists aimed to give consumers the tools to take the imaginative leap, to, in effect, defetishize commodities through visualization and other metaphors of the senses.[26]

Concerns about the misleading appearance of slave-made goods led some free produce supporters to eschew commerce altogether. Establishing what they labeled an "abstention movement," they held up the "straightforward path of self-denial" as the highest ideal. By refusing to buy altogether, they refused to collude in slavery. A number of boycotters linked self-sacrifice and virtue and paired these with a general criticism of aesthetic goods as immoral. Many free produce activists accordingly took it as an article of faith that "the natural wants of man are few, whilst his artificial wants are manifold." The movement, they believed, should discourage people from developing an interest in beauty and fashion, which stimulated such false wants.[27]

Unlike most consumer movements before and since, however, in the free produce movement there was substantial dissent from this identification of beauty and fashion with immorality. A minority in the free produce movement challenged the view that self-denial need be central. The key was not abstention per se, they argued, but the effects of one's consumption or nonconsumption on others. Where abstention had beneficial effects—if for example, it led to decreased demand for slaves—they supported it. But abstention, they claimed, was not a virtue in and of itself. Indeed, self-denial undermined the philosophy of the movement, which called on consumers to change the world by exerting market power.

These dissenting free produce activists also argued that the rhetoric of self-denial and the denigration of fashion would limit the popularity of the movement. To be successful, a market-oriented endeavor had to compete with other commercial goods, rather than count on the charitable spirit of conscientious customers. Instead of highlighting virtuous sacrifice, one free produce consumer, depressed by the sight of "coarse calicoes" and "indifferent colors" on display in free produce stores, argued that "we must rival the blood-stained productions in beauty and durability." As the granddaughter of Lucretia and James Mott wrote, in her not-so-fond recollections of childhood visits to the family store, "Free sugar was not always as free from other taints as from that of slavery; and free calicoes could seldom be called handsome, even by the most enthusiastic; free umbrellas were hideous to look upon, and free candies, an abomination." These critics suggested that extreme self-denial and indifference to fashion would undercut the market-based precepts of the movement. Only with sufficient aggregate demand could the market perform its magic. Yet when George

Washington Taylor endeavored to market slave-free clothing in the "prettiest styles," he noted with frustration that the "general cry" of movement regulars to this fashionable but virtuous clothing was that it was "not plain enough." The fashionable clothes languished in his store, suggesting that some free produce shoppers were unwilling to reconsider the ingrained opposition between virtue and fashion. These customers understood their task as "endur[ing] privations," not patronizing free labor fashions.[28]

It is instructive to compare the free produce efforts with antislavery fairs, a roughly coterminous consumerist strategy of abolitionists, whose advocates had no qualms about using fashion and aesthetics for moral ends. Begun in 1834, the fairs were most popular in New England and in Pennsylvania, where they were also supported by prominent free produce supporters. If free produce is an important progenitor of modern consumer activism, antislavery fairs helped found modern consumer society. The custom of Christmas trees and Christmas presents began with the fairs, which, because they were usually staged in mid- to late December, also initiated the practice of "holiday shopping." Indeed, Harriet Beecher Stowe described the fairs as the "most fashionable shopping resort of the holidays." Promoters of antislavery fairs did not share the free producers' ambivalence about luxury and fashion and treated them as resources rather than as the threats that Taylor's customers feared. Although some fairs sold free produce goods, and it was at the fairs that the first ethically labeled goods were sold, most items were not advertised as such. Their advertising said very little about the moral provenance of the goods sold, except to highlight their cachet, especially if they were imported from Europe.[29]

Antislavery fair organizers were much less concerned than were free produce advocates with the causal damage done by consumption. To the consternation of some free produce activists, they focused not on means, but on ends, namely, fund-raising for abolitionist organizations. For the free producer L. W. Gause, giving "all the profits to the antislavery cause" did not absolve the seller of guilt if the products were made under immoral conditions. Fair organizers cared less about purity and demanded no apologies for goods sold at the fairs or for the fact that they were explicitly marketed as luxuries. "No pains have been spared to meet the wants and gratify the tastes of the community," noted an article in the *Pennsylvania Freeman*, which never described free produce stores as stimulating and satiating the tastes of consumers.[30]

Like free produce stores, antislavery fairs promoted a consumer-powered form of abolition. But it is important to attend to the different ways in which they conceived of consumer power. Although, like the free produce activists, organizers of antislavery fairs encouraged consumers to "buy for the sake of the slave," as a poem commemorating the 1838 fair urged, the phrase had different meanings for the two groups. Rather than directly helping the slave by propping up demand for free labor alternatives to slavery, the kind of buying encouraged at the fairs would aid them indirectly by enabling antislavery organizations to flourish. Promoters of antislavery fairs advocated consumption in the service of political struggle; free producers advocated consumption *as* political struggle. The fairs did not repudiate free produce principles; indeed, some free produce activists supported the fairs. But the fair organizers also did not encourage consumers to deconstruct the chain of events resulting from their purchases. It was enough, they believed, for shoppers to raise money for the cause.[31]

V. An Uphill Work

Abolitionists turning toward immediatism in the late 1820s and early 1830s initially welcomed free produce as a legitimate and noteworthy tactic in the campaign to end slavery. Many prominent abolitionists, including William Lloyd Garrison and the Grimké sisters, supported free produce for a time. As late as 1843, Garrison, while acknowledging criticisms of free produce, continued to consider it an important arrow in the quiver of abolitionism. Free produce campaigners, for their part, claimed that abstention from slave produce should complement, not supersede, other legitimate antislavery strategies. However, they repeatedly condemned the "lamentable apathy" of abolitionists toward free produce. "Want of interest on the part of abolitionists," complained Mary Grew in a comment echoed by other free produce supporters, made the "abstinence business an up-hill work." Following the market logic to which free producers were devoted, Mary Johnson observed, in a letter to Grew, that "judging from the high price, and indifferent quality, of many kinds that we have seen, it appears very evident that the demand for [free produce goods] must be very limited." Grew, in reply, agreed that this was a "lamentable fact," as many abolitionists evidently continued to "purchase the products of the slave's unrequited labor, thus *hiring* the oppressor to continue in the commission of sin." Frustration at the manner in which most abolitionists downplayed or ignored their cause, which they believed "would sign the death warrant of slavery" if widely practiced, often blended into irritation, with Garrison (who in 1831 called the logic of free produce a "self-evident truth") singled out as the most significant betrayer of the cause: "If this champion of freedom had continued, as he began, to earnestly and powerfully advocate the disuse of slave products . . . the downfall of slavery would at this moment be nearer than it is." (The word "disuse" suggested an important continuity with

Revolutionary boycotting.) Comparing the "non-abstaining" abolitionist to the "drunkard" who preaches temperance, Sarah Pugh, an officer in the American Free Produce Association, declared that "the great mass of abolitionists . . . need an abstinence baptism." Following Pugh, free produce activists called abolitionists hypocrites for engaging in the "glaring inconsistency, (to which the eyes of so many are so strangely blinded), between an Anti-Slavery theory, and the pro-slavery practice of purchasing the fruits of the slave's extorted toil." Those who criticized slavery but continued to purchase slave-made goods, they claimed, sustained "the iniquitous system with one hand, while endeavoring to demolish it with the other." The immoral consuming practices of the hypocritical abolitionist, according to the delegates at a free produce meeting, were "sanctioning and building up the system his theory would destroy."[32]

After a brief period during which many leading abolitionists rallied around it, free produce became a target of criticism, almost all of it from abolitionists themselves, for whom it had become both "an extraneous issue" of "comparatively small importance" and a rather large annoyance. (There is little evidence that slaveholders or their political representatives paid much attention to it and no evidence that it had a discernable economic impact on them.) It is important to catalog the criticisms, because so many of these were to reappear in later debates about consumer activism, from outside the consumer movement but also especially from within. If those in favor of free produce put forward new conceptions of the politics of consumption, many of their opponents' arguments challenged the primacy as well as the efficacy of a politics of consumption. Thus, these debates, a regular feature of abolitionist newspapers, foreshadowed twentieth-century debates about the value of consumer politics.[33]

The critics called free produce impractical and inconvenient, claiming that it was futile for consumers to try to separate themselves from slavery, since the slave system interpenetrated every aspect of American life and, indeed, the world economy. "These productions are so mixed in with the commerce, manufactures, and agriculture of the world . . . so indissolubly connected with the credit and currency of the country—that, to attempt to seek the subversion of slavery by refusing to use them, or to attach moral guilt to the consumer of them, is, in our opinion, alike preposterous and unjust," wrote William Lloyd Garrison. Opponents of free produce also suggested that abolitionists would be paralyzed and unable to do their work if they followed to the letter the demanding precepts of free produce. As Elizur Wright said, "No antislavery agent or other abolitionist must now travel in stage or steam-boat, for the sheets and table cloths of the latter are of cotton. . . . No abolitionist can any longer buy a book, or take a newspaper printed on cotton paper." Related to these seeming pragmatic claims was a moral one; slaves would be better served if abolitionists spent their time in the political fight against slavery. Free produce advocates were "so occupied by abstinence as to neglect THE GREAT MEANS of abolishing slavery," claimed Garrison, who declared that since he vigorously pursued these great means, his slave-made purchases should be considered "innocently used." Free produce shoppers, he said, had a "pretext to do nothing more for the slave because they do so much" in the exhausting efforts to find non-slave-made goods and the uncomfortable job of wearing and eating them. In other words, even if it were possible to divest oneself of all slave-made goods, the quest for what one free produce advocate called "clean hands" diverted energy from the antislavery struggle by shifting the focus to what amounted to a selfish obsession with personal morality. Some critics, especially evangelicals, condemned free produce because it was based on coercing slaveholders to abandon slavery rather than changing their consciousness. Critics also made two class-based arguments. First that free labor goods were too expensive for the poor to be able to afford. Second, that the line between free and slave labor was fuzzier than the free producers assumed. In a letter of dissent sent to the Requited Labor Convention, the prominent abolitionist William Goodell urged the delegates to address the "kindred discussion of the propriety of abstinence from the products of other forms of oppression besides that of American slaveholding."[34]

Free produce activists had lengthy responses to all of these charges, but by the mid-1840s the real action in American abolition had shifted elsewhere. Garrison spoke for many abolitionists in 1850, when, conceding that he had "once regarded it in a different light," he declared that the free produce "question has lost its importance with us." Many abolitionist families went the way of Garrison's, which, according to his son Wendell, ate without scruple "Cuban and Louisianan sweetness" from a bowl inscribed, "East India Sugar, not Made by Slaves," tableware that in headier days served as a proud memento of allegiance to free produce in many abolitionist households. Abolitionists, Garrison noted, "claimed for themselves, almost in the name of the slaves, the right above all others to wear the products of their blood and travail." Abolitionist defiance of free produce reached its zenith in 1847 when, in response to a free produce motion at an antislavery convention, Wendell Phillips declared that he would happily face the "Great Judgement" attired in slave-made cotton of South Carolina. Denying that "it is morally wrong to wear slave grown cotton, or eat slave grown sugar or rice," by 1850 the elder Garrison finally came around to repudiating the fundamental premise of free produce: "The wrong concentrates," he concluded, "not on the head of the consumer." Even as the steam was running out of the free produce idea, not all abolitionists were willing to concede Garrison's point. Writing in the *Liberator* in 1848, D. S. Grandin, while recognizing the legitimacy of Garrison's arguments ("I am aware that we cannot avoid giving to some extent this kind of support to unrequited labor, without going out of the world"), nonetheless argued that free produce remained an important means of fighting slavery. This was one of the last mentions of free produce in the leading journal of American abolitionism.[35]

In the last decade before the Civil War, the free produce idea did not die, but its center of gravity shifted, once again, in two directions: to England, where free produce pamphlets, associations, lecturers, newspapers, and stores, all of which were virtually extinct in mainstream abolitionist publications the United States, abounded, and to the community of black abolitionists centered around Frederick Douglass. Arguments in favor of "free labor products" appeared in the *North Star*, long after Garrison had rejected their virtues. Similarly, advertisements for free produce stores, a common sight in the early years of the *Liberator* but a rarity by the mid-1840s, regularly appeared in *Frederick Douglass' Paper* well into the 1850s. Douglass continued to publish reports about the activity of local free labor associations. Moreover, his newspaper reported on the continued transatlantic linkages on the free produce issue. For example, it reported on the visit of Harriet Beecher Stowe and her husband, Calvin, to England in 1854, in which they separately urged the importance of the free produce weapon. Calvin Stowe noted that "as the largest consumer in the world" of slave-made cotton, the English people had a "plain duty" to abstain. And his famous wife reminded the women of that country of the successes they had won by boycotting in the past. Finally, Douglass saw fit to publish in the summer of 1855 the poetic words of Frances Ellen Watkins who described free produce as "a harbinger of hope." In what may have been a subtle rebuke of Garrison, *Frederick Douglass' Paper* publicized the claim of Henry Miles that purchasing slave-made goods was an act of hypocrisy for abolitionists.[36]

VI. The Legacy of Free Produce

Attending to the history of free produce does more than fill in a gap in the historiography of consumer activism, the supposed century-long lull between the Revolutionary boycotters and the late nineteenth-century founders of modern consumer activism. Knowledge of abolitionist consumer politics helps explain the origins of modern consumer activism and also the future shape that it took. A *longue durée* perspective helps us to sort out both the continuities and novelties in the twentieth-century consumer movement.

One significant continuity is the free produce movement's ambivalence toward consumer society. Free produce supporters recognized, however grudgingly, that the new category of person called "consumer" made their movement possible and that without commerce their efforts to promote long-distance solidarity would have been ineffectual. While zealous in their quest for individual moral purity, most free produce activists struggled with and recognized (although not to the degree that their critics thought necessary) the need to align the desire to be personally free of guilt with the broader welfare of society. Like many of their fellow citizens during the age of the "market revolution," free produce advocates viewed commerce with ambivalence. They sought to use market power without falling victim to its potential vices. Some trumpeted a full engagement in the free market, while others valorized abstinence. Stoic self-denial, the practice of "disuse," was an important strand of free produce, but unlike previous boycott movements (and most since), free produce contained other strands. In the emerging consumer culture, free produce was the first consumer protest movement that invoked the logic, and occasionally the techniques, of consumer society, that is, the new infrastructure of mass markets, advertising, and large-scale production. It used advertising (and even inaugurated the celebrity endorsement, when figures like Angelina Grimké supported the cause) and celebrated consumption, and at least a minority within the movement recognized the importance of paying attention to style and aesthetics as potentially positive forces. In defining consumers as representative citizens, it laid the groundwork for the political culture of modern America.

Other innovations of the free produce movement continue to inform modern consumer politics as well. The most important perhaps is the concept of long-distance solidarity, the notion that consumers are responsible for the results of their purchases, however far reaching and invisible to them they may be at the point of purchase. For free produce promised to take an imagined community of producers and consumers and, with real world consequences, turn them into freedpeople and emancipators. To achieve this they developed a new conception of causation, which dramatically expanded the concept of responsibility and promoted what we might call a "posthumanitarian" worldview, in which the idea of an innocent good Samaritan became unthinkable. In his place was a consumer whose every purchase set off a wave of activity, often criminal, for which she was ultimately responsible. Finally, free produce activists pioneered a politics firmly situated within the market, and indeed unimaginable outside of it.

If the emphasis in this chapter has been on the ways in which free produce abolitionists modernized consumer activism, one virtue of this history is that it sets into relief aspects of consumer politics that truly are twentieth-century phenomena. It was not until the twentieth century that consumer politics came to be characterized by a conception of "the consumer" as needing protection. Moreover, self-described consumer organizations—groups that saw their task as representing, defending, and lobbying for consumers themselves—emerged, establishing consumers as an interest group in a pluralistic society, rather than as an embodiment of that society, as they had been thought of by free produce activists. Those groups coalesced in the 1930s into something known as the "consumer movement," an organized political effort on behalf of consumers, whose chief aim was, as Helen Sorenson described it in her 1941 book *The Consumer Movement*, "protecting and promoting the consumer interest." What distinguished the "consumer movement" from previous and contemporaneous movements of consumers was precisely this emphasis on consumers themselves as the chief beneficiaries of political activism. These groups claimed to represent the "consumer interest," an interest which for the first time, became seen as within the purview of state regulation. From the Pure Food and Drug Act of 1906, through the various consumer advisory boards of the New Deal, through the president's special assistant for consumer affairs, begun under President Lyndon Johnson in the 1960s, the federal government came to understand the protection of the consumer interest as one of its duties. By contrast, none of the Revolutionary boycotters, "free produce" campaigners, or even the turn-of-the-century founders of the National Consumers League saw themselves as part of a "consumer movement." Rather, these groups mobilized consumers not for the benefit of consumers but on behalf of the nation, the slave, the worker, or the poor.[37]

It is a puzzle of the history of consumer activism that despite the fact that it has been a continuous strand in American politics, each successive generation of consumer activists tends to think it is the pioneering generation. This has allowed each generation to inaccurately understand its form of political engagement as innovative. Earlier in this chapter, I suggested that the free produce movement had been "largely forgotten" by future generations of consumer activists. In this sense, free produce parallels the relation that the Civil Rights pioneers of the New Deal era bore to their better-known postwar heirs. "Although little, if any, memory of the New Deal years informed the Civil Rights movement of the 1960s," writes Patricia Sullivan, "the activists of earlier decades tilled the ground for future change." Collective memory of American social movements is a surprisingly unstudied phenomenon. But Sullivan's insight suggests that the forgetting of free produce may not be atypical among social movements. Still, it would be a mistake to treat any of these movements as having no impact on what followed. Charles Payne has suggested that family memory abetted the "organizing tradition" in Mississippi. He has argued that a group of families which "kept the story before" family members, that is, passed on hidden traditions of resistance, played a crucial role in the Civil Rights struggle. A similar pattern may be discerned in relation to free produce. Florence Kelley, a founder of the Progressive Era National Consumers League, first learned about the importance of consumer activism from her aunt, Sarah Pugh, the free produce activist. Kelley's family kept the story before her. It is thus fittingly ironic that Robert Lynd labeled *Your Money's Worth*, the best-selling 1927 book by Stuart Chase and F. J. Schlink that set off a new wave of activism, "the Uncle Tom's Cabin" of the consumer movement. Lynd, like most twentieth-century consumer activists, was apparently unaware that many of the readers of *Uncle Tom's Cabin*, and even its author, had laid the groundwork for the modern consumer movement.[38]

Consciously or not, practitioners of consumer politics have mirrored the philosophy and methods of the free produce campaigners. The promoters of the idea of the "union label" in the late nineteenth century called on consumers to prevent "wage slavery," much the way that free producers claimed that shoppers could eliminate chattel slavery. Kelley's National Consumers League called consumer responsibility the key to improving the plight of poor workers. The leaders of the movement to boycott Japanese silk in the 1930s, like their counterparts a century before them, stressed the political significance of promoting alternative commerce, in that case nonfascist rather than nonslave, and of developing new tastes in fashion, rather than condemning fashion outright. The idea that consumers help to sustain immoral enterprises and underwrite exploitation has been central to every major boycott campaign of the recent past, including the Montgomery bus boycott and the United Farm Workers–led grape boycott.[39]

Free produce activism may have failed, but its vision of consumers as political actors and of consumer society as a contested terrain has prevailed. The anthropologist James C. Scott has argued that since "many acts of resistance may fail to achieve their intended result," we need to study "intentions" as much as "consequences." It is equally important to understand the unintended and unforeseen consequences of such "failures." Free produce activists did not seek to pioneer consumer activism, but, in retrospect, that accomplishment is more significant than their failure to achieve their intended goal of bolstering abolition. In her history of the cooperative movement, Beatrice Webb notes that the "Rochdale pioneers," the first cooperators, "unwittingly discovered" the theories that would later guide the movement. Like these cooperators, free produce activists "achieved without intending" a new conception of consumer politics, one that has become the lingua franca of consumer activists ever since. Although they did not understand themselves as such, the free produce pioneers invented modern consumer activism, a protean and tension-filled form of protest that is characterized by a view of the market as a source of power and danger, of individual shoppers as moral agents, and of consumer society as simultaneously a resource for and an impediment to political engagement. Modern consumer activists from the post–Civil War years onward have borrowed and adapted, even when they thought they had invented, the techniques and moral claims of this band of marginal abolitionists. As we will see in the next chapter, they also took from ideological enemies of the free producers: white, Southern advocates of "nonintercourse" with the North.[40]

REBEL CONSUMERISM

"We are all 'rebels,' and it is proper that we appear in the garb of rebels." So noted an article in the Atlanta-based newspaper the *Southern Confederacy* in 1862, which continued: "Therefore, go round to McPherson's and buy a rebel hat—price 50 cents. They are made in South Carolina, and are genuine rebel productions."[1]

This pronouncement is typical of the phenomenon that I call "rebel consumerism." In its claim that purchases announce one's tribal attachments, in its attempt to wed virtue and consumption, in its efforts to create an imagined community of like-minded people—"rebels"—constructed through shopping, and in its concern for the provenance and authenticity of goods, and the truth claims of advertising, it captures the tensions and appeal of the efforts of a group of white Southerners to wage a consumerist Civil War. That effort, known as the nonintercourse movement, began with passage of the so-called tariff of abominations in 1828. It was energized by the debates around 1850 over slavery extension, reached a fever pitch in the period between John Brown's Harper's Ferry raid in 1859 and secession in 1861, and attained a not entirely welcome fruition during the war itself.[2]

I did not invent the term "rebel consumerism." It is a phrase that has been embraced in recent years by advocates and critics of contemporary countercultural consumption to describe the process by which "nonstandard acts of consumption come to be seen as politically radical." Indeed, when I first chose the title for this chapter, I thought of it as a humorous and ironic pun. Nineteenth-century white Southern supporters of slavery and secession would appear to have nothing in common with contemporary ethical shoppers and "green consumers." The comparison is surprisingly apt, however, for notwithstanding enormous differences in outlook and in political orientation, both sets of rebel consumers share a defining characteristic: a tendency to treat consumption as heroic political action and indeed to frame their actions in the marketplace as alternatives to base consumption. (Contemporary commentators are correct to note that rebel consumerism began in the fifties and sixties. They have the century wrong, however, for it began in the 1850s, not the 1960s.) Rebel consumers, now and then, did not challenge the logic of consumer society so much as reproduce it, often unconsciously, through their efforts to moralize and politicize alternative forms of consumption. In this sense, rebel consumers are prototypical consumer activists who, throughout American history, have celebrated the impact and power of acts at the point of consumption as the key to the exercise of citizenship while they often decried consumption and consumer society itself. Asking their supporters to extend a "liberal (pocket) discrimination in favor of homemade [Southern] articles," rebel consumers of the antebellum period, along with their contemporaries, the free produce activists, urged shoppers to think that spending more on the goods that identified and revealed their loyalties and affiliations not only evinced proof of commitment to a cause but also tangibly aided the cause. This is a mode of consumption as identification that rebel consumers have encouraged ever since.[3]

We are not accustomed to understanding white Southern nationalists as consumer activists, as part of a political tradition that includes not only a fair number of their contemporary rivals, the abolitionists, but also consumer activists from other periods of American history. To see them this way does not require a kind of historical sleight of hand that removes them from their context. If we listen to their words, read their speeches and resolutions, and examine the organizations they created, the evidence is abundant that they promoted, if less consistently practiced, consumer politics. The Southern nonintercourse movement was one of the most popular grassroots consumer campaigns in all of American history. Why has it not been studied as such? Why have the consumer politics of Southern economic nationalists not been treated as part and parcel of their overall political vision?

Scholars of the antebellum period are partly to blame. Divided up into analysts of the North or the South, they tend to assume that differences more than similarities characterized the relationship between these regions. As a reporter for the abolitionist weekly the *National Era* noted, there were striking similarities between the consumer slogans of proponents of nonintercourse ("Non-intercourse with the North") and those of free producers ("No union with slaveholders"). There were also similarities in practices, even if they applied those techniques to anitpodal causes. Indeed, tactics adopted at almost the same moment in these two regions changed the shape of consumer activism. Although both rebel consumers and free producers failed to achieve their ends, emphasizing only these results often distorts or underestimates the significance of these movements. If the nonintercourse movement manifestly failed in its effort to create a viable Confederate republic, it nonetheless, like the free produce movement discussed in the last chapter, introduced key components of modern consumer activism.[4]

Five critical developments of the antebellum period laid the foundation of modern consumer activism. First the verb "to consume" took on its modern meaning of "to purchase," rather than "to use," or more commonly "to use up." We can see this evolution in the nonintercourse movement itself. While many of the organizations formed in 1828 included resolutions promising, in an echo of nonimportation rhetoric, that "we will neither purchase nor consume" goods, by 1860, nonintercourse associations no longer drew this distinction. Second, activists in this period invented what we now call the "buycott," the purchase of morally sanctioned goods to advance their cause. Most nonintercourse associations, which sprang up in towns and cities all over the South, urged members and fellow citizens not only to shun goods from the North but also to buy Southern goods. In these ways, the nonintercourse movement paralleled the "free produce" campaigns of Northern abolitionists. As a result—and this is the third crucial development—in both of these movements "sacrifice" took on an ambivalent status. On the one hand, movement leaders valorized self-denial not just as a virtue but as a "patriotic duty." However, activists for both causes determined that it was consumption, not sacrifice, that effectively stimulated the sorts of morally sanctioned production they wanted to encourage. The fourth development of the antebellum era is the belief that consumption makes possible "long-distance solidarity," the understanding that to consume is to initiate a process with real-world effects, even if these effects are often invisible to the consumer, who can not see the impact of her actions on the faraway workers who made them. Indeed, ever since the antebellum period it has been a commitment of consumer activists to defetishize commodities by telling the story of their creation, a story obscured by the growing distance between sites of production and consumption, artful packaging, misleading advertising, and too often, consumer activists have believed, the willful blindness or indifference of consumers to the consequences of their actions at the cash register. A related transformation was suggested by the adoption of metaphors of electricity and communication by both Northern and Southern consumer activists. They understood the mechanism for this new form of solidarity to be the web that connected consumers and citizens to each other and to the goods they bought and sold. Writing of the South, a reporter for the *National Era* proclaimed in 1859 that, "nothing startles them from their potential slumbers, but a fall in the price of rice or cotton; and, of course, little save that which acts as an electric application to the pecuniary sensorium sometimes known as the pocket nerve is worthy of communication by telegraph." The insight that consumption, new modes of communication, and new ways of conceiving of energy operated in parallel—an insight neatly highlighted by the language of the "pocket nerve" frequently used by antebellum Northerners and Southerners—shaped the ways in which future consumer activists have come to understand the nature of their relationship to each other and of the most effective ways of exercising consumer power.[5]

All five of these developments were set in motion not only by white Southern supporters of nonintercourse but also, as we saw in chapter 2, by their ideological opposites in the abolition movement, namely, the supporters of "free produce" campaigns, as well as by Northern evangelical supporters of temperance, Sabbatarianism, and other moral reforms.[6] None of these movements could claim a huge amount of popular support, although nonintercourse had more associations, prominent endorsements, and support in the mainstream press than any of the others. Free producers were a besieged sect of abolitionism, which itself represented a tiny percentage of the Northern population. Nonintercourse advocates, a subset of Southern economic nationalists, likewise represented a minority of white Southern opinion. Yet both groups had an outsized, if unacknowledged, influence on the history of consumer activism—an influence that extended into the postwar years.

I. "The Licentious Spirit of the North Must Be Rebuked"

Shortly after the first "free produce" store opened in the North in 1826, a group of elite, white Southerners inaugurated a movement similar to it in method and philosophy, if opposite in intent. Underlining the diverse, even opposing, uses to which consumer activism could be put, Southern proponents of "nonintercourse" with the North aimed to strengthen the system of slave labor, while simultaneously weakening the economic and political power of the free labor North. Employing a topsy-turvy version of the strategy invented by the free producers, they proposed to achieve their aims by boycotting Northern goods, stimulating, through increased patronage, Southern manufacturers and industry, and denying the North "any of ours to ship, spin, chew, or eat," as the *Charleston Mercury* urged in 1857. Nonintercourse supporters also promoted the wearing of homespun clothing, the hiring of Southern workers, and the opening of direct trade with Europe. The movement paralleled free produce in duration, enduring for the roughly thirty-five years prior to the start of the Civil War. Like the free produce movement, its economic impact was minimal, although its political impact in fomenting Confederate nationalism was considerable. Also like free produce, the strategy of nonintercourse was criticized as much by presumed allies, other white Southerners, as it was by opponents of slavery.[7]

Although nonintercourse proponents were philosophically and tactically close to their contemporaries in the free produce movement, they drew their primary inspiration, at least explicitly, from the American Revolutionaries, whom they sought to emulate and to whom they paid incessant homage. Nonintercourse proponents understood themselves as the successors to their heroes, who supported nonimportation, wore homespun clothing, and upheld the American virtues of manliness and simplicity. It is no coincidence that the label they chose for their movement (nonintercourse) resembled the name of the Revolutionary efforts (nonimportation). In highlighting the role of women as producers of homespun and eschewers of luxuries, nonintercourse advocates also self-consciously sought to place themselves in the Revolutionary tradition. Conversely, they compared Northerners to the Revolutionaries' wartime opponent, England. As a Jackson, Mississippi, newspaper editorialized in 1851, "Our Northern brethren, as they are called, have, on the profits of our agriculture, built another England with her palaces and her monopolies, to grind" the South, leaving it "poor and dependent." They further claimed that Northerners had inherited the unvirtuous characteristics that the Revolutionaries had attributed to the British: effeminacy, excessive fashion consciousness, and an unhealthy materialism. Toasts to surviving Revolutionaries were standard fare at nonintercourse meetings in 1828. By 1850, although few Revolutionaries survived, nonintercourse advocates regularly referred to the Revolutionary boycotters as exemplars of the kind of ideological and institutional struggle that they sought to wage. Like the Revolutionary organizations, and very much unlike free produce associations, the nonintercourse movement gained support from a number of leading politicians, editorialists, preachers, and ordinary citizens, many of whom donned homespun, joined local nonintercourse associations, and observed "fast days" in support of the cause.[8]

Also like the American Revolutionaries, proponents of nonintercourse with the North redescribed what had been one country as two, and based the distinction between these incipient nations largely on clashing patterns and systems of consumption. In the logic of nonintercourse, Southern independence, like the American independence trumpeted by the Revolutionary generation, was necessary because the two societies held different consumer values and consumer power. In the view of the Southern nationalists, by 1860 these cultural and economic differences had become tantamount to differences in national identity. Further naturalizing regional distinctions, some nonintercourse proponents even figured these cultural and economic differences in racial terms, as when they referred to Yankees as "a mischievous, meddlesome race."[9]

Proponents of nonintercourse called for an assertion of distinctive Southern consumer values and for the need to deploy Southern consumer power into twin, and to some extent conflicting, narratives of secession. Together, these narratives explained the need for Southern independence and propounded a means, short of war, to achieve it. The first narrative proposed a diagnosis of the problem that made independence necessary: different, fundamentally clashing consumer values and consumer regimes. The second proposed a cure that would make independence possible: namely, a consumer-driven expansion, diversification, and internationalization of the Southern economy that would make the South commercially and, ultimately, politically independent of the North. Nonintercourse supporters, thus, posited the somewhat contradictory claims that Northern society was corrupt because of its consumerism and that that society could only be defeated by way of an increased and refined Southern consumerism. If the cure amounted to a partial revocation of the values that prompted the calls for independence in the first place, this reflected an ever-present tension in the nonintercourse movement and, more generally, in the political economy of the capitalist, slave-labor South. It also reflected a tension that has existed among consumer activists across a wide swath of time and causes, who have embraced consumerist techniques and, in so doing, have often reenforced the very consumer society they have sought to overturn. Indeed, the presence of these tensions has provoked many contemporary critics to denigrate "rebel consumerism."[10]

But these tensions and contradictions are a critical aspect of the history of consumer activism. And they inhered in the popular narrative that supporters of nonintercourse constructed to describe the regional clash of values. In that narrative, the two regions, which were fast on their way to becoming separate nations, could be distinguished not only by their productive systems (the familiar slave-vs.-free-labor distinction) but also by their antithetical systems of consumption, with the North endorsing a set of commercial values that substituted for and were anathema to the civilization that reigned in the South. Since Southern plantation owners were not only America's wealthiest people but also its most profligate consumers, this narrative required invoking obscurantist distinctions between base consumerism, on the one hand, and the material basis of civilization, on the other, the most important of which was to deny that the purchase of human property, and the riches produced by unpaid slave labor, amounted to consumption at all.[11]

Proponents of nonintercourse helped shape modern consumer activism through their attempts to highlight the far-reaching impact of consumption, and to note that consumption was not just symbolic but performative—that is, not merely a badge of identity but an action with real-world social and political consequences. But their status as supporters of slavery, and not infrequently as owners of slaves, led to some unique tensions. Attentive to the ways in which commodities affected people and often embodied their oppression, many white Southerners were also commodifiers of people. Sometimes, they acknowledged slave trading and owning as a form of consumption. For example, Joseph Ingraham, who visited the Natchez slave market in 1834, noted that the phrase "'he is gone to Virginia to buy negroes or niggers'. . . is as often applied to a temporarily absent planter, as 'he is gone to Boston to buy goods,' to a New-England country merchant." But white Southerners more often denied that the consumption of human beings lay at the heart of their political economy. At the same time, pointing to the poverty of free laborers—their inability to consume—as proof of the moral bankruptcy of the Northern social system, supporters of slavery sometimes asserted that slaves were actually better able to consume wealth than free laborers. According to a newspaper notice in 1860, a house slave sold cotton thereby "producing nearly $250 for the cook-woman . . . a very comfortable sum to spend in luxuries, and more money than thousands of poor men and women in New England see in one sum in the whole course of their lives." The chattel slave was thus better off than the wage slave, in this view, not only because of paternalistic working conditions but because of better opportunities for consumption.[12]

Driving these tensions endemic to the nonintercourse movement was less anxiety about commerce itself than about the reality that the North was the seat of the expanding American commercial empire. Shortly after secession, the *Charleston Mercury*, a newspaper which had, from the onset of the sectional crisis, led the calls for homespun and sacrifice, proclaimed that "the relation which commerce bears to the progress and strength of a nation is intimate and vital" and promised "to chronicle every new branch of industry by our people." A writer who denounced the "jimcrackeries" of the North also believed it possible for Southerners to "supply every possible want as well as every real need at home" and "to open a thousand new branches of labor, invention, enterprise, and employment to our own sons and people." The problem, it appeared, was less the jimcrackeries (or "notions" or "nickknacks") themselves than the Northern

provenance of those jimcrackeries. Morever, the *Mercury's* Robert Barnwell
Rhett and other Southern editors proclaimed the essential importance of
"chronicling" Southern commercial developments. Like their predecessors
in the nonimportation movement, nonintercourse supporters used print
to publicize membership in their associations and to dishonor all of the
movement's enemies, from Yankee merchants to hypocritical Southerners
who talked nonintercourse but helped themselves to the full panoply of
Northern goods at the market.[13]

In spite of the claims of nonintercourse advocates that North and South
held fundamentally opposing views of commercial life, the desires of
Southern consumers, especially the wealthy slaveholding class, resembled
those of their enemies in the Northern middle class. The leading newspaper of the fire-eaters, the *Mercury*, publicized charges of Northern corruption while advertising for all manner of merchants, services, and products,
ranging from the quotidian to the luxurious (see fig. 3.1). Judging from
these ads, products from Europe and the North were particularly prized.
Moreover, the newspaper devoted many columns, as well as a good deal of
advertising space, to the latest fashion news, with an emphasis on trends
along the New York–London–Paris axis. A popular establishment called
the New York Store graced the shopping district of Greenville, South Carolina, a center of the nonintercourse campaign. The start of the war heightened the tensions between this shared set of commercial desires and its denial, as Southerners took the conflict as an opportunity simultaneously to
showcase their abstemious virtues, to develop new businesses, and to advertise new products, such as the "secession suit" offered by "Kahnweiler
& Brothers' Cheap Store" in York, South Carolina (fig. 3.2). The "secession
suit," one of many products proffered for Southern consumption, was both
analogous to and constitutive of political nationalism, like the "home manufactured Fatigue Hats" pitched in the *Mercury* early in 1861 to the growing ranks of "regiments or Rifle Companies." Turning even their founding
document into a fungible commodity, newspapers advertised that for one
dollar Southerners could purchase a lithographed copy of the "Ordinance
of Secession."[14]

Wealth, nonintercourse advocates freely admitted, was the bulwark of
Southern civilization. But due to the nature of their slave-labor-produced
capital, white Southerners, in contrast to their Northern counterparts,
claimed to stand for a culture of leisure, not of busy-ness, of accumulated
wealth, not of incessant buying and selling, of stability, not impermanence.
A common refrain, among the white Southern advocates of nonintercourse
was that the North valued wealth above all else, while the South, paradoxically, because of the vastness of its slave-produced wealth, could afford to

MORE BARGAINS STILL.

JUST RECEIVED BY RECENT ARRIVALS FROM PHILADELPHIA AND N. YORK.

200 pair Ladies' GAITER BOOTS, at 75c
200 do   do   Bl'k and Bronze Gaiter Boots, $1
1000 do   do   Morocco Ties, 50
500 do   do   do   40
200 do   Misses' Kid and Leather Ties, 37
200 do   do   Morocco Slippers, 50
300 do   Ladies' French Morocco Ties, 60
500 do   do   fine Phil.   do   85
FOR BOYS AND YOUTHS.
200 Boy's Goat BOOTEES, 1 and 2, 62½; 3, 4 and 5, 75c
100 do   Calf   do   1 to 5, $1
100 Youths' Bootees, small sizes, 40
200 do   do   do   50, 62½ and 75
1000 do Children's Bootees and Slips, 25, 37 and 50

ALSO,
Gents Patent Leather and Cloth CONGRESS BOOTS
Do col'd D'Orsey Gaiters
Do Antideluvian   do
Do Patent Cubian Ties.
ALSO,
Gents fine Phila. Sewed and Peg'd French Calf BOOTS
BESIDES
Large quantities of TRUNKS, Carpet Bags and Satchels, at
WITHERBY'S,
corner King and Society-streets.

N. B. A few of those VELVET CORN CURERS, of the same sort that we have had so great a rush for, going fast.   wfm3   June 12

HURRAH
FOR THE PALMETTO STATE,
NOW OR NEVER!

DON'T let us wait any longer for the wagon, but pitch in at once, and go to KAHNWEILER & BROTHERS' Cheap Store, and buy a
WARM SECESSION SUIT,
for the small sum of FIVE DOLLARS. Kahnweiler and Brothers are determined to sell their stock of READY MADE CLOTHING from now until the first of January, at
COST PRICES,
as they have made arrangements to manufacture their Clothing in the SOUTHERN CONFEDERACY. And being afraid that the Southern and Northern Clothing could not agree together on the same shelves, therefore, we would say that the Northern Clothing must and shall quit the Store. Please call and test the truth of what we say.   K. & B., Cheap Store.
Nov 22   47   tf

Figure 3.1. An ad in the *Charleston Mercury* for goods from Philadelphia and New York. ("More Bargains Still," *Charleston Mercury*, Jun 17, 1850, 3.)

Figure 3.2. An ad for a "warm secession suit" at a York, South Carolina, store. (*Yorkville Enquirer*, Nov 22, 1860, 3.)

prize other virtues. Denunciations of Northern "Mammonism" became a staple in the sermons of Southern ministers. The Reverend Charles Cotesworth Pinckney of Charleston, for example, called the Yankees a "keen, thrifty, speculating . . . people, money-loving and money-making." While members of the Northern middle class would have understood these adjectives as words of praise, for white Southerners they highlighted the ways in which Northerners' crass pursuit of riches blinded them to nonmonetary values.[15]

A growing number of white Southerners, mostly in the lower South, came to believe that these cultural differences, which appeared to be accelerating, demanded a response. "The licentious spirit of the North must be rebuked," declared "Cincinnatus," writing from the Barnwell district of South Carolina in 1850, as the sectional crisis once again heated up. At first, this response amounted to a rallying cry for the South to hold firm to its unique and defining values in the face of Northern commercial hegemony. Later, it amounted to a declaration of commercial independence. Many Southerners believed that this "rebuke" of Northern values could be best actualized through the practice of sacrifice and nonconsumption, which would serve the dual purposes of punishing the North in its vulnerable pocketbook and reaffirming the noncommercial and Spartan values that marked Southern distinctiveness. "A year or two of homespuns and domestics—of avoidance of Northern and European *and all other unnecessaries*, would result in a greater feeling of independence than could be procured by any number of conventions and pronunciamentoes," proclaimed a North Carolina editorialist early in 1860. By the crisis of 1860, secessionists claimed, only political independence, abetted by the tradition of nonintercourse, could secure Southern economic values, which were at the same time moral values.[16]

What made the hegemony of Northern pecuniary values particularly galling for white Southerners was that what an Atlanta newspaper called this "fat, arrogant and saucy" culture of the Yankees rested on the systematic plundering of Southern wealth. Northern merchants "have grown wealthy at the expense of their customers, their consumers," claimed a dismayed Southerner in 1835. Turning the Northern fears of a "slave power" conspiracy on its head, these Southerners argued that Northern politicians and financiers had rigged, to their region's benefit and to the South's detriment, the nation's political economy. The South possessed, as the *Southern Literary Messenger* noted, "every material necessary for the comfort and subsistence of a people." Yet Southerners had became "almost wholly dependent upon their Northern brethren for every, even the most simple, article of domestic use." This swindling was no accident but was rather the deliberate plan of Northern politicians and businessmen. "The whole policy of the Federal Government, from the beginning has been to build up and enrich the North at Southern expense," claimed an editorialist in the *New Orleans Daily Crescent*. "In this business that monster engine, a high Protective Tariff, has been chief instrument." The tariff, agreed the *Charleston Mercury*, had simultaneously "built up the great emporiums of the Northern merchant princes" while it "kept Southern cities stationary." The North's embarrassment of riches was thus an embarrassment to the South, the problem pithily summed up in the title of Thomas Prentice Kettell's popular 1860 tract, *Southern Wealth and Northern Profits*. The North, claimed an 1860 editorial in the *Kentucky Statesman*, was seeking to "obtain uncontrolled power." A Savannah editorialist despaired of his region's captivity in "the shackles of utter dependence on the North."[17]

Drawing profits from the labor of a dishonored other? Shackles? Uncontrolled power? Dependence and compulsion? These phrases must have resonated for Southerners because they recalled a set of images and a vocabulary they knew well; they were the mirror image of the abolitionist denunciation of slavery. In a sickening irony, the South, the land of slavery, had, it seemed, itself become a slave to the North, a region that, like its own slaves, both produced vast riches to be enjoyed by others and consumed little of the wealth that it created. As in all forms of slavery, coercion and humiliation undergirded this economic exploitation.[18] It is noteworthy that, as we have seen, free produce activists shared the view that power rested with Northern consumers, not Southern producers. Even *Uncle Tom's Cabin*, the locus classicus of abolitionist fiction, depicted the slave-owning Shelby family as impotent, powerless to prevent the sale of their slaves, an outcome determined by the forces of the market to which the Shelby's were inexorably beholden. Nonintercourse advocates agreed with the free producers that Northern shoppers were, in effect, slaveholders and that Southern slaveholders were, in a sense, themselves enslaved, although they put this understanding to very different use.

White Southerners, in this view, were trapped in a web of Northern finished goods, proffered by Northern merchants, whose sale lined Northern pockets. Two characteristics made this web not merely exploitative but what white Southerners repeatedly denounced as "colonial." South Carolina's George McDuffie, for example, spoke of "the colonial vassalage of the Southern states" and claimed that "they have been better colonies to the Northern States than they ever were to England." First, these patterns of consumption not only enriched the North in general but the South's political enemies in particular. As a Carrollton, Alabama, editor noted in April 1860, the North was using Southern "dollars to fatten and enrich a set of fanatics. . . . Southern money and Southern labor have indirectly . . . paid the John Browns, that have all, through their respective channels, worked for the overthrow and destruction of the peaceably disposed, easily beguiled South."[19] Against all evidence, proponents of nonintercourse treated the North as an undifferentiated region of "black Republicans" and radical abolitionists.[20] Second, these finished goods began their life as raw materials planted and/or harvested in the South. "Reproachfully as it has been said of us, it is nevertheless true, that we neither *eat, drink, sleep,* nor even *die,* without a shameful dependence upon other people," declared a South Carolinian in the *Edgefield Advertiser* in 1846. "To prove that this assertion is no exaggeration," the author asked readers to "stand upon one of the wharves of our metropolis, and behold a picture of our trade." This picture included a long description of an incoming ship, one which, of course, belonged to a Northern state. Once on board, the evidence of total Northern commercial domination became even clearer:

> Open the hatches—there is Northern flour and hops and soda and salt to make bread; but with Northern butter to butter it. Northern beef and beans, potatoes, cabbages, onions, and pork to feed our people, and Northern drinkables to wash down what they eat. Northern pans, ovens and roasters to cook our food, with Northern knives and forks to cut it up.— Northern pickles and sauces, to tickle our appetites, and even Northern dentists with Northern teeth to enable us to chew our food. We sit down in Northern chairs, to Northern tables, decked out with Northern plates, dishes and glass ware; and when we get up, call our Northern hats, gloves, and sticks; walk out over pavements made of Northern stone—footed in Northern boots, and clothed with Northern clothing. We return home at night by the light of Northern lamps, to sleep upon bedsteads with Northern bedding. We eat, drink, and are merry at Northern labor; when sick, swallow Northern medicines; and when we die, are packed up in Northern coffins, put into graves dug with Northern spades, and have Northern tablets to tell where the only thing Southern in us lies.

Northerners proudly attested and Southerners grudgingly agreed that Northern domination of the material culture of the entire life cycle of Southerners, from birth to interment, provided concrete proof that this region had "risen by commerce and manufacturers to the wealth and power of an empire." To combat this overreaching empire it was necessary for the South to create a commercial empire of its own.[21]

Until white Southerners joined action to thought, "put our theories to practice," as one nonintercourse proponent phrased it, they would continue to enrich Northern coffers. One Staunton, Virginia, resident, following the favored pattern of the enumeration of Northern goods and services that effectively imprisoned Southerners, called on all white Southerners to "resolve each for himself that not one cent shall go from the South into the services of the Aid Societies, Underground Railroads, and Freedom Shriekers of the North, either through the merchant princes, manufacturers, institutions of learning, yankee book-sellers, yankee teachers, yankee peddlers, or any other channel." Nor, nonintercourse proponents argued, were Northern products necessary. As Solon Robinson, a Southern sympathizer from Indiana, observed, "There is not a single thing now imported from the North but what can be manufactured here just as well as there, except ice, and even that, the rapidly lengthening Railroad will soon bring down from the mountains of North Carolina and Tennessee." Word had it that John Randolph "had not purchased a dollar's worth from Northern factories . . . and he never would." According to the journal of the English traveler Edward Stutt Abdy, Randolph let it be known that he "would neither eat, nor drink, nor wear anything from the north of the Patapsco," a river in Maryland roughly at the border of the Mason-Dixon line.[22]

Demonstrating the difficulty of reading the moral value of goods and services, nonintercourse proponents often had a difficult time singling out objects to be boycotted. "W.J.S.," a nonintercourse proponent from Macon, Georgia, claimed that "complete non intercourse" was "the only effective antiseptic" to Northern skullduggery. The way to stop depositing "millions of dollars annually into Northern coffers, every dollar of which is now being used to attempt a subjugation" of the South, he confidently claimed, was to follow his four-part boycott, which included

1. No more Yankee goods.
2. Take no more Yankee newspapers.
3. Buy No More Northern books.
4. Patronize no more Northern schools.[23]

Despite the regular appearance of such seemingly definitive advice, nonintercourse advocates, reflecting the reality of the complex economy of the market and transportation revolutions, were not in agreement on what constituted "Yankee goods." At various times, they suggested boycotts only of abolitionist-owned businesses, or of goods from Boston, the seat of abolitionism, or of products from the states of Massachusetts and Vermont. Others urged boycotts of Southern sympathizers with the North or with Yankee peddlers, even if they lived in the South and purveyed what they claimed to be Southern goods. Many nonintercourse advocates urged Southern tourists to avoid Saratoga, Newport, and other Northern resorts. (After the tariff of abominations in 1828, some South Carolinians called for a boycott of goods from Kentucky, which had voted in favor of this punitive tax). Ultimately, most nonintercourse advocates settled upon the general category of all goods from the North, since, as a businessman in Augusta claimed, "they are all, more or less, tainted with abolitionism."[24]

Even after settling on the North as a generic category, nonintercourse proponents felt the need to specify, calling on their supporters to eschew a wide variety of products, salespeople, and services. Among those they enumerated were farm animals, booksellers (and the books they sold; they often singled out *Uncle Tom's Cabin* as a book that should not be bought or sold in the South), candles, food (we have already heard about ice), nutmeg, popular culture and theater, preachers, medical schools, printers, schoolteachers, universities, resorts, and vehicles. In specifying Northern goods to be avoided, nonintercourse proponents and Southern entrepreneurs encouraged the purchase of Southern equivalents in a wide variety of areas. "We are striving for commercial independence, let us also strive for literary and theatrical independence," declared a notice for a Savannah theater company in 1863. Following what was already a well-established pattern in consumer activism, these Southerners believed that such actions became truly political only when they informed "the public through the press what they manufacture," as the *Charleston Courier* urged in an article announcing the formation of a nonintercourse association in Beech Island, South Carolina. And so the paper saw fit to publicize the example of a Bullock's Creek merchant who claimed never to have bought from the North.[25] In treating publicity through print as the necessary precondition for successful consumer politics, nonintercourse advocates echoed not only their predecessors in the nonimportation movement but also their enemies in free produce associations.

Precisely because of the materialism that they believed lay at the root of Northern culture, and because Northern wealth depended on the deadly combination of Southern raw materials and Southern consumers, nonintercourse advocates confidently predicted that, provided they could increase the number of Southern boycotters, their method was bound for success. If "the whole South would be roused to the whole North like that of Revolutionary times," it was very likely to win, said one observer, drawing on the nonintercourse movement's favorite inspiration. It was a confidence they shared with their enemies, free producers who also thought the compelling market forces they unleashed would lead slaveholders to turn to free labor in relatively short order. Southern dependence on the North, Southern boycotters argued, could easily be reversed if Southerners understood the power they had to weaken the Yankee economy. This power was rooted in consumer power, which had rippling causal consequences, as illustrated by the statement that with a Southern boycott, "the Yankee capitalists will be ruined; their factories emptied, the operatives turned out of employment, and reduced to starvation." Once the boycott took hold, nonintercourse proponents predicted, this disastrous chain of events would lead the Northerners to reconsider their ways, since, as the *Richmond Dispatch* claimed, "the Yankees are the last people in the world to persist in a course of action that won't pay." Southern newspapers regularly published upbeat stories about the devastating economic consequences of their actions. In 1850, the *Mercury* predicted imminent upheaval in the North due to the potential "deprivation of eight million consumers for the innumerable manufacturers of the North." A decade later, an Arkansas newspaper reported that the New York trading house of Stewart and Company "have discharged FIFTY of their employees in consequence of the reduction of their Southern trade." Article after article, often with headlines such as "Gotham Getting Scared," optimistically and apocalyptically proclaimed that the "prostration of Northern commerce is complete," observed that Northern markets were "inactive," and predicted that the North would soon "reap the Whirlwind." In a statistics-laden speech before the Virginia House of Delegates in 1860, a member of that body, James Barbour, argued that the "whole industrial system of New England would be completely prostituted if the Southern market could be closed against their manufacturers." Like other supporters of nonintercourse, he believed the North was "at the mercy of the south" because Southern consumers were the source of Northern power. Southern newspapers, mixing fact with rumor, reported all available evidence to support the claim exemplified in one headline as "Non-intercourse Physic Working." "A large Hat and Cap Factory in Connecticut is to be broken up and moved to Alabama, because it has lost its trade from the South, and its proprietors mean to regain it in the South," claimed a newspaper in Raleigh. Similarly, a Fayetteville paper reprinted rumors that "over 100 hands have been discharged from one of the largest manufactures in Philadelphia in consequence of orders from the South having been countermanded" and that a northern publisher was "suffering" from lack of Southern customers of an encyclopedia. Since the typical Yankee's primary sensory organ, according to their Southern critics, was his "sensitive pocket," nonintercourse advocates expected that Northerners would give in quickly to Southern commercial pressure. The future they envisioned was bright indeed; "While the factories of Lowell, Lynn, and Springfield will become the haunts of bats and owls," prophesied the *Richmond Enquirer* in 1859, "those of the Southern states will be vocal with the hum of life-giving trade."[26]

Nonintercourse was met with a divided response in a divided North. One response was to mock "the South's heroic resolve to ignore the North," as the New York magazine *Vanity Fair* put it, tongue firmly in cheek. As a writer in the *National Era* observed, taking the claims of self-sufficiency to an extreme, "Southern printers are going to print with Southern type on Southern paper, by means of Southern steam generated by Southern fire. Southern pedagogues will teach Southern children Southern ideas out of Southern books." Responding perhaps to the Southerner who predicted that even ice need not be bought from the North, the author concluded: "A few icebergs are to be naturalized in the South, so that Southern drinks may be cooled by Southern ice." On this front, a Boston newspaper encouraged Southerners in 1855 not to "forego ice in your mint julep." In another

satire, the *New York Tribune* mocked the enthusiasms of small-town Southerners as they were rendered in their grandiloquent resolutions. Reprinting the "spirited resolutions" of a tiny farming and oystering burg, the fictional Hobbs Hollow, the *Tribune* sought to demonstrate the absurdity both
of Southern claims that Northern markets and businesses harmed Southerners and of the outsized results that they predicted. Defining trade as
"'aggression' upon our institutions" and noting that Northern purchases
are "impoverishing us," the citizens of Hobbs Hollow—the "bravest men
on earth" in their self-satisfied description—resolved "that as 'chivalrous'
and 'generous sons' of Hobbs Hollow, we will hold no further intercourse
with said City of New York; that by withholding our oysters and vege-
tables from the fanatical consumers thereof, in said city, her population will
soon dwindle, and Hobbs Hollow will become the most prosperous portion
of the globe." The satire concluded with a resolution that "a regiment of
five men be forthwith raised to enforce our rights." A Louisville newspaper
put a Southern spin on the satires, as it personalized the regional struggle,
casting it in terms of a romance. There "is one 'union' that will stand and
hold the rest," it opined. Nonintercourse, the writer continued, "may well
touch the Northern pocket but how are we to protect the Southern heart
against the fascinating belles of Boston, New York, and Philadelphia?" Unlike the market for goods, the marriage market, in this view, was inherently
resistant to the logic of regional self-sufficiency. Then came the obligatory
comparison with the Founders: "True our fathers in the Revolution made
and carried out a similar pledge in regard to importations from the mother
country, but they never made the importation of the mothers of the country contraband," continued the article. "We propose a war of retaliation.
If the North will interfere with our Southern domestic institutions let our
young men go forth and rob the Northern homes of their most cherished
ornaments and bring them back to found more patriarchal relations among
us." Theft of women would ultimately do as much damage to the North as
the boycott by making its own reproduction impossible.[27]

   More often, Northerners (and some Southerners) responded to nonintercourse in the same way that critics of consumer activism have throughout American history, by arguing that what the *Boston Daily Advertiser*
called "the truths of political economy" would inevitably undercut the effectiveness of a boycott. "We know, both as a matter of experience and as
a matter of history, that the only place in the world in which men do not
readily carry out their political and religious opinions is the market-place,"
observed the *New York Times* tartly, applying the "sensitive pocket" theory
to its Southern originators. "We know that amongst the many follies into
which crazes, and theories, and 'isms' drive people, the folly of buying their

boots and shirts in the dearest shops is the last to take possession of their minds." Agreeing that "the laws of trade cannot so easily be set aside," the *Lowell Daily Citizen* offered as evidence the claim that "the chief matrons of the Old Dominion" put in orders to Northern merchants even at the high point of sectional crisis in 1859, when John Brown "was fairly or unfairly hung." Noting that Southern orders of shoes produced in the North showed a significant increase from the first three months of 1859, a Boston paper concluded that "people understand very well that water cannot be made to run uphill, nor trade forsake its regular channel, in deference to the prejudices of a few overheated disunionists." Pointing to the continued, even growing, strength of the Southern market for Northern goods, many articles in the Northern press sought to demonstrate this case anecdotally and statistically, to reveal that "the non-intercourse bubble" had already burst. Others used humor to make the same point about the rapacity and extensiveness with which Southerners continued to buy Northern. Speaking of the song "Dixie's Land"—"which the Southern people have adopted as a 'national air'"—an editorialist for the *New York Times* noted that "like most articles of Southern consumption, the melody was imported from the North;—Northern men being guilty of perpetrating words and music." Similarly, critics pointed out that the strongly nonintercourse *Richmond Enquirer* contained laudatory reviews of books published in New York as well as advertisements "of goods for sale of purely Northern manufacture." This was a sign, to them, that the entire movement was "just so much buncombe."[28]

In the face of these reports about the lack of support for nonintercourse, the Northern press emphasized the hypocrisy of Southerners whose actions at the cash register belied their calls for Southern commercial independence. Although "our fire-eating friends make up their minds to wall themselves in by non-intercourse," very few of their countrymen—who recognized the "mutual dependence of the two sections upon one another"—agreed. And, as Northern journalists never tired of showing, even many of the fire-eaters paid only rhetorical attention to this wall. When a newly established shoe manufactory closed in Mississippi, the *Liberator* crowed, "It speaks louder than we can say about the hypocrisy of the times. Here is a home manufactory, of articles which are usually imported from Massachusetts, in the very heart of Mississippi, which does not receive patronage sufficient to keep it going." A Boston newspaper offered a similar observation: "How dangerous it would be for South Carolina herself to declare nonintercourse with the North may be seen by the following despatch, received in New York last week, by a provision dealer. 'Please send by Saturday's steamer one hundred turkeys, twenty pair capons, twenty pair pheasants.'" According to the newspaper, the letter was signed, "Proprietor Charleston Hotel."[29] Because of such hypocritical behavior, the predictions of the "utter financial ruin of the North" were yet another of the "Southern delusions" that drove the sectional crisis, according to a New England journalist. Looking back in 1863, he reviewed the dire predictions of the nonintercourse movement: "Northern industry was to be paralyzed; Northern looms were to be stopped; Northern ships were to rot at the wharves; Northern merchants and banks were to suspend payments. The crowd of greedy Northern parasites, which had long fattened upon Southern wealth, were to be rejected forever from their posts and deprived of their ill-gotten gains. . . . Anarchy would reign in Northern cities and grass would grow in their streets." None of this came to pass, and the Northern press laid the blame squarely on the Southern radicals who fomented the movement for regional self-sufficiency with their lips while they harmed the movement with their wallets. "The very men who talk loudest at the South against patronizing northern merchants and northern institutions, in seven cases out of ten, are the most ready to make their purchases and send their produce there whenever they think they can profit by it, and patronize those institutions when they deem it their interest," claimed Frederick Douglass. "In short, they are generally the greatest humbugs of the age always excepting Barnum."[30]

Some Southerners responded in a similarly negative way to the threat and practice of nonintercourse. As early as 1828, one Columbia, South Carolina, resident was already calling nonconsumption "arrant nonsense." Doubting the practicality of coordinating the actions of "millions and millions of men," he further stated that, according to his definition, freedom included the right to "buy and sell where we please." Finally, he pointed to the difficulty in a market economy of knowing the origins of a product, and the futility of trying to find out: "If a hog, or a horse, or a mule is offered to me for sale, how am I to know whether he be from Kentucky?" "Mammon has its own world, and within it reigns supreme," argued a Richmond resident in 1850. "Merchants, as a general rule, no matter what their prejudices, will buy and sell in the most profitable markets." Agreeing with this sentiment a decade later, a writer in Asheville, North Carolina, doubted whether "the course of trade, like a man's coat, can be changed at will." By naturalizing the market, they argued that there was no possibility of altering its effects.[31]

As the war came, it became a luxury to debate about luxuries, which were no longer readily available. Newspapers continued to advertise products, but the variety was considerably reduced (see fig. 3.3). Making a virtue of necessity, white Southerners stepped up the talk of virtuous sacrifice. The coming of war, they believed, would of necessity lead to the kind of spiritual purification they admired, and which followed, in their view, from the Southern Spartan values it would call forth. After offering a paean to the sweet potato as the perfect foodstuff for a wartime economy, a resident of Fairfield, South Carolina, argued in May of 1861 that involuntary nonintercourse was accomplishing what four decades of voluntary nonintercourse had failed to do. In danger of becoming "not only a degenerate, but an effeminate race, both male and female," the South was being forced by the war to reclaim its proper manhood and womanhood, categories that for him included a strong suspicion of luxuries. A month later, a Richmond resident agreed. Through war "our people will learn the habits of carefulness and economy, which no other means will teach them." He continued, "difficult as it may be for the liberal and generous Southerner to descend to such unknown thriftiness, it is his positive duty now" not only to practice thrift himself but "to enforce it in his children and servants." Noting that economy has become a "patriotic duty," a Virginia Fourth of July orator hopefully foresaw the day when the "ornamental will be sacrificed to the useful."[32]

Northerners too claimed that the martial spirit was stemming the tide of a dangerous "extravagance and effeminacy." A meditation on the "uses of war" in the *New York Herald* argued that it had dampened the dangerous "spirit of fashion" and turned Northerners into "avowed economists." A few months later, another article in the *Herald* noted that "there is now less sham and more comfort than formerly, and very few people really regret the loss of sham friends, sham luxuries, sham houses, and sham horses." The war was apparently helping Northerners to keep it real, and several women's organizations sought to help "diminish the use of imported luxuries." Like their Southern counterparts, however, Northern merchants quickly saw the opportunities in marketing patriotic items, such as "Union cockades" and "Union bonnets."[33]

In this rhetorical, if not practical, adoption of virtuous sacrifice during wartime we see again a convergence of Northern and Southern views. For it was one of the ironies of the Southern nonintercourse campaigns that not only did it adopt the techniques of the free producers but, in the attempt to forge a unique and independent Southern nation, the campaigners also borrowed the economic language of their enemies in the consumerist North. In calling for Southern households to become producers of clothing, in imploring Southerners to diversify their economy, with factory joining farm, and, above all, in insisting that Southerners—not least enslaved men and women—embrace consumption and trade, the path to autarky mirrored the model provided by the Northern economy.

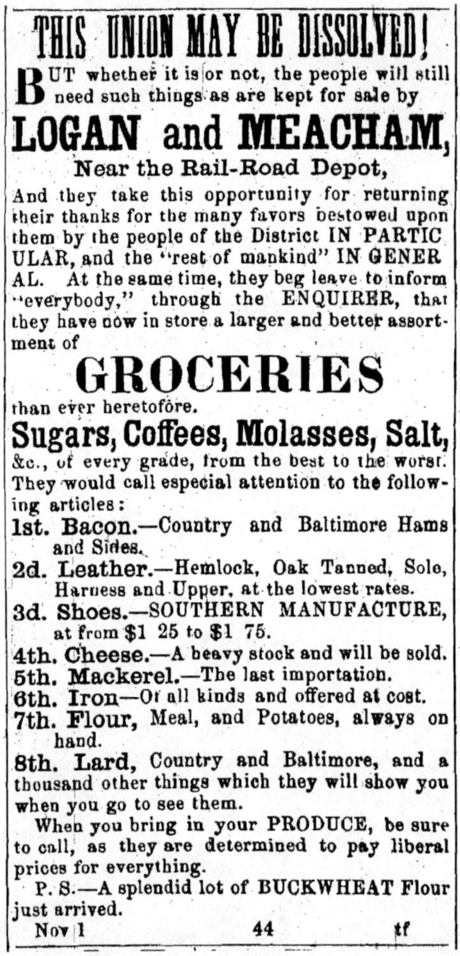

THIS UNION MAY BE DISSOLVED!

BUT whether it is or not, the people will still need such things as are kept for sale by

LOGAN and MEACHAM,
Near the Rail-Road Depot,

And they take this opportunity for returning their thanks for the many favors bestowed upon them by the people of the District IN PARTIC ULAR, and the "rest of mankind" IN GENER AL. At the same time, they beg leave to inform "everybody," through the ENQUIRER, that they have now in store a larger and better assortment of

GROCERIES

than ever heretofore.

Sugars, Coffees, Molasses, Salt,

&c., of every grade, from the best to the worst. They would call especial attention to the following articles :

1st. Bacon.—Country and Baltimore Hams and Sides.

2d. Leather.—Hemlock, Oak Tanned, Sole, Harness and Upper, at the lowest rates.

3d. Shoes.—SOUTHERN MANUFACTURE, at from $1 25 to $1 75.

4th. Cheese.—A heavy stock and will be sold.

5th. Mackerel.—The last importation.

6th. Iron—Of all kinds and offered at cost.

7th. Flour, Meal, and Potatoes, always on hand.

8th. Lard, Country and Baltimore, and a thousand other things which they will show you when you go to see them.

When you bring in your PRODUCE, be sure to call, as they are determined to pay liberal prices for everything.

P. S.—A splendid lot of BUCKWHEAT Flour just arrived.

Nov 1   44   tf

Figure 3.3. "The Union May Be Dissolved." Groceries, however, were still for sale in this ad for Logan and Meacham, merchants, in York, South Carolina. (*Yorkville Enquirer*, Nov 15, 1860, 3.)

In other ways, white Southerners promoted a consumer society in advance of the one that existed in the North, and not just in the insistence of some Southern nationalists that the slave trade be reopened. It was non-intercourse proponents who introduced the celebrity endorsement (with politicians from George McDuffie in 1828 to Alexander Stephens in 1860 ostentatiously wearing homespun) and the extravaganza (as in the dozens of "homespun" weddings, in which the bride wore—sometimes literally— domestically produced clothing), two techniques that did not become popular in Northern consumer activism until later in the century. Nonintercourse advocates also invented both the "white list"—the compendium of morally sanctioned goods, merchants, and shops—and its opposite, the "black list" of goods to be avoided; such lists became a staple of organized labor and the National Consumers League in the Progressive Era.[34] In all these ways, then, nonintercourse proponents anticipated contemporary rebel consumers.

The nonintercourse movement ended with the Confederate defeat at Appomattox.[35] But consumer politics—with the boycott as the central tool—continued to be practiced in the South after the war, helping to shape, in ways that have not been acknowledged, the course of American consumer activism. Indeed, as we will see in the next chapter, Southerners indirectly contributed to the coining of the term "boycott." During Reconstruction, advocates of "redemption" organized campaigns of social and economic ostracism against Yankee "carpetbaggers" as well as against their African American neighbors who achieved a modicum of economic and political success. In some cities, white Southerners organized boycotts of integrated streetcars. With what one observer called "an ostracism more pitiless than that of ancient Athens," many white Southerners dealt "personal and pecuniary injury to Northern business men"and others who violated the Lost Cause myths they cherished.[36] James Redpath, the journalist who coined the word "boycott" in 1880 in reference to the struggles of Irish tenants against British landlords, claimed that the tactics used by white Southerners against carpetbaggers and Republican supporters during the era of Reconstruction (actions that Redpath had witnessed as a school superintendent in Charleston) inspired him to encourage the Irish Land League to protest Captain Charles Boycott's actions through economic and social ostracism. As early as 1868, one Southern politician, Representative Ben H. Hill of Georgia, described "social ostracism" of those seeking to "establish a new order of things in the South" as an apt manifestation of the old "rebel spirit."[37]

Yet this rebel spirit differed from what came before in one crucial way. If previous boycott campaigns had been understood as weapons of the weak against the powerful—and while the nonintercourse advocates were not in any sense "weak," they depicted themselves at least as suffering at the hands of a more powerful economic forces from the North—the consumer-based politics of postbellum Southern whites clearly did not fit this pattern. As W. E. B. Du Bois observed, the white Southern revolt against Reconstruction can be understood in a general sense as a "boycott of planters against negroes" that was carried out with, among other tactics, boycotts of blacks who exercised their right to vote and boycotts of symbols of interracialism, such as schools, the Republican party, and streetcars. Some white Southerners boycotted Wanamaker's department store because its founder, John Wanamaker, in his capacity as postmaster general, hired a number of African American postmasters. He later dined publicly with the African American leader Booker T. Washington, setting off another wave of white boycotts of his establishment.[38]

Other boycotts dotted the landscape of the post-Reconstruction South. The tool was frequently employed by populists in the 1880s and 1890s, the largest of which was the Farmers' Alliance's temporarily successful boycott of Northern jute manufacturers, who had raised their prices precipitously, in the late 1880s.[39] The rhetoric and practice of the jute boycott echoed many of the features of Southern consumer campaigns in the antebellum era, including the dismissal of Northern jimcrackeries as unnecessary. Addressing his comments to Northerners, Zebulon Vance, an alliance leader, announced that Southerners had no need for "your patent medicines, your hair dyes, your wooden hams, your hickory nutmegs, your left hand razors, and your doubled bladed gimlets." Following the sartorial practices of nonintercourse supporters (and the Revolutionaries before them), populists dressed in cotton substitutes and even staged a double wedding at an Alliance Exposition in Atlanta in which twenty thousand Alliancemen watched as "both brides and grooms were attired in cotton bagging costumes." Jute boycotters referred explicitly to the Founders, as when the Georgian Tom Watson proclaimed, "It is useless to ask Congress to help us, just as it was folly for our forefathers to ask for relief from the tea tax." The jute boycotters, as C. Vann Woodward has pointed out, also faced an opposition that used tactics evocative of those used against carpetbaggers, including ostracism and counterboycotts, and they heard the usual "pocket nerve" arguments about how they would soon "feel the loss" and be unable to sustain their actions.[40]

And in July 1890, history was repeated as farce, when a group of white, Southern politicians, led by the Georgia governor (as well as former Confederate general and commander of the United Confederate Veterans) John B. Gordon called for a boycott of the North to protest the so-called force bill being debated in the Senate, which aimed to enforce African American voting rights. Unlike the nonintercourse campaigns, which lasted the length of the antebellum period, this boycott call dissipated within two weeks of Gordon's declaration. Moreover, most of the leading newspapers of the South derided rather than embraced by this effort. The force bill boycott, though itself short lived, revealed the continuing appeal of the rhetoric of Confederate consumerism. Indeed, boycott proponents frequently invoked the nonintercourse movement, reimagining it as a widely popular, highly successful endeavor, which could be reredeployed, this time successfully, since war would not again interrupt the momentum of the movement. Advocates saw the force bill protests as an opportunity to revivify the "old dream we used to hear talked of so earnestly in our old Southern Commercial Conventions." That dream, as an editorial in a Columbia, South Carolina, newspaper reminded its readers, was "to forswear Northern products and touch the North in its vital part—its pocket." Proponents of the force bill boycott drew their claims directly from the nonintercourse play-book, as did the Northerners who noted that their region would no more be "bullied . . . in 1890 than it could in 1860." Sounding as if they had been unlocked after a generation spent in a time capsule, the force bill boycott advocates called for self-sacrifice, direct trade with Europe, the support of domestic manufactures, and the eschewal of vacations in the North. Just as their predecessors had done, this group of Southern white nationalists continued to co-opt the rhetoric of abolitionism, quoting their favorite biblical passage, Colossians 2:21, which advised Christians to "touch not, taste not, handle not" impure goods, and advising Southerners to "build a wall of fire between the south and all northern commodities." Finally, con-tinuing the pattern initiated in the counterrevolution against Reconstruc-tion, they threatened to boycott black Southerners who had the audacity to support Civil Rights legislation. Northern critics also echoed their dismiss-als of nonintercourse, as when Senator Henry Cabot Lodge, the bill's lead-ing proponent, called Gordon's provocation nothing more than "the old slavery spirit threatening to boycott Northern business, trying to bully the Northern people." They also claimed that inexorable market forces meant that force bill boycotters "could no more change the natural flow of com-merce then they could make the Niagara reverse its course."[41]

Shortly after this failed boycott, designed to uphold the racial caste sys-tem, another group of Southerners used this tool on behalf of a very differ-ent goal. These were the African Americans who boycotted in towns and cities all over the South to protest Jim Crow streetcars and other public accommodations, a campaign that began with the institution of legalized segregation in the 1890s and continued through Jim Crow's dismantle-ment; indeed, these boycotts crucially contributed to that dismantlement. As we will see in chapter 5, the African American boycotts of the Jim Crow system truly represented acts of rebel consumerism, for they involved the use of consumer tactics on behalf of a universal equality that was thor-oughly rejected by their fellow citizens both North and South. Like sup-porters of nonintercourse, black boycotters called for sacrifice, alternative modes of commerce (in this case, private hacks), and consumption (or its withdrawal) as an expression of group loyalty. They, too, regularly invoked the metaphor of the pocket, turning it against the white Southerners who had habitually accused Northerners of being governed by this "sense." As a group of three African Americans in Lynchburg, Virginia, wrote in a cir-cular in 1906, "Let us attack the white man's heart and conscience—his pocket." The desegregation of the dollar, to borrow Robert Weems's phrase, thus began well before Montgomery in 1955. One can just as easily interpret the Montgomery boycott as the culmination of a long tradition of African American boycotting rather than as (in the way it is often seen) as the beginning of the modern Civil Rights movement. Indeed, a reporter who observed that "Montgomery is experiencing the most unique boycott in its history," which was being maintained with "surprising persistency" and broad participation, did so not in 1955 or 1956 but in 1900, at a time when bus boycotts were already firmly established as important mode of grassroots protest against segregation.[42]

Although the nonintercourse campaigns had a negligible economic impact, were rejected by many Southerners, and were fraught with tensions inherent in the effort to use consumption as a weapon against consumerism, they also helped shape the future of American consumer activism. Consumer activists, as we have seen, have been notoriously bad at remembering their own history. Yet understanding the contribution of nonintercourse activists to the development of modern consumer activism teaches us important lessons about the nature of this long-standing tradition. It should also warn us against the still too-common assumption that consumer activism has a single and inherently progressive political valence. If we knew more about the ideological diversity of consumer activism throughout American history, perhaps we would be less surprised by the fact that boycotting and buycotting continue to be invoked by diverse groups with diverse worldviews. A number of observers have understood the recent conservative Christian-led boycotts of Microsoft, Ford, and Disney for their gay-friendly policies as the ideological hijacking of a fundamentally progressive tactic.[43] Consumer activists, however, have always ranged across the political spectrum, sharing a view of the importance of incorporating ethics into their consumption decisions, even as they have held radically different understandings of what constitutes morality. Perhaps no historical era better illustrates this insight than the antebellum period, when small, and today largely forgotten, groups of slaveholders and abolitionists together invented modern consumer activism.

TRAVELS OF THE BOYCOTT
WHAT'S IN A NAME?

The practice at the heart of the American political tradition of consumer activism—the boycott—did not have a name until more than a century after it began. Or, rather, it had many names. In the Revolutionary era, practitioners of *nonimportation* and *nonconsumption* called on their fellow colonists to eschew British goods. Beginning in the 1820s, advocates of *free produce* promoted abstinence from slave-made goods. In the same decade, white Southern nationalists implored their compatriots to practice *nonintercourse* with the North. Throughout the antebellum era, Sabbatarians and temperance proponents asked supporters of the cause not to give their *custom* to businesses that violated their ethical standards. Those accused of unfair labor practices were *left alone*. Others spoke of making their enemies *anathema*, of *excommunicating*, *ostracizing*, or *blacklisting* them. No single word described the act of collectively withholding patronage for political, ethical, or moral reasons. Similarly, no single term existed to categorize those who partook of the practice.[1]

This state of affairs changed abruptly in 1880, with a chronology that can be detailed with unusual precision. More specifically, the name was birthed in October of that year, when the Scottish-born American radical, James Redpath, in collaboration with an Irish priest, John O'Malley, coined the eponymous phrase to describe the weapon of ostracism used by Irish peasants in County Mayo, Ireland, against an exploitative British land agent named Charles Cunningham Boycott. Within a few months it had become, according to one observer, "a very forcible phrase" in the United States, one widely adopted throughout the country. By 1886 the labor journalist John Swinton observed that the practice had "come into vogue far and wide." The boycott, as a reporter for the *Chicago Tribune* observed, looking back at the end of the decade, "spread like wildfire, or influenza, and in a short time there were boycotts on foot all the way from New York to San Francisco."[2]

Other names were proposed in these early years. As the boycott came under legal attack in the mid-1880s, one advocate, writing in *John Swinton's Paper*, declared that the action is "as old as mankind" and proposed replacing the controversial "boycott" with "taboo." Noting the exotic "Polynesian origin" of the word, and calling it a word of "terrible sound," he called for the "tabooing" of antiunion employers. Claiming that "very few have heard of the Irish gentlemen of the name," a writer in 1889 suggested replacing boycott (who was, in point of fact, English) with "Wanamaker," after the department store magnate, John Wanamaker, who, we saw in the last chapter, was boycotted by some Southerners for violating the social and political rules of Jim Crow. Without giving a reason for his choice, a writer suggested in 1885 that the word "Folger" would serve as well as "boycott."[3]

Boycott emerged as the undisputed name of choice. Initially, when set in print the new word was typically capitalized, surrounded by quotation marks, or hyphenated as "boy-cott." (A sloganeering feline *boy-cat* served as the mascot of one newspaper, the *Workmen's Advocate* of New Haven.) But these trimmings quickly disappeared, as the term entered the vernacular with extraordinary rapidity. One linguist in 1890 commented on the "instantaneous adoption of the verb." In 1881, for example, a journalist in Salt Lake City surmised that "most of our readers are doubtless aware" of the meaning of the term.[4] Within two years it had entered into not only *Webster's English Dictionary* but the language of many European and even Asian countries.[5] While the journalist Arthur Dudley Vinton, who assessed the history of the term in 1886, was correct to note the "lack of authoritative definition of the word 'boycott,'" the phrase had become ubiquitous. By the mid-1880s, people used the word in a broader sense, to mean the rejection of an idea, person, or activity; periodicals referred to a group of teenage boys boycotting a particularly coquettish girl, or girls boycotting overly flirtatious boys. By the mid-1880s, boycotting was common not only in parlance but also in practice, as the so-called labor boycott became a regular, and to many, a frightening feature of the landscape in urban America. Three newspapers with the identical name, the *Boycotter*, were founded in the mid-1880s in the diverse and geographically dispersed cities of New York, Chicago, and Topeka.[6]

Boycotts became the common currency of economic and political protest in the 1880s and 1890s, deployed on behalf of wide variety of causes by a diverse group of people, who had nothing in common other than a belief in the power of the boycott and a shared sense of how boycotts operated (see fig. 4.1). As the *New York Times* waggishly noted in 1887 in response to a pro-

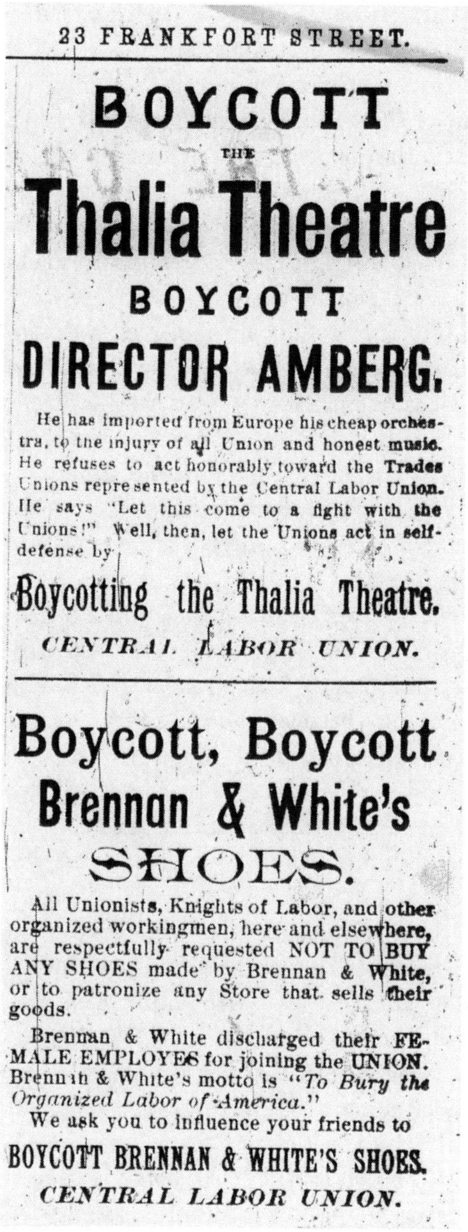

23 FRANKFORT STREET.

BOYCOTT
THE
Thalia Theatre
BOYCOTT
DIRECTOR AMBERG.

He has imported from Europe his cheap orchestra, to the injury of all Union and honest music. He refuses to act honorably toward the Trades Unions represented by the Central Labor Union. He says "Let this come to a fight with the Unions!" Well, then, let the Unions act in self-defense by

Boycotting the Thalia Theatre.
CENTRAL LABOR UNION.

Boycott, Boycott.
Brennan & White's
SHOES.

All Unionists, Knights of Labor, and other organized workingmen, here and elsewhere, are respectfully requested NOT TO BUY ANY SHOES made by Brennan & White, or to patronize any Store that sells their goods.

Brennan & White discharged their FEMALE EMPLOYES for joining the UNION. Brennan & White's motto is "*To Bury the Organized Labor of America.*"

We ask you to influence your friends to

BOYCOTT BRENNAN & WHITE'S SHOES.
CENTRAL LABOR UNION.

Figure 4.1. Announcements of boycotts in a newspaper created by boycotting printers. (*New York Boycotter*, Nov 14, 1885, 3.)

test against the Criterion Theatre, "The deadly boycott has been extended from the handlers of coal to the performers upon the lute and harp." It was not only that different professions practiced the boycott. People in different regions did too, for disparate purposes. In the South, as we have seen, the Farmers' Alliance launched a boycott against the "jute trust." Populists in the South also used the boycott as a way to protest antagonistic news-papers, and those in the mountain West boycotted Eastern financiers and merchants, and business leaders who rejected bimetallism. In 1890, as we saw in the last chapter, a group of white Southern politicians launched a boycott of Northern businesses because of perceived Northern support for the Federal Elections Law, the so-called force bill. At the turn of the cen-tury, as we will see in chapter 5, African Americans in the South regularly employed the tactic to protest the nascent Jim Crow system, especially in streetcars. Women's suffrage activists employed boycotts as well.[7]

Proponents of several of the moral causes that first emerged in the an-tebellum era continued to call for boycotts. A. B. Leonard called for a boy-cott of saloons, making the classic consumerist argument that "the money spent for drink could be used in purchasing books and newspapers." Large groups of evangelical protesters threatened to boycott the World's Colum-bian Exposition in Chicago in 1893 because it remained open on the Sab-bath. Like most of its antebellum predecessors, this boycott attempt too was a "manifest failure."[8]

Almost as soon as they adopted the phrase, Americans naturalized it. Even before Captain Boycott's death in 1897, its users no longer interro-gated the meaning of the word. They stopped thinking about the meaning of the word "boycott" "as anything but what it is," as one reporter observed in 1907. Taking seriously the view of the scholar who in 1901 declared that words like "boycott" contain "condensed histories," this chapter will seek to unpack the term in order to examine the various ways in which Ameri-cans used and debated the meaning of the word "boycott" in the first de-cades after its coinage.[9]

Proponents tended to view the development of the word "boycott" in contradictory ways. Many of them claimed that the name itself was in-significant, since the action it described was not new. Noting that it was simply an "old thing under a new name," they claimed that "the thing it-self will remain, though it may change its name as often as a snake does its skin."[10] Some boycotters and a good number of their enemies, however, saw the new word as marking a critical break with traditions of consumer ac-tivism. Both sides had a point. The boycotts of the 1880s bore a close rela-tionship to those that came previously, albeit under a wide assortment of names. Yet in that decade, the practice of boycotting changed significantly, albeit not always in expected ways. Rather than instantiating and stabiliz-ing a singular meaning, the coinage of the term set off a period of fluid-ity and debate. Moreover, although the boycotts of the 1880s were smaller, more focused, and more dispersed—as well as more frequently successful than the national boycotts of the antebellum period—boycotters of this era described their struggles as intimately interconnected. From its inception, the boycott in name and in practice was extremely controversial and the debate about its meaning was not limited to its practitioners. A diverse group of critics questioned the legitimacy, and, in short order, the legality of the practice. In many ways, this was an unresolved dialogue, with neither side yielding or accepting the points of their critics; yet we can learn a great deal about how Americans understood the politics of consumption in the late nineteenth century through an examination of the debates over the origins of the boycott, its legitimacy, as well as its power and scope. For, in spite of the difference in their views about its history, provenance, and legitimacy, both proponents and critics of the boycott posited remarkably similar views about its nature and its impact.

I. "An American Custom with an Irish Name"

We typically think of historical developments as radiating from local to global. Most phenomena, such as a religions or social movements, start in a specific locale and expand outward. Boycotts would seem to be an exception to this historical pattern. Begun as a transatlantic mode of protest during the era of the American Revolution, and continuing into the antebellum period, when, we have seen, its practitioners understood and counted on the far-reaching effects of consumption, boycotts seemed to narrow in scope and ideology in the 1880s, the decade when the term was coined, only to take on national and global proportions once again in the twentieth century. According to Michael Gordon, the most thorough analyst of the boycotts of the 1880s, the boycott was a "pre-industrial" mode of activism. The meaning of the boycott in the 1880s, Gordon argued, "differs from what it subsequently connoted." In the same vein, the sociologist James M. Jasper claims that boycotts "began as weapons of the weak for highly oppressed, tight moral communities of the kind that usually animate citizenship movements." The assumption is that early boycotts of the 1880s were local, intensive, and social, and that this stood in sharp contact to the economic, extensive, and global form that they had taken in earlier periods and came to adopt in the twentieth century as well.[11]

In many ways, the boycotts of the 1880s, in contrast to those that came before and after, fit this pattern of local, subaltern protest. The key transformation of the Revolutionary period, as we have seen, was from the use of "early modern" consumerist tactics of direct and visible confrontation to the more market-oriented strategies that came to characterize the early nineteenth-century activists. Although they targeted and punished specific people—for example, Southern merchants seeking to sell Northern goods in contravention of the nonintercourse agreements—consumer protesters aimed to make visceral the unseen, to get consumers to realize the harm they caused, but never witnessed, though unthinking acts of consumption, such as purchasing slave-made goods or British-produced tea. Consumer activists, prior to the 1880s, promoted long-distance solidarity, since they recognized that the consumers they sought to motivate typically resided far from the problems they were being asked to address or otherwise could not comprehend their complicity in the system the boycotters sought to overturn.

Beginning with the Irish boycott of Captain Boycott, however, consumer protesters specified particular, proximate people or businesses as targets (see fig. 4.2). Over the course of the 1880s and 1890s, labor boycotters targeted many thousands of firms, the vast majority of them discrete entities in one location with a recognizable owner (or owners), among them breweries, bakeries, shoemakers, hat manufacturers, clothiers, theaters, newspapers, streetcar lines, and railroads. Protesters could see the person or firm they targeted, and they often knew the proprietor, sometimes as an employee and often as a neighbor. As in the early days of the nonimportation movement, what previously had to be imagined—the source of the problem, the cause of the boycott—could now be directly witnessed. The most common form of consumer protest of the 1880s, the labor boycott, was scaled down geographically and did not require the same degree of visualization and metaphor, because the enemy was a visible business or a person or a racial or ethnic group. (The great railroad boycotts of the 1880s and 1890s, national in scope, provide a partial exception to this general claim, but they too named particular, prominent people, such as Jay Gould and George Pullman.) Thus, labor boycotters, unlike most of their predecessors, seemingly took on the particular rather than the general. They acted against George Theiss's Alhambra Concert Saloon rather than chattel slavery; the *New York Tribune* (and its despised publisher, Whitelaw Reid) rather than the British; George Ehret, the brewer, rather than the North; Brennan and White Shoes, rather than Sabbath violators; or Kaufman Brothers Clothiers rather than purveyors of demon rum. They singled out the concrete thing rather than the general category, a site rather than an idea; they condemned a specific person in a particular place and time, rather than, as previous boycotts did, a systemic problem, such as imperialism, or slavery, or northern commercial hegemony. There was no need to invoke metaphor or to imagine the distant; all citizens needed to do was to literally face the problem and act on it. In this sense, we can agree with the historian Richard Schneirov that the labor boycott of the 1880s "retained its original Irish meaning."[12]

Figure 4.2. The beginning of the personalization of the boycott: Captain Boycott's family, ostracized by the community, forced to work the fields themselves. ("The Land Agitation in Ireland," *Harper's Weekly*, Dec 18, 1880, 808.)

Yet, as is often the case with consumer activism and consumption in general, looks can be deceiving. Thousands of discrete labor boycotts took place in these years.[13] Although individual boycotts were discrete actions, each with their own causes and protagonists, boycotters made every attempt to join their causes and to enforce solidarity through publicity. The boycotts of the last two decades of the nineteenth century were a product of the movement of people, goods, and ideas characteristic of an increasingly globalizing industrial capitalism, often covering vast expanses. The boycott was not, as it is sometimes described, a desperate premodern swipe against modern capitalism but rather a product of these economic forces. The institution itself was born as part of the mixing of cultures, ideas and peoples in the modern world. Even the most local boycotts were built upon the two networks that increasingly drew the country closer together, the print nexus and the cash nexus.

The proper frame for understanding the coinage and dissemination of the word "boycott," then, is both local and global, interpersonal and economic, social and political, historical and contemporary. The name itself points to the impact of transatlantic modes of commerce and communication. Its coiner, James Redpath (fig. 4.3), derived its name from the anticolonial protest of Irish peasants against British landlords. A Scottish-born

American journalist and a classic nineteenth-century transatlantic radical, Redpath always gave credit to his friend and fellow activist John O'Malley for, in conversation with Redpath, suggesting the name. They knew that ostracism had been recommended by a number of leading Irish national-ists, several of whom claimed to be the true "promulgators" of the prac-tice. In a speech in Ennis on September 19, 1880, later taken to be an impor-tant forerunner of the boycott, Charles Stewart Parnell addressed a crowd of angry Irish peasants. When the crowd called for the murder of evicting landlords, Parnell responded that a "a more Christian or charitable way" was to ostracize land agents and he called for exiling them to "moral Cov-entry," leaving them "severely alone." Parnell later claimed that the prac-tice of boycotting "grew up subsequently to that speech." Highlighting the transatlantic nature of boycott discourse, others claimed that Michael Da-vitt invented the idea in a speech in Boston in July of that year. Some traced the idea of ostracism back still farther, to speeches by Irish nationalists in the late 1870s. Although they were delivered in particular localities, each of these speeches was widely publicized (and later recorded for posterity in the *Special Commission Report* in 1888) through a print network; moreover, each of these speeches emphasized the importance of the circuitry of com-munication and markets.[14]

Although Redpath and others addressed the specific issue of abuse of Irish agricultural workers by British land agents, Redpath made clear that his observations of consumer politics on both sides of the Atlantic shaped his thinking about what in 1880 he called "the terrible power of social ex-communication." In formulating the boycott, Redpath, who was born in Berwick-upon-Tweed in 1833 and emigrated to the United States in 1848, drew on his long experience of the consumerist actions he had participated in, been victimized by, or witnessed as an abolitionist, a Reconstruction official, a labor reformer, a foreign correspondent, and an anticolonial ac-tivist. Looking back on his career as an itinerant radical in 1883, Redpath claimed that while his focus had shifted over time, his goal remained con-sistent: "to lift up an oppressed class or help an unpopular cause or to ad-vance a boycotted truth." Redpath's biography, embodying the history of consumer activism, exemplifies the links between the antebellum and postbellum periods.[15]

Redpath claimed, as we noted in chapter 3, that the actions taken by white Southerners against carpetbaggers and their Republican support-ers during the era of Reconstruction inspired him to encourage the Irish renters to protest Boycott's actions through economic and social ostra-cism. Redpath had witnessed these practices as a school superintendent in Charleston, South Carolina, and Northern journalists, including Red-

Figure 4.3. James Redpath in the 1880s. (Thos. W. Herringshaw, *The Biographical Review of Prominent Men and Women of the Day* [Chicago: Elliott & Beezley, 1889]. Clipart courtesy FCIT, http://etc.usf.edu/clipart/18700/18753/redpath_18753.htm.)

path himself, had reported on them, notably Albion Tourgee, who served as a Reconstruction official in North Carolina. "No Northern man is welcomed in the South if he believes in the principles of the Republican party and votes and acts in accordance with his creed," as Redpath wrote in 1876. "He is ostracized in society and business by native whites."[16] Describing these acts of ostracism as an "American boycott whose history has not yet been written," the journalist Arthur Dudley Vinton in 1886 labeled the "policy of social ex-communication with which the south met the emigrants or 'carpetbaggers' from the north after the civil war" as "the immediate parent of the policy of social excommunication which the Irish adopted and to which they gave the name of boycott." Vinton noted that "this policy was first recommended to the Irish people by Mr. James Redpath" and claimed that Redpath's experience of ostracism in the South explained why the boycott should be considered "an American custom with an Irish name." Given Vinton's accurate summation, it is fitting that in one of Redpath's articles on his experiences in the South he called for the enshrinement of the principle of "ostracizing no man."[17]

Redpath's encounter with consumer activism began long before Reconstruction. Prior to the Civil War, he had witnessed or knew of other examples of consumer activism, some of which he viewed more favorably than the postbellum boycotts of Reconstruction officials. As he was preparing John Brown's biography in 1859, for example, he learned that the radical abolitionist, with whom he was closely associated in Kansas in the 1850s, had at least once ostracized an employee who had stolen "fine calfskin," instructing his colleagues to leave the man alone for several weeks after the crime. It is likely that Redpath also knew that Brown was a devotee of maple candy and that his family, in a reversal of nonintercourse sentiments, refused to bury Brown in a Southern-made coffin, transferring his body to a Northern-made casket as it was en route from Harpers Ferry to its final resting place in North Elba, New York. Moreover, in his travels in the South in 1854, Redpath met a free black "confectioner and fruiterer" in Richmond, who later moved to Philadelphia, where he may have been a free produce entrepreneur. At Redpath's next stop, Charleston, he attended the Southern Commercial Convention and heard the nonintercourse arguments of Southern fire-eaters.[18]

In the course of his career, Redpath observed and wrote about many other aspects of consumer politics, including the Rochdale system of consumer cooperation (which he supported) and the attempts by working-class organizations in California to use consumption as a tool in their anti-Chinese campaigns (which he opposed). By the time he coined the word "boycott," then, Redpath had witnessed forms of consumer politics he admired and some he disliked, in many different places and for a variety of causes.[19]

In this context, we can appreciate the aptness of Vinton's comment that "we lent the policy to Ireland and she returned it to us with a name." Vinton argued for the importance of studying "the travels of the boycott," since to freeze the practice to one place was to lose sight of its meaning, its transatlantic derivation, and its uses by the "downtrodden people of other nations." Travels of the boycott. An apt phrase. For the boycott was a traveling institution, in many senses of the word, one that developed in a transatlantic (and, we will see, transpacific) context. Not only did word of the Irish boycotts travel immediately via the various newspapers for which Redpath wrote, but the web of print culture also set off immediate responses from distant places. Less than a month after the Irish boycott had begun, an American woman telegraphed Father O'Malley with an offer to pay the arrears of the tenants, as the *Chicago Daily Inter-Ocean* reported, thereby publicizing this course of action and perhaps encouraging others to do the same. Beginning with Redpath's exhortation that "I hope no American will buy" British goods, coverage of the Irish tenant farmer's ostracism of British land agents set off sympathy boycotts of British goods among Irish-Americans. "Fifty years ago, these articles would not have been heard," observed the boycott critic E. L. Godkin late in 1880, in one of the first reflections on the origins of the word "boycott" published in the United States. "But the times have changed. The magazines go everywhere." Godkin was correct: An expanding web of print culture facilitated the rapid dissemination of the boycott.[20]

When we examine boycotters and boycottees in the first decades of its use, we see that the global movement of peoples played a role as significant as that of the global spread of ideas. Although many of the Americans who took up the boycott can accurately be described as "downtrodden," among the most targeted groups to be boycotted in the early years were a generally impoverished class of immigrants. For among the earliest and, without a doubt, the largest boycotts, "the most gigantic boycott ever known in this country," according to *John Swinton's Paper*, was anti-Chinese protests led by working-class groups in the western United States. Indeed, the first article in the *New York Times* on the boycott's migration to the United States, in the spring of 1882, noted that California workers were proposing that the Chinese be "severely left alone." Calling on fellow workers to "drive out the Chinese by refusing to hire them or buy of them," the *Times* quoted a boycott leader who, drawing on the heritage of Revolutionary boycotters, called for "a non intercourse act" against the Chinese. It is important to note that the boycott went in the other direction as well, and also at a very early date. As early as 1882, and for the next several decades, many Chinese threatened to boycott American goods because of America's treatment of Chinese immigrants and passage of the Chinese Exclusion Act.[21]

If Americans were the targets in this case, Americans frequently used the weapon against other countries as well. For example, after the Dreyfus affair, a number of American newspapers called for a boycott of the French Exposition at the World's Fair in 1899. American women also called for a boycott of "frilly" French fashions. The boycotts of Perrier and other French goods in the wake of the refusal of France to join the coalition that took part in the Iraq War in 2003 did not represent the first time that Americans had taken such action against that country.[22]

If we shift our gaze from those who were boycotted to examine those who used the boycott in the early years, we find that many early boycotters were working-class immigrants or their children, most often of Irish or German ancestry. When critics denounced boycotting, as they regularly did, as a foreign institution, they were correct to the extent that these actions were a product of global migrations. The boycott was "imported from Ireland," not just because the phrase was invented there but because people of Irish ancestry pioneered the labor boycott in the United States. If the migration of peoples played a role in the history of boycotting, the global movement in commodities and ideas did as well. Many of the products boycotted in the 1880s and 1890s had a transnational history of their own, and those that did not, such as beer, cigars, newspapers, saloons, and bakeries, usually had a transnational workforce and appealed to an immigrant audience.[23]

In addition to people and commodities, the media also played a crucial role in the remarkably rapid travels of the boycott. The name of the practice spread so quickly in large measure because of the infrastructure of print capitalism that rapidly made "boycott" a household word throughout much of the world. Redpath himself fully recognized this power of dissemination through print. Indeed, he proposed renaming the tactic of ostracism so as to publicize it more effectively. Acknowledging that Father O'Malley "was the first to utter the word," and therefore "invented" it, Redpath claimed credit for the coinage because, he said, distinguishing between orality and literacy, he was "the first who wrote it" and therefore set in motion the word's life in print. Upon hearing O'Malley's utterance, Redpath's response was the following: "I was delighted and said, 'Tell your people to call it Boycotting so that when the reporters come down from Dublin and London they will hear the word. . . . We will make it as famous as the similar word, 'Lynching' in the United States.'" Again drawing from an American case (and perhaps not coincidentally another racialized one), Redpath had in mind international urban media markets as much as the local peasantry when he promulgated the word. Indeed, Redpath claimed that he and O'Malley invented the word "boycott" because it was short and catchy, more likely to be adopted by both the press and the protesters. ("Ostracism won't do—the peasantry would not know the meaning of the word—and I can't think of any other," he had told Father O'Malley.) Redpath's prediction was correct, in no small measure due to his journalistic efforts; the Inter-Ocean, one of the newspapers for which he was a special correspondent, used the verb "boycotted" in a front-page headline shortly after Redpath coined the term.[24]

Like the boycotters who followed him, Redpath had one eye on the local context and the other on the broader world. The founder, several years earlier, of the nineteenth-century's most successful speakers' bureau, the Redpath Lyceum, he was well aware of the importance of disseminating ideas through commercial modes of communication. Far from representing "premodern" tendencies, Redpath and others in the pioneering generation of boycott advocacy were quintessentially modern in their understanding that ideas, like goods, could be publicized and "sold"; intellectual no less than other forms of property followed networked pathways. More than fifty years after the coining of the term, Carlyle W. Morgan, observing that it was "still a popular word" and depicting Redpath and O'Malley as marketing wizards rather than heroes of moral reform, observed, "Few publicity agents or propagandists have hit upon so easily tongued a term for selling anything to the masses as did these two coiners of 'boycott.'"[25]

From the beginning, boycotters publicized their actions through the media and not infrequently created their own newspapers or other forms of print publicity to do so. The route of publicity was not always transatlantic, from the British metropole to the urban northeast, or vice versa. A printed circular of 1906 produced by a group of African Americans in Lynchburg, Virginia, and later reprinted in the *Lynchburg News*, proclaimed the boycott of Jim Crow streetcars to be an "effective weapon" and drew a supporting example from Asia: "Witness, for instance the late Chinese boycott of American made goods. Dollars worked where diplomacy had failed." Here was an example not of transatlantic boycott path, but of a transpacific route, made possible by global media coverage of boycotts, the culture of reprinting pamphlets and broadsides or articles from other newspapers, and the widespread adoption of the practice.[26]

Boycotters ensured that even the most local of actions received widespread attention, through an increasingly national, and even international, media and commercial network. In an editorial addressed "To Advertisers," a New York-based boycott newspaper suggested that publicity was as important as the action itself: "Advertisers who have discontinued advertising in the *Tribune* can have that fact announced in the *Boycotter* should they wish it." The editor deemed publicizing support for the boycott to be as important as the support itself because the airing of such news redounded to the benefit of the advertisers. Local newspapers frequently published letters from readers in distant places, commenting on a particular boycott. Indeed, it was not uncommon for newspapers based far from the scene of a particular boycott not only to publish articles about it, but also to print letters from locals either supporting or denouncing the cause. A group of printers in Atlanta, for example, sent a letter to the *New York Boycotter* in 1886, announcing that they were encouraging fellow Atlantans to cancel their subscription to the boycotted *New York Tribune*. In suggesting that a sizable group of Atlantans subscribed to a New York daily, this letter reveals the spread of print capitalism and its centrality to boycotting. While the historian David Scobey is correct to note that individual boycotts often "worked best where there were as yet visible connections between the worlds of production and consumption, where buyers brought to the consumer market their personal experience of the work behind it," it is also the case that boycotters sought to create equally powerful invisible connections abetted by the use of print and market to link disparate consumers. As a group of Providence printers claimed, "We and our wives, and our families and our friends (who number some 250,000) will put our money into those channels through which our friends, our cause and our active sympathizers will receive substantial benefit." Such channels, whose vastness was suggested by the quantity of "friends" casually mentioned, could take the boycotters far afield from their home, as they promised to boycott "any man who advertises in the *Tribune*," a New York newspaper. The *New York Boycotter* reminded potential advertisers that supporting the boycott was not only a good in itself but also a savvy way to appeal to "your cash customers."[27] (See fig. 4.4.)

This aspect of the boycott was not new. Since the 1760s, as we have seen, boycotters have used the web of print and commerce to link turn distant strangers into political communities. However, in the 1880s, more than ever, friends and foes treated seemingly local boycotts as part of a broad social movement. To the dismay of opponents of the tactic, boycotters repeatedly used the media to proclaim their actions as integral links in the chain of boycotts, and to encourage citizens to support other boycotts. The sociologist James Jasper judges boycotts "too mild" because they depend upon what he calls "a silent choice, made alone, in the aisle of a crowded supermarket." What this analysis misses is that, from the Revolutionary era to our own day, boycotters have rarely been "silent," since even the most local actions have been accompanied by widespread publicity and have almost always been linked to a broader cause.[28]

Although the boycotts of the 1880s and 1890s were smaller and more diffuse than those of the 1770s or the 1830s, many boycotters took these discrete actions to be interrelated aspects of a concerted struggle for labor rights, Civil Rights, or women's rights, and they made print culture central to the circulation of these larger claims. Like boycotts themselves, the forms of print boycotters chose radiated outward from the local. The most local and direct was the phenomenon of "sandwich boards," the physical advertisement of a boycott, carried on the body of a boycotter or sympathizer directly in front of a boycotted establishment. Boycotters also produced posters and broadsides and distributed them around the neighborhood of their actions. A typical such circular listed the name of "every foul finisher, foul prouncer, and foul trimmer" associated with the boycott of the Berg Hat Factory. Moving beyond the neighborhood, labor newspapers regularly published boycott "lists," compendia of boycotts, and encouraged workers and sympathizers to support not just this or that boycott but all boycotts sanctioned by national trade unions, Central Labor Unions, or other governing bodies. Similarly, African American newspapers comprehensively cataloged the sites of Jim Crow boycotts, so that a reader in Chicago would know of every reported streetcar protest in the South. One

ADVERTISE

IN THE

BOYCOTTER.

IT REACHES THE

Working People

WHO ARE

YOUR CASH CUSTOMERS.

Figure 4.4. The *Boycotter* encouraging businesses to view advertising in the paper as an opportunity to increase profits. (*New York Boycotter*, Oct 5, 1884, 4.)

commentator referred to the transition from what he called the "sword" to the "print" boycott, or from the sandwich to the newspaper, from the direct source of confrontation to the broad dissemination of knowledge about such confrontations. Indeed, the quantity of boycotts, the degree of publicity about them, and the pressure on consumers of these media to support them quickly became a topic of discussion. One good Samaritan complained in 1885, in a manner reminiscent of today's deluged ethical shoppers, about the difficulty in keeping up with the continually growing list of boycotts. "To be a sincere and systematic boycotter now requires the carrying about of a catalogue of the different boycotted firms or articles; and, if you have a family, another catalogue is required for their use," a writer who called himself "Nobody" declared. Another critic claimed in 1900 that "the list of prohibited articles grew so long that no man could remember what to avoid." Similarly, Terence Powderly, the head of the

Knights of Labor, noted with frustration that "I have in my possession 400 boycott notices." Clearly, sympathizers were meant to see disparate boycotts as linked; hence the need for being, to use the word invoked by "Nobody," "systematic."[29]

Boycotters posited a networked world, in which individuals were, whether they were aware of it or not, connected by markets in goods, through immigration and migration patterns, and by communication networks, with an increasing number of individuals that they would never meet, in increasingly distant lands. Just as novels and newspapers created a new culture of simultaneity, in which potentially distant people shared similar experiences through reading, boycotters considered all consuming individuals part of an imagined community. However, although the community may have been imaginary, the impact of the actions of consumers was anything but fictional. Boycotters argued that consumers affected people directly through their purchasing decisions. This group was a community not merely by virtue of experiencing similar feelings, but also because their actions had a direct if, to them, invisible impact. Just as print nodes allowed ideas to travel, disseminating the term "boycott" throughout the world, market nodes distributed goods nationally and globally. The two were often related; it is not surprising that printers of the International Typographical Union were particularly avid boycotters in the 1880s. As a group of workers with a high density of unionization, and with ready access to the means of publicizing their cause, printers frequently published pamphlets and newspapers, such as the three mentioned earlier called the *Boycotter*; the New York version of which eventually came to be called the *Union Printer*. These papers served both to trumpet particular boycotts (against newspapers in these cases) and to delineate the ways in which boycotts operated to link consumers to moral causes. For boycotters, the imagined community of print capitalism was both a metaphor for the worldview they sought to popularize, an exemplar of this worldview, and a mode of popularization, since even the most local of boycotts were publicized by local, urban newspapers in stories that were often reprinted in other newspapers.[30]

Let us dwell for a moment on the difference between reading newspapers and buying goods from the market. They are similarly networked activities, dependent upon webs of production and distribution. Like consumers, readers also sat at nodes of a network, but the act of reading did not have an immediate or necessary consequence. Groups of readers may, over time, begin to think of themselves and their fellow citizens differently, but there is nothing inexorable about this process, which is deliberative and dependent upon readers' coming to similar conclusions about who constitutes their community. Buying, in the opinion of consumer activists, has a very different impact, since it sets off an inevitable chain of events, irrespective of the worldview or the consciousness of the buyer, which have direct consequences for all the people in the chain of production and distribution of that good (and perhaps on many others as well). This impact might be quite minimal if the number of boycotters is small. But the crucial point is that the process is inexorable: buying a product leads to the production of that good, the hiring of a worker to make it, and a profit to both the factory owner and seller. The only variable is the degree, which is purely a function of numbers: the more boycotters, the bigger the impact.

Readers were an interpretive community, potentially deliberative and political. Reading a novel or newspaper, and knowing that many thousands or millions of others are doing the same, may lead one to think new thoughts about nation and community. Each reader might interpret the text differently and take different messages from the simultaneous or near-simultaneous experience. Buyers were different; in some ways their actions were suprapolitical, because their intentions did not matter, or, at least, they did not matter in the same way. (This is why the question of whether boycotts provided "conscious moral satisfaction" was, for most boycotters, irrelevant; they were more concerned with the impact of their actions than in how the subjective experience of boycotting affected consumers.) For most consumer activists, the effect of purchasing (or not buying) goods was immediate and inexorable, not subject to politics as it is usually understood. So the boycott was both supremely political and at the same time beyond politics. Politicized consumers certainly aimed to make other shoppers aware of the moral stakes of their actions and to get them to change their behavior accordingly. Unlike the imagined community of the nation, the community of those affected by the web of commerce was real, in the sense that actions had direct consequences, which were no less tangible for being invisible to the shopper who stood at some remove from the producer who made the goods. It is immaterial whether buyers know the person or people who created and sold the goods they buy—in a market society, they hardly ever do—the important consideration for consumer activists is that they directly affect the lives of these people through their consumption choices.[31]

II. How to Boycott

Most of the boycotts of the 1880s started as protests against a particular person or business. But, as boycott advocates made clear, and as critics were quick to perceive, these boycotts almost invariably expanded in concentric circles beyond the boycotted business to confront those who continued to support that business. Just as printers and journalists translated the local to the national and even the international through media networks, so too did consumer activists imagine a increasingly widespread ringed network of potential supporters in commercial networks. Although boycotters of this period started with the local, they rarely stopped there. Rather, they built on the Smithian premise that consumption creates production and that global markets and divisions of labor mean that consumers may never see the site of production, which they, by their actions, call into being. Boycotters targeted ever-expanding concentric circles of enemies. Starting with the particular person or firm held to be guilty, they threatened to use the same actions against those who had dealings with that enemy, and those who had dealings with the enemy's abettor. An 1884 article on "how to boycott" the *Tribune* in the *New York Boycotter* (a printer's strike at the former paper had called the latter into being) encouraged readers to begin with the local: "Does your grocer take it? If so, tell him he must choose between the loss of your custom and stopping the paper. Does your tobacco dealer, barber, or druggist subscribe for it? If so, tell him you cannot deal with him unless he will stop it." The article continued, however, by moving beyond "your" merchant and asked supporters to stay away from all businesses implicated in supporting the *Tribune* through advertising, a list of which it helpfully included in almost every issue: "Do not buy anything that you require for your daily needs from any one who either subscribes to or advertises in the *New York Tribune*." The same newspaper advised boycotters not only to "refrain from buying the sheet," but also to "canvass among our friends and find out who takes the daily, weekly, or tri-weekly Tribune." After garnering the support of allies, the printers urged boycotters to monitor the local "stationer or cigar and newspaper dealer" and to "induce him to comply with your desire." If the dealer failed to comply, the printers urged boycotters to "trade with those who do not give aid and comfort to our enemies," regardless of their physical location. Boycotters built upon this conception of expanding concentric circles; although the key action was taken by an individual, boycotts were in this sense fundamentally social. Long before the bumper sticker phrase appeared, boycotters sought to act locally and think globally, but they recognized, in a way that the slogan does not, that acting locally had global repercussions. One aspect of boycotting, then, was that individual boycotters were asked to expand their moral policing in ever-widening circles. "The meaning of boycott is, to leave alone," noted a writer for the *Boycotter*, who went on to demonstrate examples of the extensiveness of this act of leaving alone. "When we boycott a thing we simply leave it alone. If it is a cigar, we neither buy it nor smoke it, nor buy anything else from the man who sells it. If it is a newspaper, we buy nothing from the man who advertises in it. If he is a lawyer, we give him no business. If he is an official, we refuse to vote for him or with the party that sustains him." This was a market-based version of ostracism. It is instructive that the writer starts with commodities (the cigar) and moves on to people, but, not distinguishing between the two, holds that the same principle applies to both. To boycott, in this sense, was to extend the meaning of "disuse" in both commercial and personal directions.[32]

In addition to eschewing purchases at boycotted establishments, boycotters asked local sympathizers not to provide services to the boycottee. A classic case of this collective withdrawal of services occurred in 1886. Over the opposition of the Knights of Labor, "foul" hatters who worked for the Berg Hat Factory in Orange, New Jersey, faced a community unwilling to provide them any services. One such dishonored hatter faced this situation in the extreme, in a manner that evoked the treatment accorded Captain Boycott himself: "He had gone into a barber's shop to get shaved, but the barber cried out 'foul!' and refused to lather his face. He went to a saloon to get a glass of beer, but the beer-seller refused to draw it for him. He went to a news-dealer to buy a paper, but the dealer would not sell it to him. His baker had refused him a loaf of bread, and his grocer a pound of sugar. His acquaintances refused to speak to him in the street, and when he went to church, nobody else would sit in his pew." Once again, the essence of boycotting was "leaving alone" in every sense, both interpersonal and commercial. Just as free producers redefined the slogan "No union with slaveholders" to include commerce, so too did the boycotters of the 1880s expand ostracism into the commercial realm. Claiming that boycotters had gone too far in this direction, a critic complained about the mushrooming number of people being asked to "refrain from intercourse with the boycotted man." Another opponent claimed that for boycotters to be consistent, "they must boycott all bakers, butchers, and tailors who have the hardihood to help keep those boycotted individuals alive and clothed." Carried to "its logical limits," the critic recognized, the boycott was not local at all but an inherently metastasizing form of social protest. Referring to a streetcar boycott in Cleveland, a reporter similarly noted that "the boycott is far-reaching. If the store-keeper refuses to obey the orders of the leaders of the strike the boycott is then extended to the store, and the patronage at once falls off. Some of the stores have attempted to ignore the boycott and they have suffered the consequence."[33]

The final, and most important, source of power upon which boycotters of the 1880s depended, came from the other side, in a way. Boycotters enlisted the support of consumers, not just nearby but far and wide, by asking them to eschew products from boycotted firms. The community of participants lay far beyond the site of a boycotted business or person. Instead, boycotters created an imagined community of all supporters of the cause, one far larger and more powerful than the proximate community. These were not just passive supporters either, but, to the extent that they used their purchasing power, active participants in the struggle, morally proximate even if physically distant. One labor leader, Edward King of New York, labeled the boycott "a strike by consumers," meaning an action not limited to a finite set of aggrieved employees but enlisting an unlimited set of politicized shoppers. Boycotters sought to deploy the power of large numbers. "Now brothers, certainly we are not all hat makers," commented a Knights of Labor member, John G. Carville, "but are we not the ones who wear hats?" Carville redirected this classic idiom of fraternal solidarity to an imagined brotherhood of hat wearers. Carville's shift from producerism to consumerism was one echoed by other champions of the labor boycott. While the set of hatmakers directly involved in a labor dispute was limited (as was the pool of fellow hatmakers who could extend solidarity), the group of potential purchasers of hats (or any other boycotted good) was as large as the total number of potential consumers and as wide as the marketing scope of the boycotted establishment, a range that was increasingly national and even global.[34]

So, in the labor boycott, belying the view that it was exclusively local, individual consumers looked outward, sympathetic tradespeople refused to serve dishonored individuals, and large numbers of dispersed consumers focused laserlike on particular companies or goods. In each of these cases, consumers moved beyond the immediate and the local and extended their moral focus via the use of market power. Even when its target appeared local and discrete, boycotters depended on the expanding rings beyond that particular target, rings which could, and often did, extend beyond the neighborhood, the city, the state, and even the country. This was precisely the fear that a critic voiced when he commented on the dangers of boycotts, which tended, he observed, to expand in "ever-widening circles in general society."[35]

The labor boycott, in this conception, was anything but limited. Edward King summed this up in a talk that he gave in 1886 entitled "The Boycott and Its Relation to the American Public." For King, the boycott was not "narrow" but "broad and liberal." The reason for this, he said, was that boycotts rested on "the widest of all democratic sources of authority, the purchasing public—the consumers." The boycott was nothing less than the practice of democratic citizenship, exercised by the group newly anointed as the embodiment of the people, consumers. Boycotters sought to gain the sanction of this democratic public; broad support for a boycott, in this conception, was ipso facto proof of its legitimacy. Similarly, a newspaper in Toledo emphasized that the "far-reaching power" of the boycott rested on the support of "a large number of people outside of Labor organizations"; indeed, what made the boycott a "potent weapon" was that it could be employed by every "child who had a penny for a stick of candy." Union leaders and labor intellectuals depicted the boycott as a, perhaps the, key weapon of working-class advancement precisely because it encompassed the consuming public, and often compared it favorably with the strike and the ballot. "Thoroughly organized as consumers we shall be better prepared and more thoroughly equipped for the determined assertion of our rights as producers," claimed a member of the Knights of Labor in 1889. "We can but rarely strike, we cannot often vote, but as long as breath of life finds abiding place in man we must consume." John Swinton too noted the relative success of boycotting versus other working-class strategies and suggested that its strength lay in the mustering of large numbers of consumers. "For example, take the case of the anti-Union brewer, DOELGER: the ballot could not be used against him, but the boycott brought him to terms. The Thalia Theatre or the three German papers of this city could not be reached through politics; but the boycott forced a surrender." While Swinton here contrasted boycotting with politics, most boycotters, like King, equated the two.[36]

Critics highlighted and condemned the seemingly inexorable tendency of boycotts toward expansion, which one critic called "a new sensation with respect to this modern invention of the devil." The *Dallas Morning News* editorialized that boycotters aimed to "proceed until they have established non-intercourse with the rest of the world." A few months later, putting specific substance to this charge, the newspaper denounced a boycott of an establishment, Sanger Brothers, that sold Stetson hats, a product boycotted by the Knights of Labor. While conceding the legitimacy of the boycott of the Stetson firm, the writer called the Knights' boycott of Sanger Brothers unfair, precisely because it illustrated the dangers of extending boycotts beyond the immediate offender to the broader category of all the people and businesses that enabled that offender. The newspaper illustrated:

> If sustained in this shameful abuse of power they would, perhaps, next boycott the country merchant who buys from Sanger, then the physician who buys from the country merchant, then the mechanic who employs the physician to heal his sick wife or daughter, then the blacksmith

who makes the mechanic's implements of labor, then the butcher who supplies the mechanic with his daily meat, then the stock-raiser who sells the butcher his animals for slaughter, then the farmer who sells the stock-raiser the corn upon which he fattens his cattle, hogs, and sheep, then the field hand who labors for the farmer in the production of grain— then the very Creator who made from chaos the soil upon which the laborer lives, and in which he is to find his last resting place. Where would the unholy, vicious, agrarian, communistic doctrine find a termination?

Opponents viewed the extensive boycott as a violation of American principles of freedom. But boycotters defined this expansion as the embodiment of that freedom. Not only did they urge individual consumers continually to extend their targets, from the business which was the specific source of the problem to those businesses that enabled the business originally at fault; they also encouraged far-flung consumers to target particular businesses. "The possibilities of this method of coercion are enormous when it is systematized and extended, as has now been done in some parts of the United States," editorialized the New York Times in 1885. The difficulty, according to the Times, was for boycotters to "induce other men totally uninterested in their quarrel" to join them. (Boycotters, of course, argued that there were no "uninterested" consumers since their support financed these businesses.) If successful, boycotted businesses would have no customers, a force that could have only one "logical outcome," namely, "the death by starvation of the employer who resisted a strike, through the refusal of all men to furnish him with food." This was death by boycott, the refusal of those on every node of the market to engage in commodity exchange and therefore a denial of the necessities of life in a world in which self-sufficiency no longer reigned. Writing critically of a threatened boycott of the New York market by the Brick Manufacturers' Association of New-York and New-Jersey, the Times worried that it would "put a stop to the circulation of millions of dollars" and that it would "throw about 150,000 men out of employment in New-York and vicinity." The fact that a boycott of one industry could wreak such havoc highlighted the growing power of the expanding web of politicized consumers.[37]

The reference to death by boycott implies the power, even violence, of this strategy. Both sides frequently referred to it as a weapon. James Redpath himself called it a "bloodless war." "Vigorous boycotting" will have a "crushing effect," claimed John Swinton, who was himself ambivalent about the boycott precisely because of its raw power. Recognizing it as "a powerful and dreaded weapon, but nevertheless sometimes a necessary one," a New Jersey advocate of the boycott argued that "it should never be used vindictively." A common feature of media coverage of the 1880s was to list the businesses destroyed by boycotts, and either to lament or to celebrate this powerful economic force, which *Frank Leslie's Illustrated Newspaper* condemned as a dangerous "juggernaut" (fig. 4.5). Conceding that the "boycott is a terrible engine to set in motion," one of the early issues of the *New York Boycotter* argued that the bar to initiating boycotts should be set high, since, once in motion, the boycott, with its appeal to potentially millions of consumers, contained virtually unlimited power: "How long would the wealth even of Mr. Vanderbilt last if the people as an organized body should refuse to ride on his railroads or to patronize any institution in which he was interested? There are none so rich and powerful as to stand alone." What made this form of political action so effective is that it was market based and therefore potentially could be practiced by consumers everywhere. Defining a boycott, and distinguishing it in magnitude from earlier forms of ostracism, as the process whereby "a man is severely let alone by a large number of people," the printer J. R. O'Donnell also singled out the wealthiest American, to note that "William H. Vanderbilt with his $200,000,000 could be driven into bankruptcy if all the workingmen of the country should institute a thorough boycott against the roads under the control of the millionaire." The wealthy and powerful could in the past "stand alone" in a county retreat or exclusive neighborhood, but in an age of economic interdependence self-sufficiency was impossible, even, perhaps especially, for the rich. In 1881, a journalist in Utah provided an example of the impoverishment of the rich, that he claimed to have learned from an "eastern exchange." "Yesterday, a landlord was living in a luxurious home, with hosts of servants and dependents ready to do his will. His elegant mansion stood in the midst of his broad acres that were covered with the growth of an abundant harvest. . . . To-day the scene remains, but the circumstances have totally changed." This was a metamorphosis caused by the boycott. Even the wealthy were dependent on the consumption of others; when this was withdrawn, the results were dire: "In fact, he is in danger of starving. If any grocer sells him an article of food, the dealer is included in the ban and his shop is shunned and may as well be closed. The butcher and the baker cannot serve him a chop, nor a loaf, for it they do their business is totally ruined. . . . He is more helpless than the master of a ship becalmed in mid ocean, for there is no cook in the galley, no man at the helm, no boy in the cabin, and crew have deserted, taking the boat with them." The boycott, this suggested, was a force of isolation even more powerful than the classic nineteenth-century image of alone-ness, the sailor stranded at sea.[38]

In an 1885 sermon on the "tremendous power of the new force whose use was learned from dissatisfied tenants in Ireland," the Reverend Charles

THE AMERICAN JUGGERNAUT.

Figure 4.5. The boycott depicted as a "juggernaut," more powerful than American capital-ism. (*Frank Leslie's Illustrated Newspaper*, May 1, 1886, 176.)

Hawley recalled with concern a string of recent successful boycotts: "The product of a lager beer company is boycotted until the proprietors yield to the terms imposed on them by discontented employes. A theatre is boycot-ted until the manager agrees to employ only musicians belonging to a reg-ular organization of musicians. . . . All business was lately kept at a stand-still in Galveston because a steamship company was boycotted." In all these cases, consumer power had massive economic and, from the point of view of the minister, unjust consequences. Agreeing about the dangers of aggre-gate consumer power, *Harper's* magazine labeled the boycott a "new form of terrorism" that "seeks to destroy its victims, not by the guillotine or the dagger, but by depriving them of the means of support." Frank Eno, a critic of the boycott, described a similar dynamic: "No one will work for him, no one will sell to him. He cannot even buy food; he cannot even leave that town, for no one will hire him a carriage or loan him one, or help him into it. The only thing he can do is yield to the boycotters." Boycott opponents resented that thin-skinned workers could arbitrarily inflict such dire punishment.[39] (See fig. 4.6.)

Although opponents criticized the scope and power of the labor boycott, they also used its logic and practice, along with the law, as a way of defeating specific boycotts. Foes of the boycott quickly became adept at "boycotting the boycotters." (Similarly, they selectively praised boycotts as an honorable American tradition when they endorsed the goal; such was the case when the *Atlanta Constitution* in July 1890 reprinted Arthur Dudley Vinton's article from the *New York Commercial Advertiser*, quoted earlier in this chapter, as a way of legitimating the controversial force bill boycott.) Enemies of the boycott turned to the law to punish boycotters, but they also imitated them; perhaps this is why they inevitably described the boycott as a "boomerang," a "double-edged sword," or a "weapon that shoots at both ends" that could ricochet in unanticipated directions.[40]

The most well-organized counterboycott was the remarkably well-publicized and nationally coordinated response to the seemingly minor

PUCK'S PLEASANT PROSPECT.

Figure 4.6. Coercive, violent, demanding, and prickly boycotters. (*Puck*, May 5, 1886, cover.)

boycott of Esther Gray, who owned a bakery on Hudson Street in New York City. Improbably, no boycott of the decade received as much publicity as this one, which dominated the United States newspapers in April of 1886, although a boycott of "Mrs. Landgraf," a widowed baker on Second Street, vied with the Gray boycott for national attention. When the Knights of Labor authorized a boycott of her nonunion shop, they could not have anticipated their vigorous attempts to publicize this action would be dwarfed by negative accounts that appeared not only in the major metropolitan dailies of Albany, Boston, Chicago, Denver, Milwaukee, St. Louis, San Francisco, and Los Angeles, but also in the papers of Tombstone, Arizona, Macon, Georgia, Atchison, Kansas, Raleigh, Buffalo, Bridgeport, and many other smaller towns and cities. Whereas boycott proponents, such as T. P. Barry of the Knights of Labor, declared it "utterly impossible to get out of the reach of the boycott," noted the *Atchison Daily Champion*, "the case of Mrs. Gray, the brave little New York bakeress, shows that a person may be placed beyond the reach of the boycott by public sympathy." This was an antiboycott, consumer power deployed in defense of a boycotted business, "people going of out their way to patronize it in order to express their disapprobation of the boycotting method." As a Boston newspaper crowed, "Mrs Gray is making money by hundreds of dollars because of the proscription."[41]

In the hands of its opponents, the Gray boycott was the embodiment of "boycotting gone to seed," as one headline had it, an unreasonable and unconscionable attempt by workers (most of them immigrants) to bankrupt the brave and, as she was invariably described, "plucky" widow. (Although some accounts mentioned a Mr. Gray, most described her as a widow, perhaps because it made the parallel with the widowed Langraf even stronger; two plucky women, one on the East Side and the other on the West Side, both "prospering" in spite of the unfair tactics of their enemies.) The plight of Mrs. Gray inspired dozens of editorial cartoons, and even poetry (see fig. 4.7). "The boycott of Mrs Gray's bakery has gone all over the world, and, like Byron, she has awoke and found herself famous," noted a reporter for a newspaper in Macon. "Art has been exhausted in the cent-paper illustrations but not poetry." To fill this gap, he supplied his own verse about the widow, a riff on Thomas Gray's famous eighteenth-century poem "Elegy Written in a Country Church-Yard." A sample line: "How checks and greenbacks in that bakery pour." Typical of the distance traversed by the networked media was an irate letter against the boycott from a Poughkeepsie resident to Mrs. Gray published by the *Chicago Tribune*. Even farther afield, the *Los Angeles Times* reported that Charles Crocker, the California railroad magnate, had donated fifty dollars to Mrs. Gray. Newspapers

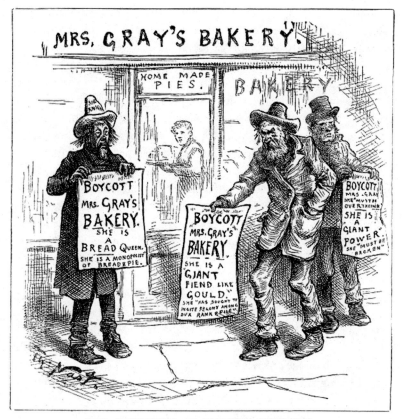

THE CHIVALRY OF MODERN KNIGHTS.

Figure 4.7. Scraggly boycotters threaten the "plucky" Mrs. Gray. ("The Chivalry of Modern Knights," *Harper's Weekly*, Apr 24, 1886, 271.)

throughout the country printed Crocker's letter, and also letters of their own from people and organizations who not only contributed to Mrs. Gray but also publicized their actions by means of letters to the editor. "The odd thing about this boycott is the strange interest that people who never heard of Mrs. Gray or her little bake-shop take in the affair," reported the *Chicago Tribune*. "No sooner was it known that the regular customers were dropping off than people from Harlem, and Fifth Avenue, and Brooklyn, and every other distant locality, rushed for this particular bakery to tell the little woman to keep up the fight and to buy of her." The *Tribune* did not pause to consider the possibility that this "strange interest" might have been abetted by the five articles on the subject it published in April of 1886. It is hard to disagree with W. A. Croffut's assessment, originally published as a letter to the *St. Paul Pioneer Press* and reprinted in the *Chicago Tribune* and the *Detroit Free Press*, that the boycott of Mrs. Gray's small bakery in an immigrant neighborhood in lower Manhattan had "stirred up the whole country." Croffut's observation, published in at least three newspapers in the Midwest, that Gray's sympathizers included shoppers who arrived "from way up town, Brooklyn, and some of 'em, they tell me, from Jersey and Connecticut," was among the many nonlocal media interventions that generated supporters far afield from the New York metropolitan area. Counterboycotters too constituted themselves as imagined communities.[42]

For many opponents, the Mrs. Gray-inspired "boycott of the boycotters" was not a repudiation of the tactic but an example of its power. A newspaper in Milwaukee noted that Gray's bakery was "getting a fine advertisement" that "resulted in a great affluence of custom to the bakery, people going out of their way to patronize it in order to express disapprobation of the boycotting method." This combination of publicity and commercial incentives mirrored the way boycotts worked; as a cartoon in *Puck* suggested, the boycott was a "business boom" for Mrs. Gray and other proprietors unfairly targeted (fig. 4.8). One reporter for the *New York Evangelist* (who assumed that boycotts were Catholic affairs), after briefly describing the history of the word "boycott," noted, "It seems a misfortune that we can't put up a monument in the language to brave Mrs. Gray, who fought and killed it." Unlike "Boycott," which referred to the victimization of the person for whom the practice was named, presumably a "Gray" would connote the vanquishing of the boycott. Other newspapers highlighted parallel cases of businesspeople for whom the boycott served as a boon to their firm. For example, the *Atlanta Constitution* (which published four articles in the month of April about Mrs. Gray, despite the fact that the action was far from the site of its readership) highlighted the story of one "Lotholz," a boycotted butcher from the North Side of Chicago, whom the reporter compared to Mrs. Gray.[43]

The opponents of the Gray boycott did more than adapt boycott techniques for their own purposes; they also used the courts to challenge the legality of the boycott. The previous year in a landmark case, Judge Arnold Krekel of the Circuit Court of the United States for the Western District of Missouri declared that boycotts were not only "foreign to our institutions" but also potentially "actionable and indictable" under the law of conspiracy. Soon critics began to distinguish between direct boycotting and the "indirect" form, which "consists of the effort by the boycotter to prevent other people from exercising their right of choice of the persons, firms, or corporations with which they shall deal." The *New York Times* concurred: the expansive boycott constituted "an agreement between persons with no direct interest to injure the business of other persons, and this agreement comes very near to the legal conception of conspiracy." The Gray case

⁀ P U C K. ⁀

THE BOYCOTT AS A BUSINESS BOOM.

Hard Times for Mr. Minzesheimer—"Beesness is no goot."

But Mr. Minzesheimer Reads the Papers—and Has an Idea.

The Idea Works—the Record of Mrs. Gray's Bakery Beaten.

"Rebecca, uf you got dem goupons gut, I'll trop down by dot office.'

Figure 4.8. "The Boycott as a Business Boom," with Mrs. Gray as a central exhibit. (*Puck*, Apr 28, 1886, 133.)

marked the most publicized application of this law, when the secretary of the Baker's Union, as well as several of the "sandwich" protesters, were indicted and fined for conspiracy. "Boycotters are the enemies of good social order; and they should everywhere be treated as criminals, who can make themselves most useful to society when safely locked up in the penitentiary," claimed a writer for the *Independent*, who, like so many other opponents, adduced the boycott of Esther Gray as exhibit number 1. "Whether it succeeds or fails it is upon its face the most detestable and abominable tyranny over the freedom of individual action." In contrast to the labor activists who understood the boycott as the essence of industrial freedom, the critics defined it as freedom's negation.[44]

III. Beyond Ostracism

Boycotters of the 1880s described the practice as a descendant of the venerable practice of ostracism, a punishment that they often claimed was as "as old as mankind." Indeed, one of the justifications they offered to those who condemned the boycott as new and dangerous was precisely that it was merely an adaptation of this age-old practice. Although the word was new, boycotters frequently claimed that the "social excommunication" at the heart of the boycott was as old as civilization itself. As William A. Hammond observed in his 1886 article on the evolution of the boycott, there was "nothing new about the boycott except the name." Writing in 1914, the labor activist Tom Fitch agreed that the boycott was "as old as history." As he explained, "The Jews boycotted the Samaritans. The Pharisees boycotted the Publicans as far as social intercourse was concerned. In Greece, following the rule of Clisthenes, the people boycotted the unsuccessful candidates for office." Embattled boycotters sought instances from American and world history to support their claim that they were merely perpetuating a tradition. In making this "old wine in new bottles" claim, the first generations of boycotters underestimated the degree to which their practice differed from traditional forms of ostracism. Boycotters did indeed seek to update ostracism, but in so doing, they developed a different understanding of how to isolate and sequester dishonored people, and also of the scope of ostracism.[45]

What made the labor boycott novel was that it combined the age-old tradition of ostracism with the American practice of market-based radicalism. In so doing, a tactic appropriate to a world of what the historian Robert Wiebe has called self-sufficient "island communities," changed. Traditional practices of ostracism understood the key act as the isolation of that person, especially in social matters. Generally, this meant having no neighborly relations with him or her. The culmination of ostracism was exile, banishment from a community. Referring to ancient Greece, commentators often mentioned the practice of Clisthenes, who devised a system whereby citizens banished dishonored compatriots from the polis.[46]

In a market-oriented world, to effectively leave someone "severely alone" required not just the actions of neighbors but also the efforts of potentially far-flung customers, employers, and suppliers. "Every dollar you spend with him only adds to the fund that is to be used against you," noted one boycott supporter, who recognized that distance from the proprietor was irrelevant from this perspective. To isolate somebody in this context meant to insure that wrongdoers were adversely affected by a range of economic actions. This required people to think like consumers as well as neighbors, that is, to understand that the consequences of their actions were not always visible or apprehensible by the senses. Indeed, boycotters frequently talked of replacing the sensory with the economic, that is, local knowledge with market impact. Calling on all "liberty-loving persons" to action, William Hammond reminded them that effective action required making boycottees "feel their shame in the only place they would be likely to experience such a sensation—their pockets." The metaphor of the pocket, borrowed from their antebellum forebears, remained a common trope in the boycotting era. "Most people acquire information through the senses," noted the *Boycotter* of a targeted publisher, "but Mr. Tousey is securing his through his pockets." The corollary to the view that businessmen acquired information through their pockets was that consumers anywhere could impart such information through market-based actions that did not require proximity. African Americans employed this metaphor in their struggles against Jim Crow streetcars in the 1890s and the first decade of the twentieth century. Demonstrating that economic affects trumped physical sensation, a group of boycotters in Lynchburg wrote, "The colored brother is learning how to strike back and when the blow is landed on the white man's pocket it will do more to wind him than if delivered on his stomach." Many black boycotters, as we will see in the next chapter, concluded that the pocket was the "most vulnerable point" of white supremacy.[47]

Emphasizing the power of the purse over the power of the senses—or more accurately constituting the "pocket nerve" as a new sense—consumer activists of the nineteenth century stressed the limits of interpersonal excommunication, notwithstanding the local contexts in which they frequently acted. The goal was not so much to shame a neighbor as to get her to change her ways; one did not need to ignore somebody personally to accomplish this. Indeed, many boycotters called the morality of such actions into question. For them, the bottom line was effectiveness, and therefore they took isolating an individual to mean taking away that person's customers, labor sources, and materials. Despite its deep roots in Western civilization, the new ostracism was a system meant to work in the modern world, and this required actions by consumers far from the scene.

Like the ostracizers of ancient Greece, the Bible, early Christianity, medieval Europe, and other epochs cited by those stressing continuity, boycotters believed that isolation was the essence of their action. They believed, following Harry Nilsson, that "one is the loneliest number." But isolation meant something different in the 1880s from what it meant in fifth-century Athens. Neighbors could continue the practice of physically "leaving alone," but, for most boycotters, the key was economic isolation. One did not need to touch a person, or even to see him, to "touch" his pocket. Taking the old and making it compatible with relations in modern society, which were as often economic as neighborly, advocates of this form of consumer activism understood it as a modernization of older forms of moral protest based upon ostracism and social excommunication.

IV. "A Tyranny Wholly Foreign"

In the late nineteenth century, critics and proponents saw the boycott not as a limited form of activism, but as an expansive and powerful one, whose tentacles extended in many directions. They recognized that even the tiniest American boycott was the product of global forces and likely to have an impact far beyond its physical locale. Individual boycotts were simply nodes on a network, which extended far and wide. The critics condemned the boycott precisely because of its expansive qualities, which made it, in the words of one enemy, "un-American, undemocratic, and irrational."[48]

Although both critics and proponents generally agreed on the chronology of the coinage of the term and on the local-global admixture characteristic of the boycott, they disagreed about the meaning of this combination, and about the provenance of the boycott. The critics saw the boycott as a new and dangerous invention, a "foreign creature" which ought immediately to "depart to the despotic lands where it belongs." They criticized the tactic as violent, un-American, illiberal, and, as we have seen, illegal, and they soon persuaded the courts to agree with them.[49] By contrast, proponents saw the coinage of the term "boycott" as the continuation of a tradition as old as the West itself and one that was constitutive of American political culture. For them, the boycott represented nothing less than the distillation of the best of the Western tradition and the embodiment of American freedom, well suited for modern conditions. The boycott generation, unique in the history of American consumer activists, sought sanction in history and regularly placed its actions in the context of the past. In many ways, in fact, the boycott battle was a fight over the legitimation of history. Each side peddled competing origin stories, which largely revolved around the question of whether the boycott was alien or homegrown, novel or traditional.[50]

In the first decade of its use, boycotters were highly self-conscious—if not always accurate—about the history of the term, although, like those that came after them, they tended to limit their recounting of boycott history in America to the Revolutionary era. (The New York Boycotter provided a good example of this neglect of early nineteenth-century boycotts when it quoted the "venerable John G. Whittier" to support the claim that "boycotting is a very ancient weapon" but noted only his mention of the "the boycotting of British tea in Boston Harbor" and not the cause that the Quaker poet prominently led as an activist and editor, free produce.) Boycotters sought the sanction of history not for antiquarian reasons but because it provided support for a tactic that a large number of powerful people in the country deemed illegitimate. Critics tried to tar the boycott with the brush of foreignness and newness. Boycotters turned to history as a means of combating these charges. Calling boycotting "no new thing" and utterly American—with a "genuine Yankee Doodle in every line and letter"— undermined the critics' key assertions. Finally, in turning to history, boycotters made a claim that seems perhaps to contradict their efforts to find the boycott deeply rooted in venerable American and Western traditions. Claiming that they borrowed the idea from employers, they described boycotts as a necessary response to the ugliest elements of modern industrial capitalism, especially capitalists' unfair efforts to stack the market. For boycotters, these varied roots were not contradictory. Boycotts, they agreed, came from many sources, and boycotters took inspiration from many of them. This form of jujitsu, in which boycotters take an action and reverse its meaning, is embedded in the history of the coinage of the term. James Redpath did not admire the actions of Southern ostracizers of carpetbaggers or the anti-Chinese groups in California. Yet he saw the power of this practice and sought to encourage Irish peasants to adapt it to their ends. Similarly, working-class boycotters hated the blacklist but nonetheless believed that they could use it from the other end, so to speak. Indeed, they argued that the power of the boycott was far greater than that of the blacklister, since working-class consumers outnumbered producers.[51]

Critics and proponents also disagreed about the nature of the boycott's power. If arguments about the provenance of the boycott stood in for debates about its legitimacy as a political tactic in the United States, discussions of the potential power of the boycott, and of its operations, set off similar questions. The key question was whether the boycott qualified as a "purely peaceful" substitute for violence, as Judge James Maguire of San Francisco had it, or whether it stood for violence itself, as the critics charged. For opponents, the boycott was, as Sanford D. Thatcher wrote in 1886 in one of the first articles on boycotting in a national periodical, "essentially inhuman as it is un-American." Like most critics of the boycott, Thatcher emphasized its power; it was a "fearfully effective" weapon "vastly more powerful than a strike." Denying liberty to the boycottee and implicating innocent people made it un-American, according to Thatcher and other critics. This was not just an abstract denial of rights but violence in a much more straightforward sense; the boycott aimed to harm and ultimately to kill. The critics thus defined the boycott as un-American in at least two senses: first, because it sprang from foreign shores (even in America it was promoted, they argued, by foreign-born peoples), and, second, because it contravened American ideals of liberty.[52]

Given the well-known role of consumer politics in the American Revolution, these critics faced a problem: how to redefine an act so widely celebrated as foundationally American as, in fact, unpatriotic. Not wanting to disclaim the signature tactic of the Founding Fathers, critics of the late nineteenth-century boycott told a story of discontinuity, in contrast to the continuity preached by boycott advocates. Agreeing that the boycott was not new, a writer for the *Christian Union* dismissed it as an "obsolete custom," one "better buried than used." Conceding that "patriotic men long ago believed in boycotting," the Civil War hero and Republican politician Benjamin Butler called it a "poor weapon," ill-suited to modern purposes. During the Pullman boycott of 1894, Walter Blackburn Harte made this claim through a mocking comparison of the noble deeds and goals of the "famous boycott and agitation of 1773–1776" with the ignoble and dangerous campaign in Chicago. These critics decried the degradation of a once-great tactic, one suited to a different time, and no longer necessary in the American republic.[53]

Opponents also sought to sever the link between history and the present, dismissing the boycott of the 1880s as foreign. Referring to an effective action in Galveston, Texas, a writer for the *New York Times* described the boycott as "the simple plan, imported, with the name, from Ireland." The next year, the same newspaper labeled boycotting "the Irish pastime," whose "alien origin" tainted it in the United States. The boycott was not only literally a "foreign institution" but was conceptually alien as well, since it "is set up here by persons who have not the faintest conception of what American citizenship is," or, as an Arizona newspaper proclaimed, it was "a piece of imported tyranny particularly repulsive to American notions." A jurist who took on the boycott, Judge Barrett, called it "essentially an un-American and anti-American offense." Labeling the boycott "an exotic on American soil," the *Chicago Tribune* editorialized that "boycotting originated in Ireland and as an incident of the struggle between foreign landlords and the peasants; it is an offshoot of misgovernment and oppression and took root only when the country was in a condition scarcely a degree removed from revolution." Although exotic flaura and fauna sometimes took root in foreign soil, they generally were potentially dangerous and always unnatural. As the *New York Times*, also using gardening metaphors, editorialized, "Boycotting is a mode of compulsion which is foreign to American soil, and it does not succeed well here." Others complained that it succeeded all too well, to the detriment of American institutions.

"There is a smell of Russian prisons about you, a stifling taint of German oppression, a stench of English repression, and a foul odor of Hungarian pauperism," complained a writer for the *Christian Advocate*, who concluded that "it isn't American and it isn't pleasant."[54] Editorial cartoonists often depicted upstanding American artisans being intimidated into boycotting by foreign-looking dandies (fig. 4.9).

By 1890, boycott opponents had generally ceased acknowledging the boycott's distinctly American roots. Condemning a proposed white Southern boycott of the force bill in 1890, the *New York Times* denounced its origins. "In spirit and purpose it is not in any sense American, but Irish, and had better be left to the light-headed and shorted-sighted people that invented it." (As we have seen, some Southern supporters of this boycott conversely latched on to the boycott's American-ness briefly during this period.) A day earlier, the *Times* denounced the action because "it has too much the spirit characteristic of the people with whom 'boycotting' originated." No longer an American idea perverted by foreigners, it was now described as a wholly foreign export; as the *New York Evangelist* had it, it was "another contribution of Ireland to America, like many other new customs which have been imported." A Protestant minister, the Reverend John Snyder, called the boycott un-American and suggested in 1894 that therefore it "has no place in a land of ballots." At a time when many native-born Americans felt threatened by the immigration wave, the boycott represented yet another unwanted import.[55]

Critics also blamed German immigrants as carriers of the boycott virus. Mrs. Gray, the baker who became for boycott opponents a symbol of the injustice of the practice, claimed that the boycott of her establishment was carried out by "the Irish and low German," and she claimed not to be overly concerned about the economic consequences of their actions, since these impoverished groups generally "used to buy our old bread." The *New York Times*, ignoring the prior migration from the United States to Ireland, suggested that the boycott had not become American in its migration from Ireland. It remained an "entirely un-American idea." Faced with the evidence of systematic boycotts "composed of and directed by Germans," which engulfed the city in 1886, the paper decided that "the wild Irish device of the boycott suffers at their hands a change into something strange and Teutonic. It would not occur to any Irishman to organize sad and solemn processions of animated sandwiches to march up and down, in front of an infected bakery for days and weeks and scatter handbills warning the public away from it. After the Irishman had smashed the windows and shied a brickbat at the boss, his mercurial temperament would need other diversion." It was not only the provenance of the boycott that was un-American.

THE ROOT OF THE MATTER.

BOYCOTTER. "You must stop work, because I have a grievance against your employer, no matter whether you have any, or whether your family suffers meanwhile. I must show my power."

Figure 4.9. An aggressive and unwholesome boycotter threatens an American artisan. ("The Root of the Matter," *Harper's Weekly*, May 8, 1886, 293.)

Its very essence was uncivilized, coercive, and "barbarous." The boycott was "essentially foreign and not American," according to *Harper's Weekly*, because it represented the "destruction of individual freedom and the establishment of mob tyranny." For George Cary Eggleston, the boycott subverted "the American idea." Frustrated that "many thousands of Americans, native and naturalized, had been seduced into acceptance" of "the perverse ideas of foreign theorists," Eggleston held that the boycott was "a tyranny wholly foreign to the spirit of American institutions and utterly subversive of human liberty." The *New York Evangelist* agreed, calling the boycott the "new tyranny." Referring to the founding document of the nation, the *Chicago Tribune* denounced the "un-American practice of boycotting" because it denied the "sacred" right of citizens to "life, liberty and the pursuit of happiness." For the *Tribune*, which ignored the inconvenient fact that the Founders were boycotters, these American values included the "privilege of buying and selling or disposing of his goods or his labor on such terms and in such manner as he sees fit," a privilege denied by boycotters. Similarly, the *Times*, pairing boycotting with the other scourge of the 1880s, labor violence, claimed that "boycotting and dynamite are intimately associated in their origin." The comparison is instructive; both, in the view of their enemies, operated outside the rule of law and used force, either physical or market based, as a means to constrain individuals.[56]

The legal and moral critiques of both boycotts and boycotting continued unabated throughout the late nineteenth century and into the Progressive Era and did much to transform the commonsense meaning of the term. "Three years ago when THE BOYCOTTER was given its title, the public understood by the term boycott 'to leave alone,'" began an 1887 article in the journal that had previously had that title. "Today it has a different meaning," and in consequence of this change in meaning, the journal announced that it was adopting a new name, the *Union Printer*. While the printers still supported the boycott of Whitelaw Reid and the *Tribune*, they now believed that name had "become an impediment." Weakened by a fierce employee counterattack and by overuse ("The appeal for a boycott has been made so often in various parts of the country as to lessen its force"), the practice had taken on "a meaning which it did not bear when it was adopted by the craft."[57]

Challenges to the morality and legality of the boycott continued, culminating in the fierce lobbying of the American Anti-Boycott Association, founded in 1902. Yet the tactic of the boycott did not die. Consumer activism did begin a major transformation in the late nineteenth century, however, one built around new conceptions of consumer representation. Ultimately, this became known as the "consumer movement," born at the dawn of the Progressive Era. But even as this new element of consumer activism emerged, the older aspects we have traced did not disappear. And the consumer movement and the boycott have existed, not always comfortably, side by side ever since as sometimes reenforcing, sometimes dueling components of consumer activism.[58]

PART II

THE BIRTH OF THE CONSUMER MOVEMENT

REMAKING CONSUMER ACTIVISM IN THE PROGRESSIVE ERA

In the early 1970s, David Thelen encouraged his fellow historians to make consumption central to their accounts of the period from roughly 1890 to 1920. Complaining that "the producer orientation has beguiled historians of the Progressive Era," Thelen argued that historians had yet to account for the fact that most Americans of the period thought of themselves primarily as consumers. In the years since Thelen's invitation scholars have examined many aspects of consumer society around 1900. Yet as a central theme, and particularly as a political issue, consumption still does not shape our conceptualization of the period.[1] Arguing that discourses and practices of consumer activism both shaped and reflected Progressivism, this chapter examines three crucial developments and transformations: the centrality of consumption to the political thought of the era; the perpetuation and remaking of the boycott, particularly as it was practiced by African American opponents of Jim Crow; and the origins of the new phenomenon of the "consumer movement," as it was developed by the National Consumers League (NCL). External forces, internal transformations, and new conceptions of consumer politics combined to remake consumer activism in this period.

I. The Progressives and Consumption

Politicians and thinkers described consumers as the classic Progressive constituency and consumption as the fundamental Progressive act. The defining texts of the era—by intellectuals such as Herbert Croly, Walter Weyl, and Walter Lippmann, the founders of the *New Republic* magazine, the economist Simon Patten, and the consumer activist Florence Kelley—identified the predicaments faced by consumers as symbolic of the problems of modern society. Indeed, Progressives claimed, with some justification, that they had coined the modern meaning of the word "consumption," transforming its popular connotation from tuberculosis, the dread wasting disease, to the fundamental economic activity of modern society. Maud Nathan, a leader of the New York branch of the NCL, told the story of how, in the first years of the organization, audiences would turn up at her lectures on consumption expecting to hear the testimony of a tuberculosis victim. "In the early years we were constantly called upon to explain what a 'Consumers' League' meant," she recalled in her 1926 autobiography, "whereas to-day it would be difficult to find any one of ordinary intelligence who has not some knowledge, however vague or slight, of the movement."[2]

Progressives identified consumers as the key to the most vexing question of their age: how could a robust practice of citizenship be reconciled with the massive economic changes that had transformed a rural, agricultural country into an urban, industrial, and global power? The answer, they believed, lay in the assertion of consumer power, guided by knowledgeable experts. Consumption and consumers illustrated a tension that Progressives saw as characteristic of their age. Although they professed democratic principles, many Progressives also believed that the resources citizens needed to navigate the increasingly complex world would not come from their ordinary fellow citizens but from experts. Consumers nicely embodied this tension, since, the Progressives believed, their actions had far-reaching effects but few fully understood how to exercise this power.

As consumer activism was being remade from the top down, however, so too was it recast from the bottom up. African Americans took the lead here, adapting older forms of consumer activism, employing but also remaking older techniques. As we will see, African Americans modernized boycotts in a number of ways, characteristic of the Progressive spirit, applying it to two realms of increasing importance, the state and culture.

Progressives so closely identified the practices of consumption and citizenship that they often described the two in overlapping terms. In the modern world "you cannot be a citizen without being a consumer as well," said the Reverend Henry Potter, a Social Gospeler and bishop of the Episcopal Diocese of New York, who considered the two words to be "copulative not antithetical."[3] Progressives believed the reverse was true as well: if citizens were consumers, consumers were also citizens. Of all the diverse groups in a pluralistic American society, consumers had the unique power to revitalize citizenship, making it relevant to modern conditions. To the Progressives, consumer power was a double-edged sword, because if consumers acted selfishly or ineffectually, their actions would inevitably diminish the meaning of citizenship and impoverish society.

Many of these ideas had been aired in the nineteenth century. But consumer citizenship took on new meaning in the first decades of the twentieth century. Progressive thinkers and politicians analogized the citizen to the consumer not in order to condemn consumers as wasteful detractors from the common good (as they were often described in the nineteenth century) or as passive spectators (as they came to be described in the post–World War II years) but to call attention to the ways in which consumption provided important, if insufficiently understood, resources to strengthen citizenship. Progressive Era consumer groups explicitly related responsible consumption to responsible citizenship: rather than personal liberation through shopping or even through low prices, they highlighted the social obligations and rights of consumers. Consumer activists made similar claims before and after the Progressive Era. But in this period, unlike most others in American history (with the brief exception of the Revolutionary boycott of England and the Southern nonintercourse movement in the antebellum period), a substantial group of political and intellectual elites shared the view that consumption was an important political act even as this group was highly suspicious of the abilities of ordinary people to master the forms of ethical consumption they championed.

No group claimed the citizen-consumer label more forcefully than the NCL, which in many ways should be considered the first Progressive organization. (The first Consumers' League, in New York City, was established in 1891, and the NCL was founded in 1899.)[45] Its range of concerns throughout the period made it a gauge—sometimes even a bellwether—of Progressive ideology, and its motto, "Investigate, agitate, legislate," could well serve as the epigraph of the Progressive movement, which similarly stressed social scientific inquiry, aggressive lobbying, and intervention by the state. The NCL had two missions: urging female consumers to be efficient and ethical shoppers and encouraging the state to protect female workers. NCL leaders, many of them among the first generation of college-educated women, undertook to gain special expertise, which gave weight to their advice to ordinary consumers and the legislators and judges they sought to influence. Thus, Florence Kelley, the executive director of the organization, studied the classics of sociology, translated Friedrich Engels into English, and became a factory inspector, responsible for studying conditions of production for women and child laborers. Other NCL leaders pioneered "sociological jurisprudence," the use of legal arguments supported by research in medicine, public health, and social science. In 1908, they succeeded in getting the Oregon Supreme Court to uphold the state's maximum hour law for women workers in the celebrated case of *Muller vs. Oregon*. NCL members believed in the importance of expertise. They did not view it, however, as an elite or arcane male preserve but as accessible to those women willing to commit the time and effort.[5]

In its diagnosis of the problems faced by consumers, its appeal for responsible consumption, its emphasis on the special role played by women in moralizing economic transactions, its call for reform within the capitalist system, its ambivalence toward the "public," and its belief that ordinary consumers best served themselves and society by following the advice of experts, the NCL anticipated, shaped, and reflected the Progressive project, one of whose main missions was making citizenship relevant to modernity by transforming it along consumerist lines. The NCL was also quintessentially Progressive in its transatlantic scope: the first Consumers' League began in England; branches also arose in Germany, Switzerland, Holland, Belgium, and France. NCL leaders, including Kelley, self-consciously participated in the international dialogue about "social politics" that the historian Daniel T. Rodgers has identified as central to the era.[6]

Although the NCL's leaders emphasized their new approach to consumer issues, they also argued that the group represented a continuation of nineteenth-century consumer activism. As we saw in chapter 2, Florence Kelley was the niece of Sarah Pugh, an ardent free produce advocate. Kelley was not alone in seeing the mission of the organization as consistent with abolitionism. The group aimed to eliminate all forms of unfree and undignified labor and placed a special emphasis on attacking "wage slavery." Occasionally, the group took on real slavery as well. Declaring that the "familiar old cruelties of the slave traffic" were being "repeated in the twentieth century," for example, the NCL urged its members to eschew chocolate produced from "slave-made cocoa."[7]

The NCL had an explicit interest in the problems and responsibilities of the consumer. But its leaders were not alone in regarding the issue of consumption as particularly relevant for their era, a time when the pundit Walter Lippmann identified "consumer consciousness" as the "real power emerging today in democratic politics." This is not to suggest that Progressives as a group were monomaniacs, concerned exclusively with consumption. Such a complex and diverse movement cannot be reduced to a single issue. Yet their discourse of consumption highlights the "tissue of connections" (to borrow Rodgers's phrase) among such Progressive keywords as "complexity," "citizenship," "causality," "gender," "efficiency," "interdependence," "responsibility," and "expertise."[8] The Progressive spirit no doubt contributed to the rise of the consumer movement; and, the consumer movement shaped Progressivism as well.

The consumer movement. This was a new idea, one that, like Progressivism itself, arose in the late nineteenth century and came of age in the first decades of the twentieth century, although it took on the name only in the late 1920s. The central idea of the consumer movement was the recognition that consumers were a distinct group with their own interests, rights, and responsibilities, one which required a lobby to protect its interests. Unlike other interests requiring lobbies, however, consumers were not a narrow minority but representative of all Americans. It became an article of faith among leaders of the consumer movement that consumers needed protection, which could be achieved via a combination of technical expertise, lobbying assistance, and an activist state. Consumer activists, as we have seen, had invoked the centrality of consumption and consumer power ever since the late eighteenth century. Highlighting the force of consumption was not the same, however, as acknowledging a separate consumer interest. In the nineteenth century, consumer activists had called upon citizens in their capacity as consumers to act collectively on behalf of a great many causes and people, but "consumers" were not among them. To be sure, they saw consumers as the central moral agents in an interconnected world of markets; but they did not posit consumers as the key group to be served by this vision of moralized consumption.

An important facet of the new vision of a consumer movement emerged in the late nineteenth century, when pundits and intellectuals began to refer to consumers as a bloc in society with unique and distinct interests. Debates about the tariff in this period were among the first in which the phrase "the consumer interest" was invoked. Other commentators believed that the rise of trade unions in the 1880s had made labor relatively more powerful than consumers. "The poor Consumer, who in previous ages was so well protected against the men who work with their hands is now abandoned to their merciless exactions," wrote Isaac Rice. "He must recoup himself elsewhere." Condemning the labor boycott as a "boomerang," Washington Gladden, the Social Gospel Congregational minister, predicted in 1886 that, if "recklessly" deployed, "there may easily arise a consumers' union, to fight them with their own fire—to patronize those whom they proscribe." Here Gladden, in one of the first uses of the term, analogized a "consumers union" to a labor union, as a group that would work to serve its own interests, which were understood to be in conflict with those of other classes in society, particularly boycotting workers. While some proponents of consumers' organizations depicted labor unions as the chief force to be counteracted, others argued that corporations represented an equally powerful force. (Of course, many muckrakers, notably Upton Sinclair, depicted big business as the far more dangerous enemy of the consumer interest than organized labor.) In 1899, M. F. Ames similarly used the phrase "consumers union" as a necessary countervailing force in a country with a growing number of "manufacturers unions and producers combinations." Others believed that cooperative groups should take the name "consumers unions," as one advocate of consumer cooperation urged in 1888. William E. Chandler believed that "it is only a matter of time when the people of the United States will form themselves into a 'consumers' union.'" In an age of organization, Chandler believed, consumers were latecomers to the lobbying that had become a necessity. The "wage workers have their labor unions. . . . The big manufacturers are organized into trusts or have trade associations. . . . But the consumers, which, of course, means the great body of the American people, have no association," observed Chandler. Actually, such groups had already formed; in the early 1870s, a short-lived Consumers' Protective Association appeared in Boston as a means of distributing milk from area farms directly to customers. The stress on consumption marked a reversal and repudiation of the traditional view that the United States was a country of "producers" and that farmers and workers represented the spiritual heart of the nation. In the opinion of these commentators, producers had devolved into a narrow but increasingly powerful interest group. Consumers, as the new representative group of the nation, needed to organize in kind, in order to protect their interests. Consumers were an unusual lobby, however, because like the "producers" of the nineteenth-century, all Americans qualified for membership in this group.[9]

A second understanding of the collective rationalization of consumer power that emerged in the Progressive Era came in the call for aggregate buying clubs. An article on "consumer's unions" in the *Youth's Companion* defined them as "purchasing associations" formed as a "means of combating the increasing cost of food." Describing the formation of a "consumers union" in Chicago, Peter Powers reported that the "object of the organization is to form a monopoly of purchasers." For these people, consumers' unions were best understood as purchasing organizations.[10]

While agreeing that consumers as a class had taken on new importance, other advocates of the organization of consumers understood the mission quite differently, as an auxiliary of the labor movement rather than an enemy. Proponents of "consumers' leagues" emphasized the consumer's moral responsibility to the workers who made the goods he or she bought. This was not an abstract ethical duty but one produced by the fact that consumers were directly responsible for the workers who made the goods. "What we hire others to do we are responsible for the doing of," declared John Graham Brooks, the first president of the NCL. This was not a new theory of consumer responsibility; as we have seen, free produce advocates made very similar claims, as did labor intellectuals and organized working people, who, in the postbellum era, also insisted that consumers were, in effect, employers, responsible for wages and working conditions. From the 1870s onward, they encouraged workers and supporters of the labor movement to purchase goods affixed with a "union label" that certified that they were made by unionized workers earning living wages.[11]

While the emphasis on consumer power and responsibility was not new, advocates of consumer leagues emphasized the difficulty of enacting ethical concerns in a national, increasingly corporate economy in which production and consumption were increasingly separated. The remedy for this separation was "organization among consumers," declared J. Elliot Ross, a supporter of the consumers' league idea. For, in this distended economy, looks could deceive. As William Clarke noted, in an 1891 plea for consumers' leagues, "It is difficult for a buyer to discover under what conditions the articles he purchases were made." As Clarke observed, "a pretty table or chair" that a shopper observed in a gleaming showroom or department store window display might have been made by poorly paid workers. Even where one could see the "folks behind the counter," as, for instance, in a department store, it was sometimes hard to assess their working conditions and wages. The goal of consumers' leagues was to help shoppers solve these ethical quandaries by arming them with information about conditions of production—"educating" them, in the preferred argot of the NCL leadership—so that they could avoid what Eliza Putnam Heaton called "starvation-made articles."[12]

Advocates of the consumer movement (or consumer unions or leagues) thus varied widely in their conception of what such a movement should stand for. Furthermore, the emergence of the consumer movement did not mean the eclipse of consumer activism. As we will see, the NCL in effect saw the one as a form of the other. And other groups continued to practice boycotts on behalf of a wide range of causes.

The context for this chapter is thus the rise of the consumer and Progressive movements. Although not perfectly coextensive, both shared a similar diagnosis of the problems they faced and a worldview that highlighted mastering complexity (with the essential assistance of experts) as the key to solving these problems. Progressive thinkers, most notably those in the NCL, regarded consumers as both central to the reinvigoration of citizenship and as symbolic of the obstacles facing modern citizens. In order to avoid the pitfalls and take advantage of the opportunities of early twentieth-century America, the NCL saw its role as teaching an ignorant, overmatched, and largely indifferent public new rules of ethical consumption. The NCL, as a public-spirited interest group, wanted not only to mobilize the aggregate consuming might of the people but also to use its expertise to govern the deployment of this power, since, in its view, ordinary consumers rarely had "sufficiently developed social consciences." Critical of and yet dependent upon consumers, the NCL was ambivalent about the "public," an ambivalence that its leaders shared with many of their fellow Progressives. At the same time, however, consumer activists continued the traditions that had begun in the Revolutionary era and also developed new causes and new targets. Ever since this period, consumer activism has reflected this dual character of top-down and bottom-up forms—an expert-led movement on the one hand and grassroots boycotters, on the other hand—with both sides diverse, and sometimes divisive, in themselves.[13]

The fact that there was a tremendous amount of discourse about consumption and citizenship during the Progressive Era does not mean that there was general agreement about what the relationship between the two should be. During this period, there was consensus about neither the meaning of citizenship nor the proper role, if any, for a consumer movement or, for that matter, consumer activism, which, while beyond the radar of many Progressive leaders, contributed critically to the political culture of the period. Conflicting visions of citizen consumers and consuming citizens characterized the era. Progressives had differing views of the consumer as a political actor, and these visions differed from those put forward by labor and grassroots groups. Such groups promoted a kind of consumer activism that was sometimes at odds with the expert-driven agenda of the NCL. For its part, the NCL, largely an organization of women (descended from women's trade union and union-label organizations of the 1880s), understood expertise (in the form of ethical consumption) as a female labor and responsibility and as a guiding hand of grassroots movements. These divisions in the consumer movement appeared from its inception, reflected tensions within the Progressive project, and presaged schisms in the twentieth-century consumer movement and, more broadly, in twentieth-century political culture, in which social movements continued to be riven by a tension between grassroots initiatives and expert knowledge. The splintering of the Progressive and consumer movements in the 1920s and 1930s was not merely the result of post–World War I developments; it was also a product of the diverse beliefs and constituencies that made up these movements even at their zenith.

II. "A Righteous Boycott"

Even as the consumer movement was being conceived, older forms of consumer activism flourished in the Progressive Era. Indeed, grassroots boycotts were as frequent in the decades after the turn of the century as they had been in the Gilded Age. Progressive Era boycotters, like their precursors, employed the weapon on behalf of a wide range of causes. As in the late nineteenth century, activists generally understood the local boycott as "a peaceful but very effective" part of a broader social movement. Even as the labor boycott faced legal difficulties, thousands of boycotts dotted the landscape of late Gilded Age and Progressive Era United States. Americans on the margins of political power, notably African Americans and women, employed the boycott frequently in these years in ways that both reflected and shaped the Progressive Era. Throughout this period, working-class women's groups organized boycotts to protest the high cost of meat and other staples. In 1902, immigrant Jewish women organized a boycott protesting the high cost of kosher meat. In 1910, Cleveland's Central Labor Union organized a consumer boycott of meat and one hundred thousand city residents signed a pledge not to eat meat for a month. Pittsburgh, Kansas City, Baltimore, and other cities also had such "cost-of-living" boycotts, protesting the high cost of food. These grassroots movements were local affairs, and depended not on permanent organizations but on individuals, usually working-class women, mobilized on an ad hoc basis to address a specific problem. At the same time, like the labor boycotters of the 1880s they depended on a print network in which seemingly local acts often added up to national campaigns for Civil Rights, for suffrage, and against the high cost of living.[14]

This magnification of specific actions was especially central to one of the most significant consumer campaigns of this period: the boycotts of segregated streetcars and other public facilities organized by African Americans in more than twenty-five Southern cities in the states of Alabama, Arkansas, Florida, Georgia, Louisiana, Mississippi, North Carolina, South Carolina, Tennessee, Texas, Virginia, and the District of Columbia.[15] These anti–Jim Crow boycotts added a new element to the arsenal of consumer activists by challenging public or quasi-public institutions. In the nineteenth century, boycotters directed their ire at private firms or individuals. But as racial segregation was mandated by state legislatures and city councils and as streetcars typically operated as public utilities, African American boycotts during the Jim Crow era took on the state more directly than had their immediate predecessors. (The Revolutionaries, of course, had challenged the sovereignty of the British government, in part by attacking its business adjutants.) As John Mitchell, the editor of the *Richmond Planet* and a leader of the campaign there noted, what made these boycotts distinct was that they involved "public conveyances which are operated by virtue of a public franchise." Rather than confronting proprietary businesses—Theiss's Saloon or Mrs. Gray's Bakery—the streetcar boycotters opposed municipally run and state- or city-chartered companies, such as the Asheville Electric Corporation, Atlanta Traction Railroad, Citizens Light and Transit Company (Pine Bluff), Columbia Electric Street Railway Company, Jacksonville Street Railway Company, Virginia Passenger and Power Company (Richmond), Savannah Electric Company, Vicksburg Railway and Light Company, Houston Electric Railway, Mobile Light and Railroad Company, and the Traction Company (San Antonio). Many other boycotters—from the nonimportation movement in the late eighteenth century through the labor movement in the late nineteenth century—eschewed merchants whom they claimed served the interests of a government they found immoral. Progressive Era African Americans, however, challenged the state (or its representatives) itself. Calling these boycotts "a very useful political weapon," one commentator modified an old trope of consumer activism by claiming that they touched "influential pockets, pockets that may even hold legislatures." This particular "pocket nerve" was firmly rooted in the public sphere. "WALK rather than swell the state's treasury," as one Richmond streetcar boycotter urged his fellows, associating streetcar patronage with public coffers rather than private enterprise. Even though most streetcar companies opposed segregation laws because of the added expense and enforcement burdens, boycotters effectively portrayed these "public utilities" as agents of the state.[16]

The pioneering scholars of early streetcar boycotts, August Meier and Elliott Rudwick, labeled them "conservative" because the boycotters aimed to return race relations to the status quo, avoided direct confrontation, and used "moderate" and "conservative" rhetoric. One can, however, interpret the politics of African American Progressive Era boycotts as considerably more radical. Even on their own terms, each of these characterizations is problematic: if the boycotters sought a return to a status quo at all, it was the brief interracial moment of Radical Reconstruction; confrontation was hardly absent from their actions; and the claim of conservative rhetoric is tautological. At a time of great repression—evidenced by lynchings and other forms of extralegal violence and disfranchisement—and general disrespect by whites, the streetcar boycotts required considerable courage and represented a significant challenge to white economic, social, and political prerogatives. An examination of their supporters (the Southern, urban, African American middle and working classes of both genders) and their claims (that the boycott could be extended to the apparatus of the state) hardly shows the boycotts to be conservative. Whereas they adopted boycotting techniques of earlier generations (the creation of solidarity through print communities, the emphasis on alternative moral commerce, and the use of "pocket nerve" rhetoric), their challenge to the hardening Jim Crow system can plausibly be viewed as radical. These episodes fit the pattern of African American politics during the Jim Crow years in which, as Glenda Gilmore has observed, "the political underwent a transformation," as women and African Americans of both sexes took on the new role "of a client who drew on services" from the government. The Jim Crow boycotts epitomized this consumer-based politicalization.[17]

Proponents of segregation described it as fully Progressive in spirit and practice, a rational, organized, top-down response to the problem of racial tensions in public spaces. Many white Southerners viewed these new legal codes as "a badge of sophisticated, modern, managed race relations." The Jim Crow boycotters, however, refused to cede the Progressive label to the segregationists. One black journalist dismissed Jim Crow as evidence of a "non-progressive movement" among white Southern business leaders and politicians, and opponents of Jim Crow dismissed the segregators as inefficient and unscientific. Another journalist described Richmond's boycotters as "the progressive, independent colored people of this city." Whereas putative Progressives depicted segregation as based on the latest scientific theories of race, the boycotters believed that old-fashioned prejudice better explained the impetus behind separate-compartment laws. For example, one segregation advocate called it "one of the safeguards against the breaking down of the barrier between the races and the amalgamation and mixing, which is the worst horror Southern white people can imagine and would be the worst disaster that could befall both races in the country." African American boycotters resented the racial subordination at the root of this vision and rejected what a group from San Antonio condemned as an arbitrary creation of a "color line as ordained by the City Council." Streetcar segregation epitomized the everyday face of state-sponsored Jim Crowism.[18]

Whites generally dismissed these claims of state-sponsored racial subordination by the streetcar companies, which were an "innocent party in the whole matter." "Why should the railway company be punished for obeying the law?" asked an editorial in a Savannah newspaper. Indeed, the white press expressed puzzlement over these boycotts and assured readers that "sensible negroes" would oppose it. Those who did boycott "have been badly advised," according to a Mobile newspaper, since the "law applies equally to whites and blacks." (The *Chattanooga Times* was not alone in singling out "Negro editors" for offering this bad advice.) Although sometimes imagining that "blacks are now taking to the new provision kindly" and no longer fear "imaginary discrimination," the white Southern press also challenged the motives and questioned the stamina of boycotters. Pensacola's boycotters will "discover that walking is not as amusing as it is said to be, and that troddling a bicycle through the sandy streets is no joke," according to one white prognosticator. Others offered similar views that African Americans would be unable to stop their reliance on "their greatest delight," what one derogater called the "poor man's carriage." The Savannah paper quoted the streetcar manager who predicted a quick end to that city's boycott. The white press occasionally printed rumors of boycotts but only to claim that such efforts were "groundless." Occasionally, they affected more concern as when they noticed that the "'want ad' columns" were "teeming" because "domestics have apparently received warnings, and injunctions not to ride on the cars." In general, the mainstream press underplayed or omitted mention of ongoing boycotts.[19]

Observing in 1933 that "the Negro has very much to fight for and very little to fight with," Kelly Miller, an eminent African American sociologist and the dean of arts and sciences at Howard University, sought to explain what he called his people's "turn to the boycott" in recent years. Noting the lack of robust institutions for the protection of black citizens, he concluded that the "boycott then is about the only effective weapon available to the Negro contendent," one, he noted, which had met "with significant success in several of our large cities." Having been frequent targets of white boycotters in the nineteenth century—a practice which continued in the twentieth century—Southern African Americans adopted the boycott in large numbers in the twentieth century. As suggested in chapter 3 and as we will see in chapter 8, the Montgomery bus boycott of 1955–1956 marked as much the culmination of a long tradition of Jim Crow streetcar protests as it did the start of the modern Civil Rights movement.[20] (See fig. 5.1.)

Celebrating the tradition of consumer activism, black boycotters made regular reference to the Revolutionaries in the eighteenth century and the labor boycotters of the nineteenth century. They did more than invoke this history, however; they also employed the rhetorical styles of previous generations of consumer activists, including the use of inspirational poetry. Like the labor boycotters, they encouraged supporters to ensure that opponents were left "severely alone." Like their antebellum precursors, they emphasized the responsiveness of "the white man's nerve center, which is his pocket." As their earlier counterparts had, the streetcar boycotters stressed the solidarity of print and market. "It is certainly a pleasure to read in the Afro-American papers that colored people are walking rather than suffer the degradation of being 'Jim Crowed' in street cars," observed an editorialist in a Baltimore newspaper. "It is also pleasant reading that the street car companies, suffering from their losses, are begging the colored people to come back and ride. When the white man's pocket is touched he is touched in his most vulnerable point." At the root of this view was the belief that economic interests trumped personal prejudice, or, in the words of John

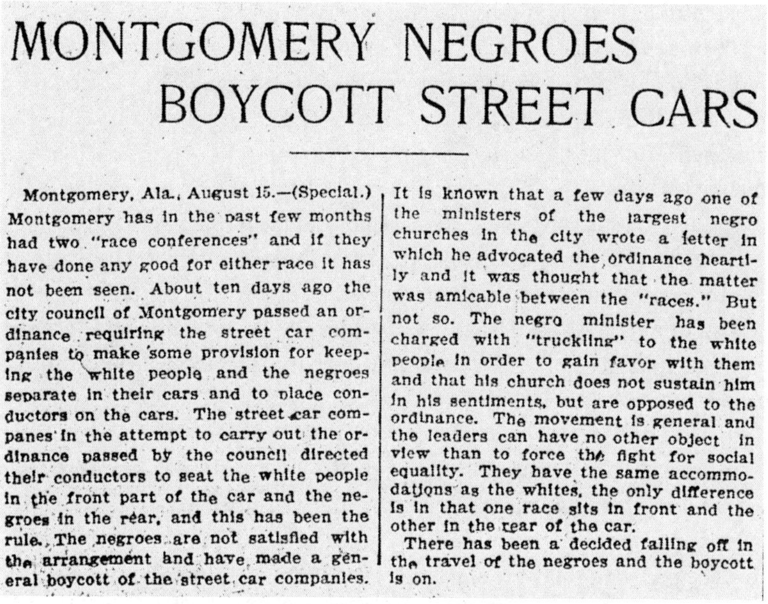

MONTGOMERY NEGROES
BOYCOTT STREET CARS

Montgomery, Ala., August 15.—(Special.) Montgomery has in the past few months had two "race conferences" and if they have done any good for either race it has not been seen. About ten days ago the city council of Montgomery passed an ordinance requiring the street car companies to make some provision for keeping the white people and the negroes separate in their cars and to place conductors on the cars. The street car companes in the attempt to carry out the ordinance passed by the council directed their conductors to seat the white people in the front part of the car and the negroes in the rear, and this has been the rule. The negroes are not satisfied with the arrangement and have made a general boycott of the street car companies.

It is known that a few days ago one of the ministers of the largest negro churches in the city wrote a letter in which he advocated the ordinance heartily and it was thought that the matter was amicable between the "races." But not so. The negro minister has been charged with "truckling" to the white people in order to gain favor with them and that his church does not sustain him in his sentiments, but are opposed to the ordinance. The movement is general and the leaders can have no other object in view than to force the fight for social equality. They have the same accommodations as the whites, the only difference is in that one race sits in front and the other in the rear of the car.
There has been a decided falling off in the travel of the negroes and the boycott is on.

Figure 5.1. The first Montgomery bus boycott. (*Atlanta Constitution*, Aug 16, 1900, 1.)

Mitchell, the editor of the influential *Richmond Planet*, "When the blow is landed on the white man's pocket it will do more to wind him than if delivered on his stomach." "We have always contended that few white men's race prejudice is so deep seated that they will stand to lose good money to satisfy it," proclaimed the *Colored American* of Washington DC. "The Caucasian's vulnerable spot is his pocket. Strike it and you've got him." Like previous boycotters, the streetcar protesters used market-based language for political purposes. Black boycotters, wrote a Mississippian, "have set an example which the colored men of the other States might profitably imitate." The Richmond businesswoman and boycott organizer Maggie Lena Walker spoke of the need to bankrupt the "jim crow business." As Walker doubtless intended to highlight, this was a spiritual and tactical profit but a financial one as well, since streetcar boycotts provided African Americans with an opportunity to engage in alternative commerce, to add "dollars to the pile of Negro institutions," as a Savannah writer put it. The surprising "persistency of the boycott" was thus simultaneously a blow against Jim Crow and a business opportunity.[21]

In the boycott tradition, the streetcar protesters also emphasized the force of their collective consuming efforts, a power that would be compounded with the citywide support of black commuters. "If the colored people would stand together and act as a unit in a matter of this kind," wrote Mitchell, discussing a streetcar boycott in Jacksonville, "they could bankrupt every street-car company in the Southland that attempted the innovation." This was so for simple economic reasons: "The success of all street-car lines depends upon the number of passengers carried. There is no other source of revenue. . . . All five cents count. When there is a lack of them, it is felt by the management and it ultimately results in a 'kick' on the part of the stock-holders, who insist upon at least having the interest on their money." Like the labor boycotters, the streetcar boycotters publicized the economic bad news that they caused. When the Richmond streetcar system, operated by the Virginia Passenger and Power Company, declared bankruptcy in 1904, the *Planet* emphasized that "the colored people were instrumental in hastening its downfall." A series of articles under headlines such as "The Street Car Co. Here 'Busted,'" identified "the refusal of the colored people to patronize the line" as the cause. The African American press highlighted the similar "financial disaster" abetted by low ridership in Montgomery and New Orleans. Even streetcar officials, such as J. W. Wilson, the president of the Mobile Light and Railroad Company, complained that the "separation ordinance has resulted in depriving his company of the patronage of the colored people."[22]

Although the streetcar boycotts were seemingly discrete, the boycotters viewed them as a coordinated attack upon the newly enshrined system of legal segregation in which state legislatures all over the South mandated that streetcar companies enforce racial separation. The African American press highlighted the importance of the print community in promoting solidarity. "Another result of the boycott is not only the loss thus sustained by the street car company, but the effect it is having upon the other cities of the state," observed a reporter in New Orleans. As the labor press had during the era of labor boycotts, black newspapers listed current boycotts, reprinted articles about faraway boycotts, and encouraged financial support for boycotters, near and distant. In a letter to the *Planet*, J. L. Birchett, the Pastor of Zion Baptist Church in New York City, described reading about distant boycotts as itself a form of solidarity. "I read with great joy the noble and manly stand which you and the noble people of Richmond have taken," Birchett wrote. "I feel the same injustice of that law perpetrated upon my race in the South as if I were directly under the hammer." The *Planet* received other letters from New York, as well as Chicago and rural Texas, in support of the boycott.[23] Within cities, circulars extended the community of boycotters, as in Lynchburg, where, as a reporter noted, "the circular by the colored committee, the exhortations of several colored preachers and the speeches delivered by some of the members of the race . . . have had considerable effect." Black boycotters sometimes extended the circle of solidarity beyond their own struggles, as when they expressed support for the Chinese boycott of the Japanese.[24]

The streetcar boycotters demanded unanimous support in the African American community. The *Planet* called for "the entire colored population or at least ninety percent of it" to "make the sacrifice and walk for a year." Black newspapers offered evidence that this advice was heeded by highlighting the empty streetcars. A Vicksburg newspaper proudly noted that black passengers "could almost be counted on the ten fingers of a man's hands." A visitor to Montgomery described the boycott of the streetcar system as "universal." "It seems that the 20,000 to 30,000 Negroes of the city, high and low, are in perfect accord," a participant in Houston wrote. "For once the Negro is together." And newspapers repeatedly remarked on the noticeable "absence of negroes from the cars" and that the lines were "deserted." "The colored people treat the street-cars," wrote Mitchell, "just as though [they] carried the germs of contagious diseases." Boycott leaders also urged supporters to participate in what later became known as "secondary boycotts" of white businessmen known to be supporters of the segregation laws. For example, black boycotters in Kansas City called for the eschewing of an ice cream shop whose proprietor was accused of supporting Jim Crow, and where "Negroes are heavy consumers of the product."[25]

The boycotters held special contempt for their fellow African Americans who rode the streetcars and punished them with community sanctions. Like their Revolutionary forebears, they upheld a strict moral economy and targeted boycott violators with both "wordy disturbances" and deeds. Boycott supporters across the South regularly threatened, jeered, and generally made "things unpleasant" for their "reviled" fellows who rode the cars. In one notable case in Savannah, two black women were arrested for "cursing and abusing Rev. E. Bland, colored, because he rode on an E. and W. Belt street car." Boycotters denounced preachers who violated the boycott in Richmond as "yellow leg chickens." They also resorted to force at times, in acts ranging from rock throwing to the physical abuse of black riders. In Jacksonville, as in other cities, "women took the lead in the matter and threatened to boycott the men of the race if they dared to ride."[26]

Some African Americans went farther still and performed acts of civil disobedience on the streetcars, acts that we generally associate with the Civil Rights movement of the 1950s and 1960s. In cities ranging from Nashville, to Savannah, to Richmond, to Pensacola, newspapers reported arrests and vigilante attacks on blacks who knowingly violated segregation statutes. Often, these protesters were, like Rosa Parks, women. The articles frequently emphasized the anger of the lawbreakers, as in the case of Annie Lee, who, while being arrested for refusing to give up her seat in the "white" section of the car, "cursed and abused" the conductor, who called a police officer to arrest her. A headline from the main Richmond newspaper quoted in the *Richmond Planet* said it all: "Made Furious by Jim Crow: New York Negress Objected to Color Line in Richmond Street Cars—Tried to Kill the Conductor—Declined to Sit in Rear, Cried To H___ With Jim Crow, and Cursed Him Long and Loud." As the article noted, the "Negress" was unapologetic; "the insulted colored female from New York made the air break into blue bubbles from the multitude of her oaths." The same paper described Laura Smith, another arrested boycotter as "black, hard-headed and inclined to have her way." Addie Ayres, a nanny for the child of a white actress, was fined for refusing to move to the back of the car, to the consternation of her boss, Mary Marble, who was the leading lady in the popular play *The Knickerbocker Story*. In other cases, prominent community members were fined or arrested, setting off renewed protests of Jim Crow. Some violators of the Jim Crow ordinances were not arrested but harassed and beaten. A white commuter, for example shoved Mrs. Mariah Howard for sitting in the white section of a Nashville car. (An interesting aspect of the implementation of Jim Crow in the early twentieth century is that not only did a large number of white people object to these laws, but several whites, including Custis Lee, the daughter of the venerated Confederate General, Robert E. Lee, were arrested or fined for violating them. To be sure, most whites were arrested not in solidarity with African Americans but because of anger and confusion about how the new Jim Crow system operated.)[27]

The most common response among black boycotters, again in keeping with the spirit of consumer activism, was to champion alternative modes of transportation. Frequently, this amounted to a call for walking. "Now, as to the 'jim crow' cars, our advice to all Negroes is—W-A-L-K," declared a Richmond editorialist, noting that it was "healthful and invigorating exercise." Commentators noted that "fish-salt and witch-hazel are in great demand and the soaking of colored folk's feet at night continues as a means of alleviating the distress of a long tramp in the morning." Boycott supporters also promoted commercial alternatives. Streetcar substitutes took many forms. Most commonly, individual entrepreneurs using horses, bicycles, carts, furniture wagons, and drays sought to serve the growing market. The black press praised these individuals as saviors, singling out heroes such as the "colored hackman" who charged less than the streetcars of New Orleans, or the "enterprising citizen" of Norfolk who put his two-horse wagon to public use. In several cities, groups of businessmen bought or leased automobiles and other forms of transportation and even organized companies (sometimes these were stock companies with several hundred investors). "Let the Negro men organize transportation companies, press buggies, carriages and herdicks into service," advised the *Nashville Clarion*, noting the moral and economic benefits of such Jim Crow substitutes. Boycott proponents greeted the substantial loss to the streetcar companies—estimated in Richmond at five thousand dollars per month—as gain for creative businesspeople in the black community. A writer for the *Baltimore Afro-American Ledger* claimed that the channeling of "a great deal of money" and facilities would uplift the race.[28]

Noting that the Lord "helps those who help themselves," boycott leaders in many cities attempted to move beyond "private conveyances" (in the form of walking, riding bicycles, or catching a ride with an enterprising neighbor) as they crafted a business-like response—a collective, well-organized buycott of transportation services. Indeed, the attempts to develop such alternative enterprises generated more "mass meeting[s] of colored citizens to arrange protest" and collective organization than the boycotts themselves. Boycotters described these alternative lines as a form of resistance, more effective than rock throwing or even Civil disobedience. "While to all appearances the Negroes of RICHMOND have quietly acquiesced in the operation of the new street-car laws," wrote a reporter for the *News Leader*, "yet there is a movement on foot by some of those who are dissatisfied." The first part of this statement was inaccurate insofar as noisy protest and rock throwing not infrequently accompanied the boycotts. But the reporter singled out the heart of the "movement," one characterized by "mass meetings," as the efforts to "to bring the operation of an auto-bus line in the city." What made it a "righteous boycott," according to the *Colored American* of Washington DC, was the opportunity simultaneously to reward friends and punish enemies.[29]

In founding alternative businesses, black Southerners generally chose corporate-sounding names that reflected the nature of ownership and also the hoped-for permanence of these new firms. Rather than the family names that graced most free produce stores, they chose impersonal labels, such as the United Transportation Company of Savannah. In Jacksonville five hundred people attended a mass meeting organized by Reverend G. B. Wilson, and several thousand dollars were raised to organize the "Colored Citizens Suffrage Transportation League." They set up a stock company with two thousand shares to fund the business. In Nashville, the Union Transportation Company, headed by R. H. Boyd, a prominent black resident, bought six automobiles (see fig. 5.2). Norfolk's boycotters organized a Metropolitan Transportation Company. In Richmond at a "mass meeting of citizens for the purposes of making a dignified and conservative protest against the action of the Virginia Passenger and Power Company in making racial discrimination upon its lines in Richmond, Manchester, and

A HINT TO THE WISE.

The Union Transportation Company of Nashville, Tenn. has solved the Jim Crow street car question.

Figure 5.2. A celebration of alternative transportation companies in Nashville. (*Indianapolis Freeman*, Oct 14, 1905, cover.)

Petersburg," leaders of four banks serving the African American population pledged "their personal and financial support to any movement having for its purpose the transit of the colored people who must ride from one section of the city to the other." A week later, the *Planet* advised commuters to use the "bus lines owned by Mr. A. D. Price, Mr. W. Isaac Johnson, Mr. A. Hayes and others." Cities without an alternative line, as in Houston, tried to organize makeshift fleets of "large passenger vans, carriages, etc.," into a usable and orderly system that would make them "independent of the street cars." Even the best capitalized of these enterprises had a tenuous economic existence, and few of them had staying power. Yet several were successful enough that W. E. B. Du Bois highlighted them in his 1907 study *Economic Cooperation among Negro Americans*. The sociologist singled out the efforts in Nashville, Wilmington, and particularly in Florida, where the North Jacksonville Street Railway, Town and Improvement Company handled 7,220 persons on its first day of operation and lasted several years. Even where they did not endure, these anti–Jim Crow businesses served a political purpose. Mass meetings often centered on raising money for and planning the organization of these alternatives, setting off energies and co-alitions that continued after the boycott momentum slowed.[30]

Despite the fact that these boycotts did not defeat Jim Crow, they none-theless offered one of the most impressive displays of consumer activism in American history and played a significant role in the history of the Civil Rights movement. They also ushered consumer activism into the twenti-eth century by expanding the purview of boycotting in a number of ways. In 1911, a group in Chicago, for example, boycotted a store in a black neigh-borhood whose owner refused to employ blacks or advertise in black news-papers. Using familiar rhetoric—"Our money should never be poured into the hand that would smite us"—they applied the boycott to a new cause and presaged the "Don't buy where you can't work" campaigns of the De-pression era. Equally important here was the recognition of the importance of advertising—an acknowledgment of consumer society that was some-times difficult for consumer activists to concede. African Americans also extended the boycott to fight lynching, which was at its height in the Pro-gressive Era. In the absence of any state action, they organized boycotts of merchants accused of being involved in extralegal violence against blacks. In 1921, the boycott movement moved outside the South to Chicago, where blacks launched a "secret boycott" against de facto Jim Crowism. (A fre-quent tension in African American boycotts was that secrecy and rumor, characteristic of subaltern protests dating back to slavery and extending to boycotts well into the twentieth century, was conjoined with the publicity that was at the root of boycotting.)[31]

African American boycotters also added novel cultural elements to the boycott that became increasingly important aspects of consumer activism. They noted that purveyors of Jim Crow, like supporters of the "Redemption" period before it, targeted visibly successful black people. "A Negro as a ser-vant is all right with them," argued John Mitchell, speaking of white elites, who selectively applied the dragnet of Jim Crow to those African Ameri-cans who "put on a Fedora or Derby hat" or wear "a late style suit of the tai-lor's finest make."[32] In this sense, black boycotters saw fashion and style as political, as markers of African American dignity and a rebuke to white su-premacy. As we will see in chapter 7, the aesthetic dimension became espe-cially important in a number of twentieth-century boycotts.

Moreover, black boycotters, understanding the importance of com-mercial leisure in the modern world, increasingly set their sights upon segregated sites of entertainment, such as movie theaters. In 1917 a group of African Americans in Birmingham boycotted a racist Judge Abernathy, who owned a "colored only" theater as a means of punishing "the baiters of our people who thrive financially upon the support of our folks." The *Chicago Defender* trumpeted, "No member of the race with a grain of self-respect would be seen going or coming out of this rotten insect's nickelodeon." To ensure this unanimity, the paper warned that those African Americans who disobeyed the boycott would be "ostracized." Boycotters also took aim at the perpetuation of racial stereotypes, as in the protest organized by the *Defender* against any newspapers that used demeaning and sexist phrases, including "mammy" "wench" or "negress." The most significant cultural boycott of the Progressive Era was the protest, sanctioned by the National Association for the Advancement of Colored People (NAACP), against the hugely popular D. W. Griffith epic film *The Birth of a Nation*. In addition, black cultural workers, especially musicians, often used the boycott as a tool against racist practices of leisure entrepreneurs.[33]

After World War I, black cultural politics morphed into protests against the perpetuation of stereotypes in all aspects of mass culture. In the 1920s, African Americans organized boycotts of other forms of racist cultural production, including one of a Jim Crow Costume Shop. A Black fraternity, Omega Psi Phi, also organized boycotts of potential vacation spots where blacks had been poorly treated. In the 1930s, blacks urged the boycott of stores in New York that sold watermelons under the name of the "Georgia Nigger Head" and against a beer company that used demeaning imagery in its advertisements. These cultural boycotts culminated late in the 1930s with boycotts in both the United States and England of another epic film of Southern revisionism, *Gone with the Wind*. Presaging anticolonial activities of the post–World War II era, a broad segment of the "colored population of the British capital"—"Africans, West Indians, Arabs, Indians, Chinese, Ceylanese, Burmese and other colonials in London"—boycotted this "anti-negro film," according to George Padmore, the Trinidadian pan-Africanist and the *Defender*'s London correspondent. The cultural boycott continued to be employed as a weapon well after World War II, as manifested by protests against the radio and television show, *Amos and Andy*. A boycott of Sambo's in the late 1970s and early 1980s forced the fast-food restaurant chain to change its name.[34]

III. Between Consumer Activism and the Consumer Movement

The NCL drew on previous traditions of consumer protest, and also from the contemporaneous bottom-up boycotts led by African American and women's groups. Like the Revolutionary boycotters, it understood consumption as an act of citizenship and as a component of national identity. The "National" in the title of the NCL also evoked corporate products, such as the National Biscuit Company, characteristic of the new nationwide mass market.[35] Like the free producers and their contemporary Jim Crow boycotters, NCL members saw consumption as a means of liberating the oppressed. From organized labor, they drew on the idea of labeling objects as a mark of their morality. With the Jim Crow boycotters and cost-of-living advocates, they recognized, and sometimes sought to unleash, the power of grassroots, women-led protest. The NCL did not invent but perpetuated a long tradition of treating consumption as political, viewing consumers of immoral goods as not merely countenancing immorality but actively promoting it, and understanding consumers as, in an important sense, owners and employers of labor and therefore employers of those who produced what they bought.

Despite these continuities, the NCL also accurately described itself as unique and new. Maud Nathan called the consumers' leagues a "revolutionary idea." NCL members set out to help others—poorly paid, working-class women, primarily—rather than themselves. In this sense, they resembled nineteenth-century boycotters. They also did so in their promotion of ethical holiday shopping practices; just as abolitionists promoted ethical consumption at antislavery fares, the NCL urged consumers to complete their Christmas shopping early so as to relieve the burden of department store workers. Unlike free produce campaigners, however, the NCL saw itself as an expert lobby as much as a moral crusade. A crucial element that separated the NCL from its predecessors (and from the leaders of streetcar and local labor boycotts), its leaders claimed, was that it operated in the far more complex economic climate of a new corporate America. "It was easy enough for the abolitionists to give up the use of sugar and cotton, because these were known to be slave-made," declared Josephine Shaw Lowell, an NCL founder (in a statement that free produce advocates would probably have challenged). Modern conditions, she believed, "are more complicated." Learning "where and how the goods they desire to purchase are made," Lowell maintained, was a task that required both moral commitment and technical expertise. In the modern world of consumption—a world of advertisers and department stores—appearances were deceiving; hence the need for the NCL, which specialized, as Kelley wrote, in looking "behind the price and appearance of products to the processes and conditions by which they are produced." Lacking the immediacy and transparency of, for example, labor boycotters protesting a merchant unwilling to recognize a union or a black community attempting to integrate streetcars, consumers in this new economic order needed experts who could chart proper consumer behavior.[36]

Also, unlike previous consumer groups, the NCL saw its job as permanent, since, in the modern world, the work of uncovering deceptive appearances was never ending. Previously, boycotts had arisen frequently but they had done so on an "as needed" basis and ended when the problem was resolved. The NCL was different; it was an umbrella organization designed to last beyond individual boycotts. (Indeed, the NCL still exists today, carrying on much the same mission that its founders developed.) The NCL's ethical crusade was a managed, scientific project; indeed, the science enabled it to be moral in a way relevant to the complex world. The problem to be solved by the NCL's turn to science was a general one: how to consume ethically in a world in which production and consumption were separated by markets of increasingly vast distances and in which pretty displays, deceptive advertising, and artful packaging further obscured the provenance of objects. The metaphor deployed by the NCL was of an ongoing war rather than of a single battle. Whereas the free produce movement set up stores and acted as small business owners, the NCL (although it maintained a few stores) took as its inspiration the managers and bureaucrats of the twentieth-century economy.[37]

With its membership peaking at around thirty thousand just before World War I, the NCL positioned itself, in a manner that became the hallmark of Progressive social movements, as a hybrid organization, part social movement and part expert lobby. Its leaders saw themselves as activists and lobbyists, a combination that, we will see in chapter 7, became increasingly fractious later in the century. Like other Progressive lobbies—and like the consumer movement of the later twentieth century—it stood for its constituency, consumers, without being wholly of them. Unlike the populists (or other mass movements) of the late nineteenth century—and unlike consumer activists of its own time—the NCL did not expect that social change would come about solely through the righteous indignation and concerted action of ordinary citizens. If it exploited what the historian Richard Hofstadter called the "vague consumer consciousness" that permeated the era, the NCL aimed to reshape rather than to reflect what it diagnosed as the misdirected and often wrongheaded manifestations of this popular consciousness. It expressed limited faith in the judgment of ordinary people, who were, according to the NCL's Maud Nathan, by and large, "indifferent and selfish," and whose lives had become too complicated for them to interpret important phenomena accurately and effectively. While it wanted consumers to heed its message and to act collectively, the NCL appealed as much to an abstract "public opinion" as to actual people. It did not champion the people as consumers but rather sought to instruct them to be better consumers. The goal of the NCL, according to Nathan, was not to uncover and promote the popular will but to shape it, to "help form a public opinion that will lead consumers to recognize their responsibilities." Positing that the old common sense was no longer effective, the NCL sought to create a new conventional wisdom for consumers: about responsibility, causality, sensibility, and rights. This effort, it believed, had to begin with a reconsideration of the place of the consumer in American society, a project in keeping with Progressive discourse.[38]

For a number of reasons, Progressives saw consumers as the representative citizens of the modern age. First, consumers highlighted the challenges presented by what the historian Arthur M. Schlesinger called "the increasing complexity of modern life," which Progressives described as characteristic of their era. As a group of "drifters" seeking "mastery," to borrow the language of Walter Lippmann's 1914 manifesto, consumers epitomized the plight that Progressives diagnosed among citizens. The motto "Caveat emptor," in Lippmann's view, applied equally to shoppers and voters. Neither could be expected to understand the complexities of modernity or to be fully engaged in public affairs. Both needed help in interpreting the economic and political phenomena around them, much of which occurred at a "subterranean" level or at great distances. As Upton Sinclair demonstrated in *The Jungle* (1906), there was a way in which the old joke about food making and lawmaking—"There are two things you don't want to see made: sausage and legislation"—was literalized in this era: the creation of both was invisible to the public and later presented to that public in pretty but misleading packages, which obfuscated the ugliness of their creation. The illusion of surfaces, whether promulgated by lying politicians or dissembling admen, equally fooled citizens and consumers. Complexity and distance rendered moot the older ideal of what Lippmann called the "omnicompetent" citizen. Nobody could be expected to comprehend the workings of the "Great Society" (the term that American Progressives borrowed from the British social theorist Graham Wallas) without the assistance of a "map of the world" provided by specialists. The desire to "clean up" politics and consumption required the assistance of experts who possessed the ability to look beneath the surface and beyond the local. Life, according to Lippmann, had become "too big, too complex, and too fleeting for direct acquaintance." What he labeled the "overmatched consumer" was a symptomatic aspect—perhaps the most glaring—of the more general problem of a grasping and befuddled citizenry searching to control complex processes that it did not fully understand. If, as Lippmann wrote, the "consumer is trying to redeem his helplessness in the complexity of the newly organized industrial world," so too, Progressives believed, were all Americans grasping to make citizenship relevant in a new century.[39]

The problems facing consumers mirrored the challenges of modern citizenship. But, Progressives believed, the cause of these problems—the increasing complexity of the modern world—also held the key for the expansion and improvement of citizenship. The same processes of economic change that made consumers ubiquitous—"overwhelmingly superior in numbers to the producers," in the words of Walter Weyl—made them potentially powerful catalysts for change. Consumers were, like workers in the Marxian schema, current victims but future saviors. Forced to rely on others—merchants, distributors, and experts, who in turn depended on them—consumers could not be autonomous. But, once mastered, Progressives believed, the logic of interdependence empowered consumers and served as an object lesson in how to redeem citizenship in a new era, one in which interdependence rather than autonomy was the watchword. As the economist Arthur Hadley declared, "Reform is likely to come through the agency of the consumer rather than from any other source." This was so, according to Maud Nathan, because the consumer had become "the lever . . . which controls . . . the great forces of the industrial world," or, as Potter declared, "in the hands of the discriminating consumer rests finally the settlement of the gravest issues of the whole industrial problem." Florence Kelley ascribed great power to consumers—he or she "ultimately decides everything"—even as she complained that they wielded that power "blindly, and in a manner injurious" to themselves and the broader society. Responsibility in the modern word, according to a religious magazine, "now rests with the all-powerful consumer."[40]

Progressives also linked the consumer and the citizen by describing the former as embodiment of the latter. If the small producer symbolized the nineteenth-century citizen, Progressives believed that the consumer would represent the citizen of the twentieth century, taking his or her place as the central figure of the republic. "In America today the unifying economic force . . . is the common interest of the citizen as a consumer," wrote Weyl, who believed that industrialization and specialization had led to both the fragmentation of the producing classes and the consolidation of the consuming classes: "The producer is highly differentiated. He is banker, lawyer, soldier, tailor, farmer, shoeblack, messenger boy." In contrast, Weyl noted, "the consumer . . . is undifferentiated." In answer to the question, "Who is a consumer?" Progressives answered, "Everyone." As an NCL pamphlet put it, "Every person who buys anything, from a bun to a yacht, is a consumer." This was a wholesale reversal of the nineteenth-century view that valorized producers as the embodiment of "the people" and denigrated consumers as wasteful speculators or otherwise unproductive idlers. While the previously universal category of the producer shattered into dozens of special interests, the consumer came to be seen as a new unifying force in the nation. Thus, even when Progressives used the language of interest groups to refer to the need for consumer organization, they averred that such an organization would fight for everyone. Since the interests of a consumers' lobby fundamentally differed from the self-interest of other lobbies, it was legitimate for them to organize and to assert power, for they did so not on behalf of a particular segment of the country but for the benefit of the nation itself. Thus, Americans approvingly quoted the French economist and advocate of consumer cooperatives Charles Gide, who declared that the consumer must "defend his interests energetically, for they are also the interests of society, therein lies their superiority."[41]

In this spirit, the NCL identified itself as a lobby based upon what Richard Hofstadter has called "high principles rather than group interests," which is how the consumer movement ever since has seen itself. Defining the NCL as a guardian of the public good, not, as its name might imply, a narrow interest group, its leaders disclaimed the view that they "should be concerned with the consumers' interest in themselves." As one advocate wrote, "the first object of the Consumers' League is not the quality of the article, but right conditions for the worker."[42] For this reason, as we will see, by the late 1920s rival consumer advocacy organizations emerged that criticized the NCL for being a "labor" auxiliary rather than a true consumer group, that is, a group that lobbied on behalf of a distinct "consumer interest."

The NCL posited that consumption, too often misconstrued as private, was in fact a profoundly public act whose powerful and far-reaching effects were little understood. Its primary mission was to convince shoppers "to do their buying in such ways as to further the welfare of those who make or distribute the things bought," wrote John Graham Brooks, the first president of the NCL. The NCL, which acknowledged that few consumers viewed shopping in these terms, harbored no illusions about the difficulty of inculcating such a vision. Florence Kelley called the job of the NCL "our never ending task," and Nathan declared that the "work of the Consumers' League will never be fully accomplished." When Walter Lippman wrote that "the art of consumption is uncultivated," he in effect described the raison d'être of the NCL. If the architects of the commercial world in advertising and marketing encouraged the fantasy of the consumer's individualistic id, the NCL wished to serve as the "shoppers' conscience," the consumers' collective superego. (A 1906 interview with Nathan revealed the extent to which the superego provided by the NCL governed her every quotidian action, from eating, drinking, and traveling to even reading the Bible, for she had recently learned that a young girl who complained about unsanitary conditions had been discharged from a Bible bindery.)[43]

Cultivating the "art" of ethical consumption (most NCL leaders preferred to see it as a science) required imbuing consumers with a new sense of civic duty. As the Consumers' League of New York put it in 1898, the goal was to "enlighten the community as to the means to remedy evils." The starting point was the belief that consumers, through a series of economic changes of which they were only dimly aware, had become the linchpin of the new economy, possessing tremendous power and responsibility. Consumer power followed on the fact that, as Reverend Potter said, "the whole industrial fabric crumbles into ruins" without consumption. "Moral responsibility" followed from the far-reaching impact of shoppers' purchases, particularly on the lives of those who produced the goods they bought. "Consumers can abolish sweatshops," declared an NCL pamphlet, revealing the vast potential it assigned to shoppers. Consumers, in other words, were capable of making the great (complex, distended) society a good (just, ethical) society.[44]

In attributing this power to consumers, Progressives, consciously or not, registered a shift in conceptions of gender roles. By analogizing citizens to consumers, Progressives were to some extent defining citizens as women. For they were asserting that shopping was not solely or even primarily an activity of the private sphere; they classified this "female dominion," like so many others during this period, as essential to the welfare of society. Indeed, they labeled what was widely seen as women's activity the key to the exercise of modern citizenship. They suggested that if the nineteenth-century citizen was an independent man, his twentieth-century counterpart was an interdependent housewife. Perhaps in reaction to this radical thought, male Progressives tended to use masculine pronouns to refer to consumers.[45] But even those who, like the NCL leadership, were comfortable calling consumers "she" asserted that female consumers were representative citizens not by virtue of their skillful exercise of consumer power but because of their haplessness. Overmatched consumers, like citizens generally, needed expert guidance to master the new political economy. But once mastered, there was limitless potential for the exercise of citizenship through consumption.

The NCL, drawing on the insights of previous consumer activists, posited that the consumer was inextricably implicated in a market-based web of responsibilities. And the league understood its job as bringing these responsibilities to light by emphasizing that the shopper, in Florence Kelley's words, "ultimately decides all production." "In the act of buying," wrote

Brooks, the consumer becomes "a creator. The shoddy buyer is a shoddy maker. In a very real sense, to buy a harmful thing is to help make that thing." Since every purchase set off an act of production, consumers were, in effect, employers of labor, "indirectly" but ultimately responsible for the well-being of producers. Consumers, according to the NCL, were not just involved in the productive process; they were the prime movers of that process. They did not merely affect workers; through their actions they "employed" them. They did not simply buy goods; they "created" them. This is why the second item on the platform of the inaugural meeting of the Consumers' League of New York in May of 1890 stated that "responsibility for some of the worst evils through which wage-earners suffer, rests with the consumers, who persist in buying in the cheapest markets, regardless of how cheapness is brought about." The "revolutionary idea" which motivated the NCL, according to Nathan, was not only that consumers held great power but also that they could not escape the logic of this power or avoid their public duty. As Potter put it, about other subjects one could say "'it has nothing to do directly with me' . . . But, my brother, you cannot do that when it comes, in our modern social mechanism, to the duties and responsibilities of the consumer. There you cannot put yourself outside of distinct and personal responsibility. No matter how modest your consumption, you are nevertheless a consumer."[46] All consumers had to exercise personal and social responsibility, since the act of purchasing made them simultaneously employers of labor and citizens of the republic. "Consumers are entitled to a clear conscience if they act as conscientious people," wrote Florence Kelley. "They can, if they will, enforce a claim to have all that they buy free from the taint of cruelty." Making consumers aware of this ever-present duty, according to the NCL, necessitated instilling a new "habit of mind." NCL's leaders, who defined their organization as first and foremost an "educational movement," considered it necessary to instruct consumers about the unfamiliar, and in some ways counterintuitive, causal chain set off by consumption. Processes that used to occur close to home now took place at a distance; transactions that were previously observable were no longer apprehensible to ordinary people, most of whom were "entirely oblivious," according to Nathan. As production moved from the home and the community and commercial transactions were mediated by abstract markets, the new economy created a system of interdependence in which the well-being of individuals depended not on face-to-face interactions but to an unprecedented degree on the actions of unseen others. Far from a private act, consumption was the fulcrum of this new economic system, for it connected the home to the market to the workplace, traversing great distances and, not infrequently, national borders. "Any form of expenditure," wrote Henry Potter, sets "in motion a whole series of influences" that binds consumers to a "vast network of producers which to-day spreads all round the world, from the tea-planters and cotton-spinners of India or China or Japan to our own, and on whom, directly or indirectly, our expenditures, indulgences, luxuries, or comforts, and the demands for them, act and react to the last and remotest extremities." In this economy, consumers became, in Florence Kelley's words, which echoed those of antebellum activists, critical "links in a chain," one which extended far beyond the cash register at the store where they shopped. The NCL's role was to alert consumers to their essential role in promoting just working conditions.[47]

The NCL's key insight was that while in an objective sense the new economy linked consumers to ever-more-distant producers, consumers were less likely than ever to be aware of these connections. Modern economic forces made consumers responsible for the plight of workers; indeed, they made them the key actors in the global market-based economic web. But these same processes blinded shoppers to this obligation. Both the rituals of urban shopping and the seductions of modern advertising identified shopping as a private act for personal pleasure and not as a performance of citizenship. This explains why the NCL believed it necessary to impart constant warnings about the social impact of consumption. Disconnected from the productive process and ill equipped to understand industrial commodities, shoppers were likely to experience consumer alienation, a blindness to and ignorance of the origins and meaning of the goods they bought. "In the vast complications of modern production and distribution," wrote Florence Kelley, "the individual purchaser at the moment of buying, cannot ascertain for himself whether the representation of the seller is accurate or not." In articulating the importance of Consumers' Leagues, the Progressive politician, secretary of war, and NCL president Newton Baker noted that, in the modern world, specialized knowledge—the ability to make sense of the complex causal chain set off by consumption—was the necessary precondition for ethical action: "Good behavior can rest only upon knowledge of the implications of conduct, and knowledge can only be acquired, under modern conditions, when high-minded and disinterested inquirers investigate and tell us what they find." The NCL sought to be the eyes and ears of consumers, whose own sensory organs were ineffectual, incapable of interpreting the meaning of goods in the commercial world. Evoking free produce rhetoric, NCL literature claimed that if objects could talk or "the personality of the workers could be impressed upon the product," consumers' own sense organs would enable them to shop ethically. But since inanimate objects could not speak or carry visual images of workers' "fatigue, their strain, their suffering," the NCL had to communicate this information to consumers, who had no way of ascertaining the truth about products on their own.[48]

The NCL encouraged shoppers to overcome the feelings of isolation that accompanied modern consumption through reliance on those trained in looking "behind the price and appearance of products to the processes and conditions by which they are produced." Shoppers, the NCL believed, too often evaluated goods on the basis of cost, looks, and, advertising messages. But these criteria alone did not provide information about what it saw as the fundamental issues: working conditions, workers' wages, and safety of products. Even if women desired to shop ethically, they had no innate ability to do so. Rather, the ability to deconstruct the meaning of industrial goods was a specialized form of expertise. As Florence Kelley asked, "What housewife can detect, alone and unaided, injurious chemicals in her supplies of milk, bread, meat, home remedies?" In doing so, Kelley echoed the Progressive Era's leading diagnostician of "drift," Lippmann, who wrote, "The simple act of buying has become a vast, impersonal thing which the ordinary man is quite incapable of performing without all sorts of organized aid." Such statements highlighted the need for expert lobbying on behalf of "overmatched" consumers. The NCL's debunking of the familiar and the obvious undermines David Thelen's claim that Progressive Era "consumer consciousness was profoundly local in orientation." Indeed, NCL leaders inveighed against the overly local orientation of most shoppers. Instead, it preached the virtues of long-distance interdependence, a form of solidarity—"an imagined community of consumers and producers" in the apt words of the historian Kathryn Kish Sklar—that was invisible to the untrained eye. In order to help the "unseen" workers who produced goods, Kelley urged consumers to rely on the advice of the NCL's "visiting committees and executive secretaries."[49]

The medium promoted by the Progressive Era NCL to transmit expertise to the masses was the "white label." (The league also worked diligently to pass protective labor legislation.) Such labels enabled consumers to rely on the judgment of trusted experts—Kelley and a team of trained investigators—on the morality in their purchasing decisions. Through these labels, according to Maud Nathan, "the public conscience was being quickened, stimulated, and made more sensitive." The idea behind the white label was, according to Sklar, to challenge "the power of anonymous market forces." To be precise, the NCL opposed anonymity more than "market forces." The NCL used the logic of the market to try to correct the injustices of a market economy. For its belief was that the market made consumer power possible. This is not to dismiss the claim of Nathan and others that the NCL had radical goals, but only to highlight that theirs was market-based activism, a species of radicalism too often dismissed by American historians as a contradiction in terms but which describes many movements for social change in the industrial era, especially consumer activism. Rather than posing an alternative to capitalism, the NCL pushed for an alternative style of capitalism. Indeed, one could argue that in its attempts to promote transparency in economic transactions, the NCL was seeking to promote a freer market for consumers. The economist Edwin Seligman, an NCL supporter, wrote that the efforts of the league would not "injure competition but raise it to a new level."[50]

IV. Consumers: Necessary but Ignorant Allies

Informing consumers of shopping's inevitable social impact was the primary mission of the NCL. But the NCL did not expect that notifying consumers of the power they exerted would automatically make ethical consumption the norm. Florence Kelley realized that her ultimate goal—a time "when there are no more indifferent purchasers"—was nowhere on the horizon. Although members sometimes claimed that "shoppers would refuse to allow conditions to exist if they only knew about them" and referred to the "dormant sense of responsibility" in shoppers, more often they decried what Kelley called "the willing ignorance of the masses" and assumed that, even if alerted to the important role they played in improving the lives of unseen working people, the vast majority of consumers would not change their ways. Maud Nathan said, with more bluntness, that shoppers often "leave their consciences at home." The NCL had no illusions about the consumers it claimed to represent; they were not only inexorably drawn to immoral "bargains" but also, in Kelley's words, "prefer not to know the truth." Even if they possessed the truth, they would make the morally wrong choice, selecting fashion or economy over ethics. As Kelley complained in her 1902 annual report, "Purchasers have cared for style and finish more than for the assurance of the league that less attractive garments were made under more righteous conditions." Moreover, "the inertia of public morality" made it difficult to "rouse a storm of indignation." The NCL thus saw its constituency, which Kelley called "the great purchasing public," as a group which both acted "blindly" and, even more disconcertingly, unethically. The typology of consumers provided in Maud Nathan's memoir reveals precious little faith in the group that she devoted her life to serving. She began with the sizable category of knowing immoralists. "Some purchasers are selfish and grasping, and care not at all whether a bargain represents the sweated toil of some hard-driven victim." Nathan described the other major category of consumers in equally unflattering terms: "Other purchasers are

merely thoughtless and have never had their attention called to these matters." A small percentage of shoppers, she acknowledged, were "conscientious and high-principled."[51] This was the exceptional group targeted for
League membership, an elite similar to the "talented tenth" among African Americans whom W. E. B. Du Bois targeted for membership in another
Progressive organization, the NAACP.

The NCL criticized even well-meaning shoppers who did not engage in
modern practices of ethical consumption because they operated according to outdated cognitive maps. The good intentions of philanthropists
were insufficient, according to the NCL. Do-gooders, who were ignorant
of the ultimate impact of their shopping, were likely to engage in what the
NCL considered to be "ill-judged" acts of "mistaken pity." The NCL singled
out two venerable activities—bargain hunting and charitable giving—
as particularly harmful because they gave the illusion of being virtuous.
While recognizing the benefits of stretching the family budget through the
search for inexpensive products, the NCL constantly warned of *The High
Cost of Cheap Goods*, as one of their pamphlets was titled. Because consumption was a market-based activity, shoppers pondering what Nathan called
"The Ethics of the Bargain Hunter" had to consider not only the benefits
of buying cheap but also the impact of the "brutal side of the bargain" on
those who made the goods. "Without bargain hunters and bargain counters there would be no sweatshops," declared the *American Woman's Home
Journal*. "Mere cheapness is not the end of life," said Potter; Brooks decried
a "cheapness which is bound up with dangerously low surroundings" for
workers. Betraying its middle-class bias, the NCL regularly condemned
what it dismissed as worship of the "almighty bargain counter" and the "almighty 99 cents." It criticized those who attempted to defend themselves
against such charges for stubbornly clinging to outmoded beliefs. As one
NCL member scolded, "Don't say, in a grandiloquent manner, that by buying ready-made clothes at a bargain counter you are aiding in the support
of many of your sex. You are not; you are simply making it possible for the
sweat shop to remain open." In the view of the NCL, the naive consumer,
not yet aware of the shopper's proper place in the causal chain, was not only
ignorant but also arrogant in thinking that her actions helped workers in
the sweatshops.[52]

The NCL also dismissed charity as ineffective. What the NCL called
"careless giving" was, it claimed, no better than "careless buying." Indeed
it was worse, since it provided the giver with a false sense of having made
the world a better place. The NCL sought to encourage moral citizens to replace charity with smart shopping for reasons of both ethics and efficiency.
Kelley made this point in 1892 when she claimed that "the evil would be

stopped" if consumers shopped ethically. The NCL pamphlet *Charity vs. the Consumers League* made the case that ethical shopping would make charity "unnecessary" by eliminating the problems that charity addressed. Ethical shopping addressed the root cause, charity only the consequences. "Charity cares for the delinquent girl," reads a typical passage of the pamphlet, but the NCL addresses the prior problem of delinquency by building a "stronger, better womanhood." While recognizing that shopping "does not yield the same satisfactory sensation" as charity, the NCL claimed that "it may be more virtuous to buy justly than to give liberally." The goal of the NCL was not to "dispense generosity but to secure justice."[53]

By noting that the altruistic citizen might not find ethical shopping as emotionally satisfying as charity, the NCL acknowledged that it was demanding thoroughgoing changes in deeply ingrained habits. NCL leaders often spoke as if they were an elect who had received such wisdom in an experience of epiphany. They highlighted the sudden shift from ignorance to knowledge as a change of consciousness that accompanied the realization of consumer responsibility. The proposition that "we create the thing that we buy is so absolutely true that all who heard it began wondering at once why they had not been conscious of this great truth," declared John Graham Brooks. A participant at the inaugural meeting of the New York Consumers' League described her realization of responsibility in similar terms: "These facts proved startling to the listeners. Many of them had never realized that such things existed. One of them said afterward: 'When I had shopped for a piece of lace, I had not realized that the saleswoman had been on her feet all day long, lifting heavy boxes; when I had run into a store at a quarter before six, to purchase some trivial accessory, I had not considered that I was keeping the saleswoman from arranging her counter for closing hour, and this detained her unnecessarily. It flashed though my mind that I had often been inconsiderate, unsympathetic, impatient.'" The epiphany was often personal and self-reflexive, as in the case of the minister who declared, "I had no conception at that time of the wider knowledge which came to me later, that a woman's duty and responsibility are not bounded by the four walls of her home." Having undergone this conversion experience, NCLers felt emboldened to scold those whom Kelley called the "unconscious" consumers as well as to enlighten them as to the error of their ways.[54]

V. The NCL and Progressivism

The NCL was, as Maud Nathan asserted, "in its very nature. . . . progressive." If it was characteristically Progressive to have great hopes for ordinary people but to be uncertain whether these same people were up to the task of realizing those hopes, the NCL indeed epitomized Progressive ideology. The NCL aimed to reconcile the view that consumers were both incompetent and all-powerful. While members of this group, along with most other fellow Progressives, deemed consumption to be a supremely important act and consumers to be the twentieth-century's most significant constituency, they did not have great faith in ordinary consumers, whom Nathan labeled "supine."[55] The NCL saw its task as giving consumers not a pat on the back but a kick in the pants.

Yet NCL leaders ultimately viewed the consuming public as a potential ally, not an enemy. They knew that the expertise they disseminated would come to nothing without public involvement; as frustrating as they sometimes found it, they saw the relationship they had with the public as symbiotic. Nathan recognized that the NCL could be effective only if consumers "throw their weight and power constantly on the side of justice and fairness." Moreover, in using the phrase "we, the shoppers," she included herself in this group. Florence Kelley, who regularly criticized the public, also described the consumer as part of an "us" rather than an "other" when she wrote, "Let us give the preference in our dealing to the merchant who employs large help; let us make it commercially valuable to a manufacturer when he follows the example of the enlightened merchant." Although it maintained a critical distance, the NCL identified itself with the great consuming public. NCL activists acted as if they were in a sibling relationship with ordinary consumers, teaching consumers things that they were fully capable of mastering.[56]

The challenge for the NCL, as for Progressives as a whole, was to ally expertise with people power. This was not the only tension that it hoped to resolve. The NCL can be understood as part of the *via media*, the middle road, that the historian James Kloppenberg identifies as the essence of Progressivism.[57] As an "in between" group, it mediated among the conflicting forces of the era: private and public, things and people, capital and labor, efficiency and justice, common sense and science, rule by experts and rule by popular will. In the process of this effort to mediate among such forces, the NCL, along with many other Progressives, believed it had come upon the key to the revitalization of citizenship. For as consumers moved from ignorance to power, thanks to the efforts of the NCL, they were simultaneously enacting their public duties as citizens of the modern world. Although the NCL's leaders looked warily at consumers, often wagged their fingers at them in disappointment, and sometimes acted condescendingly toward them, they were also unique in treating consumers as, above all, citizens of the republic. Never before or since have consumers been treated with such respect, however grudging.

When the consumer movement revived in the late 1920s and 1930s, it seemed as if the vision of the NCL had prevailed. As we will see, by the mid-1930s a growing number of consumer activists had begun to call for a revival of the other side of the consumer movement, represented not by scientists but by female grassroots protesters, and serving the interests not merely of low prices and good quality but also of the workers who made the goods they bought. At the same time, however, as in the Progressive Era, this revived consumer movement was accompanied by a recrudescence of consumer activism, of boycott campaigns, both global and local. In these decades a variety of groups battled for the legacy of Progressive Era consumer reform, and also showed that legacy to be one that included both the consumer movement and consumer activism.[58]

THE STRIKE IN THE TEMPLE OF CONSUMPTION

In September 1935 forty-one employees of a small firm in rural New Jersey walked off the job to establish a picket line. In a year of more than two thousand strikes involving well over 1 million workers, neither the size of the strike nor the proximate cause of the work stoppage—management's refusal to recognize a duly elected union—stood out. Yet it was "one of the strangest strikes in American history," as one participant declared many years later. Throughout its six-month duration, this small strike became one of the most talked-about work stoppages in a year of notable labor upheavals. Reinhold Niebuhr chaired a committee of luminaries that investigated the strike, which became one of the first to be adjudicated by the newly created National Labor Relations Board.[1]

The strike received so much attention because it occurred at Consumers' Research (CR), a product-testing and consumer education organization with more than fifty thousand subscribers. Not only was the CR strike a classic example of the "unrest in odd places" that characterized many labor actions of this period; it also pointed to a schism in the movement that many Americans had come to believe was their salvation. Before the strike, CR was, in the words of *Business Week*, "the fair-haired boy of liberalism," the vanguard of the rapidly expanding consumer movement, which, in turn, was seen as central to the movement culture of the Depression decade. Thus, what the trade journal *Sales Management* dubbed "the strike in the temple of consumption" set off shock waves because it challenged assumptions about the nature of the consumer movement, pointed to a vast schism within it, and raised doubts about the strength of the supposedly powerful alliance between liberals and radicals. "A Strike at Consumers' Research . . . is no ordinary strike. Here is an organization that has appealed to a liberal, if not a radical, public constituency," noted *Advance*, a liberal religious magazine, expressing the consensus shared by both advocates and opponents of the consumer movement. Just as the consumer movement was becoming recognized as a powerful force, the strike revealed its fractures; just when the Popular Front appeared to be coalescing, the CR strike showed it to be turning on itself.[2]

If the strike at CR called into question the solidarity of the consumer movement, it also showed that, confident pronouncements notwithstanding, there was a good deal of confusion about who exactly was a "consumer." For a society that had only recently claimed to have "discovered" the consumer—labeled by one commentator "the most popular, most sought after, the most flirted with debutante of 1934"—the realization that, as two well-known consumer activists put it, "the consumer remains a shy and elusive being" made impossible any simple definition of the "consumer interest." "Even where the existence of the consumer is admitted," Walton H. Hamilton, the director of the short-lived Consumers' Division of the National Recovery Administration, lamented, "it is charged that his interest cannot be reduced to a get-at-able question." After the CR strike, one could no longer describe the consumer movement or its constituency—American consumers—in monolithic terms.[3]

This chapter explores the significance of divisions within the consumer movement of the 1930s, schisms that "the strike in the temple of consumption" underscored. It examines how clashing conceptions of consumerism, many of which originated in the previous decade, led to the strike and how these schisms within the consumer movement, largely unacknowledged before the strike, erupted into plain view after it commenced. As the decade unfolded, two main forms of consumer organization, already foreshadowed in the first three decades of the century, emerged, the distinctions between them more clear: one stressed expertise, individualism, and the products which consumers bought; the other emphasized collective action, a social conception of consumption, and the labor which made such products. Although observers, and even proponents, initially took the movement to be a unified whole, it became clear by the mid-1930s that rival consumer organizations held fundamentally different conceptions of how, or indeed whether, consumers could or should serve the public interest, the kind of politics they should practice, and the causes for which they should stand. The divisions of the 1930s illuminate the transformation and splintering of Progressivism and foreshadow important aspects of post–World War II political culture, including interest-group liberalism, left-liberal activism, and free-market conservatism. Although strike supporters claimed that the actions of CR's management "constitute one of the most complete betrayals in the history of American liberalism," it is more accurate to say that the strike highlighted the fact that consumer activism in the 1930s, as in earlier years, had many different meanings and expressions, and that these differences could not be contained within a unified movement.[4]

I. Discovering the "Consumer Movement"

In the Depression decade, pundits and politicians claimed that for the first time Americans had discovered both the "forgotten consumer" and problems of consumption; some commentators even referred to a "New Deal" for consumers. This discovery was prompted by the actions of previously invisible consumers, who had suddenly become an "army" that was "on the march," to borrow the military metaphors favored by the press. As the journalist Stanley High put it, "Until about 1927, the American consumer— male and female—was isolated, anonymous, and generally peaceable. Today he is an army with banners. Already more than eighty organizations are instructing, warning, and mobilizing him." The consumer activist Henry Harap agreed that prior to 1927 "popular interest in the consumer was practically non-existent" and that it "was not until we had reached the depth of the depression that a full-fledged [consumer] movement was in the making." Joseph Gaer called the Depression decade the era of "the Awakening Consumer." Books, articles, and pamphlets about "organizing as consumers," "the political power of consumers," and the newly energized consumer movement abounded.[5]

This was neither the first nor the last time that Americans claimed to have discovered the consumer. In 1899, John Graham Brooks announced, "The whole question of 'consumption' is comparatively modern." Upon appointing a special assistant for consumer affairs in 1967, President Lyndon B. Johnson declared, "Consumer is a word that was hardly known in our American language three years ago." Both Brooks and Johnson had reason to claim that their era had discovered the consumer: Brooks was president of the newly formed National Consumers League; Johnson had seen the furor that surrounded the publication of Ralph Nader's *Unsafe at Any Speed* in 1965 and the "consumer movement" that followed from it. Dorothy Houston Jacobson's 1941 claim that "interest in consumer movements is new in the United States. It has grown up within the past few years," thus fits into a long tradition of forgetfulness, while also highlighting the undeniable excitement the movement generated in the New Deal era.[6]

Although consumer activists and commentators overstated the degree to which it was new, they were correct to view the consumer movement of the 1930s as "unprecedented" in its diversity and prominence. Ruth Brindze, who in the mid-1930s penned a column on "information of value to consumers" for the *Nation*, observed that "consumers have rebelled before," but added that "there has never been a consumer movement quite like the one now on the march." The 1930s was perhaps the only decade in American history when commentators could speak of "consumer society" as a potentially radical force; in the mid-1930s, J. B. Matthews, using a term that we take today to be synonymous with the interests of hegemonic, global, corporate capitalism, defined a "Consumers' Society," as an "alternative to the regency of business." If, as Warren Susman observed, "commitment" was the keyword of the Depression decade, many thousands of Americans expressed their engagement in the realm of consumption through membership in a consumer organization or cooperative, or through participation in boycotts, educational campaigns, "Don't buy where you can't work" movements, and cost-of-living strikes. While it was not the first era in American history to witness consumerist efforts to combat racism in employment and the high cost of living, in the 1930s these actions were more widespread than ever before. In addition to the maturation of product-testing organizations like CR, the Depression decade witnessed efforts to revise and improve pure food and drug and fair labor standards legislation, the first, halting attempts by the federal government to represent the consumer interest (in the Consumers' Division of the National Recovery Administration and the Consumers' Counsel Division of the Agricultural Adjustment Administration), the first widespread consumer education organizations (notably the Institute for Consumer Education at Stephens College in Columbia, Missouri) and the concomitant popularity of consumer economics courses and curricula, the first cooperative product distribution business (Cooperative Distributors), and a plethora of national as well as local organizations (including the Consumers' National Federation, founded in 1937 as an umbrella group representing more than thirty organizations), many of which hosted conferences, distributed pamphlets, and published magazines such as *Consumers' Digest*, *Consumers Union Reports*, *Consumer*, *Woman Shopper*, *Consumer Shopping News*, *Organized Consumer*, *Consumers Defender*, *Consumer Education*, and *Consumers' Guide*. "If the consumer could be saved by printed matter," wrote Dayton D. McKean in 1938, "he would be now well on his way to redemption." The consumer movement did not limit itself to the print media. The General Federation of Women's Clubs sponsored *Consumers Time*, a weekly radio show on NBC; the radio station WEVD hosted a regular *Consumer Movement Show*, with a more activist orientation. A film version of Stuart Chase and F. J. Schlink's best seller called *Getting Your Money's Worth* appeared, as did other moving picture documentaries along the lines of the "guinea pig" books, muckraking works that condemned businesses for producing unsafe products and false advertising. Morever, the Democratic platform of 1936 explicitly mentioned as a goal the need to "secure for the consumer fair value."[7]

All of this activity provided evidence of what the influential columnist Dorothy Thompson called a "growing consumer consciousness," a consciousness which manifested itself in new modes of thought and new political practices. Even enemies of the consumer movement, including the businesses it targeted, exhibited a "growing consciousness" of its power. They vigorously opposed the consumer movement and, perhaps even more revealing of the degree of their concern, attempted to co-opt it by founding their own "consumer" organizations (including the National Consumers Tax Commission and the National Consumer Retailer Council), publishing "consumer" magazines (*American Consumer* and *National Consumer News*), and adding features such as "The Consumer Wants to Know" to the trade magazine *Retailing.*[8]

The focus on consumption in the 1930s may seem surprising given the material deprivations of the Depression decade. But it was during this period that a wide variety of public intellectuals and politicians—including Hugo Black, Stuart Chase, John Dewey, Horace Kallen, Robert Lynd, Persia Campbell, Caroline Ware, and some of President Franklin Roosevelt's close associates—made a powerful set of arguments about the unprecedented significance of consumption. Singling out underconsumption as a root cause of the Great Depression, they called for the construction of a consumerist political economy and pronounced America to be entering a new era defined economically by consumption and driven politically by the might of organized consumers. Walton H. Hamilton described the development of this new order as a "quiet revolution" with many repercussions for the consumer and society. As Chase wrote, "Up to 1930 or thereabout we lived in the age of the producer. His interests were paramount. We are now entering an age when the consumers' interests are going to be paramount." In an organizational society, these intellectuals argued, it was necessary for consumers to overcome their isolation. While other constituencies have "chambers of commerce . . . labor unions, teachers federations, medical societies to represent them," Horace Kallen wrote, "as consumer, a man is simply the average unorganized citizen." At the very least, consumer advocates (and, according to polls, so did a good number of ordinary Americans as well) demanded a cabinet-level Department of the Consumer.[9]

More grandly, they believed that through the organization of their aggregate purchasing might, consumers could exert power in a corporate economy that increasingly separated ownership and control. Summing up the wisdom of the moment, John Cassels, the director of the Institute for Consumer Education, called for "a science of consumption" that would promote the "good living of the individual and the general welfare of the community." In this context, Hildegarde Kneeland, an economist, claimed, "We must have mass consumption to use the products of mass production" not just for economic reasons but because the welfare of consumers "is essential to the preservation of American democracy." The growing importance of the consumer movement comforted many observers who believed that in an ideological age characterized by class conflict and, elsewhere in the industrial world, by political violence, the universal category of consumer held out hope of stability, inclusion, and consensus. Stressing the inclusive rather than divisive nature of the consumer movement, Dorothy Thompson asserted, "We have workers, we have employers, but as consumers we really are one people." As Graeme O'Geran, wrote, "It is easy to see that the consuming class is far broader than the producing class in society. From the cradle to the grave each and every one of us is a consumer, whether we ever produce or not." J. B. Matthews and Ruth Shallcross took this argument to an extreme, declaring that the development of a consumerist society would lead to a "classless community." While none of these claims was entirely new, they were more widely circulated and acted upon in the Depression decade.[10]

Consumer activists of the 1930s traced their beginnings to the 1927 publication of *Your Money's Worth* by Chase and Schlink, the immensely popular book that Robert Lynd called "the Uncle Tom's Cabin" of the consumer movement. (Lynd's own book *Middletown*, which followed two years later and which described the residents of Muncie, Indiana, as avid but naive, "socially illiterate" consumers, also contributed significantly to the movement.) *Your Money's Worth* set off a wave of similarly themed best-selling "guinea pig" works written by a closely knit group of reformers, including *100,000,000 Guinea Pigs* by Schlink and Arthur Kallet; *Eat, Drink and Be Wary* by Schlink; *Skin Deep* by Schlink's wife and colleague, M. C. Phillips; *Guinea Pigs No More* by J. B. Matthews, also a colleague of Schlink's; and *Partners in Plunder* by Matthews and his wife, Ruth Shallcross. The main message of *Your Money's Worth* and its successor volumes was simple but powerful: ordinary consumers—ignorant of the workings of the large corporations that produced the nation's consumer goods—were being systematically bilked. Since understanding the nature of these goods was a full-time job requiring vast expertise, the solution proposed by Chase, an accountant who had served on the staff of the Federal Trade Commission, and Schlink, an engineer who had worked for the National Bureau of Standards, was for consumers to get accurate information from objective experts like themselves, men and women of science. Only by subscribing to CR, noted M. C. Phillips, could consumers be "kept posted on the continually changing nature" of products. As Schlink explained: "Being a competent consumer is not an easy profession, nor is it one in which training is ever completed. The ideal training for a 'professional consumer' would include physics, chemistry, biochemistry, nutrition, several branches of engineering, a general knowledge of the scientific basis of medicine plus an interest in the most important current fashion and style trends, and a wide knowledge of scientific literature, an omnivorous reading of business and trade journals and a knowledge of market outlets—where to buy what. Obviously, the average person, whose main job is to earn a living first, cannot—even if he were so inclined—devote his whole time or even a big fraction of it to learning how to buy." Professional consumers groups, Schlink averred, were the only hope for this overmatched "average person."[11]

Frustrated that no such organization existed, enthusiastic readers, apparently not put off by the harsh diagnosis of their condition put forward in the book, urged Chase and Schlink to organize a Your Money's Worth club. In 1928, Chase and Schlink formed Consumers' Research (CR), which began as a subscription service to interested consumers and the world's first consumer-product-testing service. CR became what *Business Week* called the first "professional consumer organization," meaning that, even though it had a large and growing membership, its agenda was set and carried out by scientifically trained experts. It saw its main function as performing laboratory tests on advertised products and determining how the facts about the product squared with the hype of the admen. It carried out this mission with zeal, and this approach was popular with its growing list of subscribers, who by 1935 numbered fifty-eight thousand.[12]

Liberals and radicals initially viewed CR as a fount of integrity, a tremendous asset to consumers, and, best of all, an amusing thorn in the side of big business. The group seemed to be the epitome of rectitude and honorable reform. The *New Republic* called CR's annual *Handbook of Buying* "the Buyers' Baedeker." An editorialist went further, calling CR a "Consumer's Heaven." The *New Yorker* paid its respects in a "Talk of the Town" piece that gently mocked CR's crusading zeal: "In this age of unalloyed hokum, it's really very comforting to be a member of an organization that treats commodities realistically instead of romantically. . . . We do feel, however, that our club goes a little far on the subject of breakfast food. The handbook advises, as an economical substitute, washed wheat bought at a seed store, and adds, somewhat cryptically, that it's a good idea to find out whether or not formaldehyde has been used in processing it. . . . Even if we knew where there was a good seed store, we shudder to think of the taxi fare going and coming, [and] the possible doctor's bills for formaldehyde poisoning. . . . Somehow a box of patent puffed wheat seems kind of handy." In "Advice to Consumers," a satiric send-up of the CR newsletter also published in the *New Yorker*, Richard Lockbridge dryly noted that an analysis of fifty-seven varieties of "dill pickles" revealed that only one of them actually contained dill, and that a scientific study of Santa Claus determined that "there isn't any." Along these lines, the magazine published a cartoon depicting Thanksgiving dinner at the Schlink's house as a sterile affair, in which the food was rated, in the style of CR's *Bulletin*, "Non Recommended," "Intermediate," or "Recommended."[13] (See fig. 6.1.)

Because the experts at CR minced no words in their critique of shoddy and dishonest business practices, they gained a reputation as annoying busybodies among business groups, one of which condemned CR as "industry's nuisance number one." *Business Week* reported that CR, "Advertising's Enemy No. 1" was largely to blame for "the current wave of consumer distrust" of business. Books with titles such as *The Poison Pen of New Jersey*, *Guinea Pigs and Bugbears*, and *Dollars and Sense* lampooned CR as a "group of radical agitators" whose "seemingly altruistic and high-sounding name" masked its desire to subvert "our form of government and our industrial system." Few business leaders dissented from the view of a Chicago editorialist who labeled CR "the pet brain child of some of our leading radicals." As the *Tide of Advertising and Marketing* noted, "CR's purpose in life . . . is to further the establishment of a 'production for use' society, to overthrow capitalists, but to have the overthrowing done by an army of embattled consumers and housewives rather than by the traditional revolutionary agent—Marx's proletariat." As the last statement suggests, the business press condescendingly declared that groups like CR were transforming previously docile female consumers and their quaint women's groups into militant activists. Referring to the comparison between *Your Money's Worth* and *Uncle Tom's Cabin*, *Business Week* noted that the latter book may have aroused "grandma's crusading zeal back in 1852, but grandma's desire to Do Something About It pales into insignificance alongside mother's when Mr. Chase . . . and Mr. Schlink . . . first told her that the soap which made her so popular at the dance was made with a little creosol, a common and cheap disinfectant recommended by the Government for disinfecting cars, barns and chicken yards." Writing in *Nation's Business*, Fred DeArmond concurred with the view that groups like CR were radicalizing women: "Women's clubs have put aside Oriental travel and the poetry of Edna St. Vincent Millay as topics for discussion and are now clamoring for speakers on 'Consumer Education.' Editors of women's magazines find that their readers want fewer recipes for summer salads and more in-

Mr. and Mrs. Schlink of Consumers' Research Sit Down to Thanksgiving Dinner

Figure 6.1. Product testing meets Thanksgiving in the Schlink household. (*New Yorker*, Nov 30, 1935, 16. Copyright The New Yorker Collection 1935 Rea Irvin from cartoonbank .com. All Rights Reserved.)

formation on consumer goods specification or social consciousness." Like many other commentators, DeArmond ignored the long history of female consumer activism, preferring instead to charge CR with fomenting this gender-based rebellion by frightening naive housewives.[14]

Acting on the principle that the enemy of my enemy is my friend, radicals and liberals trumpeted the triumphs of CR as their own. One called on "every Socialist to push this movement." They assumed that, as the *New Republic* put it, "the very function of CR in exposing fraudulent advertising and shoddy merchandise . . . would seem to demand an alliance with workers (the great mass of consumers)." Liberals and radicals took at face value the charges of CR's enemies that its leadership was dominated by "sociopolitical crusaders." Just as the fault line within liberalism and between liberals and radicals was about to surface, the *Nation* asserted that CR was "founded and operated by and for persons of liberal and radical sympathies."[15]

The brickbats of conservatives and plaudits of leftists notwithstanding, the radical label never accurately described CR. Observers mistook CR's belligerence for political militance, its condemnation of advertising for economic radicalism, and its call for a consumers' movement for unequivocal support of the Popular Front. CR's leaders were not guilty of false advertising; they never claimed to hold the political and economic beliefs that both the left and right assigned to them. The authors of *Your Money's Worth* were careful to concede that the changes they wished were "in no sense revolutionary. They imply no change in the system of law or property." As the economist and CR Board member Charles Wyand accurately observed, "Although exceedingly militant, these people seek to reform and not to reorganize the status quo."[16]

CR's leaders are best thought of as exemplars of what I call "technocratic individualist" consumerism.[17] While they claimed to champion the "consumer interest," technocratic individualists understood such an interest in rigidly circumscribed terms, as dues-paying members relying on experts like themselves to critique business practices and to highlight cost-effective, quality goods. They wanted to instill what they called "gyp consciousness" rather than any kind of consumer class consciousness. They did not see consumers as constituting the leading edge of a revolutionary social movement; rather, they declared that "consumption is a personal matter." They carefully distanced themselves from the radical social movements of the age. As early as 1930, Schlink condemned "the excesses of organized labor," and he consistently criticized the labor movement for its single-minded focus on wages, rather than on what he took to be the more pressing question of what wages could buy. When Schlink's wife, the CR executive M. C. Phillips, argued in 1936 that the "consumer issue" should be "in a clear-cut fashion, separated from the labor issue" and applauded her organization for rescuing the consumer movement "from being considered merely an appendage to the Communist, Socialist, and Labor movements, to which it has no relation," she was not marking a break with CR's prestrike views but instead signaling continuity. Against the tide of New Deal thought, which stressed an identity of interests among workers and consumers, CR called for a strict division of labor in which consumers and producers remained separate, each vigilantly guarding their own distinct interests. Charles Wyand dismissed the idea that the interests of consumers and workers were identical as "a patently absurd statement" and argued that "if not antipodal, [production and consumption] are certainly a very long way from being coincident." For CR's leaders, a consumer's movement was quite simply one that promoted the interests of shoppers, not one that tried to aid other social movements, each of which had its own distinct, often antagonistic, interests. For this reason, CR rejected alliances with other, more activist, branches of the consumer movement, including groups which fought for consumer cooperatives, consumer education, and consumer legislation.[18]

CR's leaders may have harshly criticized corporate America, but they did not indict American capitalism. As Schlink said, "Only under the free market of capitalism, with an absolute minimum of regimentation by the State, does the consumer have an opportunity to obtain the kind and quality of goods which he needs, or happens, for reasons of his own, to prefer." In a 1936 article in the *Atlantic Monthly* critical of the cooperative movement, CR board member J. B. Matthews stressed that "private competitive enterprise" was "the best . . . servant of the consumers' interests." What Schlink and his management team did not like was waste and misleading labeling, neither of which was, in their view, inherent in capitalist production. CR described its mission as one of restoring and purifying capitalism, as making the free market truly free by forcibly returning transparency to a system that had been corrupted by advertising, dishonest labeling, and other forms of sophisticated cheating. As Wyand observed of CR management shortly after the strike, "They have consistently ignored crusades involving a remote and hypothetical reorganization of the economy, preferring to attempt the practicable readjustment of current buying problems within the existing economic framework." CR's leaders were in no sense "strongly anticapitalist," although they were often depicted as such.[19]

Finally, rejecting any notion of a grassroots consumers' democracy, CR's leaders, like their predecessors in the National Consumers League (NCL), distrusted the wisdom of the average consumer, whom they understood to be ignorant, impetuous, and naive. In an odd way, CR mirrored what Roland Marchand has described as advertisers' ambivalence about consumers, whom both groups figured as irrational and female. Like the admen they despised, CR's experts saw consumers as careening between two dangerous poles: easily manipulated, on the one hand, yet stubborn adherents of their own inadequately developed and unscientific tastes, on the other.

One can see hints of this ambivalence in the hectoring first lines of *Your Money's Worth*: "Why do you buy the toothpaste you are using—what do you know about its relative merits? . . . Do you know if it has, beyond a pleasant taste, any merit at all?. . . . Have you any evidence, except blind hope, that the package of insecticide under your arm will actually rid a house of flies?" Such rhetoric warned consumers against trusting their instincts. CR saw itself as representing ordinary consumers whose lack of expertise made them incapable of understanding, much less pursuing, their interests. The only hope for ordinary consumers—whom M. C. Phillips, following her forebears in the National Consumers League, characterized as "pretty dumb as a whole"—lay in following the dictates of CR's qualified technocrats.[20] Consumers' League activists of the Progressive Era shared this assessment of consumers, but they also believed that ordinary shoppers could overcome their ignorance and that they were an essential element in the campaign for just working conditions. CR had no such social movement vision for consumers in mind.

After a brief honeymoon period, activists in the consumer movement began to criticize CR for its narrow agenda, its lack of fundamental economic critique, its top-down style of management, and its unwillingness to ally with the emerging Popular Front coalition of liberal and left-wing organizations. James Rorty, the former advertising executive turned advertising critic and an editor of the radical *Consumers Defender*, complained that Schlink and CR had "isolated themselves" from popular social movements and that "CR's policies and programs never got far enough to make any kind of fundamental economic or social sense." Rorty noted with disappointment that "CR is not a cooperative. . . . Neither has it any connection with the labor movement." It was not enough to promote a narrow agenda of consumer satisfaction; the goal should be "not the information of the consumer, but the destruction of his . . . exploiters."[21]

Such criticisms highlighted what was already manifest but not widely noted: the consumer movement did not walk in lockstep. Despite the rapid spread of consumer groups in the 1930s, to call them an "army" or even a movement was to vastly overstate their cohesiveness. To declare that consumers were "on the march" was to suggest incorrectly that they were all moving in the same direction. As significant as the proliferation of groups claiming to represent consumers was, the less discussed divisions within these groups and the fierce debates among the members about the meaning of consumerism were important as well. The consumer movement was becoming a powerful "voice of protest," conceded Fred DeArmond, but he recognized that this voice was best understood as "a conflicting medley" rather than "one clear and understandable chorus."[22]

II. Consumerism in the 1920s

For a brief time it seemed as if CR symbolized the spirit of the whole of the consumer movement. But the "medley" of consumer activism consisted of a variety of ideologically distinct groups. A key to the differences among the consumer activists was how they interpreted the meaning of Progressive Era consumerism, a protean political discourse that called for expert decision making but also stressed that each shopper had a social responsibility to consume ethically. As we have seen, most observers, and even many participants, dated the birth of the consumer movement to 1927, the year of the publication of *Your Money's Worth*. "When CR got its start in life, the term 'consumer' was not particularly fashionable," agreed Schlink. Yet the movement and the book itself represented the melding of a number of earlier precedents, including the union-label and eight-hour-day campaigns of the late nineteenth century, the Progressive Era promotion of ethical consumption by the NCL and the home economics movement, and Herbert Hoover's efforts in the 1920s to promote efficient consumption. Developments in that decade set the stage for the schisms of the 1930s.[23]

The 1920s are often understood as a time of economic abundance and political quiescence. The decade's alleged political lethargy and conservatism is frequently seen as a consequence of its affluence. With Progressive energies exhausted—weakened by an idealistic war gone awry and the domestic repression that accompanied and followed it—and with the economy booming, Americans, in this stereotypical account, turned inward. Commentators often speak of the rise of "consumer society" in the 1920s as a way to encapsulate these political and economic transformations, using the phrase to explain the economic vibrancy and political passivity that they take to characterize the decade, and also to link the two. While it may have witnessed a diminution of political energy, this decade also produced new kinds of engagements centered around the politicization of consumers and consumption.[24] One manifestation of this was what the historian Liette Gidlow has called "the commodification of political culture," in which print and radio advertising reached unprecedented levels. Older forms of consumer politics were reenergized too. A keyword search of the *New York Times* for the word "boycott" produces more than two thousand hits for the decade of the 1920s, suggesting that the practice of this action and discourse about it continued unabated, even as the Progressive Era came to an end. As in the nineteenth century, boycotters organized on behalf of causes both liberal and reactionary. While streetcar boycotts were rare, some African American boycotters turned their attention to segregated schools. Continuing the trend of cultural boycotts pioneered by

African Americans, other conservative religious groups boycotted movies and plays that they found objectionable. At the same time, the revived Ku Klux Klan organized boycotts of Catholic and Jewish merchants and proposed the "economic boycott and social ostracism" of its opponents. Moreover, the labor boycott continued in spite of legal constraints established in the Progressive Era. Seattle workers launched a nearly year-long boycott of the Bon Marché department store and also organized a successful action against the Van Herberg theater chain. Alongside older forms of boycotts, new ones were invented, such as the "Spend your money where you can work" campaigns, in which, starting in 1929, members of Chicago's African American community demanded that businesses which depended on their patronage hire black workers.[25]

As in the Progressive Era, consumer activism of this sort mingled with the "consumer movement," a phrase that was coined in the 1920s. Interestingly, some of the early uses of the phrase did not suggest, as its later use did, expertise by consumer groups but rather the efforts of businessmen to rationalize and organize consumption. William T. Ogburn, for example, described Henry Ford in 1929 as "the leader of what may be called the 'consumer's movement,'" since he was promoting efforts "to increase the market for manufactured goods by increasing wages." Both business and government began to conceive of the "consumer interest" as an important, perhaps defining, political and social force in modern America. One indication of this reorientation was the coinage in 1921 of the term "consumerism" by the economist Sidney A. Reeve. The New York Times quickly took note of this new word and agreed, long after consumer activists first made the case, that the organized "exercise of economic sovereignty" by consumers was a potentially transformative force. In a 1927 article summarizing what he called "The New Economic Gospel of Consumption," the journalist Edward S. Cowdrick noted that "the worker has come to be more important as a consumer than he is as a producer." This was also a trend that Robert and Helen Lynd observed and commented upon in their famous study of Muncie, Indiana.[26]

Recognizing their dependence on mass consumption meant that businessmen were acutely concerned with promoting purchasing power. For the most part, however, they did not see the need for independent political action on the part of consumers. Indeed, they rejected any link between consumption and citizenship. The Muncie Chamber of Commerce, for example, declared that since consumption was a "new necessity" the "American citizen's first importance to his country is no longer that of citizen but that of consumer." The consumer's job was to buy; it was the job of businessmen and advertisers to entice him to do so. This was the essence of what became known as Fordism, the model of mass consumption not as empowerment for ordinary individuals—although that may have been a by-product—but as necessary fuel for the engines of corporate capitalism.[27]

Others, however, pushed to turn consumers into politically powerful citizens. Because the mass production economy of the 1920s depended on mass consumption, some commentators came to see consumers as a new political and social force. Many businessmen took the so-called buyers' strikes of the early 1920s, in which price-conscious shoppers refused to buy what they deemed to be overpriced goods, as a warning about the need to cultivate consumers through low prices and high quality goods and about the potential power of consumers to either help or weaken their businesses. The buyers' strike, the economic theorist Ralph Borsodi warned business-men in 1927, "was a dramatic demonstration of the supreme importance" of mass consumption. Similarly, in an editorial on "embattled consumers," the *Times*, also referencing the buyers' strikes, observed that "the docile and long-suffering consumer" was finally beginning to recognize her "latent power." The renewed popularity of boycotts over a range of issues, from the high cost of milk and meat, to racist practices at stores, to unhappiness with foreign governmental policies, and even to dissatisfaction with theatrical performances and prices, demonstrated that Americans used their pocketbooks to achieve their social and political goals. Demanding the "proper coordination" of boycotts, one observer in 1920 claimed that "some means must be found of getting everybody to boycott the same thing at the same time." Some Americans began to call for a political party to promote the interests of consumers.[28]

Yet even as they recognized the fundamental importance of consumers to the economy, many commentators described the average consumer as an embattled figure. In the 1920s, experts continued to agree with the Progressive consensus about ignorant consumers. The economist Hazel Kyrk described the consumer as "the helpless victim of powerful interests." The Lynds determined that the citizens of Muncie were not knowledgeable enough to pursue their interests as consumers and labeled this problem of ignorance in the ways of consumption "the new illiteracy." Schlink and Chase compared consumers to Lewis Carroll's fairy-tale character Alice, helplessly facing "conflicting claims, bright promises, fancy packages, soaring words," armed only with an "almost impenetrable ignorance." As the prominent economist Evans Clark noted in his review of *Your Money's Worth*, Chase and Schlink built on people's lack of direct knowledge about consumption to make the case for a surrogate to serve as their figurative eyes and ears. "Our grandfathers knew a great deal about what they bought," Clark wrote. "They knew the people who made it and they knew how and where it was made. Usually the process took place in the neighborhood—if it was not performed in the home." The economist contrasted this intimate knowledge of goods with the "naivete" of contemporary shoppers. Consumers, he said, were ill equipped to judge the "latest mouth wash" and required the services of groups like CR. At the beginning of the 1920s, the radical journalist John Spargo described the revolutionary possibilities of the a new "consciousness of consumers as consumers" that he observed in myriad boycott actions. By the end of that decade, however, many commentators interpreted this new consciousness differently. Rather than focusing on what consumers *do* through collective action, it emphasized what *was being done* to them, against their will and without their knowledge. This was a defensive rather than a revolutionary consciousness, an awareness of consumer weakness rather than consumer power. The solution proposed by Chase and Schlink, and widely applauded by CR's growing number of members, was for consumers to accept guidance and leadership from expert who, unlike them, could competently judge the latest mouthwash.[29]

If their diagnosis was continuous with Progressivism, Schlink and Chase proffered innovative solutions that became lasting elements of the consumer movement: an emphasis on objective and scientific product testing and a call for an organized lobby on behalf of consumers, which they called an "impartial bureau which has the confidence of the public." At first, Schlink and Chase called for some sort of government bureau of product testing, one that could take advantage of the massive amounts of information that the Bureau of Standards (for which Schlink worked early in the decade) and other federal bureaus collected. "Signs are multiplying that this country is definitely headed for an era of consumer buying governed by set standards or specifications," said Chase, whose New York City–based club already had several hundred members by early 1928.[30]

If the main attraction for CR members was the advice they received about the relative merits of foods and other consumables, the group also maintained a strong political element. In its newsletter CR leaders regularly lobbied for increased government intervention on behalf of the consumer. CR pushed the government to develop standards that would aid the consumer. And it was one of the first organizations to call for a cabinet-level, federal Department of the Consumer. Although CR later disavowed its broad-based conception of consumer politics, in the 1920s it was—in spite of its elitism—widely seen as the vanguard of a broad-based consumer politics, which would include the full array of political strategies developed or reenergized during this decade: from boycotts, to lobbying, to political party formation.[31]

The publication of *Your Money's Worth* and the founding of CR had a transformative effect on consumer activism. Consumer activism up to that point had been a decentralized and diverse phenomenon. CR claimed to stand for the consumer movement as a whole, but it had little to do with the broader sphere of consumer activism. In the Progressive Era, the NCL understood itself as multifaceted, part expert-led advice organization and part popular movement. CR leaders rejected this dialectic, seeing themselves as the unequivocal leaders of the movement and rejecting the need for popular action, other than smart consumption guided by their expertise. Many commentators took this new vision of the consumer movement to be its beginning, rather than an adaptation and rejection of a preexisting movement.[32]

III. Social Movement Consumerism

By the mid-1930s, several rival "social movement" consumer organizations had formed to challenge the policies of the "technocratic individualists."[33] One of the first and most significant social movement organization was the League of Women Shoppers (LWS), founded in 1935. The LWS engaged CR in a battle for the legacy of Progressive reform. Challenging CR's emphasis on expertise and individualist consumption, the LWS called for a revival of an older form of female consumer activism reminiscent of the National Consumers League (NCL), which had been superseded in the late 1920s by the technocratic vision of the male-dominated CR. Whereas CR drew its valorization of experts from the Progressive tradition, the LWS stressed another side of Progressive reform, one that attributed to consumers primary responsibility for the exploitation of workers. In emphasizing activism, the LWS did not eschew science. Rather, the view of science that it espoused was consistent with its politics: it stressed the social rather than the natural sciences and, in the pragmatic tradition, understood scientific inquiry as the province of all members willing to investigate the social conditions of consumption. "We want all women who BUY to become BUY CONSCIOUS. Women should look into the conditions under which the products they buy are made and sold," the inaugural issue of the league's newspaper editorialized. The suggestion that all consumers were capable of such investigations was an affront to the technocrats at CR, who saw as its reason for being the incapacity of ordinary consumers to properly conduct such inquiries.[34]

The LWS gained more than twenty-five thousand adherents in fourteen cities by the late 1930s, owing in part to its well-known, upper-middle-class membership, which included the wives of many New Dealers, celebrities like Lillian Hellman and Margaret Bourke-White, and radicals like Jessie

Lloyd O'Connor. Equally important, however, were its tactics. The LWS conducted a series of campaigns, in which, as one member noted, it both pointed out the "facts" (as the NCL would have) and advocated mass political activity. The league specialized in organizing "buyers' strikes" led by its "mink-coat picket lines" to mobilize public opinion, and it, as we will see in the next chapter, helped lead a popular boycott of silk, which was imported from authoritarian Japan. LWS investigators also informed members about low-wage employers, about department stores that imported goods from fascist Germany, Italy, and Japan, and urged its middle-class, mostly white membership to support African American–led "Don't buy where you can't work" campaigns. The group's motto, "Use your buying power for justice," expressed its belief that consumers needed to concern themselves with the conditions under which goods were produced and to act collectively to enforce good conditions: "An individual shopper's action as a consumer passes unnoticed," declared an LWS pamphlet. "But many shoppers organized . . . bring results." Moreover, the LWS stressed that the work of consumption was largely a female labor, claiming that women performed 90 percent of the buying and noting that "the power that lies in this is tremendous." Unlike CR, which saw very little connection between production and consumption, LWS wished to reduce what the radical journalist and LWS member Mary Heaton Vorse called the "gulf between the worker and the consumer." The LWS sought as its project to "remedy the inarticulateness of consumers," in contrast to Schlink and company, who took such inarticulateness for granted and, indeed, made it the very foundation of the CR philosophy.[35]

The differences between consumer activists of the social movement and technocratic individualist persuasions, significant as they became, should not obscure the commonalities that these rival descendants of Progressive reform shared. To be sure, significant ideological differences led to the internecine warfare of the CR strike. But these two groups were so often taken to be identical for a reason: a shared genealogy led both groups to hold in common certain assumptions and political stances. Both groups inherited the Progressive suspicion of big business and expressed the need for constant vigilance against predatory practices. As organizations critical of what was uncritically celebrated by business, the media, and politicians, both groups challenged what I call "consumer triumphalism," the self-satisfied belief system that declared consumer sovereignty and a wide variety of choices to be proof of America's unique greatness. Finding more than a glimmer of hope in the possibilities of consumer activism, both groups also challenged another long-standing, and still potent, American tradition, "consumer defeatism," which defines consumer society as a totalizing and wholly negative force. "In a culture of consumption. . . . The citizen disappears into the consumer," wrote Christopher Lasch, the most prominent contemporary proponent of this view.[36]

Another similarity worth noting is that both groups rooted their consumerism in productivist assumptions. Despite their mistrust of advertisers and salesmanship, technocratic individualist and social movement consumerists of the Depression era posited economic growth as an unmitigated social good. A later generation of consumer activists would shift their focus from productivism to environmentalism. In the 1930s, however, activists articulated a vision of consumption that was thoroughly dependent on what Jean Baudrillard has called "an unbridled romanticism of productivity." Kenneth Burke's prescient 1930 claim that "the maximum consumption is made possible by the maximum possible waste . . . at least until there is nothing more to waste," was rarely echoed during the Depression era heyday of consumer activism. Although they routinely decried waste—indeed, Stuart Chase's *The Tragedy of Waste* (1925) was influential in these circles—consumerists of this period usually defined waste in terms of efficiency rather than ecological degradation. Technocratic individualist consumer activists might criticize the Ford Motor Company for producing an inferior product and social movement activists might condemn its antiunion policies, but neither group challenged Fordism, the reigning mass production/mass consumption model of political economy.[37]

In spite of these similarities, the agendas and goals of technocratic individualist groups like CR and social movement groups like LWS diverged in fundamental ways. Whereas engineers and experts ran the individualist consumer groups, activists and reformers staffed social movement organizations; whereas the experts saw themselves as representing individual consumers, the activists spoke for consumers as a class of which they were members; whereas the goal of the technocrats was consumer satisfaction and economic transparency, social movement types wished to awaken consumers' sense of responsibility and to correct the abuses of American capitalism; whereas groups like CR concerned themselves with product quality, social movement consumer groups focused on working conditions; whereas scientists for CR quietly performed quality studies in their isolated laboratories near the Delaware Water Gap, activist groups staged public protests and initiated well-publicized "investigations" into working conditions and the origins of products lining department store shelves; whereas individualists sought to separate the identities of producers and consumers, activists sought to highlight the connection between the two; whereas Schlink and his supporters rejected a broad social agenda and had no particular role in mind for the state, other than making the data it collected broadly available, social movement types sought to become an "effective force for progressive social action," organizing boycotts, educational campaigns, and calling on government to raise minimum wages as well as to enforce fair labor codes.[38] Whereas many of the individualists became early and vociferous anticommunists, the activists (while vehemently denying charges of communist infiltration) championed a Popular Front ideology of political inclusiveness. Finally, the technocrats were led by mostly male experts, while the social movement groups defined themselves as representing the interests of mostly female consumers. Gender doubtless played a role in these conflicting worldviews. Female activists of the Progressive Era had found a niche in the reform world through their embrace of social science and their claims that shopping was a fundamentally social activity. Social movement consumerists of the 1930s continued to argue that the web of the market linked female consumers to the wider world to which they bore the same caretaking relationship they undertook in their own homes.

Underlying these contrasts was a philosophical difference centering on how consumers should best understand material objects. Technocratic individualists put science to the task of examining things in themselves, while social movement activists employed social science to understand things in their context.[39] For CR, consumer goods were physical facts; for the LWS, they were social artifacts. The former examined the object in isolation to determine how closely it accorded with the description provided by advertisers and product labels. The latter group examined objects in the broad context of the labor that made it, the business that sold it, and the country in which it was made. For CR the important binary was fraud/truth; their question always was: is this object what it is purported to be? The LWS examined objects in terms of a justice/injustice binary; they asked: is this object a product of fair working conditions, honorable employers, and a legitimate government? CR believed consumers profited from understanding the object itself, while the LWS, rejecting what they regarded as a kind of fetishism of commodities, thought consumers' interests could only be adequately determined when the commodity was properly situated. CR sought to help consumers get a good buy, while the LWS aimed to use consumption to promote justice. CR's worldview served its free-market individualism, just as the LWS vision accorded with its conception of the market as a social institution which linked shoppers to each other and the wider world of workers, businesses, and governments. The individualists understood the market economy as inexorably separating people from objects, making it necessary for experts to help individuals overcome this alienation by providing objective knowledge about products. Social movement activists preferred to see the market as a web that widened the network of solidarity for conscientious consumers.

Ultimately, technocratic individualist and social movement consumerists disagreed on how consumers served the public interest and the health of the nation. In ways akin to Adam Smith's conception of the "invisible hand," the individualists believed that the public interest was best served through the cumulative actions of unorganized consumers, each of whom made decisions based on self-interest. They were not libertarians, however; in order to make such self-interested choices, they believed that a lobby was necessary to ensure that these unorganized consumers received accurate information from reliable experts. Social movement groups believed in first charting a public interest and then encouraging consumers to behave in ways that could achieve their vision. They conceived of the public interest as a moral compass to guide individual shopping decisions, whereas individualists saw it as the outcome of these decisions.

IV. The Strike

The August 1935 strike at CR brought the conflict between individualist and social movement activists into sharp relief and made it abundantly clear that advocates of these two approaches were as prone to conflict as to coalition. The strike began when CR summarily fired three employees who had helped to organize a chapter of the American Federation of Labor's Technical, Editorial and Office Assistants Union. The majority of the workforce, unhappy with the low wages they earned, the high rate of turnover, and the autocratic control exercised by Schlink (whose salary was three times higher than any other employee's) walked out in support of the fired workers.[40]

Management's actions struck observers and participants, who initially understood the strike as an almost inexplicable internecine squabble among like-minded progressives, as "a paradox," one that was variously described as "amazing," "utterly incredible," and "incongruous." "This strike just brims with irony," said the wife of Dewey H. Palmer, a CR board member turned strike leader, because CR was supposed to be "the friend of the worker-consumer." Ignoring CR's clear words on the subject, the *New Republic* noted that "the strike remains a blot on the record of an organization which should have been the first to recognize that the interests of labor and the consumer are one." Commentators from the liberal and radical media expressed surprised that "no one is making more vicious attempts at strike-breaking than J. B. Matthews, vice president of CR, a man who was once too radical for the Socialist Party." Consumers' Research, declared

Alexander Crosby, a striking worker, is the "last source from which we should have expected labor trouble." According to a letter from a committee of strike supporters, "The most astounding thing about this strike is that the people who are outdoing the coal and steel barons in their attempts to break the strike are men who once professed their friendship for labor and their devotion to social and economic reform."[41]

CR's seeming hypocrisy may have "astounded" the strikers and their advocates, but it was a great source of satisfaction to those business groups that had been the targets of Schlink's "poison pen." Trade journals could barely contain their glee, publishing articles under headlines such as "Schlink's Stand on Consumers' Research Employees' Strike Appears Inconsistent with His Other Radical Philosophy." Trade publications were not the only ones to gloat. CR "now finds itself in the position of the preacher whose conduct lags behind his eloquence," wrote one editorialist, who, like many observers, depicted the strike as a morality tale in which the do-gooder Schlink was finally getting his comeuppance. The right-wing red hunter Elizabeth Dilling pronounced herself "amused" by the "Radicals Quarrel" at CR.[42]

Interestingly, businesses, advertisers, and other critics of the consumer movement interpreted the strike as proof that, as *Sales Management* concluded, "Americans are incurably producer rather than consumer minded." Notwithstanding their own dependence on consumers and their tireless efforts to locate and describe the "typical consumer," trade journals stressed that the bitterness at CR conclusively demonstrated that, as *Advertising and Selling* claimed, "'The Consumer' is a phantom." Even in the "sacred temple of consumption itself," claimed *Electronic Refrigeration News*, "production raises its horrid and rather awkward head." Although not generally supportive of work stoppages or organized labor, these groups viewed the labor conflict at CR as confirmation that consumer identities were weak and evanescent. According to *Sales Management*, the strike "makes it a bit difficult for CR, because the existence and future of that upright organization rests upon the assumption that the consumer is a vital concept in the lives of millions." This provided "confirmation of the doubts as to whether there has ever been, except in the fleeting moments of outrage over some particularly flagrant gyp, such a thing as the consumer." To Schlink this was proof of "a tie-up between big business and the Communists" and further evidence of his own rectitude in opposing these malevolent forces. The unholy alliance of unscrupulous businessmen and opportunistic leftists was, he claimed, the real "united front." How else, he asked, could one explain "the remarkable and enthusiastic support which the 'strike' received in business publications"?[43]

If CR's enemies in the business world interpreted the strike as proof that producer identity trumped consumer identity, the striking workers drew a more complicated conclusion. As the strike wore on, it became clear to the picketers and their supporters that the strike involved more than mere workplace grievances; it was also a struggle for the soul of the consumer movement. To be sure, the workers emphasized CR's abuses at the point of production; they described the proximate causes as CR's unwillingness to pay living wages and to recognize a democratically chosen union. But as the strike progressed they also criticized the philosophy of consumerism that was practiced at CR. Indeed, relating the former to the latter, they argued that CR's narrow product-based research agenda was part and parcel of its inhumanity toward employees. No longer a Popular Front hero, Schlink began to be portrayed as a ruthless boss, a hypocrite, and an elitist, whose attempt to isolate products from people in his science came to affect his politics. "Schlink can be honest about toothpaste and shoes and face powder—but he won't be honest about the human beings who work for him," remarked John Heasty, a chemist who was the union president and one of the fired workers, highlighting the problem with CR's fetishistic approach to commodities. CR, he claimed, ignored the social relations of production—the market-based web that linked producers, consumers, and citizens—and this affected, and in his view weakened, both its employment policies and political stances.[44]

For the picketing workers—most of them college-educated engineers, scientists, and writers—the strike marked a turning point. Heasty viewed the strike as important evidence that white-collar workers, no longer understanding themselves as a "separate class" of "employees" superior to mere "workers," were "seeing the imperative need of organizing." It "was a wonderful experience for those of us who were new to the union movement," said Alexander Crosby, a CR writer and strike leader. Crosby described the strike as an "erotic picnic," noting the "great spirit of comradeliness" (which included organized attacks on strikebreakers and CR executives) and sexual energy which became part of the atmosphere of the strike for the youthful, mixed-sex workforce. He emphasized the excitement that CR's strikers felt when they were aided on the picket lines by a nearby group of hosiery workers, who were also on strike: "I think we all enjoyed having contacts with honest to god experienced union men like these hosiery workers." League of Women Shoppers members also marched in solidarity with CR picketers. Summing up the strike experience, Crosby declared: "Well, see, those were the glory days of the United Front, and it was the only time in my life when you suddenly felt that you belonged to something great and promising and that wonderful things were around the corner, that we were going to see better days in the United States."[45]

The strike's many dramatic moments—including CR's use of strike-breakers, armed detectives, and private police, and the daily arrests, skirmishes, and violence—made it a litmus test for the assertion of political beliefs. As chair of a committee that investigated the claims of both sides, Reinhold Niebuhr produced a report which found the CR management culpable and rejected charges that the strike was a communist plot. (Schlink promptly dismissed the members of the Niebuhr committee as duped fellow travelers.) "Every progressive element in the country is behind the strikers," declared the *New Masses*. Characteristic of the emboldened Popular Front culture, strike supporters organized a public "trial" at an ad hoc "Consumers and Workers Court" at Town Hall in New York City. Before an overflow crowd, the well-known radical journalist Heywood Broun played the role of "Judge," the left-leaning Congressman Vito Marcantonio served as "Prosecutor," and members of various Popular Front organizations, including the League of Women Shoppers, constituted "the Jury." Not surprisingly, this "trial" returned a verdict unfavorable to CR. Many CR subscribers registered their disapproval of management tactics by forming an Association of Consumers' Research Subscribers, led by James Gilman, the president of the Book and Magazine Guild. The association urged members to cancel their subscriptions and to write CR management in protest.[46]

In 1936, when the National Labor Relations Board found that the CR had "engaged in and continues to engage in unfair labor practices" and ordered that the fired workers be reinstated and given back pay, the workers and their advocates celebrated. But rather than return to CR, a group of strikers led by Schlink's former collaborator Arthur Kallet (who was not a CR employee but secretary of the board), formed a rival organization, Consumers Union (CU), a group which today is best known as the publisher of *Consumer Reports*. While maintaining the scientific, laboratory testing apparatus of CR, CU sought to "avoid past mistakes in the field of testing," which one CR founder described as "neglecting all consideration of the place of the worker in the so-called consumer-oriented society." It unabashedly described itself as a "pro-labor" organization: it charged a lower subscription fee than CR so that working people could afford it; it focused not just on product quality but on working conditions; it was a union shop; and it organized a "labor advisory committee" that included many union leaders, among them A. Philip Randolph, the president of the Brotherhood of Sleeping Car Porters and Homer Martin, the president of the United Auto Workers. As the first issue of *Consumers Union Reports* declared, "The directors of Consumers Union do not feel . . . that they have done their job when they have provided information which permits the saving of a few pennies, or even a few dollars. . . . All the technical information in the world will not give enough food or enough clothes to the textile worker's family living on $11 a week." Unlike CR, which "has consistently failed to cooperate with other consumers' groups," CU sought the "mass support of consumers." Within a year, CU—which effectively recruited the disgruntled CR subscribers who had joined the Subscribers' Association—had gained forty thousand adherents, and it quickly became larger than its rival, CR, which had metamorphosed in less than twelve months from the darling to the enemy of Progressive America. Even Stuart Chase, one of CR's founders, quietly shifted his allegiance to CU.[47]

V. Anticommunism

In the aftermath of the "strike in the temple of consumption," CR executives J. B. Matthews, Schlink, and M. C. Phillips all began long careers of searching for subversives in the consumer movement, which had become, they claimed, "fronts for a deliberate attack on our present economy." They loudly proclaimed the strike to be a communist-led "putsch," a "coup d'etat." Matthews, beginning his journey from the far left to the extreme right, which, before the end of the decade, would make him the director of research for the House Committee on Un-American Activities (HUAC), described the consumer movement as "a natural for the Trojan Horse tactic," with CR as exhibit number 1. Prior to the Communist Party's "united front" strategy in 1935, Matthews noted that "the attitude of the Party had been one of unconcealed contempt for organizations which had for their honest objective the advancement of consumers' interests." But after that date, consumer groups became favorite targets of Communist Party infiltration. Others agreed. Writing in the *American Mercury*, Fletcher Pratt concluded that "the consumer cause is merely another of the long list of Red rackets which are being exploited by the alert Comrades for the purpose of undermining the Capitalist system." Schlink and Matthews in particular became prominent anticommunists; in the years before the beginning of Cold War, they stood out as what we might call "premature anticommunists," two of the most vocal opponents of the Communist Party of the United States of America and of all links, real and imagined, between consumer groups and communists. In late 1939, the Dies Committee, spurred by Matthews's research, firsthand knowledge, and talent for innuendo, accused fourteen consumer organizations, all under the rubric of what I have described as social movement groups, including the LWS and CU, of being a "Consumers Red Network" of communist "transmission belts" (fig. 6.2). Despite being widely criticized, these attacks marked the beginning of the end of New Deal–era social movement consumerism. Although LWS and CU remained active during the war years, the immediate postwar years of the Cold War posed another threat to their style of consumer activism, as both groups appeared on HUAC's list of disloyal organizations.[48]

Even before that date many commentators called for a chastening of the consumer movement. In 1939, *American Consumer*, a commercial publication financed by business groups, applauded the "constructive consumer movement" which belongs to "no group, to no organization, to no proponents of this or that political thought." Those who would turn consumers against the "free enterprise order," an editorial assured, "do not make up, nor do they represent, the consumer movement." Even supporters of an activist consumer movement cautiously tried to position that movement in nonthreatening terms. In response to the HUAC charges, Stuart Chase declared, "The consumer movement is middle class and American and nonpolitical to the core." In her 1941 survey of the state of the consumer movement, Helen Sorenson, a home economist who supported CU, called for consumer organizations to define their interests narrowly rather than engaging in broad social agendas which were susceptible to "capture" by outside forces. "The point is that consumers have interests of their own which they need to defend and promote; when they are drawn off into supporting other causes or interests, they have less organization energy. . . . To this loss is added positive injury when these other interests borrow the name 'consumer' and use it as a front behind which to pursue their special ends." When Sorenson asked, "Why could we not have had one bona fide organization pursuing the true undefiled ends of testing consumers' goods?" she appeared not to recognize that social movement consumerists wanted to do more than merely serve as "undefiled" product testers. More likely she was consciously calling on CU to abandon its activist orientation, which she defined as working "on behalf of labor rather than in the consumer interest."[49]

In the very different political culture of Cold War America, social movement consumerists had a difficult time even maintaining their organizations. Some former members began to tell the tale of how they had been seduced into the movement by dissembling communists, or how they had resisted such seductions. By 1949 the LWS had ceased to exist as an independent group. Its skeletal remains merged with the Congress of American Women; one year later, an order of the Department of Justice forced this "subversive" group to disband. As we shall see, CU, while remaining

Figure 6.2. The Dies Committee labels consumer groups communist. (Rollin Kirby, *New York Post*, Dec 13, 1939, 18.)

a popular organization with nearly a million subscribers by the late 1950s, underwent decades of internecine battles over what kind of organization it should be. Proponents of a social mission vied with those who believed it should be a purely technical organization, and it oscillated between these two visions. In the wake of HUAC's 1939 allegations, CU director Arthur Kallet sought to remove suspected leftists from the board and, true to his own engineering background, to highlight product testing more than social activism. In the mid-1940s the organization dropped its coverage of working conditions. During the hot years of the Cold War, from the late 1940s through the late 1950s, the organization's president, the economist Colston Warne, who complained that CU was no longer behaving as if it were part of a "social movement," and its director, Kallet, fought over these and other issues. Finally, in 1957, the board, at the urging of Warne and others who wished to return to CU's activist roots, fired Kallet. Throughout the late twentieth century, as we will see in chapter 8, CU balanced its seemingly narrow focus on product quality and cost by playing a leading role in the national and international consumer movement and by allying itself with more socially oriented consumer activists. CU was instrumental in developing state and local consumer agencies and in founding the

Consumer Federation of America, an umbrella organization organized to nourish local consumer efforts. To many of its middle-class subscribers, remained primarily a product-testing organization very much like CR, the group that it broke away from in the heady days of the Popular Front. Former CU board member Abraham Isserman lamented in 1974 that "their attitude today is softer. They're less militant in their approach to products now." CU continues to see itself both as a purveyor of accurate information for the budget-conscious, middle-class consumer and as part of the politicized consumer movement, working for justice in the marketplace.[50]

The strike in the temple of consumption provides insight into the transformation and bifurcation of the consumer movement, the turn toward anticommunism, and the eclipse of Popular Front radicalism as well as some general lessons about political culture in the twentieth century. Looking backward from the 1930s reveals how tensions within Progressive thought became transformed into competing political ideologies. Conflicts within the consumer movement reflected different interpretations of the concept that Progressives most valorized: science. In many ways, as we have seen, the technocratic individualists, with their optimistic faith in experts and their attempt to rescue capitalism from its own worst excesses, remained steadfast Progressives. While social movement consumerists adopted the political rhetoric of the New Deal era, they too held true to the female-centered, social scientific vision of their forebears in the National Consumers League. The LWS and CU attempted to continue the Progressive Era marriage of collective action with scientific expertise. In its condemnation of a populist consumerism driven by a range of social concerns, CR severed this link.

Casting our vision beyond the Depression decade, we may gain another perspective. What began in the late 1920s as a movement of Progressivism's descendants and was transformed by radicals in the 1930s soon became a laboratory of postwar political identity. In part this was because, as in other social movements—for example, organized labor—the communism/anticommunism binary became the filter through which all consumer activity was interpreted. But this does not tell the whole story. J. B. Matthews became an apostle of modern conservatism, the "spiritual leader of the Far Right in America," in David Oshinsky's words. This was so not only because of his vehement, not to say obsessive, anticommunism—in 1953 he went to work for Senator Joseph McCarthy and in a well-publicized article accused the Protestant clergy of communist subversion—but equally because of his abandonment of any critique of free-market capitalism. The anticommunism of Matthews and his colleagues at CR led *Business Week*, with tongue in cheek, to welcome CR's executives "to the ranks of true conservatives" with "open arms and the kiss of loving brotherhood." However, the conservative label did not apply as neatly to Matthews's colleague Schlink. Although staunchly anticommunist, Schlink's politics were not so easily definable. He became something of a crank who turned against the New Deal order and was extremely critical of the kind of reformist liberalism that he detected in other consumer organizations. As Kathleen Donohue has astutely noted, "By grounding consumerism in libertarian conservative notions of personal liberty and limited government, he fashioned an ideology well suited to a capitalist system." Schlink thus showed that consumerism could be allied with a rejection of the New Deal consensus. Yet notwithstanding his anticommunism and antiradicalism, his continued friendship with Matthews (and support of McCarthy), and even his self-description as a "libertarian," he rejected the label "conservative" in large part because he continued to believe that the free market could not be trusted to govern itself without the input of expert representatives of the consumer interest. Unlike Matthews, he continued to consider himself part of the consumer movement and a critic of big business. Thus, although he would have rejected the label, in many ways, Schlink became an advocate of interest-group liberalism. While he no longer demanded a cabinet-level Department of the Consumer, he continued to believe in the need for a lobby (albeit in the private sector) to protect consumers' interests. Other consumerists, more comfortable with the liberal label, worked to formulate interest groups that represented consumers without being made up of ordinary consumers. As early as the 1940s, the economist and reformer Persia Campbell began a series of studies of the "consumer interest" in a pluralist political system. Federal recognition of a consumer interest (as manifested, for example, in President John F. Kennedy's Consumer Bill of Rights in 1962) and the existence of a consumer lobby pointed to another side of the transformation of liberal, individual consumerism into postwar interest-group liberalism. One way to describe this shift is from prewar consumer activism to postwar consumer advocacy, which is the term usually used to describe the methods of Ralph Nader and the modern consumer movement.[51]

After the eclipse of the LWS and the purging of CU, social movement consumerism suffered in the immediate postwar years. But as Michael Denning has noted in his study of the "cultural front," Popular Front ideology, while repressed, did occasionally challenge the postwar consensus, most notably during the Civil Rights movement in which consumer activism played an important tactical role. In addition, as we will see in chapter 8, the consumer movement in the postwar years was more vibrant and diverse than is usually assumed. Similarly, consumer boycotts of table grapes beginning in the 1960s became the signature strategy of the United Farm Workers' struggles for union recognition and decent working conditions. In the late 1970s, the Amalgamated Clothing and Textile Workers Union used the slogan "Don't sleep with J. P. Stevens" to encourage a boycott of the textile manufacturers products. And the post–Cold War years, as we will see in the epilogue, have witnessed a new emphasis on consumer politics, linking individuals to a variety of social justice and environmental issues. "What does your underwear support . . . pesticides and sweatshops or people and the planet?" a recent mailing from Co-Op America asks, highlighting the efflorescence of social movement consumerism. Students at many universities in the United States, Canada, and elsewhere have protested apparel makers (who produce the logo-studded clothing for students and sports fans) for violating codes of fair labor conduct and have called for a revival of ethical consumption. Other recent phenomena, including "green consumerism," living wage campaigns, boycotts of companies that rely on low-wage workers, and the "voluntary simplicity" movement, all suggest that the linking of consumption and political engagement was not an evanescent product of the radical thirties but a significant and continuing, though frequently overlooked, feature of the political culture of the United States.[52]

"MAKE LISLE THE STYLE"

On a Friday afternoon in late January 1938, a standing-room crowd of six hundred, including many of the leading society women of the District of Columbia, attended an unusual fashion show at the Wardman Park Theater. The hour-long pageant entitled "Life without Silk: From Morning to Midnight in Cotton and Rayon," sponsored by the League of Women Shoppers (LWS), aimed, quite literally, to make a cause fashionable. Directed by Lee Simonson, the well-known scenic designer, who wore a woolen necktie, the LWS organized the show to popularize the nascent campaign to boycott Japanese silk. Simonson and the DC branch of the LWS intended "Life without Silk" to "reveal the chic a woman can acquire without a thread of Japanese silk." To promote the boycott, they believed, was also to raise consciousness about socially responsible and stylish modes of nonsilk fashion.[1]

The audience members, many of them prominent boycott supporters, attended "Life without Silk" as proponents and originators of such styles. Demonstrating that "Washington women can dress smartly in clothes made of cotton, rayon, and wool—everything but silk," the pageant's participants—mostly "members of the Junior League and women prominent in the social life of the capital"—modeled nonsilk styles fit for any occasion and any time of day (fig. 7.1). A model who wore a "gayly printed morning coat of a cotton pique" was followed by others clad in suede suits and hats, "tennis costumes of rayon, with copper tunic top, zippered down the front," cashmere cocktail dresses, and flowered cotton evening gowns. "To judge by the volume of applause, it was evident that women could look smart on the beach, at the races, around a bridge table, at the dance or in an embassy garden without silk," one newspaper reported. The show had "dowagers and sub-debs alike 'ohing' and 'ahing' in admiration." The highlight of the pageant occurred when the dancer and movie star Eleanor

Powell, whom the *Washington Post* described as the "owner of what many believe to be the shapeliest legs in Hollywood," emerged on stage with those limbs "encased in cotton stockings."[2] (See fig. 7.2.)

Outside the theater, a contingent of women representing the American Federation of Hosiery Workers (AFHW), a union affiliated with the Congress of Industrial Organizations (CIO), marched in protest of the boycott.[3] Some three hundred hosiery workers had traveled by train from Reading, Pennsylvania, the heart of the country's full-fashioned hosiery industry, to challenge the premises of the silk-free fashion show. Refusing to cede the moral high ground to the LWS, the hosiery workers argued that the dictates of both ethical consumption and good fashion required not a boycott but the continued purchase of silk. Decrying the silk boycott as shortsighted and wrongheaded, the paraders, many of whom claimed to be unemployed, argued that a silk boycott would victimize American industry, particularly American hosiery workers, far more than it would hurt the Japanese economy. "Why Make Us the Victims of Foreign War?" asked one sign; "Wear Silk and Save Our Jobs," implored another (fig. 7.3). The hosiery workers claimed that there were no practicable alternatives to silk, the essence of good fashion, and that it was unrealistic as well as unfair to ask American women to discard their silk apparel. "Nothing can properly take the place of silk," declared Lillian Shearer, a union member from Reading, who spoke on the Mutual Radio Network the evening of the protests. American women, she said, would not, and should not, be expected to settle for "lower standards of dress than they now enjoy." The silk boycott, she charged, turned silk workers into fashion victims not once but twice; as workers forced into unemployment, and as consumers unable to dress fashionably. Posing for the photographers and spectators who lined Constitution Avenue, the paraders drew attention to their silk hose by holding their skirts aloft; a twenty-piece band provided musical accompaniment.[4]

Media coverage of "Life without Silk" and the hosiery workers' protest march emphasized the bodily displays of the women of the LWS and of the AFHW rather than the causes their fashions were meant to serve. *Time* described Powell's limbs as "superhuman and mordantly adept, as if animated by a baleful intelligence of their own." In a rare moment of agreement from the other end of the ideological spectrum, the *Daily Worker* emphasized the majesty of Powell's "shapely legs sheathed in cotton stockings." Jane Eads reported in the *Washington Herald* that "'Life Without Silk' was not only illustrated on the stage, but carried out in real life yesterday as some 600 women, wearing cotton or rayon stockings—in some instances none at all—flocked to see a fashion show at the Wardman Park Theater drama-

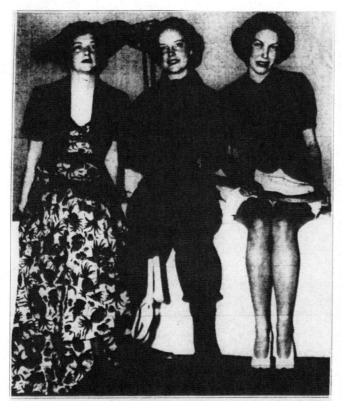

THE WASHINGTON LEAGUE OF WOMEN SHOPPERS met yesterday at the Wardman Park Hotel and held a fashion show during the afternoon. Among the members taking part were (left to right) Mrs. Sydney Manson, Martha Schoenfeld and Freda Frazier, running the gamut of fashion for summer and winter. International News Photo

ELEANOR POWELL
She boycotts silk stockings

LILLIAN SCHEARER
She disagrees with Eleanor

Figure 7.1. Members of the League of Women Shoppers participating in the nonsilk fashion show "Life without Silk." (*Washington Herald*, Jan 29, 1938, 9. International News Photo.)

Figure 7.2. The actress and dancer Eleanor Powell was one of many celebrities to endorse the silk boycott. (*Reading Eagle*, Jan 29, 1938, 1.)

tizing the Washington LWS' boycott of Japanese goods." In the *Washington Daily News*, Martha Strayer wrote that LWS membership "is well equipped in the matter of ankles but not in cotton stockings worn upon said equipment." The media singled out the exotic stylishness of America Iglesias, the "pretty" daughter of the resident commissioner of Puerto Rico, "who

PHILADELPHIA WORKERS HERE TO OPPOSE JAPANESE BOYCOTT
These Girls Paraded to White House Yesterday in Protest Against Banning Tokyo Silk

Figure 7.3. Silk-clad hosiery workers protest the silk boycott. (*Washington Herald*, Jan 29, 1938, 3. Harris Ewing Photo.)

came barelegged, in a white cotton frock" and jacket that she wore "with as much verve and style as if it were one of the more fashionable silk outfits."[5]

Reports on the AFHW counterprotest had a similar bodily emphasis, stressing what one reporter called "the sheer number of sheer hose." "The current theme in this capital city today is all about 'Legs-Legs-Legs' and how they ankle up Constitution Avenue. It was a grand parade—the greatest leg show the city has ever witnessed," noted a reporter for the *Reading Eagle*, who could not resist adding, "Lots of people didn't know what it was all about. They just stared, goggle-eyed" at the "600 legs in the sheerest silken hose." The style columnist Alice Hughes agreed that debate about silk was the cause of "a lot of leg staring." Even journalists who addressed the political differences that divided the protesting women did so in corporeal terms: "Both factions were supplied liberally with beautiful girls, chief difference being that the Pennsylvania factory workers flaunted their silk hosiery while the embattled shoppers and their models moved to and fro on legs encased in lisle," declared the *Washington Post* in an article accompanied by a series of photographs of the pro- and antiboycott contingents in seductive poses headlined "Shapely Pros and Cons of the Silk versus Cotton Debate."[6] (See fig. 7.4.)

Despite their attempts to reduce the events in the District of Columbia to a peep show, the reporters unwittingly brought to light important similarities in the political tactics of these opposing groups, tactics which both extended older practices of consumer activism and also squared off against those practices. Following a tradition traceable to the nation's Founders, the LWS and the AFHW accepted as fundamental the view that consumption was a moral and political act that linked individuals to each other and to the producers of the goods they purchased in an imagined community of mutual responsibility covering great distances, sometimes even crossing national borders. Like previous generations of consumer activists, both groups believed that wearing (or avoiding) certain kinds of clothing was not just a matter of political rhetoric but a political activity, with tangible real-world consequences. The media coverage also highlighted the ways in which both groups rejected a defining characteristic of many previous forms of American consumer activism: the degradation of pleasure and fashion and the valorization of sacrifice. The LWS and the AFHW challenged the assumption that beauty and ethics were antithetical, and, conversely, that sacrifice was, in itself, a form of morality. Instead, they demonstrated that consumers could be activists not just when they refused goods and eschewed pleasure but also when they consumed goods and enjoyed them. Unlike most previous consumer movements, which walled themselves off from popular culture, the silk boycotters and their opponents, while disagreeing about the proper course of action, used fashion-conscious, media-friendly, public-relations-savvy strategies to nourish their political engagements.[7]

By using the techniques of mass culture to advance a cause, the silk boycott, understudied and little remembered though it may be, demonstrated that ethical politics could be eminently fashionable, that good fashion could be a political statement, and that female consumers were central to both of these projects. The silk boycott, at home in the world of fashion and pleasure, did not, however, represent a singular moment in the history of consumer activism; it was rather the most visible episode in a recessive strain of that tradition. In tracing the origins of this fashionable

Shapely Pros and Cons of the Silk versus Cotton Debate

Chinese Reach Tsining Gates in New Offensive

Terrorists Hurl Bombs in Shanghai; 'Puppet' Police Beat Briton.

By the United Press

Shanghai (Saturday), Jan. 29.—Reinforced Chinese troops, smashing against extended Japanese lines in North China in a new offensive, reported today they had reached the south gate of Tsining.

Chinese terrorists in Shanghai celebrated the sixth anniversary of the first Shanghai war by hurling bombs at the Japanese consulate general, the Japanese censors' office and the pro-Japanese "great way" municipal government's police office. One Chinese was injured and damage was slight.

J. M. Leeming, Canadian-born member of the Shanghai municipal police, was beaten by police members of the Chinese "puppet" government of Shanghai when he tried to make an arrest. The incident was the latest of a series involving Britons and added to British-Japanese tension. A protest was expected.

Huge Armies Close In.

Huge armies were reported closing in on each other on the extended North China front, where bloody fighting has been raging for weeks north and south of Suchow, at the intersection of the Tientsin-Pukow and Lunghai railways.

Chinese troops, ordered by Generalissimo Chiang Kai-shek to regain territory lost by the defection of Han Fu-chu, who was executed in Hankow this week, struck back at the Japanese and began an encircling movement around Tsining

Associated Press Photos

15 Are Seized In Plot to Kill Greek Dictator

Metaxas Mobilizes Army Against Exiled Leaders of Parliament.

By the Associated Press

Athens, Jan. 28. Fifteen persons were arrested tonight as participants in what police described as a plot against the life of Greece's "strong man," Premier Gen. John Metaxas.

Meanwhile the Greek army was reported mobilized to put down possible disturbances growing out of the mass exile of leading opponents of the dictatorial government of Gen. Metaxas.

Private advices from Athens said Metaxas had arrested all former leaders of Parliament and sent them to remote islands. Metaxas warned "The dictatorial regime abandons its previous measures and enters upon a new period a period of severity without any pity . . . If necessary, other and even more severe measures will be taken."

The government statement, published in the controlled Greek press, said old parties "refused to let bygones be bygones" and "allied themselves with various criminal elements which stir up unrest as a profession."

The situation apparently came to a head when opposition leaders united in a manifesto assailing the government's financial and domestic policies and calling on the people to demand restoration of their sovereign rights.

Admiral C.C. Bloch To Take Command

Figure 7.4. The media highlighted the dueling views of the boycott with many images such as these photos of silk boycotters baring their limbs. (*Washington Post*, Jan 29, 1938, 3. AP/Wide World Photos.)

form of consumer activism, and in emphasizing continuities as well as departures from previous traditions, this chapter argues that the boycotters and their opponents articulated in a new register of pleasure the notions of consumer power and long-distance solidarity, foundational concepts which gave rise to and continue to sustain consumer activism. Their disagreement about the proper course of that activism also revealed the capaciousness of the category of political consumption, showing that fashion-friendly consumerism, like the broader category of consumer activism of which it was a part, can take different forms and sanctions no single political viewpoint.[8]

I. Did Your Stockings Kill Babies?

The movement to boycott Japanese goods began in the United States in August 1937.[9] Influenced by the romantic writings of Pearl Buck and others, many Americans had grown sympathetic to the Chinese people in the 1930s. These feelings intensified after Japan launched its undeclared war against China in July 1937. Against a country whose motto "Export or die" pointed to the degree to which it relied on global markets, the threat of a boycott posed a powerful weapon, especially during a time of worldwide Depression (fig. 7.5). Unlike the ongoing but less effective boycott of Nazi Germany, which did not single out a particular good, the antisilk campaign linked militarism to the consumption of one product. While calling attention to a wide range of Japanese imports that consumers should avoid, and launching, accordingly, a boycott of Japan's manufactured goods, most boycotters identified raw silk as "the lifeline of the Japanese militarists," the major export of "an economy built on textiles" and the United States' most economically significant Japanese imported good. They emphasized the unwitting culpability of American consumers—especially women, who reportedly bought ten to fifteen pairs of silk stockings per year—in financing war crimes through their consumption of Japanese products.[10]

The boycott quickly became what the *Nation* described as "a nation-wide movement of unprecedented proportions." In October 1937, both the American Federation of Labor (AFL) and the CIO endorsed a boycott of Japanese manufactured goods and President Franklin D. Roosevelt seemed to sanction such actions when he called for a "quarantine" of militarily aggressive nations, including Japan. In the aftermath of the sinking of the United States gunboat the USS *Panay*, on the Yangtze River in December 1937, and growing publicity about Japanese atrocities in China, the silk boycott became one of the most popular consumer campaigns in American history. That month the leading intellectuals John Dewey, Albert Einstein, and

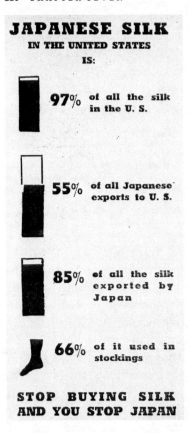

JAPANESE SILK
IN THE UNITED STATES
IS:

97% of all the silk in the U. S.

55% of all Japanese exports to U. S.

85% of all the silk exported by Japan

66% of it used in stockings

STOP BUYING SILK AND YOU STOP JAPAN

Figure 7.5. A chart demonstrating the central role that American silk purchases played in aiding the Japanese economy. (*Did Your Stockings Kill Babies* [Boston: The Boycott Japanese Goods Committee of Greater Boston, 1938], vertical file: Tamiment Institute Library, New York University.)

Bertrand Russell came out in support of the boycott. Proponents dubbed it the "people's boycott" after a *Fortune* poll in February 1938 found that well over half the country supported it. The silk boycott campaign was carried out in different parts of the country by a variegated constituency that included students, Chinese Americans, veterans and consumer groups, YMCAs, manufacturers' associations, celebrities, progressive women's groups, and liberal and leftist organizations, ranging from the LWS, to the American Friends of the Chinese People, to the Committee for a Boycott against Japanese Aggression, to the American League for Peace and Democracy, to the Communist Party. Early in 1938, R. A. Howell, a member of the American Friends of the Chinese People, called the boycott "the largest movement of its kind in history." An "imposing list of international unions, federations, councils and locals" endorsed the boycott, including the Trades Union Council in England, the Confédération Générale du Travail in France, and Jawaharal Nehru's Indian National Congress Party. That same year the boycott gained further momentum when America's six largest chain stores—F. W. Woolworth, S. S. Kresge, McCrory, S. H. Kress, the F. and W. Grand Stores, and the National Dollar Stores—announced that they would place no additional orders for Japanese manufactured goods.[11]

Drawing on the global vision that had long been central to consumer activism, boycott supporters argued that the causal chain set off by consumption did not stop at the nation's borders. Boycotters asked shoppers to adopt toward goods made in fascist countries the "same sensitiveness which causes many to refuse to buy the products of child labor or sweatshop labor." In doing so, they extended the domain of the politics of consumption. For boycott supporters, to wear silk was to contribute to Japanese atrocities and unwittingly to become what the Committee for a Boycott against Japanese Aggression called "an innocent partner in Japanese aggression." By making transparent the connection between the consumption of silk and Japanese militarism, the boycotters aimed to make such innocent ignorance impossible. Arguing that unthinking consumption of such goods would promote Japanese imperialism, they did not hesitate to postulate a direct causal link between silk purchases and murder. As one pamphlet asked, "Did Your Stockings Kill Babies?" The answer to this blunt question, according to The Boycott Japanese Goods Committee of Greater Boston, was an unequivocal yes: "If your stockings are silk . . . they helped Japan to murder thousands of babies and women, workmen, and peasants of China." Another boycott group reminded consumers that "every pair of silk stockings buys four rounds of deadly machine-gun bullets." Given that the purchase of Japanese goods made consumers accessories to murder and mayhem, the consumer's job was to "refuse to be an accomplice in the crime," by eschewing silk and other Japanese goods.[12]

Accordingly, for the boycotters, using "consumer power to effect social justice" gained new meaning. Looking carefully at products before purchasing them did not mean merely examining them for cost and quality (as the consumers' movements of the 1920s and 1930s recommended), nor did it mean only examining working conditions (as labor-friendly organizations such as the National Consumers League and the AFHW as well as the LWS itself recommended to consumers); it meant also understanding the degree to which these goods constituted the economic sinews of enemy powers, as it had for the Revolutionary and Civil War–era boycotters. As Rebecca Drucker, a member of the LWS, wrote, in supporting the boycott the league was not fundamentally altering but rather logically extending into the field of foreign-made goods its mission, summed up by the slogan, "Use your buying power for justice." The league emphasized that women, in their role as consumers, had an important role to play in this expansion of aggregate purchasing power from domestic labor relations to foreign relations. According to Robert Stark, a correspondent for the *New Masses*, the consumer was the first cause in a series of events that would weaken the Japanese economy and hence its military. Stark suggested how the chain reaction of consumption could affect foreign affairs: "When you ask for lisle . . . the salesgirl tells the buyer, the buyer tells the mill selling agent, the agent tells the manufacturer. And the manufacturer cuts down his buying of silk. Multiply your insistence by several million—and raw-silk sales will drop, crash." The same techniques of organized nonconsumption used to punish antiunion employers, Stark claimed, could be employed to weaken national economies. Indeed, some boycotters suggested extending it to the Soviet Union after that country agreed to a peace treaty with Germany in 1939.[13]

The movement's stress on the causal link between the purchase of silk and the fitness of the Japanese war machine placed a heavy burden on consumers. If the seemingly innocent act of buying stockings led directly to atrocities in distant parts of the world, ethical consumers could not be neutral about the consequences of their actions. By promulgating such a worldview, the boycott movement hoped to render moot the excuse that the consequences of consumption could not be foreseen at the time of purchase. Sometimes boycott proponents described shopping not in causal terms but as a kind of alchemy in which the very purchase of a product led it to magically and diabolically transform: "Stores display only silk stockings, satin nightgowns, pretty toys and novelties. But rub your eyes and look again, and every pair of stockings is a clip of rifle bullets, every gimcrack a blood-rusted fragment of shrapnel." This use of metonymy, evocative of the free produce movement's description of "blood-soaked" cotton or sugar that howled in pain, suggested that the consumption of silk and other Japanese products did not merely cause violence, but was itself an act of violence. The silk boycotters were not alone in the Depression decade among consumer activists in alerting consumers to their implications in criminality. For example, Tillie Olsen's 1934 poem "I Want You Women Up North to Know" alerted consumers that the "dainty children's dresses" sold at fancy department stores were "dyed in blood, are stitched in wasting flesh." But silk boycotters resorted to sensory terms to explain the logic of long-distance solidarity more frequently than any group since the abolitionist protesters.[14]

While both the AFL and the CIO voted overwhelmingly in October 1937 to boycott Japanese manufactured goods, neither organization supported the boycott on Japanese silk, the raw material that provided the livelihood for hundreds of thousands of workers in hosiery and related industries. The

AFHW was the most vociferous among the trade unions in distinguishing between the boycott on manufactured goods, which it supported, and what it deemed to be the ill-considered boycott of Japanese silk. The union asked liberal and radical consumer activists to weigh the benefits of a silk boycott against potential harm it would do to American workers. Disagreeing with the boycotters' claims of causal transparency, the AFHW argued that purchases were embedded in a complex causal matrix whose moral calculus was not readily discernable. Determining the truth about products, and consequently the morality of using them, was a complicated business, the union suggested. Indeed, rejecting the argument that silk was primarily a Japanese product, the hosiery workers' union argued that the bulk of the labor performed on silk occurred after it arrived in the United States. Emil Rieve, the union's president, claimed that, for this reason, "the silk industry is an American industry in which American capital is invested and American labor is engaged." Global trade was a fact of life, the AFHW argued; this did not make silk stockings any less American than other goods manufactured in the United States. "No modern nation is economically completely self-contained and . . . some part of its people must subsist by interdependent processes of international exchange of commodities and the flow of world trade," declared John Sayre, a critic of the boycott. He noted that the "American housewife" who "gives vent to her moral indignation . . . by refusing to purchase the silk products of peasants who live in Japan . . . ought to know that by her act she is at the same time causing unemployment to share-cropper tenant farmers of cotton in American dixie and to full fashioned hosiery workers in Pennsylvania." Sayre's comments reveal that a shared belief in the widening circle of causation set off by consumption was no guarantee that all would understand the workings of consumption's effects in the same way. The hosiery workers claimed that the boycott would harm American workers far more than it would cripple the Japanese war machine.[15]

Boycott opponents questioned the loyalty, wisdom, and judgment of the boycotters, whom they denounced as "uplifters and left-wingers" seeking an "emotional outlet" heedless of the consequences of their actions. "We level no charges against those who are promoting the Silk boycott," wrote Rieve disingenuously, before proceeding to level the following charge: "We say only that it appears to be directed by persons who either have not given sufficient thought to what they are doing or who are serving purposes not wholesome to American industry, American labor and the broad national economy of the American people." The AFHW also argued that the boycotting women were not up to the task of weighing the impact of non-consumption. Even the women of the AFHW made this sexist argument by adding a class dimension: the upscale boycotters were ignorant of the realities of working-class life. The hosiery workers claimed that these debutantes and dilettantes were, in effect, laying them off through their nonconsumption of silk.[16]

II. Cease to Support Economically What We Condemn Morally

Despite the schism between the LWS and the AFHW over the virtues of the boycott, the clash in the capital on that January afternoon in 1938 involved a surprising set of adversaries. Before the Japanese silk boycott, few observers would have foreseen conflict between these groups, one a prominent champion of labor consumerism and the other a leading proponent of consumerist labor advocacy. Both groups played a central role in reviving the consumer movement and in forging a bond between labor and consumer groups in the 1930s. No union had argued more strongly for the importance of consumerism than the AFHW, whose newspaper, the *Hosiery Worker*, was one of first periodicals of any kind to include regular columns on consumption and on the necessity of practicing politics not only on the shopfloor but at the cash register. Conversely, no consumer organization was more prolabor than the League of Women Shoppers, which described itself as an "auxiliary" of the labor movement. Jessie Lloyd O'Connor, the president of the LWS's Chicago chapter, described the organization as "an outfit formed . . . to bring consumers into understanding and sympathetic action with labor." From its founding in 1935 the league championed living wages for waitresses and domestic workers, organized boycotts of dozens of companies whose policies it determined to be antilabor, and saw its main purpose as championing the growing power of organized labor. Both groups exemplified the emerging alliance between labor and consumer advocates. And both were generally understood to be related components of the broad progressive movement, the so-called Popular Front that was at the cutting edge of social and political activism throughout the New Deal era.[17]

The LWS and the AFHW also shared similar assumptions about the ethical and political importance of consumption. Drawing on a tradition that extended back to the origins of modern consumer activism in the late eighteenth century, they understood consumption to have far-reaching consequences. Consumption was for both, above all, an act of solidarity and a mode of assisting the many people to whom the consumer, in a modern economy, was inextricably linked. Consumer activists had long argued that shoppers created a market for the goods they demanded and, in effect, "hired" the workers who made them. Consumers, thus, had great power and responsibility: power because purchasing transactions were the first cause of economic activity, setting production in motion; responsibility because purchasing decisions directly affected the livelihood of workers, the health of businesses, and even the prosperity of nations. Shoppers, therefore, had the potential to promote morality at the workplace or, conversely, to turn the workplace into the moral equivalent of a sweatshop. The silk boycotters and silk defenders shared the view that irresponsible purchasers did not merely condone exploitation but were in themselves exploiters. Shopping ethically did not merely reflect one's political beliefs but was in itself the performance of ethical politics.

Goods, consumer activists had argued since the American Revolution, had to be understood in a social context. And appearances, they claimed, could fool. Consumer activists posited a metonymy in which products, no matter how superficially appealing, if made under immoral conditions, by immoral employers, or immoral countries, embodied the evil that produced them. For the American Revolutionaries, English tea, no matter how fragrant, carried the bitter taste of oppression. For abolitionist proponents of the "free produce" movement, as we have seen, even the tastiest slave-made sugar was "smeared with the blood of the innocent and the oppressed." The Japanese silk boycotters understood themselves to be maintaining and extending these traditions of consumer politics. While silk stockings might look pretty, they could not be judged so, since the effects of wearing them were anything but lovely: as a proboycott pamphlet declared, "Never has vanity cost so much." The beauty of a good, in other words, could not be determined by an examination of the thing in isolation. The hosiery workers too positioned themselves within this tradition of uncovering the truth about products in social terms. Emil Rieve, the leader of the hosiery workers' union, argued, for example, that many goods advertised as nonsilk, and thus morally pure, alternatives, were manufactured by nonunion employers or, even worse, in fascist Germany, and thus ethically compromised. Such accusations undermined the view that lisle stockings were inherently virtuous. By ignoring the provenance of lisle stockings as well as the status of the workers who made them, Rieve charged, the boycotters violated the premises of ethical consumption they claimed to hold dear.[18]

The ethical commitments of the boycotters led them to condemn the xenophobic "Buy American" movement. Earlier consumer movements had often generated and were even motivated by antiforeign feelings. Organized labor's promotion of the "union label" in the late nineteenth century, for example, often depended on a contrast between "American" workers and dishonored foreigners. Contemporary "Buy American" sentiment of the sort promoted by the Hearst media empire was also highly xenophobic. The silk boycotters wanted to distinguish themselves from these past and present dangers. Almost every antisilk demonstration included signs bearing the slogan, "We bar Japanese goods, not Japanese people." Most boycott groups passed resolutions proclaiming that they were not motivated by nationalistic sentiment or hatred of the Japanese people. R. A. Howell of the American Friends of the Chinese People urged boycotters to avoid the taint of "economic nationalism—one of the essential features of fascism." A pamphlet produced by the American League for Peace and Democracy noted that "there is no reason for the consumers in the United States to hate the Japanese people" and called upon boycotters to avoid the "type of nationalism that fosters a feeling of superiority over other countries." Consumption could no more be ethical if it condoned ethnic hatred than if it fostered exploitative working conditions.[19]

Agreement on the political importance of ethical consumption, thus, did not guarantee consensus on specific actions that followed from this principle. The clash in the capital complicated the seemingly straightforward claim made by one boycott supporter that we should "cease to support economically what we condemn morally." There was agreement on the widened web of causation set off by consumption, but disagreement on how wide and in what direction the concentric circles extended. There was agreement on the importance of ethical consumption, but disagreement about what constituted it. There was agreement that there were no neutral or apolitical shoppers, but disagreement about what the proper form of consumerist engagement should be. There was agreement on the special importance of women in this battle, but disagreement on what role they would play. Agreeing on the importance to the political practice of ethical consumption of fashion, pleasure and sexuality, these groups disagreed on what cause these forces should be promoting.[20]

The boycott, it should be noted, precipitated other schisms. Just as it split the labor movement, the effort to punish Japan divided African Americans. A number of influential leaders, including W. E. B. Du Bois, believing that the Japanese empire was an important bulwark against white supremacy, opposed the boycott. Other African Americans, including Paul Robeson, sided with the boycotters, arguing that Japan's record in China and Korea disqualified it as moral leader of the nonwhite world; others noted that the boycott was endorsed by a variety of nonwhite peoples across the globe. Civic organizations hosted debates about the boycott, and other grassroots African American groups sought to galvanize support through leaflets, nonsilk weddings, and complaints lodged against the racial exclusion practiced by some proboycott groups.[21]

III. We Must Rival the Blood-Stained Productions in Beauty and Durability

The tactics employed by the silk boycotters and their opponents departed from the rhetoric of renunciation that had long been a staple of consumer activism. Dominant traditions of American consumer politics, as we have seen, have been leery of the elements that we commonly associate with consumer society. The nonimportation movement of the Revolutionary era, a founding event in the history of American consumer activism, for example, promoted homespun clothing both as a means to economically harm British enemies and as a way to promote simplicity. Pitting American simplicity and virtue against British fashion and corruption, the Revolutionary boycotters understood eschewing luxury as itself a statement of patriotic principles. Similarly, as we have seen, most of the antebellum advocates of free produce, boycotters of slave-made goods, defined pleasure and virtue as opposites. They proudly trumpeted their "self-denying practice" and invoked abstinence as the highest value. Many other boycott campaigns have traded on the rhetoric and practice of virtuous sacrifice. Important consumer organizations of the twentieth century, from the National Consumers League (NCL) in the Progressive Era, to Consumers' Research (CR, founded in 1929) and Consumers Union (CU, founded in 1936), to the best-selling books of Vance Packard in the 1950s, through groups associated with Ralph Nader since the 1960s have generally distrusted adornment as well. The popular (and apt) depiction of Nader as an ascetic rather than an aesthete may also be applied to earlier consumer activists, whose perspective tended toward a utilitarian suspicion of fashion.[22]

American consumer politics is not unique in this regard. Nineteenth-century British socialists, according to Noel Thompson, displayed an "uneasiness with consumption" and believed that "human liberation lay in no small measure in the simplification of desire." In Revolutionary France, sansculottes, whose very name indicated a pride in abjuring the fashions of the wealthy, promoted a "right to subsistence" but attacked a broadly defined notion of luxury as inherently counter-Revolutionary. As the historian Warren Breckman has shown, late nineteenth- and early twentieth-century German intellectuals attempted to "discipline consumption," as they sought to distinguish between productive (utilitarian) and unproductive (luxurious) acts of consumption. The Swadeshi movement in India and the National Products movement in China condemned goods of foreign provenance, in part by defining them as unnecessary, unpatriotic, and unvirtuous luxuries. None of these groups rejected increased consumption out of hand; indeed, they generally championed a higher standard of living for ordinary people. Still, in practice and in rhetoric they emphasized the dangers rather than the pleasures of consumption. Increased consumption may have been the goal, but discipline and deferral was the daily practice.[23]

This vision of consumption as a moral and political danger, while dominant, did not go unchallenged. Before the silk boycott, a countertradition, especially popular among subaltern groups, had emerged that used consumption as a resource for political engagement. African American resistance to Jim Crow, both organized and quotidian, often linked fashion and consumption to political claims. Successful black families in the urban post-Reconstruction South, according to Glenda Gilmore, "lived a deliberately conspicuous life." In proudly displaying fine table settings and luxurious wardrobes, they challenged white stereotypes about how blacks "by nature" lived. For working-class African Americans, conspicuous fashions and the display of familiarity and comfort with consumer culture served as an expression of the dignity that whites sought to deny them. From the lynching of "uppity" blacks, who had the temerity to challenge their degraded status through the display of acquisitions, to the zoot suit riots, to the Woolworth lunch counters, white supremacists often reacted with violence to such public displays of consumption.[24]

A second and roughly coterminous set of efforts to link consumption positively with politics came with the attempt of a group of working-class Americans to embed labor ideology, and even labor radicalism, in the emerging consumer culture. Through demands for an eight-hour workday, "living wages," and an "American standard of living" labor leaders and organizations sought to republicanize consumer society. For working-class women, according to Nan Enstad, the search for pleasure in popular culture—through developing distinct fashions, reading dime novels, attending movies—did not detract from their politics. Rather, these forms of consumer culture enabled them to "imagine recognition and value as workers" and as women and made possible solidarity and resistance. Similarly, women's suffrage advocates attempted to "sell suffrage" to the American people by using the developing techniques of advertising and marketing on behalf of their cause. The New York City Political Equality League, for example, asked its department of hygiene to sponsor a "suffrage temple of beauty."[25]

Until the Japanese silk boycott, however, such positive visions of fashion remained a distinctly minority view within consumer activism. For most activists, alternative consumption generally meant abstention or the purchase of ugly or uncomfortable goods, which they took to be a synecdoche for the moral worth of the cause. Adornment itself troubled the pioneering generation, as it continued to bother later consumer activists, such as the NCL members who, in the words of Josephine Goldmark, demonstrated "a considerable sense of virtue" when they endured the discomfort of "the voluminous nightgowns, chemises, and other underwear of the period made of heavy, often coarse, white cotton" that bore the league's "white label" of approval. The silk boycotters break with the antifashion tradition was particularly significant in the 1930s when the consumer movement was large and respected but still widely depicted as puritanical, humorless, and unalterably opposed to frills. As we saw in chapter 6, a cottage industry of cartoons and articles mocked the fussiness and reflexively antifashion sentiments of movement participants. The critics exaggerated only slightly: the movement sought to convince the American consumer that pleasure and fashion were as unnecessary as wasteful packaging and as nefarious as advertising and other forms of corporate manipulation. This strand of consumer activism saw consumer society—or at least its dominant characteristics—as the enemy. The silk boycotters, by contrast, made fashion central to their cause; indeed, given the performative logic they promoted, it is not too much to say that fashion was their cause.[26]

IV. Put Silk in the Doghouse

Activists on both sides of the boycott issue were well aware that they were living in an era of shifting erogenous zones. "Legs have emerged after a century of shrouding" noted the fashion commentator J. C. Flugel in 1930. As interest "has departed from the trunk and is centered on the limbs," he wrote, "ankles, calves, and knees" had become women's "chief erotic weapons." In trading on the interest in their legs, and in using them as erotic weapons in the boycott cause, the pageanteers and marchers were mimicking (or perhaps were copied by) the femmes fatales of contemporary film who, as Stella Bruzzi notes, were characterized by their legs and by their attempt to attract male attention through their limbs. James Laver, the fashion historian, noted in 1938 that the "the makers of silk stockings were enjoying a boom" based upon "the newly-discovered seductiveness of the feminine leg" (fig. 7.6). Cole Porter captured this "new erotic aesthetic" in his 1934 song "Anything Goes": "In olden days a glimpse of stocking / Was looked on as something shocking / But now, God knows / Anything goes." The AFHW illustrated this aesthetic in a cartoon entitled "Looking for the Label" that appeared in its newspaper in 1939. The cartoon depicts a group of men staring lasciviously at the legs of a department store mannequin (fig. 7.7). The fact that the male gaze was drawn to the female leg, the cartoonist seemed to be suggesting, provided a good opportunity to highlight union-label hosiery. Another AFHW cartoon highlighted the allure of union-label hosiery by showing that "Peggy O'Connor," who wears such stockings, "has many guys" (fig. 7.8). The boycotters also sought to use this

THE TENNIS COSTUME. £1 5s. 6d.
In Plain or Checked French Foulé, Cashmere Cloth, or Foulés, with Silk Lace, in bright colours, or to match, including 4 yards for Bodice.

TENNIS COSTUMES

Figure 7.6. An illustration of the ascending hemline from the 1880s through the 1930s. (James Laver, *Taste and Fashion: From the French Revolution Until Today* [New York: Dodd, Mead & Co., 1938], 224.)

Figure 7.7. A crowd of men eagerly examine a mannequin's limb for evidence of union labels. (*Hosiery Worker*, May 5, 1939, 1.)

Figure 7.8. Wearing union label hosiery was a key to popularity, according to this cartoon. (*Hosiery Worker*, Feb 9, 1940, 3.)

newfound fascination with the female leg for political gain; witness their showcasing of Eleanor Powell's famous limbs and thousands of less well-known leg barers.[27] (See fig. 7.9.)

Legs were also central to *Big Boycott of 1938*, a play (probably never performed) printed in a quarterly anthology of sketches and published by the China Aid Society, with the assistance of the American League for Peace and Democracy.[28] Indeed, the prologue was a tribute in verse to the leg, of which the authors declared it "would be a shame" to "see this lovely thing by clothes oppressed." Although there was nothing wrong with the leg "definitely nude," declared the playwrights, those who wanted it covered should be wary, since "legs, please note, are sometimes silk-encased / And silk is made in blood-bedecked Japan." The verse then shifted its focus from leg barers to leg watchers:

> Dear Audience, the opry now begins
> Your open-mouthed attention we must beg.
> If nothing else your approbation wins,
> at least you've seen a gosh-darned pretty leg.

Like much of the antisilk campaign, here was an attempt to incorporate the male gaze into the boycott movement. But female agency was not neglected either. Later in the play a salesgirl notes that "silk is out" and proclaims that "no sheer silken brassiere will shame my name." Other plays by boycott advocates had similar themes. The proboycott play *Maid in Japan* was performed in 1939, although "it dropped quickly from sight," according to the theater historian Malcolm Goldstein. Even John Cambridge of the *Daily Worker* at the height of popular culture's embrace of radical theater regretfully conceded that in spite of "its excellent theme, the need for boycotting Japanese goods," the play was weakened by "very elementary humor" and "somewhat undistinguished lyrics."[29]

Women had long been central to the American tradition of consumer activism, but the emergence of the leg-oriented aesthetic gave their actions a new visibility and resonance. With fashion widely understood as an instrument of foreign policy, antisilk boycotters assigned women power in the traditionally male arena of diplomacy. As Bryon Scott, a Democratic congressmen from California, put it, "The possibility of checking aggression rests very largely on the style consciousness of American women." Lee Simonson, the director of "Life without Silk," agreed when he said in a comment echoed by many other boycott supporters that through their nonsilk fashions, "American women must strike the first effective blow against Japanese aggression." From the opposing side, the hosiery workers' newspaper accused the boycotters of excessive "zeal and thoughtlessness" for

Figure 7.9. These Seattle women, like many other ordinary Americans, joined Eleanor Powell and other celebrities as nonsilk fashion models. (*Washington Commonwealth Federation, Sunday News*, Oct 16, 1937, 1.)

mistakenly putting foreign considerations ahead of domestic ones in their fashion choices. As the union member Lillian Shearer said, "I should like to ask them to think carefully about how they toss around the jobs which mean life to so many of us." Notwithstanding her union's own media-savvy behavior—indeed, Shearer made these comments during her radio address—she urged American "not to be misled by stunt pictures and press agent stories" of barelegged coeds or celebrities in lisle.[30]

Both the pro- and antisilk forces understood the importance of spectacle and sought to make their campaigns visually pleasing, and occasionally even titillating, to viewers. An observer of a nonsilk parade put on by the Women's Senate at Saint Olaf College noted that "lisle stockings got the 'once-over' [as the audience] eagerly craned their necks to cast critical eyes on the legs of exhibitors."[31] The organizers of a parade in Harlem, which doubled as a fundraiser for summer camp, offered prizes to paraders (both children and "stylish grown ups") and clothing designers.[32] But to promote the spectacular was not to reduce women to objectified bodies. Boycotters believed that they were, above all, political actors, drawing upon previously unclaimed resources within consumer society. They invoked sexuality, spectacle, fashion, and pleasure as political forces and rejected the usual opposition between these, on the one hand, and virtue, on the other. "We are boycotting silk, not fashion," as one antisilk group claimed. Rather than demanding sacrifice from American women, the boycotters encouraged women to engage in a simultaneously playful and serious process of creative refashioning. Stressing the importance of "making it a fashion to wear cotton, wool, or rayon clothes," they emphasized the congruence between ethics and aesthetics. Urging women to "Put Silk in the Doghouse," Leonard Sparks and Mississippi Johnson called on "women of means, working women, housewives, students, and professional people" to "start boycotting fashions which will not only keep the figurative blood and bones of Chinese babies from around their legs, but which will give them pleasure and artistic satisfaction." This was perhaps the first event in the history of consumer activism which placed "pleasure" and "artistic satisfaction" on a par with virtue, in part because, unlike some earlier boycotts, the emphasis was not on doing without but on finding pleasurable means to outdo silk fashions. This effort was political not just because women dared to demand pleasure but also because they recognized it as having both individual and social components.[33]

The recognition that silk was no ordinary fabric drove the effort to make cotton and other alternatives fashionable. Silk, all acknowledged, was a key element in women's fashion, especially in the form of stockings. A leaflet produced by the hosiery workers shortly before the boycott began declared, "Full fashion hosiery has come to be the symbol of modern women's charm." Boycotters thus had to confront and subvert the centrality of silk. Relegating this fabric to the "doghouse," as the *New Masses* urged, would be no simple matter. In the face of the difficulty of this task, boycotters portrayed their actions as benefiting both American and foreign workers and their movement as one of refashioning. As one boycott supporter said, "If enough women endure the temporary discomfort of lisle and rayon, the hosiery manufacturers will be forced to market the better substitutes which are known to exist." Boycotters described nonsilk alternatives as fun, sexy, and on fashion's cutting edge and attempted to enact these qualities in their own clothing choices to prove them so. The boycott movement sought to convince American women—who, it was said, purchased 85 percent of Japanese silk sold in the United States—not only that the cause was worthy but that eschewing silk did not mean abandoning fashion. Although they emphasized comfort and durability—as Margaret Wister Meigs wrote in a letter to the *New York Times*, "Lisle stockings are really very comfortable and one pair of nylon stockings seems to last a lifetime"—they also sought to create alternatives so stylish that, as one supporter wrote hopefully, after observing a nonsilk parade, "one would think that lisle stockings were the latest fashion decree." An LWS official said, "Women can find enough pretty things to wear without buying the products of Japan," suggesting that the quest for "pretty things" was not to be slighted as it had often been in previous consumer campaigns.[34]

Antisilk protests took a variety of forms, but almost all of them sought, in the spirit of the LWS pageant, to be fun and stylish. The first such event that gained national attention took place at Vassar College in Poughkeepsie, New York, on December 30, 1937, at the Third Annual Meeting of the American Student Union (ASU), a left-wing student organization.[35] Immediately after the delegates unanimously passed a resolution calling for a boycott of Japanese goods, Lloyd James, a student from the University of Chicago, decided that it was time for the group to take matters into their own hands. "Let's do it right now," he shouted. "Let's take off every bit of Japanese silk we have on and toss it in a big bonfire." Without waiting for a formal vote, a fire was lit and delegates came streaming outside onto the snow-covered campus of Vassar College, tossing their silk garments into the conflagration. Chanting "Make lisle the style," "Wear lisle for a while" and other slogans coined on the spot (including the less mellifluous, "If you wear cotton, Japan gets nottin'"), the men stripped off their silk shirts and neckties, and the women took off their silk stockings as well as what the *New York Times* described as "a few more intimate garments." Fully aware of the media presence, the delegates obligingly posed, dancing and singing around the silk-fed fire, as photographers snapped pictures of shirtless men and hoseless women that appeared in *Time*, *Life*, and other national journals of news and opinion.[36] (See fig. 7.10.)

Throughout 1938 and 1939, boycotters initiated hundreds of events in the spirit of the ASU bonfire. There was, for example, a silk-free "antifascist food and style show" in Seattle, an Anti Silk Fashion Parade in the Bronx; a Shun-the-Silkworm-Even-in-the-Larva-Stage Fling in Manhattan, organized pickets at the Japanese consulate and the Japanese bazaars in the Chinatown neighborhood of San Francisco, and a Cotton Ball featuring the dresses of Elizabeth Hawes and other well-known designers in New York City's Hotel Pennsylvania. A Boycott Japan event at the jam-packed Shrine Auditorium (capacity six thousand) in Hollywood, planned by Melvyn Douglas, Dashiell Hammett, and Dorothy Parker, among others, was highlighted by a "strip tease of silk stockings and silk undergarments disdainfully discarded and dropped into a red, white, and blue waste-paper basket." Students at New York University staged a dance at

LIFE ON THE AMERICAN NEWSFRONT: STUDENTS BURN CLOTHES TO SPUR SILK BOYCOTT

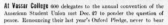
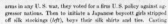

At Vassar College 600 delegates to the annual convention of the American Student Union met Dec. 27 to ponder the question of peace. Renouncing their last year's Oxford Pledge, never to bear arms in any U. S. war, they voted for a firm U.S. policy against aggressor nations. Then to initiate a Japanese boycott girls stripped off silk stockings (*left*), boys their silk shirts and ties. Casting them into a bonfire (*right*), they chanted: "Make lisle the style. Wear lisle a while. If you wear cotton, Japan gets nottin!"

Figure 7.10. Members of the American Student Union "make lisle the style." (*Life*, Jan 10, 1938, 18. Photograph on right: AP/Wide World Photos.)

which lisle hosiery was a "condition of admission." At least one couple organized an "antisilk wedding." Leading actresses on Broadway, including Frances Farmer, the star of Clifford Odets's play *Golden Boy*, and the entire cast of *The Women* let it be known in the playbill that they performed in lisle hose. In staging silk-free parades, beauty pageants, Hollywood extravaganzas, and bonfires and engaging in similar theatrical gestures, boycott groups emphasized that social responsibility could be not only fashion conscious but also trend setting. For these boycotters consumer society was not an obstacle to be overcome but an essential resource to help popularize their movement. As Sparks and Johnson urged in calling for bold nonsilk alternatives, "Inconspicuous substitutes won't do it. Something dramatic will." Calling attention to fashion and the body would not detract from the moral seriousness of the cause, they claimed. Indeed, such conspicuous consuming gestures were precisely what was necessary for the movement to succeed. These antisilk events all shared a similar spirit and focus: they aimed to merge political engagement with consumerist pleasure.[37]

By proclaiming alternative fabrics and even bare-leggedness fashionable, the show's organizers sought to dislodge silk stockings as the gold standard of style. As the *Washington Post* observed, "It would seem that the average American woman feels self-conscious if she is not wearing silk stockings. The boycott movement will not be economically important unless and until she becomes self-conscious about wearing silk."[38] In this context, fashion was no mere expression of personal taste but inescapably political in four related senses. First, what one wore became an emblem of political beliefs. For boycotters going silkless (or wearing lisle) was what Lucy Wyle called "an identification mark," a symbol of support for the cause.[39] But fashion was more than a mere statement of one's political beliefs. It was also a profoundly political activity itself. This was well illustrated by the parades, pageants, stripteases, and other events associated with this cause. According to the logic of consumer causality, wearing particular kinds of clothing had real-world effects; clothing was, thus, both symbol and action. Third, the boycotters worked to change concepts of the fashionable, from below (by grassroots activists) and from above (by department stores and designers, such as boycott supporter Elizabeth Hawes).[40] Finally, boycotters produced a politics of celebrity and spectacle that was not shallow, egotistical, or conservative. Every time that "society leaders, stars of stage and screen," such as Eleanor Powell, Sylvia Sydney, Frances Farmer, Loretta Young, or Rita Hayworth, proclaimed through word and deed that "lisle is the style," they helped publicize the movement far beyond the abilities of ordinary citizens (fig. 7.11). Similarly, Joseph Lash, an ASU member, noted many years after the event that "if you were trying to attract attention to a political position" you could do worse than to start a bonfire "in which all the girls threw their silk panties." The silk boycotters did not apologize for the spectacles they created or for seeking the endorsement of celebrities but understood these practices as central to their efforts. They saw no contradiction in using the techniques of advertising—sexuality, the photo opportunity, and the celebrity endorsement being among its prime components—in the service of the boycott.[41]

A positive view of fashion and pleasure also formed the basis for the antiboycott arguments of the AFHW.[42] The hosiery worker's union had long argued for a form of ethical consumption that legitimized the desire for pleasure on the part of the consumer while encouraging shoppers to ensure that workers were not mistreated in the process of producing such instruments of pleasure; as the title of one of its pamphlets proclaimed, *Loveliness Based on Human Misery Is Indeed Coarse*. To be truly fashionable, the union argued, clothing had to be produced in accord with standards of decency. Silk hose made by well-paid, unionized American women workers, the union argued, met these standards: "Union made full-fashioned hosiery is the symbol of the modern women's intelligent interest in the economic conditions that shape and mold her life with the same effectiveness that full-fashioned hosiery shapes and molds beauty onto her limbs." For the hosiery workers, as for their boycotting opponents, moral consumption served to harmonize aesthetics and politics. Boycott opponents, however, dismissed as quixotic efforts to change fashions as quickly and as fundamentally as the silk boycotters proposed. There was, they believed,

Figure 7.11. Rita Hayworth models a lamé evening dress and evening hose made of "fine crepe lisle." (Farm Security Administration photograph. Library of Congress. LC-USE6-D-001614.)

simply no acceptable substitute for silk. Despite the boycotters' promotion of native American fashions, lisle, and rayon, their opponents argued that American women were not prepared to accept what Lillian Shearer called "primitive" substitutes for silk stockings, to make what J. B. Matthews, a former consumer activist turned critic, called "the great sacrifice of feminine attractiveness involved in changing from silk."[43]

When not challenging the political judgment and fashion sense of the boycotters, opponents charged that the movement's reliance on publicity-generating activities and its use of sensuous imagery undermined the cause. Matthews, in a typical dismissive riff, noted that one boycott advocate "has proposed that some well-known actress make the 'dramatic gesture' of removing her gossamer hosiery in public, crying 'No more silk stockings for me while the Japanese troops remain in China.' Why stop with silk stockings? This suggestion has interesting possibilities (which the Minsky Brothers may have overlooked) of restoring the banned striptease to the burlesque of Broadway. The act might have little 'pushing' power in ridding Chinese soil of Japanese troops, but it would have great 'pulling' power at the burlesque box offices. Furthermore, the consumer movement, as communists conceive it, would experience a lot of activizing."[44] Such charges, of course, could also have been made against the hosiery workers, who initiated their antiboycott campaign with a media-friendly, leg-baring parade down Constitution Avenue.

In highlighting the centrality of women and of pleasure, and in linking fashion to politics, the antisilk boycott and the counterprotest it generated marked a distinctive moment in consumer activism. What made the Japanese silk boycott modern is that it took place *in* consumer society and was also *of* consumer society. Before the silk boycott, the consumer movement had been for the most part antagonistic to mass culture and was comfortable with consumer society only to the extent to which it produced low-cost, high-quality goods. By promoting engagement in consumer society, silk boycotters found in mass culture what previous activists had seen primarily in renunciation, the basis for a moral consumerism.[45]

Departing from the proudly minoritarian spirit of previous consumer movements, in part by resurrecting and embellishing a recessive strain of the consumer movement dating to the free produce movement that sought to reconcile beauty and morality, the silk boycott sought through its emphasis on the body, fashion, and fun not just to align itself with but to *become* popular culture. Drawing on the spirit of the new youth culture, on the popularity in the 1930s of stunts, such as "dance marathons, roller derbies . . . goldfish eating contests,"and on the culture of celebrity, the Japanese boycott movement embedded itself, for the first time in the history of the consumer movement, in the idiom of popular culture. This effort not only broke with the view of previous and future generations of consumer activists, it also challenged a position that continues to be espoused by influential scholars of consumption. Consumers, the sociologist Zygmunt Bauman has written, are "guided by aesthetic interests, not ethical norms." By placing aesthetics in the service of virtue, silk boycotters challenged such a dichotomy.[46]

If those involved in the silk boycott distinguished themselves from earlier activists by invoking pleasure rather than sacrifice, they nevertheless borrowed the philosophy of earlier boycotters. Rather than privatized consumption, the defining characteristic of the consumer society's promoters in business and advertising, the silk boycotters followed their predecessors in promulgating a public-oriented and politicized vision in which pleasure was closely tied to the social consequences of shopping. In the spirit of earlier modes of consumer activism, they claimed that an article of clothing, no matter how stylish, could not be defined as fashionable or pleasurable if those who made or sold it suffered. The surface aesthetics of a product had to accord with fair conditions of labor for it to qualify as truly beautiful. Similarly, pleasure could only be enjoyed in the absence of exploitation. Participants in the silk campaign sought through their consuming practices to promote a harmony between the beauty of a good and the ways in which it was made. As socially situated characteristics, neither beauty nor fashion could be understood in terms of the thing in itself; nor could pleasure be understood as an experience abstracted from its social context. These advocates of fashionable politics posited that the purchase of a good had an impact on the producers and distributors of the product. Ever mindful of the importance of spectatorship in a consumer society, they believed it also had an impact on the audience that would observe the use of that product.

This understanding of pleasure, defined in explicitly political terms, should be distinguished from the kinds of privatized pleasures sometimes celebrated by academic defenders of consumer society. James B. Twitchell's otherwise thoughtful analysis of consumption, for example, leaves unresolved the disjuncture between the private pleasures offered by consumer society and their social costs. In a discussion of the liberating role of consumption, Twitchell defends his purchase of a red Mazda Miata in purely personal terms before segueing guiltily into a recognition of the environmental and political problems caused by such forms of consumption. Similarly, this merger of pleasure and politics differs from the tendency of some cultural studies scholars to stress the subversive ways in which commodities have been used, but to do so in individualist terms, isolating both the user and the commodity from the social and political world of which, consumer activists claimed, they were inextricably a part.[47]

There is also a crucial distinction between situating a political movement within consumer culture, as the silk boycotters did, and being subsumed by that culture. Too often scholars take a social movement's use of consumerist language or techniques to be proof of co-optation. The silk boycott offers a different dynamic from that identified by Thomas Frank, for example, in which countercultural movements lose their bite as their message is muted, sanitized, or transformed by business and advertisers. Silk boycotters asked a largely isolationist America to embrace a campaign to improve the lives of a faraway people (and, many believed, at some cost to American workers) and ingeniously promoted it as fun, fashionable, and, above all, moral. They did so without compromising their ethical message; indeed, their message was inseparable from the popular media through which it was disseminated. Consumer society can distort or destroy grassroots political efforts, but the silk boycotters and their opponents demonstrate that it can also be a resource for a range of political practices.[48]

V. The Aftermath of the Boycott

The Japanese silk boycott marked a brief high point in the merger between consumer politics and consumer society. As war preparations intensified, government policy gradually replaced the "people's boycott," which, notwithstanding its popularity and effectiveness in curtailing key Japanese exports, could not stop the sale of war materiel, especially scrap metals and oil, to the Japanese. In 1940, Washington allowed the 1911 Treaty of Trade and Navigation to expire. As war approached, the United States imposed an embargo on Japanese goods and stopped almost all strategic goods from being exported. With these actions, the raison d'être for the boycott, which began as an alternative to government action, disappeared.[49] Another factor in the eclipse of the silk boycott was technological. The development in late 1938 of nylon, the "artificial silkworm," by the Du Pont corporation opened up what Roosevelt's aide Harold L. Ickes called "vast and interesting economic possibilities." According to the announcement made at the *New York Herald Tribune's* World of Tomorrow Forum at the World's Fair preview in 1939, stockings of the future would be "fashioned by chemists," thereby "ushering in the death blow to the oriental silk trade and likely to cause more strategic damage than would the sinking of Emperor Hirohito's navy." It was rumored that Du Pont's term Nylon was an acronym for "Now You Lousy Old Nipponese." One commentator predicted that "it won't be so difficult to popularize a boycott of Japanese silk when women can obtain stockings from the Du Pont's mechanical silkworm that are not only equally attractive but wear longer." Nylon stockings first became available to the public in May 1940, and although they were widely used only after the war, the celebration of "artificial silk" led many to conclude that the days of silk's hegemony had passed. If nylon would lead, as Ickes predicted, to "the cutting of all silk imports from Japan to the United States," a boycott was no longer necessary.[50]

But technological developments and government action tell only part of the story. Just as important was an ideological shift during the war, when many elements of the consumer movement deemphasized fashion and reverted to a stress on thrift. Jessie Lloyd O'Connor and other LWS leaders, reversing the arguments they had made during the boycott, sought to convince the public that "buying power is too great instead of too small." As the consumer advocate Caroline Ware wrote in her 1942 book *The Consumer Goes to War*, "Every purchase we make is a claim on our nation's resources. Every article we use is part of the nation's precious supplies." Ware deemed the logic of consumer society, a resource to the movement of the Depression decade, a detriment in the wartime climate of conservation. Continuing to hold that "Women do 85% of the Buying," the LWS declared that "Buying Power in War-Time is a Grave Responsibility" and urged women to discharge that responsibility by "supporting the Consumers Division of Office of Price Administration," the organization responsible for wartime rationing. By 1942, the act of donning or rejecting silk stockings became moot, as the embargo made them unavailable. In this context, the connection between conspicuous consumption and morality that had been posited by proponents and opponents of the boycott ceased to be a compelling social force. Throughout the war years, sacrifice was valorized in rhetoric, if not always in practice, and became, once again, a key element of political discourse.[51]

Despite the chastened wartime message of many consumer activists, the quest for a politics that was both pleasurable and ethical continued during the war. As Robert Westbrook has demonstrated in his ingenious analysis of the wartime cult of the "pin-up," rather than defining their military or civilian service as sacrificial, many Americans understood themselves, and their comrades, to be fighting for erotic, if domesticated, pleasures. Another mark of continuity was the emphasis in these pin-ups on the female leg. Betty Grable, whose limbs supplanted Eleanor Powell's as the most famous in Hollywood, became, like Powell, a bodily symbol of righteous pleasure (fig. 7.12). In an ironic echo of the silk boycott, newspapers ran photos of young women, "Taking 'em off for Uncle Sam," discarding their nylon or rayon stockings so that they could be recycled into war materiel.[52]

Somewhat surprisingly, Consumers Union, the prototypical utilitarian consumer organization of the 1930s, embraced the quest for pleasure even during the war, an ideological transformation that can be dated to its support of the cause of nonsilk fashions during the Japanese silk boycott.

Figure 7.12. "Betty Grable's Legs." (*Life*, Jun 7, 1943, 82. Copyright Life Inc. Reprinted with permission. All rights reserved.)

Consumer Reports devoted many articles to the search for fashionable alternatives to silk—including, during the depths of the war, leg paint (so-called stockings in a bottle), lisle, and the chemical compounds rayon and nylon. In the postwar years, Consumers Union—by far the largest branch of the consumer movement, with a membership of about half a million by the mid-1950s—did not revert to the suspicion of fashion and pleasure that had characterized its early years. In its critique of the postwar fashion trend of the "New Look," for example, its members did not condemn fashion outright, but rather denounced this style as immoral (because it used too much material in a time of scarcity) and ugly (in part because it ignored the pleasures, for the wearer and the admirer, of "a well-turned calf, a twinkling knee"). The journalist Leslie Velie, reporting from San Francisco, noted that consumers "in their new-found strength have even taken on fashion dictators. Dissatisfied with the postwar elongated skirt, they are resolutely keeping skirt buying down to keep skirt lengths up." As we will see in chapter 8, the *Reports* joined product tests with a host of fashion and pleasure-oriented materials in these years. By putting these issues side by side, Consumers Union suggested, like their pleasure-seeking predecessors, that the good society consisted not merely of efficient consumers but of pleasure-seeking consumers, and that such a society could value both social justice and fashionable, well-made clothing, both efficient products and beautiful objects.[53]

In the postwar years, then, some consumer activists, evoking the silk boycotters, continued to promote a socially oriented, pleasure-centered consumerism. Other branches of the consumer movement, as Lizabeth Cohen has documented, maintained an asceticism that was increasingly "out of step" with the zeitgeist of the postwar years. Furthermore, their increasing emphasis on individual consumer satisfaction, rather than social justice, was perfectly consistent with the advocates of what Cohen calls "the Consumers' Republic," who proclaimed privatized consumption to be a patriotic duty. Even when Ralph Nader helped spark a revival of the consumer movement in the 1960s, the asceticism remained; Nader and his followers condemned adornment as a ploy of big business. While the number of boycotts accelerated in the last quarter of the twentieth century, these actions, most notably the lengthy grape boycott organized by the United Farm Workers, were generally promoted under the rubric of virtuous sacrifice. (It is an irony of the postwar years that the pleasure-centered agenda, rejected by a significant branch of American progressives, was adopted by German enemies-turned-allies and that its symbol was nylon. Erica Carter writes of the "glamour of the American nylon" in 1950s West Germany and notes that "the stocking became a dominant signifier of freedom, democracy, and the American way of life.")[54]

The continuing tension between consumption and sacrifice appeared, most recently, in the disappointed reaction of many pundits to the suggestion by President George W. Bush and other politicians that shopping was an important way to exercise citizenship in the wake of the September 2001 terrorist attacks on the United States. These commentators found something untoward about the link between consumption and patriotism proposed by Bush (who encouraged Americans to "buy, buy, buy"), New York Mayor Rudy Giuliani (who urged them to "spend, spend, spend"), Miami Mayor Alex Panelas (who claimed "it has never been more patriotic to go shopping"), and other political leaders, especially in contrast to the sacrifices made by the World War II generation. "The Greatest generation got to save old tires, dig a victory garden, forego sugar," wrote Margaret Carlson of *Time* magazine. "The Richest Generation is being asked to shop. . . . Buying becomes our patriotic duty." John de Graaf, the maker of the popular public television series *Affluenza*, similarly expressed disappointment with the contrast between the Good Fight and the War on Terror. "In World War II, we came together through sacrifice, victory gardens, collecting scrap metal. Now we're told the way to be unified is to shop like there's no tomorrow." "Sacrifice is out. Self-indulgence is in," wrote Marie Coco of *Newsday*. "Our mothers had to give up their silk stockings. We're being asked to make a national trip to the shopping mall." Americans, as Thomas Friedman wrote, "would like to be summoned by the president to do something more than shopping."[55]

In recent years, there have been hints of a revival of a politics of virtuous pleasure. Although generally promoting products as moral rather than fashionable, and defining the two as antithetical, some branches of the antisweatshop movement have begun to market apparel as, without contradiction, "sweat free"and "stylish." The "fair trade" movement, for example, not only warns citizens about the social and environmental costs of corporate coffee, it also offers gourmet alternatives. Proponents claim that "pleasure is at the very heart" of the "slow food" movement. Similarly, some advocates of voluntary simplicity, rejecting the sufficiency of the idea that the goal should be sacrifice, have identified the quest for pleasure as politically productive and morally legitimate. These contemporary efforts to join consumer culture with political engagement recall the Japanese silk boycotters who claimed consumerist pleasures as social and moral, rather than as personal and amoral. These efforts to forge a fashionable politics provides an important counterexample and corrective to the widespread view of consumer culture as inherently incompatible with political engagement.[56]

In a profile of the controversial activist Michael Moore, Larissa MacFarquar has argued that one reason why progressives "lost the mainstream in the eighties" was their habit of "pious, ascetic griping." Moore, she writes, "wants to bring back to the left a sense that pleasure is O.K., that self-indulgence isn't always evil." Consumer activists, as we have seen, contributed in no small measure to this association of virtue with asceticism. In the Japanese silk boycott, however, they contributed another less widely heeded model—what we might call virtuous aestheticism. The activities of silk boycotters and their opponents demonstrate that consuming pleasures need not only be exploitative, nor fashion purely selfish, and that responsible consumption should not automatically be equated with self-denial. The boycotters' attempt to "make lisle the style" and the hosiery workers' counterefforts to encourage consumers to "wear silk and save our jobs" demonstrate that consumer activists can profitably combine aesthetics and ethics, while their differences warn us against assuming that this relationship necessarily produces predictable political outcomes.[57]

PART III

ADVOCATES AND ACTIVISTS

CONSUMER ACTIVISM SINCE WORLD WAR II

PUTTING THE POSTWAR "CONSUMER MOVEMENT" IN ITS PLACE

In November, 1946, little more than a year after the end of World War II, the journalist Carlisle Bergeron assessed the state of consumer activism for the *Nation's Business*, the official publication of the United States Chamber of Commerce. The chamber was no fan of the consumer movement, and Bergeron found cause for concern on many fronts. He began by noting that the radically new economic context—characterized by affluence rather than deprivation—could lead to "bafflement" for shoppers, who had grown accustomed to austerity during the previous decade and a half of depression and war. Now "with his heart filled with yearning and his pocket with dollars after five years of goods famine," the consumer—finally able to exercise pent-up demand—might make misguided decisions in the marketplace. But Bergeron also observed that "many champions were springing to [the consumer's] defense." Among these champions, he singled out the Congress of Industrial Organizations (CIO), "whose pickets have enlivened the shopping district of cities with placards urging consumers to strike against high prices." In addition, he alerted the country's business leaders that "what is loosely called the 'consumer movement' stirs again against a war-imposed somnambulance," noting that both Consumers' Research (CR) and Consumers Union (CU) were enjoying a "revival of interest." Although this movement continued to guide consumers in their "traditional" mission of "wise spending," he recognized that CU had also "been devoted to organized consumer buying strikes." He described Colston Warne, CU's president, as "an advanced New Dealer" and noted that other leaders had been labeled communists and fellow travelers. CU, Bergeron claimed, was leading the campaign for "federal health insurance" by lobbying in Washington and encouraging members to write to their representatives. He informed those business leaders who thought that the consumer movement's best days were behind it that CU's membership stood at an all-time peak of 140,000 and that its publications, *Consumer Reports* and *Bread and Butter*, reported not only on product testing and political news but also were adding new sections on personal health and popular culture. If business leaders thought the wartime respite from boycotts and consumer lobbying would continue into the postwar era, Bergeron warned, they were gravely mistaken. Economic and political elites were, he argued, better off recognizing the growing power and changing tactics of the reborn consumer movement, postwar version, which was establishing its bona fides on four fronts: product testing, boycotts, consumer protection, and seeking to serve as a guide to popular culture.[1]

If in the postwar years the consumer movement never became the singularly powerful force that Bergeron envisioned, it maintained a far more prominent place in American life in the fifteen years following the end of the war than is generally recognized. And it did so, as Bergeron noted, by using both traditional and novel tactics. Historians have acknowledged the significance of the consumer movement in the immediate postwar years, but they assume that these gains were soon halted and reversed. In this view, consumer activism, which was at a high point in the Depression decade, turned conservative in the post–World War II years, weakened by the exigencies of war and made irrelevant by the affluence that followed. As we have seen, during the 1930s, consumer activism—in the form of boycotts, "Don't buy where you can't work campaigns," educational organizations, testing organizations, cooperatives, and grassroots groups—flourished. By the early 1950s, however, the consumer movement was no longer in the headlines, many grassroots organizations no longer existed, and boycotts were much less prominent. The movement lost so much prominence that when Ralph Nader reignited consumerist politics in the 1960s, many commentators treated the movement as unprecedented. Commentators have often wondered what happened to the consumer movement in these years.

Instead of asking what happened or why the movement declined, which exhibits what David Hackett Fischer has called the "fallacy of the declarative question," it is better to put the postwar consumer movement in its place, by which I mean at least four different things.[2] This chapter puts the consumer movement in its place *contemporaneously*, that is, it situates the consumer movement among other forms of consumer activism of the 1940s and 1950s. It also puts the consumer movement in its place *conceptually*, that is, it sorts out the diversity of meanings hidden by this monolithic and singular catchphrase. Third, it puts the movement in its place *historically*, that is, it positions the consumer movement of the wartime and postwar years in broad historical context. Finally, it puts it in its place in the *colloquial* sense of relegating the consumer movement to one factor, and not even always the most important one, among many in the making of postwar consumer politics.

Consumer activism, as we have seen, is a protean form of protest reflecting important shifts in self-understandings and strategies. For example, the proper practitioners of political and ethical consumption have at different points been defined as merchants, ordinary consumers, and scientifically trained experts. Consumer activists have understood the main beneficiaries of boycotts as, at different times, the nation, slaves, workers, African Americans under Jim Crow, and, in the twentieth century, consumers themselves. The history of consumer activism is marked by debates about whether consumers should embrace or reject fashion, eschew immoral products or promote the consumption of alternatives, and employ or reject the techniques of consumer society. Rather than a linear progression, these competing conceptions have existed as tensions within particular consumer movements and across time.

Emphasizing the weakness of the consumer movement in the 1940s and 1950s is not so much wrong as incomplete. One can accurately narrate a story of the deradicalization of consumer politics and the decreasing significance of the consumer movement. The historian Gary Cross, for example, claims that in the 1950s there was a "narrowing of scope" of the consumer movement, which confined its focus to the "attributes and prices of goods." Other scholars have depicted the consumer movement as less central to postwar political culture than it was before in the Depression decade and that it would be again in the 1960s. Mark Nadel claims that because "interest and activity in consumer issues was a casualty of World War II," the consumer movement reemerged in the 1960s only after years of "quiescence."[3]

There is sufficient evidence, internal to the consumer movement and external to it, to support the declinist interpretation. Few postwar intellectuals trumpeted consumers as the saviors of society, as many had in the 1930s, including John Dewey, Stuart Chase, and Horace Kallen. Moreover, schisms within consumer organizations proved as debilitating to them as the divisions that famously hindered the labor movement in this period. The consumer movement was one of the first targeted by tactics that later came to be known as McCarthyism; anticommunists intimidated some consumer organizations and eliminated others. CU, which began in 1936 as a self-consciously labor-friendly organization, dropped its reports on working conditions in the late 1940s, and, as we have seen, the League of Women Shoppers, mercilessly red-baited and weakened, quietly folded in 1949.

Moreover, in the postwar years, CU stopped referring to its "members" and started calling them "subscribers," seemingly abandoning its movement culture in favor of a more anonymous, institutional one. "In the early days, Consumer Union was a democratic membership organization," wrote Leland Gordon, a board member, in his 1950 letter of resignation, born of frustration with what he saw as CU's increasingly technical and decreasingly political agenda. Arguing that CU had left behind its ethical mission, Gordon wrote, "A good consumer does not wish to buy merchandise which is low in price because it has been produced under conditions which exploit anyone." Business co-optation and postwar government policy, as Alan Brinkley and Lizabeth Cohen have demonstrated, oriented consumer politics toward private acts of mass consumption, thereby weakening the exclusive hold of the consumer movement on consumer politics. Another reason that this model of decline is so compelling is that consumer activists of the 1960s and 1970s generally understood their consumer movement as rising phoenixlike from the ashes of a discredited and largely forgotten movement, rather than as a new iteration of a continuous political tradition.[4]

CU grew in part because of its growing reputation for expertise in an age of expanding consumer choice and faith in experts. In 1959 a journalist compared CU to the most trusted expert of the baby boom era, noting "what Dr. Spock is to freshman parents, the Consumers Union is to bewildered housewives." In the view of some contemporaries this trust came at a cost, as CU became primarily a resource for middle-class shoppers and in the process deemphasized its radicalism. Another deradicalizing factor in the postwar years was the persistence of anticommunism. The House Committee on Un-American Activities (HUAC) listed CU on its *Guide to Subversive Organizations and Publications* continuously from 1944 to 1954. In 1951, at the beginning of Joseph McCarthy's brief reign of terror, a campaign led by local branches of the Better Business Bureau led to the banning of *Consumer Reports* in the public schools of Akron, Dayton, Cincinnati, and Detroit. CU rarely responded directly to these charges, although in 1951 the *Reports* contained a special "Letter to Readers," which was entitled "On Honesty, Policy, and Subversiveness," in which it proclaimed "the organization is not and has not been fronting for anybody, communists, New Dealers, or conservatives." The article quoted a letter from Fred Wilhelms, formerly the associate director of the Consumer Education Study of the National Education Association, who proclaimed, "If there was a stray communist in your organization, he must be one of the most frustrated men in the country. For your magazine consistently reveals a deep basic loyalty to what may roughly be called 'the American system.'" In 1953, Arthur Kallet, CU's director, was called to testify before HUAC despite CU's statement that it "re-affirms its faith in a democratic society in which the production of goods and services is guided by the free choice of consumers." In these responses to charges of subversion, CU reinforced the view that its sole focus was consumer choice and satisfaction. The questioning of CU's loyalty, however, affected the organization even after the subversive ban was lifted. Kallet, in particular, who was reputedly a former Communist Party member (a charge he denied), remained fearful of controversy and fought many internecine battles within CU to keep the focus on testing and off socially oriented projects, until his resignation from the organization in 1957. Colston Warne, CU's president and Kallet's main antagonist, recalled that many CU board members "abandoned ship" due to McCarthyism. Others feared being labeled subversive and shied away from socially oriented consumer politics. Some leaders, like Leland Gordon, quit the board because they thought the organization had caved in to the charges of subversion.[5]

Although there is abundant evidence to support the narrative of decline, this picture is incomplete and ultimately misleading.[6] Part of the reason for the declinist interpretation is that historians and commentators have promulgated a "three phase" model of consumer movement history that privileges the high points of the years 1900–1920, the 1930s and the 1960s. As we have seen, a long-term perspective that emphasizes continuity, however, reveals that a great deal happened in the "off" decades of the twentieth century, to say nothing of the eighteenth and nineteenth centuries. Moreover, a too-narrow focus on these years can lead to the elision of consumer activism with the consumer movement and to a more monolithic view of consumer politics than is warranted. For example, Michael McCann writes that "traditional consumer politics sanctioned and served citizen desires for private wealth as the greatest promise of modern society" and "was limited to concerns for more, better, and cheaper goods." Certainly, a key element of the consumer movement as it developed from the Progressive Era onward was the promotion of shopping assistance for individual consumers. As we have seen, however, this focus on price and quality of goods was a relatively late addition to consumer activism and never was its primary mission. Even at its height, the consumer movement was characterized by diverse elements, many of them firmly in the socially oriented tradition of consumer activism. Indeed in a 1948 journal article, Kenneth Dameron, a professor of business at Ohio State University and the leading contemporary academic scholar of the consumer movement, noted that it had recently taken up "new subjects," including inflation, health, nutrition, and what he called "socialized medicine." In the 1940s and 1950s, consumer activism reflected not only a conservatism born of the fear of subversion but also continuities with its past. Consumer activists also developed several novel techniques. Placing the consumer movement of the 1940s and 1950s in a longer historical time-frame while simultaneously expanding our conception of consumer politics produces a more positive picture. For when we take the long history of consumer activism dating back to the American Revolution, rather than the 1930s, to be the norm, what looks like decline in the 1940s can be understood not as defeat or even stagnation, but as the playing out of tensions some of which had been central to consumer activism from its inception, and others of which were unique to the postwar years. What looks like decline in a snapshot can be seen as oscillation when viewed from a more long-term perspective. This framework challenges two implicit, related, and wrongheaded assumptions: that the consumer movement is an easily definable entity and that it can be said unambiguously to have undergone a decline. Viewed through the long historical lens of the two-century history of consumer activism, the changes in the consumer movement in the postwar years appear less as a retreat from founding principles, a drop from peak to nadir, than as a not-unprecedented oscillation along various axes of consumer activism. Historians of the consumer movement have generally assumed the rejection of consumer society was a radical move in keeping with the true spirit of consumer activism and, conversely, have taken acceptance as evidence of the eclipse of that tradition. But the *longue durée* perspective suggests that acceptance and rejection are equally a legitimate part of that tradition. The 1940s and 1950s marks an eclipse of consumer activism itself only if one defines that tradition in overly constricting ways.[7]

This long historical perspective shows that the most important novelty in the twentieth century was the very idea of a "consumer movement" itself. Although consumer activism is a long-standing and near-continuous political tradition that in many ways set the template for mid-twentieth-century consumer politics, none of the important precursors—from Revolutionary boycotters, through abolitionist "free produce" campaigners, through late nineteenth-century advocates of labor's consumerist turn, even through the Progressive Era National Consumers League—saw themselves as part of a "consumer movement," if that phrase is understood as an organized political effort on behalf of consumers. Rather, these precursors mobilized consumers not for the benefit of consumers but on behalf of the nation, the slave, the worker, or the poor. So although there were politicized consumers aplenty, there was no consumer movement promoting or protecting the "consumer interest." What distinguished the "consumer movement" from previous and contemporaneous movements of consumers was precisely this emphasis on consumers themselves as the chief beneficiaries of political activism. It is instructive to note that Helen Sorenson's 1941 study of the consumer movement scarcely refers to the defining act of consumer activism, the boycott, which she labels the "consumer strike."[8]

Because historians of the consumer movement have not adopted a long-range perspective, they have failed to recognize this novelty and have generally seen the consumer movement of the 1930s not as new but as an extension of turn-of-the-century consumer politics. Lizabeth Cohen calls it the "second wave" of consumer politics following the "first wave" activities of the National Consumers League (NCL), and Norman Katz sees the Depression-era movement as the apotheosis of Veblenite economics, with roots in the late nineteenth century. Such depictions imply that the most new-fangled aspect of the consumer movement of the 1930s was continuous with earlier efforts in the Progressive Era (which is as far back in time as they go), just far larger in scale and public recognition. While consumer *activism* is a political tradition that dates to the American Revolution, the consumer *movement*, as we have seen, was an invention of the Progressive Era, first used as a phrase in the 1920s, and widely recognized only in the Depression decade.[9]

Only during brief periods in the 1930s and, and as we will see in chapter 9, the 1960s could one claim that the most energetic forms of consumer activism emerged from "the consumer movement." Certainly, the growth of the consumer testing agencies, CR and CU (leaving aside, as most commentators did, their mutual disdain), the establishment of several federal agencies devoted to the "consumer interest," namely, the Consumers' Counsel Division of the Agricultural Adjustment Administration and the Consumers' Advisory Board of the National Recovery Administration, and the unsuccessful but well-publicized efforts to establish a cabinet-level Department of the Consumer, as well as the expansion of consumer education efforts all speak to a new and vibrant aspect of Depression era consumer activism.[10]

If we recognize the crucial fact that consumer activism is not coextensive with the consumer movement, however, a different picture altogether emerges. There were many movements of consumers in the 1930s that were not bound by the consumer movement's parameters of product-testing, educational, and lobbying organizations and New Deal agencies. Despite the growth of Consumers Union and the development of several government agencies charged with representing the "consumer interest," probably the most important consumer movements of the 1930s were the "Don't buy where you can't work" campaigns of urban African Americans and the Japanese silk boycott led by a wide array of grassroots women's organizations and other progressive groups. In terms of mobilizing large numbers

of people, these two were by far the most significant campaigns of consumer politics in the 1930s. Nor is it insignificant that these groups, unlike much of the consumer movement, did not understand the broader
consumer society as the enemy but rather generally used it as a resource
in their struggle. Using the celebrity endorsement, the sexualized female
body, and the allure of fashion, these movements merged consumer politics with consumer culture, at a time when the most visible proponents of
the consumer movement—the testing agencies—were widely depicted as
censorious, puritanical party poopers. As we have seen, one can mark the
beginning of CU's turn away from this puritanical streak in its embrace of
the cause of nonsilk fashions during the Japanese silk boycott.

Even if we grant the primacy of the consumer movement in these years,
a couple of points need to be made. First, as commentators repeatedly
stressed at the time, even in the 1930s there was no single consumer movement. Typologies of the consumer movement abounded, and many commentators noted the tremendous diversity of groups and causes which fell
under this rubric. Although they did not parse the movement in the same
way, they all told of competing and sometimes contradictory goals, philosophies, and organizations.[11] While it is true that the New Deal consumer
agencies withered away by the early 1940s, not all aspects of the consumer
movement declined in the wartime and postwar years.

During the war, the pace of boycotts slowed considerably. They did not
stop altogether, however, and, indeed, at least two wartime boycotts had
their legality upheld by the courts. Many of the wartime boycotts reenforced aspects of antifascist mobilization. For example, one week after the
Pearl Harbor attack that brought the United States into the war, a letter
writer to the *New York Times*, Dorothy Smiley, warned of "the very grave error which a number of patriotic Americans will fall into this Christmas season in buying Japanese-made ornaments for their Christmas tree." In an extension of the language of the silk boycotters, she urged fellow citizens not
to "defile" the holiday by purchasing Japanese goods "which will aid Japan
economically in its ruthless war against the peaceful peoples of China and
the Far East." Three years later, another letter writer, Dorothy Josling, urged
New Yorkers to boycott goods from Argentina, which continued to main-
tain ties with the fascist powers, Germany and Italy. The Anti-Nazi League
urged a boycott of the *Daily News*, *Chicago Tribune*, and *Washington Times-
Herald* because of their "unbearable appeasement policies."[12]

Other boycotts evoked previous "cost-of-living" protests. During the war,
however, these actions were framed in patriotic terms. As in the past, citizens protested the high cost of milk and kosher poultry by eschewing their
purchase. The Hotel and Restaurant Workers Union urged its fifty thou-

sand members to take a "holiday" from shopping on food priced above Office of Price Administration (OPA)–sanctioned ceilings and called for the stigmatization of shopkeepers who sold the overpriced goods. In 1943, Daniel P. Woolley, the New York City markets commissioner, urged housewives to boycott certain foods whose prices were "skyrocketing." As this last case suggests, during the war, for the first time—with the exception of the Confederate support for nonintercourse with the North—government officials regularly called for boycotts of various sorts. (Prior to the war, in contrast, federal officials pointedly refused to endorse the boycott of Japan.) Government support for boycotts took a number of forms: federal offices, including the Office of Defense Transportation and the OPA, and municipal officials, including New York City's Mayor Fiorello La Guardia (who at various times called for boycotts of eggs and fish) supported and/or organized them.[13]

In the postwar era, boycotts accelerated. In the summer of 1946, a series of "buyers' strikes" kicked off the postwar boycotting era, "showing up in stores around the country" in protest of the high cost of postwar staples. The CU publication *Bread and Butter* called for a nationwide action "against unwarranted price increase[s]." Noting that consumers "learned to do without many things during the war," the CU activists implored that "they must continue to do without what they don't really need until the inflation threat is licked." Showing a historical memory that was rare among consumer activists, organizers pointed to the success of post–World War I food boycotts. In general, the buyers' strikes reminded shoppers both of their individual responsibility and collective power. "One consumer can't do this by himself," noted an organizer in October 1946. Stressing the importance of publicity, buyers' strike proponents emphasized effective techniques of communication so that shoppers would know how to act in concert and merchants would know that they were being watched.[14]

Conversely, business leaders and consumers themselves recognized the centrality of consumption to the postwar recovery. Usually, this took the form of encouraging citizens to buy goods of all sorts. In a satirical 1945 article, Leo Cherne mocked the business community's desperate pleas for a nationwide shopping spree. Cherne encouraged consumers to double their rate of eating and smoking, to wear "three shoes." In order to produce full employment, he wrote, "even death must become more extravagant. In place of every two tombstones laid in 1940, you'll have to unveil three in 1946." Little did Cherne know that in 1963 Jessica Mitford would publish a bestselling expose about high-pressure selling in the funeral home industry.[15]

Consumer politics became culturally and politically central in the postwar years, moving far beyond a small cadre of consumer organizers and the larger group of activists. As Lizabeth Cohen has documented, consumer politics became a defining interest of leading business leaders and politicians in the postwar era. The creators of what Cohen calls the "Consumers' Republic" often defined their mission in opposition to the consumer movement. They sought to enshrine consumer choice as the essence of American freedom. They also generally contrasted *consumer choice* with the *consumer movement* and vilified consumer activists (whom they labeled *consumerists*) for infringing on the sovereignty of shoppers. Moreover, as we have seen, many business leaders associated the consumer movement with communism, at worst, and left-wing New Dealism at best. Indeed, the concept of the American *free enterprise system* emerged in no small measure as a response to the consumer movement. The phrase was coined in the 1930s by anti–New Deal businessmen, and it became a fixture of political discourse in the 1950s. As late as 1970, Elisha Gray II, the chairman of Whirlpool, claimed that consumerism "threatens to destroy the free enterprise system." In a 1969 op-ed piece entitled "Free Enterprise Endangered by Wave of 'Consumerism,'" the satirist Art Buchwald made sport of these claims by noting that the consumer revolution "could get out of hand." Buchwald called for the creation of a "House Anti-Consumerism Committee" which would be charged with finding and prosecuting those anti-free-enterprise consumer advocates who sought "the violent overthrow of the National Association of Manufacturers."[16]

Another way of gauging interest in consumer politics is to examine the new significations of the word "consumerism" that emerged in the 1950s. Champions of "free enterprise" celebrated consumerism as the essence of American freedom in the 1950s and a bulwark in the Cold War. For these celebrants, the new stage of mass affluence—the hallmark of American freedom—was centrally dependent on consumption. As Robert Whitney, the president of the International Distribution Congress, said in 1955, "Without consumption, capitalism will crumble," and he offered "consumerism" as the proper name for this "new system." Later that year, a delegation of America's "top salesmen" visited the Soviet Union "to show Russia how American 'consumerism' really works." This group, the National Sales Executives, also proclaimed "consumerism" to be the appropriate name for the economy of the United States; the Russians will "hear about consumerism instead of communism," declared one delegate. The following year, Robert J. Eggert, a marketing research manager for Ford, told a columnist for the *Washington Post* that consumerism was the perfect "word for America," since it denoted choice and a high standard of living, two key elements separating Americans from Russians. The "Kitchen Debate," in which Vice President Richard Nixon confronted the Russian premier, Nikita Khruschev, about the superiority of U.S. domestic conveniences at the American National Exhibition in Moscow in July 1959, marked the culmination of this thinking.[17]

Other commentators took the existence of this form of consumerism as proof that the consumer movement was unnecessary or irrelevant. In a 1952 lecture, Charles Phillips, the president of Bates College, claimed that "the actions of consumers in recent years indicate that, in general, they are quite satisfied with the retailers' efforts to serve them—to treat them as king." His evidence: "If they were not, I think, we might find them rushing to join consumer's cooperatives or looking for aid in the Consumer Movement. In fact, they are doing neither. Consumers Union . . . has achieved a monthly circulation of but 500,000 copies." Like other champions of mass consumerism, as opposed to political consumerism, Phillips here paid backhanded tribute to the consumer movement, and although he prefaced the number with a "but," the membership figure he quoted represented a huge increase from the supposed high point of the 1930s and even the 1940s. In his book *The Powerful Consumer*, George Katona made the same point from the other side. Conceding that interest in testing agencies "has risen greatly during the last few years," he argued that this was so because such agencies assisted consumers' in their deliberations about what to buy rather than because of a broader concern about the fate of consumers in the public sphere.[18]

The popular writer Vance Packard developed another sense of the term "consumerism." Rather than celebrating American consumer practices, as the champions of free enterprise did, Packard sharply condemned what he took to be the morally deadening elements of excessive materialism. Acknowledging that business champions had coined the word "consumerism" earlier in the century, Packard aimed to shift the valence from positive to negative, and he popularized this connotation of consumerism as waste in the postwar years. The word "consumerism" was prominently featured in display ads for his 1960 book *The Waste Makers*. His obituary labeled him a prominent "opponent of consumerism."[19] This sense of consumerism remains the most common connotation, although as we will see, in the 1960s a new signification of the term arose, as synonymous with the consumer movement.

More evidence of the critical spirit of Consumers Union in the 1950s can be found in *The Waste Makers*. This bestseller held up CU (and, to a lesser extent, the much smaller CR) as one of the essential bulwarks against the excesses of postwar consumerism. Throughout the book, Packard quoted from *Consumer Reports* and from technicians and leaders of CU to develop his critique of the practices of American businesses. Packard depicted the

Reports not simply as a useful shopper's guide but also as a resource for citizens to see what was behind the curtain of corporate chicanery, an important mediator in what he called the "unequal relationship between marketer and buyer." Packard deployed the views of CU to highlight almost every issue that he brought up. He cited the *Reports*, for example, to condemn businesses for spending huge amounts of money on sales promotion (and more shelf space at supermarkets) rather than on product research. He quoted CU's leader, Colston Warne, on one of his main bugaboos, the growing problem of "built-in obsolescence" of consumer durables. Packard drew on CU's technical staff to support his criticism of the quality and design of American-made automobiles. Citing Warne's concerns about new techniques of marketers, such as supermarket trading stamps as well as old problems including products sold "in varying quantities and in containers often deceptive to the eye," Packard concluded his book by supporting the proposal of Estes Kefauver, a Democratic senator from Tennessee, for a cabinet-level federal Department of Consumers, which we will examine in the next chapter.[20]

During the two decades prior to 1960 consumer activists reenergized older forms of protest and developed many innovations that we usually date significantly later and associate with contemporary campaigns. Among them were the use of the term "buy-cott," usually taken to have been coined in the 1980s but first coined in 1940. Similarly, the attack on brand-name goods that we associate with Naomi Klein's best seller of 2000, *No Logo*, was recognized as a problem by the Brand Names Research Foundation, which hosted a conference on the topic at the Hotel Astor in New York City in 1946. The idea of a "consumers' bill of rights" was conceived not by President John F. Kennedy, who gave a well-publicized speech on the topic in 1962, but with the "Platform for Consumers" developed by the General Federation of Women's Clubs in 1940. Consumer activists in the immediate postwar period promoted a series of "Buy nothing" days, which are generally thought to be the brainchild of the contemporary Canadian "culture jamming" organization Adbusters. These protests took place all over the country in 1946 and 1947, led by "unions, veterans organizations, consumer groups, and social and fraternal organizations." A "Buy nothing" rally in New York City's Madison Square drew five thousand protesters in July of 1946. The concept of "consumer protection," although occasionally used in the Progressive Era, took on concrete meaning for the first time in the 1950s, in calls for government enforcement of the rights of individual consumers. Moreover, consumer activists continued the call, first voiced in the Depression era, for a cabinet-level Department of the Consumer. Kefauver made the first attempt to introduce legislation to this effect in

1959. Colston E. Warne, CU's president, proclaimed in 1960 that such a department was "inevitable," noting the growing consensus that consumers "should have some agency in government charged with protecting their interests."[21]

Although no single campaign drew the national participation of the Depression-era silk protests, numerous boycotts took place in these decades. These took a variety of forms and served many causes. Meat boycotts led by women's groups, which had been practiced since the first wave of concern about the "high cost of living" early in the century, continued throughout the postwar decades. Cultural boycotts of the sort initiated by African Americans in the Progressive Era persisted in the postwar years as well, although in the 1950s these were generally led by conservative Christians unhappy with the permissiveness of Hollywood films. In the prevailing mood of anticommunism, several boycotts of Soviet-made goods were organized. And opponents of anticommunist hysteria sought to organize a boycott of Senator Joseph McCarthy's home state of Wisconsin.[22]

The tradition of African American consumer activism also remained strong in the postwar years. One of the leading African American politicians of this period, Adam Clayton Powell, endorsed boycotts as a "tool of the new negro militancy," and this tool was employed for many causes. Continuing the tradition of cultural boycotts, black leaders urged Americans to eschew the "anti-Negro and un-American" film *Song of the South*. A reader of the *Amsterdam News* called in 1950 for a boycott of the New York Yankees until the team employed black players. Another letter writer called in 1952 for employing the "only weapon we have, an economic boycott" against oranges produced in the Jim Crow South. In the wake of the murder of the black teenager Emmett Till, a rally of twenty thousand in New York City promoted a boycott of goods from Mississippi, the state where he was killed. African Americans also organized a protest in 1949 against a bowling tournament in Atlantic City, New Jersey, which banned blacks. Holding signs that read, "Let All Americans Bowl," the protestors initiated—in the North, it should be noted—the demands for consumerist Civil Rights that became familiar with the Woolworth's lunch counter protests in Greensboro and elsewhere in 1960. From November 1949 until February 1951, the *Crisis*, the magazine of the NAACP, carried a column called "Your Dollar's Worth," which was syndicated by CU. Toward the end of the 1950s, several African American organizations called for a boycott of South African goods, in protest against that country's apartheid government.[23]

By far the most prominent boycott of the postwar years—and indeed in all of U.S. history—is the one in Montgomery that set off the modern Civil Rights movement. As noted in chapter 5, the Montgomery bus boycott of 1955–1956 should be understood in light of the long tradition of Jim Crow streetcar boycotts stretching back to the turn of the century. Indeed, in 1953, before Montgomery, Civil Rights groups organized bus boycotts in Memphis and Baton Rouge. As in other episodes of consumer activism, the postwar bus boycotters exhibited little historical memory. These actions were widely understood as new; even the Civil Rights leaders who initiated them believed themselves to be originators of the bus boycott idea. Evoking the earliest American consumer protests, boycott leaders called for the ostracism of those who did not support the boycott. The Montgomery protest, in particular, used older methods, including the use of the print media to create a national community of boycott supporters, such as the women in Boise, Idaho, whose letter of support to Reverend Martin Luther King, Jr., was published in the *Pittsburgh Courier*. Celebrity endorsements, such as those by Harry Belafonte and Duke Ellington, who performed at a benefit concert in New York City, also played a role in publicizing the boycott. By far the most important factor in the success of this 381-day boycott was the unanimity and bravery of Montgomery's black community, but the creation, through publicity, of a national community of supporters helped sustain it as well.[24]

As these examples of continuity and expansion suggest, consumer activism was alive and well in the postwar years. Even for CU, which is often taken as the epitome of the consumer movement and is usually described as less radical in the 1940s and 1950s than it was in its founding years of the late 1930s, transformation is probably a better description than stagnation. CR, CU's rival, saw its membership grow to one hundred thousand in the mid-1950s, but it leveled at roughly that figure through the early 1970s. CU's growth, on the other hand, was steady and impressive. It is hard to square the story of decline with the rapidly expanding membership figures for CU, which, according to *Business Week*, "has flourished in the postwar boom" (fig. 8.1).

"From 1944 to 1949 the *Reports* became a unique American institution and the only on-going success of the consumer movement," according to Norman Katz. Yet Katz and others see this circulation growth as evidence not of the strength of the movement but of the weakening of its founding principles. *Consumer Reports*, Cohen writes, "would increasingly stray from its original militant commitment . . . to become a kind of buying guide to consumer durables for a more and more affluent, educated professional, middle class audience. [The magazine] became a fitting manual for the purchasers as citizens who peopled the Consumers' Republic." Doubtless, many readers turned to the *Reports* primarily for help in making big-ticket purchases. And to be sure, CU became less of a social movement of engaged

Consumers Union:

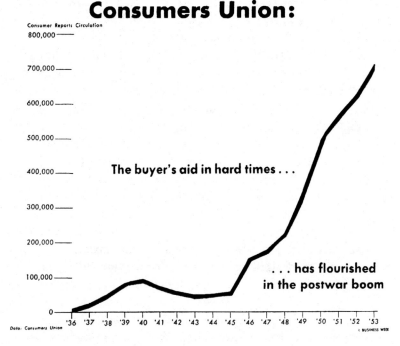

Figure 8.1. A 1954 Chart from *Business Week* showing the rapid rise in CU membership. ("Feeding Advice to Hungry Customers," *Business Week*, Mar 20, 1954, 144.)

individuals and more of a lobby on behalf of the consumer interest. But CU defined that interest broadly and, in the postwar years, promoted a series of measures whose beneficiaries went far beyond its primarily middle-class membership. In the late 1940s and early 1950s this much-enlarged CU advanced a political agenda that was at least as progressive as the liberal wing of the Democratic Party. CU vigorously argued for the continuation of the OPA and other government programs to fight inflation and to regulate the advertising industry.[25]

Particularly notable were CU's long-term efforts to promote compulsory health insurance as "the best means so far proposed to make adequate medical care available to the whole population." Shortly after the war ended, CU put its weight behind the campaign for the Wagner-Murray-Dingell plan, first proposed in 1943 and resubmitted in late 1945, to add health insurance to the Social Security system. CU urged its members to write to Congress to fight the "million-dollar lobbies" that vigorously opposed the bill. This lobby of national health insurance opponents, led by the American Medical Association, used language later adopted by opponents of the consumer movement in the 1960s and 1970s, especially in its focus on the "bureaucracy" it would engender. In March of 1947, the CU board called for "consumer resistance" to government and business leaders who had failed to restore "the purchasing power of the great mass of consumers."[26]

The narrative of CU's decline and/or deradicalization is analytically inadequate not only because of the organization's liberal politics but also due to its efforts in the realm of sexuality and popular culture. In areas outside the bounds of politics, CU came to reject some of the anticonsumerist strains of the older consumer movement, a rejection signaled even during the war by its advocacy of reproductive freedom and sexual pleasure. One of CU's largely forgotten and courageous political battles in these years was its effort to disseminate its pioneering *Report on Contraceptive Materials*, first published in 1943 as a companion volume to its sexuality guide, *Your Marriage: A Guide to Happiness*. In order to mail this *Report*, CU's legal team had to appeal court rulings which blocked its distribution. Dr. Harold Aaron, one of the journal's regular medical commentators, called for a mass movement to demand legalized abortion in 1947. In addition, throughout 1946, the year that Dr. Benjamin Spock's *Baby and Child Care* is said to have revolutionized the field, *Consumer Reports* published the pediatrician Joseph Lander's column, which, in addition to discussing thumb-sucking, jealousy, and toilet training, also included frank and nonjudgmental treatments of masturbation. In 1948, the *Reports* denounced advertisers for producing unrealistic female body images. In debunking the claims of the manufacturers of "bust enlargement creams," the *Reports* not only showed the creams to be ineffective but also challenged the claims of advertisers for creating the demand for the product in the first place: "Breasts, enticingly curved, ripely proportioned and rigidly controlled, are essential features of American advertising." The *Reports* challenged its readers to look behind the premises of such advertising campaigns.[27]

Criticizing unrealistic notions of beauty was not the same as criticizing beauty itself. In the late 1940s, *Consumer Reports* instituted a column, "The Shape of Things," by the well-known industrial designer Elliot Noyes, on product design. Throughout the late 1940s and early 1950s, Noyes discussed the aesthetics of alarm clocks, automobiles, chairs, heaters, lamps, radios, stereo cabinets, stools, sunglasses, televisions, toasters, and washing machines. Noyes treated everyday objects, including the kitchen sink, which he discussed in an April 1950 column, as worthy of aesthetic interest.[28]

Throughout the 1950s, *Consumer Reports* also published a number of prescient articles in the muckraking tradition. In 1956, for example, it produced an article, "The Safe Car," about the dangers of American automobile design, three years before Ralph Nader published his first exposé of the industry in the *Nation*, which had a similar title, and almost a decade before *Unsafe at Any Speed* made the issue a topic of national concern. A year later, the *Reports* examined the problem of air pollution, well before the environmental movement gained prominence. Although CU is often condemned for its individualist approach to consumer issues, it is notable that the article stressed "the absence of a rapid-transit system" in Los Angeles and called for citizen lobbying to promote mass transit and government regulations on business, as important ways of keeping pollution in check. An August 1960 article discussed the dangers of pesticides and food additives, two years in advance of Rachel Carson's environmental classic *Silent Spring*. These articles demonstrated exactly the sort of public-spirited consumption that John Kenneth Galbraith claimed was lacking among American citizens in his famous 1958 book *The Affluent Society*. Indeed, they directly addressed two issues of concern for Galbraith: sprawl and pollution. In all these ways, CU anticipated the new directions that American liberalism would take in the 1960s and 1970s. The focus on concerns such as sexual freedom, environmental degradation, consumer protection, and auto safety—quality-of-life issues that the political scientist Jeffrey M. Berry has labeled "postmaterialism"—is best understood not as a retreat from the commitments of the 1930s but as the harbinger of new and enduring forms of liberal politics.[29]

Despite the tensions within CU about the degree to which the organization should emphasize product testing or promote a public-spirited understanding of consumer power, the organization demonstrated throughout the 1950s that it could do both. The organization grew dramatically in this period and became national in scope, in part by its use of savvy advertising, which upset many of its old-guard supporters. "CU's appeals were by no means untruthful," writes Norman Katz, summarizing the critique, "but they did imitate some of the techniques developed by private industry to sell consumer goods." Such criticisms followed a long line of condemnation for those consumer activists who chose to act within rather than outside consumer society. However, the organization's willing use of advertising to expand its constituency shows that the image of CU as ascetic and "out of step" with the society around it needs rethinking. CU recognized that consumer society provided resources for its struggle to change the mind-set of American consumers.[30]

The *Reports* also was part of the postwar wave of the popularization of the ideas of Sigmund Freud. One of Joseph Lander's columns in 1948, for example, praised Dale Carnegie's new book, *How to Stop Worrying and Start Living*, but criticized him for ignoring "the irrational forces of the unconscious." In 1951, the *Reports* condemned L. Ron Hubbard's critique of psychiatry in his 1950 book *Dianetics*, which in 1952 became formalized as the religion of Scientology. It noted that "irrational cults" of this sort flourished because of the "the absence of rational organization of psychiatric resources and in view of the enormous deficiency of psychiatric personnel and facilities" and called for an inexpensive and "rational" system of mental health care. Given its roots in the Veblenite tradition of efficiency, standardization, and product testing, CU's main journal, *Consumer Reports*, took a surprising turn away from its utilitarian, pleasure-denying roots in the postwar years, not only emphasizing sexuality and contraception in its health columns, but also engaging in popular culture in a variety of new ways. CU's turn in this direction can be explained, as Norman Katz did in his impressive 1977 dissertation, as evidence of the middle-classness of CU, an organization that was now guided by the apolitical interests of its well-heeled membership, rather than one that sought to do the guiding. But such an interpretation is unsatisfactory. There is no evidence that the editors—or the readers, who, judging from the letters column and periodic surveys of readers, generally approved of this embedding of the magazine and the movement within popular culture—saw these moves as causing a retreat from other political commitments. Rather than harrumphing about the sterility of "mass culture," as did many postwar intellectuals, the editors of *Consumer Reports* brought a critical appreciation of that culture to its readers.[31]

The adoption of elements of consumer society should not be seen as a departure from the fundamental nature of consumer activism. It did, it is true, mark a rejection of the mainstream of the "consumer movement" in the decade of its inception. Even in the 1930s, however, as we saw in the last chapter, the politics of pleasure played an important role. The generally ascetic Consumers Union reported in one of the first issues of the *Reports* on the locus of urban cheap amusements: Coney Island.[32] CU's emphasis on consumer pleasures thus marked a renewal of a mode of consumer activism that dated back to its origins in the free produce movement and that refused to see aesthetics and ethics as mutually irreconcilable. To reject the puritanism that characterized one pole of consumer activist tradition was not necessarily to succumb to conservatism. Nor was it to turn its back on the legacy of consumer activism. Rather, it was to embrace a recessive strain of consumer activism, one that linked pleasure and politics, a strain that was, as we have seen, present as well in the 1930s.

In the postwar years, CU's product tests and medical advice were seamlessly joined not only with political commentary but also with record, movie, and television reviews. Sometimes its popular culture analysis blended into politics, as when it expressed concern about Hollywood's monopolization of television.[33] This is not to say that such a mixture was necessarily radical. But it is to suggest that CU recognized the fine line between celebrating the virtues and benefits offered by consumer society and succumbing to its false promises. While celebrating sexuality and fashion and sharing opinions of movies, musical recordings, and television sitcoms, the CU membership continued to fight for what it saw as a fairer and more just political economy. Moreover, by putting these issues side by side in *Consumer Reports*, CU suggested that the good society consisted not merely of efficient consumers but of pleasure-seeking consumers, and that such a society could value both justice and aesthetics, both compulsory health insurance and fashionable, well-made clothing. CU's efforts to turn the consumer movement away from the ascetic and toward the aesthetic not only sheds light on its inadequately explained popularity in the postwar decades but also provides perhaps an unacknowledged basis of that strand of 1960s protest politics that similarly rejected the pious asceticism of the Old Left and sought to develop a mode of politics that was simultaneously moral and pleasurable.

Changes within the consumer movement from the 1940s through the 1950s suggest that decline is not the sole, or even the main, story. And the relation between consumption and politics in the broader culture demonstrate that assessing consumer politics solely through the lens of the consumer movement is similarly mistaken. For, in a variety of ways, consumer culture itself (as opposed to the organized consumer movement) became a resource, in ways foreshadowed by the silk boycotters of the 1930s consumer movement, for postwar politics. The Civil Rights movement, youth culture, the counterculture, the women's movement, and environmental activism all developed in dynamic relation with the broader consumer culture. As the historian Andrew Hurley has astutely observed, "Postwar abundance inspired Americans to re-articulate their aspirations and frustrations in the language of consumerism." To claim that there was a direct line between popular culture and political engagement, that postwar popular culture was inherently "radical," would be wrong; plenty of racist white teenagers listened to Elvis Presley and even Chuck Berry; many suburbanites sought the pleasures of postwar life without feeling the duty to contribute to the public good, many advertisers promoted what Ruth Rosen has called "consumer feminism" as a way to sell products rather than to promote equality. And it is also true that some postwar radicals developed powerful critiques of consumer society. But to deny that that culture also at times nourished political engagement is equally wrongheaded.[34]

Both consumer activism and the consumer movement changed significantly in the postwar years. The blinders of a focus on the narrowly defined consumer movement can lead us to miss the importance of the numerous and prominent boycotts that shaped the landscape of postwar America.[35] While it is true in some ways that the consumer movement was less prominent, CU's rapid membership growth and continuing activism demonstrate its continuing popularity. Finally, even if, as measured by the pronouncements of intellectuals, the consumer movement lost a degree of prominence, consumer politics did not. The writings of Vance Packard, John Kenneth Galbraith, and David Riesman, which critiqued consumer culture, as well as the youth culture, which largely embraced it, show that consumer politics did not disappear in the immediate postwar decades.

During the 1930s, commentators and participants began to speak for the first time of a "consumer movement." Alongside grassroots consumer protest, this movement—which included product-testing organizations, policy groups, and government agencies—energized consumer activism in the Depression decade. During World War II and the postwar years, the consumer movement remained a significant, though not the only, form of consumer activism, drawing strength from its surprising convergence with consumer society. Meanwhile, consumer society itself became a resource for a number of social and political movements, revealing that the story of consumer politics can not be limited to a single consumer movement.

Putting the consumer movement of the two-decade period between 1940 and 1960 in its place does not diminish its historical significance. Rather, it helps to specify the achievements of this movement and to link it up with other related postwar transformations from which it has been needlessly cordoned off. Doing so calls into question the standard depiction of consumer movement as an episodic phenomenon of the 1930s and 1960s and more properly positions it at the frequent intersections of politics and consumption in postwar America. Such a perspective also provides context for the revival of the consumer movement in the 1960s and 1970s, as well as for the counterattack against it, a campaign that, like the consumer movement itself, changed with the times.

THE RISE AND FALL OF THE CONSUMER PROTECTION AGENCY

THE ORIGINS OF AMERICAN ANTILIBERALISM, 1959-1978

For some time now "liberalism" has been a dirty word in American politics. Democratic candidates for political office have, at least since Jimmy Carter in 1976, reflexively shunned the label "liberal," preferring to describe themselves as "competent," "pragmatic," "populist," moderate practitioners of a "third way," and even "progressive"—anything but liberal. For over thirty years, their opponents in the Republican party have employed the word to alienate Democrats from mainstream America. Despite disclaimers by Democrats, they have been effectively portrayed by Republicans as liberals, and pusillanimous ones at that, since they have been unwilling to embrace this manifestly accurate description. Moreover, many on the Right have defined liberalism as not just misguided but perverse, "not only wrong, but cruel," in the words of William Bennett, the conservative intellectual and former cabinet secretary. In his widely distributed memorandum *Language: A Key Mechanism of Control*, Newt Gingrich, the architect of the Republican takeover of the House of Representatives in 1994, encouraged GOP candidates to use "liberal" as a term of opprobrium, and to pair it, whenever possible, with words such as "pathetic," "sick," and "traitor." For Gingrich and his followers, liberalism figured less as a set of beliefs about politics and society than as a dangerous pathology. If, as the *New York Times* reported in 2007, there is a "liberal resurgence" currently taking place in the United States, this renaissance is in a very early stage, since liberalism is recovering from nearly two generations of disrespect. Indeed, the *Times* and other media outlets continued to note throughout the presidential campaign of 2008 that few politicians "have returned to using the word 'liberal.'"[1]

In 1950, Lionel Trilling claimed in *The Liberal Imagination* that "liberalism is not only the dominant but even the sole intellectual tradition" in the United States. Even the archanticommunist Joseph McCarthy used the term in a positive sense in the early 1950s. (Most liberals, notably those in Americans for Democratic Action, were strongly anticommunist.) Shortly after Lyndon Johnson crushed Barry Goldwater in the presidential election of 1964, James MacGregor Burns wrote that "this is surely a liberal epoch as the late 19th century was a conservative one." Yet little more than a decade later, liberalism had replaced communism in the rhetoric of Republican leaders and in the minds of many ordinary Americans as the most dangerous internal threat facing the country. William E. Simon's 1978 best seller *A Time for Truth* condemned liberalism as "the new Despotism," making the analogy to communism plain. By 1995, few could argue with the conservative Congressman Dick Armey's claim that liberalism was, like the communist ideology that had crumbled in the recent past, in its "death throes."[2]

How did liberalism lose its central place in postwar American culture? The question of "who killed liberalism," according to the historian H. W. Brands, is the "unsolved mystery of American politics." Unlike most such mysteries, however, the problem is not that we have no perpetrators in mind, but rather too many. And in the standard analysis, most of these protagonists were internal to liberalism itself. Debates about the extension of Civil Rights, Vietnam, cultural radicalism, and the New Left (which viewed liberals as part of the "system" it sought to overturn) all contributed to the break up the "New Deal coalition" by 1980 and marked the end of the era of liberal dominance in the United States.[3] We tend to think of the collapse of liberal hegemony as having two acts: first, the unraveling of the liberal consensus, which began in the 1960s, and, later, the emergence of the New Right, which began in the late 1970s and achieved prominence in the 1980s and dominance in the 1990s. In this account, the conservative counterattack came only after the liberal implosion.

Without discounting the significance of internal factors in the liberal collapse, this chapter offers an additional perspective on the erosion of liberalism in the 1960s and 1970s, one that examines the coalescence of a new, aggressive, and effective antiliberal political style and rhetoric. This campaign preceded the liberal crack-up and materially contributed to it. Indeed, it helps explain how by the end of the 1970s, as Bruce Schulman has noted, "a vague antiliberalism had been transformed into an avowed conservatism." Antiliberalism took several forms, among the first of which was developed by Southern politicians such as George Wallace, who equated the Civil Rights movement with liberalism. An equally important and far less studied element of antiliberalism emerged in the campaign against "consumerism," a word signifying the excesses of the consumer movement, redeployed by Arthur E. Larkin, Jr., the president of the General Foods Corporation, and quickly adopted by other opponents of the movement in the business community in the mid-1960. (As we have seen, the term was first used in the 1920s, and new significations emerged in the 1950s and early 1960s. As we will see, late in the 1960s critics of consumer-movement-style consumerism sought to claim this "broadly used and poorly-defined" word for themselves.) The consumer movement came to be seen by many conservatives, businessmen, and politicians as exemplifying the flaws of American liberalism and so as standing in for the twentieth-century liberal project as a whole. Conservatives launched a decade-long campaign against proposed legislation for a federal Consumer Protection Agency (CPA), from the late 1960s through the late 1970s. (In various incarnations, the proposed agency was also labeled the Agency for Consumer Protection and the Agency for Consumer Advocacy.) Although the fight over the CPA is little remembered today, it was front-page news throughout much of the 1960s and 1970s, and it sheds light on both the decline of Great Society liberalism and the rise of a new and ascendant style of conservatism.[4]

Famous people got involved on both sides of the issue. In favor of the CPA were Ralph Nader, Esther Peterson, the most prominent consumer representative in American government, as well as leading members of the Democratic Party and liberal Republican senators, such as Jacob Javits and Charles Percy. Opposing the CPA were members of the Old Right, such as Patrick Buchanan, William F. Buckley, James J. Kilpatrick, young conservatives like George Will, as well as many people who would soon be identified with the New Right, notably Ronald Reagan. Famous personalities, however, were only one element of the multifaceted opposition to the CPA. Indeed, the opposition was organized by a relatively unknown but well-financed lobby—made up of business leaders, politicians, intellectuals, and pundits—that developed tactics which presaged those employed by the New Right. Signature elements of this campaign, which the veteran congressional leader Tip O'Neill called the most "extensive lobbying" he had witnessed in his quarter of a century in Washington, included contributions by conservative think tanks; using of the media to delegitimate liberal programs; creating phony grassroots (now dubbed *astroturf*) organizations; and, perhaps most important, inventing a conservative populist discourse that charged liberals with being out-of-touch elitists, and that challenged the very premises of midcentury liberal political culture, namely, the governmental obligation to protect and improve society.[5]

The CPA's legislative history was a model of frustration for its supporters. In every session from the Ninety-first Congress (1969–1971) through the Ninety-fifth Congress (1977–1979), a bill to create the CPA came tantalizingly close to passing. Several times, when a majority of Congress was prepared to pass it, the legislation became bottlenecked with cloture motions by a "stubborn minority" on the powerful House Government Operations Committee. When it did pass the House and the Senate in 1975, President Ford vetoed it, although he had supported the measure as a congressman. By the time the strong CPA supporter Jimmy Carter took office in 1977, the anti-CPA lobby had gained enough traction that the bill again got stuck in Congress without ever reaching Carter's desk. Well before Ronald Reagan was elected president in 1980, both supporters and detractors recognized that the bill was no longer viable.[6]

The lobby against the CPA—"one of the biggest victories ever won by business opponents of proposed legislation"—provided a model, and a portent, for the strategies and rhetoric that brought the New Right into prominence. It is precisely for this reason that the defeat of the CPA was, in the words of Ralph Nader's biographer, a "watershed event." By depicting the CPA as a synecdoche for liberalism in general, opponents of the CPA not only defeated the bill, they succeeded in deflating American liberalism, which for four decades had been closely allied with the consumer movement. Moreover, the anti-CPA effort laid the groundwork for what Jeffrey H. Joseph, of the U.S. Chamber of Commerce and a leader of that effort, called the "legislative bonanza" for the business community and the conservative movement in the Reagan years.[7]

The defeat of the CPA, and the concomitant delegitimation of the consumer movement, came as a shock to American liberals and consumer advocates. Polls throughout the 1960s and 1970s consistently revealed strong support for consumer protection in general and for a dedicated federal agency in particular. The leading proponent of the CPA in the 1970s, Ralph Nader, was a national hero, consistently ranked among the most admired Americans for his courageous stance in taking on General Motors in his 1965 book *Unsafe at Any Speed*. Nader aggressive lobbied for what he called "the most important consumer legislation in history." Consumers Union (CU), the nation's leading product testing service, expanded tremendously, doubling in membership (to 2 million) between 1966 and 1972. (One fan dubbed the organization "the Dr. Spock of a consumer nation.") Versions of the CPA bill passed the House and Senate five times in seven years. It was endorsed, albeit sometimes tepidly, by presidents from Johnson to Carter, and by the leadership of the House of Representatives, including the powerful Speaker Tip O'Neill, as well as by 150 consumer, labor, elderly, and citizen groups. Despite the ferocity of the anti-CPA lobby, proponents fully expected the eventual establishment of the agency, especially after the election of Jimmy Carter, who had expressed strong support for the agency, had met with Nader at his Plains, Georgia, home during the presidential campaign of 1976, and even labeled himself a "consumer activist," leading Patrick Buchanan to worry that, as president, Carter would feel the need before making any appointments to "clear it with Ralph."[8]

Advocates of the CPA, however, should not have been surprised by the defeat of their agency. What was more surprising was the change in the language and tactics developed to defeat the bill. A politicized business lobby had emerged early in the postwar years, and it became remarkably effective in striking down fundamental elements of the New Deal order. These loosely related groups developed many of the modern techniques of conservative lobbying, including the savvy use of advertising and publicity. But until the business lobby took on what it had begun to call "consumerism," it did so largely in the language of anticommunism.[9] The antiliberal techniques and rhetoric of the opposition in the 1970s were new, and they set the terms of political discourse for the remainder of the twentieth century.

In the wake of the defeat of the CPA, one commentator opined that the consumer movement had once seemed poised to "join the ranks of Apple Pie and motherhood." Not long before, even die-hard Republicans had appeared to bow before the force of the consumer movement: Richard Nixon proposed a Buyer's Bill of Rights in 1969, and Ronald Reagan, as governor of California, signed a bill in 1971 creating a statewide version of the CPA. "Consumerism—Upton Sinclair and Rachel Carson would be glad to know— is a healthy development that is here to stay," claimed *Time* magazine in 1969, which pronounced the "growing power of consumerism." What happened? How was it that by the late 1970s, as Robert Reich observed, "consumer protection is everywhere in retreat"? As was liberalism itself, a once uncontroversial, widely popular idea was suddenly under attack as fundamentally unsound, dangerous, and even un-American. This parallel was not coincidental; conservatives attacked liberalism obliquely by first taking direct aim at consumerism. The defeat of the CPA was unquestionably a symptom of what David Broder—a bellwether of the conventional wisdom—called "America's changing political mood." "Consumerism was . . . appealing . . . in the early 1970s," Broder conceded. "But now that cause has been blunted by the fear of a meddlesome, bureaucratic big government." As Broder's language suggests, the campaign against the CPA marked an early stage of the great antiliberal offensive. The keywords of that offensive depicted consumer protection efforts as counterproductive, overbearing, elitist, bloated, and out of touch, and contrasted the government-centered and social vision of CPA proponents with the wisdom and strength of individual, ordinary people operating in an unencumbered free market.[10]

I. The Consumer Movement and Liberalism

Until the 1960s, the most frequent line of criticism of the consumer move-ment was that it was a "front" for communism. Prior to World War II, the most widely publicized investigation of the newly created House Commit-tee on Un-American Activities (HUAC) in 1939 was its report on the con-sumer movement, or what it called the "Consumers' Red Front." During the age of McCarthy in the 1950s, critics continued to condemn consumer movement activists for their alleged communist connections. By the 1960s, except in the eyes of a few extremists, the association of consumerism with communism had diminished. Critics no longer suggested that the move-ment was subversive or communist inspired, as they had from the 1930s through the 1950s. Rather, in the view of the critics, the consumer move-ment was not just wrongheaded but dangerous simply because it was pro-moted by liberals, and liberalism itself had come to stand in opposition to American values, as they were defined by conservatives. So when in 1974 James Kilpatrick called the pending CPA legislation a "profoundly un-American bill," he did not mean that it was unpatriotic because it was com-munistic, which had been the meaning of the phrase since the creation of HUAC in the 1930s. Rather, he used that phrase and referred to the "com-missars" who would potentially run the CPA to suggest that liberalism had supplanted communism as the leading internal threat to the republic. In the 1950s, the reference to commissars would have produced an image of gruff Soviet apparatchiks. But Kilpatrick used the word to connote a do-gooding and arrogant American liberal.[11] Critics of the consumer move-ment in general and of the CPA bills in particular developed a style of vir-ulent antiliberalism, one that set the template for conservative rhetoric in the last third of the twentieth century, which insisted that liberalism ran against the American grain. To remember that two decades earlier, conser-vative thinkers, such as Russell Kirk, had despaired because they took the United States to be fundamentally and thoroughly liberal is to recognize the magnitude and significance of this dismissal of liberalism as beyond the pale of American politics.

The attempt of critics to associate the consumer movement with lib-eralism was not fanciful. Liberalism and consumer activism are both broad concepts with internal divisions and meanings that have changed over time. Although the two share origins in the late eighteenth century, the main currents of consumer activism and liberalism have not always been in sync. For example, consumer activists have consistently rejected the public-private distinction characteristic of modern liberalism. The two movements have, at times, been closely aligned, often undergoing parallel shifts. Both had great faith in the market in the nineteenth century, a time when liberals stressed the benefits of laissez-faire and when consumer activists pursued what I have called "market perfectionism." Both grew more comfortable with state intervention in the twentieth century, as the goal of individual freedom and social health came to require, in the view of both liberals and consumerists, the regulation of businesses. The alliance between liberalism and the consumer movement was never stronger than in the postwar era of the New Frontier and Great Society. Sometimes this was an uneasy alliance. But from Senator Estes Kefauver's call for a federal Department of the Consumer in 1959, through John F. Kennedy's enunciation of a Consumer's Bill of Rights in the 1962, to Lyndon Johnson's hiring of a White House adviser on consumer affairs, the consumer movement formed a central element of the liberal movement. Although Ralph Nader consistently refused to identify with a political party, the movement associated with him, from the mid-1960s through the 1970s, was closely identified with liberalism. Indeed, to the frustration of many New Leftists, Nader remained a reformer in the Progressive tradition and not an anticapitalist radical in the sense that they understood it.[12]

The consumer movement was especially allied with interest-group liberalism. A defining goal of the consumer movement was scientific product testing, to provide consumers with accurate information about the goods and services they bought. As we saw in chapter 6, another defining goal of the consumer movement was to gain federal recognition of "the consumer interest." Progressives first called for a federal Department of the Consumer in the 1920s. This call was revived in the postwar years, and by the 1960s embodied in the bills promoting a Consumer Protection Agency. Just as the government represented the interests of farmers, businessmen, workers, and bankers, consumer advocates called for government representation of the consumer interest. As Senator Kefauver wrote, "The fundamental logic behind the proposal is that most of the other departments, including the Department of Commerce, the Department of the Interior, the Department of Agriculture, and the Department of Labor represent the American people in their capacities as producers. There is no department to represent them in their capacity as *consumers*." "Our whole history shows how various groups have been moving toward recognition in our society," Esther Peterson explained, by way of justifying a federal consumer agency. "First the farmers wanted in, then the labor movement, they're wanting in, and the Civil Rights movement, they're wanting in, and the women's movement, they're wanting in. Now it's the consumers. And my thinking is that we'd be very smart if we recognized this and began to tailor things toward that type of acceptance." Formal representation for consumers amounted to a place at the table in a pluralistic society.[13]

Several developments in the 1960s indicated that consumers were well on the way to achieving this representation. On March 15, 1962, President John F. Kennedy presented to Congress his Consumer's Bill of Rights, which comprised four rights: to safety, to be informed, to choose, to be heard. Later that year, he appointed a Consumer Advisory Council, as a subgroup of his Council of Economic Advisors. That council urged Kennedy to appoint a special assistant to the president for consumer affairs, a position that was created by President Lyndon Johnson, who appointed Esther Peterson to the job in 1964. All of this foretold what *Consumer Reports* declared in 1964 to be a "new era in consumer affairs." Moreover, the pace of legislation aimed at consumer protection accelerated rapidly in that decade. A chart in a 1971 book on consumerism which listed "significant consumer legislation" enacted since the nineteenth century showed that thirty of the thirty-seven important bills had passed after 1950 and that twenty-four bills had become law during the 1960s. Another way of measuring the importance of the consumer interest is that major metropolitan newspapers had a regular consumers' affairs beat. Alongside those who covered labor and business, reporters at major metropolitan dailies began to cover the consumer beat, most notably the "dean of consumer reporting," Morton Mintz of the *Washington Post*, who was among the first to cover the Thalidomide scandal in 1962 and to recognize the importance of Ralph Nader. In addition, Stanley Cohen, Frances Cerra, John D. Morris, and Sidney Margolius reported consistently on the consumer movement. Although he continued to be opposed to government programs, the consumer advocate F. J. Schlink pronounced 1967 "the year of the consumer." In 1969, *U.S. News and World Report* observed that the country was in the midst of a "consumer revolution."[14]

Accompanying the turn toward interest-group politics and increasing recognition in the media, the consumer movement in the postwar years also qualified as a popular social movement. Membership in CU expanded rapidly, doubling from 1 to 2 million between 1966 and 1972. Alongside the technocratic, Progressive elitism that had been a hallmark of the movement from the beginning, in these years, contrary to its staid reputation as a narrow-minded watchdog of the interests of middle-class shoppers, CU, continuing the turn we have seen in the late 1940s and 1950s, promoted a range of liberal causes—such as a regular column in the *Reports* called "The Docket: Notes on Government Actions Taken to Enforce Consumer Protection Laws." It provided a grant to the Union and Henry Street Settlements in New York City to study the spending patterns of low-income urban residents, organized an international consumer movement, and published a paperback edition of Rachel Carson's *Silent Spring.* Summarizing some of these achievements in 1963, Colston Warne proclaimed that "the consumer movement is not just a testing organization." Moreover, while they were distinct from the consumer movement, popular consumer campaigns—from the Montgomery bus boycott in 1955–1956, to the so-called housewives boycott of 1966 (to protest high grocery prices), to the United Farm Workers' grape boycott of the 1970s, to the meat boycott of 1973—also found many allies in that movement.[15]

In the postwar years, consumer activism also took on a new name: "consumerism." Although this connotation of the word was repopularized in the mid-1960s by the movement's detractors, many consumer activists took pride in that label. Consumerists were a diverse lot, but by and large they pushed against the limits of personal politics. They challenged the view that the consumers' quest for personal purity, which for a century and a half had been a goal of consumer activists, should be the sole aim of consumer activism. Moreover, they recognized the limits of product-testing organizations, which had flourished since the 1930s. Beyond individual and organizational politics, consumerists came to argue that it was necessary for the consumer movement to seek political standing in the nation-state. For most of its history, consumer activists, intoxicated by the power of what I have elsewhere called "market-based radicalism," had made few demands of the federal government. The push for the CPA showed the consumer movement to be in a new phase, one which recognized the importance of federal recognition and protection.

Another side of the consumer movement was reinforced by Great Society liberalism. This was the questioning of abundance for its own sake and of consumption as an inherently good thing. A little-remembered aspect of Lyndon Johnson's famous 1965 speech advocating "the Great Society"— a text usually taken to be the locus classicus of what Robert Collins has dubbed "growth liberalism"—is that he implored Americans to consider the limits of consumerism, in the sense that Vance Packard had popularized several years previously. The "demands of commerce," LBJ urged, must be considered alongside "the desire for beauty and the hunger for community." He envisaged the Great Society as "a place where men are more concerned with the quality of their goals than the quantity of their goods," and an environment in which "leisure is a welcome chance to build and reflect, not a feared cause of boredom and restlessness." This questioning of consumption was perfectly in keeping with the consumer movement and gave impetus to the environmental, health food, and countercultural movements of the 1960s, all of which existed, albeit sometimes uneasily, within the broad tent of American liberalism. Emphasizing the ethical limits of personal autonomy even in an affluent society, and simultaneously acknowledging the limits of personal power in the marketplace, liberals of this era saw the federal government as an honest broker capable of protecting equally the health of individuals and of society.[16]

The critics who associated the consumer movement with liberalism were correct to do so. Liberalism has many varieties, but the consumer movement allied itself with almost all of the tendencies of New Frontier and Great Society liberalism. It was the genius of the opposition to articulate this link and to attack both liberalism and the consumer movement as two aspects of the same related problem or, more accurately, set of problems, namely, big government, elitism, snobbery, a lack of faith in ordinary people, and a corresponding desire to limit individual freedom.

II. CPA Opponents and the Rise of Conservative Populism

From its founding in the 1920s, the stock-in-trade of the consumer movement had been its claim to stand up for the little guy (and gal). Some consumer advocates, especially those in the product-testing area, did this in the posture of technocratic elitists who deciphered what ordinary people could not understand about the secrets of packaging and who could demystify the false claims of advertisers. Others believed that consumer representation in government would provide an important impetus to active citizenship. They encouraged individuals to air their grievances publicly and to act collectively to achieve social change. Still others foresaw the consumer movement as a social movement, on par with labor, Civil Rights, and the burgeoning feminist and environmentalist campaigns. Whatever their attitude toward individual consumers, all agreed that the consumer movement's most important function was to represent the unheard voice of the consumer, and to protect her or him. As Kefauver said in 1959, the consumer was a "forgotten man" or a "forgotten woman" in American life: consumers "should be in the driver's seat," claimed the senator, but instead they were belittled and ignored. Dexter Masters, a longtime consumer advocate and the director of Consumers Union, echoed the remark in 1962, calling the consumer the "law's forgotten man," who was in need of vigorous representation. Ralph Nader's challenge to General Motors in the mid-1960s embodied the "David and Goliath" narrative avidly promoted by the consumer movement.[17]

The genius of the conservative critique of CPA legislation was to turn these claims on their head. Critics of consumer legislation developed a style of rhetorical jujitsu in which they both denigrated consumer advocacy and claimed to be the true consumerists: it was they, not the putative consumer advocates, who truly had the consumers' best interests at heart. The leading opponents in this well-financed campaign against the CPA, supported by many of America's largest corporations and trade groups, developed a political style that I call "conservative populism," which became an enduring legacy of their campaign and in the following decades became the dominant style of American conservatism and, for a time, even the face of the Republican Party. Whereas the original populists, in C. Vann Woodward's words, "spoke for the little man against the establishment," the anti-CPA forces claimed to speak for the ordinary Americans by defining the consumer movement and the countervailing power of government regulation offices as the establishment and by denying their own lofty perch in that very establishment. This was not the first time that free-market mania and what the historian Michael Kazin calls the "populist persuasion" had come together in American history, but it was by far the most successful and enduring version of this unlikely marriage, one that the critic Thomas Frank has aptly labeled "market populism."[18]

From almost its beginnings, the revived consumer movement alarmed opponents, who vowed to launch a counterattack. As early as 1967, Sidney Margolius reported that the "business backlash has been unusually sharp and surprisingly effective" and by 1970 some industrialists were speaking openly of their attack strategies. Critics employed a myriad of rhetorical devices to delegitimate the CPA idea. This rhetoric did not spring forth spontaneously. Ever since the consumer movement had emerged in the 1930s, business groups had organized to weaken its power, creating counterorganizations, attacking the motives and personnel of consumer groups, and predicting the terrible consequences of consumer protection. With the reemergence of the consumer movement in the 1960s, business groups once again organized. As early as 1964, the advertising trade journal *Printers Ink* called the flourishing consumer movement an "ominous phenomenon." A business lobbyist recoined the term "consumerism" in 1966 as a means of delegitimating the movement, the "ism" making it seem a cousin of other dangerous ideologies, such as communism. A flurry of critiques followed, voiced in trade journals, at conventions, and in business magazines. But it was the legislation for the CPA put forward beginning in 1969 that drove critics to formal organization. The anti-CPA lobby poured several million dollars into the campaign to defeat the bill; by contrast, the three main institutional supporters of the bill (the Consumer Federation of America, Ralph Nader's group Congress Watch, and the National Consumers League) spent a total of $352,000.[19]

Several key organizations played an especially prominent role in organizing the opposition, notably the U.S. Chamber of Commerce, the Business Roundtable, the Grocery Manufactures Association, the National Association of Manufacturers, and the American Enterprise Institute (AEI). (For two editorial cartoons depicting the imbalance of power between the business lobbyists and the consumerists, see figs. 9.1 and 9.2.) These groups formed a kind of executive council organized by the veteran Republican lobbyist and Proctor and Gamble executive Bryce Harlow and chaired by Emmett Hines, a lobbyist for the construction company Armstrong and Cork. The job of this council, the Consumer Issues Working Group (CIWG), was to develop wide-ranging strategies to defeat the bill, including letter-writing campaigns, the placement of paid advertisements attacking the legislation (fig. 9.3), hiring well-known people to argue against the bill, and paying the North American Precis Syndicate to submit identical "op-ed" pieces and editorial cartoons to hundreds of small-town newspapers. (One small-town Texas newspaper, which like thousands of other such papers published a press release produced by the powerful Hill and Knowlton lobbying firm as an editorial, credited the "HK News Service," apparently unaware that there was no such entity.) A particularly bald-faced expression of these tactics can be found in the *Business Responsiveness Kit* to the CPA, which it derided as the "Nader Enabling Act," produced by the U.S. Chamber of Commerce in 1971. The kit included the sections "The Need for Grass Roots Business Protests" and "Forming a Consumer Protest Group" and noted that "an effective grass roots business program can usually be organized most efficiently with effective trade or business associations at its core." This turned the meaning of "grassroots" on its head: these programs were not formed spontaneously at the local level but were rather the products of a system, created from the top down, to let politicians know what the "folks back home" think by manufacturing such opinion. The booklet included advice on whom to contact as well as a scorecard of key congressional committee members and where they stood on the CPA bill. The goal of these "grassroots" campaigns, the kit said, was to show that CPA proponents sought to "undermine basic premises of capitalism and government."[20]

Several months before the publication of the *Business Responsiveness Kit*, in August of 1971, Lewis F. Powell, Jr., a corporation lawyer, former president of the American Bar Association, and soon-to-be Supreme Court justice, prepared a memorandum for the U.S. Chamber of Commerce on related issues. In what became known as the "Powell Memo"—the confidential letter was leaked to the press after Justice Powell was confirmed—he condemned what he saw as the "frontal assault" on the "free enterprise system," one that was, in his view, being met with by "apathy" in the busi-

Figure 9.1. A cartoon depicting the powerful business lobby steamrolling CPA supporters. (Ben Sargent.)

ness community. Powell singled out Ralph Nader as "perhaps the single most effective antagonist of American business" and noted that "thanks largely to the media," he "has become a legend in his own time and an idol of millions of Americans." Powell counseled aggressive actions on the part of the chamber and the rest of the business lobby, a strategy that included a staunch defense of the "free enterprise" system by scholars, a call to monitor and critique the media, and the building of organizations that could fight against that system's enemies in the consumer movement and elsewhere. The chamber's *Responsiveness Kit* of early 1972 was very likely the first manifestation of Powell's action plan. Insofar as Powell's advice was followed by what came to be called the New Right, which built around think tanks and the war of ideas as well as the aggressive condemnation of liberalism alongside an equally passionate defense of free enterprise, we can recognize that

LOVE IS ...

Figure 9.2. Lobbyists convince Congress to oppose CPA legislation. (*Boston Globe*, Feb 12, 1978.)

the battle against the consumer movement and the CPA was an early salvo in the conservatives' long war of the 1970s against liberalism.[21]

The anti-CPA lobby's biggest success came in the promotion of a series of talking points and keywords, which spread as memes throughout the country and appeared repeatedly—and not infrequently verbatim—in op-eds and political speeches. The *Wall Street Journal* did not exaggerate when it observed that the bill was "killed by words." CPA critics used a number of related buzzwords to defeat the bill: in the eyes of its enemies the bill was not simply bad; it was a "colossal disaster" and a "monstrously bad bill." Indeed, one critic claimed that it was "an affront to the American people." These phrases, which, in sum, amounted to a repudiation of American liberalism, became familiar aspects of conservative discourse in the 1980s and even part of the mainstream in the era of Newt Gingrich and, later, Karl Rove. In tracing the keywords that the CPA opponents used, we can unpack the elements of this now-familiar but then-emergent discourse. Although the proposed agency was relatively modest (with an initial budget of $15 million per year), opponents depicted it as exemplifying a new kind

Figure 9.3. A full-page ad against CPA legislation. (*New York Times*, May 19, 1977, B7. U.S. Chamber of Commerce.)

of bureaucracy. Indeed, "bureaucracy" was the favored word used by critics to describe the CPA, and it stood in for (or was paired with words that suggested) a number of related accusations. According to critics, the authorization of a consumer protection agency would result in "big government," a favorite symptom of which was "red tape and lawyers." Such, according to its critics, was the inefficient nature of bureaucracies, with their "onerous" and "mind-numbing" regulations. The CPA bill would lead to "immense harassment of employers," concluded the *Nation's Business*, which noted that it "could not help but be a source of major new regulatory and paperwork demands."[22]

But the opponents went further than merely condemning the excessive paperwork the CPA might generate. What made it a "bureaucratic nightmare," according to Kilpatrick and other critics, was the form of the CPA's regulation. The CPA bill would produce not just a lumbering and inefficient body, but a dangerous one, with inappropriate and excessive powers: a "meddlesome" and "out of control" body, a "superagency," to use the terms that the critics frequently employed, and which they sometimes amplified to a "monster superagency" or "the granddaddy of all agencies." Critics agreed that the CPA would hold what they variously (and creatively) framed as "irresponsible power," "unbridled power," "absolute power," and "enormous power." The CPA would produce a group of potentially "despotic" and dangerous "super snoops." According to the U.S. Chamber of Commerce, the CPA bill marked "the most serious threat to free enterprise and orderly government ever to be proposed in Congress."[23]

What made this "superagency" particularly dangerous, according to the critics, was that its raison d'être was fundamentally flawed, and its chief flaw was precisely what invited dangerous bureaucratic overreach. The problem was that, as the AEI claimed in its 1971 report, "there is not a single consumer interest." Consumers, the critics emphasized, were a diverse lot, with different preferences, meaning that the idea of a consumer interest was a fiction, and a dangerous one since it willfully ignored the fact of human diversity. The "orthodoxy of the consumer advocacy movement," editorialized the *Dallas Morning News* in 1977, is that "we all think alike. We have the same interests." This was "the most impudent kind of nonsense," according to the editorialist, and reason enough to oppose the CPA. The former Watergate prosecutor Leon Jaworski, who was hired by the Business Roundtable as a consultant in their anti-CPA lobbying efforts, asked rhetorically in an opinion piece (which did not note that he was being paid to promote this opinion), "Can a Consumer Czar Represent Us All?" His answer was no, and his question suggested that anyone with the temerity to think they could would perforce act like a czar. "Who is 'the consumer'?"

asked Senator Robert Taft of Ohio. "Who is this mythical 'every man'? I do not believe there is a composite every man out there in this complex, ever-changing nation of individuals. What is in the interest of one consumer in one set of circumstances may well be contrary to the interests of another consumer in another set of circumstances." (This was an old tactic, dating back to the earliest attempts to represent the consumer interest in government. "What is a consumer! Show me a consumer!" These words, bellowed in a rage, were addressed to Mary Harriman Rumsey by General Hugh Johnson, President Roosevelt's crusty National Recovery Administration director, during the early days of the New Deal.) The leader of this agency would have to "somehow divine" the consumer interest, editorialized the *Wall Street Journal*, since such a thing manifestly did not exist. Particularly of concern, according to the editorial, was that the agency was "being fashioned to Mr. Nader's specifications."[24]

The problem was one of democratic legitimacy, claimed the critics. By attempting to, in Pat Buchanan's words, "establish themselves as the ultimate judges of what is the true consumer interest," the CPA was engaging in nothing more than a power grab. With the establishment of the CPA, unelected, arrogant, and power-hungry consumer advocates—dismissed as "self-appointed consumerists," "self-styled consumerists," "self-appointed police," or "professional consumerists"—would seek to judge what they could not. Placing the government imprimatur on their judgments could lead to dangerous, even totalitarian, consequences, since the agency would provide a vehicle by which a small number of people would have excessive authority. According to the Yale Law School professor Ralph Winter, the consumer advocate was "the self-appointed vigilante of the economic system." The proposed agency, in the words of one trade association, "would provide a vehicle by which a small number of people would have authority to determine unilaterally what the 'consumer's interest' is." Senator Sam Ervin took these criticisms to an extreme when he claimed that "the truth is, the bill would give such vast powers to the administrator of the consumer agency that there is only one Being in this entire universe who can exercise those powers with wisdom, and that is the Lord, God Almighty." Seeking to divine the consumer interest, even where that interest did not exist, expressing the whims of self-styled experts, and aiming to impose that interpretation on the country, consumer advocates qualified as elitists with a totalitarian bent, according to the critics. The power wielded by these undemocratic bureaucrats, the bill's opponents claimed, while illegitimate, would be very real and overly excessive. Consumer protection, claimed Henry Hazlitt, a columnist for the *Los Angeles Times*, has the "odor of medieval statism," with the power to "control, hobble, and harass" all under the benevolent "guise of "protecting consumers." The CPA, according to the AEI, would "harass business in its unreasonable, single-minded pursuit of the consumer interest." "Exuberant consumerists," editorialized the *Wall Street Journal*, using even a stronger word than harassment, "would terrorize American industry."[25]

A final element of the undemocratic nature of the CPA, according to the bill's opponents, was that the agency represented, in effect, a coronation of Professional Consumerist Number One, namely, Ralph Nader. Rather than seeing CPA legislation as the culmination of a forty-year struggle for government representation, they dismissed it as the result of the whim of Ralph Nader and his obedient acolytes in Congress. They labeled CPA legislation the "Nader Enabling Act" or the "Nader Appreciation Bill" and claimed that it was fashioned to his specifications by liberal Congressmen and bureaucrats in the agency who would "instinctively serve him."[26]

The flip side of bureaucratic arrogance and overreach, according to the critics of the consumer movement, was the assumption of incompetence on the part of ordinary consumers. The very call for an agency on behalf of consumers was an expression of the bureaucrats' elitism and lack of faith in the abilities of their countrymen and women. Ronald Reagan, the ex-governor of California, criticized the consumerists—whom he compared to Orwell's "Big Brother," in several op-ed pieces and radio commentaries in 1975—for "promoting the notion that people are too dumb to buy a box of corn flakes without being cheated. . . . .The professional consumerists are, in reality, elitists who think they know better than you do what's good for you." The business columnist Louis Rukeyser offered a similar analysis: CPA proponents assume that "the shopper is a dumb bunny incapable of finding the supermarket exit without a taxpayer-supported Big Brother looming overhead." A group of senators who opposed the CPA also rejected the view, which they claimed was implicit in CPA legislation, "that all consumers are mental midgets who must look to Washington to find out how to manage their personal lives from some bureaucratic consumer 'representative' who will have neither the time nor the knowledge to shop for and cook a decent supper." If only dumb consumers needed protection, then it followed that intelligent consumers did not require it. But, according to the advertising executive Arthur Fatt, the consumer movement sees "the typical consumer as a moron, incapable of exercising even the most elementary judgement in the marketplace." The result was that it sought to take "the consumer into protective custody." Such language about the stupidity of the consumer became a leitmotif of the bill's critics: the CPA proponents, they claimed, took the consumer to be "gullible," a "poor slob," and an "uninformed dullard." The celebration of ordinary Americans became a component of conservative antielitism and an element of its populism. Congressman Tom Hagedorn sneered that the CPA, if it came into existence, would "probably choke on its own profundity." If consumer advocates were snobs, it was easy to dismiss their beliefs and proposal as tainted. By extension, conservatives in this period applied the same elitist label to liberalism, and they continue to denounce it as "a doctrine of condescension."[27]

Here was the essence of conservative populist rhetoric: aggrieved like the populists of old, yet much sunnier about human nature. Whereas the nineteenth-century populists saw the government as a necessary countervailing force against the vagaries of the free market, these market populists located hope for ordinary people precisely in that market. The *Washington Star* editorialized that proponents of the CPA believe that consumers "stand naked in the marketplace before greedy, abusive, insensitive merchants." This was, of course, precisely the assumption of the original populists. In the new populism, the real danger lay in the false protectors of the consumer interest; it was elitist to presume that the consumer "is incapable of protecting himself." The president of a large advertising agency told the economics reporter Sylvia Porter that "the consumer is not nearly as defenseless as committees may dream." Using gendered language typical of this rhetoric, he claimed that the typical consumer may be a "sweetheart" but "she's a tough shopper in the marketplace." He concluded in an attempt at light-heartedness by joking that "what we really need in Washington is a Cabinet level department to protect the manufacturer from the consumer." If the consumer was a sovereign queen, why create an agency in her name?[28]

The feminizing of the consumer movement through such rhetoric, which reduced the consumer movement to a bunch of "angry housewives"—too often exhibiting what the *Wall Street Journal* dismissed as "Consumer Hysteria"—became an enduring component of conservative populism as well. Esther Peterson's critics dismissed her work as the "politics of the pantry," a feminine and insubstantial form of politics. Peterson—known as "Mrs. Consumer"—Jimmy Carter's consumer affairs adviser, and thus the leading government lobbyist for the CPA, was treated with remarkable sexism by the bill's critics. Referring to the campaign for the CPA, Richard L. Lesher, the president of the Chamber of Commerce, claimed that her efforts, and by implication the movement she helped lead, were ultimately "the saga of a woman scorned." Yet these same critics imagined that the consumer movement would open up a new space for the assertion of female political power, an outcome they feared no less. While continuing to decry "Big Brother," critics sometimes reversed the gender of the power-hungry and despotic bureaucrat who might potentially "protect" consumers. Their new bogeyman was not an intrusive brother but an overbearing maternal figure, what they called "a national nanny" who represented the trend of "big motherism." The conservative columnist Emmett Tyrell, for example, denounced the "violent struggle to create a Consumer Protection Nanny." Compounding the objection to being "protected" by a bureaucrat, then, was the fear that superempowered women might be doing the protecting. Current right-wing critiques of the "nanny state" can be traced to this gendered dismissal of consumer protectionism.[29]

A subtle but significant change came over the discourse of the opposition in the final years of the CPA struggle. Opponents stopped referring to the average American as a consumer and began to label that person a "taxpayer," whose besieged figure became iconic in conservative populism. In 1961, the U.S. Chamber of Commerce acknowledged in the first sentence of its critical statement on consumer protection that "all Americans are consumers," and it expressed concern that such protection "would only encumber the consumer with an additional tax burden." By 1977, conservatives no longer readily recognized the centrality of the consumer identity, which they had dismissed as a fiction. Indeed, they emphasized the divergence between the "consumer interest," a concept which they otherwise rejected, and the "public interest." The key metric to judge legislation became the "higher costs to the taxpayer," which also militated against "regulation," "paperwork," and "bureaucracy," insofar as they added to the "tax burden." The following year, 1978, kicked off the great American tax revolt with the passage of Proposition 13 in California, which dramatically slashed property taxes (and correspondingly cut public services) in a state that had been a leading laboratory of postwar liberalism. Although the line of causality may not be direct, there is no doubt that the lobby against consumerism helped lay the groundwork for the "taxpayerism" that came to dominate American political life in the late twentieth century. Consumer groups quickly recognized the dangers of the taxpayer revolt to their cause.[30]

III. Rebranding Consumerism

Having dismissed the main goal (CPA legislation), rejected the underlying premise (the "consumer interest"), undermined the key institutions (the "consumer movement"), and lambasted the political leaders ("consumerists") of what had been one of the most successful social movements of the postwar years, critics engaged in a wholesale condemnation of "consumerism." This condemnation, they claimed, was actually in the consumer's interest. Indeed, the business-conservative alliance against the consumer movement sought to rebrand the term "consumerism" as one congenial to their free-market ideology. In this vision, consumerism meant simply encouraging individuals to consume a lot and to establish the personal realization of preferences in the marketplace as a social good. After having spent a decade or more weakening what Tom Hagedorn called "the so-called consumer movement," by the mid- to late 1970s many conservatives now sought to co-opt it in the form of an inverted style of consumerism. Mary Bennett Peterson's 1972 claim that "free enterprise is the consumer's best servant" metamorphosed in the 1980s into a full-blown theory of "laissez-faire consumerism," which was marked, for example, by President Reagan's proclamation of National Consumers' Week.[31]

This rebranding effort took a variety of forms. One strategy, we have seen, was to esteem the intelligence of the ordinary consumer. The assertion that liberals thought ordinary people dumb has a history as long as the consumer movement itself. In 1964, *Printers Ink*, the advertising trade journal, charged that consumer activists took consumers to be "ignorant." This charge, cemented during the decade-long struggle against the CPA, remains a staple of right-wing populist rhetoric. Rush Limbaugh charged in the early 1990s that liberals believe "the average American is an idiot—stupid, ignorant, uninformed, unintelligent." This alleged arrogance defined those whom President Ronald Reagan called "liberal elites."[32]

To the extent that there was a consumer interest, according to conservative populists, it was merely the aggregation of such individual choices in the free market. What advocates of CPA legislation took to be consumer protection its opponents took to be the smothering of consumer choice, the essence of consumer sovereignty for them. The true friend of the consumer was not the group that Senator Robert Taft of Ohio dismissed as the "elite cadre in Washington," but those who opposed consumer protection. Indeed, headlines from op-eds (many of them written by lobbyists and CIWG operatives) called the CPA an "Anti-Consumer Agency." Ralph K. Winter made the same point when he titled his 1972 AEI pamphlet *The Consumer Advocate versus the Consumer*. The consumer's best friends, it turned out, were emphatically not those who acted in her name, for as Mary Bennett Peterson wrote, "those the Movement is designed to protect can actually wind up as its victims." In spite of polls that showed an overwhelming majority of Americans favoring the CPA, critics expressed confidence that consumers did not want "protection," a word that they almost always surrounded with quotation marks.[33]

Co-optation of the language of the consumer movement to defeat its aims took other forms as well. Many business leaders encouraged their peers to understand rather than reject consumerism. As early as 1969, in a "special report," *Business Week* advised its readers that they "would do well to listen" to consumerists and encouraged businesses to respond creatively to the challenge. Similarly, a special issue of *Fortune* noted that "consumerism will be around for years to come, perhaps growing stronger," and that businesses had better engage this force. Yet another business periodical editorialized in 1970 that "the vast majority of businessmen have now come around to the view that many consumers do have legitimate grievances." The key, according to these assessments, was for businesses to see consumerism as a business opportunity. "Why Fight Consumerism?"as a writer for an agricultural trade journal asked, when "it can help sell more dairy products if producers play their cards right." Speaking before the ur-trade organization, the National Industrial Conference Board, in 1970, the Federal Trade Commission official Mary Gardiner Jones called consumerism "a blessing in disguise" for business. The CEO of General Foods, James L. Ferguson, shared a similar message at an advertising convention in 1974. What he called phase 1 of consumerism had been characterized by "excesses, distortions, misunderstandings," but there was no reason why corporations could not take advantage of phase 2 by making the term their own. One of the ways they did this was by privatizing the concept of consumer affairs. Rather than concede that consumer protection was the purview of the state or the nonprofit sector, businesses began to set themselves up as its arbitrators. By the time Ferguson made his remarks, 149 companies had full-time consumer affairs departments.[34]

Another form of co-optation was rhetorical rather than institutional. Some critics of the consumer movement borrowed the anarchic and liberatory language of the New Left and couched opposing the CPA not as a defense of conventional business interests but as a form of radical individualism. In a 1977 opinion piece published in the *New York Times* with the title "Consumer Liberation," Robert Quittmeyer, the president of Amstar, a sugar refiner, claimed that it was time to "liberate consumers from their self-appointed 'protectors' in and out of government." Since the "root of regulatory impulse is often arrogance," a blow against regulation was also a move toward egalitarianism. Consumer freedom was a good thing, argued Quittmeyer. But he called for adding a new form of liberation to the list: the freedom "not to be treated as incompetent." The following year, an editorial in the *Christian Science Monitor* echoed Quittmeyer's rhetoric. The piece began by urging, in faux-Marxian style, "Consumers of the world, unite!" The *Monitor* urged them to do so by refusing to answer "to the name 'consumer.'" The editorial questioned whether Americans really want "to be lumped into a faceless crowd of 'consumers.'" Noting that "the time for consumers has gone," the editorial implored its readers to reject the category and its political consequences: "Let's forget about consumer agencies, consumer actions, consumer reports. Let's define ourselves as what we want to be." The message here was that consumers should "unite" only to assert their limitless and essential individualism and that they should express this individualism by refusing to see themselves as part of a collectivity called "consumers." Consumer liberationists took this offensive labeling to be more damaging to the consumer interest than the well-documented corporate depredations that had given rise to the consumer movement in the first place.[35]

Consumer liberationists valorized choice and framed consumer protection as the usurpation of a fundamental right. "We have doubts about whether the backers of the CPA . . . are philosophically attuned to the consumer's interest," editorialized the *Wall Street Journal* in 1977. "Do they really want consumers to have a wide choice of products or services or do they want more laws?" The editorial concluded by critiquing "Naderists and others who style themselves 'consumerists,'" suggesting that a true consumerist would not subjugate choice to regulation. Rather than submitting to an agency to decide what consumers should have, William Buckley argued, consumers should be free to make those choices without interference. Freedom of choice ultimately was the fundamental issue of concern for consumers, proclaimed the new consumerists. In providing proof that consumers did not care for "protection," one of the new consumerists, Roger Klein, used choice-based analysis to prove his point: "Indeed, if consumers really desire more product information, why isn't *Consumer Reports* more popular than *Playboy*?" Klein undoubtedly offered an extreme and dogmatic view of consumer sovereignty, but all free-market consumerists shared his understanding of purchases as "votes" and his dismissal of other forms of recognizing, measuring, and protecting the consumer interest as an important component of the public good.[36]

IV. Consumer Activism Comes Full Circle

Long before there was *consumerism* and well before there was the *consumer movement*, there was *consumer activism*. Collective action on the part of consumers has been a consistent and long-standing element of American political culture. From the nonimportation movement preceding the American Revolution, through abolitionist boycotts of slave-made goods in the early nineteenth century, through labor boycotts of unscrupulous employers in the later part of that century, through the great Civil Rights boycotts of the 1900s, consumer activism has accompanied, and sometimes preceded, all of the major social movements of American history.

Consumer activism not only came before the consumer movement, it has also outlasted it. By 1979, activists had abandoned as a "lost cause" their decade-long battle to create a CPA. This came as a decisive blow to the consumer movement, which had put all its marbles in the passage of the CPA, a defeat from which it has never fully recovered. By some measures, such as membership in CU, which in the twenty-first century is at an all-time high of more than 5 million, the consumer movement may be seen as an important force in American life. But as a force for social change, with consumer protection at the forefront and with government representation as the goal, the movement is far less central than it was in the period from its birth in the 1930s through the 1970s. Since the final defeat of the CPA in 1978 there have been no serious proposals from liberals, and seemingly little popular demand, for a federal consumer protection agency. In his 2002 memoir, Ralph Nader, long since alienated from the liberal establishment to which he and his movement were once central, argued that the Democrats' refusal to reintroduce the bill was proof of their political cowardice. But neither does the call for a CPA, or some equivalent agency, appear in his blueprint of ten "First-Stage Goals for a Better America."[37]

In the aftermath of the defeat, consumer advocates tried to make the best of a bad situation by predicting a resurgence of their movement. Early in Ronald Reagan's first term as president, Ralph Nader predicted that this administration would be "his next Corvair." He expressed optimism that Reagan's "'disastrous, anticonsumer policies' would galvanize citizens to rebuild the stalled consumer movement, much as . . . *Unsafe at Any Speed*, heated up consumer issues for a decade." Writing in the *Chicago Tribune*, James Worsham wishfully fantasized that "Ronald Reagan may be just about the best thing to happen to the consumer movement since the Great Society." Other consumerists cited a 1983 Harris poll that suggested a renewed faith in the importance and necessity of the movement. Such hopes for the revival of a consumer movement have proved unfounded. The consumer movement never regained the central place in American culture and politics that it held in midcentury, and especially in the 1960s and 1970s, when presidents from Kennedy to Carter willingly displayed their consumerist bona fides, or were forced to do so, and when thirty major consumer protection laws were passed.[38]

The weakening of the consumer movement did not, however, spell the death of consumer activism. If this period revealed the daylight between consumer activism and the consumer movement, this was not so much a new development as a reversion to consumer activism as it had been practiced for most of its long history. If we imagine consumer activism and the consumer movement as circles in a Venn diagram, the intersection between the two was enormous, if never complete, during the postwar years. But as the circle describing the consumer movement has shrunk in the past several decades, the intersection between the two sets has also been significantly reduced. Many leaders of the consumer movement, unaware that consumer activism came first, initially misunderstood this dynamic. Helen Nelson, a veteran member of the Consumers Union board, the Consumer Advisory Council for Presidents Kennedy and Johnson, and a consumer adviser to the California Governor Pat Brown, said in 1970 that "the consumer movement started from the White House and is still looking for its grass roots." Unlike most social movements, she continued, consumerism was "not a grass roots activity." To the extent that the consumer movement represented an admixture of technical expertise and professional lobbying, Nelson was correct.[39]

In the post-CPA era, however, consumer advocates exhorted the movement to find a new direction. Recognizing that the CPA struggle had been primarily a top-down affair, led by Ralph Nader and prominent politicians, many called for a return to grass roots organizing. Others, such as Michael Pertschuk, a veteran consumer activist and former head of the Federal Trade Commission, hoped that the movement would delink itself from the increasingly polarizing figure of Ralph Nader. Consumerism, he claimed was a "truly popular cause." But, he observed, even at the height of the CPA battles that cause had not translated into a "movement." A more critical observer of the consumer movement noted that "such fire as may be found in the consumer movement comes entirely from its leaders, not from the grass roots." The critic Robert Shapiro observed that "the consumer movement exists almost exclusively in the person of Ralph Nader." The alleged movement, he claimed, was "more aspirational than descriptive." As much as they may have hated to admit it, in the wake of the CPA debacle, many consumer activists were forced to agree with Max Brunk, a professor of marketing at Cornell University and a critic of the movement, who declared, "Consumerism is a movement of activists who champion issues which appear to be beneficial to consumers, it is not a movement of consumers themselves."[40]

Even during the height of the consumer movement, some consumer activists warned against the dangers of focusing exclusively on a single bill. As early as 1970, a grassroots organization in Philadelphia, the Consumer Education and Protection Association (CEPA), charged that Nader's vision was unnecessarily limiting. The CPA and consumer advocacy as a whole, declared CEPA's newspaper, "cannot be a substitute for organizing and building the vast consumer movement the country needs." In 1977, Max Weiner, CEPA's founder and leader, called for a renewal of an older form of consumer activism, based on popular campaigns for social justice. "The movement must be turned to the mobilization of millions of consumers in battles for their immediate needs and long-range objectives," declared Weiner. "Consumer advocates must be called back to the firing line. The movement must stop hanging around 'the highest rooms of government' and go 'back to the streets.'" Weiner was not alone in decrying consumer *advocacy*—what he called purely "legalistic channels and legalistic methods"—in favor of a more widespread and democratic activism. Robert Shapiro shared this view in 1982, when he criticized the consumer movement for its refusal fully to embrace participatory democracy. "Comparing the consumer movement to the great movements in our history—abolitionist, labor, prohibitionist, Granger, feminist—suggests a significant difference in the degree, if not the kind, of personal and emotional involvement of the grass roots adherents. People who subscribe to *Consumer Reports* may or may not be participating in a movement; certainly the nature of their participation is discernibly less ardent than, say, that of civil rights marchers." If Shapiro were more aware of the history of consumer activism, he would have known that consumer activism was, in fact, central to each of the social movements he mentioned. (Indeed, groups like CEPA were continuing the tradition, even as he wrote.) Consumer politics was not necessarily or inherently top down; indeed, for most of its history, consumer activism has depended precisely on the "personal and emotional involvement" that Shapiro found lacking in the consumer movement.[41]

Several months before Shapiro's article appeared, a legal case revealed that consumer activism of the sort he commended was an ongoing element of American history. In a landmark 1982 decision, *NAACP vs. Claiborne Hardware*, the United States Supreme Court, for the first time, unambiguously upheld the right of Americans to organize boycotts to achieve, social, political, and economic change. This case began in 1966, when a meeting of several hundred African Americans in the local branch of the Civil Rights organization launched a boycott of white merchants in Port Gibson, Mississippi. The aim of the boycott was to force the merchants and other elites in the area to support equality and racial justice. As it had been for the Montgomery Bus Boycotters, a major goal for the boycotters was simple civility on the part of the merchants, as reflected by the demand that the white businesspeople refrain from calling African Americans "boy, girl, shine, uncle and any other offensive term." In 1969, some white merchants filed suit in Mississippi Chancery Court for injunctive relief and damages against petitioners (including the NAACP, Mississippi Action for Progress, and a number of individuals who had participated in the boycott, including Charles Evers, the field secretary of the NAACP in Mississippi and a principal organizer of the boycott). The chancery court held the NAACP and other petitioners liable for all respondents' lost earnings during a 7-year period from 1966 to the end of 1972. Eventually, the Mississippi Supreme Court rejected some of the chancery court's finding but upheld the imposition of liability on the basis of the common-law tort theory. Claiming that fear of reprisals caused some black citizens to withhold their patronage from respondents' businesses, the court held that the entire boycott was unlawful and affirmed petitioners' liability for all damages "resulting from the boycott" on the ground that petitioners had agreed to use force, violence, and "threats" to carry out the boycott. At issue in particular were the merchants' claims that the boycott leaders had coerced their fellow citizens to support the boycott and that they had threatened violence against those who did not participate. Recognizing that coercion and violence often play a role in long-term struggles for social change, the Supreme Court held that a "few violent acts" by the boycotters were not sufficient reason for them to be deemed illegal.[42]

Although many Americans (including Robert Shapiro) and even most consumer activists evinced little knowledge of the political tradition of boycotting, it is notable that the NAACP and the court took great care to place this boycott of Mississippi merchants in the context of what the law professor Leonard Orland called the "200-year tradition of economic protest" in the United States. Indeed, in its petition for writ of certiorari, the NAACP provided a more thoroughgoing history of American consumer activism than many history textbooks of the time, linking the actions of Civil Rights protesters to a continuous stream of politics, from Revolutionary boycotters, to free produce activists, to Consumers' Leagues boycotts of sweatshops, and even to contemporary church-led boycotts of companies trafficking in obscenity. Defending his clients against charges of coercion, Lloyd Cutler began his oral argument by placing the Mississippi boycotters in this tradition as well. "These boycotts were enforced by many of the same methods of surveillance, denunciation, and ostracism used in Claiborne County, and occasionally there were episodes of violence, such as the Boston Tea Party," noted Cutler. "Thomas Jefferson, John Dickinson, and other leaders of the colonial boycotts regarded" occasional violence as well as "surveillance, denunciation, and ostracism," as well as the far more common "peaceful acts, such as meetings, parades, speeches," as elements of "the enforced colonial boycotts," the esteemed Washington DC attorney told the justices. At this point one of the justices asked Cutler to flesh out the "analogy to the Boston Tea Party," especially whether the colonial boycotters viewed themselves as responsible for the "loss of tea." Cutler responded by further elucidating the Founders' conception of coercion and

responsibility. Persuaded by these arguments about the historical centrality of boycotting, the Supreme Court reversed the Mississippi court in every respect and ruled that the "politically motivated boycott" was "guaranteed by the constitution."[43]

Those who called for a revival of an older style of activism were in effect challenging the model of interest-group liberalism that gave rise to the
CPA campaign. Though they shared the conservative populists' criticism
of the top-down model of consumerism, they just as firmly rejected the
approach of these free-market liberationists. A key difference from both
interest-group liberals and free-market conservatives lay in consumer activists' conception of the thick bonds of moral obligation and ethical responsibility that linked individuals to each other through markets and
empowered them to act. For these activists, the CPA proponents too narrowly located such power and responsibility in the federal government,
when consumers, acting collectively, were also capable of fomenting social
change. These activists equally rejected the thin conception of social relations posited by the laissez-faire consumerists, who minimized, and even
denied, the ethical obligations of consumers, disclaimed the existence of a
"consumer interest," and, at the extreme, as in the famous claim of the British prime minister Margaret Thatcher, rejected that there was such a such
thing as society beyond an agglomeration of individual self-seekers.[44]

Consumer activists, who, with the conservative populists, emphasize
the importance of individual consumer choices, and, with the consumer
advocates, recognize the weakness of individual consumers vis-à-vis big
business, have multiplied in the 1990s and 2000s. As the epilogue shows,
in terms of the sheer quantity of campaigns and percentage of the population involved, consumer activism has flourished as never before in the
last fifth of the twentieth century and first decade of the twenty-first century. Socially responsible consumption—whether in the purchase of "fair
trade" coffee, "no sweat" clothing, or environmentally friendly goods and
services—has gone from marginal to mainstream. Moreover, the proliferation of boycotting and buycotting has been enormous, used by the political Left and the Right, by secular and religious groups. However diffuse
these movements, they have reestablished the central underlying ideals of
consumer activism: the bonds of causality and responsibility that link individuals to each other in networks of long-distance solidarity. And though
Great Society liberalism was defeated in large measure because of its association with consumerism (and vice versa), there is reason to believe that this
new wave of consumer activism may contribute to an emergent liberalism,
one which uses the nexus of the market and the internet to remind people
that consumption is a vital component of citizenship in a global society.

CONSUMER ACTIVISM COMES FULL CIRCLE

In the 1970s, the media, overly focused, like many consumer advocates, on the ups and downs of the consumer movement, precipitously foretold the victory of consumerism as a powerful social force and then, only a few years later, just as quickly pronounced its death. In 1972, the editors of the business magazine *Fortune* predicted that "consumerism will be around for years to come, perhaps growing stronger." "With much of the country angry about rising food prices and the high cost of living," wrote Edward Cowan in the *New York Times* the following year, "there is in the air the possibility that consumerism will become a mass movement of untold economic and political power." Throughout the media, such predictions were widely echoed in the early 1970s. Yet by 1977, a year before the final defeat of the Consumer Protection Agency (CPA) bill, *Time* magazine declared the era of consumer activism over; it was, the magazine pronounced in a headline, an "idea whose time has passed." By the early 1980s, *Time*'s Walter Isaacson advised consumer advocates to "retrench for hard times." The brief reign of the consumer movement was apparently over before it ever came to pass.[1] (See fig. E.1.)

To be sure, the late 1970s and the 1980s, with the defeat of the CPA and the turn against market regulation, the consumer movement struggled. But even in this relatively dormant period important events occurred. Most of these were in the realm of consumer activism rather than under the aegis of the consumer movement. Indeed, it was precisely in this period that labor and student groups joined boycotts against the J.P. Stevens textile company (for its bold antiunion stance) and Nestlé (for aggressively marketing infant formula in the Third World), and they joined the ongoing economic protests, first organized by the African National Congress in 1959, against the apartheid government of South Africa. Into the 1970s,

Figure E.1. The cartoonist Edward Sorel's "Ralph Nader's Retreat from Washington," modeled after the famous Meissonier painting *The Retreat from Moscow*, which appeared in *Money*, June 1978, just as the CPA idea was collapsing. Many observers believed the death of the CPA would mark the end of consumerism. (Source: Edward Sorel. Credit: Edward Sorel.)

Civil Rights protesters continued to occasionally employ the boycott, and labor unions used it in their battle against Coors, the antiunion beer manufacturer, and against nonunion grape and lettuce growers. Globally, the era was rife with well-publicized geopolitical boycotts, most notably the boycott of Israel organized by the Arab League, the ongoing boycott of South

Africa, especially after the Soweto massacre, the African athletes' boycott of the 1976 Olympic Games, and the 1980 boycott of the Moscow Olympics by the American team.[2]

Throughout American history, consumer activism has waxed and waned but never disappeared. Because of the poor social movement memory of most consumer activists and of Americans more generally, nearly every boycott outbreak has been understood as the "rebirth" of a moribund tradition. And in the latter part of the 1980s and especially in the 1990s—continuing through the first decade of the twenty-first century—consumer activism became prominent once again. The *Wall Street Journal* pronounced 1990 "the year of the boycott." In 2000, the *New York Times* took note of the slew of boycotts, including NAACP boycott of South Carolina, the boycott of Paramount by gay rights groups for producing the *Dr. Laura* television show, the Southern Baptist boycott of Disney, and a number of labor boycotts, notably of Kaiser Aluminum. In the post-9/11 world, this tendency toward political consumerism has accelerated. "Talk about all kinds of boycotts is filling the air," wrote Clyde Haberman in the *New York Times* in 2003. He argued facetiously that people were making "the ultimate American sacrifice: keeping their money instead of showering it on something they do not need in the first place."[3]

Not only did the number of boycotts increase substantially in this period; the modes of publicity became more effective as well, with the creation of periodicals whose mission it was to catalog and disseminate the boycott message. "Boycotts are way up from the 60s and 70s," noted the consumer activist Todd Putnam, who in 1989 founded the first of these boycotting journals, the *National Boycott Newsletter*. In 1990 one journalist, noting several hundred simultaneous boycotts, proclaimed that the boycott had penetrated society more deeply than ever before. It is plausible to speculate that the number of boycotts increased thanks to the publicity provided by Putnam's magazine and other boycott outlets. Beginning in 1984, Putnam, the Seattle-based founder and director of the Institute for Consumer Responsibility, brought out his *Newsletter* (this periodical morphed in the late 1980s into *National Boycott News* and, with a new editor, Zachary Lyons, in 1993 into the *Boycott Quarterly*) to help conscientious consumers keep track of current boycotts and also to seek through print to link them into a coherent movement. When these print publications ceased operating in 1998, a number of Web-based resources continued to systematize and promote current boycotts.[4]

These publications sought to buck up consumer activists, to show them that they were not alone, that victory was possible, and, perhaps evincing a belated recognition of the power of historical memory, that others had come before them—"Consumer boycotts have been used as tools for change for literally hundreds of years," as one article noted. They stressed "the power of the pocketbook," the need to press for political change through economic means, or what they called "grassroots democracy in the marketplace." They also sought to highlight the role of modern communications in speeding up the pace of boycotts and making them more winnable. "Boycotts used to take years. Now they take weeks," as one author noted in 1994. They listed the companies that faced ongoing boycotts and noted the products they made. One 1994 issue of *Boycott Quarterly* enumerated more than one hundred companies and listed seven pages of tainted products to be avoided. Organizers of a boycott of companies that treated animals poorly encouraged "caring consumers" to unite.[5]

Another factor in the increase in boycotts, one abetted by the proliferation of newsletters cataloging boycotts and cajoling potential participants, had to do with the combination of a decreased willingness of politicians to regulate businesses and an increased faith in market relations. "After eight years of Reagan," Putnam said, "I think people are feeling more than ever that government won't do anything." By that time, according to Putnam, more than 120 boycotts were occurring. Less than a decade later, one survey in 1997 enumerated more than 800 active boycotts.[6]

The increase in boycotts, combined with the relative weakness of other forms of radical politics, has led some commentators to argue that our age is witnessing a revival of the notion of the concept of citizen-consumers. As Margaret Scammell has recently claimed, "the act of consumption is becoming increasingly suffused with citizenship characteristics and considerations." Scamell argues that "the site of citizens' political involvement is moving from the production side of the economy to the consumption side." A more historically informed vantage might suggest that citizenship has not moved from one side to the other. It has always been practiced in both realms, although, to be sure, at times, including the recent past, the emphasis has been weighted toward the consumerist side. As Steven Miles has written, "Consumerism is arguably the realm within which the tensions of late twentieth-century social life in the developed world are most graphically played out"[7]

In the late 1990s, not only did the number of boycotts and buycotts grow but consumer activists also organized them around many seemingly new issues, such as animal rights. Students and labor activists organized boycotts of sweatshop-made goods, drawing attention to poor working conditions of workers, not only in the United States but globally. The "fair trade" movement, begun in 1997, emphasized buying goods, most notably coffee, from humane and environmentally aware purveyors in less developed countries. That decade also saw the rise of the "slow food" movement, one of many efforts emphasizing the ethics of eating. Many of these movements sought, in a manner reminiscent of their predecessors, to "get behind the label" of culinary false advertising. A number of environmentally inflected movements used consumer tactics as well, emphasizing the close relationship between overconsumption and ecological depredations. Proponents of "simple living" or "voluntary simplicity" emphasized the importance of leaving a small carbon footprint by limiting purchases. Conversely, "green consumerists" stressed the importance of buying environmentally friendly products. The NAACP in 1994 launched a boycott of the state of South Carolina for flying the Confederate battle flag on the grounds of the Capitol. A large number of faith-based groups came to emphasize the importance of the spiritual politics of consumption.[8]

Commentators in the 1990s and 2000s also took stock of what they called the "new tactics" of contemporary boycotters. Todd Putnam observed that some groups "are taking out full-page ads in popular newspapers and magazines. . . . Boycott organizers seem to have learned two lessons: To succeed, it helps to get the message to as many people as quickly as possible, and it helps to aim the boycott not only at consumers but also at the companies' image." Other new tactics he identified included "attracting sympathy with sympathetic celebrities, and publishing newsletters to keep boycotters up to date." Putnam was undoubtedly correct to note the diffusion of new kinds of boycotts in the 1990s. Yet his discussion of techniques revealed, once again, the degree to which contemporary boycotters lack awareness of their historical predecessors. For none of the techniques discussed by Putnam were new. Revolutionary boycotters, as we have seen, were notorious publicizers of lists (indeed, intimidation by public naming was one of the issues that emerged again in the *NAACP vs. Claiborne Hardware* case). Southern nonintercourse supporters used the celebrity endorsement and newsletters, and even newspapers of boycotts, such as the three newspapers called the *Boycotter* of the 1880s, go back well more than a century. Just as activists of the 1990s repopularized "buycotts" and "Buy nothing" days without inventing them, so too did they bring to the fore and adapt old tactics.[9]

While many of the boycott causes in the 1990s and 2000s appear novel, most of them can be traced back in boycott history. For example, free produce newspapers consistently emphasized kindness to animals (as well as temperance). Many of the fair trade products are descended from the "white label" goods of the National Consumers League. The NAACP-led boycott of South Carolina can be linked to a more-than-century-long tradition of Civil Rights consumer activism. And simple living, as the historian

David Shi has shown, is not so much a new idea as a variation on an old American theme.[10]

Nor are the impulse to boycott or the modes of publicity quite as novel as boycott advocates think. From the beginning, consumer activists have highlighted the rippling and radiating impact of individual practices of consumption. They have stressed the ways in which the purchases of consumers had a range of potential consequences on other people, environments, and nations, and have encouraged consumers to keep those consequences in mind even as advertisers and marketers discouraged them from doing so. Since the turn of the twenty-first century, however, commentators and activists have emphasized radiation from the other side of the commodity chain, from the outside world to the individual. In doing so, they have shifted the question from the ethics of consumption (how do my actions impinge on other people, ecosystems, and nations?) to the personal affects of consumption (how does what I buy change me?). Whereas many consumer activists urge citizens to reduce the "carbon footprint" of their actions, this group emphasizes consumption's (often) toxic impact on the self. Two recent examples include Morgan Spurlock's 2004 documentary that demonstrated the deleterious impact of subsisting on a diet solely of McDonald's food for a month, and David Ewing Duncan's 2006 essay analyzing the 321 toxins in his body and tracing many of them to particular consuming practices (such as bottled water and shampoo). But what is new here is more a matter of emphasis than of framework. Consumer activists, as we have seen, have stressed the "chain" of consumption, noting that individuals are inexorably connected to each other through their purchases. In the past, they had occasionally complained that consumers focused too much on their own end of the chain. "I aimed at the public's heart, but by accident I hit it in the stomach," as Upton Sinclair lamented of the impact of The Jungle. Sinclair wanted to draw attention to the horrible working conditions of Chicago's packinghouse workers, and instead readers focused on the condition of their food. As he later reflected, "The slaves of Packingtown went on working and living as they were described doing in The Jungle and nobody gave a further thought to them." Similarly, as chapter 6 showed, many of the "guinea pig" books of the 1930s focused on the negative personal consequences of the purchases of consumer products. If the focus of a good number of recent consumer campaigns has been on personal health, activists have also emphasized the other side of the equation. Nineteenth-century free producers emphasized the metaphorical "poison" that immoral consumers absorbed, meaning that the goods were tainted by their associations with cruelty to the producers. Twentieth-century activists literalized the metaphor, emphasizing the quite real toxins contained in commodities, stressing the harm they do to those who imbibe or ingest or wear the good. The recent controversy over Chinese-made goods provides an instructive lesson in the shift in these causal chains. In the 1990s, the focus of consumer groups was on the working conditions of Chinese laborers (some of them prisoners) who made the toys that fill Western emporiums. More recently, the focus has shifted to the impact of "poison toys" made in China on consumers in the United States. As a 2007 article in the *New York Times* noted, "A lot more parents are looking carefully at what they buy and where it comes from." Unlike earlier consumer activists, they scrutinized goods more for concern about their side of the commodity chain than for the producing side of that chain.[11]

A large percentage of activist politics in the contemporary world focuses on consumption and consumers as potential agents of change. Yet the scholarly consensus still holds that by and large consumption and politics are negatively correlated. Politics is almost completely omitted from Mark Patterson's *Consumerism and Everyday Life*, for example, except when he asserts consumerism's "effective dampening of political action." The sociologist James Jasper claims that "this form of political protest becomes a relatively thoughtless routine" and suggests that consumer boycotts can be effective only when they are "combined with other tactics that are more emotionally expressive." A similar message is conveyed by the title of Benjamin Barber's recent book, *Consumed: How Markets Corrupt Children, Infantilize Adults, and Swallow Citizens Whole*. Like other critics of consumer society, Barber holds out hope only for "consumer resistance," a politics that rejects the logic of consumer society.[12]

But what qualifies as consumer resistance? Is it a "Just say no" attitude toward shopping? Some elements of this spirit have emerged, such as the guerilla theater of the Reverend Billy and his "Church of Stop Shopping" and the "Buy nothing" days organized by the Canadian group Adbusters throughout the industrialized world in the midst of the holiday shopping season. Yet even in these seemingly straightforward cases of rejection, the story gets complicated. Both the Reverend Billy and Adbusters use techniques of consumer society in order to challenge consumerism. Indeed, Kalle Lasn, the founder of Adbusters, coined the term "culture jamming" to describe this process of subverting consumerism. Some critics have claimed that, in using such techniques, they have made their movements "a form of consumerism." For example, Ken Conca analyzed the sales pitches, product tie-ins, omnipresent logo, and promotional materials through which the environmental group the Sierra Club seeks to expand its membership, to demonstrate the ways in which they reinforce rather than reject consumerist principles. Other critics have noted that both

Adbusters and antisweatshop activists have taken to promoting and marketing their own brands of sneakers and other consumer goods.[13]

Rather than condemning these groups for hypocrisy, it is more helpful to place them in the context of the history of consumer activism, in which we have seen, from the very beginning, engagement with the techniques of consumer society. Indeed, in this context—the context of what I have referred to as "market-based radicalism"—we might emphasize the potential radicalism of these forms of consumer politics. At a time when many commentators decry the weakening of American citizenship and blame this condition on the increasing commercialization of our culture, the history of consumer activism suggests another way of understanding the relationship between commerce and citizenship. Advertisers promote a privatized, apolitical vision of the joys of shopping, and, purveyors of the artifacts of our consumer society celebrate the personal pleasures they bring without attending to their environmental and social costs. The fact that so many Americans are not only ardent consumers but avid consumer activists, however, suggests that they see consumption not only as a private pleasure but also as a public good. At a time when cynicism about the political process is high—not least because *it* has become increasingly commercial—the enduring appeal of consumer activism is that it promises citizens, in their capacity as shoppers, a kind of power and responsibility that seem largely unavailable through conventional politics.

APPENDIX

	Members	Opposition	Beneficiary	Methods	Institutional Forms
American Revolution (1760s–1770s)	Merchants	Loyalists, some merchants	The emerging nation	Homespun, boycott, ostracism, vigilance committees	Merchant's associations, vigilance committees
Abolition (1820s–1860s)	Free produce advocates (Quakers, free blacks), supporters of antislavery fairs	Many abolitionists, white Southerners	Slaves	Boycott, free produce stores	Free produce societies and stores
Confederate nationalism (1820s–1860s)	Firebrand editorialists, politicians	Other Southerners, Northerners who ridiculed it	The South	Nonintercourse, homespun	Associations, vigilance committees
Labor boycott era (1870s–1900s)	Union members, consumers, and correspondents	Employers, antiboycott leagues, judges	Themselves, Irish peasants	Widely publicized local boycotts	Trade unions, labor newspapers
Progressive Era consumer activism (1890s–1920s)	National Consumers League women, Southern African Americans	Many businesses, supporters of Jim Crow	The working poor, especially women, African Americans	Boycott, white label, exposé	Muckraking, committees, labor leagues, alternative transportation companies

Vision of Consumption	Significance	Continuities and Breaks	Memory of Predecessors	Connections with Earlier and Later Movements and Events
Largely negative: equated sacrifice with virtue, but supported home industry and recognized that consumption could bring the new nation together	Invented long-distance solidarity; pioneered the virtual world	Broke with moral economy of consumer activism; continued moral economy of bread riots, ostracism, and communal punishment		Drew on early modern techniques of consumer activism; related to nonintercourse campaigns of the early 19th century, and to the Non-Intercourse Act of March 1, 1809—an act to interdict the commercial intercourse between the United States and Great Britain and France, and their dependencies
Conflicted: valorized abstention but also supported purchases	Set the modern template	Broke with the idea that the consumer activist was a figure of ridicule; opened up the possibility of aesthetic virtue	Invoked the American Revolution often	
Mixed: proudly critiqued the North for being overly consumerist, but at the same time called on the South to step up its consumerism to end the colonial relationship	Showed that consumer activism as technique and philosophy can be used by groups with totally different agendas	Reconceived the South as a nation	Frequently invoked the American Revolution	Coterminous with free produce, with many similarities
Saw commerce and print as twin weapons of solidarity	Made consumer activism local for the first time, but also applied techniques in new ways	Deployed consumer activisim for the benefit of the members themselves for the first time		Linked in philosophy and techniques backward to free produce and forward to the National Consumers League
Saw consumption as a source of power	Was the first to lobby the state, and the first to claim expertise and to investigate; was the first to turn the boycott to the state and mass culture	Was similar in many ways to free produce and antislavery fairs (both of which shared a concern with Christmas shopping); used social science	Learned from the free produce activist Sarah Pugh, Florence Kelley's aunt, and from the example of white ostracism during Jim Crow	Set the template for the "consumer movement" and the turn toward the state

(continued)

	Members	Opposition	Beneficiary	Methods	Institutional Forms
Origins of the consumer movement (late 1920s–1930s)	A new breed of scientifically trained experts and their supporters	Business interests	The "consumer"	Testing products, investigating, lobbying for a Department of the Consumer	Consumers' Research, Consumers Union
Silk boycott (1937–1940)	Broad spectrum of antifascist protesters, including China lobby, League of Women Shoppers, and American Student Union	Many businesses, American Federation of Hosiery Workers, silk-based organized labor	The Chinese	Boycotts of silk, making other styles fashionable	Boycott committees, events (fashion shows, beauty pageants, parades)
Consumer movement in war and postwar years	Consumers Union	Many business leaders and politicians	The consumer interest	Testing, publications, lobbying (in support of a Consumer Protection Agency)	
Anticommunism to antiliberalism	Business organizations, politicians, journalists		American free enterprise	Exposé of individuals, critique of methods	House Un-American Activities Committee, business groups
The rebirth of consumer politics (1960s–1970s)	Consumers Union, Naderites, Consumer Education and Protection Association, United Farm Workers, Consumer Protection Agency	Business and politicians opposing "consumerism"	Ripped-off consumers, unrepresented consumers	Reports, grassroots actions, politics (the Consumers Party)	Nader organizations
The new consumer activism (1990–present)	Grassroots groups (antiglobalization), antisweatshop and living wage advocates, conservative groups seeking to weaken liberal media, simple living advocates, environmentalists			Boycotts, green products	Boycotts, Adbusters, simple living groups, Center for the New American Dream

Vision of Consumption	Significance	Continuities and Breaks	Memory of Predecessors	Connections with Earlier and Later Movements and Events
Saw consumption as utilitarian and opposed fashion	Was the first movement devoted to the welfare of consumers, to a "consumer interest," and placed an emphasis on quality and cost that made the interests reconcilable if not identical	Built on National Consumers League, but with the focus on consumers	Referred to progressivism	Existed at the time as the continuing National Consumers League, the League of Women Shoppers, and other grassroots groups
Sought to marry aesthetics and virtue	Was the high point of virtuous aestheticism	Revived virtuous aestheticism	Referred occasionally to boycotts of Confederate goods	
Supported consumer society but also called for beauty and social justice	Vastly increased membership	Moved away from utilitarianism in the postwar years	Showed little memory of previous movements	
Equated consumption with freedom in the Cold War struggle, but held that consumption could also make the country soft and irresolute	Shows in a negative way how the consumer movement became a window into the rise and fall of twentieth-century liberalism			
Varied, but generally took an ascetic view of consumption				
Varied	Shows continuing appeal of long-distance solidarity			

NOTES

Abbreviations Used in Notes

AC	*Atlanta Constitution*
AHR	*American Historical Review*
AMP	August Meier Papers MG 340, Schomburg Center for Research in Black Culture, New York Public Library, New York, NY
AN	*New York Amsterdam News*
BG	*Boston Globe*
CD	*Chicago Defender*
CDIO	*Chicago Daily Inter Ocean*
CLMP	Consumer's League of Massachusetts Papers, Schlesinger Library, Radcliffe Institute, Cambridge, MA
CM	*Charleston Mercury*
CMA	Consumer Movement Archives, University Archives and Manuscripts, Kansas State University, Manhattan, KS
CRA	Records of Consumers' Research, Inc., Special Collections and University Archives, Rutgers University, New Brunswick, NJ
CRe	*Consumer Reports*
CSM	*Christian Science Monitor*
CT	*Chicago Tribune*
CUA	Consumers Union Archives, Yonkers, NY
FDP	*Frederick Douglass' Paper*
GUE	*Genius of Universal Emancipation*
JAH	*Journal of American History*
JSP	*John Swinton's Paper*
LAT	*Los Angeles Times*
MNS	Scrapbooks, Maud Nathan Papers, Schlesinger Library, Radcliffe Institute, Cambridge, MA
NBN	*National Boycott News*
NS	*Non-Slaveholder*
NYT	*New York Times*
NYTr	*New York Tribune*

PF   *Pennsylvania Freeman*
PG   *Pennsylvania Gazette*
RHR   *Radical History Review*
RP   *Richmond Planet*
WMQ   *William and Mary Quarterly* 3rd ser.
WP   *Washington Post*
WSJ   *Wall Street Journal*

Preface

1. Nicholas von Hoffman, "The Consumer Is Not a Customer," *CT*, May 7, 1977, S11.

2. The labor protests were aimed at Maggio Inc., a carrot grower, JP Stevens, and Coors: "UFW Launches a Strike and Boycott," *LAT*, Apr 30, 1977, A21; Bayard Rustin, "Rustin's Roost," *Los Angeles Sentinel*, Apr 14, 1977, A6; "Coors Boycott Launched," *LAT*, Apr 11, 1977, A1. "A Gay Activist Campaign," *WP*, Apr 8, 1977, B10; "Boycott over ERA Proposed," *LAT*, May 1, 1977, E2. "Japanese Boycott: How Productive? U.S. Environmental Groups Rethinking Decision as Many Japanese Oppose Whale, Dolphin Killings," *CSM*, Apr 1, 1977, 34; Neil Amdur, "Coalition Set Up for Boycott of South Africa," *NYT*, May 24, 1977, 47; John F. Burns, "Young, in Johannesburg, Urges Boycott by Blacks: Economic Boycott Urged by Young," *NYT*, May 23, 1977, 1; "Carter Signs a Compromise Bill on Arab Boycott," *NYT*, Jun 23, 1977, 67.

3. Marian Burros, "Consumer Unrest Staggering," *WP*, May 17, 1977, D8; Marlene Cimons, "Mrs. Peterson Returning to the Consumer Fray," *LAT*, Apr 17, 1977, C2; "Consumer Protection Bill Approved by House Panel," *NYT*, May 11, 1977, 8; "Making the Case for Consumers," *NYT*, May 31, 1977, 20; Jack Anderson and Les Whitten, "Big Business vs. Consumer Agency," *WP*, May 4, 1977, B11; "Plan to Create Consumer Unit Backed by Carter: His Support Boosts Chances New Agency Will Come into Existence This Year," *WSJ*, Apr 7, 1977, 3.

4. Lynne Duke, "Proliferating Boycotts Turn Buying Power into Political Clout," *WP*, Apr 14, 1991, A1.

5. Over the course of the twentieth century, as the historian Lizabeth Cohen has observed, the concepts of citizen and consumer "often were in tension" and were frequently contrasted as polar opposites. But Cohen also notes the categories "sometimes overlapped." Lizabeth Cohen, "Citizens and Consumers in the Century of Mass Consumption," in *Perspectives on Modern America: Making Sense of the Twentieth Century*, ed. Harvard Sitkoff (New York: Oxford University Press, 2000), 145-162. This was also true in the period from 1760 to 1900.

6. George Will, "An Inalienable Right to a Big Car?" *WP*, Apr 17, 1977, 31.

7. See Richard Blake, "'Girlcot' Not Intended," *National Boycott News*, Spring/Summer 1988, 5.

Introduction

1. Caroline Heldman, "Political Consumerism in American Politics" (PhD diss., Rutgers University, 2002). See also Heldman's "Consumer Activism Project" at http://web .whittier.edu/academic/politicalscience/tcap.htm (accessed May 31, 2008). More recently,

The Civic and Political Health of the Nation: A Generational Report states that 55 percent have boycotted at some point in their life, with 38 percent doing so in the past year; 45 percent have buycotted at some point, while 35 percent have done so within the past year. Put together, this means that 73 percent of Americans have engaged in consumer activism in the past year. See http://www.civicyouth.org/research/products/Civic_Political_Health .pdf (accessed May 31, 2008).

2. Ralph Nader, *Speech Sponsored by the Berkeley Co-op*, Aug 26, 1971 (Richmond, CA: Consumer Cooperative of Berkeley, 1971), 12, Brooks/Warne Collection, box 1, folder 41, CMA.

3. The phrase "the inclusive community of the affected" is from the translator's introduction to Hauke Brunkhorst, *Solidarity: From Civic Friendship to a Global Legal Community*, trans. Jeffrey Flynn (Cambridge, MA: MIT Press, 1999), x; Thomas Haskell, "Capitalism and the Origins of the Humanitarian Sensibility, Part I," in *The Antislavery Debate: Capitalism and Abolitionism as a Problem in Historical Interpretation*, ed. Thomas Bender (Berkeley: University of California Press, 1992), 107-135, quotation on 128.

4. Michael Lamb and Benjamin Lundy, "Produce of Free Labor: Circular," *GUE*, Aug 5, 1826, 388. Phillips is quoted in Louis S. Gerteis, *Morality and Utility in American Antislavery Reform* (Chapel Hill: University of North Carolina Press, 1987), 2. For similar use of "chain" imagery among free producers see "How Do You Know," *NS*, Jun 1853, 37; and W.C.B., "Abolition Consistency," *National Enquirer*, Mar 1, 1838, 98-99. Horace Meyer Kallen, *The Decline and Rise of the Consumer: A Philosophy of Consumer Cooperation* (New York: D. Appleton Co., 1936), 54; Stuart Chase, *The Economy of Abundance* (New York: Macmillan, 1934), 115-132; Helen Sorenson, *The Consumer Movement: What It Is and What It Means* (New York: Harper & Brothers, 1941), 3-5; Martin Luther King, Jr., "Letter from Birmingham Jail," in *Why We Can't Wait* (New York: HarperCollins, 1964), 65; Viviana A. Zelizer, "Circuits within Capitalism," in *The Economic Sociology of Capitalism*, ed. Victor Nee and Richard Swedburg (Princeton: Princeton University Press, 2005), 289-321, quotation on 316.

5. See, for example, Andrew Scasz, *Shopping Our Way to Safety: How We Changed from Protecting the Environment to Protecting Ourselves* (Minneapolis: University of Minnesota Press, 2007).

6. *Did Your Stockings Kill Babies* (Boston: Boycott Japanese Goods Committee of Greater Boston, 1938). All of this is to say that consumer activists believed the answer to Zygmunt Bauman's question was clearly yes. See his recent book, *Does Ethics Have a Chance in a World of Consumers?* (Cambridge, MA: Harvard University Press, 2008).

7. Shannon Stoney uses the phrase "proximal empathy" in a critique of Peter Singer's philosophy that appeared in a letter to the *Princeton Alumni Weekly*, Mar 9, 2005, http://www.princeton.edu/~paw/archive_new/PAW04-05/10-0309/letters.html #Letters3 (accessed Jun 6, 2008).

8. Robert Wright argues that "the 21st century may even witness what you could call the death—or at least the decline—of moral distance," something consumer activists described as early as the nineteenth century. "The Death of Moral Distance," *Slate*, Dec 30, 1999, http://www.slate.com/id/68014/ (accessed May 31, 2008).

9. The first quotation is from David M. Henkin, *The Postal Age: The Emergence of Modern Communications in Nineteenth-Century America* (Chicago: University of Chicago Press, 2006), 2; Warne's 1936 comments are quoted in "In the Beginning," *CRe* (Mar 1996): 9; "Does It Touch the 'Pocket Nerve,'" *Signal* (Evanston, IL), May 25, 1882, 6. The *Enquirer* is quoted in "Refuge of Oppression," *Liberator*, Dec 23, 1859, 1.

10. "Boycott Bad Landlords, Is Mrs. Craigie's Plan," *NYT*, Jan 31, 1906, 2.

11. Raymond Williams, "Consumer," in *Consumer Society in American History: A Reader*, ed. Lawrence B. Glickman (Ithaca: Cornell University Press, 1999), 17–18; *Voluntary Simplicity: Responding to Consumer Culture*, ed. Daniel Doherty and Amitai Etzioni (Lanham, MD: Rowman & Littlefield, 2003).

12. Amy Cortese, "Wearing Eco-politics on Your Sleeve," *NYT*, Mar 20, 2005, BU 7.

13. http://www.choosetheblue.com/main.php (accessed Nov 10, 2006).

14. Monroe Friedman, "A Positive Approach to Organized Consumer Action: The 'Buycott' as an Alternative to the Boycott," *Journal of Consumer Policy* 19 (1996): 439–451. Neil McKendrick, John Brewer, and J. H. Plumb, *The Birth of a Consumer Society: The Commercialization of Eighteenth-Century England* (Bloomington: Indiana University Press, 1982); T. H. Breen, *The Marketplace of Revolution: How Consumer Politics Shaped American Independence* (New York: Oxford University Press, 2004). Kalle Lasn, *Culture Jam: How to Reverse America's Suicidal Consumer Binge—and Why We Must* (New York: Harper, 2000).

15. *1897 Sears Roebuck Catalogue*, ed. Fred L. Israel (New York: Chelsea House, 1993). Readers are encouraged to visit the warehouse on 4; testimony from customers can be found on 39, 85, 147, 177, 181, 189, 335, 541; and on 336 and 369 Sears gives away the secrets of his competitors and encourages readers to distrust local merchants.

16. Kathleen G. Donohue, *Freedom from Want: American Liberalism and the Idea of the Consumer* (Baltimore: Johns Hopkins University Press, 2003); Robert M. Collins, *More: The Politics of Economic Growth in Postwar America* (New York: Oxford University Press, 2002).

17. Naomi Klein, *No Logo: Taking Aim at the Brand Bullies* (New York: Picador, 2000).

18. For an excellent examination of antiboycott activity see Daniel R. Ernst, *Lawyers against Labor: From Individual Rights to Corporate Liberalism* (Urbana: University of Illinois Press, 1995). Open letter from Lee Scott, the company's president and CEO, "Wal-Mart's Impact on Society: A Key Moment in Time for American Capitalism," *New York Review of Books*, Apr 7, 2005, 6–7.

19. For examples of overviews of consumer activism that skip from the eighteenth to the twentieth century, see Martin Daunton and Matthew Hilton, "Material Politics: An Introduction," in *The Politics of Consumption: Material Culture and Citizenship in Europe and America*, ed. Martin Daunton and Matthew Hilton (Oxford: Berg, 2001), 28; Lizabeth Cohen, *A Consumers' Republic: The Politics of Mass Consumption in Postwar America* (New York: Knopf, 2003), 21. I neglected the period before the 1870s in my quest to locate the origins of consumer politics in the late nineteenth century. Lawrence B. Glickman, *A Living Wage: American Workers and the Making of Consumer Society* (Ithaca: Cornell University Press, 1997).

20. Daniel Boorstin, *The Americans: The Democratic Experience* (New York: Vintage, 1974).

21. "The Boycott in New Hands," *Denver Evening Post*, Aug 21, 1899, 4. James Scott treats boycotts a form of everyday resistance in *Weapons of the Weak: Everyday Forms of Peasant Resistance* (New Haven: Yale University Press, 1985), 292–293.

22. Robyn Muncy, *Creating a Female Dominion in American Reform, 1890–1935* (New York: Oxford University Press, 1991).

23. Esther Peterson and Winifred Conkling, *Restless: The Memoirs of Labor and Consumer Activist Esther Peterson* (Washington DC: Caring Publishing, 1997).

24. I used the phrase "consumer regime" in Lawrence Glickman, "Twentieth-Century

Consumer Activism and Political Culture in America and Germany," in *Eigeninteresse und Gemeinwohlbindung: Kultursspezifische Ausformungen in den USA und Deutschland,* ed. Roland Becker, Andreas Franzmann, Axel Jansen, and Sascha Liebermann (Constance: UVK, 2001), 115–136, esp. 117–118. For a more expansive discussion of the concept see Victoria De Grazia, *Irresistible Empire: America's Advance through Twentieth-Century Europe* (Cambridge, MA: Harvard University Press, 2005).

Chapter 1

1. Beth A. Salerno, *Sister Societies: Women's Antislavery Organizations in Antebellum America* (Dekalb: Northern Illinois University Press, 2005), 19. Members of the Louisiana Anti-Lottery League claimed their actions to be "as righteous as . . . the boycotting of Revolutionary Tories by the Patriots in our war of independence." "The Anti-Lottery Campaign," *Christian Union,* Nov 28, 1891, 1053. On the Tea Party reenactments: "The Buyers' Strike Spreads," *Bread and Butter,* Aug 3, 1946, 3; Steven V. Roberts, "Grape Boycott: Struggle Poses a Moral Issue," *NYT,* Nov 12, 1969, 49.

2. Susan Ariel Aronson, *Taking Trade to the Streets: The Lost History of Public Efforts to Shape Globalization* (Ann Arbor: University of Michigan Press, 2001), 2. Observers of the World Trade Organization protests in Seattle in 1999 "forgot that the Seattle protests were not the first time that trade policy was made in the streets," according to Tom Hayden, who claimed that these protests were "like the Boston Tea Party." "The Battle in Seattle," *WP,* Dec 5, 1999, B1.

3. T. H. Breen, *The Marketplace of Revolution: How Consumer Politics Shaped American Independence* (New York: Oxford University Press, 2004), 19.

4. Just as we speak of this as a time of economic and political transition, so too was it a time of transition (rather than invention) for consumer politics. For a parallel formulation see Barbara Clark Smith, "Social Visions of the American Resistance Movement," in *The Transforming Hand of Revolution: Reconsidering the American Revolution as a Social Movement,* ed. Ronald Hoffman and Peter J. Albert (Charlottesville: University Press of Virginia, 1996), 34. Richard Ely, *The Labor Movement in America* (New York: Thomas Y. Crowell, 1886), 297. George Kibbe Turner, "What Organized Labor Wants: An Interview with Samuel Gompers," *McClure's* 32 (Nov 1908): 25–31. Gompers made these comments in a section of the interview entitled "The Boycott and the Boston Tea Party." For an elaboration of the birth metaphor in relation to the concomitant rise of consumer society, see Neil McKendrick, John Brewer, and J. H. Plumb, *The Birth of a Consumer Society: The Commercialization of Eighteenth-Century England* (Bloomington: Indiana University Press, 1982), 2, 4–5, quotation on 5.

5. Breen, *Marketplace of Revolution,* xvi, 197; T. H. Breen, "Narrative of Commercial Life: Consumption, Ideology, and Community on the Eve of the American Revolution," in *Consumer Society in American History: A Reader,* ed. Lawrence B. Glickman (Ithaca: Cornell University Press, 1999), 111.

6. Adam Hochschild, *Bury the Chains: Prophets and Rebels in the Fight to Free an Empire's Slaves* (Boston: Houghton Mifflin, 2005), 195. Breen, too, emphasizes novelty: the fact that the word "boycott" did not exist, he claims, "need not deter us" from using the term to describe their actions. *Marketplace of Revolution,* xvi. See also John R. Alden, *A History of the American Revolution* (New York: Knopf, 1969), 97. These formulations are typical of

the way in which historians of this period assume that the term carries no particular significance in terms of the way it was practiced.

7. Sidney Tarrow, *Power in Movement: Social Movements, Collective Action, and Politics* (New York: Cambridge University Press, 1994), 40; J. Franklin Jameson, *The American Revolution Considered as a Social Movement* (Princeton: Princeton University Press, 1973; 1926), 54.

8. John E. Archer, *Social Unrest and Popular Protest in England, 1780–1840* (New York: Cambridge University Press, 2000), 28, notes that food riots, which he calls a "form of consumer protest," "were the most common and widespread form of popular collective action in the eighteenth century, accounting for two out of every three disturbances." E. P. Thompson, "The Moral Economy of the English Crowd in the Eighteenth Century," *Past and Present* 50 (Feb 1971): 76–136, quotation on 132 (Tawney is quoted here as well). Jonathan Swift, *A Proposal for the Universal Use of Irish Manufacture* (1720), in *Miscellanies, in prose and verse*, vol. 5 (London: Charles Davis, 1735), 201–213, quotations on 203, 204. Martyn J. Powell, *The Politics of Consumption in Eighteenth-Century Ireland* (New York: Palgrave Macmillan, 2005), 183–184.

9. Thompson, "Moral Economy," 79; Barbara Clark Smith, "Food Rioters and the American Revolution," *WMQ* 51 (January 1994): 3–38, esp. 11; Phyllis Whitman Hunter, *Purchasing Identity in the Atlantic World: Massachusetts Merchants, 1670–1780* (Ithaca: Cornell University Press, 2001), 104.

10. Toni M. Massaro, "Shame, Culture, and American Criminal Law," *Michigan Law Review* 89 (Jun 1991): 1880–1944, esp. 1912–1916; Pauline Maier, *From Resistance to Revolution: Colonial Radicals and the Development of Opposition to Britain, 1765–1776* (New York: Norton, 1972/1991), 73–74; Ann Fairfax Withington, *Toward a More Perfect Union: Virtue and the Formation of American Republics* (New York: Oxford University Press, 1991), 222; Robert Middlekauff, *The Glorious Cause: The American Revolution, 1763–1789* (New York: Oxford University Press, 1981), 187–188.

11. *PG*, Feb 22, 1775.

12. Quoted in Maier, *From Resistance to Revolution*, 73.

13. *Pennsylvania Journal*, Nov 28, 1765, cited in Maier, *From Resistance to Revolution*, 73–74.

14. "Boston, December 6," *PG*, Dec 15, 1773.

15. Benjamin H. Irvin, "Tar, Feathers, and the Enemies of American Liberties, 1768–1776," *New England Quarterly* 76 (Jun 2003): 197–238; Withington, *Toward a More Perfect Union*, 229.

16. Massaro notes that "shaming as a form of social control occurs more within small societies that are characterized by intimate, face-to-face associations, interdependence, and cooperation." "Shame, Culture, and American Criminal Law,"1916.

17. These examples are drawn from Maier, *From Resistance to Revolution*, 282–83. Interestingly, some contemporary scholars of the ethics of boycotting place a premium on ensuring that boycotted groups recognize past errors and renounce them. As Claudia Mills writes, "Someone who gives up wrongful behavior in order to avoid economic loss from a boycott is not guided by the change of heart needed to reenter fellowship with those who have previously shunned him." See "Should We Boycott Boycotts?" *Journal of Social Philosophy* 27 (Winter 1996): 136–148, quotation on 146. See also Monroe Friedman, "Ethical Dilemmas Associated with Consumer Boycotts," *Journal of Social Philosophy* 32 (Summer 2001): 232–240.

18. In *Marketplace of Revolution*, Breen argues that the colonists use of the terms demonstrates the modernity of their beliefs. This claim is problematic since he quotes colonists using the word "consumer" rarely (he uses the term repeatedly). Moreover, the uses of the term "consumption" in the book almost always connote the older sense of the term. Breen claims that "their actions gave new meaning to the word *consume*" (310). But the example from which he draws this conclusion—a bonfire is set up to burn "that baneful and despised article, T E A"—shows not a new understanding but a very old one; indeed, the article states that the tea was "consumed by fire," a literalization of the original meaning of the term. John Brewer has made a similar point in a review entitled "The Birth of Consumerism," *Times Literary Supplement*, Oct 21, 2004, 3. Brewer notes that the word "consumer" appears only once in the book (265), and in this case the connotation of the term is clearly pejorative, when, in 1769, "Philo Americanus" described consumers as "the bane of their country."

19. Jon Butler notes that the first wave of this process began in 1680–1740. *Becoming America: The Revolution Before 1776* (Cambridge, MA: Harvard University Press, 2000), 154–155.

20. "Postscript to the Pennsylvania Gazette, No. 2375," *PG*, Jun 29, 1774.

21. In "Postscript to the Pennsylvania Gazette, No. 2375," for example, "we do in like manner covenant that we will not buy, purchase, or consume, or suffer any person, for or under us to purchase or consume, in any manner whatever, any goods, wares, or merchandize which shall arrive in America from Great Britain." At several points in this resolution, the Boston group uses the phrase "purchase or use." "Proceedings of the Continental Congress," *PG*, Nov 2, 1774. "Hartford, January 1," *PG*, Feb 8, 1770. "Postscript to the Pennsylvania Gazette, No. 2393: Continuation of the Proceedings of the Congress," *PG*, Nov 2, 1774. John Dickinson, *The Farmer's Letter to the Inhabitants of the British Colonies* (Philadelphia, 1767), in *The Political Writings of John Dickinson, 1764–1774* (Philadelphia: Historical Society of Pennsylvania, 1895), 1:134–284. The quoted passage is from letter VII, 206.

22. "Postscript to the Pennsylvania Gazette Friday Evening, Five o' Clock, December 24, 1773," *PG*, Dec 24, 1773. Breen argues that the nonconsumption movement of that period marked a turning point from nonimportation, in part because of the emphasis on the role of individual consumption in the patriotic cause. This is true, as far as it goes, but it must be understood that even in this period agreements encouraged people "not to purchase or consume" prohibited articles, suggesting a continuity of meaning in the years leading up to the Revolution. See, for example, "New London, September 29," *PG*, Oct 12, 1774.

23. "Philadelphia, March 1," *PG*, Mar 1, 1775. "Boston Ladies' Boycott Agreement," *Boston Evening Post*, Feb 12, 1770, 4.

24. *Massachusetts Gazette*, Dec 23, 1773, quoted in Francis S. Drake, *Tea Leaves: Being a Collection of Letters and Documents Relating to the Shipment of Tea to the American Colonies in 1773 by the East India Company* (Boston: A. O. Crane, 1884), LXVII. Alfred F. Young, *The Shoemaker and the Tea Party: Memory and the American Revolution* (Boston: Beacon Press, 1999). Young's claim that the term "tea party" was not used in print until 1834 is incorrect. See, for example, "Boston Tea Party," *New-York Mirror*, Feb 4, 1826, 223. For concern about the taking of tea see Benjamin Woods Labaree, *The Boston Tea Party* (New York: Oxford University Press, 1964), 144–145.

25. Hewes's recollections can be found in James Hawkes, *A Retrospective of the Boston Tea-Party with a Memoir of George R. T. Hewes* (New York: S. S. Bliss, 1834), 40–43. His discussion of his actions aboard the ship are on 39. See also Hewes's recollections reprinted in Drake, *Tea Leaves*. When Hewes returned home, his wife, referring to the tea, asked him, "Did you bring home a lot of it?" Drake, *Tea Leaves*, LXXIV.

26. Drake, *Tea Leaves*, LXXXVII. For an excellent analysis of the Withington incident see Breen, *Marketplace of Revolution*, 294–296.

27. Barbara Clark Smith, "The Politics of Price Control in Revolutionary Massachusetts, 1774–1780" (PhD diss., Yale University, 1983), 131. For an earlier use of the label "anticommercial" see Edmund S. Morgan, "The Puritan Ethic and the American Revolution," *WMQ* 24 (1967): 3–43, quotation on 11.

28. The phrase "ascetic morality" is from Withington, *Toward a More Perfect Union*, xv. See also 26. Woody Holton, *Forced Founders: Indians, Debtors, Slaves, and the Making of the American Revolution in Virginia* (Chapel Hill: University of North Carolina Press, 1999), 77–78, 99. "Superfluities" is from Middlekauff, *Glorious Cause*, 180. The Articles of the Association can be found in many sources. I am quoting from the eighth article as it appeared in *PG*, Nov 2, 1774. According to Michael Zakim, this support for domestic industry shows that the colonists, in contrast to what we often assume, were "far less concerned with ascetic self-denial than with encouraging American arts and manufacturers." *Ready-Made Democracy: A History of Men's Dress in the American Republic, 1760–1860* (Chicago: University of Chicago Press, 2003), 17. However, as Drew R. McCoy demonstrates in his study of Jeffersonian political economy, we should not read support for certain kinds of manufacturing as an endorsement for a regime of mass consumption. Early national politicians of all stripes continued to believe only in the production of domestic necessities and that luxuries should be produced in Europe (and consumed only infrequently in the United States). *The Elusive Republic: Political Economy in Jeffersonian America* (Chapel Hill: University of North Carolina Press, 1980).

29. "New London, September 29," *PG*, Oct 12, 1774. Morgan, "Puritan Ethic and the American Revolution," 13, 9. Herman Plejj, *Dreaming of Cockaigne: Medieval Fantasies of the Perfect Life*, trans. Dianne Webb (New York: Columbia University Press, 2001); Hal Rammel, *Nowhere in America: The Big Rock Candy Mountain and Other Comic Utopias* (Urbana: University of Illinois Press, 1990); Jesse Lemisch, "Nader vs. the Big Rock Candy Mountain," *New Politics* 8 (Summer 2001): 12–19.

30. "William Jackson" 1768, Early American Imprints, 1st ser., no. 11120; Abraham H. Van Vleck, "To the Public," Aug 4, 1775, Early American Imprints, 1st ser., no. H589 (American Antiquarian Society and Newsbank, 2002), http://readex.com.

31. Gadsden is quoted in *The Lessons of Freeman, Etc.: Essays on the Nonimportation Movement in South Carolina*, ed. Robert M. Weir (Columbia: University of South Carolina Press, 1977), xix. Gary B. Nash, *The Unknown American Revolution: The Unruly Birth of Democracy and the Struggle to Create America* (New York: Viking, 2005), 143. Smith, "Politics of Price Control in Revolutionary Massachusetts, 1774–1780," 96. On Lexington see *PG*, Dec 24, 1773.

32. Morgan, "Puritan Ethic and the American Revolution," 9. "Distinguishing mark" is from Breen, *Marketplace of Revolution*, 20, who notes that for most of the newly emerging public watching for evidence of cheating by merchants was "as far as it went" (229). The observation about the slow incorporation of the general populace is from Maier, *From*

Resistance to Revolution, 116. See the version of the Association published as "Postscript to the Pennsylvania Gazette, No. 2393." Richard H. Dana, "An American View of the Irish Question," *Forum* (Aug 1892): 709-717. Ray Raphael, *People's History of the American Revolution: How Common People Shaped the Fight for Independence* (New York: New Press, 2001), 31.

33. Drake, *Tea Leaves*, LXX.

34. Withington, *Toward a More Perfect Union*, 264.

35. Labaree, *Boston Tea Party*, 162-163. Labaree notes that there was a vigorous debate about the legitimacy of selling, buying, and drinking smuggled tea in the wake of the Tea Party. "The Following Acts Were Passed the Last Sessions of the General Assembly," *New-Haven Gazette and Connecticut Magazine*, Jul 6, 1786, 164, which used the phrase "consumers of goods" as synonymous with buyers.

36. McCoy, *Elusive Republic*, 9.

37. "Postscript to the Pennsylvania Gazette, No. 2393."

38. David Jaffee refers to an "Anglo-American consumer network" in "The Ebenezers Devotion: Pre and Post-revolutionary Consumption in Rural Connecticut," *New England Quarterly* 76 (Jun 2003): 239-264, quotation on 246. See also the reference to the "transatlantic marketplace" in Paul G. E. Clemens, "The Consumer Culture of the Middle Atlantic, 1760-1820," *WMQ* 62 (Oct 2005): 577-624. On the "bonds of commerce," see McCoy, *Elusive Republic*, 86. Hopkins is quoted in David Waldstreicher, *Runaway America: Benjamin Franklin, Slavery, and the American Revolution* (New York: Hill & Wang, 2004), 176. The merchants are quoted in Arthur M. Schlesinger, *The Colonial Merchants and the American Revolution, 1763-1776* (New York: Frederick Ungar, 1957), 31. See also Thomas M. Doerflinger, "Philadelphia Merchants and the Logic of Moderation, 1760-1775," *WMQ* 40 (Apr 1983): 197-226, quotation on 213. Drayton is quoted in Weir, *Lessons of Freeman, Etc.*, xxix.

39. As Cary Carson writes, "The consumer revolution would make comrades of ladies and gentlemen half a world away while leaving near but unequal neighbors worlds apart." Cary Carson, "The Consumer Revolution in Colonial America: Why Demand?" in *Of Consuming Interests: The Style of Life in the Eighteenth Century*, ed. Cary Carson, Ronald Hoffman, and Peter J. Albert (Charlottesville: University Press of Virginia, 1993), 483-697, quotation on 502.

40. The Smith and Jefferson passages are quoted in McCoy, *Elusive Republic*, 66, 12. Joyce Appleby, *Liberalism and Republicanism in the Historical Imagination* (Cambridge, MA: Harvard University Press, 1992), esp. 36-37, 42, 49; Edmund S. Morgan and Helen M. Morgan, *The Stamp Act Crisis: Prologue to Revolution* (Chapel Hill: University of North Carolina Press, 1953/1962), 32.

41. Smith, "Social Visions of the American Resistance Movement," 55; McCoy, *Elusive Republic*, 76.

42. John Adams to Hezekiah Niles, Feb 13, 1818. Quoted in Merrill Jensen, *The Founding of a Nation: A History of the American Revolution* (New York: Oxford University Press, 1968), xii. As Smith has written, "Participants sometimes knew of actions elsewhere and viewed each episode as part of a wider drama." "Food Rioters and the American Revolution," 3.

43. Kevin Gilmartin, *Print Politics: The Press and Radical Opposition in Nineteenth Century England* (New York: Cambridge University Press, 1997), 108. David M. Henkin, *City Reading: Written Words and Public Spaces in Antebellum New York* (New York: Columbia University Press, 1998), 84-85. On the Charleston meeting see "Charlestown (South Carolina) November 25," *PG*, Dec 22, 1773. On the rapid spread of the news see Labaree, *Boston Tea*

Party, 152. "Now London, September 29." Breen, *Marketplace of Revolution*, 236 (the phrase "distant strangers" is on 214, 234, 237).

44. "Commercial connexions" is from "Postscript to the Pennsylvania Gazette, No. 2393." The Bostonians are quoted in Maier, *From Resistance to Revolution*, 121. "At a meeting of Delegates from the Towns in the Counties of Hartford, New London and Windham, and part of the County of Litchfield, held at Hartford on the 15th of September, 1774," *PG*, Oct 12, 1774.

45. The Charlestonians are quoted in "Charlestown (South Carolina) November 25." Article 14 is quoted in "Postscript to the Pennsylvania Gazette, No. 2393," *PG*, Nov 2, 1774.

46. At a slightly later date, as Gilmartin points out, the "circulation of alternative products" began in the early nineteenth century in England with the sale of Henry Hunt's Radical Breakfast Powder. *Print Politics*, 108. On calls for substitutes and encouraging the brewery industry see Morgan and Morgan, *Stamp Act Crisis*, 33. Morgan, "Puritan Ethic and the American Revolution,"12. On giving up goods see *PG*, Jan 9, 1766, cited in Schlesinger, *Colonial Merchants and the American Revolution*, 77; Labaree, *Boston Tea Party*, 27; Mary Beth Norton, *Liberty's Daughters: The Revolutionary Experience of American Women, 1750-1800* (Boston: Little, Brown, 1980), 159. The phrases are from Smith, "Politics of Price Control in Revolutionary Massachusetts, 1774–1780," 136, 131.

47. Charles Tilly, "Major Forms of Collective Action in Western Europe, 1500–1975," *Theory and Society* 3 (Autumn 1976): 365–375, quotation on 372. Tilly notes that by 1820 this practice had essentially ended in England and by 1850 it had done so in Germany and France. Thompson, "Moral Economy," 80. 136. Benedict Anderson, *Imagined Communities: Reflections on the Origins and Spread of Nationalism* (New York: Verso, 1983), 6. For an important essay on the shift in the meaning of the market see Jean-Christophe Agnew, "The Threshold of the Market: Speculations on the Market," *RHR*, 21 (Fall 1979): 99–118.

48. Withington, *Toward a More Perfect Union*, xv. Gordon S. Wood, *The Radicalism of the American Revolution* (New York: Knopf, 1992), 326, 327. Blodget is quoted on 337. On the "liberating" aspects of the market see Waldstreicher, *Runaway America*, 97. Breen, *Marketplace of Revolution*.

49. Carson, "Consumer Revolution in Colonial America," 487. As Drew McCoy has shown, many republicans believed in the importance of commerce (of a particular kind) as a means of maintaining human connections in an increasingly distended society. *Elusive Republic*, 87 (also 75 for the Priestley comment).

50. Charles Tilly, *Social Movements, 1768-2004* (Boulder, CO: Paradigm Publishers 2004), 32. William Montgomery Meigs, *The Life of John Caldwell Calhoun* (New York: Neale Publishing Company, 1917), 370.

51. Tilly, *Social Movements*, 32.

52. Tarrow, *Power in Movement*, 40–41.

Chapter 2

1. Charles G. Sellers, *The Market Revolution: Jacksonian America, 1815-1846* (New York: Oxford University Press, 1991). "On Boycotting: Using Your Dollars for Change: The Power of the Pocketbook," *NBN* 2 (Spring/Summer 1988): 11–13, quotation on 11. Putnam's examples from the 1930s are drawn from the labor, rather than the consumer, movement.

2. John Greenleaf Whittier, "Introduction," in *The Journal of John Woolman* (Boston: James R. Osgood & Co., 1871), 1. Elias Hicks, *Observations on the Slavery of the Africans and Their Descendants and on the Use of the Produce of their Labour* (New York: Samuel Wood, 1814). Claire Midgley, "Slave Sugar Boycotts, Female Activism and the Domestic Base of British Anti-slavery Culture," *Slavery and Abolition* 17 (Dec 1996): 137–162. M. De Warville, "On Replacing Surgar of the Cane by the Sugar of Maple," *New York Magazine, or Literary Repository*, Aug 1792, 486. George Clinton, *Remarks on the Manufacturing of Maple Sugar: With Directions for Its Further Improvement* (William Morton: Philadelphia, 1792). See, in general, Wendy A. Woloson, *Refined Tastes: Sugar, Confectionery, and Consumers in Nineteenth-Century America* (Baltimore: Johns Hopkins University Press, 2002). Herbert Heaton, "Non Importation, 1806–1812," *Journal of Economic History* 12 (Nov 1941): 178–198. W. E. B. Du Bois was thus wrong to suggest that "Wendell Phillips alone suggested a boycott on Southern products." The idea was promoted long before Phillips, who, as we will see, later turned against free produce. W. E. B. Du Bois, *Black Reconstruction in America, 1860–1880* (New York: Russell & Russell, 1935), 25.

3. Lindsay Swift, *William Lloyd Garrison* (Philadelphia: George W. Jacobs, 1911), 72.

4. "Clean hands" is from "Hints," *Liberator*, Jul 30, 1831. "Buy for the Sake of the Slave" is from "Go, Relieve the Sufferings of the Slave," *Liberator*, Jan 4, 1839, 4. Augusta Rohrbach, *Truth Stranger than Fiction: Race, Realism, and the U.S. Literary Marketplace* (New York: Palgrave Macmillan, 2002), 8–9.

5. Adam Hochschild, *Bury the Chains: Prophets and Rebels in the Fight to Free an Empire's Slaves* (Boston: Houghton Mifflin, 2005), 7.

6. The Sabbatarian phrase is in Paul E. Johnson, *A Shopkeeper's Millennium: Society and Revivals in Rochester, New York, 1815–1837* (New York: Hill & Wang, 1978), 85. "American Democracy and Slavery," *Eclectic Review*, Nov 1857, 424–444, quotation on 442. Edward B. Bryan, *The Rightful Remedy: Addressed to the Slaveholders of the South* (Charleston, SC: Southern Rights Association by Walker & James, 1850).

7. The Presbyterians are quoted in Richard R. John, *Spreading the News: The American Postal System from Franklin to Morse* (Cambridge, MA: Harvard University Press, 1995), 180. Bertram Wyatt-Brown, "Prelude to Abolitionism: Sabbatarian Politics and the Rise of the Second Party System," *JAH* 58 (Sep 1971): 316–341; Robert H. Abzug, *Cosmos Crumbling: American Reform and the Religious Imagination* (New York: Oxford University Press, 1994), 110–111.

8. William Ellery Channing, "Associations," *Christian Examiner* 34 (Sep 1829): 105–140, quotations on 106.

9. The first quotation is from an antiantislavery pamphlet by William Fox, "An Address to the People of Great Britain, on the utility of refraining from the use of West India Sugar and Rum" (London, 1791), cited in Charlotte Sussman, *Consuming Anxieties: Consumer Protest, Gender, and British Slavery, 1713–1833* (Berkeley: University of California Press, 2000), 41. Adam Smith, *An Inquiry into the Nature and Causes of the Wealth of Nations* (Chicago: University of Chicago Press, 1996), vol. 2, bk. 4, chap. 8, 179. "Conscientious consumer" is from "Free Produce Convention," *Liberator*, Nov 15, 1839, 2. The phrase is also used in "Free-Labor Goods," *Friend's Intelligencer*, Feb 25, 1860, 790. As Elizabeth B. Clark has noted, the chain symbolized both the shackles of enslaved workers and the "essence of sympathy" linking people to each other. "'The Sacred Rights of the Weak': Pain, Sympathy, and the Culture of Individual Rights in Antebellum America," *JAH* 82

(Sep 1995): 463–493, quotation on 482. The purchaser of slave-made goods becomes "one indispensable link in the chain of causes which perpetuates the system," according to L. W. Gause, "Free Produce," *PF*, Feb 2, 1854, 1.

10. Channing, "Associations," 140. "Involved in the guilt" and Beecher are quoted in John, *Spreading the News*, 183, 181. The "Pioneer Line" is discussed in Johnson, *Shopkeeper's Millennium*, 85–87.

11. Ruth Nuermberger, *The Free Produce Movement: A Quaker Protest against Slavery* (Durham: Duke University Press, 1942), 119. For the reasons why George Washington Taylor kept his free produce store open until 1867, see W. P. Garrison, "Free Produce among the Quakers," *Atlantic Monthly* 22 (Oct 1868): 485–494.

12. Levi Coffin, *Reminiscences of Levi Coffin, the Reputed President of the Underground Railroad*, 3rd ed. (Cincinnati: Robert Clarke & Co., 1898), 265, 269. Nuermberger calls the period from 1838 to 1844 the high point of the movement, in *Free Produce Movement*, 59; on Garrison's early support for free produce see 101–102. The first notice for a free produce store is Michael Lamb and Benjamin Lundy, "Produce of Free Labor: Circular," *GUE*, Aug 5, 1826, 388. "David L. Child, Esq.," *National Enquirer*, Apr 29, 1838, 4. On the free produce wedding of the Welds see "Angelina Grimké to Weld," May 6, 1838, in *Letters of Theodore Dwight Weld, Angelina Grimké Weld, and Sarah Grimké, 1822–1844*, ed. Gilbert H. Barnes and Dwight L. Dumond (New York: D. Appleton-Century, 1934), 2:665. Benjamin Quarles, *Black Abolitionists* (New York: Oxford University Press, 1969), 74–76; Carleton Mabee, *Black Freedom: The Non-violent Abolitionists from 1830 through the Civil War* (New York: Macmillan, 1970), 187. Joan D. Hedrick, *Harriet Beecher Stowe: A Life* (New York: Oxford University Press, 1994), 241–242; Harriet Beecher Stowe, *Sunny Memories of Foreign Lands* (London: Low, 1854), 2:62, 77–79, 99, 105. See also J.E., "Free Articles," *Liberator*, May 14, 1831, 78, which declaimed that "every individual who disapproves of slavery is bound to abstain from using the productions of slave labor"; and the ad for "Free Groceries," *Liberator*, Oct 29, 1831.

13. Information in this paragraph is drawn from Nuermberger, *Free Produce Movement*, 60–82, 93, 95, 97, 119; Julie Roy Jeffrey, *The Great Silent Army of Abolition: Ordinary Women in the Antislavery Movement* (Chapel Hill: University of North Carolina Press, 1998), 22. The quotation is from *Report of the Board of Managers of the Free Produce Association of Friends, New York Yearly Meeting* (New York, 1853), 1. On the difficulties of running a free produce store, see George W. Taylor, *Autobiography and Writings of George W. Taylor* (Philadelphia: by the author, 1891), 42. Free produce advocates complained about a lack of support from their core constituencies. *Freedom's Journal* of New York City, a paper owned and edited by free blacks, condemned "the free coloured population of the United States" for "*adding to the labors and groans and stripes of two thousand of their enslaved brethren*" through consumption of slave-made sweets. "What Does Sugar Cost?" *Freedom's Journal*, Oct 19, 1827, 127.

14. On the use of labels see "Anti-slavery Fairs," *NS*, Dec 1847, 277. The quotation is from "Free Produce Convention," 2. For an example of the scholarly consensus see Richard Ohmann, who argues that "the very concept and word [consumer] appeared only" in the late nineteenth century. *Selling Culture: Magazines, Markets, and Class at the Turn of the Century* (London: Verso, 1996), 48. Women operated at least four free produce stores. Nuermberger. *Free Produce Movement*, 119; Harriet Beecher Stowe, "An Appeal to the Women of the Free States of America on the Present Crisis in Our Country," *PF*, Mar 2, 1854, 1.

Lewis C. Gunn, "Address to Abolitionists," in *Minutes of Proceedings of the Requited Labor Convention, Held in Philadelphia on the 17th and 18th of the Fifth Month and by Adjournment on the 5th and 6th of the Ninth Month, 1838* (Philadelphia, 1838), 34.

15. Garrison, "Free Produce among the Quakers."

16. The slogan is found in an undated pamphlet by "E. Harris, printer" in the Taylor Family Papers, Special Collections, Haverford College. The first chain quotation is from Gause, "Free Produce"; the second is from "Slave-Grown Sugar," *Christian Observer*, Mar 1825, 146–151, quotation on 147.

17. "Consumers," *GUE*, Feb 1831, 169. For earlier formulations of this point see "The Objection to the Use of Prize Goods Examined," *GUE*, Jan 1825, 61–65; "Mr. Garrison's Lectures on Slavery," *Christian Watchman*, Oct 29, 1830, 176, in which he argued that Northern consumers were responsible for slavery.

18. On the extermination of slave labor, see Adam Hodgson, "A Letter to M. Jean Baptiste Say, on the Comparative Expense of Free and Slave Labour, Continued," *Freedom's Journal*, Aug 31, 1827, 75. Benjamin Lundy, *A Plan for the Gradual Abolition of Slavery in the United States* (Baltimore: by the author, 1825). In *GUE*, the phrase "free produce" was not used until 1829, three years after Lundy opened the first store in August 1826 selling the "produce of free labor." "Free Products Again," *GUE*, Sep 16, 1829, 12; "Free Produce Society," *GUE*, Oct 30, 1829, 58. *Minutes of Proceedings of the Requited Labor Convention*, 13.

19. On "unpaid toil," see "Duty of Abstinence," *NS*, Jan 1846, 2. For examples of such language see "Address to the Friends of the Anti-slavery Cause on the Disuse of Slave-Labour Produce," *Anti-slavery Reporter*, Nov 1, 1847, 161–162; Henry Grew, "Free Labor Produce," *NS*, Jul 1, 1847, 162–165; Gunn, "Address to Abolitionists,"26; *The Letters of John Greenleaf Whittier*, ed. John B. Pickard (Cambridge, MA: Harvard University Press, 1975), 2: 217. Joseph A. Dugdale, "Original: Slave-Grown Produce," *Philanthropist*, Jan 18, 1843, 1. On the "ultimatum" see BERA, "Dialogue No. 1," *Liberator*, Aug 25, 1832, 134. The block quotation is from the undated pamphlet by "E. Harris," Taylor Family Papers. Harriet Beecher Stowe, *A Key to Uncle Tom's Cabin* (Boston: Jewett, 1854), 7, 255. See, for example, *Uncle Tom's Cabin* (London: Wordsworth, 1995; 1854), 123–124. Later in the novel (156), Marie St. Clare claims that "we mistresses are the slaves."

20. Ralph Waldo Emerson, "John Brown (6 January 1860)," in *Emerson's Antislavery Writings*, ed. Len Gougeon and Joel Myerson (New Haven: Yale University Press, 1995), 123. Whether abolitionists possessed the "sentiment of mercy" that Emerson detected in them, free produce advocates saw them as treating the slaves mercilessly if they bought slave-made goods. Free produce activists also invoked real Southern slaveholders and defenders of slavery, such as when Lucretia Mott "quoted the opinions of Hayne, Cooper, and Calhoun, severally of South Carolina, that the Southern planters are but the agents of the North in maintaining the slave system." "Sketches of the Sayings and Doings at the New England Anti-slavery Convention," *Liberator*, Jun 4, 1847, 91. The quotation "We are but your servants" is from "Prospectus," *NS*, Jan 1846, 1. Grew quoted in "Sketches of the Sayings and Doings at the New England Anti-slavery Convention." "Commercial union" is from "Fragmentary Labor," *PF*, Oct 29, 1846, 2. Benjamin Kent and Lydia C. Hambleton, "Union Free-Produce Society," *Liberator*, Aug 4, 1848, 124. "Prop and stay" is from "The Disuse of Slave Produce and the Abolition of Slavery," *NS*, Oct 1849, 198. "Stimulated" is from Sarah Pugh, "Annual Report of the Executive Committee of the American Free

Produce Association," *PF*, Nov 3, 1841, 4. On the "guilt" of consumers see W.C.B., "Abolition Consistency," *National Enquirer*, Mar 1, 1838, 98–99.

21. "Furnishing products" is from "Products of Slave Labour," *NS*, Apr 1847, 84–89. Jean Fagan Yellin, *Women and Sisters: The Antislavery Feminists in American Culture* (New Haven: Yale University Press, 1989), 13. On the connection between consumption and the sexual abuse of slaves, see "On the Disuse of Slave Produce," *NS*, Feb 1847, 33–35. Thomas L. Haskell, "Capitalism and the Origins of the Humanitarian Sensibility, Part I," in *The Antislavery Debate: Capitalism and Abolitionism as a Problem in Historical Interpretation*, ed. Thomas Bender (Berkeley: University of California Press, 1992), 111. Haskell notes of the starving stranger, a concept he develops on 127–128, that "being causally involved does not mean we regard ourselves as the cause" (131), marking a key difference from the conception of causality promoted by the free producers.

22. "Free-Produce Association—Philadelphia (U.S.)—Extracts from the Last Report," *NS*, Jul 2, 1849, 109. Henry Miles, "The Free Labor Movement," *FDP*, Sep 21, 1855; Frances Ellen Watkins, "The Free Labor Movement," *FDP*, Jun 29, 1855.

23. Gause, "Free Produce." The quotation about commerce and conscience is from "Disuse of Slave Produce," *Anti-slavery Reporter*, Jan 1, 1847, 1–2. Samuel Rhoads, "Free Produce," *Liberator*, Mar 1, 1850, 36. For an astute reading of the "commercial jeremiad" of early abolitionists see Philip Gould, *Barbaric Traffic: Commerce and Antislavery in the Eighteenth-Century Atlantic World* (Cambridge, MA: Harvard University Press, 2003).

24. On "Free Enterprize," see "Products of Slave Labour," 88. The "great lever" quotation is from *Minutes of the Twentieth Session of the American Convention for Promoting the Abolition of Slavery, and Improving the Condition of the African Race: Convened at Philadelphia, on the Second of October, 1827,* 41. Daniel Murray Pamphlet Collection (Library of Congress) http://hdl.loc.gov/loc.rbc/lcrbmrp.t1502 (accessed May 31, 2008). On the "productions of requited labor," see W.C.B., "Abolition Consistency." Samuel Rhoads, *An Address to Our Fellow Members of the Religious Society of Friends: On the Subject of Slavery and the Slave-Trade in the Western World* (Philadelphia: Free Produce Association of Friends, 1849), 13. Wm. Henry Hobbey, "Letter to William Lloyd Garrison," *NS*, Sep 1847, 202–205, quotation on 203.

25. "How Do You Know?" *NS*, Jun 1853, 37; Sussman, *Consuming Anxieties*, 17; Snelling quoted in Garrison, "Free Produce among the Quakers," 486.

26. "True colors" is from "Free-Labor Produce: Report of the New York Association," *Anti-slavery Reporter*, Sep 2, 1850. Garnet is quoted in Joel Schor, *Henry Highland Garnet: A Voice of Black Radicalism in the Nineteenth Century* (Westport, CT: Greenwood Press, 1977), 117. The other description is from "Slave Labor Produce," *NS*, Jun 1853, 46; Watkins, "Free Labor Movement." She made a similar point in her poem "On Free Produce," in *A Brighter Coming Day: A Frances Ellen Watkins Harper Reader*, ed. Frances Smith Foster (New York: Feminist Press, 1990), 44.

27. On "self denial" see "Abstinence from the Fruits of Unrequited Toil," *PF*, Aug 30, 1838, 1. On the self-denial of the movement's progenitors, including John Woolman, Benjamin Lundy, and Elias Hicks, see Elizabeth M. Chandler, "John Woolman," in *The Remembrancer* (Philadelphia: T. E. Chapman, 1841), 27–30; "Biography of Benjamin Lundy," *PF*, Oct 5, 1839, 3; Garrison, "Free Produce among the Quakers," 491–92. "Artificial wants' is from an unsigned letter, *PF*, May 28, 1840, 4.

28. "Coarse calicos" is from D.W.J., "Free Labour Goods," *NS*, Apr 1848, 74. Mott's granddaughter is quoted in *James and Lucretia Mott: Life and Letters*, ed. Anna Hallowell (Boston: Houghton, Mifflin, 1884), 88. Taylor's experiment with style is discussed in Nuermberger, *Free Produce Movement*, 98. "Privations" is from J.P.M., "Slave Labor Products," *PF*, Mar 22, 1838, 1. An ad for Taylor's store, emphasizes the quality of the food and clothing and the "fine Chintz umbrellas." "Free Labour Goods," *Friends' Review*, Nov 13, 1847, 128.

29. The Boston fairs successfully subsidized the *National Anti-slavery Standard*. Betty Fladeland, *Men and Brothers: Anglo-American Antislavery Cooperation* (Urbana: University of Illinois Press, 1972), 358. Supporters of the Philadelphia Fair included "Lucretia Mott, Charlotte Forten, Lydia White, Gay, McKim, and Sarah Pugh." "Anti-slavery Fair," *PF*, Dec 2, 1852, 195; Jeffrey, *Great Silent Army of Abolition*, 120, 122. Stephen Nissenbaum, *The Battle for Christmas* (New York: Knopf, 1996), 187. Deborah Van Broekhoven, 'Better than a Clay Club': The Organization of Women's Antislavery Fairs, 1835–60," *Slavery and Abolition* 19 (Apr 1998): 24–5l. Stowe is quoted in Lee Chambers-Schiller, "'A Good Work among the People': The Political Culture of the Boston Antislavery Fair," in *The Abolitionist Sisterhood: Women's Political Culture in Antebellum America*, ed. Jean Fagan Yellin and John C. Van Horne (Ithaca: Cornell University Press, 1994), 249–274, quotation on 268. "Ladies' Sale of Fancy Articles," *National Enquirer*, Dec 17, 1836, 59. The fairs strove for "a sense of abundance, and a quality of prettiness," observes Beverly Gordon in *Bazaars and Fair Ladies: The History of the American Fundraising Fair* (Knoxville: University of Tennessee Press, 1998), 42.

30. Nell Irvin Painter notes that the boycotts of slave produce and the fairs illustrate that abolitionists "placed great importance on how they spent their money," but they represent two distinct ways of thinking about the social impact of consumption. "Representing Truth: Sojourner Truth's Knowing and Becoming Known," *JAH* 81 (Sep 1994): 461–492, quotation on 474. Gause, "Free Produce." "Thirteenth Anti-slavery Fair," *PF*, Dec 7, 1848, 2.

31. "Go, Relieve the Sufferings of the Slave." Julie Roy Jeffrey notes that the fairs "entangled abolitionist women in the world of fashion and taste" and led to a "clash between standards of Christian plainness, self-denial, rural usefulness and urban elegance, self-indulgence, and frivolity." *Great Silent Army of Abolition*, 118, 120, 153.

32. David Brion Davis notes that "the decline of faith in gradualism had been marked in the mid-1820s by enthusiasm for a boycott of slave produce." "The Emergence of Immediatism in British and American Antislavery Thought," *Mississippi Valley Historical Review* 49 (Sep 1962): 209–230, quotation on 226. On the role that free produce played in the conversion of the Grimké sisters, see Gerda Lerner, *The Grimké Sisters from South Carolina: Pioneers for Women's Rights and Abolition* (New York: Schocken, 1967), 99–100. William Lloyd Garrison and Maria Weston Chapman, "To the Friends of the American Anti-slavery Society," *Philanthropist*, Jun 7, 1843, 1–2. "Lamentable apathy" is from "Free Produce Convention," 2. Mary Grew is quoted in "Free Produce Association," *Liberator*, Nov 24, 1843, 1. The letters between Johnson and Grew can be found in "Correspondence: Between the Buckingham Female A.S. Society, and the Female A.S. Society of Philadelphia," *GUE*, Oct 1837, 91. "Self-evident truths" is from Kent and Hambleton, "Union Free-Produce Society." "Death warrant" is from W.C.B., "Abolition Consistency." The critique of Garrison is from Rhoads, "Free Produce." Pugh, "Annual Report of the Executive Committee of the American Free Produce Association." "Glaring inconsistency"

is from "American Free Produce Association," *PF*, Oct 28, 1847, 3. "Iniquitous system" is from J.P.M., "Slave Labor Products." The hypocritical abolitionist is from "Annual Meeting of the American Free Produce Association," *PF*, Oct 29, 1846, 2.

33. "Extraneous issue" is from William Jay, "Slave Labor Productions," *Liberator*, Jun 18, 1836, 98. "Small importance" is from "Products of Free Labor," *Liberator*, Mar 5, 1847, 38. Garrison almost certainly wrote this unsigned article.

34. Garrison quoted in "Slavery Abolished by Abstinence from Its Products," *NS*, May 1846, 76–78, and "Products of Slave Labour." Elizur Wright, Jr., "On Abstinence from the Products of Slave Labor," *Quarterly Anti-slavery Magazine* 1 (Jul 1836): 393–400, quotations on 397, 399. "Clean hands" is from W.C.B., "Abolition Consistency." Goodell is quoted in *Minutes of Proceedings of the Requited Labor Convention*, 19.

35. The quotations from the elder Garrison are from "The Free Produce Question," *Liberator*, Mar 1, 1850, 1. Garrison, "Free Produce among the Quakers," 492. Phillips quoted in "Sketches of the Sayings and Doings at the New England Anti-slavery Convention." D. S. Grandin, "Free Labor Produce," *Liberator*, Sep 1, 1848, 139.

36. On England see Schor, *Henry Highland Garnet*, 117; Fladeland, *Men and Brothers*, 369. William Goodell's 1852 history of abolition did not mention free produce. *Slavery and Antislavery: A History of the Great Struggle in Both Hemispheres; with a View of the Slavery Question in the United States* (New York: Negro University Press, 1968). L. Mabbett, "Slave Labor Products vs. Free Labor Products," *North Star*, Jun 15, 1849. See the free produce advertisements in *FDP* on Dec 18, 1851 and Mar 4, 1852. S. Humphrey and Henry Miles, "Communicated the Free Labor Movement," *FDP*, Jun 9, 1854; Henry Miles, "The Free Labor Movement," *FDP*, Apr 20, 1855 (in this piece, Miles condemned those who did not seek accord between their "practice and profession"); and the letter to the editor by Marcus Stickney, *FDP*, May 18, 1855, which notes that the village of Lockport, NY, had received pledges from ninety-eight people to "support a Free Labor Produce Store." "Prof. Stowe and the Cotton Question," *National Era*, Oct 27, 1853, 170; Stowe, "An Appeal to the Women of the Free States of America." Watkins, "Free Labor Movement." George Washington Taylor continued to advertise free labor goods late into the war. See "Free Labor Sugar," *Friends' Review*, Aug 27, 1864, 9.

37. Helen Sorenson, *The Consumer Movement: What It Is and What It Means* (New York: Harper & Brothers, 1941), 111. On the ebb and flow of this duty, see Michael Pertschuk, *Revolt against Regulation: The Rise and Pause of the Consumer Movement* (Berkeley: University of California Press, 1982).

38. Patricia Sullivan, *Days of Hope: Race and Democracy in the New Deal Era* (Chapel Hill: University of North Carolina Press, 1996), 275; Charles M. Payne, *I've Got the Light of Freedom: The Organizing Tradition and the Mississippi Freedom Struggle* (Berkeley: University of California Press, 1995), 206–235; Kathryn Kish Sklar, *Florence Kelley and the Nation's Work: The Rise of Women's Political Culture* (New Haven: Yale University Press, 1995), 22. Lynd quoted in "The Consumer Movement," *Business Week*, Apr 22, 1939, 40.

39. For a contemporary example see "Do Cocoa Plantation Slaves in West Africa Produce Your Favorite Chocolate?" at http://www.antislaverysociety.addr.com/chocolates1.htm (accessed May 31, 2008).

40. James C. Scott, *Weapons of the Weak: Everyday Forms of Peasant Resistance* (New Haven; Yale University Press, 1985), 290; Beatrice Webb, *The Discovery of the Consumer* (New York: Cooperative League, 1928), 6, 12–13.

Chapter 3

1. "Fashionable," *Southern Confederacy* (Atlanta), Jul 2, 1862, 3. For another example of dress as an emblem, calling on all members of the group to wear "a badge on the left side of their hat," see "Southern Rights Association of Orangeburg District," *CM*, Jan 3, 1851.

2. On Southern boycotts after the John Brown raid see Richard H. Sewell, *A House Divided: Sectionalism and the Civil War, 1848–1865* (Baltimore: Johns Hopkins University Press, 1988), 71.

3. The first quotation is from Joseph Heath and Andrew Potter, *Nation of Rebels: Why Counterculture Became Consumer Culture* (New York: HarperBusiness, 2004), 108; Thomas Frank, *The Conquest of Cool: Business Culture, Counterculture, and the Rise of Hip Consumerism* (Chicago: University of Chicago, 1997). Common Sense, "Manufacturing of the South," *Southern Cultivator* 18 (Oct 1860): 303.

4. "More Madness," *National Era*, May 3, 1849, 71. James C. Scott, *Weapons of the Weak: Everyday Forms of Peasant Resistance* (New Haven: Yale University Press, 1985), 292–293.

5. On the resolutions, see, for example, from *CM*: "Anti-tariff Meeting," Aug 20, 1828, 2; Oct 7, 1828, 2; "Southern Rights Association of St. Johns and St. Stephens Parishes," Feb 4, 1851, 2. On "patriotic duty," see "What Shall We Wear?" *Staunton Spectator*, Jun 4, 1861, 2. "Charleston: Its Educational Institutions and Literature," *National Era*, Feb 17, 1859, 25.

6. For a comparative study of these efforts see Lawrence B. Glickman, "'Through the Medium of Their Pockets': Sabbatarianism, Free Produce, Non-intercourse, and the Significance of 'Early Modern' Consumer Activism," in *The Expert Consumer: Associations and Professionals in Consumer Society*, ed. Alain Chatriot, Marie-Emmanuelle Chessel, and Matthew Hilton (Hants, UK: Ashgate, 2006), 21–36.

7. See, for example, Yardley Taylor, "Southern Patronage to Southern Industry," *Southern Planter* (Richmond), Mar 1861, 160; "Non Intercourse," *CM*, Jul 3, 1857. William W. Freehling calls nonintercourse a "feeble gesture" in *Prelude to Civil War: The Nullification Controversy in South Carolina, 1816–1836* (New York: Harper & Row, 1965), 147.

8. Referring to "Mrs. Washington draped in homespun . . . arrayed in fabrics manufactured at home," one newspaper noted that "anterior to the Revolution" homespun was similarly popular. "Homespun Parties," *Dallas Herald*, Feb 8, 1860, 1. Many articles contained headlines such as "The Spirit of '76," *CM*, Sep 20, 1850, 2. "Commercial and Social Non-intercourse," *Mississippian and State Gazette* (Jackson, MS) Mar 21, 1851. An 1828 dinner in support of the campaign for Southern homespun, for example, concluded with a tribute to Thomas Taylor, a "venerable old patriot of the Revolution" who "seconded the call from appearing in clothes of Southern manufacture on the Fourth of July next." "Dinner to Messrs. Martin and McDuffie," *CM*, Jun 25, 1828, 2. "The Fast: A Suggestion," *CM*, Jun 10, 1861, 1; "The Day," *CM*, Jun 12, 1861, 1; Rev. R. H. Lafferty, *A Fast Day Sermon: Preached in the Church of Sugar Creek, Mecklenbrug County, N.C., Feb 28th, 1862* (Fayetteville: Congregation and Presbyterian Office, 1862).

9. "Extortion by Southern Manufacturers," *Semi-weekly Raleigh Register*, Nov 13, 1861, 2.

10. See, for example, the opening anecdote in Heath and Potter, *Nation of Rebels*, 1–2, in which the authors critique alternative ethical marketing as merely reinforcing capitalist domination. For a thoughtful meditation on antebellum Southern economic tensions see Douglas R. Egerton, "Markets without a Market Revolution: Southern Planters and Capitalism," *Journal of the Early Republic* 16 (Summer 1996): 207–221.

11. Drew Gilpin Faust, *The Creation of Confederate Nationalism* (Baton Rouge: Louisiana State University Press, 1988). On the conspicuous consumption of the slave-owning class see Daniel Walker Howe, *What Hath God Wrought: The Transformation of America, 1815–1848* (New York: Oxford University Press, 2007), 60–61.

12. Ingraham is quoted in Robert H. Gudmestad, *A Troublesome Commerce: The Transformation of the Interstate Slave Trade* (Baton Rouge: LSU Press, 2003), 17. "Negro's Crop," *Yazoo Democrat*, Mar 17, 1860, 2. For excellent treatment of these themes see Kathleen Hilliard, "Spending in Black and White: Race, Slavery, and Consumer Values in the Antebellum South" (PhD diss., University of South Carolina, 2006); Walter Johnson, *Soul by Soul: Life inside the Antebellum Slave Market* (Cambridge, MA: Harvard University Press, 1999), 117–134.

13. The three quotations are from *CM*: "Commercial Independence of the Confederate States, No. 1," Apr 8, 1861, 1; "Southern Made Gold Foil," Apr 12, 1861, 1; "Home Resources," Jun 15, 1861, 1. A writer from Muscogee County, Georgia, calling himself "Common Sense" also denounced the proliferation of "nicknacks." "Manufacturing at the South," *Southern Cultivator* 18 (Oct 1860): 303.

14. The *Mercury* had a New York fashion correspondent, whose regular column continued to appear even after the war began. See, for example, the regular Fashion Letter by "G.H.S.H.," with a New York dateline, which appeared in 1860 and 1861. "New York Hats by a New York Hatter," *CM*, Mar 14, 1850, 2. For additional evidence on this point see Jonathan Daniel Wells, *Origins of the Southern Middle Class, 1800–1861* (Chapel Hill: University of North Carolina Press, 2004), 62. The secession suit was advertised in *Yorkville Enquirer*, Nov 22, 1860, 3. "Charleston Made Fatigue Hats," *CM*, Feb 16, 1861, 2. The secession document was advertised in *CM*, Apr 6, 1861, 2.

15. Kenneth Moore Startup, *The Root of All Evil: The Protestant Clergy and the Economic Mind of the Old South* (Athens: University of Georgia Press, 1997), 142; Pinckney is quoted in Faust, *Creation of Confederate Nationalism*, 42. See also Eugene Genovese, *Political Economy of Slavery: Studies in the Economy and Society of the Old South*, 2nd ed. (Middletown, CT: Wesleyan University Press, 1989), 30.

16. "Non-intercourse," *Fayetteville Observer*, Jan 16, 1860 (originally published in *Wilmington Journal*).

17. *Atlanta Intelligencer* quoted in Weymouth T. Jordan, *Rebels in the Making: Planters' Conventions and Southern Propaganda* (Tuscaloosa, AL: Confederate Publishing Co., 1958), 116. For a similar claim see "Shoe and Leather Manufacturing Company," *CM*, Mar 27, 1861. On Northern merchants see "Slavery," *Southern Literary Journal and Magazine of Arts* 1 (Nov 1835): 188. "Southern Rights Associations," *Southern Literary Messenger*, Mar 1851, 178. "Sumner's Statistics," *New Orleans Daily Crescent*, Jun 15, 1860, in *Southern Editorials on Secession*, ed. Dwight Lowell Dumond (New York: Century Co., 1931), 127. The same volume includes "The Contest of 1860," *Kentucky Statesman*, Jan 6, 1860 (9), and *Savannah Republican*, Feb 6, 1860 (31–32). "The Bitter Bit," *CM*, Mar 29, 1861. Thomas Prentice Kettell, *Southern Wealth and Northern Profits* (Tuscaloosa: University of Alabama Press, 1860/1965). Senex, "Are We Dependent on the North?" *CM*, Jun 1, 1861, 1. For an excellent treatment of Southern fears along these lines, see Harold Woodman, *King Cotton and His Retainers* (Lexington: University of Kentucky Press, 1968), esp. chap. 12, "The Dependent South."

18. Anne Sarah Rubin, *A Shattered Nation: The Rise and Fall of the Confederacy, 1861–1868* (Chapel Hill: University of North Carolina Press, 2005), 87. For Northern recognition of

this irony in which slaveholders complained of being enslaved (while claiming that slavery was a benign institution) see "The Slaveholder's Heart," *Anti-slavery Record* 3 (Mar 1837): 1–12.

19. Jordan, *Rebels in the Making*, 114. McDuffie quoted in Leonidas, "For the Mercury," *CM*, Jul 17, 1828, 2.

20. For excellent treatment of this phenomenon see David S. Reynolds, *John Brown: Abolitionist* (New York: Vintage, 2005).

21. "Our State: Its Depressed Condition, the Remedy," *Edgefield Advertiser*, Nov 4, 1846, 1. Thanks to Michael Reynolds for sharing this article with me.

22. "The Homespun Movement," *Staunton Vindicator*, Jan 13, 1860, 2; Solon Robinson, "Another Letter to the North," *CM*, Jan 21, 1850, 2. On the Patapsco see Edward Strutt Abdy, *Journal of a Residence and Tour in the United States of North America* (London: John Murray, 1835), 1:394.

23. W.J.S., *Daily Morning News*, Mar 7, 1861 (originally published in *Macon Telegraph*).

24. On boycotts of resorts: Clement Eaton, *A History of the Old South: The Emergence of a Reluctant Nation* (New York: Macmillan, 1975), 434. Massachusetts: "Coming to the Point," *FDP*, Jul 6, 1855. Vermont: "Slavery and State Madness," *North Star*, Feb 8, 1850. Kentucky: "Dinner to Messrs. Martin and McDuffie." Abolitionists: Franklin, "The Rightful Remedy," *CM*, Oct 30, 1850, 2. The Augusta merchant is quoted in "A Boston Drummer," *FDP*, Jun 26, 1851.

25. For boycotts of animals: "Communicated for the Mercury," *CM*, Aug 15, 1828, 2; book sellers, schoolteachers, and universities: "The Homespun Movement"; *Uncle Tom's Cabin*: Joseph Carlyle Sitterton, *The Secession Movement in North Carolina* (Chapel Hill: University of North Carolina Press, 1939), 117; Boston and candles: "Incendiarism," *North Star*, Oct 31, 1850; food : "Our State: Its Depressed Condition"; ice: Robinson, "Another Letter to the North,"; nutmeg: "North and South," *CM*, May 2, 1850, 2 (originally published in *Mobile Tribune*); Yankee preachers and vacation destinations: "Spirit of Alabama Women," *Yazoo Democrat*, Feb 25, 1860, 2; printed matter: Alice Fahs, *The Imagined Civil War: Popular Literature of the North and South, 1861–1865* (Chapel Hill: University of North Carolina Press, 2001), 23–25; vehicles: "Non-intercourse," *CM*, Dec 17, 1850, 2. Amicus, "The Stage," *Savannah Republican*, Jun 6, 1863, 2. "Non Intercourse," *Charleston Courier*, Jul 12, 1860. J. G. Davidson, "Non-intercourse," *Charleston Courier*, Jan 31, 1860.

26. On the revolutionaries see *Boston Daily Atlas*, Dec 17, 1850. On the causal chain see "Non-intercourse between the North and the South," *National Era*, May 17, 1849, 78. "Will They Persist in This War!" *CM*, Apr 26, 1861, 4 (originally published in *Richmond Dispatch*). Pilgrim, "Disunion," *CM*, Apr 17, 1850, 2. "Practical Non-intercourse," *Old-Line Democrat* (Little Rock), Feb 2, 1860, 3. The dire predictions from *CM* include "Gotham Getting Scared," Apr 3, 1861, 1; "The Condition of the North," Jun 19, 1861, 1; "Commerce of New York," Apr 18, 1861, 1. Dr. Alexander Jones, "The Future under Supposed Permanent Separation," Apr 13, 1861, 3; "They Will Reap the Whirlwind," Mar 19, 1861, 1. Barbour is quoted in "Non-intercourse with the North," *Staunton Vindicator*, Mar 2, 1860, 2. "Non-intercourse Physic Working," *Weekly Raleigh Register*, Jan 11, 1860. The reporter also noted, referring to the large department store, "The great Stewart, too, is discharging clerks on account of loss of trade." "The Effect of Non-intercourse," *Fayetteville Observer*, Jan 5, 1860. The *Enquirer* was quoted in "Non-intercourse, the First Remedy," *Ripley Bee* (Ripley, OH), Dec 10, 1859.

27. "The Non-intercourse Dodge," *Vanity Fair*, Feb 11, 1860, 101. "Non-intercourse," *National Era*, Oct 31, 1850, 174. "Nullification and Retaliation," *Liberator*, Jul 6, 1855 (originally published in *Boston Courier*); "Alarming Spread of Non-intercourse," *National Era*, Dec 12, 1850, 197 (originally published in *NYTr*); "Non-intercourse," *New York Observer and Chronicle*, Jan 12, 1860, 14 (originally published in *Louisville Journal*).

28. "Non-intercourse to Be Dropped," *Boston Daily Advertiser*, Dec 20, 1859. "The South and Non-intercourse," *NYT*, Feb 15, 1860, 4. Frederick Douglass agreed that radical Southerners were "the last to carry into effect any such project, if there is even danger of prejudice to the pocket nerve." "Southern Trade," *FDP*, Feb 25, 1853. "Non-intercourse," *Lowell Daily Citizen and News*, Feb 4, 1860. The same paper told the anecdote of a hypocritical Virginia women who said she would eschew the North and two days later sent a request for silk and dress patterns from a Northern shop. "Non Intercourse," *Lowell Daily Citizen and News*, Dec 30, 1859. "Non-intercourse Exploded Again," *Boston Daily Advertiser*, May 10, 1860. "The Non-intercourse Bubble," *Boston Daily Advertiser*, Jan 19, 1860. See also "How 'Non-intercourse' Works at the South," *Franklin Repository and Transcript*, May 16, 1860, 8. "Songs for the South," *NYT*, Jun 16, 1861, 4. For the critique of the *Enquirer* see "Inconsistency," *Liberator*, Dec 30, 1859, 207 (originally published in *New York Commercial*).

29. The first quotations are from "Non-intercourse," *North American and United States Gazette* (Philadelphia), Dec 6, 1860. "Non Intercourse," *Liberator*, Mar 30, 1860, 52. "No Repudiation," *Boston Daily Advertiser*, Jan 15, 1861, 2.

30. "Article IV: Financial Aspects of the Rebellion," *New Englander* 22 (Jan 1863): 54–79, quotation on 54. "Southern Trade."

31. Colleton, "To the Editors of the Columbia Telescope," *CM*, Jul 9, 1828, 2. See also Leonidas, "No. V," *CM*, Jul 18, 1828, 2. "The Money Argument," *National Era*, May 1, 1851, 70 (originally published in *Richmond Republican*). "Non Intercourse," *Asheville News*, Dec 29, 1859.

32. "Letter from the Country," *CM*, May 28, 1861, 1. "Economize," *Staunton Spectator*, Sep 17, 1861, 1 (originally published in *Richmond Examiner*). "What Shall We Wear?"

33. "The Uses of War," *New York Herald*, Oct 30, 1861; "The Great Rebellion a Great Revolution," *New York Herald*, Nov 24, 1861. For calls for female sacrifice, see the pamphlets *The Women's Patriotic Association to Diminish the Use of Imported Luxuries* (Chicago, 1864); *New England Women's League, for Diminishing the Use of Luxuries during the War*, "To the Women of New England" (Boston, 1864). On cockades and bonnets see Fahs, *Imagined Civil War*, 43.

34. *The Anti-slavery History of the John Brown Year* (New York: Anti-slavery Society, 1861), 197. On Southern consumerism see Jan Ellen Lewis's perceptive "Slavery and the Market," *Reviews in American History* 28 (Dec 2000): 539–546.

35. Die-hard economic nationalists continued to promote autarkic rhetoric, even after the war ended. "Reader, if you have a dollar to spend, be sure to spend it with your own people," urged H. Rives Pollard, editor of the journal *Southern Opinion* in 1867. Quoted in Rubin, *Shattered Nation*, 182.

36. Heman Lincoln, "Shall the North or the South Rule?" *Independent*, Oct 21, 1880, 1, who noted that ostracism extended to former Confederates, such as James Longstreet. "Injury" is from "Intolerance of Opinion in the South," *Zion's Herald*, Jan 28, 1875, 28. O. O. Howard, "The Rising People," *Independent*, Aug 27, 1868, 1; H. C. Northcott, "A Voice from the South," *Christian Advocate*, Apr 1, 1869, 102; Thomas Wentworth Higginson, "Who Is Responsible for the Carpet-Baggers," *Independent*, Feb 12, 1874, 1; Miss Eliza

Woodworth, "Fraternity," *Zion's Herald*, Dec 23, 1875, 402. For a proostracism article see "Shall We Go South?" *Southern Planter and Farmer*, Feb 1870, 121. Jubal Early objected to the Robert E. Lee monument in Richmond in 1890 because it was composed of Maine Marble. David Blight, *Race and Reunion: The Civil War in American Memory* (Cambridge, MA: Harvard University Press, 2001), 267.

37. The boycott, noted one writer, is "not, he says, an Irish invention, but was introduced into Ireland by . . . Mr. James Redpath, who had seen its working in the South during the reconstruction period." "The Outlook," *Christian Union*, Jul 31, 1890, 131. See, for example, James Redpath, "The Coming Contest," *Independent*, Mar 2, 1876, 3; James Redpath, "The Stake in America," *Independent*, Mar 23, 1876, 1. Redpath's debt to his Southern experience with boycotts, "whose history has not yet been written," is discussed in Arthur Dudley Vinton, "The History of Boycotting," *Magazine of Western History* 5 (1886): 211–224, esp. 224; and Arthur Dudley Vinton, "As to Its Origin: Something about the Term Boycott," *AC*, Jul 29, 1890, 9. Eric Foner notes that the boycott "stemmed in an ironic way from the abolitionist experience." "Class, Ethnicity and Radicalism in the Gilded Age: The Land League and Irish America," in *Politics and Ideology in the Age of the Civil War* (New York: Oxford University Press, 1981), 182. "The Rebel Spirit," *New York Observer and Spirit*, Aug 6, 1868, 254.

38. W. E. B. Du Bois, *Black Reconstruction in America, 1860–1880* (New York: Russell & Russell, 1935), 532. See also 371, 386, 406, 450. On ostracism of Reconstruction officials and "a white boycott of Charleston's integrated streetcars" see Eric Foner, *Reconstruction: America's Unfinished Revolution, 1863–1877* (New York: Harper & Row, 1988), 137, 371. On the department store boycott see from the *Dallas Morning News*, "Dines with Whites: Booker T. Washington Is the Guest of John Wanamaker at Dinner in Saratoga," Aug 15, 1905, 2. "Wanamaker Incident," Aug 21, 1905, 5. "A Good Word for Wanamaker," Aug 27, 1905, 14. "To Boycott Wanamaker: Chapters of Daughters of Confederacy Take Action," Sep 18, 1905, 2. "A Sane Northern View," *AC*, Aug 27, 1905, B4, reported that Northern newspapers generally sympathized with the white South's outrage. On the boycott of Wanamaker for his actions in the post office, see "White Supremacy," *Harper's Weekly*, Sep 7, 1889, 715; "A Disappointed Kicker: Why the Arizona Editor Is Determined to Boycott John Wanamaker," *WP*, Sep 1, 1889, 16 (originally published in *Detroit Free Press*); "The Postmaster General Boycotted," *AC*, Feb 25, 1890, 1; *Independent*, May 1, 1890, 12.

39. On the jute boycott see Michael Schwartz, *Radical Protest and Social Structure: The Southern Farmers' Alliance and Cotton Tenancy, 1880–1890* (Chicago: University of Chicago Press, 1988), 262–265; William F. Holmes, "The Southern Farmers' Alliance and the Jute Cartel," *Journal of Southern History* 60 (Feb 1994): 59–80. "Boycotting the Merchant," *AC*, May 25, 1889, 3; "Boycott Jute Bagging and Use Cotton," *Charlotte News*, May 8, 1889, 3. "The Whole South to Join in a Boycott against the Trust," *Dallas Morning News*, Sep 9, 1888, 3; "Cotton Bagging: Southern Farmers Resolve to Boycott the Jute Trust," *Wheeling Register*, Aug 9, 1889, 1. Later Southern populists organized boycotts of merchants who supported the Democratic Party: "Resorting to the Boycott," *Macon Telegraph*, Sep 11, 1895, 4.

40. Vance is quoted in "The Deadlock Broken," *Columbus Daily Enquirer*, Jan 9, 1889, 1. The wedding is mentioned and Watson is quoted in Lawrence Goodwyn, *The Populist Moment: A Short History of the Agrarian Revolt in America* (New York: Oxford University Press, 1978), 88; Robert McMath, Jr., *American Populism: A Social History, 1877–1898* (New York:

Hill & Wang, 1990), 96. C. Vann Woodward, *Origins of the New South, 1877–1913* (Baton Rouge: Louisiana State University Press, 1951), 259. The last quotation is from "No Sectional Boycott," *WP*, Nov 27, 1888, 4.

41. Henry Cabot Lodge, "Federal Election Bill," *North American Review* 151 (Sep 1890): 257–266, quotation on 264. On Gordon see Blight, *Race and Reunion*, 262, 272, 282, 353, 361. The claim that the absence of war would help the movement is made in "The Question of a Boycott," *New Orleans Daily Picayune*, Jul 23, 1890, 4. "Commercial Secession," *Columbia Daily Register*, Jul 24, 1890, 2. Others agreed that the "pocket book of our northern friends was their vulnerable part." "Strike the Tender Spot," *AC*, Jul 24, 1890, 2. See also on the "highly sensitive" pocket nerve of Northerners, "Atlanta Is All Right," *AC*, Jul 29, 1890, 4. "Bullying out of Place," *NYTr*, Jul 24, 1890, 6. The old arguments are made in "The Boycott Is the Thing," *AC*, Jul 22, 1890, 1. For a statement that could have been taken verbatim from a nonintercourse tract see W. A. Knowles, "How to Boycott," *Southern Cultivator*, Sep 1, 1890, 445. For the biblical quotations see Southern Democrat, "To Meet the Force Bill," *AC*, Jul 21, 1890, 4. On threats against African Americans see "How the South Feels about It," *NYT*, Jul 7, 1890, 4. On the power of market forces see "Passing Notes and Bric-a-Brac," *Belford's Magazine* 5 (Sep 1890): 629–636, quotation on 635–636.

42. For other African American–led boycotts, some of which occurred before 1890, see Steven Hahn, *A Nation under Our Feet: Black Political Struggles in the Rural South from Slavery to the Great Migration* (Cambridge, MA: Harvard University Press, 2003), 186 (on Union League–organized boycotts among freedpeople), 356 (on boycotts by steamboat companies of exodusters), and 422 (on Colored Alliance boycotts of local merchants). African American consumer activism was not confined to the South. See, for example, "For Drawing Color Line Ministers in Boston to Boycott a Hotel," *Milwaukee Sentinel*, Feb 1, 1896, 5; "Hotel Boycott," *Boston Daily Advertiser*, Oct 24, 1896, 6. In the latter case, fifty "colored musicians" could not get a hotel in Hartford and sought to organize a boycott. "Street Car Receipts Fall Off," *AC*, Sep 20, 1900, 4. See also "Montgomery Negroes Boycott Street Cars," *AC*, Aug 16, 1900, 1. Robert E. Weems, Jr., *Desegregating the Dollar: African American Consumerism in the Twentieth Century* (New York: New York University Press, 1998).

43. Carol Eisenberg, "Christian Right Exhorts Consumer Crusades," *Newsday*, Dec 14, 2005, at http://www.corpwatch.org/article.php?id=12971 (accessed Jun 18, 2008).

Chapter 4

1. For these and other examples, see "Taboo!" *JSP*, Jul 18, 1886, 1.

2. "Boycott and 'Boycotting,'" *CDIO*, May 21, 1881, 10; John Swinton, "Justifiable Boycotts," *Independent*, Apr 8, 1886, 4; "The Decay of the Boycott," *CT*, Dec 20, 1889, 4.

3. "Taboo!"; "Wanamakered," *Belford's Magazine* 4 (Aug 1889): 405; "We Stick to 'Boycott,'" *Boycotter*, Mar 21, 1885, 3. See also "The Boycott in Politics," *Milwaukee Sentinel*, Oct 28, 1886, 4.

4. For an example of the hyphen, see "A Voice from Roanoke," *RP*, May 7, 1904, 4. For descriptions of the changing ways of presenting the word see "About People," *Outlook*, Jul 24, 1897, 764. Eventually, the "marks of neologism disappeared" according to the *Friends Intelligencer*, Jul 31, 1897, 538. See from the *Workmen's Advocate*, "Ye Gentle Boy-

Cat," Aug 8, 1886, 4; and "Ye Boy-Cat," Jul 11, 1886, 4. The linguist is quoted in "The 'Man in the Street' as Grammarian," *Litttell's Living Age*, May 24, 1890, 510. "Boycotting," *Deseret Desert News*, Oct 12, 1881, 583.

5. For the spread of the verb into French, Dutch, German, and Russian and the suggestion that the word need not be capitalized see "About People." See the German language article "Baerum War die Tribune Boycotter," *Boycotter*, Jun 14, 1884, 1.

6. Arthur Dudley Vinton, "The History of Boycotting," *Magazine of Western History* 5 (Nov 1886): 211–224, quotation on 212. On gender boycotts see, for example, "Amherst Boycotts Smith," *NYTr*, Apr 4, 1907, 4; "They Will Boycott the Young Men," *Memphis Commercial Appeal*, Oct 21, 1895, 2.

7. "A Theatre Boycott," *NYT*, Feb 2, 1887, 8. The alliance leader L. L. Polk called for boycotts of newspapers that "seek to impair our strength and unity" and urged farmers to also boycott their advertisers. Quoted in C. Vann Woodward, *Origins of the New South, 1877–1913* (Baton Rouge: Louisiana State University Press, 1951), 194–195. Silver, "Boycott the Goldbug Papers," *Rocky Mountain News*, Jul 1, 1893, 4; "Propose a Boycott: Silver Men Will Touch the Pockets of the East," *St. Paul Daily News*, Jul 15, 1893; A. C. Fisk, "To Boycott the East Silver Men Now Threaten to Divert Shipping to Gulf Ports," *Milwaukee Sentinel*, Aug 6, 1893; "Now It's a Boycott: New Plan of Campaign Threatened by Free Silver Advocates," *CDIO*, Aug 6, 1893, 6; "To Boycott the East Bimetallists to Meet and Adopt a Policy of Commercial War," *Milwaukee Sentinel*, Aug 17, 1893, 5. "Women Take Up Boycott," *NYTr*, Jan 29, 1910, 14.

8. A. B. Leonard, "Boycott the Saloon," *Christian Advocate* (New Orleans), Jan 21, 1886. S.R., "The 'Sun' and the Boycott," *Liberty*, 14 (Dec 1903); "An International Boycott," *Youth's Companion*, Jul 27, 1916, 414. The "manifest failure" quotation is from "An Ineffective Boycott," *CDIO*, Jun 27, 1893, 4. See also "A Religious Boycott," *Atchison Daily Globe*, May 6, 1893; "The Sunday Boycott," *Sunday Oregonian*, May 6, 1893, 4; "A Sabbatarian Boycott," *CDIO*, May 20, 1893, 5.

9. "Made Immortal by a Word," *WP*, Nov 10, 1907, M4; Ralph David Bretterton, "Dialects," *Living Age*, Apr 6, 1901, 24.

10. The first quotation is from *Boycotter* (Topeka), Dec 18, 1885, 2; the second is from "Taboo!"

11. Michael Gordon, "The Labor Boycott in New York City, 1880–1886," *Labor History* 16 (Spring 1975): 184–229, quotation on 207; Michael Allen Gordon, "Studies in Irish and Irish-American Thought and Behavior in Gilded Age New York City" (PhD diss., University of Rochester, 1977), 355; James M. Jasper, *The Art of Moral Protest: Culture, Biography, and Creativity in Social Movements* (Chicago: University of Chicago Press, 1998), 266. For a description, more in line with my view, of the boycott as market oriented rather than preindustrial see David Scobey, "Boycotting the Politics Factory: Labor Radicalism and the New York City Mayoralty Election of 188[6]," *RHR* 28–30 (Sep 1984): 280–325.

12. B.N., "The Jay Gould Boycott," *Puck*, Apr 21, 1886, 19; Horace White, "Pullman Boycott," *Nation*, Jul 5, 1894, 5. "Boycott! Boycott! Peter Doelger's Lager Beer," *JSP*, Sep 20, 1885; "Boycott, Boycott: Garry Brothers and Brennan and White Shoes," *JSP*, Jan 17, 1886, 3. Richard Schneirov, *Labor and Urban Politics: Class Conflict and the Origins of Modern Liberalism in Chicago, 1864–97* (Urbana: University of Illinois Press, 1998), 124.

13. For an analysis of several hundred recent boycotts see "Boycotting: Its Employment in the United States within Two Years," *Bradstreets*, Dec 19, 1885, 394–398. There were

1,352 boycotts between 1885 and 1892. See Samuel P. Orth, *The Armies of Labor: A Chronicle of the Organized Wage-Earners* (New Haven: Yale University Press, 1919), 178.

14. *The Special Commission Act, 1888: Report of the Proceedings Before the Commissioners Appointed by the Act* (London: London Times, 1888), IV: 263–273. This section is labeled, "The Land War: Boycotting: Promulgation by Davitt and Mr. Parnell." See 266, 271, 265.

15. James Redpath, "Mr. Redpath's Letter", *CDIO*, Oct 29, 1880, 1. "Topics of the Week," *Redpath's Weekly*, Dec 1, 1883, 3. As the *Inter-Ocean* observed, "Mr. Redpath is a natural agitator. He took part with John Brown in the Kansas movement. . . . His writings in the South since reconstruction have attracted national attention, and he is widely known as a man of radical views on social and economic questions." *CDIO*, Oct 25, 1880, 4.

16. Quotation is from James Redpath, "The Stake in America," *Independent*, Mar 23, 1876, 1. Albion Tourgee, "About Carpet-Baggers," *NYTr*, Jan 31, 1881, 2. See also Tourgee, *A Fool's Errand, by One of the Fools* (New York: Fords, Howard & Hulbert, 1879), 134, 159. For instances of Tourgee being boycotted in the South see Otto H. Olsen, *Carpetbagger's Crusade: The Life of Albion Winegar Tourgee* (Baltimore: Johns Hopkins Press, 1965), 56, 193; Mark Elliott, *Color-Blind Justice: Albion Tourgee and the Quest for Racial Equality* (New York: Oxford University Press, 2006), 139–140. On the ostracism of a Reconstruction official and labor radical see Dominic Candeloro, "Louis Post as a Carpetbagger in South Carolina: Reconstruction as a Forerunner of the Progressive Movement," *American Journal of Economics and Sociology* 34 (Oct 1975): 423–432; Sarah Woolfolk Wiggins, "Ostracism of White Republicans in Alabama during Reconstruction," *Alabama Review* 27 (Jan 1974): 52–64.

17. Redpath's debt to his Southern experience is discussed in Arthur Dudley Vinton, "As to Its Origin: Something about the Term Boycott," *AC*, Jul 29, 1890, 9 (originally published in New York *Commercial Advertiser*); and Vinton, "History of Boycotting," 224. An irony is that Redpath went to Ireland as an employee of Whitelaw Reid's *NYTr*, the newspaper that later became the target of one of the most visible boycotts of the 1880s. See Charles F. Horner, *The Life of James Redpath and the Development of the Modern Lyceum* (New York: Barse & Hopkins, 1926), 255. The "American custom" quotation is from Vinton's entry "Boycott" in *Appletons' Annual Cyclopaedia and Register of Important Events of the Year*, new series (New York: D. Appleton, 1891), 15:73–75, quotation on 75. Redpath's rejected ostracism in "The Coming Contest," *Independent*, Mar 2, 1876, 3.

18. Redpath learned of this act of ostracism as he was preparing Brown's posthumous biography in an 1859 letter he received from Brown's former employee. James Foreman to James Redpath, Dec 28, 1859, in *John Brown: The Making of a Revolutionary*, ed. Louis Ruchames (New York: Grosset & Dunlap, 1969), 171–176. These incidents are described in David S. Reynolds, *John Brown, Abolitionist* (New York: Vintage, 2005), 41, 292, 399. Redpath's travels to Virginia and South Carolina are discussed in John McGivigan, *Forgotten Firebrand: James Redpath and the Making of Nineteenth-Century America* (Ithaca: Cornell University Press, 2008), 7.

19. For criticism of the anti-Chinese movement see James Redpath, "In Jack Cade's Camp," *Independent*, Mar 11, 1880, 2. James Redpath, "Christian Social Reconstruction," pt. 4, "Co-operation of Consumers," *Zion's Herald and Wesleyan Journal*, Aug 8, 1867; James Redpath, "Christian Social Reconstruction," pt. 5, "Management of Co-operative Stores," *Zion's Herald and Wesleyan Journal*, Aug 22, 1867. Later, he also endorsed the eight-hour day. See "Eight-Hour Problem," *CT*, May 2, 1886, 26.

20. Vinton, "As to Its Origin." O'Malley turned the offer down, noting that it was the British landlord's responsibility to settle with the tenants. Redpath's speech "What I Know about Boycotting," given at Cooper Union in New York City, is quoted in "Pleas for the Irish," *CT*, Jan 14, 1881, 12; "Patriotism vs. Prices: The St. Louis Land League Resolve to Boycott English Manufacturers," *St. Louis Globe-Democrat*, Oct 31, 1881, 3. Thomas N. Brown notes that eight thousand Philadelphians joined this boycott in *Irish-American Nationalism, 1870-1890* (Philadelphia: Lippincott, 1966), 168. For a later boycott, see M. Philbin, "Boycott John Bull," *Irish World and American Industrial Liberator*, Dec 10, 1898, 10. On the attempt of a group of Irish-American trade unionists to organize an American Federation of Labor boycott of British goods after World War I see "A Warning to Irish Extremists," *NYT*, Jun 15, 1921, 10. For an overview of World War I–era boycotts see Elizabeth McKillen, "American Labor, the Irish Revolution, and the Campaign for a Boycott of British Goods: 1916–1924," *RHR* 61 (1995): 35–61. E. L. Godkin, "The Genesis of Boycotting," *Nation*, Dec 23, 1880, 437–438, quotation on 438.

21. "A Gigantic Boycott," *JSP*, Jul 11, 1886, 1; "A Gigantic Boycott," *Workmen's Advocate*, Jul 18, 1886, 3. This practice was not limited to the West. The *Christian Recorder*, Jan 14, 1884, notes a boycott of the Chinese in Natick, MA; "White Laundrymen Combine to Boycott the St. Louis Patrons of Chinese Rivals," *New Orleans Daily Picayune*, Jul 17, 1892, 15. The Central Labor Union of New York called for a boycott of the Chinese to "prevent the coming East of the Chinamen who have been boycotted in the West." "Boycott the Chinese," *NYT*, Mar 1, 1886, 5. The "leave alone" quotation is from "American Boycotters," *NYT*, May 7, 1882, 8. On Chinese boycotts see "Chinamen Are Angry," *NYT*, Jan 5, 1882, 5.

22. "Boycott the French Exposition," *Denver Evening Post*, Sep 10, 1899; "Boycott France! Whole World Rings with Execration of Dreyfus's Verdict," *Boston Daily Advertiser*, Sep 11, 1899; "'The Dreyfus Blot': Movement to Boycott the Paris Exposition Unless Justice Prevails," *Arkansas Democrat*, Sep 12, 1899; "The Dreyfus Boycott," *Weekly Rocky Mountain News*, Sep 21, 1899, 4. "Shall American Women Boycott French Frills?" *Milwaukee Journal*, May 21, 1898, 5.

23. "Latest Definitions," *Life*, Apr 8, 1886, 206.

24. James Redpath, *Talks about Ireland* (New York: by the author, 1881), 82. The 1947 film *Captain Boycott* (Universal-International Pictures), captures this well. The character based on O'Malley, Father McKeogn, ends the movie by uttering the verb "to boycott." "Boycotted: Thirteen Landlords and Land Agents Formally Boycotted by the Agitators Sunday," *CDIO*, Nov 15, 1880, 1.

25 Horner, *Life of James Redpath and the Development of the Modern Lyceum*; Carlyle W. Morgan, "The Wide Horizon; Boycott for Peace?" *CSM*, Feb 16, 1938, 20.

26. "Street Car Law," *Lynchburg News*, Jun 9, 1906, 6.

27. "To Advertisers," *Boycotter*, Jan 5, 1884, 2. J.A.W., "Good Work in the South," *Boycotter*, Feb 15, 1886, 1. (The author was the chair of the boycotting committee of the Atlanta Typographical Union.) Scobey, "Boycotting the Politics Factory," 299. "Defense of Boycotting," *Boycotter* (New York), Jan 5, 1884, 4 (originally published in *Providence Telegram*).

28. Jasper, *Art of Moral Protest*, 264.

29. On the Berg boycott see "A Factory in Siege: Lively Work of the Orange Boycotters," *JSP*, Apr 5, 1885, 1. On the transition from sword to print see "The Boycott: Its Present Status in America," *Boycotter*, Aug 14, 1886, 1. "Nobody," "'Nobody' on Boycotting and

Blacklisting," *JSP*, Aug 23, 1885, 2. "Tired of Boycotts," *Youth's Companion*, Mar 15, 1900, 134. Powderly quoted in "Record," *New Princeton Review*, Nov 1886, 426.

30. Leo Wolman, *The Boycott in American Trade Unions* (Baltimore: Johns Hopkins University Press, 1916), 90–91. I draw the concept of simultaneity from Thomas J. Schlereth, *Victorian America: Transformations in Everyday Life, 1876-1915* (New York: HarperCollins, 1991), 201.

31. "Moral satisfaction" is from Jasper, *Art of Moral Protest*, 264. As Benedict Anderson notes, citizens of modern nations "will never know most of their fellow members." *Imagined Communities: Reflections on the Origin and Spread of Nationalism*, rev. ed. (London: Verso, 1983), 7.

32. "Do You Take the *Tribune*? If So, Stop It," *Boycotter*, May 31, 1884, 2. "Boycott the Tribune," *Boycotter*, Mar 29, 1884, 1. "Boycotting as a Remedy," *Boycotter*, Apr 26, 1884, 1 (originally published in *Toledo Record*).

33. "Factory in Siege." "Refrain from intercourse" is from T., "The Boycott and Its Limit," *Liberty*, Dec 3, 1887, 4. "Logical limits" is from "Practical Effects of the Boycott," *New York Evangelist*, Nov 18, 1886, 3. On the Cleveland situation see "The Boycott," *Boston Daily Advertiser*, Aug 18, 1899, 4.

34. "King on the Boycott: An Institution Backed by the Bible," *Boycotter*, Aug 28, 1886, 1. Carville is quoted in Gordon, "Studies in Irish and Irish American Thought and Behavior," 551.

35. "General Boycotting Reduced to Absurdity," *Dallas Morning News*, Dec 8, 1885, 4.

36. "King on the Boycott." For another description of the boycott as a "consumer's strike" see Hayes Robbins, *The Labor Movement and the Farmer* (New York: Harcourt, Brace & Co., 1922), 135. "A New Phase of the Boycott," *Boycotter*, Dec 5, 1885, 1 (originally published in *Toledo News*); "The Ballot, the Strike and the Boycott," *Journal of United Labor*, Feb 21, 1889; "Butler on the Boycott," *JSP*, Feb 14, 1886, 1.

37. The first quotation is from "Current Topics," *Albany Law Journal*, Aug 12, 1899, 60. "General Boycotting Reduced to Absurdity." G.F.A., "More about Boycott," *Dallas Morning News*, Feb 6, 1886, 6. "Boycotting," *NYT*, Nov 7, 1885, 4; "What a Boycott May Do: Throw Thousands out of Work and Cause a Loss of Millions," *NYT*, Aug 7, 1890, 8.

38. On the boycott as a weapon see, for example, Washington Gladden, "Is It Peace or War?" *Century Illustrated Magazine* 32 (Aug 1886): 565. Redpath quoted in "The Outlook," *Christian Union*, Jul 31, 1890, 131. "The Boycotters: An Attempt to Find out the Real Result of Boycotting," *JSP*, May 11, 1884, 1. The New Jersey advocate is quoted in "From the Trenton Sunday Advertiser," *Boycotter*, Jan 9, 1886, 2. On the "terrible engine" see "Organized Boycotting," *Boycotter*, Jan 5, 1884, 2. O'Donnell quoted in "Parade and Protest," *Boycotter*, Apr 26, 1884, 1. "Boycotting," *Deseret Desert News*, Oct 12, 1881, 583.

39. Rev. Charles Hawley, "The Power of the Boycott," *New York Evangelist*, Dec 17, 1885, 8; "The Boycott," *Harper's Weekly*, Apr 24, 1886, 258; Frank Eno, "The Boycott," *Golden Era*, Jun 1886, 383–385, quotation on 384.

40. "Boycotting the Boycott," *NYTr*, Oct 25, 1903, 10. Boycotting as a double-edged weapon: "A Blow at the Boycott," *NYT*, May 6, 1889, 4. "Weapon that shoots at both ends": "The Word Boycott Is to Be Put in the new Dictionaries," *North American* (Philadelphia), Jan 15, 1886. Boycotting as a boomerang: "Books and Authors," *Christian Union*, Aug 12, 1886, 22; "The Boycott: A Boomerang," *Charities and the Commons*, Jan 4, 1908, 1372–1373.

41. "Boycotting a Widow: Mrs. Landgrof Suffering from the Quarrel of Two Unions,"

NYT, Apr 18, 1886, 2. For a treatment of the Gray boycott as epitomizing the problems of boycotts writ large see Orth, *Armies of Labor*, 178–179. "A Test Case," *Tombstone Epitaph Prospector*, Apr 22, 1886, 3 (originally published in *NYT*); "The Boycott: Opinions of Influential Journals on This Modern System of Tyranny," *Tombstone Epitaph Prospector*, Apr 23, 1886, 3. *Atchison Daily Champion*, Apr 18, 1886; *Milwaukee Sentinel*, Apr 15, 1886, 4; *Boston Daily Advertiser*, Apr 21, 1886, 4.

42. "Boycotting Gone to Seed," *NYTr*, Apr 14, 1886, 4. "Plucky Esther Gray: The Brave Little Woman Who Defies the Boycotters," *CT*, Apr 17, 1886, 12. (This article is the source of the "strange interest" quotation.) For another description of Gray as "plucky and famous" see Demot Enmot, "Our New York Letter," *Albany Law Journal*, May 8, 1886, 380. "The Boycotting Must Go: An American Community Will Not Tolerate It: Practical Sympathy for the Oppressed: Mrs. Landgraf Prospering as Well as Mrs. Gray," *NYT*, Apr 24, 1886, 8. "The Mrs. Gray's Elegy," *Macon Weekly Telegraph*, Apr 23, 1886, 3. This was not the only poem inspired by Mrs. Gray. See H. C. Dodge, "Boycotting versus Stone-Cutting," *Puck*, May 5, 1886, 146. "Mrs. Gray Wins: The Foreign Boycotters Cease Annoying Her," *CT*, Apr 19, 1886, 3. "Beating the Boycott: A Plucky Woman's Fight-Letter from Charles Crocker," *LAT*, Apr 14, 1886, 1. A number of such letters are included in "Mrs. Gray and the Boycott," *St. Louis Globe-Democrat*, Apr 17, 1886, 4; "Eight Boycotters Caught: Arrested for Annoying Mrs. Gray," *NYTr*, Apr 15, 1886, 1; "Violence in the Bakery: Throwing Cakes in Mrs. Gray's Shop," *NYTr*, Apr 16, 1886, 2, which reported contributions from Massachusetts, Pennsylvania, and elsewhere. W. A. Croffut, "The Un-American Boycott: A Foreign Invention: Its Advocates Going to Rule This Country," *CT*, Apr 22, 1886, 9; W. A. Croffut, "Boycott of Esther Gray: Sights and Scenes about the Brave Little Woman's Bakery," *Weekly Detroit Free Press*, Apr 24, 1886, 4.

43. Gray's "business continues to be unusually large," according to "Is Boycotting a Conspiracy?" *BG*, Apr 16, 1886, 2. The phrase "boycotting the boycotters" is from *Raleigh News and Observer*, Apr 18, 1886; *Milwaukee Sentinel*, Apr 15, 1886, 4; "Some New Words for Webster," *New York Evangelist*, Aug 5, 1886, 7; "The Boycotted Butcher," *AC*, Apr 18, 1886, 5. See also "Wants to Be Boycotted," *LAT*, Dec 6, 1903, A4.

44. For Krekel's decision see "Boycotting in the United States," *Central Law Journal*, Oct 23, 1885, 326. See also Gordon, "Studies in Irish and Irish-American Thought and Behavior," 566. On "indirect boycotts" see "Two Kinds of Boycotting," *Century* 32 (Jun 1886): 320–322. "The Boycott," *NYT*, Feb 9, 1886, 4. "Fined for Boycotting: Mrs. Gray Wins a Victory at the Court: Justice Duffy to Make a Test Case: A Walking Delegate Arrested," *NYTr*, Apr 16, 1886, 5; "Getting into the Courts: Legal Aspect of the Boycott at Mrs. Gray's Bakery: A Fine and a Warning for the Sandwich Men," *NYT*, Apr 15, 1886, 8; "A Lull in the Boycotts: Thirteen of Mrs. Gray's Persecutors Said to Have Been Indicted," *NYT*, Apr 20, 1886, 8. "The Boycott System," *Independent*, Apr 22, 1886, 20. See also "Boycotters Punished," *Harper's Weekly*, Jul 17, 1886, 450–451.

45. William A. Hammond, "The Evolution of the Boycott," *Forum*, Jun 1886, 369–376. The "old as mankind" quotation is from this article. Tom Fitch, "What Is Boycotting?" *LAT*, Feb 20, 1914, sec. 2, p. 4. "Early Record of Boycott: English and Scottish Weavers Resorted to It in 1752," *WP*, Sep 1, 1908, 6 (originally published in *Indianapolis News*); "Boycott No Modern Invention: Interesting Details of a Labor Trial in New York in 1809," *CT*, Aug 5, 1894, 11; "An Old Time West Point Boycott," *CT*, Aug 10, 1889, 5; "Before the Boycott," *AC*, May 9, 1886, 8; Henry Frankel, "He Thinks Boycotting Was Practiced in Ancient

Times," *CT*, May 4, 1886, 4. Richard Ely traced the boycott to "time immemorial" and Canterbury in 1327 in *The Labor Movement in America* (New York: Thomas Y. Crowell, 1886), 297. Leo Wolman cited as precedent a boycott imposed in Baltimore in 1833 at a meeting of "the citizens generally" upon master hatters who had combined to cut the wages of journeymen: *Boycott in American Trade Unions*, 23. An untitled article in the *Christian Advocate*, Aug 5, 1886, 488, found that an instance of boycotting in 1820 in Custhanas, Brazil.

46. Robert Wiebe, *The Search for Order, 1877-1920* (New York: Hill & Wang, 1967), 44. 'The Power of the Boycott," *Boycotter*, Dec 12, 1885, 2 (originally published in *New York Sun*). On the ancient history of ostracism see Sara Forsdyke, *Exile, Ostracism, and Democracy: The Politics of Expulsion in Ancient Greece* (Princeton: Princeton University Press, 2005).

47. The first quotation is from "Boycotting as a Remedy." Hammond, "Evolution of the Boycott," 376. "Don't Read any of Frank Tousey's Publications," *Boycotter*, Jan 31, 1885, 2. "Boycotted Street Cars," *RP*, Apr 7, 1900, 4; *Baltimore Afro-American Ledger*, Jun 18, 1904, 4.

48. Rev. John Snyder, "The Boycott: Banish the Hateful Word from the Vocabulary," *LAT*, Aug 27, 1894, 4 (originally published in *St. Louis Globe-Democrat*). In a different context, Sven Beckert has observed that "global links are important to examining even the most local articulations of capitalism" in "Comment on Nelson Lichtenstein, 'Supply Chains, Workers' Chains, and the New World of Retail Supremacy,'" *Labor: Studies in the Working-Class History of the Americas* 4 (Spring 2007): 45–48, quotation on 45.

49. This story is expertly told in Daniel R. Ernst, *Lawyers against Labor: From Individual Rights to Corporate Liberalism* (Urbana: University of Illinois Press, 1995).

50. "Boycott the Boycott," *St. Louis Globe Democrat*, Apr 28, 1886, 6 (originally published in *NYTr*).

51. Whittier is discussed in *Boycotter*, Jul 31, 1886, 2; "The Boycott and Its Uses," *Boycotter* (Topeka), Feb 12, 1886, 4. "Yankee Doodle" is from "King on the Boycott."

52. "Legality of the Boycott: An Open Letter from Judge James G. Maguire of San Francisco," *JSP*, Aug 8, 1886, 1. Sanford D. Thatcher, "Boycotting," *New Englander and Yale Review*, Dec 1886, 1038–1042, quotations on 1041, 1040.

53. *Christian Union*, Aug 26, 1886, 2; "Butler on the Boycott"; Walter Blackburn Harte, "A Review of the Chicago Strike of '94," *Arena* 10 (Sep 1894): 497–533, quotation on 501.

54. "Boycotting," *NYT*, Nov 7, 1885, 4; "The Boycotted Bakery," *NYT*, Apr 13, 1886, 4; "Boycott: Opinions of Influential Journals on This Modern System of Tyranny." On Judge Barrett, see "Boycotters Punished." "The Boycott. A Double-Edged Sword," *CT*, Apr 16, 1886, 4. Editorial in *NYT*, Jan 26, 1885, 4. "The Fable of the Boycott," *Christian Advocate*, May 6, 1886, 292.

55. *NYT*, Jul 25, 1890, 4; *NYT*, Jul 24, 1890, 4. "The Religious Press," *New York Evangelist*, Jan 7, 1886, 3; Snyder, "Boycott."

56. The first quotations are from "The Boycotted Bakery," *New York Evangelist*, May 6, 1887, 7; "Our Un-American Citizens," *NYT*, Apr 25, 1886, 8; "The Boycott," *NYT*, Dec 26, 1885, 4; "The Lesson of the Day," *Harper's Weekly*, May 8, 1886, 290. George Cary Eggleston, "The American Idea," *New Princeton Review*, Nov 1887, 317–328, quotations on 323; "The New Tyranny," *New York Evangelist*, May 6, 1887, 7; "The Boycott. A Double-Edged Sword"; *NYT*, Jan 26, 1885, 4. "The boycott is an anomaly in a land governed by principles of personal liberty and individual right that hold sway in America." "Boycotting," *WP*, Feb 11, 1886, 2.

57. "The Union Printer," *Union Printer*, Nov 13, 1886, 2.

58. "23,000 March for Right of Boycott," *NYT*, Oct 27, 1912, 15.

Chapter 5

1. David Thelen, *The New Citizenship: Origins of Progressivism in Wisconsin, 1885-1900* (Columbia, MO: University of Missouri Press, 1972), 1, 2. Several recent surveys of the era mention consumer culture but do not emphasize the politics of consumption: Steven J. Diner, *A Very Different Age: Americans of the Progressive Era* (New York: Hill & Wang, 1998); Shelton Stromquist, *Reinventing the People: The Progressive Movement, the Class Problem, and the Origins of Modern Liberalism* (Urbana: University of Illinois Press, 2006); Michael McGerr, *A Fierce Discontent: The Rise and Fall of the Progressive Movement in America, 1870-1920* (New York: Free Press, 2003).

2. Maud Nathan, *The Story of an Epoch-Making Movement* (Garden City, NY: Doubleday, Page & Co., 1926), 23-24.

3. Henry C. Potter, "The Citizen and the Consumer," in *The Citizen in His Relation to the Industrial Situation* (New York: C. Scribner's Sons, 1902), 125-126.

4. There is no agreement about either of these dates. Some date the Consumers' League of New York to 1888 and the NCL to 1898. Mary Gay Humphreys, "The Consumers' League," *Harper's Bazaar*, Jun 21, 1890, 1-2; "The Consumers' League," *Christian Union*, Feb 26, 1891, 277; William Clarke, "A Consumers' League," *Christian Union*, Sep 12, 1891, 44.

5. On Kelley's career see Kathryn Kish Sklar, *Florence Kelley and the Nation's Work: The Rise of Women's Political Culture* (New Haven: Yale University Press, 1995). On women's claims to expertise in this era see Robin Muncy, *Creating a Female Dominion in American Reform, 1890-1935* (New York: Oxford University Press, 1991). On women, expertise, and the law see Nancy Wolloch, *Muller v. Oregon: A Brief History with Documents* (New York: Bedford Books, 1996).

6. "Moralizing Shoppers," *CT*, Jan 7, 1900, 36. *The Consumers' League in Europe*, NCL Bulletin no. 4 (Boston: NCL, Jan 1913); Nathan, *Story of an Epoch-Making Movement*, 89-103; Daniel T. Rodgers, *Atlantic Crossings: Social Politics in a Progressive Age* (Cambridge, MA: Harvard University Press, 1998).

7. "Don't Drink Slave Cocoa," *Friends' Intelligencer*, Dec 4, 1909, 779-780.

8. Walter Lippmann, *Drift and Mastery: An Attempt to Diagnose the Current Unrest* (New York: M. Kennerley, 1914), 73, 71. For a similar argument about the relationship of the Social Gospel movement to consumer society, see Susan Curtis, *A Consuming Faith: The Social Gospel and Modern American Culture* (Baltimore: Johns Hopkins University Press, 1991). Daniel T. Rodgers, "In Search of Progressivism," *Reviews in American History* 10 (Dec 1982): 113-132.

9. For two excellent overviews see Daniel R. Ernst, "Free Labor, the Consumer Interest, and the Law of Industrial Disputes, 1885-1900," *American Journal of Legal History* 36 (Jan 1992): 19-37; and Peter Edward Samson, "The Emergence of a Consumer Interest in America, 1870-1930" (PhD diss., University of Chicago, 1980), which mentions the "Consumers' Protective Association" (53) and quotes Amos G. Warner on 272-273. Debating the tariff transformed the consumer from an "individual unit" to a person forced to "think and act in the aggregate, proclaimed one observer." "Politics of the Trust Question," *NYT*, Oct 6, 1911, 12. For a critique of the "pettiness of the consumer's interest," see "The

Tariff," *NYT*, Aug 27, 1904, 6. Isaac L. Rice, "The Consumer," *Forum*, Jul 1892, 594–602. Washington Gladden, "Is It Peace or War?" *Century* 32 (Aug 1886): 565, quoted in "The Industrious Crisis," *Christian Recorder*, Aug 5, 1886, and also in Boom, "Labor and Capital: The Golden Rule Applied: Better than 'Boycott,'" *Wheeling Register*, Sep 4, 1886, 3. M. F. Ames, The Middlemen Must Go," *Massachusetts Ploughman and New England Journal of Agriculture*, May 27, 1899, 1. "Union of Consumers: Former Senator Chandler's Proposal Is Criticised in Boston," *WP*, Nov 7, 1908, 6.

10. "Consumer's Unions," *Youth's Companion*, Feb 27, 1913, 110; Peter Powers, "'Consumers' Union' Has Unique Plans," *Wilkes-Barre Times*, Nov 6, 1908, 4.

11. Brooks is quoted in "Consumer Duties," *Outlook*, Oct 30, 1897, 512. Lawrence B. Glickman, *A Living Wage: American Workers and the Making of Consumer Society* (Ithaca: Cornell University Press, 1997), 110–11.

12. J. Elliot Ross, *Consumers and Wage-Earners: The Ethics of Buying Cheap* (New York: Devin-Adair Co., 1912), 109; Clarke, "Consumers' League," 488–489. "The Folks behind the Counter," *NYTr*, Jul 2, 1905, 10; Eliza Putnam Heaton, "Women Help Women Consumers' League against Starvation-Made Articles," *Galveston Daily News*, Jan 15, 1889, 6. See also "To Push Union Labels a Branch of the Consumers' League to Be Formed Here," *Milwaukee Journal*, Dec 1, 1893, 8; "League of Consumers," *Denver Evening Post*, Sep 3, 1896, 8; Martha Bensley Bruere, "Educating the Consumer," *Outlook*, Sep 7, 1912, 29.

13. Ross, *Consumers and Wage-Earners*, 109.

14. A keyword search of the *NYT* shows that 2,636 articles between 1880 and 1899 used the word "boycott"; between 1900 and 1919 2,873 articles used the term. "Peaceful but effective" is from "On the Right Track," *RP*, Apr 30, 1904, 1 (originally published in *Baltimore Afro-American Ledger*). Paula E. Hyman, "Immigrant Women and Consumer Protest: The New York City Kosher Meat Boycott of 1902," *American Jewish History* 70 (Sep 1980): 91–105; Kimberly Nusco, "The South Providence Kosher Meat Boycott Of 1910," *Rhode Island Jewish Historical Notes* 14 (2003): 96–126. Dana Frank, "Housewives, Socialists, and the Politics of Food: The 1917 New York Cost-of-Living Protests," *Feminist Studies* 11 (Summer 1985): 255–285. Some African American boycotts were similarly local in character. See, for example, "Negroes Boycott White Man: Won't Cook or Wash for Legislator Who Pushed 'Jim Crow' Bill," *NYT*, Mar 18, 1904, 1. Eric Rauchway, "The High Cost of Living in the Progressives' Economy," *JAH* 88 (Dec 2001): 898–924.

15. See by the pioneering scholars August Meier and Elliott Rudwick: "The Boycott Movement against Jim Crow Streetcars in the South, 1900–1906," *JAH* 55 (Mar 1969): 756–775; "Boycotts of Segregated Street Cars, 1894–1906: A Research Note," *Phylon Quarterly* 18 (1957): 296–297; "Negro Boycotts of Jim Crow Streetcars in Tennessee," *American Quarterly* 21 (Winter 1969): 755–763; and "Negro Boycotts of Segregated Streetcars in Florida, 1901–1905," *South Atlantic Quarterly* 69 (1970): 525–533.For an excellent overview of the boycott in three Southern cities see Lynne Blair Murphy, "'A Right to Ride': African American Citizenship, Identity, and the Protest over Jim Crow Transportation" (PhD diss., Duke University, 2003). See also Stephen Edward Cresswell, *Rednecks, Redeemers, and Race: Mississippi after Reconstruction, 1877–1917* (Oxford: University Press of Mississippi, 2006), 86. David E. Alsobrook, "The Mobile Boycott of 1902: African American Protest or Capitulation," *Alabama Review*, Apr 2003, 83–103. On the DC streetcar boycott of 1915 see Linda Gordon, "Black and White Visions of Welfare: Women's Welfare Activism, 1890–1945," *JAH*, 78 (Sep 1991): 581.

16. The "street car company can do nothing to change the law which has been enacted by the legislature." "Negroes Boycott the Street Cars," *Daily Arkansas*, Jun 2, 1903, 3. "Separation of Races on Streetcars," *Florida Times-Union*, May 3, 1905, 3; "Jim Crow Bill Passed by Council," *Florida Times-Union*, Oct 18, 1905, 8; "Jim Crow Law in Pensacola: Court Commission Holds It Valid," *Florida Times-Union*, Nov 25, 1905, 1. On the Louisiana legislature's passage of a segregation law see "Editorial Notes," *Christian Advocate* (New Orleans), Nov 6, 1902, 1. Mitchell's claims can be found in "Editorial Notes," *RP*, Apr 9, 1904, 4. On his role in the boycott see Ann Field Alexander, *Race Man: The Rise and Fall of the "Fighting Editor," John Mitchell, Jr.* (Charlottesville: University of Virginia Press, 2002), 133–142. "Pocket nerve" is from "Political Boycotts," *Independent*, Aug 17, 1905, 404. "'Jim Crow' Street Cars," *Colored American*, Apr 16, 1900, 10 (originally published in *St. Luke's Herald*, Richmond, VA). "Public utility" is from "Boycotting the Street Cars," *San Antonio Daily Express*, Mar 17, 1904, 4.

17. Meier and Rudwick, "Boycott Movement against Jim Crow Streetcars in the South," 770–771. On radical uses of conservative rhetoric in Richmond see Alexander, *Race Man*, 137. Glenda Elizabeth Gilmore, *Gender and Jim Crow: Women and the Politics of White Supremacy in North Carolina, 1896–1920* (Chapel Hill: University of North Carolina Press, 1996), 147. See also Elsa Barkley Brown, "Womanist Consciousness: Maggie Lena Walker and the Independent Order of Saint Luke," *Signs* 14 (Spring 1989): 610–633, esp. 618 on Walker's support for the 1904 Richmond streetcar boycott. Robin D. G. Kelley, "'We Are Not What We Seem': Rethinking Black Working-Class Opposition in the Jim Crow South," *JAH* 80 (Jun 1993): 75–112, esp. 103. Kelley considers boycotts to be part of the "everyday posing, discursive conflicts, and small-scale conflicts" that are an important aspect of the "infrapolitics" of the Jim Crow era.

18. On segration as modern see Edward Ayers, *The Promise of the New South: Life after Reconstruction* (New York: Oxford University Press, 1992), 145. "A Black Paradise: Race Separation the Country's Salvation," *Raleigh News and Observer*, Apr 3, 1907, 3. The progressive quotation is from "Saturday, April 9, 1904," *RP*, 1. On Jim Crow as "non-progressive," see "'Jim Crow' Street Cars," *Cleveland Gazette*, Jul 29, 1905, 2. On segregation as a "safeguard" see "Negroes and Street-Cars," *RP*, Apr 30, 1904, 1. "Negroes Boycott the Compartment Street Cars: Resent the Separation of the Races and Are Keeping off the Cars: Boycott Complete but Peaceful," *San Antonio Daily Express*, Mar 16, 1904, 8.

19. "The Law Is Working Well," *Savannah Morning News*, Sep 14, 2006, 6. "Sensible negroes": "The 'Separate Race' Law," *Chattanooga Times*, Jul 17, 1905, 4. "Race Separation in the Street Cars," *Mobile Daily Register*, Nov 5, 1902, 4. "Negro Editors and Separate Law," *Chattanooga Times*, Jul 25, 1905, 4. "Imaginary discrimination": "Color Line Observed: No Trouble in Wilmington over the Enforcement of the Jim Crow Street Car Law," *Raleigh News and Observer*, Apr 3, 1907, 3. "Pensacola's Street Car Boycott by Negroes," *Mobile Daily Register*, May 17, 1905, 4. "Greatest Delight": *Charlotte Daily Observer*, Apr 13, 1907. "Poor man's carriage": "Boycotting the Street Cars." "No Trouble Enforcing Law: Only One Arrest So Far," *Savannah Morning News*, Sep 15, 1906, 4. "Want ads": "Drove Negro Passenger from a Street Car," *San Antonio Daily Express*, Mar 20, 1904, 13. On the silence of the white press see Meier and Rudwick, "Boycott Movement against Jim Crow Streetcars in the South," 759, n. 38.

20. Kelly Miller, "We Turn to the Boycott," *CD*, Dec 30, 1933, 11. "Boycott the Postmaster," *Wisconsin State Register*, Sep 25, 1897; "Race Issue Raised in House Restaurant:

Southern Congressmen Walk Out When Negro Official and Guest Are Served," *NYT*, May 15, 1909, 2.

21. "A Voice from Roanoke," *RP*, May 7, 1904, 4, not only references the Founders but uses the old spelling "boy-cott." For examples of poetry see O. M. Steward, "Richmond's Jim Crow Cars," *RP*, Apr 30, 1904, 1; J. Conway Jackson, "The Jim Crow Kyar," *RP*, Jun 6, 1904, 1. "Severely alone": Hustler, "No Race Compromise," *Savannah Tribune*, Sep 8, 1906, 4. "Nerve center": "Jim Crow Street-Cars," *RP*, Apr 9, 1904, 4; *Baltimore Afro-American Ledger*, Jun 18, 1904, 4; "Notes in General," *The Friend: A Religious and Literary Journal*, Aug 26, 1905, 55. "Boycotted Street Cars," *RP*, Apr 7, 1900, 4. "Money in Their Pockets," *RP*, May 7, 1904, 1 (originally published in *Clarksdale Mississippi Journal*). *Colored American*, Nov 10, 1900, 8. "Have Set the Right Example," *RP*, May 7, 1904, 1 (originally published in *Mound Bayou Mississippi Demonstrator*). Walker is quoted in Murphy, "'Right to Ride,'" 159. For a later use of the phrase see "Urges Boycott of Jim Crow Business," *CD*, Mar 23, 1946, 3. "Savannah Jim Crow Cars," *Savannah Tribune*, Sep 29, 1906, 4. "Persistency": "Avery Law Killed by Judge R. M. Call," *Florida Times-Union*, Jul 26, 1905, 5. On black businessmen profiting from boycotts of white merchants in other contexts see Gilmore, *Gender and Jim Crow*, 125. For suggestive comments about the potentially radical use of market-based language see Richard F. Teichgraeber III, *Sublime Thoughts/Penny Wisdom: Situating Emerson and Thoreau in the American Market* (Baltimore: Johns Hopkins University Press, 1995).

22. "The Situation in Florida," *RP*, Jun 10, 1905, 4; "The Street Car Co. Here 'Busted': Didn't Earn Enough to Meet the Interest on Its Bonds," *RP*, Jul 23, 1904, 1; "The Street-Car Situation," *RP*, Aug 29, 1904, 1. "The New Orleans Street Car Situation," *Southwestern Christian Advocate*, Apr 23, 1903, 8; "Editorial Notes," *Christian Advocate*, Jun 12, 1902, 1. Wilson is quoted in "Ignoring the Separation Ordinance," *Mobile Daily Register*, Dec 2, 1902, 4.

23. "The Streetcar Boycott in Houston," *Christian Advocate*, Dec 17, 1903, 1. "New Car Law Is in Effect," *Journal and Tribune* (Knoxville), Jul 6, 1905, 5, noted that residents of that city were aware of events in Nashville. J. L. Birchett, "Colored Folks Yet Walking," *RP*, May 7, 1904, 1. The letters from other cities are cited in Murphy, "'Right to Ride,'" 179. One of the criticisms of the historian August Meier and Elliot Rudwick's pioneering research on Jim Crow boycotts was that their article manuscript relied too heavily on "papers out of state." Letter from Martin Ridge, managing editor of the *JAH*, to August Meier, Aug 7, 1968. Meier replied that it was only through these out-of-state accounts that "we first encountered the majority of the boycotts and first came to realize the extent of the movement." Meier to Ridge, Aug 13, 1968. Both letters can be found in box 90, folder 2, AMP.

24. "Street Car Law," *Lynchburg News*, Jun 9, 1906, 6. On the Chinese boycott see "Editorial Article 2—No Title," *CD*, Sep 18, 1915, 8.

25. "Jim Crow Street-Cars," *RP*, Apr 9, 1904, 4. A later issue reported that "between eighty and ninety per cent of the colored people who have used the street-cars are now walking." See "'Jim Crow' Street-Car Law Set to Catch Negroes: Only White Folks in the Trap," *RP*, Apr 30, 1904, 1. "The 'Jim Crow' Situation," *Daily Herald* (Vicksburg), Jun 5, 1904, 3. E. A. Dale, "'Jim Crow' Street Cars," *Cleveland Gazette*, Mar 16, 1901, 2. Dale noted that receipts had fallen by 47 percent. "Come Back and Accept Your Humiliation," *Southwestern Christian Advocate*, Dec 24, 1903, 1. On the deserted cars see "Separation of Races," *Mobile Daily Register*, Nov 4, 1902, 5; Birchett, "Colored Folks Yet Walking." "She Wanted

Air, But It Cost $10: Negro Fined for Disregarding Jim Crow Law on Trolley Car," *RP*, Jul 23, 1904, 1. "Negroes Draw Color Line: Boycott San Antonio Ice Cream Man Who Signed Jim Crow Petition," *Kansas City Rising Sun*, May 20, 1904, 1. Playing up its economic clout, an ad in the paper read, "It pays to advertise in the *Rising Sun* for it reaches more homes of colored people than any other paper in the state."

26. "Wordy disturbances": "New Orleans Separate Cars," *Mobile Daily Register*, Nov 4, 1902, 3. Examples of African Americans harassing other African Americans can be found in "Negroes on the Lonsdale Line Causing Considerable Trouble," *Knoxville Journal and Tribune*, Jul 9, 1905, 9; "Boycott on the Cars," *Mobile Daily Register*, Nov 11, 1902, 8; "Cars Separated Yesterday," *Augusta Chronicle*, May 21, 1900, 5. On the minsters: "Police Are Now Taking a Hand," *Savannah Morning News*, Sep 17, 1906, 8; "Boycotting Street Cars," *RP*, Apr 7, 1900, 4. Rock Throwing: "Cars Were Stoned: Fourth Ward Negroes Resented Separation," *Houston Daily Post*, Nov 1, 1903, 1; "Boycott Still in Force: Few Negroes Ride," *Houston Daily Post*, Nov 2, 1903, 3. Physical violence: "Because he Rode on a Street Car: Negro Was Disemboweled," *Savannah Morning News*, Sep 17, 1906, 8; "Drove Negro Passenger from a Street Car." On Jacksonville see "Editorial Notes," *Christian Advocate*, Jan 30, 1902, 1.

27. Annie Lee: "Race Ordinance Is Again to Fore," *Savannah Morning News*, Feb 3, 1907, 3. The long headline is from *RP*, Jun 6, 1904, 1. Laura Smith: "She Wanted Air, But It Cost $10." Addie Ayres: "Colored Women Fined Ten Dollars," *RP*, Aug 29, 1904, 1. "Virginia Jim Crow Laws and Ignorant Conductors: E. C. Brown, Business Man, Arrested Fined for Not Giving Up Seat," *New York Age*, Aug 1, 1907, 8; "Separation Case: Andrew Patterson Fined for Violating Ordinance," *Florida Times-Union*, Dec 6, 1905, 5. Typical of the white press coverage, the paper noted only that a "colored lawyer" defended Patterson but that "Attorney Odum" represented the city. "Results of Jim Crowism: Colored Woman Dragged and Beaten on the Jim Crow Car," *RP*, Aug 12, 1905, 1 (originally published in *Nashville Clarion*). "Separation Law Ignored," *Mobile Daily Register*, Dec 2, 1902, 5. The story about Lee is from *Montgomery Advertiser*, Jun 19, 1902, 10; clipping is cited in box 90, folder 1, AMP. "Jim Crow Street-Cars," *RP*, Apr 16, 1904, 1; "The Jim Crow Street-Car," *RP*, Apr 23, 1904, 1; "'Jim Crow' Street-Car Law Set to Catch Negroes"; "'Equal Rights before the Law: The 'Jim Crow' Street Car," *RP*, Aug 29, 1904, 1. In New Orleans, a white man, Julius Weis, "one of the wealthiest cotton merchants," was arrested for sitting in the section reserved for blacks. "Violated Separate Car Law," *Mobile Daily Register*, Dec 2, 1902, 3.

28. "'Jim Crow' Street Cars," *Colored American*, Apr 16, 1900, 10 (originally published in *St. Luke's Herald*). See also Birchett, "Colored Folks Yet Walking."; "Street-Car Company 'Busted.'" "Colored Citizens Are Walking," *Danville Register*, Jun 20, 1906, 2; "Is Great Falling Off in the Negro Traffic: Many Walking Since New Law Became Effective," *Ledger-Dispatch* (Norfolk), Jun 15, 1906, 15. "Witch hazel": "She Wanted Air, But It Cost $10." "The Jim Crow Street-Car"; "Streetcar Boycott Continued Sunday: But Few Colored People Rode on Cars of the Jacksonville Electric Company," *Florida Times-Union*, Jul 3, 1905, 8; "Jim Crow Effective," *Savannah Tribune*, Sep 15, 1906, 4. "Editorial Notes," *Christian Advocate*, Dec 13, 1903, 1; "Negroes Continue Boycott of Cars: Wagons Hauling Colored Passengers to Piedmont Heights," *Ledger-Dispatch* (Norfolk), Jun 26, 1906, 9. "Results of Jim Crowism." On the potential "gain" see "Boycotted Street Cars." "On the Right Track."

29. Public conveyances: "Fighting 'Jim-Crowism' in Nashville," *Literary Digest*, Oct 7,

1904, 474. "Mass meeting": *Savannah Tribune*, Sep 22, 1906, 4, which noted "'Lily White' street cars are among the popular sights these days, caused by the proud colored citizens who are determined not to be 'Jim Crowed'." "Negroes May Whirl by Us in Automobiles: Disgruntled 'Afro-Americans' Talk of Testing New Trolley Car Regulations in Court: Should They Fail There They Will Resort to 'Horseless Carriages,'" *News Leader* (Richmond), May 20, 1904, 1, 8, quotation on 1. "A Righteous Boycott," *Colored American*, Mar 17, 1900, 2.

30. Union Transporation Company: Murphy, "'Right to Ride,'" 232. Jacksonville: P. A. Jackson, "From Florida," *RP*, Jun 10, 1905, 1; "Negroes Boycott Street Car Line," *NYT*, Nov 20, 1901, 10. "Negroes to Ride in Autos: Buy Machines in New York to Fight Nashville Street Railway," *Chattanooga Daily Times*, Sep 18, 1905, 2; "Fight Jim Crow Law: Memphis Negroes Raise a Fund of $5,000 to Test the Statute through All Courts," *Nashville American*, Jul 31, 1905, 1. "A Protest That Counts," *Indianapolis Freeman*, Oct 7, 1905, 1; "Money to Fight Jim Crow Law: Negro Business Men's League May Contest: Boycott Advised," *Nashville Banner*, Aug 1, 1905, 7. "Real 'Jim Crow' Buss Operates," *Norfolk Landmark*, Aug 4, 1906, 3. "Citizens Protest: Will Not Ride the Street Cars," *RP*, Apr 23, 1904, 1. "Negroes and Street-Cars." Houston: "Streetcar Boycott in Houston." "Cooperation in Transportation" in *Economic Cooperation among Negro Americans*, ed. W. E. B. Du Bois (Atlanta: Atlanta University Press, 1907), 164.

31. "Boycott, Boycott, Boycott! A Shoe and Gents' Furnishing Store in the Neighborhood Refuses to Employ Us and Does Not Advertise in Any of Our Papers," *CD*, Nov 11, 1911, 1. B. L. L. Brown, "New Method of Curbing Lynching: Boycott of White Merchant Who Refused to Swear That He Was Not a Party to a Certain Mob Has Effective Results," *CD*, Dec 25, 1915, 6. This article described a boycott in Henderson, KY. "South's Labor Starts Boycott on Jim Crowers: Secret Movement Now on Foot in Cities Where Discrimination Rules," *CD*, Nov 12, 1921, 3. Another case of this rhetoric of secrecy occurred when the Montgomery businessman H. A. Loveless set up a hack line but denied that his intent was to challenge the streetcar company. "Separate Accommodation Law: Loveless Denies He Will Compete with Car Companies," *Montgomery Advertiser*, Aug 18, 1900, 2. On rumors and secrets see Steven Hahn, *A Nation under Our Feet: Black Political Struggles in the Rural South from Slavery to the Great Migration* (Cambridge, MA: Harvard University Press, 2003); Patricia A. Turner, *I Heard It through the Grapevine: Rumor in African-American Culture* (Berkeley: University of California Press, 1993), esp. 92; Gary Alan Fine and Patricia A. Turner, *Whispers on the Color Line: Rumor and Race in America* (Berkeley: University of California Press, 2001). See also "Boycott Rumor Is Denied," *Atlanta Daily World*, Apr 13, 1940, 1.

32. "Voice from Roanoke."

33. On protests of segregated sites see Alsobrook, "Mobile Boycott of 1902," 95. "Boycotted: Judge Abernathy, Who Joined the Jackass Club, Gets Kicked in the Pocketbook," *CD*, Apr 7, 1917, 1. In all likelihood they were referring to Judge H. B. Abernathy of the Municipal Court of Birmingham. See Thomas McAlary Owen, *History of Alabama and Dictionary of Alabama Biography* (Chicago: S. J. Clarke Publishing Co., 1921), 3:4–5. See also "Negroes Boycott White Man." "Mammy," *CD*, Feb 3, 1917, 10. On the boycotts of *The Birth of a Nation* see Thomas Cripps, *Slow Fade to Black: The Negro in American Film, 1900–1942* (New York: Oxford University Press, 1977), 61–64; David Blight, *Race and Reunion: The Civil War in American Memory* (Cambridge, MA: Harvard University Press, 2001), 397; Gilmore, *Gen-*

der and Jim Crow, 137; Janet Steiger, "The Birth of a Nation: Reconsidering Its Reception," in *The Birth of a Nation*, ed. Robert Lang (New Brunswick: Rutgers University Press, 1994), 195–213, esp. 207. For a compilation of African American protests see Boston Branch of the NAACP, *Fighting a Vicious Film: Protest against "Birth of a Nation"* (Boston, 1915). See also John Hammond Moore, "South Carolina's Reaction to the Photoplay, *The Birth of a Nation*," *Proceedings of the South Carolina Historical Association*, 1963, 30–40. The "Black Pattis Troubadours," a group of fifty "colored musicians," threatened to boycott a hotel in Hartford that would not provide lodging. "Hotel Boycott," *Boston Daily Advertiser*, Oct 24, 1896, 6. For another example, see "For Drawing Color Line Ministers in Boston to Boycott a Hotel," *Milwaukee Sentinel*, Feb 1, 1896, 5, about a black minister, Benjamin W. Arnett of Wilberforce, Ohio, who was refused at "three leading hotels" in Boston.

34. "Students Boycott Movie Performance," *CD*, Feb 27, 1926, 2; "Omega Fraters Boycott Jim Crow Costume Shop," *CD*, Apr 7, 1928, 4; Henry Trammer, "To Boycott Miami," *CD*, Oct 23, 1926, A2. "Urge Boycott of Watermelon with Offensive Name," *CD*, Jul 20, 1935, 5; "This Sign Made Us Hot," *Pittsburgh Courier*, Jun 4, 1938, 5. William H. Gaulden, "'Gone with the Wind,' Vicious," *AN*, Jan 13, 1940, 14; William H. Gaulden, "Fight Still Rages over 'GWTW,'" *AN*, Feb 24, 1940, 14; "Chicagoans Picket 'Gone with the Wind': More than 100 Urge Boycott of Epic Film," *CD*, Feb 3, 1940, 9. African Americans were joined in these boycotts by communists, members of the Grand Army of the Republic, and the Daughters of Union Veterans. See "Red Paper Condemns 'Gone with the Wind,'" *NYT*, Dec 24, 1939, 14; "War Movie Scored by G.A.R. Veterans," *NYT*, Sep 1, 1939, 25; B. R. Crisler, "The Cinema Carries On," *NYT*, Sep 10, 1939, X4. "Red Paper's Critic Scorns Tan 'Gone with Wind' Order," *AC*, Dec 22, 1939, 1. George Padmore, "Londoners Boycott 'Gone with the Wind,'" *CD*, May 18, 1940, 5. For a boycott of the film by British theater owners owing to high rental prices see "Britain Boycotts 'Gone with Wind,'" *NYT*, May 1, 1940, 23. "'Amos 'n' Andy,' 'Beulah' Blasted by NAACP Board," *Atlanta Daily World*, Jun 30, 1951, 1; J. Benjamin Horton, "Makes Attack on Amos and Andy Program," *Atlanta Daily World*, Oct 3, 1951, 2. Gerald Horne, "Boycott as a Weapon, a Lesson of Sambo's," *AN*, Jan 2, 1982, 35.

35. Susan Strasser, *Satisfaction Guaranteed: The Making of an American Mass Market* (New York: Pantheon, 1989); Richard S. Tedlow, *New and Improved: The Story of Mass Marketing in America* (New York: Basic Books, 1990). See the logic developed by Florence Kelley in "The National Federation of Consumers' Leagues," *Independent*, Dec 14, 1899, 3353.

36. "Christmas Shopping Easier This Year: Campaign of Consumers' League Begins to Make Itself Felt among Department Stores," *NYT*, Dec 5, 1909, C6. Lowell is quoted in Jacqueline Dirks, "Righteous Goods: Women's Production, Reform Publicity and the National Consumers' League, 1891–1919" (PhD diss., Yale University, 1996), 166.

37. For the Web site see http://www.nclnet.org (accessed May 31, 2008), which invites people to "rediscover" the NCL and "to promote economic and social justice for consumers and workers in the United States and abroad." William James's 1906 essay "The Moral Equivalent of War" made a similar point about the need to apply the martial spirit to social problems. *Pragmatism and Other Essays* (New York: Pocket Books, 1963), 289–301.

38. Membership figures are discussed in Dirks, "Righteous Goods," 62–63. Richard Hofstadter, *The Age of Reform: From Bryan to F.D.R.* (New York: Knopf, 1955), 172. Nathan, *Story of an Epoch-Making Movement*, 13. Nathan, "The Consumers' League," *Alumnae News* (n.p., n.d.), in MNS. For a similar formulaton of the NCL's role in shaping public opinion see "The Consumers' League," *Outlook*, Mar 30, 1907, 730–731.

39. Schlesinger quoted in Michael E. McGerr, *The Decline of Popular Politics: The American North, 1865–1928* (New York: Oxford University Press, 1986), 189; Potter used the word "subterranean" in "Citizen and the Consumer," 126; Lippmann, *Drift and Mastery*, 75.

40. Walter E. Weyl, *The New Democracy: An Essay on Certain Political and Economic Tendencies in the United States* (New York: Macmillan, 1912), 250. As Lippmann wrote, through new economic conditions "the solidarity of the consumer is made possible." *Drift and Mastery*, 74. Hadley is quoted in Kathryn Kish Sklar, "The Consumers' White Label Campaign of the National Consumers' League, 1898–1918," in *Getting and Spending: European and American Consumer Societies in the Twentieth Century*, ed. Susan Strasser, Charles McGovern, and Mattias Judt (New York: Cambridge University Press, 1998), 17–35, quotation on 25. Nathan, *Story of an Epoch-Making Movement*, 125; Potter, "Citizen and Consumer," 155–156. Kelley, *Some Ethical Gains through Legislation* (New York: Macmillan, 1905), 210. "Our Responsibility as Buyers," *Congregationalist*, Nov 16, 1899, 730.

41. Weyl, *New Democracy*, 250; *The National Consumers' League: First Quarter Century, 1899–1924* (New York, 1924), 1; Charles Gide, *Principles of Political Economy* (Boston: D. C. Heath, 1904), 700–701. Nathan, *Story of an Epoch-Making Movement*, 126.

42. Hofstadter, *Age of Reform*, 257–258. Erma Angevine, *Roots of the Consumer Movement: A Chronicle of Consumer History in the Twentieth Century* (Washington DC: National Consumers League, 1979). For a similar analysis see Kathryn Kish Sklar, "Two Political Cultures in the Progressive Era: The National Consumers' League and the American Association for Labor Legislation," in *U.S. History as Women's History: New Feminist Essays*, ed. Linda Kerber, Alice Kessler-Harris, and Kathryn Kish Sklar (Chapel Hill: University of North Carolina Press, 1995), 36–62, esp. 42. "First object" is quoted in Dirks, "Righteous Goods," 89.

43. John Graham Brooks, *The Consumers' League* (Cambridgeport, MA, 1899), 3. Kelley quoted in Sklar, "Consumers' White Label Campaign," 27; Nathan, *Story of an Epoch-Making Movement*, 124. Lippmann, *Drift and Mastery*, 67. "Shoppers' Conscience," Feb 18, 1897, unidentified clipping, MNS. Interview quoted in Dirks, "Righteous Goods," 167.

44. "Consumers' League," *Annals* 11 (May 1898): 435; Potter, "Citizen and the Consumer," 126. As Florence Kelley wrote, "Any article must cease to be produced if consumers cease to purchase it." *Some Ethical Gains through Legislation*, 206. "Moral responsibility" is from Brooks, *Consumers' League*, 3. "Consumers Can Abolish Sweatshops" (Boston, n.d.), in "Consumers' League of Massachusetts Early Publications," box 16, folder 253, CLMP.

45. Muncy, *Creating a Female Dominion in American Reform*. The Reverend David Greer discussed consumer power in masculine terms. However, when he offered a critique of consumers he abruptly switched pronouns: "The consumer . . . is the employer and it is upon him, or rather upon her (for the chief offender in this case is the shopping woman) that the responsibility lies." "Extracts from the Address Delivered at the Annual Meeting of City of NY by the Rt. Rev. David H. Greer, Bishop of New York," 266, in CLMP.

46. Kelley, *Some Ethical Gains through Legislation*, 209; Brooks, *Consumers' League*, 3–4; Ross, *Consumers and Wage-Earners*, 118. The first item stated that "all workers should receive not the lowest, but fair living wages." Nathan, *Story of an Epoch-Making Movement*, 149. Potter, "Citizen and Consumer," 125.

47. Florence Kelley, *Modern Industry in Relation to the Family, Health Education, Morality* (New York: Longmans, Green, 1914), 132. Both quotations are from "The Home Club,"

Outlook, Aug 7, 1897, 916; Nathan, *Story of an Epoch-Making Movement*, 13; Potter, "Citizen and Consumer," 160

48. As Potter wrote, the "result of industrial development has been . . . the severance or weakening of the personal nexus a) between employers and employed, and b) between sellers and buyers." "Citizen and Consumer," 31–32. Kelley, *Some Ethical Gains through Legislation*, 211; Newton Baker, foreword to Nathan, *Story of an Epoch-Making Movement*, xiv. Examples of these visual and verbal discussions can be found in Dirks, "Righteous Goods," 166, 283.

49. "Behind the price" is from Dirks, "Righteous Goods," 166; Kelley is quoted in Blanche Wiesen Cook, *Eleanor Roosevelt* (New York: Viking, 1992), 1:64; Lippmann, *Drift and Mastery*, 69. David Thelen, "Patterns of Consumer Consciousness in the Progressive Movement: Robert M. LaFollette, the Antitrust Persuasion, and Labor Legislation," in *The Quest for Social Justice*, ed. Ralph M. Aderman (Madison: University of Wisconsin Press, 1983), 21. I would also challenge Sklar's characterization of the league as "a moral arbiter anchored in an earlier era." In fact, the NCL was self-consciously modern. "Two Political Cultures in the Progressive Era," 44. Florence Kelley, "The Responsibility of the Consumer," *Annals of the American Academy of Social and Political Science* (Jul 1908), 108–112; Sklar, "Consumers' White Label Campaign,"17.

50. Sklar, "Consumers' White Label Campaign,"27. Seligman is quoted in an unidentified clipping in the MNS. Nathan, *Story of an Epoch-Making Movement*, 85–86. Nathan wrote that the NCL was "in line with the thought of the leading economists of the day" (23).

51. The first and third Kelley quotations are from in Sklar, "Consumers' White Label Campaign," 27, 32. The second and fourth are from Kelley, *Some Ethical Gains through Legislation*, 212, 210. "Dormant" is from "High Society to Aid Overworked Shopgirls," *New York Evening Journal*, Dec 10, 1898. See also "Consumers' League," *Annals* (May 1898): 435; Kelley, "Responsibility of the Consumer." The first Nathan quote is from "No Shopping Conscience," *NYT*, Apr 17, 1906, 3. The second is from Nathan, "Consumers' League." "Inertia" is from "The Brutal Side of the Bargain," in *Kate Field's Washington* (n.d.), 149, in NNS.

52. Brooks's phrase "mistaken pity" is quoted in "Home Club." "Ill-judged" and the Nathan quotation are from "Do Bargain Counters Encourage . . . [rest of title not legible]," *American Woman's Home Journal*, in MNS. *The High Cost of Cheap Goods* (n.p., n.d.), in box 16, folder 253, CLMP. See also Dr. A. Doual, "Perilous 'Cheap': Cheap Production Makes Cheap Producers," *Workmen's Advocate* (New Haven, CT), Sep 3, 1887. Potter, "Citizen and Consumer," 152; Brooks, *Consumers' League*, 16–17. Final quotation is from "The Consumers' League," undated clipping in MNS.

53. The first quotations are from "Home Club," 916. Kelley is quoted in Sklar, *Florence Kelley and the Nation's Work*, 221. "Millions Are Given Every Year to Charity/What Do You Do to Make Charity Unnecessary!" undated pamphlet in box 16, folder 253, CLMP. The final quotation is from "Brutal Side of the Bargain."

54. Brooks is quoted in "Home Club," 916. The New York member is quoted in *A History of the Consumers' League of Kentucky* (1941), in Consumers' League of Kentucky Records, 1901–1951, Sophia Smith Collection, Smith College, Northampton, MA. Minister quoted in Nathan, *Story of an Epoch-Making Movement*, 19. Kelley, *Some Ethical Gains through Legislation*, 209.

55. Nathan, *Story of an Epoch-Making Movement*, 124, 125.

56. Nathan, *Story of an Epoch-Making Movement*, 124, 13. Kelley, "Responsibility of the Consumer," 111. I find the sibling analogy more descriptive of the NCL attitude than maternalism, the term that is often applied to Progressive Era women's activism. See, for example, Seth Koven and Sonya Michel, "Womanly Duties: Maternalist Policies and the Origins of Welfare States in France, Germany, Great Britain, and the United States, 1880–1920," *AHR* 95 (Oct 1990): 1076–1108.

57. James T. Kloppenberg, *Uncertain Victory: Social Democracy and Progressivism in European and American Thought, 1870–1920* (New York: Oxford University Press, 1986).

58. During the 1930s the League of Woman Shoppers worked closely with the NCL on a number of campaigns, and the groups briefly considered a merger. Landon R. Y. Storrs, *Civilizing Capitalism: The National Consumers' League, Women's Activism, and Labor Standards in the New Deal Era* (Chapel Hill: University of North Carolina Press, 2000), 235.

Chapter 6

1. Florence Peterson, *Strikes in the United States, 1880–1936* (Washington DC: Government Printing Office, 1938), 41, 45. Colston E. Warne interview by Sybil Shainwald, Spring 1971, transcript, 632, Colston E. Warne Oral History, CUA.

2. The phrase "unrest in odd places" is from Irving Bernstein, *Turbulent Years: A History of the American Worker, 1933–1941* (Boston: Houghton Mifflin, 1970), 126. "Editorially Speaking," *Business Week*, Dec 14, 1935, 43. "Strike in 'The Temple of Consumption,'" *Sales Management*, Sep 15, 1935. "Who Is John Heasty?" *Advance*, Dec 1, 1935, 117–118. This journal was published in Boston by the Congregational Publishing Society.

3. On the consumer as "debutante," see Jeanette Eaton, *Pictorial Review* 35 (Feb 1934): 2. On the "elusive consumer," see M. C. Phillips and F. J. Schlink, *Discovering Consumers* (New York: John Day, 1934), 7; John Chamberlain, "Who Is the Consumer?" *Common Sense* 3 (Jun 1934): 15–16. Walton H. Hamilton, "The Consumer's Front," *Survey Graphic* 24 (Nov 1935): 524–528, 565, 567.

4. Consumers' Research NY Strike Aid Committee to "Friends," "CR Strike, AFL Labor Corr. 1935," Oct 19, 1935, box 4, folder 1, Arthur Kallet Papers, CUA.

5. Kathleen McLaughlin, "New Deal in Buying Seen as Women Back Consumers Movement," *NYT*, May 23, 1937, 86. The phrase "forgotten consumer" can be found in *Nation*, Nov 6, 1935, 526. Articles entitled "Consumers on the March" include Colston E. Warne, *Nation*, Jun 5, 1937, 645–646; Ruth Brindze, *Independent Woman* 18 (Jan 1939): 6–8, 22–23; Mary Taylor, *CSM*, Weekly Magazine section, Jun 22, 1938, 3. The image of the "mighty army of consumers" had been used previously, but it became a far more common phrase in the 1930s. For examples from the Progressive Era, see David Thelen, "Patterns of Consumer Consciousness in the Progressive Movement: Robert M. LaFollette, the Antitrust Persuasion, and Labor Legislation," in *The Quest for Social Justice*, ed. Ralph M. Aderman (Madison: University of Wisconsin Press, 1983), 31. Stanley High, "Guinea Pigs, Left March," *Forum and Century* 102 (Oct 1939): 153–157. Henry Harap, "What Is the Consumer Movement?" *Frontiers of Democracy*, Nov 1940, 48–50, quotation on 48. Joseph Gaer, *Consumers All: The Problem of Consumer Protection* (New York: Harcourt, Brace, 1940), 5; Clark Foreman and Michael Ross, *The Consumer Seeks a Way* (New York: W. W. Norton, 1935), 189–207; "The Political Power of Consumers," *Consumers' Digest* 5 (Feb 1939): 37; Edward A. Filene, *The Consumer's Dollar* (New York: John Day, 1934).

6. John Graham Brooks, *The Consumers' League* (Cambridgeport, MA, 1899), 4–5. Box 1, folder 1, John Graham Brooks Papers, Schlesinger Library, Harvard University, Cambridge, MA. Johnson quoted in "Who Is the Consumer?" *Consumer Bulletin* 51 (Feb 1968): 23. Ralph Nader, *Unsafe at Any Speed: The Designed-In Dangers of the American Automobile* (New York: Grossman, 1965). Dorothy Houston Jacobson, *Our Interests as Consumers* (New York and London: Harper & Brothers, 1941), 1.

7. The word "unprecedented" is from Stuart Chase, "Consumer Takes Stage Center," *New York Post*, Aug 14, 1934, 18. Brindze, "Consumers on the March"; Ruth Brindze, "Facts for Consumers," *Nation*, Nov 6, 1935, 541. J. B. Matthews, *Guinea Pigs No More* (New York: Covici, Friede, 1936). For a similar view, see Seba Eldridge, "Socialism via the Consumers," *Common Sense* 3 (Feb 1934): 18–23. Warren Susman, *Culture as History: The Transformation of American Society in the Twentieth Century* (New York: Pantheon, 1984), esp. 166, 172. While Susman describes "participation and belonging" to groups as the essence of "commitment," he does not mention consumer organizations and uses the term "consumerism" to connote the triumph of commercial values. For a dismissive treatment of the consumer movement, see Ellis W. Hawley, *The New Deal and the Problem of Monopoly: A Study of Economic Ambivalence* (Princeton: Princeton University Press, 1966), 198–204. On the "Copeland-Tugwell" pure food and drug bill, see Arthur M. Schlesinger, Jr., *The Coming of the New Deal: The Age of Roosevelt* (Boston, 1958), 355–359; and Inger Stolle, *Advertising on Trial: Consumer Activism and Corporate Public Relations in the 1930s* (Urbana: University of Illinois Press, 2006). For taxonomies of consumer organizations, see Helen Sorenson, *The Consumer Movement: What It Is and What It Means* (New York: Harper & Bros., 1941), 111–136; Kenneth Dameron, "The Consumer Movement," *Harvard Business Review* 17 (Spring 1939): 271–289. *Consumer Education*, the magazine of the Institute for Consumer Education, regularly listed consumer activities and organizations. On the radio program see *Consumer Education* 1 (Nov 1939): 6. "Today on the Radio: Outstanding Events on All Stations Morning Afternoon Evening," *NYT*, Jul 29, 1937, 27. Dayton D. McKean, "Your Money's Worth," *Forum and Century* 3 (Oct 1938): 197–202, quotation on 198 (this page also mentions the Democratic platform). For a list of films by the consumer movement see Jacobson, *Our Interests as Consumers*, 311. The Dies Committee later claimed that the film was produced by "an organization set up by the Communist Party." See "Dies Report Charges Communist Influence in Consumer Groups," *Printers' Ink*, Dec 16, 1939, 15–16, 84, 86, 88, 92–93, quotation on 16.

8. Dorothy Thompson, "We, the Consumers," *New York Herald Tribune*, Aug 27, 1936, 17. The phrase "awakened consumer consciousness" was used in *Drug Trade News*, Aug 28, 1939, 18. The American Retail Federation sponsored an influential study of the consumer movement: Werner K. Gabler, *Labeling the Consumer Movement* (Washington DC: American Retail Federation, 1939). "Searchlight," *Consumer Education* 1 (Dec 1939): 5; "Old-Timers," *Consumer Education* 1 (Mar 1939). Consumer activists were constantly being warned of the dangers of "bogus" consumer organizations. See, for example, "Consumers vs. Stooges," *Hosiery Worker*, Apr 1, 1938, 2.

9. A history of calls for a cabinet-level department is traced in Richard J. Leighton, "Consumer Protection Agency Proposals: The Origin of a Species," *Administrative Law Review* 25 (Summer 1973): 269–312. A Gallup poll on the consumer movement showed that 45 percent of the population favored a federal Department of Consumer Affairs. See "Consumer Organizations: The Consumer Movement, 1936–1938," box 148, folder 8, CRA.

10. Richard Wightman Fox, "Epitaph for Middletown: Robert S. Lynd and the Analysis of Consumer Culture," in *The Culture of Consumption: Critical Essays in American History, 1880–1980*, ed. Richard Wightman Fox and T. J. Jackson Lears (New York: Pantheon, 1983), 103–141. For a synopsis of the ways in which the "Great Depression did stimulate the growth of consumer consciousness," see John S. Gilkeson, Jr., *Middle-Class Providence, 1820–1940* (Princeton: Princeton University Press, 1986), 339–340; Olivier Zunz, *Why the American Century?* (Chicago: University of Chicago Press, 1998), 107. As Senator Hugo Black wrote, "enough income must be distributed to American wage earners to enable them to buy American goods." "My Views on the Short Work Week," *Common Sense* 4 (Feb 1935): 22–23. On the political significance of debates about consumption in the 1930s see Michael Bernstein, *The Great Depression and Economic Change: America, 1919–1939* (New York: Cambridge University Press, 1987); Alan Brinkley, *The End of Reform: New Deal Liberalism in Recession and War* (New York: Knopf, 1995); Meg Jacobs, "Democracy's Third Estate: New Deal Politics and the Construction of a 'Consuming Public,'" *International Labor and Working-Class History* 55 (Spring 1999): 27–51; Landon R. Y. Storrs, *Civilizing Capitalism: The National Consumers' League, Women's Activism, and Labor Standards in the New Deal Era* (Chapel Hill: University of North Carolina Press, 2000), 21–22. Hamilton, "Consumer's Front." Chase, "Consumer Takes Stage Center"; Chase, "The Age of Distribution," *Nation*, Jul 25, 1934, 93–95; Chase, *The Economy of Abundance* (New York: Macmillan, 1934). John Dewey expressed similar sentiments in "The Need for a New Party," pt. 1, "The Present Crisis," *New Republic*, Mar 18, 1931, 115–117. Horace Meyer Kallen, "Consumers Organize!" *Christian Century*, Jun 27, 1934, 858–860; Kallen, *The Decline and Rise of the Consumer: A Philosophy of Consumer Cooperation* (New York: D. Appleton Co., 1936). On consumers in a corporate economy, see E . J. Lever and J. J. Schalet, "Consumers, Unite!" *New Republic*, Nov 15, 1933, 20–21. Cassels's call for a "science of consumption" can be found in Institute for Consumer Education, *Next Steps in Consumer Education: Proceedings of a National Conference of Consumer Education Held at Stephens College, Apr 3–5, 1939* (Los Angeles: Ward Ritchie, 1939). For a concurring opinion, see Charles S. Wyand, *The Economics of Consumption* (New York: Macmillan, 1937), viii. Kneeland's call for mass consumption can be found in "Economist to Give Lecture," *WP*, Apr 7, 1939, 19. A similar argument was made in the 1938 *Report on Economic Conditions in the South*. See *Confronting Southern Poverty in the Great Depression*, ed. David L. Carlton and Peter A. Coclanis (Boston: Bedford Books, 1996), 78–80. Thompson, "We, the Consumers." Others put the point slightly differently: "broadly speaking, labor and the consumer are identical." "Labor and the NRA," *New Republic*, Dec 20, 1933, 169. Graeme O'Geran, "The Confused Consumer," *Daily Register*, Mar 2, 1938, 1–2. J. B. Matthews and R. E. Shallcross, *Partners in Plunder: The Cost of Business Dictatorship* (New York: Covici, Friede, 1935), 77.

11. Stuart Chase and F. J. Schlink, *Your Money's Worth: A Study in the Waste of the Consumer's Dollar* (New York: Macmillan, 1927). Lynd quoted in "The Consumer Movement," *Business Week*, Apr 22, 1939, 40. The "guinea pig" books include Arthur Kallet and F. J. Schlink, *100,000,000 Guinea Pigs: Dangers in Everyday Foods, Drugs, and Cosmetics* (New York: Vanguard Press, 1932); F. J. Schlink, *Eat, Drink and Be Wary* (New York: Covici, Friede, 1935); Matthews, *Guinea Pigs No More*; M. C. Phillips, *Skin Deep: The Truth about Beauty Aids: Safe and Harmful* (New York: Vanguard Press, 1934); Matthews and Shallcross, *Partners in Plunder*. For a complete list of such books see Charles F. McGovern, *Sold American: Consumption and Citizenship, 1890–1945* (Chapel Hill: University of North Carolina Press, 2006),

245-246, 442, n112. M. C. Phillips is quoted in Norman David Katz, "Consumers Union: The Movement and the Magazine, 1936-1957" (PhD diss., Rutgers University, 1977), 36. Schlink discusses the "professional consumer" in "Off the Editor's Chest," *Consumers' Research Bulletin* 4 (Feb 1938): 1.

12. "Memorandum for the Establishment of the Consumers Foundation," container 2, subject file "Consumers' Research Folder: Correspondence, Memoranda, Clippings, and Documents, 1928-31," Stuart Chase Papers, Library of Congress, Washington DC. On the growth of CR see from *NYT* "Consumers' Group Grows," Dec 8, 1929, N10; "Consumers' Group Grows: Membership in Testing Bureau Has Reached 5,700 Since Jan. 1," Oct 19, 1930, 48. The first *Consumers' Research Bulletin* appeared in Apr 1929. Chase served as president of the organization until the early 1930s, but the position was largely ceremonial; CR was Schlink's brainchild from the beginning. "Consumer Movement," 40. "How a book may develop into an institution is illustrated by the history of the Consumers' Club . . . an outgrowth of *Your Money's Worth*," noted an article produced by the International Labor News Service. "Work of the Consumers' Club," May 25, 1929, "Publicity-Press Clippings," box 88, folder 1, CRA. As Warne wrote in 1937, "the most spectacular consumer-protective development of recent years has been the rise of testing laboratories to assess the merits of competing merchandise." "Consumers on the March," 645.

13. CR's success was "due to liberal and radical support," according to the CR employee and strike leader John Heasty. See "The Amazing Situation in Consumers' Research," *Advance*, Dec 1, 1935, 110. "The Buyer's Baedeker," *New Republic*, Nov 26, 1930, 32-33. "Consumer's Heaven," *Bergen Co. Sunday Leader*, Mar 15, 1931, clipping in MC3, box 87, folder 1, CRA; "Talk of the Town," *New Yorker*, Jan 24, 1931, 10-11. Richard Lockridge, "Advice to Consumers," *New Yorker*, Oct 19, 1931, 25. For a later generation of spoofs of CU, in the 1950s, see Norman Isaac Silber, *Test and Protest: The Influence of Consumers Union* (New York: Holmes & Meier, 1983), 33.

14. On CR as a nuisance, see "Thunder on the Left," *Tide of Advertising and Marketing* 9 (Sep 1935): 22-23. "CR: Comedy Relief," *Business Week*, Oct 12, 1935, 30. Frank Dalton O'Sullivan, *The Poison Pen of New Jersey* (Chicago: O'Sullivan Publishing House, 1936); G. L. Eskew, *Guinea Pigs and Bugbears* (Chicago: Research Press, 1938); Charles E. Carpenter, *Dollars and Sense* (New York: Doubleday, Doran & Co, 1928). The quotations are from O'Sullivan's preface. Carpenter described *Your Money's Worth* as "basically communist propaganda" (xiii). Although not exclusively focused on CR, another venomous critique of the consumer movement was George E. Sokolsky, *The American Way of Life* (New York: Farrar & Rinehart, 1939). "Mr. Schlink's Money's Worth," *Chicago Daily News*, Sep 12, 1935. "Subject of CR," *Tide of Advertising and Marketing* 9 (Oct 1935): 72. "Consumer Movement," 47-50. Fred DeArmond, "Consumer Clans Are Gathering," *Nation's Business* 26 (Jan 1938): 41-44.

15. On the importance of the consumer movement for socialists see Richard M. Briggs, "Consumers' Research," *New Leader*, Mar 14, 1931, 8. "The Strike at Consumers' Research," *New Republic*, Oct 9, 1935, 230-231. For the characterization of CR as crusaders, see Fletcher Pratt, "The Consumer Sees Red," *American Mercury* 39 (Nov 1935): 313-320, esp. 314. "The C.R. Strike," *Nation*, Dec 4, 1935, 637.

16. Chase and Schlink, *Your Money's Worth*, 3. Wyand, *Economics of Consumption*, 393. As one astute journalist recognized, CR "was radical only in the sense that it was a help to the little man and a nuisance to business. Its director, F. J. Schlink, had no political

connections and believed in government by the technological elite." Richard H. Rovere, "J. B. Matthews: The Informer," *Nation*, Oct 3, 1942, 316.

17. Charles McGovern has characterized CR as "populist" and as expressing "antimarket," "anticommercial" beliefs and an "activist republican derived vision." What CR opposed, I contend, were admen, businessmen, and others who distorted the market, thus impeding a just system of commerce. Nor do I find a call for "consumer protest and activism" central to its ideology. Similarly, I am less convinced than is Kathleen Donohue that Schlink underwent an abrupt political transformation from left to right as a result of the strike. While agreeing that the strike heightened his anticommunism, I see him undergoing a more gradual and subtle shift from an early twentieth-century Progressive to a mid-twentieth-century interest-group liberal. McGovern, *Sold American*, esp. 190, 198, 204; and McGovern, "Consumption and Citizenship in the United States, 1900-1940," in *Getting and Spending: European and American Consumer Societies in the Twentieth Century*, ed. Susan Strasser, Charles McGovern, and Matthias Judt (New York: Cambridge University Press, 1998), 37-58, esp. 53-54; Kathleen Grace Donohue, "Conceptualizing the Good Society: The Idea of the Consumer and Modern American Political Thought" (PhD diss., University of Virginia, 1994), 338-342. Kathleen G. Donohue, *Freedom from Want: American Liberalism and the Idea of the Consumer* (Baltimore: Johns Hopkins University Press, 2003), 230-241.

18. Mary Kay, "The Development of Gyp-Consciousness: What Consumers' Research Is Doing," *Churchman*, Jul 4, 1931, 10. On "consumption as a personal matter," see Charles S. Wyand, "Wages vs. Purchasing Power," *Consumers' Digest* 2 (Aug 1937): 66-70, esp. 69. Schlink's comments are from *Consumers' Research Confidential Bulletin*, Nov 1930. In 1933 CR's board clearly stated that it would not take into account the social conditions of production in evaluating products. See Sybil Schwartz, "The Genesis and Growth of the First Consumer Testing Organization" (M.A. thesis, Columbia University, 1971), 157-158. M. C. Philips to Ferdinand Lundberg, Apr 28, 1936, "Strike—AFL—William Green, 1935," box 418, folder 1, CRA. Charles S. Wyand, "Consumers and the Labor Movement," *Consumers' Digest* 2 (Oct 1937): 71-75, esp. 72-73. Wyand made the same point in *Economics of Consumption*, 394. On CR's refusal to make alliances, see Schwartz, "Genesis and Growth," 123. Schlink noted that "there was considerable pressure in the early days . . . to make us into some sort of cooperative, or at least to have us affiliate with various cooperative organizations and sell or sponsor cooperatives' products and services." "Off the Editor's Chest," *Consumer Bulletin* 46 (Apr 1963): 2.

19. For Schlink's support for the free market, see "Consumers' Is Anti-red, Says F. J. Schlink," *Washington Star*, Dec 14, 1939. J. B. Matthews, "The Cooperatives: An Experiment in Civilization," *Atlantic Monthly*, 158 (Dec 1936): 705-715, esp. 715. Wyand, *Economics of Consumption*, 393. Arthur Kallet used the phrase "strongly anticapitalist" and also called Schlink "pro labor" and "quite radical." Arthur Kallet interview by Sybil Schwartz, Dec 7, 1970, Arthur Kallet Oral History, CUA. Kallet and others who called Schlink anticapitalist provided few specifics to support this view. The strongest evidence I have found of Schlink's putative radicalism were his vote for Norman Thomas in the 1928 presidential election and his visits to Brookwood Labor College in the early 1930s. I believe the former is evidence of his belief in planning and efficiency rather than hisanti anticapitalism; Brookwood provided a forum for Schlink to attempt to spread his ideas. McGovern, *Sold American*, 198; E. J. Lever interview by Colston Warne and Sybil Shainwald, Jul

31, 1971, E. J. Lever Oral History, CUA. For similar assessments, see Schwartz, "Genesis and Growth," 68.

20. Roland Marchand, *Advertising the American Dream: Making Way for Modernity, 1920-1940* (Berkeley: University of California Press, 1985). For a similar interpretation see McGovern, *Sold American*, 208-217. Phillips is quoted on 211. Chase and Schlink, *Your Money's Worth*, 1. For the view that people were "only partially rational bundles of impulses and habits shaped in response to an unsynchronized environment" see Robert S. Lynd with Alice Hanson, "The People as Consumers," in *Recent Social Trends in the United States*, 2 vols. (New York: McGraw-Hill, 1933), 2:866.

21. James Rorty, "What's Wrong with Consumers' Research," *Consumers Defender*, Oct 1935, 5-6, 15; Rorty, "Notes on the CR Strike," *American Spectator* 3 (Nov 1935): 16. The comment on the "destruction" of exploiters is quoted in "J. B. Matthews, Dies Committee Report (1939)," "Personnel—J. B. Matthews-Dies Committee Report?" box 43, folder 30, CRA.

22. DeArmond, "Consumer Clans Are Gathering," 44. Similarly, Joseph Gaer wrote, "What we call 'the consumer movement' today is really a strange assortment of activities." *Consumers All*, 113.

23. Schlink's comment is from "Off the Editor's Chest," *Consumer Bulletin* 46 (Apr 1963): 2. On Hoover and the 1920s see Kendrick A. Clements, *Hoover, Conservation, and Consumerism: Engineering the Good Life* (Lawrence: University of Kansas Press, 2000).

24. For explication of this argument see Lawrence B. Glickman, "Rethinking Politics: Consumers and the Public Good in the 'Jazz Age,'" *OAH Magazine of History*, Apr 2007, 16-20. See also Meg Jacobs, *Pocketbook Politics: Economic Citizenship in Twentieth-Century America* (Princeton: Princeton University Press, 2005); Lawrence M. Lipin, *Workers and the Wild: Conservation, Consumerism, and Labor in Oregon, 1910-30* (Urbana: University of Illinois Press); Joe Renouard, "The Predicaments of Plenty: Interwar Intellectuals and American Consumerism," *Journal of American Culture* 30 (Mar 2007): 54-67.

25. Liette Gidlow, *The Big Vote: Gender, Consumer Culture, and the Politics of Exclusion, 1890s-1920s* (Baltimore: Johns Hopkins University Press, 2004), esp. 161-193; August Meier and Elliott Rudwick, "Early Boycotts of Segregated Schools: The Case of Springfield, Ohio, 1922-23," *American Quarterly* 20 (Winter 1968): 744-758; "Propose Boycott for Indecent Plays," *NYT*, Oct 18, 1927, 11. See from the *NYT* "Call Mass Meeting for Fight on Klan," Jan 19, 1923, 8; "Predicts Defeats of Ex-Gov. Walton," Aug 10, 1924, 30; "W. A. White to Run as Foe of the Klan," Sep 21, 1924, 1; "Hundred Floggings in Georgia County," Mar 14, 1927, 1. The department store boycott is treated in Dana Frank, *Purchasing Power: Consumer Organizing, Gender, and the Seattle Labor Movement, 1919-1929* (New York: Cambridge University Press, 1994), 108-138.

26. William T. Ogburn, "Our Standard of Living Viewed as Going Higher," *NYT*, Aug 25, 1929, XX11. Sidney Armor Reeve, *Modern Economic Tendencies* (New York: Dutton, 1921). Reeve's work was analyzed in "Books and Authors," *NYT*, May 29, 1921, 46; and Richard J. Walsh, "Consumerism vs. Commercialism," *Nation*, Mar 15, 1922, 321-322. Edward S. Cowdrick, "The New Economic Gospel of Consumption: Revolutionary Changes Brought About by Our Highly Geared Production Machine," *Industrial Management*, Oct 1927, 209-211; Robert S. Lynd and Helen Merrell Lynd, *Middletown: A Study in Modern American Culture* (New York: Harcourt Brace Jovanovich, 1929), 88.

27. Muncie Chamber of Commerce is quoted in Lynd and Lynd, *Middletown*, 88.

28. "Should Concentrate Boycotts," *NYT*, Feb 2, 1920, 16. Ralph Borsodi, *The Distribution Age: A Study of the Economy of Modern Distritubtion* (New York: D. Appleton & Co., 1927), 276. For contemporary analyses of the "buyers' strikes," see J. H. Collins, "Coming, Another Buyers' Strike?" *Saturday Evening Post*, Jun 23 1923, 29; P. D. Vroom, "Is There a Buyers' Strike?" *Colliers*, Jul 16 1921, 5-6; "How to Break the Buyers' Strike," *Literary Digest*, Mar 26 1921, 7-9; "Should the Buyer Cease from Striking?" *Literary Digest*, Jan 22 1921, 72. "Embattled Consumers," *NYT*, Dec 27, 1927, 18. "'Buy Now' Begins with Consumer," *NYT*, Nov 2, 1930, N18. On the call for a "consumers party," see, for example, the letter to the editor from C. E. Nixdorff, *NYT*, Feb 15, 1927, 15.

29. Kyrk and Spargo are quoted in Jacobs, *Pocketbook Politics*, 81, 71. The Lynds are quoted in Chase, *Economy of Abundance*, 272. Chase himself wrote of "the increasing ignorance of the consumer," in "Society Adrift," in *Socialist Planning and a Socialist Program*, ed. Harry W. Laidler (New York: Falcon Press, 1932), 4. (Colston Warne, the future president of CU, and J. B. Matthews both have essays in this collection.) Chase and Schlink, *Your Money's Worth*, 2. Evans Clark, "Bridging the Gap between Producer and Consumer," *NYT*, Jul 10, 1927, BR3.

30. They are quoted in "Let the Buyer Beware," *NYT*, Mar 23, 1926, 26; and "Progress in Raising Buying Standards," *NYT*, Feb 19, 1928, 47. The latter noted: "Similar clubs are being formed or are contemplated in university towns in Virginia and Pennsylvania and in a small city in Michigan."

31. Stuart Chase and F. J. Schlink, "Few Billions for Consumers (Government Testing and Standards)," *New Republic*, Dec 30 1925, 153-155; F. J. Schlink, "Improving Purchasing Methods through Specifications," *American City* 42 (Apr 1930): 157-158. "Wanted, a Consumers' Advocate," *Nation*, Feb 6 1929, 151; "Cabinet Department Urged for Consumer," *NYT*, Dec 12, 1933, 17.

32. Harap, "What Is the Consumer Movement?" 48.

33. Katz employs the terms "gradualist" and "radical" to describe the different points of view, but, while helpful at drawing a distinction, these terms do not capture the nature of the fundamentally different worldviews. The word "gradualist" suggests that those I call "technocratic individualist" supported the same kind of change as the "social movement" activists, only over a longer period of time; the key difference, however, was not temporal but philosophical. "Consumers Union," 9.

34. The LWS was one of many "social movement" organizations to emerge in this period. For other examples see Kathleen Newman, *Radio Active: Advertising and Consumer Activism, 1935-1947* (Berkeley: University of California Press, 2004). A number of African American and working-class organizations promoted grassroots consumer efforts to support union-made products, and to fight racial discrimination and the high cost of living. See, for example, Otto Hall and Ben Davis, Jr., "The Struggle on the Consumers Front, a Weapon for Educating the Negro People," *Daily Worker*, Oct 27, 1935; "Labor Tie Urged on Consumer," *Hosiery Worker*, May 20, 1938, 4. On African American consumer politics: Kimberley L Phillips, *AlabamaNorth: African-American Migrants, Community, and Working-Class Activism in Cleveland, 1915-45* (Urbana: University of Illinois Press, 1999), 190-225. Cheryl Greenberg, *"Or Does It Explode?" Black Harlem in the Great Depression* (New York: Oxford University Press, 1991), 114-139; Darlene Clark Hine, "The Housewives' League of Detroit: Black Women and Economic Nationalism," in *Visible Women: New Essays on American Activism*, ed. Nancy A. Hewitt and Suzanne Lebsock (Ur-

bana: University of Illinois Press, 1993), 223–241; Andor Skotnes, "'Buy Where You Can Work': Boycotting for Jobs in African American Baltimore, 1933–1934," *Journal of Social History* 27 (Summer 1994): 735–761; Gary Jerome Hunter, "'Don't Buy from Where You Can't Work: Black Urban Boycott Movements during the Depression, 1929–1941" (PhD diss., University of Michigan, 1977). See also the article on an NAACP-organized "boycott of Kroger stores in Toledo because of their failure to employ Negroes in stores which were patronized chiefly by Negro customers." *World Tomorrow,* Jan 4, 1933, clipping in box 149, folder 7, CRA. As Landon Storrs demonstrates, the NCL had shifted its focus from grassroots activism in the Progressive Era to government lobbying for labor standards in the New Deal period. *Civilizing Capitalism.* For the editorial, see *Woman Shopper* 1 (Aug 1935): 1.

35. The women in the league prominently mentioned in the media included Mrs. Leon Henderson, wife of the WPA economic analyst; Mrs. Mordecai Ezekial, whose husband was economic adviser to Agriculture Secretary Henry Wallace; Mrs. Gifford Pinchot; Mrs. Edwin Colman, daughter of Senator Burton K. Wheeler; Mrs. Henry Morgenthau; Mrs. William O. Douglas; Mrs. Donald Richberg; Mrs. John Collier; and Mrs. James Landis. If they were married, the women's own first names were rarely mentioned: Virginia F. Durr was listed as Mrs. Clifford Durr. First names were used for single women: the head of the Women's Bureau of the Department of Labor, for example, was typically called Miss Mary Anderson. On the LWS's merging of "facts" and collective action, see Helene Frankel, "Mr. Schlink of N.J.," *Woman Shopper* 1 (Nov 1935): 1. The phrase "mink-coat picket lines" is from an LWS pamphlet (n.p., n.d.), Minneapolis League of Women Shoppers Papers, Minnesota Historical Society, Minneapolis, MN. Abraham Isserman used the phrase "mink coat brigades" in an interview by Sybil Shainwald, Feb 3, 1973, Abraham Isserman Oral History, CUA. LWS members were described as "fur-coated" in "New Dealers' Wives Picket in Pants Strike," *WP,* Mar 18, 1937, 5. On "Life without Silk" see chap. 7. Kathleen McInerny, the executive secretary of the LWS, and also a CU board member, described wearing a cotton wedding dress and noted: "I had all my bridesmaids in cotton dresses and cotton stockings—very antisilk. Completely non-silk." Kathleen McInerny interview by Sybil Shainwald, Nov 12, 1972, Kathleen McInerny Oral History, CUA. On the power of aggregate shopping, see the pamphlet for the New Jersey League of Women Shoppers, "Front Organizations, 1935–1970," box 533, folders 9–12, CRA. The LWS was not alone in using the 90 percent figure: advertisers had long used it as well. Thomas J. Schlereth, *Victorian America: Transformations in Everyday Life, 1876–1915* (New York: HarperCollins, 1991), 141; McGovern, *Sold American,* 36. Vorse quoted in *Washington Star,* Apr 26, 1938. On the remedy for the inarticulateness of consumers, see *Washington Star,* Jan 29, 1938.

36. Christopher Lasch, "The Culture of Consumption," in *Encyclopedia of American Social History,* ed. Mary Kupiec Cayton, Elliot J. Gorn, and Peter W. Williams (New York: Scribner, 1993), 2:1381–1390, quotation on 1388.

37. Jean Baudrillard, *The Mirror of Production,* trans. Mark Poster (St. Louis: Telos Press, 1975), 17. Kenneth Burke, "Waste: The Future of Prosperity," *New Republic,* Jul 16, 1930, 228–231. Stuart Chase, *The Tragedy of Waste* (New York: Macmillan, 1925). On Chase, waste, and efficiency see Robert B. Westbrook, "Tribune of the Technostructure: The Popular Economics of Stuart Chase," *American Quarterly* 32 (Autumn 1980): 387–408.

38. The quotation is from the pamphlet *What Is the League of Women Shoppers?* (New

York, n.d.), folder, "League of Women Shoppers U.S." Tamiment Library, New York University, NY.

39. On the association between women, social science, and reform in the 1930s see Storrs, *Civilizing Capitalism*, 29. For an argument about a parallel distinction between female "social work" and male "social insurance," see Linda Gordon, "Social Insurance and Public Assistance: The Influence of Gender in Welfare Thought in the United States, 1890-1935," *AHR* 97 (Feb 1992): 19-54.

40. Schlink earned $7,000 per year; the next highest salary was $2,080. Important primary sources on the strike include *Decisions and Orders of the National Labor Relations Board* (Washington DC, 1937), 2:57-77; Reinhold Niebuhr and Roger N. Baldwin, "Report of the Investigating Committee on the Strike at the Plant of CR," box 418, folder 8, CRA; "The 'United Front' against CR," *Consumers' Research Bulletin* 2 (Nov 1935): 24; CR's pamphlet *The Strike at Consumers' Research* (n.p., n.d.); Heasty, "Amazing Situation in Consumers' Research," 110-111; J. B. Matthews, *Odyssey of a Fellow Traveler* (New York: Mount Vernon Publishers, 1938), 259-269; J. B. Matthews, "Consumers' Research Replies to Mr. Heasty," *Advance*, Mar 1, 1936, 268-270; Arthur Kallet, "Consumers' Research on Strike," *New Masses*, Sep 17, 1935, 10-13. See also Donohue, *Freedom from Want*, 186-192; Silber, *Test and Protest*, 19-23; Katz, "Consumers Union," 68-82; McGovern, *Sold American*, 303-313; Schwartz, "Genesis and Growth," 148-183.

41. The quotations are from *Nation*, Sep 18, 1935, 309. Alexander L. Crosby, "Consumers' Research Fights the Union," *Nation*, Sep 25, 1935, 356-357; Arthur Kallet, "Partners in Strike Breaking: Consumers as Workers vs. Consumers as Employers," *Common Sense* 4 (Sep 1935): 22-23; *New Republic*, Oct 9, 1935, 230-231. Palmer's wife is quoted in *New York World-Telegram*, Sep 11, 1935, 6. *New Republic*, Jan 29, 1936, 322. Consumers' Research NY Strike Aid Committee to "Friends," Oct 19, 1935, box 4, Kallet Papers.

42. "Thunder on the Left," 22-23; "When the Mighty Fall," *Advertising and Selling*, Sep 12, 1935, 5. "CR: Comedy Relief"; "Kallet vs. Schlink," *Business Week*, Sep 7, 1935, 8, which noted that "most of the 60,000 subscribers . . . are presumably liberally inclined." "Schlink's Stand on Consumers' Research Employees' Strike Appears Inconsistent with His Other Radical Philosophy," *Electronic Refrigeration News*, Sep 18, 1935. The editorial appeared in *Camden Courier Post*, Sep 14, 1935. Elizabeth Dilling, *The Roosevelt Red Record and Its Background* (Chicago: the author, 1936), 314-315.

43. For efforts to locate the "typical consumer," see "A Trade Journal Discovers Consumers," *Consumers' Research Bulletin* 1 (Nov 1934): 6; "Business Cultivates Consumers," *Consumers' Research Bulletin* 2 (Jan 1935): 13; *New York World-Telegram*, Apr 11, 1936, 3A; *New York Herald Tribune*, Jan 14, 1939, 30; *NYT*, Jan 5, 1940, L27; "Mrs. Typical Consumer," *Consumer Education*, Jan 1, 1939; *Tide of Advertising and Marketing*, Feb 1, 1941, 12. The quotations are from "When the Mighty Fall," 22-23; "Schlink's Stand on Consumers' Research Employees' Strike"; "Strike in 'The Temple of Consumption.'" On the "tie-up" between business and communists, see Schlink to John R. Commons, Apr 20, 1936, "Strike 1936," box 418, folder 14, CRA; "The 'United Front' against CR." The influential columnist Walter Winchell noted that CR's bosses "blame the strike on both Reds and Capitalists, which, even if not true, isn't a bad fantasy." *Daily Mirror*, Sep 24, 1935.

44. "Consumers' Research Strike: Both Sides of the Argument," *New York Post*, Sep 13, 1935. Arthur Kallet concurred: "Schlink goes to great extremes to learn the truth about the goods which he reports to his subscribers but the fine balance he displays as to prod-

ucts is lacking in his dealings with human beings." This was quoted to him as a statement he made during the strike. Kallet interview, CUA.

45. Heasty, "Amazing Situation," 110. See the LWS report, "Investigation of Strike at Consumers' Research," box 533, folder 12, CRA. Alexander Crosby interview by Norman Katz, Nov 19, 1974. Alexander Crosby Oral History, CUA.

46. Niebuhr and Baldwin, "Report of the Investigating Committee on the Strike at the Plant of CR." "Niebuhr Committee Reports on Consumers' Research," *Christian Century*, Dec 11, 1935, 1581; "Fixing the Blame at CR," *New Republic*, Nov 13, 1935, 62; "The Autocrats of C.R.," *New Masses*, Dec 3, 1935, 3. The other members of the Niebuhr Committee, labeled "prominent liberals" by *New Masses*, were Norman Thomas, Prof. George S. Counts, Prof. William L. Nunn, Rev. Herman F. Reissig, Helena N. Simmons, secretary of the Consumers League of New Jersey, James Waterman Wise, and Vincent J. Murphy, the secretary of the New Jersey State Federation of Labor. For Schlink's reaction to the report see *New York Herald Tribune*, Nov 28, 1935, 4; "The 'Impartiality' of the Niebuhr-Baldwin Committee, Dec 5, 1935," box 418, folders 9–10, CRA; J. B. Matthews to Roger Baldwin, Nov 20, 1935, box 418, folder 8, CRA. In this single-spaced, seven-page point-by-point response to the Niebuhr report, Matthews noted, among other things, that Susan Jenkins, one of the strike leaders, worked for *New Masses* (and was married to Slater Brown, one of its editors), and that Arthur Kallet, under the name Edward Adams, wrote for the *Daily Worker* and other Communist Party publications, including *Health and Hygiene*. On "progressive" support for the strikers, see *New Masses*, Dec 3, 1935, 4. On the mock trial, "Mass Trial AFL, Local 20055 v. J. B. Matthews and F. J. Schlink, Directors of Consumers' Research," which was held at Town Hall, Oct 24, 1935, 8:30 p.m., see the announcement in *New Masses*, Oct 22, 1935; "Guilty! People's Court Condemns CR Board Members," *IPA News Bulletin*, Nov 1935, in box 421, folder 42, CRA. James Gilman to Consumers' Research Subscribers, Oct 30, 1935, box 421, folder 24, CRA.

47. *Digest of Decisions of the National Labor Relations Board* (Washington DC: Government Printing Office, 1935), 2:69; "Research Concern Told to Rehire 3," *NYT*, Jan 29, 1936, L25. The quotation about "past mistakes" is from Colston Warne to CU supporters, Mar 6, 1936. The letter noted that CU would be a "democratic organization" and would be aimed at people with "modest budgets." The quotation about the "place of the worker" is from Dewey Palmer to Colston Warne, Jan 29, 1936. Both letters are in "CU Correspondence/Documents, 1936–1955," box 4, folder 1, Kallet Papers. On labor solidarity, see the CU pamphlet *Workers as Consumers: How Consumers Union Serves Labor* (n.d., n.p.), "CU Labor Advisory Committee," box 4, folder 3, Kallet Papers. *Consumers Union Reports* 1 (May 1936): 2. "Labor Unions Endorse Plans for Consumer: Organization Is Outgrowth of CR Strike," *Progressive*, Apr 11, 1936; "The Week," *New Republic*, Feb 12, 1936, 2. "The union will offer consumer information not only on quality and price but also on the labor conditions under which goods are produced and distributed." CU also sold abridged editions of its monthly reports for one dollar rather than the customary two dollars—these editions left out "luxury items like automobiles, radio-phonographs." "Consumer Movement," 40–41; Wyand, *Economics of Consumption*, 394. On CU's appeal for "mass support," see *Nation*, Sep 18, 1935, 309. On the growth of CR, see Warne, "Consumers on the March," 646. Abraham Isserman declared that CU represented a "very positive manifestation of . . . the New Deal." Isserman interview by Norman Katz, Oct 8, 1974, Isserman Oral History. Stuart Chase interview by Colston Warne, Oct 17, 1969, Stuart Chase Oral History, CUA.

48. On the strike as a "putsch" and "coup," see Schlink to Arleen Kaufmann, Apr 21, 1936; and Schlink to E. E. Devendorf, Jul 23, 1936, "Strike—Background—Union and Left-Wing Connections of the Union, 1936–1944," box 418, folder 4, CRA. J. B. Matthews, "A New Way for Making Suckers out of Consumers," *Consumers' Digest* 3 (Feb 1938): 70–80. Pratt, "Consumer Sees Red," 314–315, 317; M. C. Phillips, "Are Consumers Being Used as a Red Front?" *Consumers' Digest* 9 (Feb 1941): 53–59. On Matthews's early anticommunism, see Matthews, *Odyssey of a Fellow Traveler*. In a Jul 10, 1947, letter to Matthews, M. C. Phillips wrote, "Aren't you entertained by the fact that everybody and his brother are now trying to capitalize on your pioneering [anticommunist] work? It must feel good to be in high fashion." "Schlink, F. J. and Mary Kay, 1938–1950," box 679, J. B. Matthews Papers, Rare Book, Manuscript and Special Collections Library, Duke University, Durham, NC. The other groups named as part of the "red network" were the New York Consumers' Council; the Greenwich Village High Cost of Living Conference; the City Action Committee against the High Cost of Living, New York City; the Consumers' National Federation; the United Conference against the High Cost of Living, Chicago; the Committee for Boycott against Japanese Aggression; the Milk Consumers' Protective Committee; the Consumer-Farmer Milk Co-operative; the Central Action Committee against the High Cost of Living, Detroit; the City Action Committee against the High Cost of Living, the Bronx; and the United Conference against the High Cost of Living, Los Angeles. "Consumers' Red Network," *Business Week*, Dec 16, 1939, 17–18. For the full text of Matthews's report to the Dies Committee, see "Consumer Groups Called 'Red,'" *American Consumer* 7 (Dec 1939): 14–19. Matthews's report on Consumers Union for HUAC contains many examples of his use of circumstantial evidence to proclaim guilt: he compiles lists of "fellow traveling" organizations to which CU's leadership belonged. See his manuscript "Consumers Union," box 168, folder 9, J. B. Matthews Papers. A lengthy Jan 1940 FBI report on the consumer movement, which claimed that it was "dominated by members of the Communist Party, communist sympathizers, and radicals," can be found in the Esther Peterson Papers, Schlesinger Library, Harvard University, Cambridge, MA. For challenges to the accuracy of Matthews's report see Walter Goodman, *The Committee: The Extraordinary Career of the House Committee on Un-American Activities* (New York: Farrar, Straus & Giroux, 1968), 83–85. See also the two exhaustive articles by Landon R. Y. Storrs: "Red Scare Politics and the Suppression of Popular Front Feminism: The Loyalty Investigation of Mary Dublin Keyserling," *JAH* 90 (Sep 2003): 491–524; and "Left-Feminism, the Consumer Movement, and Red Scare Politics in the United States, 1935–1960," *Journal of Women's History* 18 (Fall 2006): 40–67. Most of the founders of CU admitted that there was, in Abraham Isserman's words, a "left-wing influence" but differed on the extent of Communist Party involvement in the strike; all denied that the party played a dominant role in the strike or in CU policy. Isserman himself said that "some of it was C.P.; some of it was not C.P." Arthur Kallet said, "I don't know whether some of the people on the staff had any associations with the Communist organizations but certainly the Communist Party itself had nothing to do with it." Alexander Crosby said that there was a "strong CP influence" at the office. Kathleen McInerny noted that "there were people who were strongly pro-Communist, but they didn't twist your arm—this was during the United Front days and everybody was working in the inner left with all sorts of groups." All quotations from Isserman, Kallet, Crosby, and McInerny Oral Histories, CRA. Among the critics of the Dies report were President Franklin D. Roosevelt and his wife, Eleanor:

"President Shows Displeasure with Methods of Dies," *St. Louis Post-Dispatch*, Dec 13, 1939. HUAC Member Jerry Voorhis denounced the report as "purely and simply the opinion of J. B. Matthews." "Voorhis Attacks Dies, Matthews," *NYT*, Dec 12, 1939. For Drew Pearson's dismissal of the report, see "Consumer Groups Irate over Red Charge, Plan to Ask Probe of Dies," *St. Louis Post-Dispatch*, Dec 22, 1939. These articles are reprinted in a special insert in *Consumer Education*, vol. 2 (Jan 1940). From *NYT* see "Dies Investigator Says Reds Utilize Consumer Groups," Dec 11, 1939, 1; "Finds No Red Aims in Consumer Drive," Jan 17, 1940, 34; "Dies to Hunt Reds in Consumer Units," Oct 31, 1939, 13. Just two days earlier, the *Times* observed that "the days of stamping consumer groups 'red' and 'subversive' appear to be over." C. F. Hughes, "Consumer Movement Recognized," Oct 29, 1939, F8; "Red Charges Denied by Consumer Group," Dec 13, 1939, 19; "Backs Consumer Groups," Dec 16, 1939, 24.

49. "The Constructive Consumer Movement Is Honest and Sincere," *American Consumer* 7 (Dec 1939): 1. Stuart Chase, "The Years Between," *Consumer Education* 1 (Nov 1939): 7. Sorenson, *Consumer Movement*, x–xii. For the backlash against consumer groups, see George H. Tichenor, "War on Consumers," *Forum and Century* 103 (Jan 1940): 28–31.

50. Dewey Palmer, a strike leader and an important figure in both CR and CU, told J. B. Matthews that while he could not "accuse Arthur Kallet and Dexter Masters of being communists . . . their often expressed sympathy for Russia and Stalinism" left him with "but one obvious conclusion." Howard Rushmore, a former employee of the *Daily Worker*, told Matthews that in his newspaper he often reprinted *Consumer Reports* articles, which were supplied to him by CU executives. The "primary idea" was "like the basic principle of all Consumer 'fronts,' the destruction of democracy." In what may be one of the earliest uses of the phrase, Matthews claimed that the *Daily Worker* was told by Communist Party of the United States of America leadership that "anything from CU is politically correct as far as we're concerned." "Consumers Union of US, Inc., 1939–1948," box 168, folder 9, J. B. Matthews Papers. For a recantation from a former LWS member, see Helen Woodward, "How I Joined a Red Front," *Freeman*, May 17, 1954, 594–596. The celebrity ex-communist Elizabeth Bentley, the "Red Spy Queen," had worked briefly for CU in 1937 and claimed in the early 1950s to have observed subversive activity there. See "Memorandum to the File, Jun 10, 1953, "Consumers Union, Correspondence/Documents, 1936–1955," box 1, folder 1, Kallet Papers. Amy Swerdlow, "Congress of American Women," in *Encyclopedia of the American Left*, ed. Mari Jo Buhle, Paul Buhle, and Dan Georgakas (New York: Garland, 1990), 161–162. Kallet's coworkers claimed that his left-wing past made him "highly insecure," but they also noted that his abiding interest in the consumer movement lay in the technical dimension. As a result of the Dies investigation, noted Kathleen McInerny, "Arthur may have very well retreated to a technical view, which was his first love." They also noted that Kallet was, like Schlink, an imperious person with whom it was difficult to get along. See interviews with Colston Warne (from whom the "highly insecure" quotation is drawn), Abraham Isserman, Leland Gordon, Kathleen McInerny, and Sidney Margolies, CUA. David Caplovitz, *The Poor Pay More: Consumer Practices of Low-Income Families* (New York: Free Press, 1963). Colston E. Warne, *The Consumer Movement: Lectures by Colston E. Warne*, ed. Richard L. D. Morse (Manhattan, KS: Family Economics Trust Press, 1993), 151–221. Demonstrating that there was still a wide gulf between CU and its enemies from CR, Ruth Matthews, J. B.'s third wife and widow (Ruth Shallcross was his second wife), described the Consumer Federation of America as "the

culmination of agitation on the part of left-wing critics of business." Ruth I. Matthews to John A. Clements, Nov 7, 1967, "Consumer Lobby, 1967," box 168, folder 7, J. B. Matthews Papers. Isserman's "less militant" quotation is from Katz, "Consumers Union," 311. In 1973, the journalist and former CU board member Sidney Margolies criticized the organization, claiming that Consumers Union was "still too preoccupied with connoisseurship, with expensive stereo equipment, camera equipment . . . while it never gets into the problems of cooperative housing, mobile housing. . . . It should be more activist about consumer goods." Sidney Margolies interview by Sybil Shainwald and Patrick Mahoney, Sep 8, 1973, Sidney Margolies Oral History, CUA. In 1999, promotional materials from CU had these words on the cover: "It's not only about money. It's also about . . ." Anticipating the word "ethics" or "responsibility," one opened the leaflet to find that the other things turned out to be "Cell Phones," "Your Home Office," and "Shape Up!" "Dear Friend," letter from *CRe*, received in Feb, 1999 (in author's possession).

51. David M. Oshinsky, *A Conspriracy So Immense: The World of Joe McCarthy* (New York: Free Press, 1983), 318–320; Matthews, "Reds and Our Churches," *American Mercury*, 77 (Jul 1953): 3–13. "Editorially Speaking," 43. Donohue, "Conceptualizing the Good Society," 338–339. The economist Richard Morse also linked consumerism to conservative politics: "The consumer movement actually has been a vital force in preserving, protecting, and advancing capitalist free enterprise." Warne, *Consumer Movement*, 296–297. Schlink described himself as a "libertarian economist" in a letter to "Ruthie and J. B." Matthews, Apr 18, 1958. In a Jul 4, 1967, letter to Ruth Matthews, M. C. Phillips admitted to having "a confused picture of exploring how CR fits into the conservative picture." Both letters are in "Schlink, F. J. and Mary Kay, 1955–1967 and nd," box 679, J. B. Matthews Papers. Persia Campbell, *The Consumer Interest: A Study in Consumer Economics* (New York: Harper, 1949); Campbell, *Consumer Representation in the New Deal* (New York: Columbia University Press, 1940). Allis R. Wolfe, *Persia Campbell: Portrait of a Consumer Activist* (Mount Vernon, NY: Consumers Union, 1981). Works on interest-group politics that discuss the consumer movement include Frank Baumgartner and Beth L. Leach, *Basic Interests: The Importance of Groups in Politics and Political Science* (Princeton: Princeton University Press, 1998); Elisabeth S. Clemens, *The People's Lobby: Organizational Innovation and the Rise of Interest Group Politics in the United States, 1890–1925* (Chicago: University of Chicago Press, 1997); Ronald J. Hrebenar and Ruth K. Scott, *Interest Group Politics in America* (Englewood Cliffs, NJ: Prentice-Hall, 1982). For a description of Nader as a "consumer advocate," see Thomas C. Reeves, *Twentieth-Century America: A Brief History* (New York, 2000), 192. In his 2000 campaign for the presidency, Nader became, in John Judis's words, "more revolutionary than reformer." He notes that the shift from advocacy to activism marked a shift in Nader's approach, which Judis labels a "betrayal" of his "life's work." He writes: "For the last four decades . . . Nader has loomed large in American politics precisely because, unlike so many other radicals, he has not merely ranted about the system. He has tried to fix it. He founded the modern consumer movement." John B. Judis, "Seeing Green: Ralph Nader Betrays Himself," *New Republic*, May 29, 2000, 25–27.

52. Michael Denning, *The Cultural Front: The Laboring of American Culture in the Twentieth Century* (New York: Verso, 1996). Susan Ferriss, *The Fight in the Fields: Cesar Chavez and the Farmworkers Movement* (New York: Harcourt Brace, 1997). On the Stevens strike, see the epilogue. Co-op America publishes *National Green Pages: Products and Service for People and the Planet.*

Chapter 7

1. "Shoppers Plan Fashion Show: 'Life without Silk' Theme of Women's League Planned Exhibit," *WP*, Jan 19, 1938, 13.

2. "Rustling of Silk Turns to a Roar on Battle's Eve," *WP*, Jan 28, 1938, 1, 5; Jane Eads, "600 D.C. Women Attend Pageant of Silkless Styles: Wardman Presentation Given by Shoppers' Boycott," *Washington Herald*, Jan 29, 1938, 9; "D.C. Women Push Ban on Silk Goods," *Washington Times*, Jan 29, 1938.

3. The AFHW was a semiautonomous member of the United Textile Workers Union and, later, the Textile Workers Organizing Committee and its successor, the Textile Workers Union of America. Clete Daniel, *Culture of Misfortune: An Interpretive History of Textile Unionism in the United States* (Ithaca: Cornell University Press, 2001), 24–25, 89.

4. "Boycott Factions to Demonstrate: Pro-silk and Anti-silk Drama on Today's Program," *Washington Evening Star*, Jan 28, 1938; "Proposed Boycott against Japan," *Congressional Digest* 17 (1938): 101–128. Shearer's speech is quoted on 126–127.

5. On Powell's legs see "Capital Arena of Embattled Silk Factions," *WP*, Jan 29, 1938, 3; *Time*, Jan 3, 1938, 30; "Eleanor Powell Joins in Boycott of Silk Hosiery," *Daily Worker*, Jan 29, 1938, 4. Eads, "600 D.C. Women Attend Pageant of Silkless Styles"; Martha Strayer, "Shoppers' League a Bit Remiss in Boycotting Silk Stockings," *Washington Daily News*, Jan 19, 1938. On Iglesias see "D.C. Women Push Ban on Silk Goods."

6. "Silk Stocking Parade Makes Capital Goggle: Women Hosiery Workers March in Washington to Protest Boycott," *Reading Eagle*, Jan 29, 1938, 1; Alice Hughes, "A Woman's New York," *WP*, Jan 14, 1938, X17; "Capital Arena of Embattled Silk Factions"; "'Save Our Jobs': Silk Workers Fight Boycott against Japan," *Washington Herald*, Jan 29, 1938, 3; "Shapely Pros and Cons of the Silk versus Cotton Debate," *WP*, Jan 29, 1938, 3. For a similar photo spread, which contains dueling snapshots of Eleanor Powell and Lillian Shearer, see "Beliefs Differ," *Reading Eagle*, Jan 29, 1938, 1.

7. For a brilliant treatment of a contemporary example of the rejection of earlier models of sacrificial virtue see Dana Frank, "Girl Strikers Occupy Chain Store, Win Big: The Detroit Woolworth's Strike of 1937," in *Three Strikes: Miners, Musicians, Salesgirls and the Fighting Spirit of Labor's Last Century*, by Howard Zinn, Dana Frank, and Robin D. G. Kelley (Boston: Beacon Press, 2001), 57–118.

8. The silk boycott is not mentioned in Monroe Friedman's twentieth-century overview, *Consumer Boycotts: Effecting Change through the Marketplace and the Media* (New York: Routledge, 1999). For brief examinations, see Dana Frank, *Buy American: The Untold Story of Economic Nationalism* (Boston: Beacon Press, 1999), 98–99; Judy Yung, *Unbound Feet: A History of Chinese Women in San Francisco* (Berkeley: University of California Press, 1995), 238.

9. It is more accurate to say the movement was reignited in 1937. See, for example, a letter to the editor calling for a boycott of Japan for violating the Kellogg-Briand Pact in 1932. Grover Clark, "A Consumers' Boycott: Direct Action by Our People Might Have Influence on Japan," *NYT*, Mar 23, 1932, 20. "A So-Called Unofficial Boycott," *CSM*, Mar 12, 1932, 18, suggested a "national consumers' boycott" of Japan. Boycott proponents cited the fact that the First Lady wore a cotton dress to a White House reception. See "Use Mrs. Hoover in Japanese Silk Boycott Appeal," *CT*, Feb 25, 1932, 2.

10. An editorial in *the Nation* was widely acknowledged to be the starting point of the boycott. "Boycott Japanese Goods!" *Nation*, Aug 28, 1937, 211–212. See also Freda

Utley, "Japan Fears a Boycott," *Nation*, Oct 2, 1937, 341–342. Harold Isaacs describes the period from 1937 to 1944 as an "Age of Admiration." *Scratches on our Minds: American Images of China and India* (New York, 1958), 71. David Kennedy, *Freedom from Fear: The American People in Depression and War, 1929–1945* (New York, 1999), 400–401. For an example of the romantic view of the Chinese and "their conspicuous good qualities" see "The Boycott Road to War," *American Mercury*, Feb 1938, 219. Gerald Horne suggests that many African Americans supported the Japanese in *Race War: White Supremacy and the Japanese Attack on the British Empire* (New York: New York University Press, 2004). See R. A. Howell's articles from *China Today*: "World's Greatest Boycott," Mar 1938, 4–5. Howell, "The Boycott Movement," Nov 1937, 204–205; "The Consumers Boycott against Japanese Goods," Dec 1937, 217–220; "Boycott Committee Asks All Tokio Goods Barred," *Daily Worker*, Feb 25, 1938. Walter LaFeber, *The Clash: U.S.-Japanese Relations throughout History* (New York: Norton, 1997), 162, 185–187; "U.S. Labor Favors Japan Boycott," *Chinese Digest*, Nov 1937, 7, 15; Esther Carroll, "Boycott Japanese Goods: Aid China!" *China Today*, Nov 1937, 198, 211. In other fascist countries, lamented the *Nation*, "there is no one commodity like silk which can be singled out for attention." "The Shape of Things," *Nation*, Dec 18, 1937, 675. "City College Men Back Defense War: 481 Favor Consumer Boycott against Japan," *NYT*, Apr 12, 1938, 12. Samuel Untermeyer, "Why Not Extend Our Anti-German Boycott to Japan," *Anti-Nazi Bulletin*, Nov 1937, 6–9. On the anti-Nazi boycott movement see Moshe Gottlieb, "The Anti-Nazi Boycott Movement in the United States: An Ideological and Sociological Approach," *Jewish Social Studies* 35 (Jul–Oct 1973): 198–227; W. Orbach, "Shattering the Shackles of Powerlessness: The Debates Surrounding the Anti-Nazi Boycott of 1933–41," *Modern Judaism* 2 (1982): 149–169. "May Picket Stores in Boycott Drive against Japan," *Retailing*, Dec 27, 1937, 4. Jeffrey L. Meikle, *American Plastic: A Cultural History* (New Brunswick: Rutgers University Press, 1995), 137; Angela J. Latham, *Posing a Threat: Flappers, Chorus Girls and Other Brazen Performers of the 1920s* (Hanover: University Press of New England, 2000), 41.

11. For intellectuals' support of the boycott see "Boycott Urged on Japanese," *LAT*, Dec 14, 1937, 1. "Shape of Things." Howell noted that "over 800 delegates from 21 countries representing 25 international organizations with a combined membership of well over 100,000,000 people" attended a conference on the boycott in London. "World's Greatest Boycott," 4–5. Carroll, "Boycott Japanese Goods," 198. For an example of the phrase "people's boycott" see Ann Rivington, "Make Mr. DuPont Help China!" *China Today*, Dec 1939, 15–16. On widespread support for the boycott and the chain stores' decision to stop buying Japanese products, see "The Boycott Is Winning," *Nation*, Jan 8, 1938, 33–34. George Gallup found that an "overwhelming majority" of Americans favored a boycott. "Boycott of Japan's Goods and Arms Embargo Favored," *LAT*, Jun 16, 1939, 2 .

12. The quotation on sensitiveness is from "Should We Boycott Japanese Goods?" *Christian Century*, Oct 13, 1937, 1353. *Did Your Stockings Kill Babies* (Boston: Boycott Japanese Goods Committee of Greater Boston, 1938); "Boycott Pressed as Curb on Japan," *NYT*, Feb 13, 1938, 3; "Abetting the Crime," *Current History* 48 (May 1938): 50. H. J. Galland warned the "women of America" that their purchase of silk "finances the murder of Chinese children." "Where Is the Boycott Now?" *China Today* 5 (Jan 1939): 9, 15. The columnist Eugene L. Meyer claimed that "when we wear silk we are wrapping ourselves in the blood and bones of bombed Chinese babies." Quoted in Leonard Sparks and Mississippi Johnson, "Put Silk in the Doghouse: A Review of Fashions and Their Origins Proves

That It Is Possible to Start a Big Swing for China and against Japan," *New Masses*, Nov 30, 1937, 13.

13. On consumption and social justice see "Shoppers Plan Fashion Show"; Rebecca Drucker, "League Thumbs-Down Fascist Goods," *Woman Shopper*, Dec–Jan 1939, 1; Robert Stark, "Is the Boycott Slipping? Silk Stockings Still Support Japan's Army," *New Masses*, Sep 20, 1938, 10–12. After the Nazi-Soviet pact some urged the expansion of the boycott: "Boycott Extended to Russian Goods" *NYT*, Dec 13, 1939, 17.

14. *Who Bought the Bomb?* (New York: American Boycott against Aggressor Nations, 1938), 22. "Pro and Con: Should We Boycott Japan," *Reader's Digest* 32 (Feb 1938): 107–112, quotation on 112. Tillie Olsen, "I Want You Women Up North to Know," *Feminist Studies* 7 (Autumn 1981): 367–370. The poem is based on a letter by Felipe Ibarro in *New Masses*, Jan 9, 1934.

15. Fred Held, an AFHW organizer, claimed that the hosiery industry employed 100,000 workers and gave indirect employment to another 250,000 workers "engaged in transportation, distributing, merchandising and related industries." "Held Hits at Silk Ban," *Hosiery Worker*, Feb 25, 1938, 1; Rieve quoted in *Why Cut Off Our Nose? (What Price Boycott?)* (San Francisco: Far Eastern Affairs Pamphlets, 1938), 5; John Nevin Sayre, "Boycott: A False Remedy," *Christian Century*, Nov 10, 1937, 1388–1389, quotation on 1389.

16. "'Save our Jobs'"; "Held Hits Silk Ban"; Rieve quoted in *Why Cut Off Our Nose?* 5.

17. O'Connor lecture, May 1, 1942 in General Files, Chicago, 1938–1942, Spring 1942, Chicago LWS, in US League of Women Shoppers Papers, Sophia Smith Collection, Smith College, Northampton, MA

18. J. Passmore Edmonds quoted in "Free-Labor Produce," *Anti-slavery Reporter*, Nov 1, 1848, 176. The "vanity" quotation is from *Who Bought the Bomb?* 22. "Rieve's Report to the Convention," *Hosiery Worker*, May 6, 1938, 6.

19. The sign is mentioned in "500 in Parade Back Boycott of Japan," *NYT*, Dec 12, 1937, 3; "Civic Groups Urge Boycott of Japan," *NYT*, Dec 19, 1937, 38; R. A. Howell, "The Boycott Movement Grows," *China Today*, Jan 1938, 233–234, 243–244; *Why and How to Boycott Goods "Made in Japan"* (New York: American League for Peace and Democracy, 1938), 11; Frank, *Buy American*, 58–63.

20. E. Stanley Jones, "An Open Letter: To the Christian People of America and Great Britain," *Christian Century* 29, Nov 10, 1937, 1386–1388, quotation on 1387.

21. For comments in favor of the boycott: "Support Anti-Japan Boycott," *CD*, May 14, 1938, 6; "Japanese-Made Products Are Boycotted," *Atlanta Daily World*, Dec 30, 1937, 3; "Birmians Asked to Boycott Japan," *Atlanta Daily Word*, Nov 2, 1937, 5; Annabelle Brown, "Says United Asia Will Give Hope to Africans," *Afro-American*, Feb 5, 1938, 4; "The Case for Japan," *Afro-American*, Jan 15, 1938, 4; Du Bois to Waldo McNutt, Feb 25, 1939, in *The Correspondence of W. E. B. Du Bois*, vol. 2, *Selections, 1934–1944*, ed. Herbert Aptheker (University of Massachusetts Press, 1976), 184–185. Against the boycott: Louis W. Hann, "Dislikes Editorial," *Afro-American*, Feb 26, 1938, 4; "Sino-Jap Dispute Explained to Harlemites," *AN*, Feb 5, 1938, 4; Gamewell Valentine, "Capacity Crowd Hears Argument: Chinese and Japanese Notables Stage Friendly 'Clash' in Sisters' Chapel," *Atlanta Daily World*, Jan 19, 1938, 1. For similar views see, for example, the Communist Party pamphlet *Japanese Imperialism and the Negro People* (Pittsburgh, 1934); John Chen Tome, "Chinese Differs with Editorial on Japanese," *Afro-American*, Jan 22, 1938, 4; "Paul Robeson Aiding China against Japan," *CD*, Nov 27, 1937, 24. "Colored Crew Halts Sailing of Jap Vessel," *CD*, Jan 14, 1939, 24;

"Mexican Workers Boycott Jap Goods," *CD*, Feb 12, 1938, 12. For an excellent overview of this issue see Marc Gallicchio, *The African American Encounter with Japan and China* (Chapel Hill: University of North Carolina Press, 2001), esp. 90; and Horne, *Race War*. On "Japan's low-budget operation to influence black American public opinion" see David Levering Lewis, *W. E. B. Du Bois: The Fight for Equality and the American Century, 1919–1963* (New York: Henry Holt, 2000), 390. By the end of World War II, Du Bois had recanted his position. See "Japanese Colonialism," "Shanghai," and "Japan, Color and Afro-Americans," in *W. E. B. Du Bois: A Reader*, ed. David Levering Lewis (New York: Henry Holt, 1995), 83–87. In the last essay from 1945 he wrote that "the experience of Japan has proven . . . that domination of one people by other and selfish races, bad as it is, is no whit better than domination within a race by elements whose aims and ideals are antisocial" (86).

22. For a brief in favor of voluntary simplicity as challenging the assumption that "consumption and happiness are joined at the hip," see Michael Maniates, "In Search of Consumptive Resistance: The Voluntary Simplicity Movement," in *Confronting Consumption*, ed. Thomas Princen, Michael Maniates, and Ken Conca (Cambridge, MA: MIT Press, 2002), 199–235.

23. Noel Thompson, "Social Opulence, Private Asceticism: Ideas of Consumption in Early Socialist Thought," in *The Politics of Consumption: Material Culture and Citizenship in Europe and America*, ed. Matthew Hilton and Martin Daunton (Oxford: Berg, 2001), 51–68, quotation on 52. In the same volume see Rebecca L. Spang, "What Is Rum? The Politics of Consumption in the French Revolution," 33–49. Warren Breckman, "Disciplining Consumption: The Debate about Luxury in Wilhelmine Germany, 1890–1914," *Journal of Social History* 24 (Spring 1991): 485–506; Karl Gerth, *China Made: Consumer Culture and the Creation of the Nation* (Cambridge, MA: Harvard University Press, 2003).

24. Glenda Elizabeth Gilmore, *Gender and Jim Crow: Women and the Politics of White Supremacy in North Carolina, 1890–1920* (Chapel Hill: University of North Carolina Press, 1996), 12–13. On the importance of "dressing up" as a collective and political act, see Tera W. Hunter, *To 'Joy My Freedom: Southern Black Women's Lives and Labors after the Civil War* (Cambridge, MA: Harvard University Press, 1997); Shane White and Graham White, *Stylin': African American Expressive Culture from Its Beginnings to the Zoot Suit* (Ithaca: Cornell University Press, 1998); Kathy Peiss, *Hope in a Jar: The Making of America's Beauty Culture* (New York: Metropolitan Books, 1998), 90, 266.

25. Lawrence B. Glickman, *A Living Wage: American Workers and the Making of Consumer Society* (Ithaca: Cornell University Press, 1997). Nan Enstad, *Ladies of Labor, Girls of Adventure: Working Women, Popular Culture, and Labor Politics at the Turn of the Century* (New York: Columbia University Press, 1999), 8. Margaret Finnegan, *Selling Suffrage: Consumer Culture and Votes for Women* (New York: New York University Press, 1999); Elisabeth S. Clemens, *The People's Lobby: Organizational Innovation and the Rise of Interest Group Politics in the United States, 1890–1925* (Chicago: University of Chicago Press, 1997), 208.

26. Josephine Goldmark, *Impatient Crusader* (Urbana: University of Illinois Press, 1953), 62–63.

27. The phrase "shifting erogenous zones" is used by the fashion historians Robert H. Lauer and Jeanette C. Lauer in *Fashion Power: The Meaning of Fashion in American Society* (Englewood Cliffs: Prentice-Hall, 1981), 17. J. C. Flugel, *The Psychology of Clothes* (New York: International Universities Press, 1930), 161–162. Stella Bruzzi, *Undressing Cinema:*

Clothing and Identity in the Movies (New York: Routledge, 1997), esp. 135–138. "Historically, the relationship between women's legs, sexual politics, and eroticism has been complex" (135). James Laver, *Taste and Fashion: From the French Revolution until Today* (New York: Dodd, Mead & Co., 1938), 130–131. The lyrics to "Anything Goes" are at http://www.stlyrics.com/lyrics/anythinggoes/anythinggoes.htm (accessed on May 12, 2008). For another leg picture see "Girls Burn Silk Stockings in Protest," *LAT*, Dec 31, 1937, 2.

28. *Big Boycott of 1938, Contemporary Scene*, vol. 1 (Summer 1938). The lyrics were by Joe Schmul, Mike Stratton, and Saul Aarons, and the music by Aarons. For excellent analysis see Eric Winship Trumbull, "Musicals of the American Workers' Theatre Movement—1928–1941: Propaganda and Ritual in Documents of a Social Movement" (PhD diss., University of Maryland, 1991), esp. chap. 5. Thanks to Dr. Trumbull for sending me a photocopy of this hard-to-find play.

29. John Cambridge, "'Maid in Japan' Breaks New Ground in Progressive Theatre," *Daily Worker*, Feb 21, 1939, 7. Malcolm Goldstein, *The Political Stage: American Drama and Theater of the Great Depression* (New York: Oxford University Press, 1974), 174.

30. Scott quoted in "Proposed Boycott against Japan," 114–116. Shearer is quoted on 126–127. Simonson quoted in Martha Strayer, "The Debs Wore Some Silk but It Was Fabric Spun by Chinese Worms," *Washington Daily News*, Jan 29, 1938. For similar comments see "Should We Boycott Japanese Goods?"; Stark, "Is the Boycott Slipping?" 10; "Senator Norris Backs Boycott against Tokio," *Daily Worker*, Dec 31, 1937, 1; Hua Liang, "Fighting for a New Life: Social and Patriotic Activism of Chinese American Women in New York City, 1900 to 1945," *Journal of American Ethnic History* 17 (Winter 1998): 22–38; "Shape of Things"; "Silk Hose Ban Scored by AFHW," *Hosiery Worker*, Jan 14, 1938, 1; "Labor, Industry Attack Silk Ban," *Hosiery Worker*, Jan 28, 1938, 1.

31. "Cotton Is King as Women Give Up Japanese Silk Hose," *Manitou Messenger*, Apr 4, 1939.

32. "Cotton Parade Date Now Close at Hand" *AN*, Apr 30, 1938, 9; "Cotton Is Paraded for Camp's Benefit," *AN*, May 14, 1938, 9.

33. Eads, "600 D.C. Women Attend Pageant"; Sparks and Johnson, "Put Silk in the Doghouse," 13. See Rob Schorman, *Selling Style: Clothing and Social Change at the Turn of the Century* (Philadelphia: University of Pennsylvania Press, 2003), 14; Hilary Radner, *Shopping Around: Feminine Culture and the Pursuit of Pleasure* (New York: Routledge, 1995), xi. T. H. Breen suggests that the Revolutionary boycotters sought to make simplicity a new fashion in *The Marketplace of Revolution: How Consumer Politics Shaped American Independence* (New York: Oxford University Press, 2004), 214.

34. "Proposed Boycott against Japan," 114–116. See also the similar comments by Senator George Norris in "Silk Industry to Fight Boycott," *Washington Evening Star*, Jan 28, 1938. *Loveliness Based on Misery Is Indeed Coarse* (Philadelphia: American Federation of Hosiery Workers, 1938). See Fred Davis, *Fashion, Culture and Identity* (Chicago: University of Chicago Press, 1994), 88. "Women Warned of Silk Stocking Shortage If a Boycott Is Invoked against Japan," *NYT*, Oct 7, 1937, 17; "Cotton Is King as Women Give Up Japanese Silk Hose." Meigs is quoted in "Says Boycott Cut Silk Use," *NYT*, Aug 11, 1940, 49.

35. It is worth noting that during this same convention ASU members used the boycott for another purpose: to protest a movie theater owner's association that had "recently ruled against showing films which show colored people in roles other than the traditional caricatures." "Students Boycott Movie Theaters for Color Line," *Afro-American*,

Jan 8, 1938, 22. See also "Student Groups Join Boycott," *Atlanta Daily World*, Jan 21, 1938, 1.

36. "War and Peace," *Time*, Jan 10, 1938, 42; "Students Burn Clothes to Spur Silk Boycott," *Life*, Jan 10, 1938, 18; "Students Demand Boycott on Japan," *NYT*, Dec 31, 1937, 3; Harry Raymond, "Students Burn Silk Hose in Big Bonfire," *Daily Worker*, Dec 31, 1937, 4.

37. "'Made in Japan' Becomes Taboo: Women Shoppers Boycott Japan," *Washington Herald*, Jan 19, 1938, 7; Sparks and Johnson, "Put Silk in the Doghouse." On the Hollywood protest see Mary Bein, "Hollywood Chants 'Boycott Japan,'" *China Today* 5 (Jan 1939): 8–9. On the diversity of the groups involved in the movement see Nathan M. Becker, "The Anti-Japanese Boycott in the United States," *Far Eastern Survey*, Mar 1, 1939, 49–55; Howell, "Boycott Movement Grows," 233–234, 243–244; "Anti-silk Ceremony: Miss Jackson to Wed Edward Strong," *AN*, Jun 4, 1938, 8. On the NYU dance and Broadway's use of lisle see "Shape of Things."

38. "Life without Silk," *WP*, Jan 28, 1938, 8.

39. Lucy Wyle, "Communism and Stockings," *New York Evening Post*, Dec 4, 1939; Stanley High, "Communism Presses Its Pants," *Saturday Evening Post*, Jul 9, 1938, 5, 6, 30, 32–36. Joanne Finkelstein writes that throughout history people have read "an individual's politics or morality from the way she dresses." *Fashion: An Introduction* (New York: New York University Press, 1996), 70. The boycott calls into question Anne Hollander's pronouncement that "the relation between the politics and the form that fashion takes always remains somewhat uncertain, since people often wear things for perverse reasons or without reasons." *Sex and Suits* (New York: Knopf, 1994), 16.

40. In reviewing the history of "fashions and their origins" Sparks and Johnson noted that "the popular creation of fashions is nothing new" and listed a series of twentieth-century precedents, including the hair bob. Lee Simonson concurred and noted that "it doesn't take a very large group of women to change the fashion to cotton, wool, or rayon." Similarly, commentators noted that a few men donning "woolen ties in attractive Navajo weaves" could potentially set off a masculine renunciation of silk. Sparks and Johnson, "Put Silk in the Doghouse," 13; "Pro and Anti-silk Question Argued by Demonstrations," *WP*, Jan 28, 1938; *Who Bought the Bomb?* 7.

41. The celebrities are mentioned in Judy Yung, *Unbound Feet*, 238; "The Student Movement of the 1930s," Joseph P. Lash, interview at http://newdeal.feri.org/students/lash.htm, paragraph 24 (accessed on May 12, 2008).

42. They also sought to invoke the celebrity of the First Lady, as when they spread rumors that Eleanor Roosevelt purposely broke the boycott: "Japanese 'Tickled' by Mrs. Roosevelt: Her Purchase of a Kimono on Coast Is Viewed in Tokyo as 'Dropping' of Boycott," *NYT*, Apr 7, 1940, 36.

43. *Loveliness Based on Human Misery Is Indeed Coarse*; J. B. Matthews, "A New Way for Making Suckers out of Consumers," *Consumer's Digest* 3 (Feb 1938): 70–80, quotations on 78–79.

44. Matthews, "New Way for Making Suckers out of Consumers," 77.

45. For an overview of condemnation of consumption see David Shi, *The Simple Life: Plain Living and High Thinking in American Culture* (New York: Oxford University Press, 1985).

46. The quotation on dance marathons is from Warren Susman, "The Culture of the 1930s," in *Culture as History: The Transformation of American Society in the Twentieth Century*

(New York: Pantheon, 1985), 162. See also Michael Denning, *The Cultural Front: The Laboring of American Culture in the Twentieth Century* (New York: Verso, 1996); Michael Rogin, "How the Working-Class Saved Capitalism: The New Labor History and *The Devil and Miss Jones*," *JAH* 89 (Jun 2002): 87–114; Paula S. Fass, *The Damned and the Beautiful: American Youth in the 1920s* (New York: Oxford University Press, 1977), 257–259; Zygmunt Bauman, *Work, Consumerism and the New Poor* (Buckingham: Open University Press, 1998), 31.

47. James B. Twitchell, *Lead Us into Temptation: The Triumph of American Materialism* (New York: Columbia University Press, 1999), 274–286. For a critique of celebrations of consumerist pleasure that ignore "the difficult and seemingly unsolveable problems of sweatshop economies and child labor" see Angela McRobbie, "A New Kind of Rag Trade?" in *No Sweat: Fashion, Free Trade, and the Rights of Garment Workers*, ed. Andrew Ross (New York: Verso, 1997), 275–289. For an examination of the "ecological footprint" of ordinary acts of consumption, see John C. Ryan and Alan Thein During, *Stuff: The Secret Lives of Everyday Things* (Seattle: Northwest Environment Watch, 1997).

48. Thomas Frank, *The Conquest of Cool: Business Culture, Counterculture, and the Rise of Hip Consumerism* (Chicago: University of Chicago Press, 1997). For perspectives which differ from mine, see Ken Conca, "Consumption and Environment in a Global Economy," in *Confronting Consumption*, 133–134; and, in the same volume, Marilyn Bordwell, "Jamming Culture: Adbusters' Hip Media Campaign against Consumerism," 252–253.

49. Talk of the boycott continued into late 1940: "Japan's Union with Axis May Intensify Boycott," *NYT*, Oct 1, 1940, 39. In July 1941 the assets of Japan were frozen. "Freezing of Foreign Funds in U.S.," in *The Public Papers and Addresses of Franklin D. Roosevelt*, comp. Samuel I. Rosenman (New York: Random House, 1941), 9:133. For an inside account of deliberations about the embargo of Japan see Harold Ickes's diary entry for Sep 28, 1940, in *The Secret Diary of Harold L. Ickes* (New York: Simon & Schuster, 1954), 3:339–340.

50. Entry for Nov 5, 1938 in *The Secret Diary of Harold L. Ickes*, 2:497. Nylon as an acronym is from Meikle, *American Plastic*, 139. Susannah Handley, *Nylon: The Story of a Fashion Revolution* (Baltimore: Johns Hopkins University Press, 1999), 31–39; Raymond Calpper, "Artificial Silk Worm Developed by Du Pont," *New York World-Telegram*, Jan 17, 1939. See also "Sales Begin Today of Nylon Hosiery," *NYT*, May 15, 1940, 31; "Answers to the Stocking Problem," *NYT*, Aug 3, 1941, D7.

51. Caroline Ware, *The Consumer Goes to War: A Guide to Victory on the Home Front* (New York: Funk & Wagnalls, 1942), 1, 5. The quotations from Jessie Lloyd O'Connor and the LWS are from an untitled 1942 pamphlet of the Chicago LWS, Sophia Smith Collection, Northampton, MA. On wartime rationing see Amy Bentley, *Eating for Victory: Food Rationing and the Politics of Domesticity* (Urbana: University of Illinois Press, 1998); Meg Jacobs, "'How About Some Meat': The Office of Price Administration, Consumption Politics, and State Building from the Bottom Up, 1941–1946," *JAH* 84 (Dec 1997): 910–941; Mark H. Leff, "The Politics of Sacrifice on the American Home Front in World War II," *JAH* 77 (Mar 1991): 1296–1318.

52. Robert Westbrook, "'I Want a Girl, Just like the Girl that Married Harry James': American Women and the Problem of Political Obligation in World War II," *American Quarterly* 42 (Dec 1990): 587–614; "Betty Grable's Legs," *Life*, Jun 7, 1943, 82–86. On the discarding of stockings during wartime see Meikle, *American Plastic*, 148. As Robin D. G. Kelley has pointed out, however, unauthorized attempts to find "pleasure in the new music, clothes and dance" by black "hep cats" led them to be ostracized and punished. Robin

D. G. Kelley, "The Riddle of the Zoot: Malcolm Little and Black Cultural Politics during World War II," in *Race Rebels: Culture, Politics, and the Black Working Class* (New York: Free Press, 1994), 161–181, quotation on 163.

53. On the silk stocking replacements see from *CRe* "Stockings in a Bottle," Aug 1942, 201–202; "Bottled 'Stockings,'" Jul 1943, 181–182. See the editorial "The New Look and the Shell Game," *CRe*, Oct 1947, 374; D.W.S., "Cheers for the Article on the New Look!" *CRe*, Feb 1948, 51. Lester Velie, "The Customer Is Right Again," *Collier's*, May 31, 1947, 17, 86. Such critiques apparently led to the refashioning of the New Look. See Virginia Pope, "Refinements Due in New Look in '48," *NYT*, Jan 1, 1948, 26.

54. Lizabeth Cohen, *A Consumers' Republic: The Politics of Mass Consumption in Postwar America* (New York: Knopf, 2003), 130; Erica Carter, "Alice in the Consumer Wonderland," in *West Germany under Construction: Politics, Society and Culture in the Adenauer Era,* ed. Robert Moeller (Ann Arbor: University of Michigan Press, 1997), 347–371, quotation on 366; Carter, *How German Is She? Postwar West German Reconstruction and the Consuming Woman* (Ann Arbor: University of Michigan Press, 1997), 165–167.

55. Margaret Carlson, "Patriotic Splurging," *Time*, Oct 15, 2001, 76; Marie Coco, "It'll Take More than Shopping to Heal America's Wounds," *State*, Sep 29, 2001, A11. Claudia Smith Brinson, "The Problem with 'Buy, Buy, Buy,'" *State*, Nov 13, 2001, D1, 6; R. W. Apple, Jr. "Nature of Foe Is Obstacle in Appealing for Sacrifice," *NYT*, Oct 15, 2001; Thomas J. Friedman, "Ask Not What . . . ," *NYT*, Dec 9, 2001, IV:13; Jill Vardy and Chris Wattie, "Shopping Is Patriotic, Leaders Say," *National Post* [Canada], Sep 28, 2001.

56. On fair trade and slow food, see the epilogue. Paul Wachtel, "Alternative to the Consumer Society," in *Ethics of Consumption*, ed. David Crocker and Toby Linden (Lanham, MD: Rowman & Littlefield, 1998), 199. Stephanie Mills, *Epicurean Simplicity* (Washington DC: Island Press, 2002). On "stylish" clothes, see Jim Hightower, "Dressed for Success," *Nation*, Jun 24, 2002, 8. In contrast, and more typically of the consumer movement, Jeremy Larner pits moral goods against fashionable ones in his essay on the "No Sweat Apparel" Web site: "My Fashion Statement," Mar 19, 2003, http://www.nosweatapparel.com/news/bulletin52.htm (accessed May 12, 2008).

57. Larissa MacFarquar, "The Populist: Michael Moore Can Make You Cry," *New Yorker*, Feb 16–23, 2004, 133–145, quotation on 137. Jesse Lemisch, "Nader vs. the Big Rock Candy Mountain," *New Politics* 8 (Summer 2001): 12–19. For an insightful critique of the Left's "romance of parsimoniousness and asceticism," see Jesse Lemisch and Naomi Weisstein, "Cornucopia Isn't Consumerism," *Against the Current*, Jan/Feb 1992, 31–34. I take Jane Bennett to be expressing this point when she claims that "the attempt to sever ethics from aesthetics because of the dangers carried by the latter spells the probable defeat of ethics." *The Enchantment of Modern Life: Attachments, Crossings, and Ethics* (Princeton: Princeton University Press, 2001), 149.

Chapter 8

1. Carlisle Bergeron, "Buyer's Watchdogs Bark Again: As Goods Come Back to Market, Organizations Which Aim to Guide the Consumer Spring into Action," *Nation's Business* 34 (Nov 1946): 55–57, 80–82.

2. David Hackett Fischer, *Historians' Fallacies: Toward a Logic of Historical Thought* (New York: Harper Collins, 1970), 24–28.

3. Gary Cross, *An All-Consuming Century: Why Commercialism Won in Modern America* (New York: Columbia University Press, 2000), 135. Mark V. Nadel, *The Politics of Consumer Protection* (Indianapolis: Bobbs-Merrill, 1971), 31–32. Declension has been the emphasis of the scholars who have looked most carefully at consumer politics in the 1940s. Lizabeth Cohen uses the words "marginalized," "stalled," "stagnated," and "collapsed" in *A Consumers' Republic: The Politics of Mass Consumption in Postwar America* (New York: Knopf, 2003), 129–132, 347. Meg Jacobs claims that the movement moved to the "margins of American politics" in this period. *Pocketbook Politics: Economic Citizenship in Twentieth-Century America* (Princeton: Princeton University Press, 2005), 252. Norman D. Katz, "Consumers Union: The Movement and the Magazine, 1936–1957" (PhD diss., Rutgers University, 1977). I embraced the declinist position in Lawrence B. Glickman, "The Strike in the Temple of Consumption: Consumer Activism and Twentieth-Century American Political Culture," *JAH* 88 (Jun 2001): 99–124.

4. Leland J. Gordon, "Letter of Resignation," *CRe* 15 (Jan 1950): 43. Cohen, *Consumers' Republic*; Alan Brinkley, *The End of Reform : New Deal Liberalism in Recession and War* (New York: Knopf, 1995).

5. Joan Cook, "Harried Shoppers Rely on a Research Group," *NYT*, Nov 30, 1959, 25. For excellent analyses of the red-baiting of consumer activists and organizations in the postwar era, see Landon R. Y. Storrs, "Red Scare Politics and the Suppression of Popular Front Feminism: The Loyalty Investigation of Mary Dublin Keyserling," *JAH* 90 (Sep 2003): 491–524; Storrs, "Left-Feminism, the Consumer Movement, and Red Scare Politics in the United States, 1935–1960," *Journal of Women's History* 18 (Fall 2006): 40–67. Annelise Orleck, "'We Are That Mythical Thing Called the Public': Militant Housewives during the Great Depression," *Feminist Studies* 19 (Spring 1993): 165–166. Colston E. Warne, *The Consumer Movement: Lectures by Colston E.Warne*, ed. Richard L. D. Morse (Manhattan, KS: Family Economics Trust Press, 1993), 141–142; the "abandoned ship" reference is on 148; "Consumer Unit Cleared: House Group Deletes Union from Its Subversive List," *NYT*, Feb 7, 1954, 16. On anticommunism, the banning of *CRe*, and CU's statement see Katz, "Consumers Union," 260, 325, 328; "A Letter to Readers: On Honesty, Policy, and Subversiveness," *CRe* (Oct 1951): 474–476. "Consumer's Report," *Time*, Aug 12, 1957. See the interview of Colston E. Warne by Sybil Shainwald (Spring 1971), and Norman Silber's interview with the CU official, A. J. Isserman (Oct 8, 1974), who claimed that he was "unceremoniously fired" by Kallet in 1948 for defending communists in the labor movement. Both at CUA.

6. My main source for the claims that follow is an analysis of *CRe* (called *Consumers Union Reports* until 1942) from its founding in 1936 through the 1950s, and of *Bread and Butter*, a monthly publication of CU that started in 1942 and in 1947 merged into the magazine. See "The New Consumer Reports," *CRe*, Apr 1947, 86, the first issue to incorporate *Bread and Butter*.

7. For versions of three-phase periodization see Robert N. Mayer, *The Consumer Movement: Guardians of the Marketplace* (Boston: Twayne, 1989); James S. Haskins, *The Consumer Movement* (New York: Franklin Watts, 1976), 5; *Consumer Protection*, ed. Lester A. Sobel (New York: Facts on File, 1976), 141. Michael W. McCann, *Taking Reform Seriously: Perspectives on Public Interest Liberalism* (Ithaca: Cornell University Press, 1986), 135; Cohen, *Consumers' Republic*, 129. Kenneth Dameron, "Consumer Meeting Agenda: A Study in Consumer Interests," *Journal of Business of the University of Chicago* 21 (Apr 1948): 98–119, quotation on 114. On "fallacies of narration" see Fischer, *Historians' Fallacies*, chap. 5.

8. Helen Sorenson, *The Consumer Movement: What It Is and What It Means* (New York: Harper & Bros., 1941), 111. See the preface to this book by John D. Black of Harvard University, who emphasizes the newness of "a group of consumers working for consumers" and contrasts the consumer movement with the work of the National Consumers League, which he characterizes as "an agency working on behalf of labor rather than in the consumer interest" (x). "Consumer strikes" are mentioned on 7–8, 119.

9. Katz writes that the consumer movement "grew logically from a body of thought which had evolved slowly from the writings of Thorstein Veblen at the turn of the twentieth century." "Consumers Union," 201; Cohen, *Consumers' Republic*, 129.

10. For excellent analyses of the consumer initiatives in the National Recovery Administration and the Agricultural Adjustment Administration see Kathleen G. Donohue, *Freedom from Want: American Liberalism and the Idea of the Consumer* (Baltimore: Johns Hopkins University Press, 2004). On calls for a cabinet-level Department of the Consumer, see Chester Bowles, *Tomorrow without Fear* (New York, 1946), 83; Henry Harap, "What Is the Consumer Movement?" *Frontiers of Democracy*, Nov 1940, 48–50. "Department of the Consumer in the President's Cabinet," ed. E. M. Phelps, *University Debaters' Annual*, vol. 1933–1934, 159–193.

11. For one example of this genre see "What about the Consumer Movement?" *Advertising Age*, Jan 8, 1940, 23–28, which described the consumer movement as in reality "a multitude of movements of individual and organized consumers working vaguely toward similar ends, but often using diametrically different approaches" (23).

12. See from *NYT* "Boycott by Union Is Declared Legal," Oct 15, 1944, 46; "Court Refuses Ban on Milk Boycott," Jan 18, 1945, 34; "68 White Pupils Boycott Hillburn School Opened to Negroes, Enter Private Classes," Oct 19, 1943, 21; Dorothy Smiley, "Boycott-Extension," Dec 14, 1941, E9; Dorothy Josling, "Goods from Argentina," Nov 20, 1944, 20. "League Defends Call to Boycott Paper," Sep 2, 1942, 16.

13. The following are from *NYT*: "Milk 'Boycott' in Jersey," Jan 10, 1945, 26; "Retail Boycott On in Kosher Poultry," May 8, 1945, 20. "Boycott of Stores Urged on Workers," May 19, 1943, 22. "Food Boycott Urged," Apr 28, 1943, 16. "Back ODT 'Boycott' of Furniture Show," Dec 31, 1942, 23. An OPA boycott is discussed in "Boycotts Planned on Produce Tie-Ins," Apr 6, 1945, 18. "La Guardia Criticized on Egg Boycott Talk," Feb 9, 1943, 16; "Boycott of Fish Urged by Mayor," Apr 24, 1944, 16. For an instance of the head of New York City's Department of Purchase calling for a boycott see Jefferson G. Bell, "Buyers for City Boycott Poultry," Feb 1, 1944, 24.

14. "A Consumers Strike Soon? Return of the Careful Shopper," *United States News*, May 17, 1946, 14–15. See also Charles Grutzner, "Buyers' Strike Due to Cut Living Costs," *NYT*, Jun 27, 1946, 1; "To Boycott Restaurants: Buyers Strike Group Calls for 'Holiday' Today and Friday," *NYT*, Jul 31, 1946, 22; Arthur Felt, "The Deep South: Signs of Buyers' Strike amid the Rush in New Orleans," *NYT*, Dec 15, 1946, E6. See from *Bread and Butter*, which made the buyers' strikes a regular page 3 feature: "A National Buyers' Strike: Don't Buy in a Suckers' Market," Jul 13, 1946, 3; "The Buyers' Strike Spreads," Jul 20, 1946, 3; "Think Before You Buy," Oct 26, 1946, 3–4; "Organizing a Buyers' Strike," Jul 27, 1946, 3.

15. Leo Cherne, "We Can Buy Postwar Prosperity," *Science Digest* 17 (Feb 1945): 1–5. See also Sumner H. Slichter, "The Postwar Outlook for Business: Consumer Needs and Purchasing Power," *Vital Speeches of the Day* 11 (Dec 1, 1944): 122–124. Jessica Mitford, *The American Way of Death* (New York: Simon & Schuster, 1963).

16. The first use of "free enterprise system" I have found was by the Republican congressman Bertrand H. Snell: "Snell Pits Past against New Deal," *NYT*, Aug 26, 1935, 1. Alf Landon used the term in his 1936 campaign: "Text of Gov. Landon's Speech in Maine," *CT*, Sep 13, 1936, 12. See also Elizabeth A. Fones-Wolf, *Selling Free Enterprise: The Business Assault on Labor and Liberalism, 1945-1960* (Urbana: University of Illinois Press, 1994), 25-27; Wendell L. Wilkie, *Free Enterprise* (Washington DC: National Home Library Foundation, 1940); Daniel T. Rodgers, *Contested Truths: Keywords in American Politics since Independence* (New York: Basic Books, 1989), 216. The Gray quotation is from Philip H. Dougherty, "Advertising: What Makes the Going Great," *NYT*, Oct 28, 1970, 85. Art Buchwald, "Free Enterprise Endangered by Wave of 'Consumerism,'" *WP*, Oct 7, 1969, A19.

17. See, for example, Russell Porter, "Free Enterprise Urged for World," *NYT*, May 19, 1956, 5. Whitney is quoted in "Boom Held Likely to Last for Years," *NYT*, Jun 5, 1955, 41. "U.S. Sales 'Team' Plans Soviet Visit," *NYT*, Sep 10, 1955, 3; Brendan M. Jones, "Top U.S. Salesmen Vie for Team to Teach Russians How to Pitch," *NYT*, Oct 30, 1955, F1. Eggert is quoted in J. A. Livingston, "Business Outlook . . . : 'Consumerism' Suits U.S," *Washington Post and Times Herald*, Sep 28, 1956. 47. The following year, the newspaper credited Livingston with coining the term. "Arguing with a Communist ," *Washington Post and Times Herald*, Jul 24, 1957, A10. For a similar statement from the mid-1960s see George Romney, "Consumerism: We Must Share Our Progress," *Vital Speeches of the Day* 35 (Jun 1, 1965): 489-494. There are many treatments of the "kitchen debate," include Karal Ann Marling, *As Seen on TV: The Visual Culture of Everyday Life in the 1950s* (Cambridge, MA: Harvard University Press, 1995), 243-276; Elaine Tyler May, *Homeward Bound: American Families in the Cold War Era* (New York: Basic Books, 1988), 10-29. For excellent explications of the meaning of free enterprise in this context see Eric Foner, *The Story of American Freedom* (New York: Norton, 1998), esp. 263-273.

18. Charles F. Phillips, "The Consumer Is King," *Vital Speeches of the Day* 19 (Dec 1, 1952): 121-124; George Katona, *The Powerful Consumer: Psychological Studies of the American Economy* (New York: McGraw-Hill, 1960), 241.

19. Vance Packard, *The Waste Makers* (New York: David McKay, 1960), 22-23. "Books—Authors," *NYT*, Jun 23, 1960, 27. See the display ad, *NYT*, Oct 12, 1960, 32. Packard's use of the term is also highlighted in Orville Prescott, "Books of the Times," *NYT*, Sep 30, 1960, 25. Richard Severo, "Vance Packard, 82, Challenger of Consumerism, Dies," *NYT*, Dec 13, 1996, B16. George S. Day and David A. Aaker noted (incorrectly) in 1970 that "the term consumerism appears to be uniquely associated with the past decade" and called Packard "one of the earliest adopters of the term." "A Guide to Consumerism," *Journal of Marketing* 34 (Jul 1970): 12-19. For an overview see Daniel Horowitz, *Vance Packard and American Social Criticism* (Chapel Hill: University of North Carolina Press, 1994), esp. 149.

20. Packard, *Waste Makers*, 252, 14, 59 (see also 124, 127), 88, 96, 251, 59.

21. Buycotts were a strategy used by boycott opponents. The San Francisco Employers Council urged people to buy the from the Euclid Candy Company boycotted by the CIO Warehouseman's Union. "'Buy-Cotts' Urged in Dispute," *NYT*, May 18, 1940, 13. Naomi Klein, *No Logo: Taking Aim at the Brand Bullies* (New York: Picador, 2000); "Hawkes Flays Bid to Destroy Brands," *NYT*, Feb 6, 1946, 36. "Platform for Consumers," *Nation's Business* 28 (Jan 1940): 9-10. "Public Is Shunning High Price Butter," *NYT*, Jul 14, 1946, 1; "'Buy Nothing Day' Parade," *NYT*, Jul 27, 1946, 2; "Mead Assails Foes of Price Controls: At 'Buy Nothing' Day Rally in Madison Square Park," *NYT*, Aug 9, 1946, 11. On "Buy Nothing Day"

in the 1990s and after 2000 see the epilogue. In 1953, New York's Liberal Party called for a State Consumer Protection Commission: "Consumer Protection Urged," *NYT*, Jan 19, 1953, 14. Mark T. Walsh, "Protecting Consumers: Work Done by Attorney General Lefkowitz Is Stressed," *NYT*, Oct 18, 1958, 20. Colston E. Warne, "Protecting the Consumer," *Challenge*, Nov 1960, 22–27, quotation on 22.

22. See from *NYT* "Housewives in Nation Begin Meat Boycott," Aug 4, 1948, 24; "Housewives Boycott Meat," May 25, 1951, 33. "Plan Film Boycott: Los Angeles Catholics Decide on Protest during February," Feb 4, 1947, 34; "Catholic Boycott of Sex Film Urged," Dec 5, 1949, 20; "Baptists to Fight 'Improper' Films," May 11, 1947, 53. "Boycott of Reds' Goods Urged," Dec 16, 1953, 45; A. H. Raskin, "A.F.L. for Boycott of 'Slave' Goods," May 21, 1954, 23. "M'carthy Foes Urge Wisconsin Boycott," Nov 28, 1954, 37.

23. Powell is quoted in Frank S. Adams, "A Spokesman for the 'New Negro,'" *NYT*, Feb 3, 1946, BR2; James A. Hagerty, "Powell Threatens a Boycott of Both Parties by Negroes," *NYT*, Aug 4, 1952, 1. "Song of the South Pickets Are Jailed," *AN*, Mar 1, 1947, 1. Ray Johnstone, "We Can Jive Yankees, Reader Says, 'Boycott,'" *AN*, Nov 11, 1950, 8. For protest against another segregated institution see "Will Negroes Boycott a Jim Crow Army?" *Newsweek* Aug 10, 1948, 4. Mrs. Harold Laskey, "New Yorkers Urged to Boycott Dixie Oranges," *AN*, Feb 2, 1952, 14. "Boycott Is Urged in Youth's Killing; Rally of 20,000 Here Cheers Call for Action against Mississippi Goods," *NYT*, Oct 12, 1955, 62. The bowling protest is described in "Along the NAACP Battlefront," *Crisis*, Apr 1949, 117. "American Groups Urge Boycott of South Africa," *Africa Report* 5 (Jun 1960): 14. For an overview see Robert E. Weems, Jr., "African-American Consumer Boycotts during the Civil Rights Era," *Western Journal of Black Studies* 19 (1995): 72–79.

24. In the historian August Meier's interviews with the Reverend T. J. Jemison, the Baton Rouge boycott leader, as well as E. D. Nixon, Fred Gray, and Joanne Robinson, leaders of the Montgomery protest, they claimed not to know of the history of earlier streetcar boycotts and believed that they were originating the idea. Folder 4, AMP. "Negro Protest Planned: Leaders Warn of Bus Boycott in Memphis," *NYT*, Dec 26, 1953, 21; "Bus Boycott Effective: Negroes Use Other Transport in Baton Rouge Dispute," *NYT*, Jun 21, 1953, 65. "Bus Boycott on Race Issue 90% Effective," *WP*, Jun 21, 1953, M14; "Baton Rouge Transit Company Is Boycotted," *Atlanta Daily World*, Jun 20, 1953, 1; "Bus Boycott Halted after Concessions," *AN*, Jul 4, 1953, 1. "Baton Rouge Bus System Feels Boycott Aftermath," *Pittsburgh Courier*, Jul 25, 1953, 21. *Daybreak of Freedom: The Montgomery Bus Boycott*, ed. Stewart Burns (Chapel Hill: University of North Carolina Press, 1997), 11, 18, 129, 199. See also J. Mills Thornton III, *Dividing Lines: Municipal Politics and the Struggle for Civil Rights in Montgomery, Birmingham, and Selma* (Tuscaloosa: University of Alabama Press, 2002); *The Montgomery Bus Boycott and the Women Who Started It: The Memoir of Jo Ann Gibson Robinson*, ed. David J. Garrow (Knoxville: University of Tennessee Press, 1987); Tom Gardner and Cynthia Stokes Brown, "The Montgomery Bus Boycott: Interviews with Rosa Parks, E.D. Nixon, Johnny Carr and Virginia Durr," *Southern Exposure* 9 (1981): 12–21.

25. "Feeding Advice to Hungry Customers," *Business Week*, Mar 20, 1954, 144–148. CR's membership remained at only 111,000 in 1971, when CU's was close to 2 million. Katz, "Consumers Union," 242, 309. See also 247, 255–256. Cohen, *Consumers' Republic*, 131. For a similar view, see Cross, *An All-Consuming Century*, 135.

26. From *CRe*: The first quotation is from "National Health Insurance," Apr 1950, 146, 179. Dr. Ernst P. Boas, "Medical Care for All: The Wagner-Murray-Dingell Plan,"

Jan 1946, 26–27; "Compulsory Health Insurance: An Answer to the Objection that Passage of the Wagner-Murray-Dingell Bill Would Interfere with 'Personal Freedom,'" Mar 1946, 82. Hugh Leavell, "The British Health Service: Is It a Model for US?" Oct 1949, 462–464. "Million dollar lobbies" is from "Write That Letter!" Apr 1946, 86. "The AMA and National Health Insurance," Apr 1949, 175–178. Andrew J. Biemiller, "The Need for Health Insurance," Apr 1949, 174. Biemiller was a Democratic representative from Wisconsin. "The AMA and the Doctor," Sep 1949, 408–409. "Bureaucracy in Medicine: The Wagner-Murray-Dingell Bill has Adequate Safeguards against the 'Evils' of Bureaucracy," Apr 1946, 119–120. "Consumer Resistance Needed," Mar 1947, 58.

27. The push for sex education in *CRe* began even before the war. See the ad "CU Is Now Offering to Its Members for a First Time a Special Edition of *Your Marriage: A Guide to Happiness*" by Norman E. Himes, Sep 1941, 248–249. In an editorial CU announced that its board had voted to appeal in the courts the ban on the mailing of CU's *Report on Contraceptive Materials*. "A Forbidden Subject," May 1943, 115. Excerpts from CU counsel Abraham Isserman's legal brief were included in "For the People: CU to Appeal Mailing Ban to Courts," May 1943, 132–134. Letters of support and opposition from members were published in "For the People: CU members Comment on Court Action," Jul 1943, 190–191. In 1944, an appeals court affirmed CU's right to distribute its *Report on Contraceptive Materials*. See "CU Wins Court Decision," Oct 1944, 255. The editors saw fit to mention this victory in their summary of the achievements of CU's first decade: "Ten Years of Consumers Union," Feb 1946, 30. Harold Aaron, "The Tragedy of Abortion," Aug 1947, 308–309. Joseph Lander, M.D., "Auto-eroticism in Children," Jul 1946, 194–195. "Hormone Cream for Bust Development," Aug 1948, 368.

28. Noyes's column ran from April 1947 through the early 1950s.

29. "The Safe Car," *CRe*, Apr 1956, 168–171; Ralph Nader, "The Safe Car You Can't Buy," *Nation*, Apr 11, 1959, 310–313. "Air Pollution," *CRe*, Jul 1957, 344–346. Pesticides: Norman Isaac Silber, *Test and Protest: The Influence of Consumers Union* (New York: Holmes & Meier, 1983), 127. John Kenneth Galbraith, *The Affluent Society*, 40th anniversary ed. (New York: Houghton Mifflin, 1998), 187, 188. Jeffrey M. Berry, *The New Liberalism: The Rising Power of Citizen Groups* (Washington DC: Brookings Institution Press, 1999), 34–60. Warne titled the chapter on this period "New Directions in the Consumer Movement, 1953–1966." Warne, *Consumer Movement*, 151–194. Warne also stressed the growing international dimension of the movement in this era.

30. Warne pointed out that the organization became less New York centered in these years. See Warne, *Consumer Movement*, 149. "Out of step" is from Cohen, *Consumers' Republic*, 130. Katz, "Consumers Union," 310–311. I take Katz to be making a similar point on 261, where he notes that CU "never backed away from an activist orientation," and on 341, on how even the product-testing branch of CU took an interest in "matters of public concern."

31. On Freud and American culture see Andrew R. Heinze, *Jews and the American Soul: Human Nature in the Twentieth Century* (Princeton: Princeton University Press, 2004); Nathan G. Hale, *The Rise and Crisis of Psychoanalysis in the United States: Freud and the Americans, 1917-1985* (New York: Oxford University Press, 1995). Joseph Lander, M.D., "Comfort for Worriers," *CRe*, Oct 1948, 463–464; and Lander, "Psychotherapy: The Hard-to-Get-At Tensions," *CRe*, Mar 1949, 132–133. "A Critical Appraisal of a Best-Selling Book That Originated in the Realm of Science Fiction and Became the Basis for a New Cult," *CRe*,

Aug 1951, 378–380. See also "A Sign of Our Times," 380. L. Ron Hubbard, *Dianetics: The Modern Science of Mental Health* (New York: Hermitage House, 1950).

32. "Coney Island," *Consumers Union Reports*, Aug 1936, unpaginated two-page article. Although this piece showed that CU was not averse to advising its members about city pleasures, it was also critical of the unhealthy refreshment stands and the pollution, even while acknowledging that "there's nowhere else a nickel will take them." CU lab analysts studied the food and drink there and were unimpressed: "Briefly and bluntly, the laboratory analysis showed that sewage-laden sea water is no more contaminated than are some of the ice-creams."

33. See the following from *CRe*: "CU Movie Poll," Feb 1948, 94–95; "How Good Are the Programs?" Feb 1949, 88–89; "A Survey of What's to Be Seen on Television," Mar 1951, 138–139; "Radio and Television," Apr 1951, 185–186. An Eliot F. Noyes column discussed the aesthetics of radio consoles: "The Shape of Things," Feb 1950, 59. Phillip Miller, "Records," Oct 1951, 477–478. "The Hollywood/TV Invasion," Feb 1949, 86–87. This article appeared in the section of the magazine titled "For the People: Government Actions Affecting the Consumer."

34. Andrew Hurley, *Diners, Bowling Alleys, and Trailer Parks: Chasing the American Dream in Postwar Consumer Culture* (New York: Basic Books, 2001), xvi; Ruth Rosen, *The World Split Open: How the Women's Movement Changed America* (New York: Penguin, 2000), 312.

35. For evidence of pre-Montgomery consumer activism see James Farmer's discussion of the attempt to integrate a roller skating rink in Chicago in the late 1940s in Howell Raines, *My Soul Is Rested* (New York: Putnam, 1977). 27–34.

Chapter 9

1. Bennett is quoted in Dan Balz and Ronald Brownstein, *Storming the Gates: Protest Politics and the Republican Revival* (Boston: Little Brown & Co., 1996), 271. The authors describe the effort to make liberalism "an object not of fear but ridicule" on 342. "Language: A Key Mechanism of Control," at http://web.utk.edu/~glenn/GopacMemo.html (accessed on May 14, 2008). Thanks to Dan Carter for alerting me to this document. Mark Leibovich, "The L Word: Leftward Ho," *NYT*, Feb 18, 2007, 4:1, 4. See also Patricia Cohen, "Proclaiming Liberalism and What It Now Means," *NYT*, Jun 2, 2007, B7, 13. Evidence of that revival might be the manifesto (cosigned by many others) by Todd Gitlin and Bruce Ackerman, "We Answer to the Name of Liberals," *American Prospect*, Nov 2006, 25–26; and Eric Alterman's *Why We're Liberals: A Political Handbook for Post-Bush America* (New York: Viking, 2008). Robin Toner, "Obama's Test: Can a Liberal Be a Uniter," *NYT*, Mar 25, 2008, A1, 19, quotation on A19. See also Alec MacGillis, "In Obama's New Message, Some Foes See Old Liberalism," *WP*, Mar 26, 2008, A1. For an analysis of the success of conservatives at "framing" these issues, see George Lakoff, *Don't Think of an Elephant: Know Your Values and Frame the Debate* (White River Junction, VT: Chelsea Green Publishing, 2004). Interestingly, Lakoff eschews the word "liberal" in favor of "progressive." Another possible sign of the liberal resurgence was the return of "socialism" as a term of derision for Democratic policies during the presidential campaign of 2008 and beyond. See Mark Leibovich, "'Socialism!' Boo, Hiss, Repeat," *NYT*, Mar 1, 2009, WK1, 3.

2. Lionel Trilling, *The Liberal Imagination: Essays on Literature and Society* (Garden City, NY: Anchor, 1950), vii. Louis Hartz made a similar point in *The Liberal Tradition in America*

(New York: Harcourt, Brace, 1955). John Lukacs, "The Triumph and Collapse of Liberalism," *Chronicle of Higher Education*, Dec 10, 2004. Lukacs notes that the word "liberal" has become "a bad word for millions of Americans." Burns is quoted in Rick Pearlstein, *Before the Storm: Barry Goldwater and the Unmaking of the American Consensus* (New York: Hill & Wang, 2001), xi. Simon is quoted in Godfrey Hodgson, *The World Turned Right Side Up: A History of the Conservative Ascendency in America* (Boston: Houghton Mifflin, 1996), 207. See also on Vice President Spiro Agnew's condemnation of "liberal intellectuals" in *The Rise of Conservatism in America, 1945–2000. A Brief History with Documents*, ed. Bruce Laurie and Ronald Story (Boston: Bedford, 2007), 77–79. Armey quoted in Balz and Brownstein, *Storming the Gates*, 131.

3. H. W. Brands, *The Strange Death of American Liberalism* (New Haven: Yale University Press, 2001), vii. See also Ralph Brauer, *The Strange Death of Liberal America* (Westport, CT: Praeger, 2006), which does not mention the consumer movement. Carl Oglesby, a leader of Students for a Democratic Society, condemned liberals in his 1965 speech "Let Us Shape the Future," http://www.sdsrebels.com/oglesby.htm (accessed on May 14, 2008). For outstanding analysis of these issues see Allen J. Matasow, *The Unraveling of America: A History of Liberalism in the 1960s* (New York: Harper & Row, 1985).

4. Bruce J. Schulman, *The Seventies: The Great Shift in American Culture, Society, and Politics* (New York: Free Press, 2001), 194. Dan T. Carter, *The Politics of Rage: George Wallace, the Origins of the New Conservatism, and the Transformation of American Politics*, 2nd ed. (Baton Rouge: Louisiana State University Press, 2000). Merrill Folson, "Business Is Warned of U.S. Controls," *NYT*, Nov 23, 1966, 42. Arthur E. Larkin, Jr., the president of the General Foods Corporation, "urged businessmen tonight to build backfires to combat the 'consumerism' that he said Congressmen were promoting to woo the consumer." He condemned any "federal brand of consumerism." The quotation, from Michael O'Connor of the Super Market Institute, is in Annette Ashlock Stover, "Questions of Consumerism," *CT*, Jun 5, 1970, A4. Richard M. Abrams discusses the conservative "counterrevolution" and loosely links it to the consumer movement in *America Transformed: Sixty Years of Revolutionary Change, 1941–2001* (New York: Cambridge University Press, 2006), 262.

5. "Tip O'Neill's Statement before the Final Vote on the Consumer Bill," *Congressional Record*, in box 129, folder 11, CMA. Walter T. Anderson, "Astroturf: The Big Business of Fake Grassroots Politics," *Jinn*, vol. 5 (Jan 1996), at http://www.pacificnews.org/jinn/stories/2.01/960105-astroturf.html (accessed on May 14, 2008).

6. "Stubborn minority" is from "A Voice for Consumers," *WP*, Aug 20, 1974, A18. Consumer activists "appear to have abandoned the decade-old battle to create a special agency to lobby the Government for consumer causes." "Creation of Agency to Press U.S. for Consumers May Be Lost Cause," *NYT*, Jan 14, 1979, 38.

7. "Biggest victories" is from George Schwartz, "The Successful Fight against a Federal Consumer Protection Agency," *MSU Business Topics* 27 (Summer 1979): 45–57, quotation on 55. See also Kim McQuaid, *Big Business and Presidential Power* (New York: William Morrow, 1982), 296–301. Justin Martin, *Nader: Crusader, Spoiler, Icon* (New York: Perseus, 2002), 193. Joseph referred to the time in the 1970s "when Washington business lobbyists banded together to resist the efforts of consumer advocate Ralph Nader" as the key turning point. William J. Lanouette, "Business Lobbyists Hope Their Unity on the Tax Bill Wasn't Just a Fluke," *National Journal*, Oct 24, 1981, 1896–1898, quotation on 1896. Similarly, Patrick J. Akard notes, the anti-CPA drive "became the model for future lobbying

382 NOTES TO PAGES 279-81

efforts by the corporate community in the 1970s." "Corporate Mobilization and Political Power: The Transformation of U.S. Economic Policy in the 1970s." *American Sociological Review* 57 (Oct 1992): 597–615, quotation on 605. For some examples of that legislative bonanza, such as the 1977 "lemon law," which permitted used-car dealers not to disclose problems about the cars they were selling, see Abrams, *America Transformed*, 257–262.

8. "Most important consumer legislation" is from Gerald Gold, "A Strong Federal Protection Agency?" *NYT*, Sep 27, 1973, 35. "Dr. Spock" is from Susan Kastner, "Why Don't They Rate Candidates?" *Toronto Star*, Oct 16, 1988. See chap. 8 for a similar comparison from 1959. Mark Green, "Why the Consumer Bill Went Down," *Nation*, Feb 25, 1978, 198–201. Philip Shabecoff, "Carter Plans Push for Bill to Create Consumer Agency," *NYT*, Jan 19, 1978, B5. On Aug 9, 1976, Carter addressed Nader's Public Citizen Forum, promising strong consumer policies if elected. See "Carter and Consumers," *Congressional Quarterly* 1976, 2206, cited in Mary Ann Keeffe, *The Proposed Consumer Protection Agency: Legislative History and Arguments Pro and Con*, Congressional Research Service, 77-113E, Apr 15, 1977, 32. Patrick Buchanan, "Gimme That Old-Time Incentive," *CT*, Aug 12, 1976, A4.

9. Jeffrey M. Berry, *The New Liberalism: The Rising Power of Citizen Groups* (Washington DC: Brookings Institution Press, 1999), 88; Elizabeth A. Fones-Wolf, *Selling Free Enterprise: The Business Assault on Labor and Liberalism, 1945–1960* (Urbana: University of Illinois Press, 1994), 43. As Fones-Wolf shows, the campaign against Taft-Hartley Bill was an early omen of the postwar conservative style. The National Association of Manufacturers spent $3 million in a public relations drive which "featured full-page ads in 287 daily papers in 193 key industrial centers." See also Kim Phillips-Fein, "Top-Down Revolution: Businessmen, Intellectuals, and Politicians against the New Deal, 1945–1964," *Enterprise and Society* 7 (Dec 2006): 686–694; and Phillips-Fein, *Invisible Hands: The Making of the Conservative Movement from the New Deal to Ronald Reagan* (New York: Norton, 2009).

10. "Apple pie" is from "Whatever Happened to Consumerism," *CSM*, Feb 14, 1979, 24 (originally published in *Houston Chronicle*). Kenneth M. Boyd, "Will Nixon Protect Consumer Rights?" *WP*, Jan 14, 1969, A14; "Nixon Asks Congress to Reinforce FTC, Create an Agency to Protect Consumers," *WSJ*, Oct 31, 1969, 2. On Reagan's proconsumer past see Brad Knickerbocker, "The Reagan Odyssey," *CSM*, Oct 2, 1980, 13. However, it should be noted that one of Reagan's first actions as governor was to fire Helen Nelson, the state's consumer counsel. See Sidney Margolius, "Consumer Rights: The Battle Continues," in *The Consuming Public*, ed. Grant S. McClellan (New York: H. W. Wilson, 1968), 190–197, esp. 193. "Toward a Just Marketplace," *Time*, Nov 7, 1969. Robert B. Reich, "Toward a New Consumer Protection," *University of Pennsylvania Law Review* 128 (Nov 1979): 1–40, quotation on 1. David S. Broder, "America's Changing Political Mood: Time of Expected Government Activism Becomes Graveyard of Liberal Legislation," *LAT*, Feb 15, 1978, E7.

11. James J. Kilpatrick, "Administrator or Commissar?" *LAT*, Aug 16, 1974, B7. For two examples of latter-day anticommunism see Leon Hartman, *The Scandal of Consumers Union* (1962); and Hartman, "How Red Is Consumers' Union?" (July 10, 1960), in box 8, folder 6, Richard L. D. Morse Papers, CMA.

12. David Vogel notes that "consumerism was an intrinsic part of the liberal agenda of the second half of the 1960s." *Fluctuating Fortunes: The Political Power of Business in America* (Basic Books, New York: 1978), 40. Similarly, Norman D. Katz has written, "Consumerism as an ideology had moved from the non-aligned left to the mainstream of American liberal thought." See "Consumers Union: The Movement and the Magazine, 1936–1957"

(PhD diss., Rutgers University, 1977), 342. Gary Gerstle, "The Protean Character of American Liberalism," *AHR* 99 (Oct 1994): 1043-1073. The documentary *An Unreasonable Man*, directed by Henriette Mantel and Steve Skrovan (IFC First Take Films, 2006), captures the frustration of some leftists with Nader well.

13. For a thorough legislative history see Richard J. Leighton, "Consumer Protection Agency Proposals: The Origin of a Species," *Administrative Law Review* 25 (Summer 1973): 269-312. Estes Kefauver, "A Voice for Consumers," *Progressive*, Jan 1959, cited in "Consumers Act of 1959," *Congressional Record*, Mar 26, 1959, 4784-4790. Louise Sweeney, "Esther Peterson," *CSM*, Jul 17, 1979, B1.

14. The term "consumer's bill of rights," was also used in Mario Pei, *The Consumer's Manifesto: A Bill of Rights to Protect the Consumer in the Wars between Capital and Labor* (New York: Crown, 1960). John F. Kennedy, "Special Message to the Congress on Protecting the Consumer Interest," Mar 15, 1962. The text of this speech can be found at http://www.presidency.ucsb.edu/ws/index.php?pid=9108 (accessed May 14, 2008). "President Names Consumer Panel: Dean at Cornell Is Chairman of Advisory Council," *NYT*, Jul 19, 1962, 16. See Esther Peterson, "Recommendation," Dec 13, 1963, Consumer Advisory Council, Council of Economic Advisors, box 14, folder 18, Richard Morse Papers, CMA. "New Era in Consumer Affairs," *CRe*, Mar 1964, 143-144. "Appendix 1: Significant Consumer Protection Legislation Enacted, 1872-1971," in *Consumerism: Viewpoints from Business, Government, and the Public Interest*, ed. Ralph M. Gaedeke and Warren W. Etcheson (San Francisco: Canfield Press, 1972), 372-375. See also Lizabeth Cohen, *A Consumers' Republic: The Politics of Mass Consumption in Postwar America* (New York: Knopf, 2003), 357-363, esp. the chart on p. 360. Tony Blinken, "The Consumer News You Never See," *Washington Monthly*, Jul-Aug 1985; "John D. Morris, Editor, 60, Dead" *NYT*, Apr 9, 1975, 46; Frances Cerra, "Sidney Margolius Is Dead at 67: Early Consumer Affairs Writer," *NYT*, Feb 1, 1980, B7. For a story on a later generation of mostly television consumer reporters see Natalie Pompilio, "Reporters with a Cause," *American Journalism Review* 21 (Dec 1999): 16. "Year of the Consumer," *Consumer Bulletin* 50 (Jan 1967): 31-32; "Consumer Revolution," *U.S. News and World Report*, Aug 25, 1969, 43-46. See also "Consumers Union Puts on Muscle," *Business Week*, Dec 23, 1967.

15. See, for example, "The Docket: Notes on Government Actions Taken to Enforce Consumer Protection Laws," *CRe*, Jan 1963, 8. In the same issue see Colston E. Warne, "Consumers Union and the Consumer Movement," 41. The grant ultimately resulted in David Caplovitz, *The Poor Pay More: Consumer Practices of Low-Income Families* (New York: Free Press, 1963). Priscilla Coit Murphy, *What a Book Can Do: The Publication and Reception of "Silent Spring"* (Amherst: University of Massachusetts Press, 2005), 179. Dolores Huerta, a leading official of the UFW, received a Trumpeter's Award from Consumers Union. http://www.lasculturas.com/aa/bio/bioDoloresHuerta.htm (accessed on May 14, 2008). Grace Lichtenstein, "Consumer Activists Urge Meat Boycott for April 1-7," *NYT*, Mar 17, 1973, 28.

16. Robert M. Collins, *More: The Politics of Growth in Postwar America* (New York: Oxford University Press, 2002), chap. 2. For Collins's excellent analysis of this speech, see 64. See, for example, Jerry Voorhis, "The Consumer Movement and the Hope of Human Survival," *Journal of Consumer Affairs* 11 (Summer 1977): 1-16; Eric Bentley, "For the Right to Wear Our Hair Long," *NYT*, Aug 30, 1970, 69; Eric Larrabee, "Leisure for What?" lecture delivered at Sarah Lawrence College, May 6, 1961, box 156, folder 27, CMA.

17. Kefauver cited in "Consumers Act of 1959," 4789. Dexter Masters, "The Consumer and Government: Variations on a Theme by Veblen," address delivered at the Consumer Research Institute, San Francisco State College, Aug 28–30, 1962, box 156, folder 49, CMA.

18. C. Vann Woodward, "The Ghost of Populism Walks Again: The New Populists," *NYT Magazine*, Jun 4, 1972, 16, 17, 60, quotation on 17. Michael Kazin, *The Populist Persuasion: An American History* (New York: Basic Books, 1995); Thomas Frank, *One Market, under God: Extreme Capitalism, Market Populism and the End of Economic Democracy* (New York: Doubleday, 2000). I believe this phenomenon began earlier than Frank does. Jonathan Chait used this term to describe the campaign style of Hillary Clinton in her quest for the Democratic nomination for the presidency in the spring of 2008. "Let Them Eat Arugula: Hillary Sure Has Become a Populist These Last Few Weeks—a Conservative Populist," *New Republic*, May 8, 2008.

19. Margolius, "Consumer Rights," 191; Jerry M. Flint, "Auto Industry, Changing Strategy, Opens Counterattack on Environmental and Consumer Movement," *NYT*, Nov 18, 1970, 29. "Is She Ignorant?" *Printers Ink*, Sep 11, 1964, front cover, 71. For an excellent analysis see John B. Judis, *The Paradox of American Democracy* (New York: Pantheon, 2000), 139–140.

20. Morton Mintz, "Producers' Lobbying Assailed," *WP*, Sep 17, 1973, A19. Benjamin Rosenthal claimed a "group dominated by the Grocery Manufacturers of America" was waging "one of the greatest lobbying jobs in my memory" to try to "kill or maim" the CPA, and he called its actions "dishonest and underhanded." *Consumer Protection Organization Acts: Business Responsiveness Kit* on the "Nader Enabling Acts" (Washington DC: U.S. Chamber of Commerce, 1971). S. 1177, H.R. 10835. Jan 17, 1972, box 129, folder 12, CMA. The kit noted that "Nader is very popular—according to a recent national poll, he is among the ten people in the world whom Americans admire most."

21. The memo was dated August 23, 1971, and sent to Eugene B. Sydnor, Jr., Chairman, Education Committee, U.S. Chamber of Commerce. Portions of the memo, but not the passage about Nader, are quoted in Laurie and Story, *Rise of Conservatism in America*, 84–88. For the full text see http://www.progressiveu.org/node/121/print (accessed May 14, 2008). Mark Schmitt persuasively claims that the importance of this memo has been overstated in "The Legend of the Powell Memo," http://www.prospect.org/cs/articles?articleId=9606 (accessed on May 14, 2008).

22. An analysis of the campaign by anti-CPA forces found that about a fourth of the unsigned "editorials" opposing the bill were verbatim reproductions of the "model editorials" sent out by the lobbyists. See the letter from Wm. R. Fasse to Esther Peterson, Jun 27, 1977, which includes the report by one "Tom Low." Box 129, folder 11, CMA. Ronald G. Shafer, "Consumer Bill Killed by Words," *WSJ*, Oct 27, 1972, 8. "Colossal disaster" is from Bryce N. Harlow, "Remarks on Consumer Protection Agency Legislation," Jan 24, 1972, New York City, box 2, folder 22, http://www.ou.edu/special/albertctr/archives/HarlowInventory/Harlow012472.pdf (accessed on May 14, 2008). "Monstrously bad bill" is from James Kilpatrick, "Consumer Bill Bad Medicine for All," *Topeka Daily Capital*, Aug 9, 1974. Kilpatrick also called it a "very bad bill" in "Consumer Proposal Should Be Warning to Business," *LAT*, Oct 3, 1974, C5. "Affront" is from Keeffe, *Proposed Consumer Protection Agency*, 40. On red tape: Jane R. Wagner, "Consumer Agency: Is This Finally the Year?" *Congressional Quarterly* 35 (Feb 5, 1977): 205–206. On big government: "A Consumer Bill Gets Consumed," *CT*, Feb 13, 1978, C2. U.S. Senate, *The Consumer Protection Act of*

1977: *Hearings before the Committee on Governmental Affairs on S. 1262*, 95th Cong., 1st sess., Apr 19 and 20, 1977 (Washington DC: Government Printing Office, 1977). Incomplete photocopy from CMA, which includes long lists of "Newspapers which have carried editorials opposing independent consumer protection agency (as of Dec 1, 1976)," listed by state on pp. 116–124. "Onerous" and "mind-numbing" is from "Perfectionism, Consumer Style," *WSJ*, Jul 2, 1970, 16. "Consumer Protection: What's at Issue," *Nation's Business* 65 (Jun 1977): 18–20.

23. Kilpatrick, "Consumer Bill Bad Medicine for All." John W. Riehm of the Consumer Affairs Committee of the U.S. Chamber of Commerce used the term "meddlesome" in U.S. House of Representatives, *Agency for Consumer Protection: Hearings before a Subcommittee of the Committee on Government Operations on H.R. 6118*, 95th Cong., 1st sess., Apr 20 and 21, 1977 (Washington DC: Government Printing Office, 1977), 213. "Out of control" is from James G. Reynolds, "Proposed Agency Not Needed to Protect Consumers," *WSJ*, May 26, 1977, 16. "Monster superagency" is from American Enterprise Institute for Policy Research, *Consumer Agency Bills* (Washington DC: American Enterprise Institute, 1971), 15. *Consumer Protection Organization Acts: Business Responsiveness Kit.*

24. The AEI quotation is from American Enterprise Institute for Policy Research, *Consumer Agency Bills*, 15. "Such a Nerve," *Dallas Morning News*, Apr 12, 1977. Leon Jaworski, "Can a Consumer Czar Represent Us All?" *Washington Star*, May 6, 1977, A11. Congressmen also highlighted the "diversity of interests of consumers." Statement of Philip Crane (R-IL), in U.S. House of Representatives, *Agency for Consumer Protection*, 305. Taft is quoted in James J. Kilpatrick, "Agency Would Add to Bureaucracy," undated clipping, box 129, folder 10, CMA. Johnson is quoted in Esther Peterson, "Address before the National Board of the Coat and Suit Industry," Feb 26, 1964, Miami Beach, 1, box 156, folder 17, CMA. "Mr. Nader's New Year's Wish," *WSJ*, Apr 10, 1974, 16.

25. Patrick Buchanan, "Ford Plays 'President,'" *CT*, May 11, 1975, A6. Other critics conceded that a consumer interest might exist but claimed that it didn't always coincide with the public interest. See, for example, Stephen Chapman, "Pluralism Run Amok," *New Republic*, May 21, 1977, 36–39; William A. Staples, "The Business View of the Agency for Consumer Advocacy," *Akron Business and Economic Review*, Winter 1977, 22–24. The "police" phrase is from, Julius Duscha, "Stop! In the Public Interest," *NYT Magazine*, Mar 21, 1971, 4. Ralph K. Winter, Jr., *The Consumer Advocate versus the Consumer* (Washington DC: American Enterprise Institute, 1972), 1. "Appliance Group Warns of 'Super' Consumer Agency," Association of Home Appliance Manufacturers, press release, May 17, 1973, box 129, folder 12, CMA. Ervin quoted in Shafer, "Consumer Bill Killed by Words," 8. Patrick Cox argued, "The best-known 'consumer advocates' frequently take stands that are close to totalitarian in their reliance on compulsion." "Free-Market Consumer Advocate," *Reason*, Jan 1981, 54. Henry Hazlitt, "Consumer 'Help' . . . Help!" *LAT*, Jul 5, 1967, A6. The AEI is quoted in American Enterprise Institute for Policy Research, *Consumer Agency Bills*, 15. "The Rack, the Boot, the Lash," *WSJ*, Jul 19, 1972, 10.

26. Schwartz, "Successful Fight against a Federal Consumer Protection Agency," 51; "Clothing the Consumer," *Washington Star*, Apr 8, 1977; "Mr. Nader's New Year's Wish"; Harlow, "Remarks on Consumer Protection Agency Legislation," 2.

27. Ronald Reagan, "Consumerists Out: Will Return," *Manhattan Mercury*, Jan 26, 1975. See also James J. Kilpatrick, "Big Brother Is Out to See Our Freedom Go Up in Smoke," *LAT*, Sep 12, 1973, B7. Louis Rukeyser, "Consumer Agency an All-Consuming Idea, but

No Good," *Topeka Capital*, Feb 24, 1978. Minority report of Sam Ervin, Sam Nunn, and William Brock (R-TN) on S. 707, from *Congressional Record*, Jun 13, 1974, S10518. Quoted in American Enterprise Institute for Policy Research, *The Proposed Agency for Consumer Advocacy* (Washington DC: American Enterprise Institute, 1975), 13. Arthur Fatt, "Let's Take the Politics out of Consumerism," *Nation's Business*, Jan 1969, 82–86, quotation on 82. "Gullible," is quoted in Keeffe, *Proposed Consumer Protection Agency*, 40. "Poor slob" is from Roger Klein, "Consumerism Gets the Brush-Off," *NYT*, Nov 26, 1972, F12. "Dullard" is from L. S. Matthews, "Guilty Until Proven Innocent," *Vital Speeches of the Day 37* (Jun 1, 1971): 505–509. Hagedorn is quoted in U.S. House of Representatives, *Agency for Consumer Protection*, 199. "Condescension" is from George Will, "Obama's Gaffe Shows His Elitism," *State*, Apr 15, 2008, A9.

28. "Clothing the Consumer." "Incapable" is quoted in Keeffe, *Proposed Consumer Protection Agency*, 40. Ad agency head is quoted in Richard L. D. Morse, "Consumers Welfare in the Jet Age," talk delivered at the Michigan Home Economics Association, May 3, 1963, 5, box 131, folder 1, CMA.

29. "Consumer Hysteria," *WSJ*, Oct 26, 1971, 20. Esther Peterson and Winifred Conkling, *Restless: The Memoirs of Labor and Consumer Activist Esther Peterson* (Washington DC: Caring Press, 1997), 130. "Mrs. Consumer," *Newsweek*, Nov 2 1964, 78. Lesher is quoted in George Lardner, Jr., "Business Group Raps Peterson," *WP*, May 20, 1977, A6. "Someone Does Need a Nanny," *WP*, Mar 16, 1979, A18; "The FTC as National Nanny," *WP*, Mar 1, 1978, A22. The "big motherism" quotation is from Carl Madden of the U.S. Chamber of Commerce, quoted in Cohen, *Consumers' Republic*, 373. R. Emmett Tyrell, Jr., "The Error of Their Ways," *WP*, Jan 19, 1981, A19. For a recent iteration see David Harsanyi, *Nanny State: How Food Fascists, Teetotaling Do-Gooders, Priggish Moralists, and Other Boneheaded Bureaucrats Are Turning America into a Nation of Children* (New York: Broadway, 2007).

30. *Congressional Issue Study: A Federal Department of Consumers ... and Related Proposals*, 87th Congress, 2nd Session (Washington DC: Chamber of Commerce of the United States, n.d.), box 129, folder 11, CMA. Staples, "Business View of the Agency for Consumer Advocacy," 22–24. For similar statements, see the letter to the editor, Michael M. Bates, "Consumer Protection," *CT*, Sep 30, 1977, B2, which expressed concern about the "burden of the consumer and the taxpayer." See also Reynolds, "Proposed Agency Not Needed to Protect Consumers." For excellent analysis of the taxpayer revolt and its connection to New Right conservatism see Schulman, *Seventies*, 205–215. "Proposition 13: Who Really Won?" *CRe*, Sep 1979, 546–548.

31. Hagedorn used the phrase in U.S. House of Representatives, *Agency for Consumer Protection*, 198. Mary Bennett Peterson, "How Consumerism Backfires: Those the Movement Is Designed to Protect Can Actually Wind Up as Its Victims," *Nation's Business 60* (May 1972): 31; Michael deCourcy Hinds, "Laissez-Faire Consumerism," *NYT*, Aug 21, 1982, 9. Suggesting the degree to which conservatives were able to jump on the bandwagon of consumerism, the legal philosopher Ronald Dworkin wrote in 1978 that "consumer protection appeals equally to consumers who call themselves liberal and those who say they are conservative." See "Liberalism," in *Public and Private Morality*, ed. Stuart Hampshire (New York: Cambridge University Press, 1978), 113–143, quotation on 114. Molly Sinclair, "Consumer Groups Don't Buy Reagan's National Consumers' Week," *WP*, Apr 24, 1983, A15.

32. "Is She Ignorant," front cover, 71. Rush Limbaugh, *The Way Things Ought to Be* (New

York: Pocket Books, 1993). These quotations are drawn from Walter Goodman's review, "The Way Things Ought to Be," *NYT Book Review*, Feb 21, 1993, 35. Goodman perceptively calls this rhetoric "right wing populism, an American perennial." "Reagan's Address: Hailing Fruits of the Party's Dream in 1980," *NYT*, Aug 16, 1988, A16. It is fascinating that he condemned these elites for their resistance to "change," a position that, before Reagan, had been the hallmark of conservatism.

33. Taft is quoted in "Consumer Bill Splits Ohio's Two Senators," *Voice of the Consumer* 5 (Aug 1974): 1. A series of editorials with such names can be found in U.S. House of Representatives, *Establishing an Agency for Consumer Protection: Hearings before a Subcommittee of the Committee on Government Operations on H.R. 7575*, 94th Cong., 1st sess., Jun 17, 18, 19, and 20, 1975 (Washington DC: Government Printing Office, 1975), 293, 297. Winter, *Consumer Advocate versus the Consumer.* Peterson, "How Consumerism Backfires," 30–31; Mary Bennett Peterson, *The Regulated Consumer* (Los Angeles: Nash, 1971). As early as 1969 Mary Feeley asked, "I wonder just how much the average consumer really wants to be" protected. "Is Consumer Protection Cry Empty?" *CT*, Jun 5, 1969, 12. Rukeyser, "Consumer Agency an All-Consuming Idea, but No Good."

34. "Business Responds to Consumerism," *Business Week*, Sep 6, 1969, 94–108. The previous year, the editors had warned that businessmen should not assume that a Republican administration would mean an end to consumerism. "Marketing Outlook," *Business Week*, Dec 7, 1968, 64. Editors of Fortune, *Consumerism: Things Ralph Nader Never Told You* (New York: Harper & Row, 1972). "Legitimate grievances" is from "The Challenge of Consumerism," *Dun's Review* 95 (Apr 1970): 112. Dick Braun, "Why Fight Consumerism?" *Farm Journal* 96 (Aug 1972): A4. Similar points were made in Morris B. Rotman, "Consumerism Is Us! A Constructive Influence," *Vital Speeches of the Day* 38 (Jul 15, 1972): 589–592; and Mae D. Aucello, "Facing Up to Consumerism: If Business Does Not Respond to Consumer Needs, the Government Will," *USA Today* 108 (Mar 1980): 49–50. Mary Gardiner Jones, "Consumerism: A Blessing in Disguise," address before the eighteenth annual marketing conference of the National Industrial Conference Board, Oct 14, 1970, box 156, folder 8, CMA. James L. Ferguson, "Consumerism Revisited," 1974, address at the annual meeting of the American Association of Advertising Agencies, White Sulphur Springs, WV, May 17, 1974, box 155, folder 12, CMA. "Response Found to Consumerism," *NYT*, Jan 21, 1974, 37; "Consumers Spur Industry Response: Spending for Consumerism," *NYT*, Jan 7, 1973, 3: 49. For treatment of a parallel form of co-optation, see Warren Belasco, *Appetite for Change: How the Counterculture Took on the Food Industry*, 2nd ed. (Ithaca: Cornell University Press, 2006).

35. Robert Quittmeyer, "Consumer Liberation," *NYT*, Apr 11, 1977, 25. "Stop Calling Us Consumers!" *CSM*, Feb 8, 1978, 28. For a cogent critique of the discourse of consumer liberation on both the Left and the Right see George Will, "Happiness Is a Buick Electra," *LAT*, Apr 17, 1977, E7.

36. "The CPA's Problem," *WSJ*, Apr 20, 1977, 24. "Consumerism and Consumers," *National Review*, Jun 6, 1975, 595. Klein, "Consumerism Gets the Brush-Off."

37. "Creation of Agency to Press U.S. for Consumers May Be Lost Cause." Ralph Nader, *Crashing the Party: Taking on the Corporate Government in an Age of Surrender* (New York: St. Martin's Press, 2002), 302, 319.

38. Nader is quoted in Michael deCourcy Hinds, "Nader Expanding Consumer Efforts," *NYT*, Sep 7, 1981, 31. For a similar view that Reagan "may just be about the best thing to

happen to the consumer movement since the Great Society" see James Worsham, "Consumer Advocates Starting to Regroup," *CT*, Mar 22, 1981, A1, 6. See also *Warning: Reagonomics Is Harmful to Consumers* (Washington DC: National Consumers League, 1982). The Harris poll is mentioned in Michael Pertschuk, "The Case for Consumerism," *NYT Magazine*, May 29, 1983, 26, 30-33, 36. Pertschuk, like Nader, believed that "President Reagan, by stimulating consumer reaction, has done for the consumer movement of the 1980s what the consumer advocate Ralph Nader did two decades earlier," quotation 26. Victoria Irwin, "Consumerism Fights to Survive Budget Cuts, Waning Interest," *CSM*, Jun 3, 1986, 6.

39. Sheila Wolfe, "Consumers Lack Organization," *CT*, Jul 26, 1970, 5.

40. Ralph Blumenthal, "Consumer Leaders, in Reappraisal, Seek New Initiatives," *NYT*, Feb 15, 1978, A21; Merrill Brown, "Consumerists Look to Cover Grass Roots," *WP*, Jan 11, 1981, L4; Lucia Mouat, "Consumers on the March," *CSM*, Jan 27, 1978, 14; Marlene Cimons, "Consumerists Head Back to Grass Roots," *LAT*, Feb 17, 1978, G1. Pertschuk, "Case for Consumerism," 30. Robert B. Shapiro, "Exile Overlooks Doubts That Limit Consumer Cause," *Legal Times*, Dec 20, 1982, 12. Max E. Brunk, "The Meddlesome Seventies: The Consumer," *Vital Speeches of the Day* 37 (Jan 15, 1971): 200-204.

41. "Nader Urged to Use Influence for Consumer Organization: No Shortcut to Consumer Power," *Consumers Voice*, Mar 1970, 4. Max Weiner, "Which Way for the Consumer Movement?" a series of articles reprinted from *Consumers Voice* (Philadelphia: CEPA, 1977), box 188, folder 5, CMA. "Oct 11, 1968 Interview with Weiner by Marion B. Warner," box 3, Max Weiner Papers, Historical Society of Pennsylvania, Philadelphia. Shapiro, "Exile Overlooks Doubts That Limit Consumer Cause."

42. The text of the Supreme Court's decision can be found at http://supreme.justia.com/us/458/886/case.html (accessed on May 14, 2008). For superb analysis of the Civil Rights movement in the area, which puts the boycotts in context, see Emilye Crosby, *A Little Taste of Freedom: The Black Freedom Struggle in Claiborne County, Mississippi* (Chapel Hill: University of North Carolina Press, 2005); and Aryeh Neier, "Mississippi Relives Its '60s," *Nation*, Sep 23, 1978, 265-267. For excellent assessments that I have drawn on in the following passages see Michael C. Harper, "The Consumer's Emerging Right to Boycott: *NAACP v. Claiborne Hardware* and Its Implications for American Labor Law," *Yale Law Journal* 93 (Jan 1984): 409-454; Thomas A. Johnson, "N.A.A.C.P. Loses $1.2 Million Lawsuit for 1966 Boycott in Mississippi Town," *NYT*, Aug 12, 1976, 33; "N.A.A.C.P. Wants Court to Bar Boycott Damages for Merchants," *NYT*, Sep 7, 1980, 54; Daniel Jacobson, "Rule on Boycott Seen as Landmark Decision," *AN*, Nov 28, 1981, 2; Fred Barbash, "Decision Reversed in Mississippi Case: Justices Uphold Political Boycott as Social Protest," *WP*, Jul 3, 1982, A1, 11; Art Harris, "In Town of Boycott, No More Cutting in Line," *WP*, Jul 3, 1982. p. A12; "The Port Gibson Protest," *WP*, Jul 10, 1982, A22; Chester A. Higgins, "Boycott Decision Has Wrought Miracle Changes in Port Gibson," *Crisis*, Oct 1982, 19-22.

43. Leonard Orland, "Protection for Boycotts," *NYT*, Jul 31, 1982, 27; Harper, "Consumer's Emerging Right to Boycott," 419, n. 51. The text of the oral argument can be found at: http://www.oyez.org/cases/1980-1989/1981/1981_81_202/argument/ (accessed on May 14, 2008).

44. For a lengthy and explicit statement of that challenge see Robert D. Holsworth, *Public Interest Liberalism and the Crisis of Affluence: Reflections on Nader, Environmentalism, and the Politics of Sustainable Society* (Boston: Schenkman Books, 1980). After Reagan's election, some consumer activists emphasized the need for "a return to the more traditional role of consumer groups," which meant "less emphasis on legislation." See Marjorie

Coeyman, "Consumer Groups Gird for Reagan," *CSM*, Dec 24, 1980, 11. See also "NAACP to Resurrect Economic Boycott Tactic," *CT*, Jun 30, 1982, A8. Kilpatrick, "Consumer Bill Bad Medicine for All." Thatcher said, "There is no such thing as society," in "Aids, Education and the Year 2000!" *Women's Own Magazine*, Oct 31 1987, 8–10.

Epilogue

1. Editors of Fortune, *Consumerism: Things Ralph Nader Never Told You* (New York: Harper & Row, 1972), vii; Edward Cowan, "If Consumer Leagues Spring Up: Boycotts' Results Are Hard to Predict," *NYT*, Mar 25, 1973, 195. "Idea Whose Time Has Passed," *Time*, Jun 13 1977, 16; Walter Isaacson, "Let the Buyers Beware: Consumer Advocates Retrench for Hard Times," *Time*, Sep 21, 1981. See also Larry Kramer, "The Tide of Consumer Influence Is in the Grip of Strong Undertow," *WP*, Jan 13, 1980, G12.

2. For an overview of boycotts in this period see Monroe Friedman, "Consumer Boycotts in the United States, 1970–1980: Contemporary Affairs in Historical Perspective," *Journal of Consumer Affairs* 19 (Summer 1985): 96–117. On student consumer politics see "Harvard President Rebuffs Pleas by Activists to Support Boycotts," *NYT*, May 21, 1979, B7. "Labor Opens Boycott Drive against J. P. Stevens," *NYT*, Jul 25, 1977, 47. Timothy J. Minchin, *"Don't Sleep with Stevens!" The J. P. Stevens Campaign and the Struggle to Organize the South, 1963–80* (Gainesville: University Press of Florida, 2005). B. Drummond Ayers, Jr., "Blacks Stage Boycott in S. Carolina County," *NYT*, Dec 3, 1976, 18; Molly Ivins, "Union's Survival Is at Stake in 14-Month Strike," *NYT*, Jun 12, 1978, A16; "Support for U.F.W. Boycott," *NYT*, Jun 27, 1979, C16. Gil Feiler, *From Boycott to Economic Cooperation: The Political Economy of the Arab Boycott of Israel* (New York: Routledge, 1998); Steve Cady, "22 African Countries Boycott Opening Ceremony of Olympic Games," *NYT*, Jul 18, 1976, 130.

3. Janet Bodnar and Melynda Dovel, "Whatever Happened to the Consumer Movement? While No One Was Watching, It Got Bigger and Stronger," *Changing Times* 43 (Aug 1989): 45–49; Jeanne Mackin, "Consumer Movement Is Alive and Well," *Human Ecology* 19 (Fall 1990): 27. Steven Greenhouse, "A Weapon for Consumers: The Boycott Returns," *NYT*, Mar 26, 2000, WK4. Arthur S. Hayes and Joseph Pereira, "Facing a Boycott, Many Companies Bend," *WSJ*, Nov 8, 1990, B1; Guy Halverson, "Consumerism Bounces Back in U.S.," *CSM*, Jun 19, 1990, 9. Clyde Haberman, "NYC Boycott This! (Pardon Our French)," *NYT*, Feb 18, 2003, B1. For three overviews see Randy Shaw, *Reclaiming America: Nike, Clean Air, and the New National Activism* (Berkeley: University of California Press, 1999); Leslie Savan, "Activism in the Checkout Line: The Rising Tide of Boycotts," *Village Voice*, Jun 6, 1989, reprinted in *Utne Reader*, Sep/Oct 1989, 87, 89; Lawrence B. Glickman, "Boycott Mania: As Business Ethics Fall, Consumer Activism Rises," *BG*, Jul 31, 2005, D12.

4. Mark Stencel, "The Boycott Comes of Age," *WP*, Sep 26, 1990, F1. In addition, other lists were contained in the shorter-lived *Boycott Action, Bunny Hugger's Gazette*, and *Label Letter*. "Other Boycott Publications," *Boycott Quarterly*, Spring 1994, 67. The first issue of *Boycott Quarterly* noted that it had replaced *National Boycott News*, which "provided a forum for the many boycotts to present their cases to responsible consumers when the mainstream media ignored them." See "Boycott Victories Abound!" *Boycott Quarterly*, Spring 1994, 2. For a brief history of these publications see Monroe Friedman, *Consumer Boycotts: Effecting Change through the Marketplace and the Media* (New York: Routledge, 1999), xv. The url for *Ethical Consumer's* list of boycotts is http://www.ethicalconsumer.org/

boycotts/boycotts_list.htm. Another group, the Institute for Consumer Responsibility (ICR), founded in 1999 to promote consumer responsibility, maintains a boycott list at http://www.onemovement.net/boycotts.html http://boycottcity.org/index.php (accessed on May 14, 2008).

5. "Power of the pocketbook" is from "On Boycotting: Using Your Dollars for Change: The Power of the Pocketbook," *NBN*, Spring/Summer 1989, 11–13, quotation on 11. "Boycotts used to take years" is found in "Boycott Victories Abound!" 2. A similar point is made in Rafael D. Pagan, Jr., "A New Era of Activism," *Futurist*, Spring–Summer 1989, 12–16. "On-Going Boycotts," *Boycott Quarterly*, Spring 1994, 54–60. The same issue (60–66) contained a list entitled "The Products They Make." See also "Continuing Boycotts," *NBN*, Spring/Summer 1989, item 2, "The Coca-Cola Company,"17–19 (no. 3 is "The Ford Motor Company," 19–21; 4 is "The Shell Oil Company," 21–30; 5 is "Chilean Products," 31–32; 6 is "Tobacco Subsidiaries," 32–34; 7 is "Cultural Performances and Sports Engagements in South Africa," 34; 8 is "Krugerrands," 34–35; 9 is "Banks and Loaning to South Africa," 35; 10 is "Penthouse," 35; 11 is "Adolph Coors, Inc.," 35); and "Boycott Victories," *NBN*, Spring/Summer 1989, 172–175. This issue even had a section entitled "Partial Victories" (176), which noted that Benetton had agreed in Nov 1988 to no further animal testing after a three-month boycott. Christine Jackson, "Beastly Boycotts: PETA Takes Out More Animal Abusers in 1993," *Boycott Quarterly*, Spring 1994, 8–9, subhead "Caring Consumers Unite."

6. Putnam is quoted in Savan, "Activism in the Checkout Line"; Sankar Sen, Zeynep Gürhan-Canli, and Vicki Morwitz, "Withholding Consumption: A Social Dilemma Perspective on Consumer Boycotts," *Journal of Consumer Research* 28 (Dec 2001): 399–417; Sarah Ferguson, "Boycotts R Us," *Village Voice*, Jul 8, 1997, 44–46.

7. Margaret Scammell, "The Internet and Civic Engagement: The Age of the Citizen Consumer," *Political Communication* 17 (Oct 2000): 351–355, quotation on 351. See also Néstor García Canclini, *Consumers and Citizens: Globalization and Multicultural Conflicts*, trans. George Yudice (Minneapolis: University of Minnesota Press, 2001). Canclini argues that consumption provides "new openings for expanding citizenship." Steven Miles, *Consumerism as a Way of Life* (New York: Sage, 1998), 4–5.

8. On the revival of antisweatshop protests see Steven Greenhouse, "Two Protests by Students over Wages for Workers," *NYT*, Jan 31, 1999, 12; Liza Featherstone, *Students against Sweatshops: The Making of a Movement* (London: Verso, 2002); Daniel E. Bender, *Sweated Work, Weak Bodies: Anti-sweatshop Campaigns and Languages of Labor* (New Brunswick: Rutgers University Press, 2004).On sweatshop-free goods: Amy Brecount White, "Putting an End to Sweatshops: Individual Consumers Really Can Make a Difference," *WP*, Sep 30, 1997, E5. John M. Coski, *The Confederate Battle Flag: America's Most Embattled Emblem* (Cambridge, MA: Harvard University Press, 2005), 248–250. On fair trade coffee: Kim Bendheim, "Business; Global Issues Flow into America's Coffee," *NYT*, Nov 3, 2002, C6; Laure Waridel, *Coffee with Pleasure: Just Java and World Trade* (Montreal: Black Rose Books, 2001). See also the information at the "Fair Trade Action Guide" which describes the products it purveys as "great looking," "vibrant," and "gourmet" at www.fairtraderesource.org and http://www.equiterre.qc.ca/ (accessed May 31, 2008). On getting "behind the label" see Peter Singer and Jim Mason, *The Way We We Eat: Why Our Food Choices Matter* (New York: Rodale, 2006), 92–110. On slow food, see Michael Pollan, "Cruising on the Ark of Taste," *Mother Jones*, May–Jun 2003, 74–76; Florence Fabricant, "A Faintly Amused

Answer to Fast Food," *NYT*, Nov 15, 1989, C10; Carlo Petrini, *Slow Food Nation: Why Our Food Should Be Good, Clean, and Fair*, trans. Clara Furlan and Jonathan Hunt (New York : Rizzoli Ed Libris, 2007); Victoria de Grazia, *Irresistible Empire: America's Advance through Twentieth-Century Europe* (Cambridge, MA: Harvard University Press, 2005), 458–482. On simple living: Duane Elgin, *Voluntary Simplicity: An Ecological Lifestyle That Promotes Personal and Social Renewal*, rev. ed. (New York: Bantam, 1989); and http://www.simpleliving .net/main/ (accessed on May 14, 2008). On green consumerism: *The Green Lifestyle Handbook: 1001 Ways You Can Heal the Earth*, ed. Jeremy Rikfin (New York: Henry Holt, 1990); Barry Meier, "It's Green and Growing Fast, but Is It Good for the Earth?" *NYT*, Apr 21, 1990, 48. On religion: John F. Kavanaugh, *Following Christ in a Consumer Society: The Spirituality of Cultural Resistance*, 25th anniversary ed. (New York: Orbis, 2006).

9. Todd Putnam, "Boycotts Are Busting Out All Over," *Business and Society Review* 85 (1993): 47–51, quotation on 49. "New Zealand BUYcott," *NBN*, Spring/Summer 1989, 191.

10. See, for example, "Preventing Cruelty to Animals," *NS*, Aug 1846, 126; David Shi, *The Simple Life: Plain Living and High Thinking in American Culture* (New York: Oxford University Press, 1985).

11. *Super-size Me*, directed by Morgan Spurlock (Samuel Goldwyn Films, 2004); David Ewing Duncan, "The Pollution Within," *National Geographic*, Oct 2006, at http://www7 .nationalgeographic.com/ngm/0610/feature4/index.html (accessed May 14, 2008). See also Rachel Saltz, "What You Consume, You Should Consider," *NYT*, Oct 29, 2007, B7, about the play *Milk-n-Honey*, which encourages theatergoers to think about what they eat. Upton Sinclair, *The Profits of Religion: An Essay in Economic Interpretation* (Pasadena: by the author, 1918), 194. For a later version of a similar issue see L. A. Kauffman, "New Age Meets New Right: Tofu Politics in Berkeley," *Nation*, Sep 16, 1991, 294–296. Eric Schlosser, *Fast Food Nation: The Dark Side of the All-American Meal* (New York: Perennial, 2002). Andrew Adam Newman, "What's a Parent to Do?" *NYT*, Sep 29, 2007.

12. Mark Patterson, *Consumerism and Everyday Life* (New York: Routledge, 2006), 28. See also the section on the politics of logos, 217–219; James M. Jasper, *The Art of Moral Protest: Culture, Biography, and Creativity in Social Movements* (Chicago: University of Chicago Press, 1999), 264; Benjamin Barber, *Consumed: How Markets Corrupt Children, Infantilize Adults, and Swallow Citizens Whole* (New York: Norton, 2007).

13. On the Reverend Bill Talen and his "Church of Stop Shopping" see Constance L. Hayes, "Preaching to Save Shoppers from 'Evil' of Consumerism," *NYT*, Jan 1, 2003, C1; *What Would Jesus Buy?* produced by Morgan Spurlock and directed by Rob VanAlkemade (Warrior Poets Releasing, 2007). On "Buy nothing" days in the 1990s and 2000s see Carey Goldberg, "Buy Nothings' Discover a Cure for Affluenza," *NYT*, Nov 29, 1997, A8; Keiko Nasao, "Buy Nothing Day," *Dollars and Sense*, Jan 1, 2002, 6; Sari Botton, "The 60's Spirit to a 90's Beat," *NYT*, Nov 26, 1995, CY8. Kalle Lasn, *Culture Jam: How to Reverse America's Suicidal Consumer Binge—and Why We Must* (New York: Harper, 2000). See also the Adbusters Web site: http://adbusters.org/ (accessed Jun 11, 2008). Ken Conca, "Consumption and Environment in a Global Economy," in *Confronting Consumption*, ed. Thomas Princen, Michael Maniates, and Ken Conca (Cambridge, MA: MIT Press, 2002), 133–154, quotation on 133. For a good overview see, in the same volume, Michael Maniates, "In Search of Consumptive Resistance: The Voluntary Simplicity Movement," 199–236. Julian Sanchez, "Anti-consumerist Capitalism: Culture Jammers, Sneaker Peddlers," *Reason*, Nov 2003, at http://www.reason.com/news/show/28915.html (accessed May 14, 2008).

INDEX